THE ASSASSINATION OF JOHN F. KENNEDY

THE ASSASSINATION OF JOHN F. KENNEDY

A COMPREHENSIVE HISTORICAL AND LEGAL BIBLIOGRAPHY, 1963-1979

Compiled by DeLloyd J. Guth and David R. Wrone

GREENWOOD PRESS
WESTPORT, CONNECTICUT • LONDON, ENGLAND

Library of Congress Cataloging in Publication Data

Guth, DeLloyd J   1938-
    The assassination of John F. Kennedy.

    Includes indexes.
    1. Kennedy, John Fitzgerald, Pres. U.S.,
1917-1963—Assassination—Bibliography. I. Wrone,
David R., joint author. II. Title.
Z8462.8.G87   [E842.9]   016.973922'092'4
ISBN 0-313-21274-0 lib. bdg.   79-6184

Library of Congress Catalog Card Number: 79-6184
ISBN: 0-313-21274-0

First published in 1980

Greenwood Press
A division of Congressional Information Service, Inc.
88 Post Road West, Westport, Connecticut 06881

Printed in the United States of America

10 9 8 7 6 5 4 3 2 1

Contents

Preface		*vii*
Introduction		*xi*
Abbreviations		*xli*
Chronologies and Maps		
Chronology of Assassination		xliii
Chronology of Lee Harvey Oswald		xlv
Map 1.	General Assassination Scene	xlix
Map 2.	Dealey Plaza	l
Map 3.	Oswald and Oak Cliff, Dallas	lii
Map 4.	Places Associated with Oswald in New Orleans	liv
Section I:	The Evidence and the Litigants	1
PART I:	Unpublished Sources	3
(1)	Archives and Libraries	3
(2)	Private Collections	9
PART II:	Published Sources, Excluding the Warren Report	12
(1)	Federal	12
(2)	Non-Federal	32
PART III:	Local Judicial Records	34
PART IV:	Federal Judicial Records	36
(1)	Suits Involving Publication of Evidence	36
(2)	Suits Concerning Oswald's Possessions	37
(3)	Federal Litigation Associated With the Garrison Inquiry	40
(4)	"Freedom of Information Act" Litigation	45

PART V: Photographic Evidence   67
    (1)   Oswald in New Orleans   67
    (2)   The Assassination Scene in Dallas   68
Section II: Published Books and Periodicals   79
PART I: Bibliographies and Research   81
PART II: The Action   84
    (1)   Dallas Before and After   84
    (2)   Oswald the Suspect   88
    (3)   Executive Investigations: The Warren Commission
          in Progress   97
    (4)   The Warren Report   107
    (5)   Critics and Defenders of the Warren Report   109
    (6)   Guns and the JFK Autopsy   127
    (7)   Audio-Visual Materials: Tapes, Photos, Films, Records   133
PART III: The Reaction   140
    (1)   President Lyndon B. Johnson's Transition to Office   140
    (2)   Immediate Reactions: Popular and Official   143
    (3)   Memorials and Eulogies   154
    (4)   News Media   163
    (5)   Studies of Public Reactions   174
    (6)   Assassinations in General: Political and Psychological
          Studies   177
PART IV: Later Inquiries   181
    (1)   Executive Investigations: The Rockefeller Commission,
          the CIA and Cuba   181
    (2)   Congressional Investigations: Schweiker, Abzug,
          Pike-Edwards, and Downing-Gonzalez-Stokes Committees   184
    (3)   The New Orleans Investigation: Jim Garrison   188
    (4)   Manchester-Kennedy Book   197
    (5)   Other Secondary Research   205
PART V: Related Topics   221
    (1)   Police Officer Tippit and His Family   221
    (2)   Oswald the Family Man: Marina and Marguerite   222
    (3)   Oswald's Murder: The Ruby Trial   226
    (4)   Fiction Related to Events in Dallas: A Selection of
          Novels, Plays and Films   233
    (5)   TV Special Programs: A Selection   238
    (6)   The Surviving Kennedys   240
Section III: The New York Times Daily Reports, 1963-1978   243
               Supplemented by The Washington Post, 1978   394

Index of Names (Sections I, II, and III)   399
Index of Correspondents: The New York Times   435
Index of Correspondents: The Washington Post   443

Preface

Try as hard as we can to remember him living, the world best knows President John F. Kennedy dead. Try to recall that vivaciously bareheaded President-elect, braving Washington's wintry Inauguration Day. Instead, one's own head cannot rid itself of those skull-shattering bullets fired a thousand days later.

Knowing the end makes it impossible to remember accurately what preceded and followed it. Haunted, shamed by that killing in Dallas, Americans carry the further burden of knowing that his murder was only the first. After Malcolm X came Martin Luther King, Jr., and then Senator Robert F. Kennedy, and then attempts against Governor George C. Wallace and President Gerald R. Ford. Who could still say that U.S. politics gave the world a model for reasoned debate and peaceful transfer of political power? Who in the world, after Vietnam and Kent State, after the Lockheed and Watergate scandals, after history's first humiliating resignations of a vice-president and then a president, who would not see this in the shadow of that sunset of 22 November 1963?

To the public it remains the number-one murder mystery. To politicians it has meant a crisis turned into a universal skepticism about public institutions. And now, sixteen years later, a generation of new Americans enters adulthood and politics without the blighted, disjointed memories that America's most notorious homicide carved onto older minds. But what unites newer and older minds is the fact that neither knows with any certitude how this president came to be killed. For the young, this question can be either a matter of idle indifference or a fascinating historical puzzle that recedes into the past to join mysterious deaths, like the princes in Richard III's Tower. For the older, however, it remains a historical enigma, as much for the fact as for its impact on one's own American faith and values.

What about Oswald, Ruby, the Warren Commission, the FBI, the CIA, Manchester, Garrison, and numerous congressional investigations?

Taken as a whole, they have reduced the issues, without anyone's intending it, to the common denominator of credibility, to faith or doubt in government, to distrust for police investigations, rather than to matters of *evidence*. After sixteen years, all have been found wanting. Could this killing have been executed by one unstable gunman? If Oswald was not alone, who . . . ? how . . . ? why . . . ?

What, if anything can one securely believe?

It is with this problem, and in the context of what's been done and undone during the first sixteen years, that we offer this comprehensive bibliography, particularly for the newer generation of students. We want this work to organize and promote truly public, serious investigations into the murder itself and into the multiplicity of reactions to it. Because lawyers and journalists virtually controlled the JFK killing, as an issue and a story, the extant literature dictated our focus on law, litigation, and especially the media.

The first section, therefore, opens to the reader the abundance of historical evidence, some still classified but much now available. In the JFK murder case, questions of governmental obstruction and incompetence since 1963 have forced a series of lawsuits against officials and their agencies, mainly under the Freedom of Information Act. The threat and the courtroom reality of private litigation against public officials has now become the sole avenue to evidentiary truth. In this area, the U.S. Justice Department has inverted normal adversary procedures, converting its mandated role as federal prosecutor into that of the defender of police secrecy and ineptitude. Investigation of this murder, therefore, has been left to private citizens such as Harold Weisberg and his legal counsellor, James H. Lesar. We have taken full cognizance of all such efforts in Section I because such litigation remains the major instrument for establishing the evidence.

We wish to lift the subject out of a quagmire of often bizarre speculations, official disinformation, and exploitation by the likes of Mark Lane. To be reminded of how bizarre and shameless a literature has developed, one need only glance through the titles listed in Section II. They abundantly exemplify a secondary literature that has been out of control since 1963, with only a scattering of serious, even scholarly, contributions. We agree with those who will see "rubbish" in many entries, with some of it written by the crass or the crazy. Much of this is the product of the disjointed times that have followed the killing, but all document the diversity of perspectives on that event.

Because this material is organized by subject, which can disrupt the mind's focus on the flow of events, we have supplied a chronological corrective with Section III. Here we give every news story by its precise headline as it appeared in *The New York Times,* in the order of publication. We have added all entries from *The Washington Post* for 1978 for two reasons: (1) that was the year of a serious printers' strike that disrupted *The New York Times,* with only a "Strike Supplement" produced between August and November for the microfilmed record, and (2) we have the impression that *The Washington Post* during the past few years increasingly provided the broader and deeper coverage for this particular subject.

This project began in February 1978 with the support of a six-month Federal CETA assignment in the Area Research Center at the University of Wisconsin-Stevens Point. Subsequently, DeLloyd J. Guth continued to compile the bibliographical materials that comprise Sections II and III. Section I has been the work primarily of David R. Wrone, whose scholarly research into the subject began over a decade ago. The Introduction is a joint effort, and the indexes were compiled by Guth. We retain equal responsibility for the structure, layout, selection, and arguments contained in this book.

No work of this scale and depth could be executed from start to publication in under two years without outside help. Our primary debts are to our wives, Katherine Ratliff Guth and Elaine Alley Wrone. Both arranged much released time for us from normal domestic tasks. Katie drew all four maps, while Elaine proofread much of the final copy.

We have been blessed with excellent typists, thanks mainly to the University of Missouri-St. Louis's History Department, where DeLloyd J. Guth taught in 1978-1979. Their chairman, James D. Norris, now Dean of the College of Liberal Arts and Sciences at Northern Illinois University, provided us with a departmental secretary, Julie Andrew, to type the primary draft for Sections II and III. She typed from the innumerable 3" x 5" cards that required painstaking organization. The final professional version, which is here published by photolithographic process, was typed expertly by Barbara Harrington, also resident in St. Louis.

Within the University of Wisconsin-Stevens Point, we have also had important support. Arthur M. Fish, Curator in the UW-SP's Area Research Center, provided a home base for compiling the bibliography, amid his huge collection of state and federal documents. We gratefully acknowledge the general hospitality extended to us by Burdette W. Eagon, Acting Vice-Chancellor for Academic Affairs, and by Allen F. Barrows, Director of Public Services in the UW-SP's Learning Resources Center. Also, the UW-SP's History Department provided funding for telephone expenses and the costs of photocopying the final typescript.

Finally, we have had consistent support from Greenwood Press. In particular we would like to thank Arthur H. Stickney and Margaret Brezicki for their invaluable assistance.

Throughout we have designed this reference work to serve teachers, students, researchers, and the concerned public. We welcome all comments, corrections, and addenda from our readers.

DeLloyd J. Guth and
David R. Wrone

1 October 1979
Stevens Point, Wisconsin

Introduction

Novus ordo saeculorum, a new order of the ages, reads the motto on the Great Seal of the United States. It captures what three centuries emblazoned before the world's eyes: America, located where Europe's western and Asia's eastern frontiers converged, where generations of hopeless, hapless, landless poor sought to redeem their misfortunes. From Thomas Jefferson's day through the early 1960s, American political rhetoric has sustained such hopes, emphasizing human renewal and the frontier spirit. With the arrival of "The New Frontier" in 1961, such rhetorical expressions of collective idealism found their culminating enthusiasm.

The murder of President John F. Kennedy jolted that image and reality, inside and outside the United States. Subsequent if unrelated assassinations, then Vietnam and Watergate have seemed sounding bells that many heard as heralding the end for that *pax Americana* forged by World War II. America's forefathers had celebrated its distance from the Old World's order, seen as tainted by monarchy, class, conspiracies, and cynicism about the capabilities of common humanity. Even more, America had traditionally defined its destiny as ruled by a written constitution and the impartial enforcement of law.

But that act of 22 November 1963, jeopardized this New World's self-perception and challenged its very commitment to pluralism, publicity, law, and competitive democracy. Agonizing self-appraisal continued despite the 1964 presidential Warren Commission's *Report,* and probably because of it. The Commission had acted as a hasty substitute for due process of law, offering little more than an official quietus manufactured for domestic consciences and foreign skeptics. Four years later, Garrison's bungled investigation and the Kennedy-Manchester imbroglio became mere publicity-seeking interludes before new killings and new questions. In retrospect, American idealism began to die on the streets of Dallas. Sixteen years later, for most people the question "who killed Kennedy?" remains open and confused.

As part of a November 1963 political fence-mending effort, President Kennedy had taken his full entourage into Texas, making various appearances and speeches. Late in the morning of 22 November, Air Force One landed at Love Field on the outskirts of Dallas, where a motorcade waited to take him through the city's center for lunch at the Trade Mart. There he planned to deliver a moderating speech against political extremism, racialism, and the mood for witch-hunting and scapegoating. He rode openly in the rear seat with Mrs. Kennedy; Governor and Mrs. John B. Connally sat forward in the jump seats; two Secret Service men occupied the front seat, one driving. Moving down Main Street the limousine entered Dealey Plaza, where it immediately turned hard right onto Houston Street, went one short block, slowed almost to a stop, turned very sharply left onto the curving Elm Street, where it passed beneath the seven-story Texas School Book Depository. Shots rang out. It was 12:30 P.M., Central Standard Time.

President Kennedy was clearly struck as he clutched for his throat, then the top of his head exploded as he slammed down into his wife's lap. Directly in front of him Governor Connally received five wounds and spun into his wife's arms. Several score feet away, standing near the triple underpass, citizen James T. Tague was sprayed by fragments created by a bullet that smashed into the curbstone at his feet. At 1:00 P.M. President Kennedy was pronounced dead at Parkland Hospital.

At 1:50 P.M., Lee Harvey Oswald, an employee at the Texas School Book Depository, was arrested in the Texas Theater, a cinema in another section of Dallas. Hours later Captain J. Will Fritz, Dallas's chief homicide inspector, charged Oswald with murdering Police Officer J. D. Tippit, who had been shot dead between the Texas Theater and the Texas School Book Depository sometime before 1:10 P.M. That night, at about 1:30 A.M. on the 23rd, Dallas police formally accused Oswald of the murder of President Kennedy. One day later, the operator of a Dallas striptease club, Jack Ruby, shot and killed Oswald while police tried to transfer Oswald from the city to the county jail, under a blaze of media publicity and live television lighting.

In the prevailing law, murder of a United States president remained ordinary homicide limited to state and local jurisdiction. Dallas's chaos and the manifest incompetence of all law officers in the circumstances, whether local or federal, translated instantly into a national anxiety about the rule of law. A magisterial funeral in Washington, followed with macabre irony by the traditional Thanksgiving holiday, restored order without confidence. President Lyndon B. Johnson hastened to appoint a special presidential, blue-ribbon commission headed by the Chief Justice of the U.S. Supreme Court to inquire into the events and the law.

Knowledge of the origin, operation, and conclusions of the Warren Commission must precede any understanding of the swirls of controversy that still surround President Kennedy's murder. Its twenty-seven published volumes[1] effectively preempted the subject, shifting investigations away from the act itself over to Warren Commission data and its inadequacies. Its influence remains today a silent hand from the past, actively shaping perimeters of public belief and exerting intense pressure upon politicians and government attorneys. Every federal inquiry, both executive and legislative, into the murder and its attendant questions has accepted the Warren Commission's conclusions as the premise upon which to launch its probe. Senator Richard Schweiker, for example, specifically acknowledged the validity of the Commission's findings, then said that his inquiry would search out how a foreign conspiracy had actually operated through the person of Oswald.[2] The latest inquiry, by the House Select Committee on Assassinations, initially stated that one of its tasks would be to make the Warren Commission's findings "persuasive." Only on the last day of public hearings, during the Christmas season of 1978, did it openly stumble upon audio evidence of conspiracy that could not be refuted. The House Committee still accepted the mass of Warren Commission data, without challenge to specific items or comprehension of the circumstances in which all of it was compiled.[3]

Few realize even today that during the first days following the murder the world came close to nuclear war, at least according to the latest expert on the subject. American forces entered a "red alert" phase, the highest state of readiness for a preemptive nuclear strike.[4] Vital federal intelligence channels clogged under the sheer mass of data being frantically transmitted. The new president, known for occasional impetuosity, proceeded with a commendable caution in his first hours and days, fearful of every international implication. In the midst of a constantly deteriorating situation, tension mounted as numerous bits of wrong or trivial information reached the White House. The CIA's Mexican substation immediately reported Oswald as Castro's hireling,[5] while the FBI could produce *five volumes* of "facts" less than three weeks after the murder, on behalf of the Warren Commission.[6] Opinions became truths, fiction achieved factuality, prejudices became official insights, and blame began to stick to everyone and everything.

Domestic conditions heightened the potential for rash reactions. Under the glare of camera lights and before several hundred reporters, Dallas officials announced their capture of a "communist" who had killed the president. The media saturated the public with "facts" of Oswald's "communist" activities and Marxist beliefs. In Congress, several members moved for investigations, vying with each other for the chairmanship of proposed committees. Anticommunist hysteria in the United States, which predated the Russian Revolution, had cyclically reared its fevered head against presidents elected from the Democratic party. But cultivating it daily in the wake of Kennedy's murder, as many editors, reporters and politicians did, only exalted the conspiracy-minded and exacerbated the conduct of foreign policy. Added to perils of revived witch-hunting, no one knew with any certainty, despite unprecedented coverage by newsmen, what precisely had transpired in Dallas and why.

To allay fears and restore public confidence in law and elected officials, the executive branch directed that the murdered Oswald be identified as the sole killer. Oswald was dead; there could be no trial. In a 26 November 1963 memorandum to Presidential Assistant Bill Moyers, the Deputy Attorney General Nicholas Katzenbach defined the prosecution's position: "The public must be satisfied that Oswald was the assassin; that he did not have confederates who are still at large; and that the evidence was such that he would have been convicted at trial."[7] This day, then, while President Kennedy's requiem mass and burial were taking place, his own presidential appointees had begun the policy of burying the issues of fact, of guilt, and of law.

President Johnson implored Earl Warren, the Chief Justice, to head the presidential commission, arguing that only men with highest public respect could still the nation and abate any domestic military threat. In his memoirs, Chief Justice Warren stated that he took this chairmanship with extreme reluctance, only after President Johnson made an emotional appeal to his love of country. To refuse, it was suggested, could mean "40,000,000 lives lost" in a nuclear war.[8]

Johnson appointed six other members to his commission. Two Senators: John Sherman Cooper, Republican from Kentucky, and Richard Russell, Democrat from Georgia; two Congressmen: Gerald R. Ford, Republican from Michigan, and Hale Boggs, Democrat from Louisiana; the former head of the CIA, Allen Dulles; and a New York banker, John J. McCloy, completed the blue-ribbon panel. It remains a monument to Johnson's masterly political skills. Cooper, Ford, and Dulles neutralized the opposition Republican party; McCloy and Dulles reassured the financial-governmental nexus; and Southerners Boggs and Russell blocked any attack from the political right. Warren's acceptance immediately quieted the nation's liberals, especially the Eastern base of Kennedy supporters and university academicians, thereby eliminating from later controversies the single most effective potential sector of dissent to commission procedures and results. Silence and apathy have greeted the entire subject of President Kennedy's murder ever since, among serious scholars generally and with U.S. historians in particular. Even that contemporary critic of federal policy and bureaucracy, I. F. Stone, placed himself well inside lines drawn by Johnson's choice of Warren. The Chief Justice's record for civil liberties and race relations was enough for Stone to "letter-whip" mercilessly the critics of the commission, facts notwithstanding.[9]

Like most federal committees, the Warren Commission worked through its own staff. The seven members, being busy public officials with full-time interests elsewhere, had little time and expertise for the exacting research requisite to a criminal case. They selected a staff of eighty-four and named as chief legal counsel J. Lee Rankin, a former Solicitor General of the United States. The commission did not, however, assemble a body of criminal law specialists, inspectors, and field investigators, choosing instead to rely entirely on several federal agencies, mainly the FBI. This decision to farm out the entire investigation doomed the Warren Commission inquiry from the start. No one at the time dared suggest that an objective inquiry ought, at some point, to include scrutiny of Hoover's FBI. *Quis custodiet ipsos custodes?*[10]

Thus, on 9 December 1963, the Warren Commission laid its inquiry upon the Procrustean bed of the FBI's five-volume report. So anxious was the commission to adhere to the FBI's hasty hodge-podge of data that Hoover's eyes and ears inside the Commission, Congressman Gerald Ford, soon promised a final *Report* for that winter.[11] In fact, those five FBI volumes contained less than 500 words on the murder itself, being almost entirely a psychological profile of Oswald with much biographical detail about his pre-Marine Corps youth. Then the FBI departed from its usual investigatory practice and drew, in effect, a judiciable conclusion: Oswald alone and unaided, for his own political and psychological motives, killed President Kennedy. Such a bold departure from set procedure shocked Rankin, the commission's chief counsel,[12] but his reaction did not prevent him from countenancing this and other revealing prejudgments.

The list of these deliberate official manipulations of evidence is long and has been exposed elsewhere, but several examples urge at least passing notice. The FBI's immediate Oswald fixation extended to the absurdly different ways with which they, and the commission's agents, treated the two widows. Jacqueline Bouvier Kennedy, an eye-and-ear witness to murder if there ever was one, was interviewed for about ten minutes six months afterwards. Marina Oswald, who was diapering daughters in Irving, Texas, when Kennedy died, was put under FBI "house arrest," interrogated for weeks, and then made into a star witness, testifying before news cameras and *in camera*, to the Warren Commission and later congressional committees. Then there were such FBI omissions as one of the bullet wounds on Presi-

dent Kennedy's body, as well as any mention of Tague's wound, both excluded either through imcompetence or by fear that such wounds might
require more than one assassin. In such ways did Hoover fulfill the Katzenbach-
Moyers directive, leaving the Warren Commission to orchestrate it fully and
publicly.

The commission clearly knew of continuing FBI attempts to monopolize
all assassination inquiries. Dallas police and the Texas Attorney General's
office had been firmly, immediately squelched by the FBI, aided by Warren's
personal intervention.[13] Even the Secret Service were left to watch from the
sidelines. Hoover's FBI obsessively sought control, not only occasionally
through Gerald Ford but also in a general climate of trepidation that is now
known to have developed among the commissioners. On 22 January 1964,
the Warren panel held a secret executive session that would surface only
later in a stenotypist's notes:

Dulles:	*. . . Why would it be in their [FBI] interest to say he [Oswald] is clearly the only guilty one? . . .*
[Rankin]:	*They would like to have us fold up and quit.*
Boggs:	*This closes the case, you see. Don't you see?*
Rankin:	*They found the man. There is nothing more to do. The commission supports their conclusions, and we can go on home and that is the end of it. . . .*
Boggs:	*I don't even like to see this being taken down.*
Dulles:	*Yes. I think this record ought to be destroyed.*[14]

The commission's control over its own record, defeated by accidental survival in this instance, did lead to other deliberate suppressions. For one
notorious example, two pages of Senator and Commissioner Russell's
dissent from the lone-assassin theory were expunged, which utterly enraged
the terminally ill Russell when he discovered it.[15]

The Warren Commission's *Report,* then, remains of lingering paradoxical
value. Although its conclusions bear little conviction and less credibility,
it remains an invaluable catalogue for much of the murder case's data, provided that its users see it for what it is: the product of "an investigation
which has satisfied the Commission that it has ascertained the truth concerning the assassination of President Kennedy. . . ."[16] Sadly for the commission's historical status and even more so for the truth itself, such satisfaction has proven contrivedly premature.

What, then, can a citizen know about the murder of President John F.
Kennedy, nearly two decades later?

The past is always knowable only by present evidence, and we now have
much more evidence than the Warren Commission sought, selected, or
considered.[17] For one thing, the sheer quantity of information and opinion
available has created a pressing problem, which this bibliography addresses

in Sections II and III. But this measures only the literary responses during the first sixteen years. Even the most astute inquirer can become lost on the mountain of books, articles, and journalists' reports, all shouting their explanations for the murder into valleys empty of evidence. Unfortunately, most of this has created a cacophony of competing, often contradictory, echoes. Ultimate answers, when available, can be obtained only from the primary evidence, patiently and persistently accumulated. It is for this reason that all readers must first realize, by way of Section I, where most of the documents currently reside and how difficult it has often been, by recourse to federal law courts, to extract that evidence from governmental agencies.[18]

Among academic professionals in our society, historians ought to be the best trained for work with the evidence. They ought to combine reason and skepticism in their comprehensive perspective, in their attempt to put a past man or a past event back together after dissection into parts by economists, lawyers, journalists, psychologists, scientists, litterateurs, moralists, and so on. But scholars generally, and our fellow historians particularly, have remained aloof from problems created by the JFK murder and subsequent investigations. Only the Regius Professor of Modern History at Oxford University, Hugh Trevor-Roper, offered professional scrutiny of Warren Commission documents.[19] Since then, most historians have avoided the entire problem of evidence, accepting the published Warren *Hearings* as the sum total of obtainable data, while reasoned skepticism has been developed mainly by an ex-poultry farmer, several Washington lawyers, a Texas newspaper editor, two university philosophers, and several ex-graduate students.

One reason that serious scholars have absented themselves from the assassination's literature is the Warren *Report*'s preemption of the subject, with its simple verdict against one man "perpetually discontented with the world around him."[20] Rather than closing the case, this verdict openly invited theories of conspiracy. Oswald having been found guilty, the burden of proof shifted so that doubters must first prove Oswald "not guilty." To suggest this would raise the question "if not Oswald, then who did it?" Thus far, the best answer is that audio, ballistics, photographic, and eyewitness evidence gathered by and since the Warren Commission strongly suggests more than one gunman, which is all that the U.S. House Select Committee asserted in December 1978.[21]

Although it takes two or more individuals to make a conspiracy, at least in the eyes of the law, this does not necessarily mean that "more than one gunman" equals a conspiracy in fact. It has been argued that Dealey Plaza that day attracted two or more individuals armed and motivated independently for the same act.[22] Unlikely as this may be, the record of bitter political hatred enveloping places like Dallas in 1963 raises two immediate points: the fact of this violent climate is neutral to the question of conspiracy, but the entire matter remains the unknown, unresearched context for the murder itself. Numerous murder threats against President Kennedy came in the weeks preceding 22 November from groups active in that vicinity: the National States' Rights party, the Minutemen, anti-Castro militants, religious bigots, and other radical paramilitary, racialist organizations. Anti-Kennedy hysteria was hardly limited to Dallas. The president's 2 November visit to Chicago was dropped because of local threats, and then his 18 November motorcade through Miami had to be cancelled at the very last moment for similar reasons.[23] Neither the FBI nor the Warren Commission investigators showed more than routine interest in such coincidences of fact: they were too busy reconstructing a left-wing psychological profile, focused on Oswald.[24]

The specter of some prearranged conspiracy easily haunts the case and its researchers, and it takes only the mere hint of conspiracy to drive most scholars away, into other topics. The word itself connotes a sort of intellectual bankruptcy, at least in the academic world and especially in this murder case, because other suspects have never been named. Explanations based on conspiracy are usually associated with irrational, prejudiced reactions, in sharp contrast to a prosecutor's clear, scientific, dispassionate reconstruction of homicidal fact. But after revelations about the workings of the Ku Klux Klan, American corporations courting Nazi Germany's cartels, Watergate, organized crime, CIA vs. KGB, or effective fabrications like the *Protocols of Zion,* conspiracies seem to strain the modern credibility less.

We are convinced that, in the JFK case, two conspiracies did exist. The first killed Kennedy and the second, conducted by essentially honorable men, has served to subvert and obscure this truth. The first was a conspiracy among individuals as yet unidentified. The second, an institutional conspiracy, grew from that mutually inclusive self-protective, group-protective identity that individuals can be expected to develop as members of any company or bureau. The White House, the FBI, the Justice Department, the Department of State, congressional committees, and even the National Archives, all under siege from public shock and skepticism after 22 November 1963, quietly closed ranks within and among their agencies in order to restore confidence at home and abroad. Such a motive may laudably justify members conspiring to reinforce national institutions, but the result has hardly served the muse Clio's search for truth. We at no time wish to suggest that individuals in any and all agencies conspired among themselves. That would constitute individual conspiracy prosecutable at law. What we do conclude is that members of governmental institutions worked primarily to protect their own agencies and secondarily to sustain confidence in the federal government generally, with only a tertiary concern for solving this murder case.

The literature since Dallas, on the other hand, possesses a uniform impulse to resolve the crime and its attendant mysteries. Yet certain facts may never be known, thanks in large part to the institutional conspiracy begun by

FBI and Warren Commission agents. Why did Oswald go to Mexico City that September? Why did Oswald go to the Texas Theater? Why was no transcript made and preserved from Oswald's twelve and more hours of police interrogation? How did President Kennedy's brain disappear after the Washington autopsy? Did law enforcement officers ever entertain explanations and suspects other than Oswald? We simply have no hard answers, to these and hundreds of other questions, although we now know that witnesses available at the time, who might have aided investigators, were either ignored or rudely rebuffed and a large amount of physical evidence was similarly treated. The impulse to resolve the crime continues in many often over-eager authors and despite so much culpable ignorance of actual evidence.

The assassination's literature can be divided into six categories: (1) works sustaining the official conclusions, (2) works entirely irrational, (3) works riddled with subjectivity and unsubstantiated theory, (4) the exploitative literature, (5) sinister publications, and (6) works focused on evidence about the murder that strive for objectivity.

The first category includes both conventional and psychological works sustaining official conclusions in the Warren *Report.* Conventional accounts, premised on Oswald's guilt from start to finish, include David Belin's *November 22, 1963,* [25] Jim Bishop's *The Day Kennedy Was Shot,* [26] William Manchester's *The Death of a President,* [27] Priscilla McMillan Johnson's *Marina and Lee,* [28] and diverse biographies of the Oswald family, memoirs of leading figures, and several minor studies on physical evidence from the crime. Typical of such articles are those by Dr. John K. Lattimer, a New York urologist,[29] and Professor Luis Alvarez, a California Nobel Laureate in physics.[30] The former, asserting authority in ballistics, proclaimed after studying the Warren Commission autopsy materials that they proved Oswald killed President Kennedy. From X-rays and photographs alone no one can determine who pulled any particular trigger. Lattimer conveniently ignored the bullet(s) associated with the wounding of citizen James T. Tague, evidence which in itself shatters the official findings.[31] Alvarez studied the Zapruder film and asserted that that evidence affirmed official findings of Oswald's sole guilt. He too isolated the object of his study from contextual evidence, ignoring the trees that blocked the first shot, occurring around frame 190, he claimed, and also ignoring Tague.

In psychological studies the authors flee from the world of fact into the mental interstices of figures associated with the murder, mainly the dead Lee Harvey Oswald. These accounts are found mainly in articles, but Renatus Hartogs' and Lucy Freeman's *The Two Assassins*[32] and Robert Thompson's *The Trial of Lee Harvey Oswald,* [33] a screenplay for the American Broadcasting Company, are representative book titles. The former claimed to have "studied" Oswald's fifth-grade report card, which indicated his mental instability and predisposition to kill Kennedy; but they did not present a single fact in critical context to link Oswald to the murder. Thompson converted Jack Ruby into an All-American hero driven by noble motives. The truth, conveniently excised by Thompson and ABC for the illusion, instead shows Ruby to be a "punk pining to be a hood,"[34] consumed by sensuality and crudity.

The titles in the irrational category embrace every conceivable explanation that unbridled imaginations can conjure up. The more outrageous examples include Pat Matteo, *This Captive Land,*[35] in which Kennedy is killed to prevent his escape from a miniature atomic bomb; Thothnu Tastmona, *It Is As If . . . ,*[36] connects the case to origins with the nineteenth-century Mormon leader Brigham Young; and Bernard M. Bane, *Is John F. Kennedy Alive . . . ,*[37] ponders that very question. Sybil Leek, whose credentials include being "a certified witch," wrote with Bert Sugar, *The Assassination Chain,*[38] in which an evil link is found among various political murders. Robert Shea and Robert Anton Wilson, *Illuminatus . . . ,*[39] seek an explanation in ancient Egypt. Neal Wilgus, *The Illuminoids,*[40] finds the Order of the Illuminati, or masonic conspiracy, behind the murder.

The irrational literature typically assumes the conclusions of the Warren Commission to be valid in terms of Oswald's participation, but it seeks larger motives and devices that manipulated his lonesome act. Oswald's guilt is constantly reaffirmed, when it should be questioned as rigorously as any other fact. The irrational publications often appeal to some pseudo-scientific fad in popular thought, like necromancy or astrology, and can usually be found in the supermarket newspapers. Lincoln Lawrence's *Were We Controlled?*[41] even argues that a posthypnotic suggestion triggered radio transmissions operating through a neurological implant in the robot Oswald, causing him to kill Kennedy. William Smith's *Assassination by Consensus*[42] sinks in the same water, arguing that "psychic displacement" operated by a mastermind worked its design through more inferior minds. All of this, of course, drifts well beyond James Bond's world of evil conspiracies into some sort of certifiable madness.

The subjective category includes the literature of those who dissent from the Warren Commission's findings and have tried, at least, to wrestle with problems of evidence pertinent to the murder itself. Such writers do not blindly accept the official version and do show some critical analysis, but their literature remains saddled by theoretical assumptions and their fundamental question puts the who before the what. The prime question, we insist, is still: *what* happened on Dealey Plaza on 22 November 1963? After that factual base comes the question "who shot Kennedy?" We must reluctantly concede that we may never know the answer with reasonable certitude.

This third category, the subjective, can be broken into several subgroups. One theorizes that the murder was the work of the international Communist movement, although proponents often differ as to the methods employed. In Carlos Bringuier's *Red Friday*[43] and in Revilo P. Oliver's series of articles,[44] Oswald is simply a Communist agent. Michael Eddowes, *The Oswald File,*[45] changes the emphasis and baldly asserts that his exhaustive search of all documents proves that JFK's killer was a Soviet fake sent into America to fulfill diabolical ends. All such works beg the two questions that ought to be put first: What is the evidence implicating Oswald? Does any of it connect *any* Oswald to the murder?

Edward Jay Epstein's *Legend*[46] continues to exploit the Oswald theme, modifying it to make him a Soviet agent converted to spying while stationed in Japan. To carry forward this thesis, Epstein ignores his critics as well as nonconforming court records. For example, to make Oswald a defector to his new Soviet masters, Epstein reports that he left London on 9 October 1959 to reach Finland on the 10th. But according to the passport stamps, he actually left London on the 10th and arrived in Finland on the 10th, a feat impossible according to all contemporary commercial airline schedules but not beyond the fertile machinations of American intelligence agencies. Like Bringuier, Oliver, Eddowes, and others, Epstein attempts to hammer into the public mind the assertion without proof that Oswald killed Kennedy.

There is a substantial subgroup of theorists who try to prove, from the other side of the political spectrum, that the CIA killed Kennedy. Michael Canfield and Alan Weberman's *Coup d'Etat,*[47] Fletcher Prouty's *The Secret Team,*[48] and Sid Blumenthal and Harvey Yazijian's *Government by Gunplay*[49] represent this evidence-stretching effort. Aside from numerous factual errors and repeated distortions of evidence, the characteristic feature of this subgroup is their avoidance of the actual murder and of its bungled police investigation. Their hot chase after the CIA chimera is often connected with another subgroup of subjective writers.

Did organized crime kill Kennedy? This theory always had its followers, but beginning in the mid-1970s a series of volumes appeared that purported to find proofs, including those connected to Judith Campbell Exner. Typical expressions are Peter Noyes, *Legacy of Doubt,*[50] Seth Kantor's *Who Was Jack Ruby?,*[51] the Assassination Information Bureau's *Clandestine America,*[52] and Peter Dale Scott's *Crime and Cover-Up.*[53] Organized crime has become America's *"diabolus ex machina,"* released in times of heightened public awareness to explain major crimes and minor social ailments. Elusive, without structure, and without a single body of facts, the accusation nevertheless finds most recent, albeit partial, endorsement in the U.S. House Select Committee on Assassination's *Final Report.*[54]

Still another subgroup in subjectivity makes Chief Justice Earl Warren the malefactor, distorting all evidence to make this wish come true. The two best examples are Edward Jay Epstein's *Inquest*[55] and Mark Lane's *Rush to Judgment.*[56] Presented to the uninformed as a work of dispassionate scholarly dissent, *Inquest* actually upholds the basic findings of the Warren Commission by dismissing its failures as the fault of its chairman, who allegedly went against the findings of his own staff and the FBI. Epstein used FBI reports as well as the files of some staff members in his attack. This brief and fierce polemic actually exculpates Hoover's Bureau, although that may not have been Epstein's intent.

Lane's *Rush to Judgment* provides a classic example of subjective gimmickry, with its scholarly cosmetic of 4,500 footnotes, containing hundreds of substantial errors and repetitions. Quotations within the text have been quietly changed in over two hundred instances from original documentary versions; important material has been excised from the evidence in order to highlight the trivial or to mislead. Ultimately the book charges Warren with the crime of cover-up, while exonerating the FBI. For example, one entire chapter, based on the testimony of Nancy Perrin Rich, who worked in Ruby's night club, pretends proof of an Oswald-Ruby link. Lane never noted that Rich gave three entirely different sets of testimony to investigators, that she suffered several mental breakdowns, and that she had habitually appeared at famous trials offering to testify.[57]

One further subgroup has sifted the facts through a left-wing sieve to conclude that Kennedy died as a result of a right-wing conspiracy. Excellent illustrations of this subjectivity imposed upon reality are: Jim Garrison's *Heritage of Stone,*[58] Mort Sahl's *Heartland,*[59] Carl Oglesby's *Cowboy and Yankee War,*[60] and the later writings of Joachim Joesten.[61] Hugh McDonald, *Appointment in Dallas,*[62] posits a mysterious person lurking in another building who actually shot Kennedy and then framed Oswald as the "patsy" Oswald claimed to be when interrogated. Richard Popkin's *The Second Oswald*[63] plausibly assumes that a man posing as Oswald laid a track of damaging evidence around Dallas in the weeks before the murder. The evidence in no way precludes such an Oswald counterfeit, but Popkin's explanation still rests on acceptance of the Warren Commission's assertion of the real Oswald's role. Popkin more accurately might have entitled his valuable book "The Fake Oswald."

The fourth category, the exploiters, identifies a phenomenon extant since the week of the murder, ranging from the greedy merchants of grief, peddling JFK memorabilia, to the publishing financiers making ceaseless promotions of the official findings. The Warren Commission orchestrated five private publishers for versions of its *Report,*[64] coordinating the official release to make maximum impact and profits. The first exploiters, however, were Kennedy hagiographers who flooded the nation with special-edition newspapers, tabloids, trinkets, commemorative books, and memorial volumes. Reprints, collector's specials, and glossy inserts fell in scores from the national journals and local newspapers, none at reduced prices. *Four Days in November,*[65] assembled by the editors of United Press International and American Heritage Publishing Company, contained lavish color photographs and an inaccurate text. Its sales copies reached into the hundreds of thousands, with additional income derived from their record promotion and a movie spin-off. The entire success story bore the marks of a necrophiliac sell by an advertising agency: a garish, tasteless celebration of sacrificial death. Similar ventures served publishers well in packaging and selling the "martyred" president to the public.

From a long list of the publishing industry's promotional books, *The Death of a President* by William Manchester exemplifies best their impact and the sheer gall of their commercialism.[66] The book is perhaps what Norman Mailer means by "faction," because it certainly is not history based on evidence and professionalism. One promotional tease after another, with a stream of prepublication press releases, was coupled with regular television news coverage once the Kennedys intervened. Despite reviewers and critics who treated it mercilessly, media magic transformed this error-laden volume into a sort of popular truth. In fact, it was little more than a narrative skeleton of the Warren *Report,* fleshed out with numerous insider interviews.

Like wolves among ewes, major publishing houses have indiscriminately worked the entire fold, lavishly also promoting various books by Warren *Report* dissenters. The books by Anson, McDonald, and O'Toole exemplify this, with regional radio and newspaper saturation promising new discoveries and proofs. Hugh McDonald, in *Appointment in Dallas,* claimed to have interviewed the real assassin. His original manuscript had this real assassin hiding in a judge's chambers overlooking Dealey Plaza, but the published book put him at a window in a women's restroom.[67] Similar wizardry reached its most sophisticated exploitation with George O'Toole's *The Assassination Tapes.*[68] The book was actively marketed by the company manufacturing an "evaluator machine," which supposedly measured voice patterns for covert stress to prove that a conspiracy killed Kennedy. With numerous major errors O'Toole employed the faulty machine to test old video and audio tapes of witnesses to conclude that Oswald was framed. Police and sheriffs' departments across the land received advertisements for the instrument that had allegedly solved the crime of the century. But even this is child's play compared with the antics of Mark Lane.

Two books, two films, lectures, records, and articles have kept pace with sixteen years of changing fads in popular consciousness. When initial public skepticism focused on Chief Justice Warren, Lane's *Rush to Judgment* crudely misquoted documents, gave inaccurate footnotes, and skillfully selected facts literally to frame Warren.[69] When Garrison's investigation in New Orleans captured national headlines, Lane adjusted his writings and lectures with broad assertions that he was the district attorney's confidant.[70] At the height of student unrest, Lane staffed a booth at collegiate fairs, pushing his literature and his lecturing services to youthful minds seeking a better world.[71] When exposés of the CIA began piling up in the late 1960s, Lane's articles and speeches discovered that Kennedy had really been killed by the CIA.[72] When political and media winds shifted in the early 1970s against the late J. Edgar Hoover's FBI, Lane found proofs of FBI guilt.[73] This only begins to document Lane as the leading opportunist in the sorry literary history of this murder mystery.

In *A Citizen's Dissent,* Lane alleged that the British Broadcasting Company did not pay him a "single farthing" when, in fact, he had received one of their largest fees, over \$40,000.[74] When he co-produced, with Emile de Antonio, the film version of *Rush to Judgment,* he pirated its sound track, provoking litigation by his irate co-producer.[75] When Lane put Donald Freed to work on a jointly written novel, *Executive Action,*[76] he knew they were exploiting an excellent plot line. Lane had been in New Orleans when the typescript for the James Hepburn book *Farewell America* had been delivered to District Attorney Garrison by Herve Lamarre, a person associated with French intelligence.[77] As of 1975, the filmed version of *Executive Action* had earned \$15,000,000.[78]

Only Lane's initial article, published in December 1963 in the *National Guardian,* written with that weekly's editorial aid, contributed substantially to data publicly available immediately after the murder.[79] But his credibility began to collapse soon after, as he offered himself to any bidder as the instant JFK expert, whether on campus or in Congress. Perhaps in this case the CIA got it right when their secret study of Warren *Report* critics concluded that Lane instinctively went for the capillaries, not the jugular.[80] The CIA obviously saw no adversarial threat from Lane's limited vision and faulty scholarship, but he has served governmental agencies well by obscuring basic evidence, upstaging serious researchers, publicizing tangential issues, and generally avoiding anything that required hard work for no profit and little publicity.[81]

Our fifth category, labeled sinister, includes those publications about the murder that focus on intelligence-gathering agencies and, in some cases, were written under their surreptitious sponsorship. These include Camille Gilles' *400,000 . . . ,* but the foremost example is James Hepburn's *Farewell America,* published in Liechtenstein in 1968, printed in Belgium, and distributed in Canada,[82] but not in the United States, by individuals associated with SDECE, France's CIA. With potential libels on every other page, the author (or authors?) allege collaboration between right-wing oilmen and rogue CIA elements for the Kennedy kill. Commentaries on the book demonstrate little critical awareness and no comprehensive knowledge of the evidence and usually end up embracing the book's assumptions. Warren Hinckle's articles and one chapter in his *If You Have a Lemon . . .* display an intimate knowledge of the book, but the chronology as well as essential facts are in fundamental error.[83]

The works of critics responsible to the evidence and to the truth comprise our final category of Kennedy murder-literature. These authors show knowledge of the complex factual base, the duty to treat the murder objectively and without distraction, and the need to stay free from theoretical distortions. This category can be subdivided between those early authors writing before the official published findings of the Warren Commission and those later researchers who started from the findings and evidence of the commission in launching their studies.

The early writers published a few articles, including the Mark Lane effort noted earlier, and three books: Thomas Buchanan's *Who Killed Kennedy?*,[84] Joachim Joesten's *Oswald: Assassin or Fall Guy*,[85] and Leo Sauvage's *The Oswald Affair*.[86] They remain substantially sound within the context of pre-Warren *Report* materials, and each is based on painstaking research and analytical argument; but all bear the subconscious marks of a pressing controversy and the murder of an uncommon man. They are essential reading for anyone interested in the mystery itself or in the mystery's later history.

After publication of the Warren *Report,* critics produced various articles, short studies and books, the most valuable being the works of Sylvia Meagher, Harold Weisberg, and Howard Roffman. There are also many valuable articles and book reviews in the monthly journal *The Minority of One.* Raymond Marcus published a short monograph *The Bastard Bullet,* which carefully analyzed the Zapruder film and remains a minor classic for its objectivity.[87] Sylvia Meagher's *Subject Index* to the Warren Commission's volumes has given students their essential tool for mastering that wilderness of published evidence.[88] It was her *Accessories after the Fact,* though, that provided a model for scholarly method.[89] It carefully scrutinized the *Report* and the twenty-six volumes, making orderly sense of the chaotic official evidence and providing intelligent, critical commentaries.

Weisberg's *Whitewash,* addressed to the general public, demonstrated that the Warren Commission failed because it accepted unquestioningly the theory, largely manufactured by the FBI, that Oswald killed the president.[90] Weisberg had served in the 1930s as an investigator for a Senate committee uncovering American fascist penetration of the government and Nazi influence in the Americas. During World War II he had been with the Office of Strategic Services and had also worked as an analyst for the State Department. Weisberg coupled this experience with his firm belief that the original documents ought to serve as the base upon which to build an account of the murder.

Weisberg has persisted in his attack, publishing *Whitewash II, Photographic Whitewash, Whitewash IV, Oswald in New Orleans,* and *Post Mortem.*[91] This last volume, published privately as were all but two, gives an unparalleled examination of the evidence relating to the JFK autopsy, with hundreds of pages of documents photographically reproduced. All of this, plus his score of FOIA suits, makes Weisberg the premier authority, and even governmental agents who are most annoyed by him must consult his work.

Roffman's *Presumed Guilty* defined the autopsy and ballistic evidence to show that the commission could not link Oswald to the crime with such evidence, given the questions asked and the techniques that they employed. The metallic fragments inside the president and the fragments of bullets outside his body were not matched, despite the existence of several scientific tests that could have done so conclusively.[92]

The single most important characteristic making these critics responsible is their common goal to define, secure, and expose documentary evidence in this murder case, most of which governmental agencies choose to keep controlled and secret. Much has been accomplished by lawsuits brought under the Freedom of Information Act, mostly by Harold Weisberg and his legal counsel, James H. Lesar. These suits, at the very least, force agencies out of their ordinary cocoons of self-regulating, hence publicly irresponsible, bureaucracy into open legal and judicial accountability. This process has also blocked the destruction or dispersal of countless files and preserved hundreds of cubic feet of basic evidence, to be placed before the public. Section I of our bibliography provides detailed briefs of the sort of litigation required, showing the extraordinary difficulties that federal agencies and bureaucratically supportive federal judges can create for ordinary citizens. One important published example of such documents is David R. Wrone's *Legal Proceedings . . . ,* based on evidence that Federal Civil Action 2052-73 forced from federal files.[93]

In this context of misplaced bureaucratic self-preservation, no one ought to be surprised to learn that the latest congressional reopening of the JFK murder case ignored much of the mass of materials compiled outside of Warren Commission evidence. The House Select Committee on Assassinations paid virtually no attention to evidence brought into the public domain by Freedom of Information Act litigation and shunned contact with responsible critics. Their entire investigation showed a marked preference for a selection of highly visible witnesses rather than for the documentary evidence and those few experts who know it best. We therefore must conclude our remarks with a brief analysis of this most recent official report on President Kennedy's death.

On 22 July 1979, after a six-month delay, the House Select Committee on Assassinations issued the *Final Report* of its two-year investigation into the murders of President John F. Kennedy and Dr. Martin Luther King, Jr. The 686-page paperback official printing is divided into five parts: Part I contains 261 pages on the murder of Kennedy; Part II has 250 pages on the murder of King; Part III is twenty pages of recommendations; Part IV is thirty pages of separate remarks by committee members, including the important dissent by Rep. Christopher Dodd; and Part V is 171 pages of appendices and references.[94]

One week prior to official publication, G. Robert Blakey, chief counsel for the HSCA, gave the Bantam Publishing Company an exclusive advance copy and received $3,000 from them to write a fifteen-page introduction for their printing of the *Final Report*.[95] In July, the government completed their publication of the remaining twenty-seven volume appendix to the HSCA *Final Report*. Twelve volumes concern the Kennedy murder, thirteen volumes pertain to the killing of King, and two volumes focus on legislative and administrative reforms. None of the volumes is indexed, and only brief word-clues on the face of each suggest the contents to the reader.

The HSCA's *Final Report* and its twelve volumes of Kennedy documentation are blatantly, yet curiously, inconsistent with the final conclusion endorsing a conspiracy in Dallas. If anything, the bulk of their testimony and evidence remains true to the HSCA's originally stated purpose, to make the Warren *Report* "persuasive."[96] But then, as if in a mere afterthought to several sections of the *Final Report,* the reader is urged to reject the Warren *Report*'s cornerstone: Oswald, the lone assassin.

Obviously, the HSCA had gone public at the last moment over the audio evidence confirming a front gunman facing Kennedy. In fact, it was Warren *Report* critics Mary Ferrell, Gary Mack, and Penn Jones, Jr., who brought the tape and other data to the attention of the HSCA.[97] Another critic,, Robert Groden, painstakingly located a key witness for the HSCA staff.[98] This not only exemplifies the level of the HSCA's competence as researchers but also its refusal to follow its congressional mandate to investigate the performance of earlier federal investigators. In 1964 the FBI claimed to have studied certain audio tapes and to have found no pertinent evidence on them.[99] The Warren Commission even printed versions of them.[100] Apparently no HSCA member or staff investigators thought to question the FBI on this fundament for conspiracy.

Instead, the *Final Report* reassured its readers that *"the Warren Commission conducted a thorough and professional investigation into the responsibility of Lee Harvey Oswald for the assassination."*[101] It then proceeded to knock down several "strawmen" theories left and right, at rather tiresome length, most of which we have noted in our categories of the irrational, subjective, exploitative, and sinister literature. So it was that sideshow dramas about "the umbrella man" and the Soviet-substituted, Oswald look-alike were demolished in a fanfare of media publicity from Capitol Hill. Yet, at crucial points in the *Final Report*, the HSCA would have us turned halfway around from the Warren *Report* to embrace the suggestion of "more than one gunman!"

In such bewildering circumstances, it is appropriate for us to examine briefly some key elements in the official explanations, now mainly updated from the Warren *Report* by the HSCA for 1979. We must limit attention to several vital parts of this official case and the ways it uses and abuses evidence. We are not in the business of exculpating anyone, including Oswald. Rather, we wish only to measure the present HSCA's case by the total evidence available. We will examine seven points here.

First, with regard to the JFK autopsy report, the HSCA's *Final Report* states:

> The secrecy that surrounds the autopsy proceedings, therefore, has led to considerable skepticism toward the Commission's findings. Concern has been expressed that authorities were less than candid, since the Navy doctor in charge of the autopsy conducted at Bethesda Naval Hospital destroyed his notes. . . .[102]

This is not true. The problem began with the fact that the Warren Commission used a second draft, not the original autopsy report. The Navy doctor, J. J. Humes, burned the first autopsy protocol immediately after Oswald's murder by Ruby. That death eliminated the need for a trial, his testimony and cross-examination. The second draft was later changed, then modified again in the offices of a Navy admiral. The Warren Commission then masked the destruction of this original document by asserting that Humes' notes had been burned. In fact, the doctor destroyed his holographic draft, but he turned in his second draft, along with his notes, to federal agencies. These notes then disappeared, but the actual chain of evidence remains for anyone desiring to see it.

On Sunday, 24 November 1963, Humes executed two certificates. One stated that he had burned preliminary draft notes. The other, addressed to Captain J. H. Stover, his Commanding Officer, stated in part: "Autopsy notes and the holograph draft (i.e., the second one) of the final report were handed to Commanding Officer . . . at 1700, 24 November 1963."[103] The next day, Admiral Galloway, Commanding Officer, National Naval Medical Center, transmitted by hand to Admiral George C. Burkley, Physician to the President, the protocol and "the work papers in the case of John F. Kennedy," recording this transaction with a memorandum.[104] On 26 November, Robert Bouck of the Secret Service accepted this from Burkley, signing a receipt for the "autopsy report and notes of the examining doctor which is described in a letter of transmittal Nov. 25, 1963, by Dr. Gallaway *[sic]*."[105] Here the record of the chain of possession ends, and these vital notes disappear from history. Humes however testified in 1964 before the Warren Commission that: "In the privacy of my own home, early in the morning of Sunday, November 24, I made a draft of this report. . . . That draft I personally burned. . . ."[106] The commission ignored the destruction and preferred to cover up the disappearance; HSCA did the same.

This leads to the related matter of the HSCA's false assertion that ". . . neither the members of the Warren Commission, nor its staff, nor the doctors who performed the autopsy, took advantage of the X-rays and photographs of the president that were taken during the course of the autopsy.[107] This claim goes back to the Warren Commission's lone-assassin theory, which required that the alleged three bullets all came from behind and high to the right; one of them missing, one passing through Kennedy and Connally inflicting seven wounds, and the last shattering Kennedy's skull.[108] The single bullet that inflicted so many wounds had to have penetrated the president's body at a steep-enough angle to exit at his necktie knot and continue downward to hit Connally near his armpit. The commission had put the entry hole at the back of Kennedy's neck; but the HSCA found that the bullet hole in the autopsy was actually where various critics, particularly Weisberg and Roffman, had said it was: in the back.[109] To reconcile their contradiction of the Warren Commission's version, the HSCA concocted the tale of ignorance just quoted.

Again, the chain of evidence puts the lie to all of this. The Warren Commission and its staff did have access to the X-rays, photographs, and other documentary evidence that placed the bullet entry hole on the back and too low to enable the single bullet to transit two bodies and cause seven wounds. In the minutes of the executive session of 27 January 1964, Chief Counsel J. Lee Rankin informed the members of the commission: ". . . it seems quite apparent now, since we have the picture of where the bullet entered in the back, that the bullet entered below the shoulder blade to the right of the backbone. . . ."[110] On 21 June 1966, the Secret Service issued an untitled press release that stated in part: "The X-ray films were used for the briefing of the Warren Commission's staff on the autopsy procedure and results."[111] Secret Service Chief Tom Kelley, then an Inspector, told Harold Weisberg that he had shown the films to the staff.[112] Staff member Arlen Specter stated, in an interview with *U.S. News & World Report* on 10 October 1966 that: "I was shown one picture of the back. . . ."[113] In another interview, this time with Joseph Whalen, the biographer of President Kennedy's father, Specter admitted that he had seen the autopsy films at the time.[114] Why should the HSCA try to bury all of this?

The third, and related, illustration is the falsification of the description of President Kennedy's shirt collar. The "slits" on his shirt collar may appear to be of minor significance, but in fact they are a major part of the simple and concrete evidence. In order to embrace the single-bullet theory, the Warren Commission as well as the HSCA had to prove that the bullet that transited the president's neck proceeded on a steep-enough downward angle to line up with the governor's back wound. Only by lowering the exit wound to the level of the necktie knot could that downward angle fit their preconceived solution for the transit. The slightest variation in angle will completely negate the commission's attempt to tie the lone assassin and his hardworking single bullet to the murder. The HSCA, too, put all of its argument on this line.

The HSCA's team of medical specialists described the president's shirt collar through which the bullet had to pass, in order to hit the governor's back, in this manner:

> Examination of the shirt reveals a slit-like defect in the upper left front portion, 1.4 centimeters below the topmost buttonhole. This defect measures 1.4 centimeters in length, with its long axis parallel to the long axis of the body. There is a corresponding slit-like defect 1.5 centimeters below the center of the button on the right. This defect measures 1.5 centimeters in length and is also parallel to the long axis of the body (See fig. 3, a photograph of the shirt)[115]

All of this will, of course, sustain the single-bullet theory and its requisite transit, as intended. The photograph of the shirt collar, however, was taken from fifteen feet away, rendering it indistinct, perhaps also as intended.

That slit below the buttonhole is indeed parallel to the long axis of the body, but it also extends halfway into the neckband. The slit on the button side is perpendicular to the body axis and below the seam of the neckband and shirt, much closer to the edge than the other. The primary problem is that the slits do not coincide when the shirt is buttoned! Moreover, these slits were devoid of any traces of metal typically found when a bullet passes through cloth.[116] In fact, these slits were made by the Parkland Hospital emergency room staff in Dallas following surgical procedures by which they hurriedly but deftly cut away the shirt with scalpels. The attending physician, Dr. Charles James Carrico, and the duty nurse verified that this is precisely what they did.[117] Carrico testified to the Warren Commission that the bullet hole in the throat was above the shirt collar. When asked by Commission member Dulles to demonstrate where, precisely, the wound was, Carrico pointed it out on his own body, and Dulles responded: "I see. And you put your hand right above where your tie is?"[118] Needless to say, the resultant angle renders the single-bullet theory inoperable and demolishes the official case on this point.

Fourth, the HSCA *Final Report* reasserted the Warren *Report*'s claim that Oswald's palm print was found on the stock of the rifle discovered on the sixth floor of the Texas School Book Depository building.[119] But the HSCA omitted the fact that the print had been mailed into FBI headquarters by the Dallas police days after the rifle had left Dallas for laboratory testing; the Dallas officer who lifted the print from the stock refused point-blank to execute an affidavit for the Warren Commission stating where the print had originated.[120]

Fifth, the Warren Commission had claimed that Oswald carried the disassembled rifle into the building in a paper sack found on the sixth floor near the alleged scene of the crime.[121] An array of scientific data was then mustered to prove that "several" fibers discovered on the sack came from a blanket found among Oswald's possessions in a garage where the rifle was allegedly stored. The rifle "could have picked up the fibers from the blanket and transmitted them to the paper bag" but the commission, as well as HSCA's clear assertion of its findings, did not report the fact that the Dallas police took no precautions at all to keep the several articles of evidence from coming into contact with each other prior to examination.[122] Likewise, the HSCA simply eliminated the testimony of Book Depository employee Dougherty, who waited just inside the building's entrance that morning and emphatically swore that Oswald entered empty-handed.[123] Furthermore, to assert that the sack could accommodate the disassembled rifle parts is to contravene the sack's linear measurement.[124] To charge that Oswald's fingerprints were on the empty sack proves nothing. Oswald worked on the sixth floor during preceding weeks; his prints ought to be there and elsewhere. What the HSCA did not report is the fact that the fingerprints of police officers who picked up the sack and carelessly handled it did not appear when it was tested,[125] which surely suggests something about their testing procedures.

Sixth, the HSCA Final Report repeated the Warren *Report*'s conclusion that Oswald fired three shots, two of which had to occur prior to the movement of the presidential limousine behind the Stemmons' Street sign in the Zapruder film, at frame 210. The shot that they state was fired "at about frames 188-191" is the bullet that is said to have caused seven wounds on two men.[126] No mention is made of the live oak trees in front of the Book Depository that blocked the vision of any sniper from that alleged lair between Zapruder frames 170 and 210.[127] Frames 188-191, then, could arguably even eliminate Oswald, or anyone else, firing from that particular location at that particular point in time. Obviously this would require the presence of another assassin, or other assassins, firing from another location, or other locations, at that very same time. Once again, we are forced to wonder at the methods and purposes of the recent HSCA investigation.

Seventh, the omission of James T. Tague from the *Final Report,* as well as from the twelve volumes and the entire investigation, sufficiently discredits the HSCA's commitment to truth. Incredibly, such an extensive congressional probe did not call as a witness, nor even investigate, one of the victims of the crime. The *Final Report* does not even mention his name.[128] Just thirty minutes from HSCA's staff offices, on Judiciary Square, there are innumerable legal records from the FBI's testing of the material dug from the curbstone hit that caused citizen Tague to bleed that day.[129] Did it not seem important to official investigators, in 1964[130] and 1978, to know where exactly Tague stood, the location of his wound, and the whereabouts of later photographs that he took of all of this? That curbstone, apparently struck by one of the bullets, is now in the National Archives, with the shattered area neatly plastered over.[131] After someone had tidied up that bit of primary evidence, the FBI subsequently cleaned its files of key analytical reports on the curbstone itself.[132]

As if these seven points are not enough to undermine confidence in the HSCA's recent investigation, several additional and more general observations must be made. The most obvious failure is the congressional refusal to make an honest inquiry into the FBI's role in the original probe, which is all the more serious if we recall the Warren Commission's own misgivings about FBI pressures. It is compounded by the fact that the FBI controlled all security clearances for Warren Commission and HSCA staff and consultants. Perhaps a few more examples of the FBI's curious ways with the evidence will suffice.

Mrs. R. E. Arnold, in a handwritten statement for the FBI, stated that she saw Oswald on the first floor at about 12:25 P.M., which is five minutes before the gunshots and over ten minutes after an armed figure was seen on the upper floors by outside witnesses. When the FBI typed her original statement, the time changed to 12:15.[133]

Several score prisoners crowded the windows of the top floor of the Dallas Criminal Courts Building to view the motorcade. What they saw, from perhaps the best vantage point in the entire Dealey Plaza, had urgent value to any investigation of the murder, but their attempts to submit testimony to what they saw were firmly turned away. When at least one prisoner pressed the matter through his attorney, the FBI returned his request to testify that he saw two men in the alleged sniper's lair, none of them fitting the description of Oswald, with the annotation "not pertinent."[134]

Akin to this is the example of Charles Bronson, who took slides and motion pictures of the assassination. He made his film and slides available to the FBI on Monday, 25 November 1963. The FBI viewed them promptly, after the Eastman Kodak Company finished processing them in Dallas, and evaluated them. The FBI Special Agents said the pictures were "not sufficiently clear" for identification purposes and "these films failed to show the building from which the shots were fired." In 1978 Earl Golz of the *Dallas Morning News* and Gary Mack of Ft. Worth radio station KFJZ located Bronson, who made the pictures available to photographic experts and to a reluctant HSCA. The film clearly shows the Texas School Book Depository and what appears to be two figures in the windows of the alleged sniper's lair.[135]

This leads us to a final observation about the FBI in the context of the HSCA's recent investigation, specifically with regard to the case against Oswald. Some relationship clearly existed between the two in New Orleans between May and September 1963. For example, the FBI never at any point told anyone associated with the official investigation of Kennedy's killing that the address Oswald stamped on his New Orleans literature[136] was the same address used by an anti-Castro group and coincidentally as well by a close associate of the FBI. Oswald used 544 Camp, which was one side of the same corner building having the dual address of 531 LaFayette.[137] The anti-Castro Cubans worked out of offices at 544 Camp, while a certain Guy Banister kept an office at 531 LaFayette. By May 1963, Banister was a freelance detective and former FBI agent, maintaining close contact with local FBI ex-colleagues. The unpublished record, which was muddied by Garrison's grand inquisition, did establish the meetings held in Banister's office with the anti-Castro groups. David Ferrie, a shadowy figure in right-wing fringe groups around New Orleans, also met with such groups and had a "close" relationship with Banister.[138] These anti-Castro groups operated as paramilitary units, no doubt waiting for the next invasion call. Whether connected specifically to them or not, Banister also acted in certain gun-smuggling projects in and outside New Orleans.[139] The FBI reported none of the Banister associations to the Warren investigators, and the HSCA discounted the entire topic by invoking a sort of devil theory that made "organized crime" the culprit.[140]

The FBI also never reported or explained the appearance in Oswald's address book of three nonexistent addresses.[141] Some have suggested that these may possibly relate to intelligence connections, as coded locations. In addition, the FBI never identified the person associated with Oswald at several handbill operations in New Orleans, when the two openly circulated pro-Castro literature. These Oswald activities were recorded on the films by Martin, Doyle, WWL, and WDSU-TV.[142] The FBI privately examined all of the films but managed, for some inexplicable reason, to excise, blur, and modify those portions that showed Oswald's associate.[143] Finally, the FBI never identified the "other" person's fingerprint, only Oswald's, on the handbill or flyer they passed around on the Dumaine Wharf.[144] Obviously the entire tale remains to be told, but we believe that Oswald's New Orleans adventures will provide keys to future doors. For that reason, we have supplied a map that identifies some of Oswald's known locations in New Orleans during the four months prior to his fatal move to Dallas.

While much of this account remains circumstantial, coincidental, and covert, there are also some substantial links between Oswald and the CIA still overlooked in the latest official study by the HSCA. The ex-Attorney General Nicholas Katzenbach testified before the HSCA, with regard to political assassinations generally, that "whenever they [CIA] wanted a book suppressed they came to me and I told them not to do it."[145] Tenuous as this undoubtedly is, it at least suggests a CIA working-interest, an exerted control in the unfolding tragedy of U.S. political assassinations that began anew in 1963. Their desire to control aspects of such stories within domestic news media and publishing houses at that time is now so well exposed as to require no further comment. With specific reference to the case against Oswald, the former CIA Director Allen Dulles, a Warren Commission member, secretly met with the CIA officials to help them prepare for the commission's questions and to suggest to them how they could limit responses concerning Oswald.[146] The CIA also withheld crucial photographic intelligence from the commission in 1964, after secretly obtaining a print of the Zapruder film and submitting it quietly to the National Photographic Interpretation Center for technical analysis. That study found that shots occurred at times which excluded Oswald as a *lone* assassin.[147] None of this critical information ever came before the Warren Commission but although it surfaced in the Rockefeller Commission's investigation of the CIA, reported in 1975, the point conveniently sank without trace and remained submerged for the HSCA's study.[148]

We remain painfully aware of the ignorance that still surrounds this murder case. We reluctantly must assert, after a careful study of the HSCA's *Final Report,* that this most recent official version does not satisfy the need for a thorough inquiry into *what* happened that day in Dallas. It does, however, mark a major erosion in this case among federal agencies. Perhaps in time the HSCA's halting endorsement of a probable conspiracy will be seen as excessive scrupulosity rather than political timidity. Their *Report* takes a first official step away from the Warren *Report,* and we hope that the next step will be into the context of the case, to explain how every major institution, except for the federal judiciary, has failed to meet its subsequent obligation to the American public in this case.

While the media became mainly docile mouthpieces for officialdom, our legislative and executive branches were showing themselves manifestly unable to investigate themselves, much less the killing of a president. Only our federal law courts, with their adversary procedure and the Freedom of Information Act, have permitted the citizenry to break through deliberate clouds of official obfuscation. No one dares gainsay the special role that their decisions have played, in most cases, for the freeing of this murder mystery from bureaucratic bondage. Future scholars will owe their first debt to the access to the evidence that federal judges and private litigants have forced.

We are confident that more affirmative answers will some day emerge to the questions of what happened and who did it. Only the full primary evidence, once it emerges into the light of day, will provide a systematic map for the road back from Dallas. When that happens, the United States can again realize the meaning in its motto on the reverse side of its Great Seal: *Annuit Coeptis.*[149]

NOTES

1. *See* [102, 684].
2. *See* [85], p. 1.
3. *See* [79, 80], and especially [80], p. 329, *"The Warren Commission conducted a thorough and professional investigation into the responsibility of Lee Harvey Oswald for the assassination."*

4. William R. Corson, *The Armies of Ignorance: The Rise of the American Intelligence Empire* (New York: Dial, 1977).

5. *See* [2].

6. *See* [91].

7. *See* [85], p. 23.

8. *See* [531], p. 358.

9. *See* [745, 877].

10. Who will investigate the investigators?

11. *See The New York Times* [3392].

12. *See* [110], p. 234.

13. *See* [571] and the Dallas documents reproduced in [109], pp. 13, 141-65.

14. *See* [110], p. 236, and also in [973], pp. 486-87.

15. *See* [109], pp. 131-32, where the faked pages are photographically reproduced, and [110], pp. 109-10.

16. *See* [684], p. 18.

17. The Warren Commission's nine months and fifteen million dollar budget produced 300 cubic feet of paper, now in the National Archives, Washington, D.C. Secondary writers such as David Belin [699], Priscilla Johnson McMillan [2423], Jim Bishop [2160], and Alfred Newman [726] do not stray from official explanations because they rely entirely and credulously on Warren Commission evidence.

18. For example, beyond Warren Commission evidence, 500 cubic feet of FBI files are relevant, especially from its Dallas and New Orleans offices, along with hundreds of cubic feet each from other official agencies, private investigators, FOIA litigants, and state or local records.

19. *See* [389, 719, 882-84].

20. *See* [684], p. 423.

21. *See* [80], pp. 104-9; [735], pp. 333-39.

22. *See* [880], where Thompson posits three; Congressmen Samuel Devine and Robert Edgar of the HSCA raised this possibility in their separate views [80], p. 651.

23. *See* the Thomas Vallee file in CD 149, especially the 10 December 1964 report; the Joseph Adams Milteer documents, NA, are partially reproduced in Weisberg, *Frame Up* (New York: Outerbridge & Dienstfrey, 1971), pp. 468-88.

24. *See* the letter of 23 July 1964 from J. Edgar Hoover to J. Lee Rankin, General Counsel WC, CD No. 1286, which in part states: "Regarding your request concerning the John Birch Society and 'Minutemen,' this is to advise this Bureau did not conduct any investigation of those organizations or its members in the State of Texas during 1963." This is disingenuous, to say the least, because the FBI had many research reports on file for John Birch Society members and Minutemen members threatening the life of Kennedy; for example, file 1107, pp. 1055-56 and file CR 301, p. 315.

25. *See* [699].

26. *See* [2160].

27. *See* [2026].

28. *See* [418].

29. *See* [936-92].

30. *See* [1081].

31. *See* the background to Lattimer's articles as well as additional critique in [973], pp. 386-402, and [993, 999].

32. *See* [382].

33. *See* Robert E. Thompson, *The Trial of Lee Harvey Oswald* (New York: Ace Books, 1977).

34. Interview with Harold Weisberg, June 1978, based on his extensive interviews and documentary research.

35. *See* [2194].

36. *See* [2220].

37. *See* [2157].

38. *See* [1725]. Columnist Jack Anderson praised the volume for its objectivity and insights *[sic]* and wrote a blurb for the introduction.

39. *See* [2628].

40. *See* [2636].

41. *See* [1723].

42. *See* [2218].

43. *See* [1890].

44. *See* [1488, 1490, 1496, 3498].

45. *See* [2168]. The HSCA's treatment of this book from several scientific perspectives is sound; *see* [79], vol. 8.

46. *See* [381]; 18 H 162, 26 H 32.

47. *See* [1774].

48. *See* [1780].

49. *See* [1717].

50. *See* [2202].

51. *See* [2480].

52. *See* [307].

53. *See* [1781].

54. *See* [80], p. 222.

55. *See* [703].

56. *See* [719].

57. *See* [2485] and Garry Wills, "A Word for the Warren Commission," *The Washington Star,* 1 May 1975, p. A-5.

58. *See* [1894].

59. *See* [1899].

60. *See* [1732].

61. *See* [2182-83].

62. *See* [2188].

63. *See* [727].

64. *See* [688-95] and *The New York Times* [3739-94].

65. *See* [1539].

66. *See* [2026].

67. *See* [2188]; copy of original manuscript in Harold Weisberg "McDonald" files; *see* [30].

68. *See* [2203]. An example of his factual errors is his reference on page 35 to the original and final autopsy reports. Actually there were not two but five different versions; *see* [973].

69. *See* [719].

70. *See* [1915, 1931, 1800].

71. Interviews with student leaders, Madison, Wisconsin, by David R. Wrone.

72. *See* [1800].

73. Merrill Perlman, *The Southern Illinoian,* "Lane . . . ," January 1976, is representative of many reports of his campus speeches. Lane said: "Oswald and Jack Ruby, the man who killed Oswald, were both FBI agents."

74. *See* [718]. *See* "Television Hired Film Agreement No. HF 9981," 23 November 1966, BBC; correspondence in [23], *The New York Times* [4102]. Another example of the numerous errors is found in footnote 19, page 14. The footnote reads: "See index to Basic Source Materials in possession of Commission, National Archives." This is false. The greatest single impediment to JFK research in the National Archives is the total lack of any index. The cited material actually appears in facsimile reproduction in [532], p. 39, which obviates the use of a finding note.

75. *See* [23] and the folders on the film contained there.

76. *See* [2607].

77. *See* [1899]. Interviews with Bernard Fensterwald, Jim Garrison and Harold Weisberg. Weisberg was in Garrison's office the day Lamarre first called on the district attorney.

78. *The New York Post,* 8 December 1977.

79. *See* [421].

80. *See* [2].

81. A basic article is: Bob Katz, "Mark Lane: The Left's Leading Hearse-Chaser," *Mother Jones* 4 (August 1979): 22-32.

82. *See* [2172]; several critics have received copies of untitled typescripts and letters that appear to have intelligence origins; *see* [1776], interviews with critics, including one who viewed the film version and spoke with the person called Lamarre at SDECE offices in Paris, conducted by David R. Wrone.

83. *See* [1797, 1895].

84. *See* [527].

85. *See* [383].

86. *See* [728, 729].

87. *See* [972].

88. *See* [697].

89. *See* [722].

90. *See* [735].

91. *See* [532, 1075, 736, 1901, 973].

92. *See* [389].

93. *See* [110].

94. *See* [80]; Assistant Public Printer, C. A. LaBarre, in letter of 23 October 1979, to David R. Wrone, states 12,333 copies were printed; of [79], JFK appendix volumes, the following numbers were printed: 1:5099; 2:5380; 3:5299; 4:5349; 5:5808; 6:5513; 7:5411; 8:5439; 9:5210; 10:5692; 11:5340; 12:5262.

95. *The Washington Post,* 19 July 1979.

96. *See* [70, 71] and the interview with Congressman Richardson Preyer, chairman of the subcommittee on the assassination of John F. Kennedy, appearing in *The New York Times* [5062].

97. In Penn Jones, Jr., *The Continuing Inquiry* [308], 22 August 1977, Mack summarized his study of Ferrell's original discovery. The HSCA hired the prestigious scientific testing film of Bolt, Beranek & Newman to analyze the audio tape. This firm reported that their study of the tape proved inconclusive. In March 1978 the original, badly worn dictabelt plus a good copy of it surfaced in Dallas. The HSCA decided to restrict the location and number of tests performed in Dealey Plaza to the north grassy knoll and the Texas School Book Depository. On 11 September, Bolt, Beranek & Newman reported a fifty-fifty chance of a grassy knoll gunshot. On 28 December, Mark Weiss and Ernest Aschkenasy, acoustical experts using more refined techniques, appeared before the HSCA and demonstrated a 95 percent probability for the north grassy knoll gunshot. But they had not been permitted to perform their tests at locations on Dealey Plaza other than with respect to the north grassy knoll. A majority of the HSCA accepted their findings and ignored the implications of the unfinished task.

98. Interview with Robert Groden, by David R. Wrone.

99. *See* CE 1974, 23 H 832-940, with no reference to other versions.

100. There were three *different* versions of the tapes introduced into evidence: CE 1974, 23 H 832-940; Sawyer Exhibits A and B, 21 H 388-400; CE 705, 17 H 361-494.

101. *See* [80], p. 329.

102. *See* [80], p. 32.

103. J. J. Humes, CERTIFICATE, 24 November 1963, to Captain J. H. Stover, WC Records NA, reproduced in [973], p. 525; 17 H 47.

104. Admiral Galloway, Commanding Officer, National Naval Medical Center, to George C. Burkley, White House Physician, Memorandum 25 November 1963, WC Records NA, reproduced in [973], p. 526.

105. Receipt, Robert I. Bouck, Secret Service, 26 November 1963, WC Records NA, reproduced in [973], p. 527.

106. 2 H 373; confirmed by J. J. Humes, CERTIFICATE, 24 November 1963, 17 H 48, and in WC Records NA, holograph approval on certificate by Admiral George Burkley, Physician to the President, reproduced in [973], p. 524. Five versions of the autopsy existed: the burned original; the holograph second with "GGB" initials on the margin in two places is in WC Records NA and reproduced in [973]; pp. 509-23; the holograph copy *sans* initials is in WC volumes as CE 397, 17 H 30-44; the holographic alterations of the second draft, CE 397; and the final printed copy which differs slightly, CE 387, 16 H 979-983.

107. *See* [80], p. 41.

108. *See* [80], pp. 34-38.

109. *See* [79], vol. 7.

110. *See* [110], p. 212.

111. *See* [973], p. 555.

112. "Kelley" file, Weisberg Archives.

113. *See* [447].

114. "Whalen" file, Weisberg Archives.

115. *See* [79], p. 89.

116. *See* [973], p. 353.

117. 6 H 136, 139, 21 H 203-204; interview of Weisberg with Carrico, [973], pp. 358, 375-76.

118. 3 H 361-362.

119. *See* [80], p. 49.

120. *See* [735], pp. 73, 79-84; [532], pp. 38-39.

121. *See* [389], pp. 151-174.

122. *See* [389], p. 171; CE 738; Warren *Report,* p. 137.

123. 6 H 376-377.

124. *See* [389], p. 173.

125. *See* [735], p. 62.

126. *See* [801], p. 87.

127. *See* [735], pp. 97-109.

128. *See* [80], p. 71.

129. *See* [165, 168].

130. The WC paid no attention to the curbstone until 7 July 1964; testimony and depositions from eyewitnesses and Tague appear in the 26 volumes, e.g., 21 H 474, 17 H 547, and 15 H 699, and in its *Report,* p. 116. The staff and the FBI took extreme care to obfuscate the *Report*-destroying implications of the evidence. The FBI did not mention the Tague shot in its five-volume report to the commission on 9 December 1963, CD 1 [91].

131. One of the pictures, snapped by professional journalist Tom Dillard on 22 November 1963 appears in Shaneyfelt Exhibit 29, 21 H 479; the patched curb is in the NA available for public viewing.

132. *See* [168].

133. *See* the discussion in [389], pp. 184-87. As Roffman notes, p. 276, even the FBI modification removes Oswald from the scene of the crime and demolishes the official findings. "The Warren Commission stated in its Report that it knew of no Book Depository employee who claimed to have seen Oswald between 11:55 and 12:30 on the day of the assassination. This was false, as . . . the FBI report [on Mrs. Arnold] from the commission's files reveals. The [Warren] Report never mentions Mrs. Arnold. . . ."

134. Earl Golz, *Dallas Morning News,* 26 November 1978.

135. Ibid., DFO 89-43-493.

136. According to Secret Service Agent A. E. Gerrets, 22 H 828.

137. *See* the photograph of the now demolished building in [1893] and the discussions of the organizations frequenting it in [1901]; *see map 4.*

138. *See* [1901] for discussion, particularly at pp. 327-48. Haynes Johnson of *The Washington Star,* a Pulitzer Prize-winning reporter with many informants among the Cuban leaders, is the source for the Banister intimacy with the anti-Castro associate, Ferrie; *see* [1901], pp. 329-30.

139. *See* [1901], especially pp. 329, 351; Haynes Johnson, *The Washington Star,* 26 February 1967, front page.

140. An illustration of the deception practiced by the FBI is found in WC file 75, folio 683, where FBI Agent Ernest C. Wall, Jr., reported on 25 November 1963:

> GUY BANISTER, Guy Banister Associates, Inc., 531 Lafayette Street, New Orleans, was telephonically contacted on November 25, 1963, and advised that SERGIO ARCACHA SMITH of the Cuban Revolutionary Council, who was the head of that organization in New Orleans, Louisiana, some time ago, had told him on one occasion that he, SMITH, had an office in the building located at 544 Camp Street. Mr. BANISTER stated that he had seen a young Cuban man with SMITH on a number of occasions in the vicinity of 544 Camp Street, but could not recall the name of this young man.

See [1901], p. 331.

141. The book is found in 16 H 67; the addresses are partially discussed in [1901], p. 79; *see* map of New Orleans; research in New Orleans by David R. Wrone.

142. Based on files assembled by Weisberg as well as his affidavits submitted in FOIA Civil Action No. 78-420 [181].

143. Tourists who filmed the Canal Street operation informed Harold Weisberg of this, as did persons associated with the filming of the Trade Mart operation. Their interviews, e.g., Patrick Doyle's, are in his files. His research was utilized in his affidavits in Civil Action No. 78-420 [181]. These references, plus the film itself, plus the viewing of the film by journalist Earl Golz, demonstrate a change was made. For example, the Doyle film was returned with many frames missing and on a different commercial film base than used by Doyle; the edges of the film depicting the associate which appeared originally as clear and distinct are now blurred, and so forth. *See* [181].

144. Document released to Weisberg as a result of his Privacy Act request. The FBI processing blurred the finding number, but the serial number is NO 100 16601 and the report is dated 10/19/70.

145. *See* [79], vol. 3, p. 663.

146. CIA Document No. 657-831. *See* [2]. Reproduced with discussion in [1075], pp. 304-10, 312.

147. *See* [1075], pp. 295-304, where the few pages of the study released are reproduced. The Warren Commission clearly knew of the National Photographic Interpretation Center and its reputation for excellence, but the commission did not seek their aid. Had it done so, and if the CIA's commissioned project can be trusted, then the single-assassin theory would have suffered serious damage.

148. It never appeared in the report submitted by the Rockefeller Commission [101] but was the subject of a staff inquiry: *see* [1075], p. 295.

149. He has favored our undertakings: from Virgil, *Aeneid,* 9. 625.

Abbreviations

ACLU	American Civil Liberties Union
CD	Commission Document (in WC Records, NA)
CE	Commission Exhibit (in WC Records, NA)
CIA	Central Intelligence Agency
CJ	Chief Justice
CR	Congressional Record
FBI	Federal Bureau of Investigation
FOIA	Freedom of Information Act
H	Volume in the twenty-six volumes of *Hearings before the President's Commission* appendix to the Warren *Report* often cited as 24 H 425 or volume 24, page 425.
HSCA	House Select Committee on Assassinations
JBK	Jacqueline Bouvier Kennedy
JFK	John Fitzgerald Kennedy
LBJ	Lyndon Baines Johnson
LHO	Lee Harvey Oswald
NA	National Archives
PA	Privacy Act
RFK	Robert Francis Kennedy
SS	Secret Service
TSBD	Texas School Book Depository
WC	Warren Commission
WR	Warren *Report*

Chronology of Assassination

22 Nov. 1963 (Friday): Central Standard Time
- 11:55 A.M. JFK motorcade leaves Love Field, Dallas
- 12:30 P.M. JFK shot; Gov. Connally, bystander Tague wounded [LHO's movements after leaving TSBD disputed]
- 1:00 P.M. JFK pronounced dead at Parkland Hospital [Time of Police Officer Tippit's murder and identity of his murderer(s) disputed]
- 1:50 P.M. LHO seized in Texas Theater
- 2:38 P.M. LBJ sworn in as 36th president
- 5:05 P.M. Air Force One lands at Andrews Air Force Base

23 Nov. 1963 (Saturday)
- 1:30 A.M. LHO charged with the murder of JFK

24 Nov. 1963 (Sunday)
- 11:21 A.M. LHO shot by Jack Ruby while in police custody
- 1:07 P.M. LHO dies at Parkland Hospital

25 Nov. 1963 (Monday)
- Funeral of JFK

29 Nov. 1963 (Friday)
- LBJ appoints seven-member commission headed by CJ Warren to investigate the assassination

9 Dec. 1963 (Monday)   .

        FBI delivers its five-volume report on the assassination

27 Sept. 1964

        WC releases its *Report* to the public.

Chronology of Lee Harvey Oswald

18	Oct.	1939	LHO born in New Orleans
		1945	Moves to Dallas/Fort Worth
	Summer	1952	Moves to New York City
	Jan.	1954	Moves to New Orleans
	July	1956	Moves to Fort Worth
24	Oct.	1956	Joins the United States Marine Corps
11	Sept.	1959	Released from active duty
14	Sept.	1959	Arrives in Fort Worth
17	Sept.	1959	Arrives in New Orleans
20	Sept.	1959	Departs via ship to Europe
8	Oct.	1959	Arrives in Le Havre, France
10	Oct.	1959	Departs London's Heathrow Airport
10	Oct.	1959	Arrives Helsinki
15	Oct.	1959	Crosses Finnish-Soviet border enroute to Moscow
30	April	1960	Marries Marina Prusakova
15	Feb.	1962	Daughter June born
1	June	1962	Boards train in USSR enroute to Holland and home
2	June	1962	Crosses Soviet-Polish border
4	June	1962	Leaves Holland via liner for U.S.
13	June	1962	Arrives Hoboken, N.J.
14	June	1962	Arrives Fort Worth; lives with brother Robert
1-14	Oct.	1962	In Dallas—residence not known

10	Oct.	1962	First day at work, Jaggers-Chiles-Stovall graphic arts firm in Dallas
15-19	Oct.	1962	Moves into YMCA, Dallas
20-21	Oct.	1962	Unknown
22	Oct.-		
3	Nov.	1962	At work in Dallas, residence unknown
3	Nov.	1962	Rents apartment at 602 Elsbeth Street, ground rear
3	Mar.	1963	Moves to apartment at 214 W. Neely Street, top floor
6	April	1963	Last day of work at Jaggers-Chiles-Stovall, discharged
24	April	1963	LHO leaves Dallas; family moves to Irving to stay with Ruth Paine
25	April	1963	LHO in New Orleans, stays with relatives 757 French Street
9	May	1963	Takes job at William B. Reily Coffee Co., 640 Magazine Street, rents apartment at 4907 Magazine
11	May	1963	Family joins LHO in New Orleans
	mid-June	1963	LHO handbill operation at Dumaine Street wharf where USS Wasp was docked
19	July	1963	Fired from Reily Coffee Co., allegedly for "poor working habits"
9	Aug.	1963	Arrested for disturbing the peace during fracas connected with Canal Street handbill operation
12	Aug.	1963	Fined ten dollars
16	Aug.	1963	Literature operation outside Trade Mart
27	Sept.	1963	Travels to Mexico; family removes to Irving, Texas
3	Oct.	1963	LHO returns to Dallas; registers Downtown YMCA
4-6	Oct.	1963	Visits Irving, Texas, where wife and child are living
7	Oct.	1963	Rents room 621 N. Marsalis from Mrs. Mary Bledsoe
12	Oct.	1963	Visits Irving, Texas
14	Oct.	1963	Rents apartment at 1026 N. Beckley; Irving neighbors inform Marina and Ruth Paine of job possibilities at TSBD where the brother (Wesley Frazier) of one works
15	Oct.	1963	TSBD hires LHO
16	Oct.	1963	First day at TSBD
18-21	Oct.	1963	LHO travels to Irving from work with Frazier

20	Oct.	1963	Rachel, second daughter, born
21	Oct.	1963	LHO travels to TSBD with Frazier and returns to Irving
22	Oct.	1963	LHO travels to TSBD with Frazier
25-28	Oct.	1963	Travels to Irving with Frazier
28	Oct.	1963	Travels to TSBD with Frazier
1	Nov.	1963	Rents P.O. Box 6225 at Terminal Annex Post Office, Dallas
1-4	Nov.	1963	Travels to Irving with Frazier
4	Nov.	1963	Returns to TSBD with Frazier
8-12	Nov.	1963	Travels to Irving with Frazier
12	Nov.	1963	Returns to TSBD with Frazier
15-16	Nov.	1963	Unknown
21	Nov.	1963	Travels to Irving with Frazier
22	Nov.	1963	Returns to TSBD with Frazier
			1:50 P.M. CST arrested in Texas Theater, Dallas
24	Nov.	1963	Murdered in Dallas police station by Jack Ruby

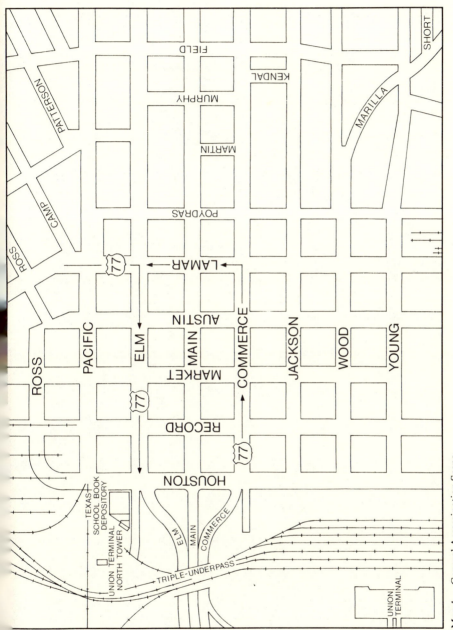

Map 1.   General Assassination Scene

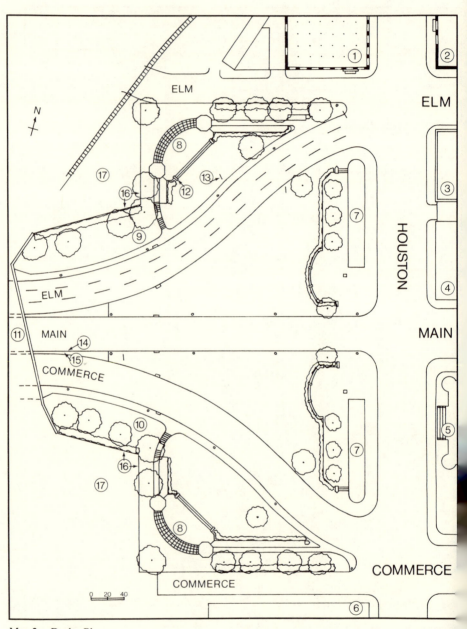

Map 2.   Dealey Plaza

1. Texas School Book Depository. Alleged assassin's lair on the sixth floor, easternmost window
2. Dal-Tex Building
3. Dallas County Records Building
4. Dallas County Criminal Courts Building
5. Old Court House
6. United States Post Office Building
7. Peristyles and Reflecting Pools
8. Pergolas
9. Grassy Knoll North
10. Grassy Knoll South
11. Triple Underpass
12. Position of Abraham Zapruder
13. Stemmons Road Sign
14. Approximate Location of Curbstone Hit [see 973 and 21 H 478-482 for photographs]
15. Position of James T. Tague
16. Stockade Fences
17. Parking Lots

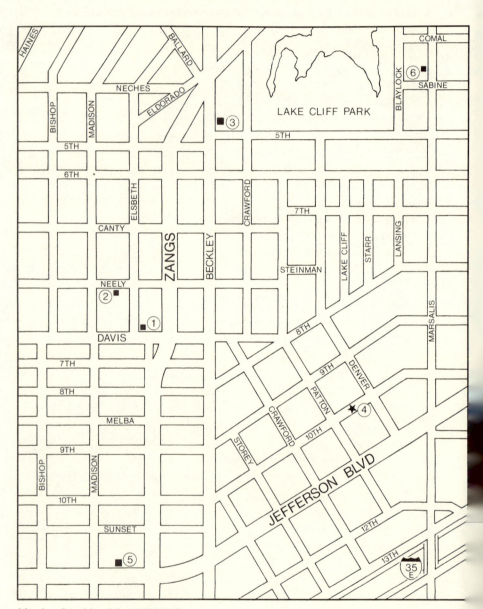

Map 3.   Oswald and Oak Cliff, Dallas

1. 602 Elsbeth. From 3 November 1962 to 3 March 1963 LHO rented an apartment
    for his family. The unresolved controversy raised by Meagher [722, 90-93] on
    Dallas Police prior knowledge of LHO relates to this address.
2. 214 W. Neely. From 3 March to 24 April 1963 LHO rented an apartment for his
    family.
3. 1026 N. Beckley. On 7 October 1963 LHO attempted to rent a room but none
    was available. On 14 October he rented a single room from the owner, Mrs. A. C.
    Johnson, whose housekeeper was Earlene Roberts. It was a ground floor, 5' x 12'
    room with a window front that ran the length and opened out on the neighbor's
    driveway. See Roffman's discussion [389] of it and Gene Daniel's photograph of
    the housekeeper hanging curtain rods; a reproduction is in Roffman [1055].
4. Location of the murder of Dallas Police Officer J. D. Tippit. Precisely when and
    by whom is disputed.
5. Texas Theater where LHO was arrested about 1:50 P.M. while watching the film
    War is Hell.
6. 621 N. Marsalis. LHO rented a single room at the rooming house of Mrs. Mary
    Bledsoe, 7-12 October 1963. She later claimed to have seen him during his
    alleged flight on 22 November and testified before the WC [see Meagher 722,
    and especially Weisberg 735].

Note: All evidence relating to the alleged route LHO traveled in Oak Cliff on 22 November
        1963 is in dispute [see Weisberg 735, Meagher 722 for discussion].

        Jack Ruby lived in the Marsala Apartments, 223 Ewing, two blocks east of Marsalis
        between 11th and 12th.

Map 4.   Places Associated with Oswald in New Orleans

1. Federal Building fronting LaFayette Park, contains a postal substation where LHO rented a postal box.
2. Federal Building also contains offices of federal agencies that share a common lobby with postal substation.
3. Crescent City Garage, 618 Magazine. Adrian Alba's garage that serviced FBI and SS cars and where LHO loafed.
4. William B. Reily Coffee Co., 640 Magazine. Next door to Crescent City Garage. LHO worked here 10 May-19 July, 1963.
5. Jones Printing Co., 422 Girod. Opposite side entrance of Reily Coffee Co. Firm where LHO's Fair Play for Cuba Committee leaflets were printed.
6. The Newman Building on a corner with dual addresses. Photograph is found in Flammonde [1893]. Contains four places of interest:

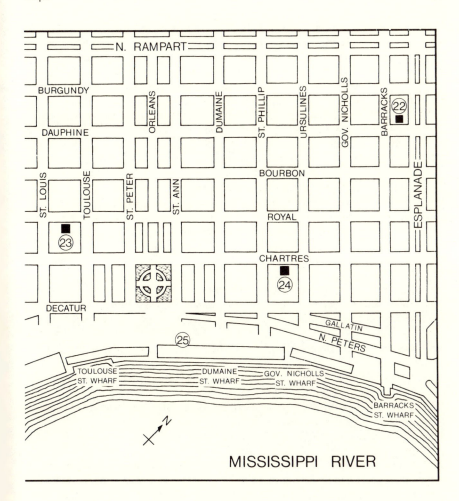

Guy Banister Associates, Inc., entrance on 531 LaFayette side, office of con-servative detective associated with anti-Cuban activity in New Orleans. Hale Boggs Federal Office Building now occupies site. (Boggs was a WC member.)

Mancuso's Restaurant, on the corner of Camp and LaFayette, where Banister's employer Jack S. Martin was seen with David Ferrie, Sergio Arcacha Smith, and Carlos Quiroga.

Entrance on 544 Camp Street is the return address stamped on LHO's Fair Play for Cuba Committee leaflets.

The second floor also contains rooms rented by anti-Cuban groups.

7.   402 St. Charles. Corner building with dual addresses. On 20 January 1961, a

man signing himself as "Oswald" placed a bid for ten Ford trucks and gave this as his address and Friends of Democratic Cuba as his organization [see Weisberg 1901].

8. Parking lot where a car LHO is said to have used was parked.

9. Old International Trade Building, Gateway Building, where LHO ran a handbill operation on 16 August; it was the area most associated with this activity. New Orleans businessman Clay Shaw had offices here. Building now demolished. Photographs in James & Wardlow [1896]. For LHO distributing leaflets see 21 H 139. Motion picture is in [191-192, 194].

10. Waterburg Drug Store, 536 Canal. Coffee shop reported by many to have been frequented by the real LHO. Source of fake story of threat on Nixon's life that arose during the waning days of Watergate.

11. Cigali Building, Corner building with dual addresses, 107 Camp. Advertising offices of Ronnie Caire, organizer and headquarters of Crusade to Free Cuba Committee formed to raise funds for Cuban Revolutionary Council. Listed in LHO's address book.

12. LHO residence, 126 Exchange. On second floor LHO lived here from May 1955-Spring 1956.

13. Pool Hall, 132 Exchange. LHO frequented it.

14. Silver Dollar flophouse, between 619 and 601 Iberville. Where Ricardo Davis sent his buckos and where a figure in the Garrison inquiry hid from the District Attorney's men.

15. Casa Roca, 107 Decatur. Store owned by Carlos Bringuier and visited by LHO several times.

16. Habana Bar and Lounge, 117 Decatur. Owned by Oresta Pena. Where "one" LHO threw a spectacular drunk scene.

17. Coffee Shop, Corner of Iberville and Decatur; "one" LHO was repeatedly reported to have frequented it in the early mornings.

18. Ward Discount, 709 Canal. Site of LHO's 9 August 1963 handbill operation [see film 189, 190].

19. Maritime Building. Offices of INCA, right-wing organization whose officer Ed Butler had radio debate with LHO and later merchandised the incident.

20. Pere Marquette Building. G. Wray Gill's law offices were located here. David Ferrie worked for him as a part-time investigator.

21. Law Offices of Dean Andrews. Colorful figure in the Garrison inquiry who was, he said, asked to do legal work for LHO.

22. Clay Shaw's residence, 1313 Dauphine.

23. WDSU-TV and radio stations, 520 Royal. Where LHO appeared for radio debates and interviews.

24. Provincial Motel, 1024 Chartres. James Earl Ray stayed here.

25. Dumaine Street Wharf. LHO picketed at *USS Wasp* and ran a handbill operation here between 13 June and 16 June 1963. Wharf now changed to part of waterfront development.

Note: LHO's address in the summer of 1963 was 4907 Magazine, several miles west of the map area. David William Ferrie lived on the second floor of 3330 Louisiana Avenue Parkway, also to the west, and across the river [see Flammonde 1893 and James & Wardlow 1896 for photographs].

Section I:
The Evidence and the Litigants

Part I: Unpublished Sources
(1) ARCHIVES AND LIBRARIES

1. <u>Assassination Information Bureau</u>. 1322 18th Street, N.W. #21, Washington, D.C. 20036.

Papers of an organization of critics, include twenty feet of miscellaneous clippings, articles, documents, and unpublished manuscripts; all HSCA and WC volumes; four feet published materials and press handouts of the HSCA. By appointment only during business hours and on an individual basis; [See 307].

2. <u>Central Intelligence Agency</u>. Freedom of Information Act and Privacy Act Coordinator; Central Intelligence Agency, Washington, D.C. 20505.

The CIA has reviewed and approved the release of 936 documents on the assassination of JFK constituting 3,747 pages accompanied by a 310 page index indicating what is released and what is withheld in each segment. Copies are officially neither deposited in an archives or library nor available to an inquirer until a request in writing is filed under the Freedom of Information Act and directed to the FOIA/PA Coordinator. An awkward arrangement for use in facilities external to the Agency's headquarters is promised. Copies can be purchased by mail at conventional costs for electrostatic reproductions.

The complex and extraordinary legal battle of critics to force the JFK documents from the CIA is partially found in FOIA suits, especially Harold Weisberg's. The released documents are but part of the CIA's JFK holdings which

presumably will continue to be reviewed and released
under critics' pressure. In themselves the documents
show how the CIA monitored foreign reception of the WR,
the impact of critics upon the foreign press, suggestions
for refuting the critics, and related topics.

3. Collector's Archives. Box 114, Beaconsfield, Quebec,
Canada.

A private collection of film, photographs, slides, and
recordings on JFK that distributes them commercially.
Lists available; [See 289].

4. Federal Bureau of Investigation. Freedom of Informa-
tion-Privacy Acts Branch. Chief, Freedom of Information-
Privacy Acts Branch, Records Management Division; Federal
Bureau of Investigation, J. Edgar Hoover Building, Pennsylvania Ave. N.W., Washington, D.C.   20535.

Possesses no records on FOIA requests relating to the
subject of the JFK assassination, according to officers
of the Division contacted by telephone, May 1979.

5. Federal Bureau of Investigation Freedom of Informa-
tion/Privacy Acts Reading Room. Supervisor, Federal Bureau
of Investigation FOI/PA Reading Room; J. Edgar Hoover Building, Pennsylvania Ave. N.W., Washington, D.C.   20535.
Phone (202) 324-5520. Open 9-4 working days.

Room in FBI headquarters building where records released
under the Freedom of Information and Privacy Acts will,
upon appointment, be brought and made available for
public use. As of mid-1979 those available in the reading room relating to the JFK assassination totaled:
120,728 pages released from the FBI Headquarters' files;
6,986 pages released from the Dallas Field Office files;
3,276 pages released from the New Orleans files. These
are periodically augmented as new files are released.
A constantly updated FOIA Preprocessed List issued by
the Supervisor and available upon request lists the
subject categories of released records. Requests for
access, which is by appointment only, must be made
either in writing or by telephone, with 48 hours advance
notice, and must provide: (1) name; (2) a contact telephone number; and (3) the subject one wishes to research.
In the austere, converted classroom the reader is free
to make any notations he or she wishes or to have
electrostatic copies made at conventional cost.

The complex history of the decade-long fight by critics
to pry the records from the FBI is to be found partially
in the Freedom of Information Act suits, especially the
significant Harold Weisberg suits. The voluminous
correspondence of Weisberg with Department of Justice
attorneys and officials concerning the obfuscations,
elliptical FBI responses, delays, tangential issues

raised to thwart release, and the constant fight to uncover hidden records should also be consulted.

See IBM-NYT [108], Carrollton [104] for commercial efforts
to publish selections. [See 4992, 4997, 4999, 5000-5002,
5004-5005, 5007, 5010.]

6. Georgetown University Library. Director, Special
Collections Division; Georgetown University Library, Georgetown University. 37 & O Streets, N.W., Washington, D.C.
20057.

Contains material relating to the JFK assassination
compiled by independent researchers. Three linear feet
of Richard Billings' papers, including one and one-half
feet of photographs by a journalist who covered the
trials of New Orleans District Attorney Jim Garrison;
one-half foot of Robert B. Cutler's papers; four feet
of Richard E. Sprague's papers, but not his photographic
files; audio tapes of the Nov. 1973 Assassination Symposium held at Georgetown University.

NATIONAL ARCHIVES AND RECORDS SERVICE.

7. (a) Administrative Files Relating to Warren Commission
Records and Kennedy Autopsy Materials. National Archives and
Records Service, Washington, D.C. 20408.

Possesses 53 files containing varying amounts of material
relating to the administration of records associated with
the assassination investigations by several components of
government grouped into the following units:

Legislative, Judicial, and Fiscal Branch Records;
Civil Archives Division Records;
Office of Presidential Libraries Records;
Office of the Archivist Records.

Requests for access ought to be addressed to the unit
having custody of them.

8. (b) Office of the General Counsel of the General Services Administration. Office of the General Counsel, National
Archives and Records Service, Washington, D.C. 20408.

The records of the legal aspects of the National Archives'
custody of JFK materials are held here, including litigation concerning assassination records, such as FOIA suits,
correspondence with some critics, declassification of certain materials, and related issues.

9.   (c) Records of the President's Commission on the
Assassination of President Kennedy. National Archives and
Records Service, Washington, D.C. 20408.

The WC officially deposited its records in the National
Archives where they are housed in a special records
group.   Public Law 89-318, 79 Stat. 1185, provides for
the preservation of the entire body of evidence considered by the WC.   On 31 Oct. 1966 the Attorney General
[87] designated some minor items for acquisition and
deposit, but failed to include key records held by the
FBI and other agencies.   Some records of the WC are in
private hands, e.g. Edward J. Epstein's Inquest [703]
used many WC files possessed by a former WC staff
10.   counsel Wesley Liebeler.   In 1970 the National Archives
issued a Preliminary Inventory of the Records of the
President's Commission on the Assassination of President
Kennedy, Washington, D.C., compiled by Marion Johnson
11.   which in 1973 was superceded by his 158 page compila-
tion Inventory of the Records of the President's
Commission on the Assassination of President Kennedy,
Washington, D.C., Government Printing Office.   It is
actually a sparse, summary inventory.   Some factual
inaccuracy appears, e.g. the 16 mm Wolper film is described as the work of a single amateur photographer when
actually it is a selection from the Dallas Cinema Associates collection of film.   The WDSU film includes the
WWL film.   Many opinions of investigators, conclusions,
and controversial descriptions are listed as facts.
The bulk, pages 23-158, a "List of Numbered Commission
Documents and Parts of these Documents Published in
Commission Exhibits in Volumes XXII-XXVII of the Hearings
of the Commission," is restricted to those printed by
the WC, and omits the other CDs held in the record group.
The Inventory is without much value to an inquirer lacking subject-matter knowledge.

12.   (d) The Gerald R. Ford Presidential Library.   In the
Gerald R. Ford Presidential Library Records, National Archives
and Records Service, Washington, D.C. 20408.   To be trans-
ferred to the Gerald R. Ford Presidential Library, Ann Arbor,
Michigan, 48106, upon its completion.

Papers of a WC member, his aids, associates, agencies,
and commissions associated with his political life.   As
president, Ford appointed a special Commission on CIA
Activities within the United States, chaired by Vice-
President Rockefeller [101], which investigated several
aspects of controversies surrounding the assassination
of JFK.   Its records as well as its finding aid are
security classified.

13.   (e) The Lyndon Baines Johnson Presidential Library.
Austin, Texas.   78705.

   Contains essential White House Special Files compiled by
   various aids for the President's private use, including
   LBJ's personal diary, appointment books, and file on the
   WC; also, 38 relevant oral histories, such as WC members
   John J. McCloy and Earl Warren.   Published guides and
   brochures available.

14.   (f) The John F. Kennedy Presidential Library.   380
Trapelo Road, Waltham, Mass.   02154.

   Contains the records, papers, films, tapes, and related
   material of the JFK presidency, including the papers and
   oral histories of various aids, associates, and federal
   agencies.   Interspersed among some records and some oral
   histories are scattered comment and reflection on the
   assassination.   The collection policy is restricted to
   JFK's life and career.   Consistent with that emphasis,
   they do not make an effort at present to collect materials
   on his death and the controversies surrounding it.   See
   the library's irregular publication, with supplements,
   Historical Materials in the John F. Kennedy Library.
   Waltham, Mass., John Fitzgerald Kennedy Library, 1975,
   64 pp.

15.   Office of Privacy and Information Appeals.   Director,
Office of Privacy and Information Appeals, Office of the
Associate Attorney General; Department of Justice, Washing-
ton, D.C.   20530.

   A temporary non-public repository holding records on
   the processing of appeals under the FOIA and PA.   No
   subject matter guide or index to JFK or other historical
   cases exist, because they are handled by case name only
   and fused with all others.   Federal archivists review,
   retain and destroy records at stated intervals of
   usually five years.

16.   Richard B. Russell Memorial Library.   The University
of Georgia, Athens, Georgia.   30602.

   The papers of WC member Russell contain six linear feet
   of documents on Kennedy Assassinations with the majority
   relating to the assassination of JFK and the WC's investigation.   They are arranged in two groups: (A.) Subject
   File, 1963-1970, of correspondence, evidential material,
   reports, testimony transcripts, book manuscript drafts
   and proofs, and memoranda; (B.) Miscellany File, 1963-
   1969, of books, magazine articles, newspaper clippings
   and related topics.

17. <u>Southeastern Louisiana University Library</u>. Kennedy
Assassination Materials, Special Collections Room, Linus A.
Sims Memorial Library; Southeastern Louisiana University,
Hammond, Louisiana   70402.

> Collection of JFK materials open to the public.   Contains
> the published volumes of the WC; the CIA Assassination
> Files, approx. 4,000 pages; FBI Assassination Files,
> approx. 100,000 pages; transcripts of HSCA Hearings,
> approx. 5,000 pages; transcript of Clay Shaw trial;
> audio-visual materials; various secondary sources,
> including some rare items;   [See 27].

18. <u>Texas State Archives</u>. Texas State Library Building,
Box 12927, Capitol Station, Austin, Texas   78711.

> Contains the working papers of the Texas Attorney Gen-
> eral's inquiry into the assassination comprising twenty
> volumes, including correspondence, transcripts, and
> photographs amounting to one and one-half linear feet.
> Copies appear in the National Archives and have been
> microfilmed and distributed commercially [106].   A few
> miscellaneous newspapers are preserved.

19. <u>United States House of Representatives</u>.   Records of
all committees.

> Records of all House committees are closed for 50 years,
> including those of the HSCA.   They are excluded from the
> provisions of the FOIA and are under the control of the
> Clerk of the House of Representatives.

20. <u>University of Wisconsin-Stevens Point Library</u>.
Assassination Collections, Learning Resources Center, University of Wisconsin-Stevens Point, Stevens Point, Wi.   54481

> Includes books, magazines, federal publications, films,
> photographs, and slides relating to the JFK assassination
> as well as Martin Luther King, Jr.'s assassination.   Vide
> tapes and audio cassettes of an Assassination Symposium
> held at the University in Nov. 1976 [1054-1059].   Papers
> of JFK critics Jenifer and James D. White [31], 50 linear
> feet plus tapes and cassettes.   Several hundred audio
> cassettes plus initial boxes of Harold Weisberg [30], a
> major JFK critic and author whose papers will be deposite
> here.   Cassettes include his interviews with critics and
> JFK figures, conversations, talk shows, radio journalist
> reports including Art Kevin's, and related subjects.   A
> box of records of the JFK critic and Washington attorney
> James H. Lesar [28].   Miscellaneous files.

(2) PRIVATE COLLECTIONS

The papers of several individuals associated in varying
degrees with the JFK assassination, its investigation,
and public discussion are listed and briefly described.
Because this is an expanding field still under Congressional and Judicial inquiry, the list cannot be
complete. Some persons with papers did not respond to
the editor's queries and therefore are not included. At
the same time a few substantial collections remain in
the hands of private individuals who, in order to protect
their privacy and to shield them from inordinate demands
on their time and energies, do not wish to make their
names public. A List of Private Papers is maintained by
David R. Wrone, Professor of History, University of
Wisconsin-Stevens Point, Stevens Point, Wi. 54481, and
is available to serious researchers who have done extensive work in the documentary base.

21. Billings, Richard. Papers. 3 linear feet. Director,
Special Collections Division, Georgetown University Library,
37 & O Streets, N.W., Washington, D.C. 20057.

A journalist who covered the trials of New Orleans District Attorney Jim Garrison.

22. Cutler, Robert B. Papers. ½ foot. Director, Special
Collections Division, Georgetown University Library, Georgetown University, 37 & O Streets, N.W., Washington, D.C.
20057.

A critic's papers relating to his study of the flight
path of bullets which the WC alleges were fired in the
JFK assassination.

23. de Antonio, Emile. Papers. 4 boxes plus electronic
and photographic items. Archives Division, The State Historical Society of Wisconsin, 716 State Street, Madison, Wi.
53706.

Correspondence, records, photographs, and tape recordings
of radical documentary film maker who directed and co-
produced with Mark Lane the film Rush to Judgment.
Included are one box of biographical information; one
box of general correspondence relating to JFK matters;
one box on the film Rush to Judgment with folders on
script, production notes, technical production, record
albums, and publicity. He provides a severe criticism
of Lane. One folder on Lord Bertrand Russell and the
English JFK critics concerns de Antonio's futile efforts
to make a Russell documentary under the corrupting influence of Lane.

24. Dulles, Allen W. Papers. 5 boxes. Manuscript Division, Princeton University Library, Princeton University, Princeton, N. J. 08540.

WC member and former head of the CIA. Five boxes relating to the WC are found among his papers, including correspondence, statements, recollections, reports, interviews, testimony transcripts, drafts of WC publications, articles, lists, and legal documents, including the subpoena from Jim Garrison's New Orleans office. Written permission for access must be obtained.

25. Gertz, Elmer. Papers. 78 containers. Manuscript Division, Library of Congress, Washington, D.C. 20540.

Attorney for Jack Ruby in the appeals proceedings as well as for Gordon Novel in legal cases associated with the Jim Garrison probe in New Orleans. The papers have articles, notes, commentaries, and some book proofs by Wills [2485], Lane [718], Belli [2475], Kaplan and Waltz [2478], Garrison [1894], and Judge Joe Brown's unpublished manuscript, as well as Gertz' Moment of Madness [2476]. 61 containers relate to Ruby's legal affairs, including photostats of trial transcripts, copies of briefs filed by various parties, newspaper clippings, correspondence, interviews, and scrapbooks. 15 containers relate to Novel's legal difficulties, including court proceedings, photocopies of material re Novel, case files, depositions, press material, newspaper clippings, tapes, and business files. Two containers relate to Clay Shaw's suits against Garrison, including correspondence, court proceedings, newspaper clippings, and printed material.

26. Jones, Penn, Jr. Papers. 56 feet, plus books and film. Box 1140, Midlothian, Texas. 76065

Critic, author of four volumes [711-714], former publisher of weekly newspaper, editor of The Continuing Inquiry, a monthly newsletter on the investigation of JFK's assassination [308], his files contain four legal-size drawers of correspondence from critics and the public; 36 feet of clippings and documents; 100 tapes; 800 books, including some rare volumes; plus film.

27. Kurtz, Michael L. Papers. Tapes and photographs. History Department, Box 809 University Station, Southeastern Louisiana University, Hammond, Louisiana. 70402

Professor of history and critic who possesses a personal collection of cassette interviews with various figures in the JFK controversies, including many who were not interviewed by WC or HSCA, plus documents, photographs, and other materials; [See 1061].

28. Lesar, James H. Papers. 30 file drawers plus clippings. Not open to the public. To be deposited in Assassination Collection, University of Wisconsin-Stevens Point, Wi.
54481. For information contact David R. Wrone, History Department, University of Wisconsin-Stevens Point, Wi. 54481.

   Files of attorney engaged in numerous FOIA and other legal actions associated with the JFK and MLK investigations.

29. Sprague, Richard E. Papers. 4 feet. Director, Spe-
cial Collections Division, Georgetown University Library,
Georgetown University, 37 & O Streets, N.W., Washington,
D.C. 20057.

   A critic's papers relating to the JFK assassination. It
   does not include his photographic files.

30. Weisberg, Harold. Papers. Excess of 200 file drawers,
plus tapes, books, film. To be deposited in Assassination
Collection, University of Wisconsin-Stevens Point, Stevens
Point, Wi. 54481. For information contact David R. Wrone,
History Department, University of Wisconsin-Stevens Point,
Stevens Point, Wi. 54481.

   Documents, records, correspondence, research files,
   tapes, cassettes, film, books, articles, and manuscripts
   developed by major critic, 1963-1979. In excess of 200
   file drawers of documents, records, and correspondence,
   including the Headquarters Files, Dallas Field Office
   Files, and New Orleans Field Office Files of the FBI and
   including several indexes, e.g. a 40 linear foot index
   in the Dallas Field Office Files. Many drawers of FOIA
   suit records, extensive correspondence, memoranda, and
   analyses concerning the actions of Department of Justice,
   FBI, CIA, National Archives, and other government agencies; 15,000 letters received from the public; several
   hundred tapes and cassettes relating to debates, interviews, phone interviews, talk shows, etc., book manuscripts, aides' memoire and memoranda; correspondence
   with critics; and related topics.

31. White, Jenifer and James D. Files, 50 feet plus
tapes and books. Director, Assassination Collection, Learning Resource Center, University of Wisconsin-Stevens Point,
Stevens Point, Wi. 54481.

   Files of books, magazines, tapes, records, correspondence, and organized, mounted newspaper clippings deal-
   ing with assassinations and related events, 1963-1976.
   Compiled by San Francisco citizen and her husband, an
   editor with the Associated Press. 40 linear feet of
   mounted newspaper clippings from national daily as well
   as minor press, plus daily AP wire copy, arranged by
   subject, primarily relating to JFK, but with substantial
   coverage of Watergate, intelligence operations, extremist

groups, and associated topics. Eight foot card file,
JFK notes; two foot card file, Garrison case chronology;
four foot card file, Garrison case name index with anno-
tations and cross references; 44 tapes, assassination
debates, interviews, commentaries, talk shows, etc.,
1963-1976. 5,000 pages (carbon), Harold Weisberg correspondence and memoranda to others, 1970-1977. 31 selected
tapes, Senate Watergate and House Judiciary Committee
hearings; 44 cassettes, daily Pacifica Radio summary,
including many corridor interviews, analyses, and reviews.

Part II: Published Sources, Excluding the Warren Report
(1) FEDERAL

32. U.S. Congress. House. Committee on Government Operations. National Archives--Security Classification Problems
Involving Warren Commission Files and Other Records. Hearings
before the Subcommittee on Government Information and Individual Rights Subcommittee of the Committee on Government
Operations, House of Representatives, on the implementation
of the Freedom of Information Act and Executive Order 11652,
94th Cong., 1st sess., 1975. 98 pp. Committee Print.

The Abzug Subcommittee Hearings.

Abruptly cancelled inquiry by Chairwoman Bella Abzug into
the peculiar circumstances of the security classification
of Warren Commission records in light of the Freedom of
Information Act's operation and the requirements of Exe-
cutive Order 11652 [96]. Witnesses included David W.
Belin, former staff member of the Warren Commission and
Executive Director of the Rockefeller Commission, James
B. Rhoads, Archivist of the United States, and Marion
Johnson, Archivist in charge of the Warren Commission
Records in the National Archives.

Much of the subcommittee's staff development of the
"Chronology of custodianship, etc., of autopsy data . . . "
and "records relating to Warren Commission investigation
missing from Archives collection," both printed in appendices, as well as the preparation of many questions for
the hearings, rests on the unattributed assistance of
critic Harold Weisberg and James H. Lesar, attorney associated in several legal actions to obtain classified WC
data. Although listed as a witness, Lesar was not called.
In a prepared statement printed in an appendix, Lesar
presents information that casts doubt on the testimony of
some of the witnesses. Weisberg's correspondence [30]
contains extensive discussion and memoranda on the
committee's work.

33. U.S. Congress. House. Committee on Government Operations. U.S. Government Information Policies and Practices--
Security Classification Problems Involving Subsection (b) (1)
of the Freedom of Information Act (Part 7). Hearings before
a Subcommittee of the Committee on Government Operations,
House of Representatives, 92d Cong., 2d sess., 1975.
Committee Print.

   Pages 2610-2612 contain testimony of James B. Rhoads,
   Archivist of the United States, with prepared statements
   entitled: "The Warren Commission Records and the Freedom
   of Information Act," and "Guidelines for Review of
   Materials Submitted to the President's Commission on the
   Assassination of President Kennedy."

34. U.S. Congress. House. Committee on the Judiciary.
FBI Oversight. Circumstances Surrounding Destruction of the
Lee Harvey Oswald Note. . . . Hearings before the subcommittee on civil and constitutional rights of the Committee
on the Judiciary, House of Representatives, 94th Cong., 1st
sess. Oct. 21, Dec. 11, 12, 1975. Serial No. 2, Part 3.
Committee Print. 250 pp.

The Edwards Subcommittee Hearings.

Long-delayed publication of subcommittee hearings chaired
by Congressman Don Edwards. Four issues connected with
the controversy surrounding the investigation of JFK's
assassination are addressed: 1. Whether Lee Harvey
Oswald "early in November 1963" delivered a threatening
note to the Dallas FBI office which Special Agents later
destroyed. 2. The validity of the allegation of William
Walters, former clerk of the New Orleans FBI office, that
on November 17, 1963, a teletype was received warning the
FBI there would be a threat on JFK's life. 3. Whether
Jack Ruby was a paid informer for the FBI. 4. Whether
the allegation that the FBI withheld information from the
Warren Commission was true. Witnesses included Associate
Director of the FBI James B. Adams, Special Agents James
P. Hosty, Jr., Kenneth C. Howe, J. Gordon Shanklin, and
Dallas FBI office receptionist Nanny Lee Fenner. During
the televised hearings, critic Mark Lane appeared with
Chairman Edwards, silently assisting him; he also helped
coach Edwards' staff.

The FBI witnesses presented no evidence other than their
testimony to assert that Oswald in fact did leave a note
at their office and SA Hosty destroyed it. Ruby in fact
had been a low-level informer for the FBI many years
before the assassination. Since not a shred of evidence
could be uncovered to support the Walters allegation,
the FBI concluded it was never sent. The FBI further
asserted that they cooperated fully with the WC.

Held at a time of intense public agitation for a congressional investigation into assassinations, the Edwards

inquiry in effect gave the FBI the vehicles of the national video, press, and magazines to present its position on vital issues without the substantial rebuttal that responsible and informed critics might offer.

Exhaustive detail on Oswald's allegedly threatening note, and Congressional examination of the witnesses, carefully excluded the fact the WC had been informed in 1964 that notes on Oswald in the office had been destroyed. The inquiry throughout presumed Oswald's guilt in the assassination and, to reinforce the public mind, now added a putatively latent strain of violence to his character coupled with a left-wing ideological orientation.

In previous lectures Lane presented and endorsed the Walters' allegation with embellishments. The FBI focused exclusively on their teletype system to refute Walters. Edwards and Lane effectively isolated this issue from numerous assassination threats made by ultra-rightist groups which were never investigated by the WC and largely ignored by the FBI. This permitted the larger question of massive dereliction of duty in this area to be avoided. Weisberg Post Mortem [973] mentions internal right-wing threats.

The FBI controlled and intimidated the WC. This is clearly revealed not only in FBI records but also in WC documents. Formerly classified WC executive session transcripts obtained under FOIA litigation reveal the commissioners realized that the FBI was channeling the investigation to protect itself. They did not believe that Oswald was the lone assassin but they were being forced to accept it. In the 22 Jan. 1964 session WC chief counsel J. Lee Rankin says of the Commission's plight that the FBI "would like to have us fold up and quit."; [See 4815, 4816, 4823, 4824, 4829, 4831, 4833, 4834, 4855].

35. U. S. Congress. House. Miscellaneous Resolutions by Congress and Number. 88th Congress. Directing an investigation of the Department of State. H. Joint Resolution 812, 88th Cong., 1st sess., 1963.

27 Nov. 1963 Introduced and sent to Committee on Rules: CR, CIX, Part 17, 22857.

36. Establishing a joint committee to conduct an investigation and study of the recent assassination of the President of the United States and of certain other matters pertinent thereto. H. Joint Resolution 814, 88th Cong., 1st sess., 1963.

27 Nov. 1963 Introduced and sent to Committee on Rules: CR, CIX, Part 17, 22857.

37. <u>Authorizing the Commission established to report upon</u>
<u>the assassination of President John F. Kennedy to compel the</u>
<u>attendance and testimony of witnesses and the production of</u>
<u>records</u>. H. Joint Resolution 838, 88th Cong., 1st sess.,
1963.

4 Dec. 1963 Introduced and sent to Committee on the
Judiciary: <u>CR</u>, CIX, Part 18, 23339.

38. <u>Authorizing the Commission established to report upon</u>
<u>the assassination of President John F. Kennedy to compel the</u>
<u>attendance and testimony of witnesses and the production of</u>
<u>evidence</u>. H. Joint Resolution 852, 88th Cong., 1st sess.,
1963.

7 Dec. 1963 Introduced and sent to Committee on the
Judiciary: <u>CR</u>, CIX, Part 18, 23752.

10 Dec. 1963 Reported with <u>H. Report</u> 1013, without
Amendment, "Authorizing subpoena power for Commission
in the assassination of President John F. Kennedy," 3
pp.: <u>CR</u>, CIX, Part 18, 24005. Printed in <u>House Reports</u>,
88th Cong., 1st sess., Miscellaneous Reports on Public
Bills, VI: 12545.

17 Dec. 1963 Laid on the table: <u>CR</u>, CIX, Part 19,
24788.

39. <u>Authorizing the Commission established to report upon</u>
<u>the assassination of President John F. Kennedy to compel the</u>
<u>attendance and testimony of witnesses and the production of</u>
<u>evidence</u>. H. Joint Resolution 853, 88th Cong., 1st sess.,
1963.

9 Dec. 1963 Introduced and sent to Committee on the
Judiciary: <u>CR</u>, CIX, Part 18, 23752.

40. <u>To Provide that information relating to the assassina-</u>
<u>tion of the late President John F. Kennedy shall be made</u>
<u>public</u>. H. Joint Resolution 926, 88th Cong., 2d sess., 1964.

18 Feb. 1964 Introduced and sent to Committee on the
Judiciary: <u>CR</u>, CX, Part 3, 3060.

41. 89th Congress. <u>To establish a joint committee to</u>
<u>determine the necessity of a congressional investigation of</u>
<u>the assassination of President Kennedy</u>. H. Concurrent Reso-
lution 1023, 89th Cong., 2d sess., 1966.

28 Sept. 1966 Introduced and sent to Committee on Rules:
<u>CR</u>, CXII, Part 18, 24157-61, 24201.

42. 90th Congress. <u>To establish a joint committee to</u>
<u>determine the necessity of a congressional investigation of</u>
<u>the assassination of President Kennedy</u>. H. Concurrent Reso-
lution 312, 90th Cong., 1st sess., 1967.

13 April 1967   Introduced and sent to Committee on Rules: <u>CR</u>, CXIII, Part 7, 9538.

43.   <u>94th Congress.   Creating a select committee to conduct an investigation and study of the circumstances surrounding the deaths of John F. Kennedy, Robert F. Kennedy, Martin Luther King, and the attempted assassination of George Wallace.</u>   H. Resolution 204, 94th Cong., 1st sess., 1975.

19 Feb. 1975   Introduced and sent to Committee on Rules: <u>CR</u>, CXXI, Part 3, 3670.

16 April 1975   Draft brief supporting bill by students at University of Virginia: <u>CR</u>, CXXI, Part 8, 10384-87.

14 May 1975   Statement of Bill co-sponsor Rep. Spellman of Maryland, Petition of Students at University of Maryland, including a copy of the January 22, 1964 Warren Commission Executive Session transcript: <u>CR</u>, CXXI, Part 11, 14438-40.

17 July 1975   Statement of Bill sponsor Rep. Gonzalez of Texas; critique of Warren Commission findings: <u>CR</u>, CXXI, Part 18, 23278-80.

18 Sept. 1975   Statement of Bill sponsor, list of co-sponsors: <u>CR</u>, CXXI, Part 29, 29348; 19 Nov. 1975, <u>ibid</u>.

20 Nov. 1975   Statement of Bill sponsor: <u>CR</u>, CXXI, Part 29, 37530.

44.   <u>Creating a select committee to conduct an investigation and study of the circumstances surrounding the death of John F. Kennedy</u>.   H. Resolution 432, 94th Cong., 1st sess., 1975.

30 April 1975   Introduced and sent to Committee on Rules: <u>CR</u>, CXXI, Part 10, 12481.

18 Mar. 1976   Statement of Rep. Mineta of California supporting Bill: <u>CR</u>, CXXII, No. 39, H2097.

2 July 1976   Statement of Rep. Harris of Virginia supporting Bill: <u>CR</u>, CXXII, No. 106, E3751.

45.   <u>Creating a select committee to conduct an investigation and study of the circumstances surrounding the deaths of John F. Kennedy, Robert F. Kennedy and Martin Luther King, and the attempted assassination of George Wallace</u>.   H. Resolution 455 (H. Res. 204), 94th Cong., 1st sess., 1975.

12 May 1975   Statement of Bill sponsor Rep. Gonzalez, list of co-sponsors; introduced and sent to Committee on Rules: <u>CR</u>, CXXI, Part 11, 13752, 13766.

6 Nov. 1975   Statement of Bill co-sponsor Rep. Koch of New York: Rockefeller Commission correspondence: <u>CR</u>, CXXXI, Part 27, 35448.

46. Creating a select committee to conduct an investigation and study of circumstances surrounding the deaths of John F. Kennedy, Robert F. Kennedy, and Martin Luther King, and the attempted assassination of George Wallace. H. Resolution 456 (H. Res. 204), 94th Cong., 1st sess., 1975.

12 May 1975 Statement of Bill sponsor Rep. Gonzalez, list of co-sponsors; introduced and sent to Committee on Rules: CR, CXXI, Part 11, 13752, 13766.

47. Creating a select committee to conduct an investigation and study of the circumstances surrounding the death of John F. Kennedy. H. Resolution 498, 94th Cong., 1st sess., 1975.

22 May 1975 Introduced and sent to Committee on Rules: CR, CXXXI, Part 12, 15949.

48. Creating a select committee to conduct an investigation and study of the circumstances surrounding the death of John F. Kennedy. H. Resolution 574, 94th Cong., 1st sess., 1975.

26 June 1975 Introduced and sent to Committee on Rules: CR, CXXI, Part 16, 21030.

18 Mar. 1976 Statement of Rep. Lagomarsino of California in support of Bill: CR, CXXII, No. 39, H2097.

49. Creating a select committee to conduct an investigation and study of the circumstances surrounding the deaths of John F. Kennedy, Robert F. Kennedy, and Martin Luther King, and the attempted assassination of George Wallace. H. Resolution 593 (H. Res. 204), 94th Cong., 1st sess., 1975.

11 July 1975 Introduced and sent to Committee on Rules: CR, CXXI, Part 17, 22425.

50. Creating a select committee to conduct an investigation and study of the circumstances surrounding the death of John F. Kennedy. H. Resolution 669, 94th Cong., 1st sess., 1975.

1 Aug. 1975 Introduced and sent to Committee on Rules: CR, CXXI, Part 21, 27045, 27132-35.

51. Creating a select committee to conduct an investigation and study of the circumstances surrounding the deaths of John F. Kennedy, Robert F. Kennedy, and Martin Luther King, and the attempted assassination of George Wallace. H. Resolution 721 (H. Res. 204), 94th Cong., 1st sess., 1975.

18 Sept. 1975 Introduced and sent to Committee on Rules: CR, CXXI, Part 23, 29382.

52. Creating a select committee to conduct an investigation and study of the circumstances surrounding the death of John F. Kennedy. H. Resolution 742, 94th Cong., 1st sess., 1975.

26 Sept. 1975 Introduced and sent to Committee on Rules: CR, CXXI, Part 24, 30436.

53. Creating a select committee to conduct an investigation and study of the circumstances surrounding the death of John F. Kennedy. H. Resolution 743, 94th Cong., 1st sess., 1975.

26 Sept. 1975 Introduced and sent to Committee on Rules: CR, CXXI, Part 24, 30436.

54. Creating a select committee to conduct an investigation and study of the circumstances surrounding the death of John F. Kennedy. H. Resolution 848, 94th Cong., 1st sess., 1975.

6 Nov. 1975 Introduced and sent to Committee on Rules: CR, CXXI, Part 27, 35458.

55. Creating a select committee to conduct an investigation and study of the circumstances surrounding the death of John F. Kennedy. H. Resolution 849, 94th Cong., 1st sess., 1975.

6 Nov. 1975 Introduced and sent to Committee on Rules: CR, CXXI, Part 27, 35458.

56. Creating a select committee to conduct an investigation and study of the circumstances surrounding the deaths of John F. Kennedy, Robert F. Kennedy, and Martin Luther King, Jr., and the attempted assassination of George Wallace. H. Resolution 873, 94th Cong., 1st sess., 1975.

19 Nov. 1975 Introduced and sent to Committee on Rules: CR, CXXI, Part 29, 37350.

57. Creating a select committee to conduct an investigation and study of the circumstances surrounding the death of John F. Kennedy. H. Resolution 879, 94th Cong., 1st sess., 1975.

20 Nov. 1975 Introduced and sent to Committee on Rules: CR, CXXI, Part 29, 37546.

58. Creating a select committee to conduct an investigation and study of the circumstances surrounding the death of John F. Kennedy. H. Resolution 949, 94th Cong., 1st sess., 1975.

19 Dec. 1975 Introduced and sent to Committee on Rules: CR, CXXI, Part 32, 42018.

59. Creating a select committee to conduct an investigation and study of the circumstances surrounding the deaths of John F. Kennedy, Robert F. Kennedy, and Martin Luther King, and the attempted assassination of George Wallace. H. Resolution 1035 (H. Res. 204), 94th Cong., 2d sess., 1976.

17 Feb. 1976 Introduced and sent to Committee on Rules:
CR, CXXI, Part 3, 3301.

60. Creating a select committee to conduct an investigation
and study of the circumstances surrounding the death of John
F. Kennedy. H. Resolution 1116, 94th Cong., 1st sess., 1976.

30 Mar. 1976 Introduced and sent to Committee on Rules:
CR, CXXII, No. 46, H2582.

61. U.S. Congress. House. Providing for the acquisition
and preservation by the United States of certain items of
evidence pertaining to the assassination of President John F.
Kennedy. Public Law 89-318. 89th Cong., 1st sess., Oct. 22,
1965, H. Resolution 9545.

29 June 1965 Introduced and sent to Committee on the
Judiciary: CR, CXI, Part 11, 15204.

19 Aug. 1965 Reported with H. Report 813, Amendment,
"Preserving evidence pertaining to the assassination of
President Kennedy," 6 pp.: CR, Part 16, 21103. Printed
in House Reports, 89th Cong., 1st sess., Miscellaneous
Reports on Public Bills, V, 12665-5.

7 Sept. 1965 Text of Bill Enrolled, rules suspended,
amended, passed House: CR, CXI, Part 17, 23002-04.

8 Sept. 1965 Referred to Senate, Committee on the Judiciary: CR, CXI, Part 17, 23104.

4 Oct. 1965 Reported as S. Report 851, "Preserving evi-
dence pertaining to the assassination of President
Kennedy," 4 pp.: CR, CXI, Part 19, 25873. Printed in
Senate Reports, 89th Cong., 1st sess., Miscellaneous
Reports on Public Bills, VI, 12662-6.

13 Oct. 1965 Passed over in Senate: CR, CXI, Part 20,
26829.

15 Oct. 1965 Passed over in Senate: CR, CXI, Part 20,
27076.

18 Oct. 1965 Statement of John J. King opposing Bill,
Senate passage: CR, CXI, Part 20, 27262-63.

20 Oct. 1965 Bill enrolled by Speaker of the House;
signed by Vice-President, Senate: CR, CXI, Part 20,
27539.

20 Oct. 1965 Enrolled and signed by the Speaker of the
House: CR, CXI, Part 20, 27784.

21 Oct. 1965 Bill presented to the President: CR, CXI,
Part 21, 27907.

22 Oct. 1965 Returned as signed by the President on 2 Nov. 1965: <u>CR</u>, CXI, Part 21, 28657.

62. U.S. Congress, House. Select Committee on Assassinations. Resolutions, Reports, Committee Prints in Chronological Sequence. <u>Creating a select committee to conduct an investigation and study of the circumstances surrounding the death of John F. Kennedy and the death of Martin Luther King, Jr., and of any others the select committee shall determine.</u> H. Resolution 1540, 94th Cong., 2d sess., 1976.

14 Sept. 1976 Introduced and sent to Committee on Rules: <u>CR</u>, CXXII, No. 138, H10069.

15 Sept. 1976 Reported with <u>H. Rept. 94-1566</u>: "Creating a select committee to conduct an investigation and study of the circumstances surrounding the death of John F. Kennedy and the death of Martin Luther King, Junior, and of any other the select committee shall determine." 2 pp. Printed in <u>House Reports</u>, 94th Cong., 2d sess., Miscellaneous Reports on Public Bills, XII, 13134-12.

17 Sept. 1976 Bill considered and passed House: <u>CR</u>, CXXII, No. 141, H10356-66.

63. <u>Report together with additional and supplemental views of the Select Committee on Assassinations: Results and Recommendations of the Select Committee on Assassinations.</u> H. Rept. 94-1781, 94th Cong., 2d sess., Dec. 31, 1976. v, 18 pp.

The Downing Report.

Report of committee chaired by Thomas N. Downing, broken into six parts: i. an introduction where the guilt of Oswald is set forth as already established; ii. review of the committee's initial inquiries into issues tangentially related to Oswald; iii. a sparse description of preliminary investigation and analyses; iv. staff and budget requests totaling $6,531,000; v. a recommendation to the 95th Congress that the committee be continued; vi. additional and supplemental views of members, including those of members C. Thone and C. Dodds which faintly echo the public outcry against committee irregularities such as the lack of rules, improper notification of members for meetings, and the absence of systematic record keeping.

The committee discerned the task of a newly constituted committee to be one of seeking what possible assistance Oswald had had. It accepted the fidelity of the original FBI investigation, but suggested the CIA was culpable in failing to transmit all its information to the FBI. It stated that the primary purpose for continuing the inquiry was the need to allay the public's suspicions that a conspiracy slew JFK and had not been discovered.

In its four months the committee accomplished little.
It accepted the basic conclusions of the WC and the
investigations conducted by the FBI and worked on its
stated task of not investigating the murder of JFK but
making the official findings of Oswald's guilt palatable
to the public. To this end the committee endorsed bizarre and unconstitutional methods, requesting funds in
their budget for miniphone recording devices for surreptitious listening and voice stress evaluators to record
and interpret voice patterns of unsuspecting persons
from which inferences on veracity would be drawn. Large
salaries were budgeted for modestly qualified staff members and $250 per day living expenses for "investigators."

That the original investigation had to be investigated
in order to lay a clear and objective evidentiary foundation was never considered. The influence of Mark Lane
upon the committee and its staff and on its operating
philosophy and direction of its inquiry was accurately
portrayed in an article in the NYT [4974], written with
Harold Weisberg's assistance.

64. Providing funds for the expenses of the investigators
and studies to be conducted by the Select Committee on
Assassinations. H. Resolution 1557 (H. Res. 1540), 94th
Cong., 1st sess., 1976.

21 Sept. 1976 Introduced and sent to Committee on House
Administration: CR, CXXII, No. 143, H10760.

30 Sept. 1976 Bill considered and agreed to: CR,
CXXII, No. 150, H11891.

65. Providing for funds for the Select Committee on
Assassinations. H. Resolution 9, 95th Cong., 1st sess.,
1977.

4 Jan. 1977 Introduced and sent to Committee on Rules:
CR, CXXIII, No. 1, H82.

11 Jan. 1977 Statement of Rep. Bauman of Maryland
regarding Bill: CR, CXXIII, No. 4, H260.

24 Jan. 1977 Request of Rep. Delaney of the Committee
on Rules to have additional time to file reports on
the Bill, Rep. Bauman objects: CR, CXXIII, No. 12, H493.

26 Jan. 1977 Statement of Rep. Dellums of California
supporting Bill: CR, CXXIII, No. 14, H561.

1 Feb. 1977 Statement of Rep. Kelly of Florida opposing
Bill: CR, CXXIII, No. 18, H742.

7 Feb. 1977 Statement of Rep. Holt of Maryland opposing
Bill: CR, CXXIII, No. 22, E565.

66. Creating a Select Committee on Assassinations. H.
Resolution 222, 95th Cong., 1st sess., 1977.

1 Feb. 1977 Reported with H. Rept. 95-3, "Creating a
Select Committee on Assassinations," 3 pp.; introduced
and sent to Committee on Rules: CR, CXXIII, No. 18,
H764, H770.

2 Feb. 1977 Bill agreed to, committee members appointed:
CR, CXXIII, No. 19, H800-807.

3 Feb. 1977 Statement of Rep. Barnard of Georgia opposing
Bill; statement of Rep. Stokes supporting Bill: CR,
CXXIII, No. 20, E556-57.

67. Providing for the consideration of the resolution
(H. Res. 222), Creating a Select Committee on Assassinations.
H. Resolution 230, 95th Cong., 1st sess., 1977.

1 Feb. 1977 Reported with H. Rept. 95-4, "Providing for
consideration of House Resolution 222," 1 p.: CR,
CXXIII, No. 18, H764.

2 Feb. 1977 Debated, agreed to: CR, CXXIII, No. 19,
H790-800.

68. "Rules of Procedure of the Select Committee on
Assassinations [promulgated 7 Mar. 1977]," CR, 16 Mar. 1977,
H2221.

69. Committee Meetings. Hearings before the Select
Committee on Assassinations, House of Representatives, 95th
Cong., 1st sess. Committee Print. Mar. 9, 11, 16 and 23,
1977. iii, 60 pp.

Heavily publicized sessions with witness testimony Mar.
11, J. A. Blackwell, Criminal Court Clerk, and Charles
Koster, Deputy Clerk, Memphis, Tenn., pp. 10-34; Mar.
16, Santo Trafficante, Jr., pp. 37-41.

70. "Executive Session, March 17, 1977." Select Committee
on Assassinations, House of Representatives, 95th Cong., 1st
sess., March 17, 1977. Typescript. 119 pp.

Restricted minutes mistakenly distributed at press conference. The bulk of the discussion concerns the
committee's efforts to orchestrate public meetings, news
releases, public postures on staff issues, and the
necessity to promote positive press and television
coverage of hearings in order to influence House members
reluctant to fund the committee. The discussion includes
an analysis of the Trafficante hearings where he invoked
the protective amendments of the Constitution rather than
testify. They speculated that Trafficante's refusal
would give them press coverage. Not wishing to "rehash"
the WC's work or discuss its findings, they wanted to

move into areas the WC had not penetrated, such as the role of organized crime; [See 5062, 5066-7, 5114-5116].

71. Report of the Select Committee on Assassinations [pursuant to mandate of H. Resolution 222]. H. Report 95-119, 95th Cong., 1st sess., Mar. 28, 1977. Committee Print. v, 14 pp. The Stokes Mandated Report.

Prior to providing funds, the House required the Select Committee to establish rules, scale down its budget, correct its proposals to trample civil liberties, and file a report. Chairman Louis Stokes' report falls into five parts: i) introduction; ii) the conduct of committee business where a budget of $2,796,650 was proposed and the eavesdropping machinery eliminated; iii and iv) the status of the JFK and King investigations; and v) conclusion, where he states the committee "intends to conclude a thorough, professional investigation of the assassinations by establishing the facts to prove or disprove, once and for all, the disparate theories that have arisen since the murders took place in Dallas and Memphis."

The Select Committee's purpose was not to investigate the assassination of JFK, which would require an inquiry into the primary evidence and the operation of the WC with federal investigative agencies, but to confine itself with "theories" of who assisted Oswald. Oswald was presumed guilty.

72. To provide for the continuation of the Select Committee on Assassinations. H. Resolution 433, 95th Cong., 1st sess., 1977.

23 Mar. 1977 Referred to Committee on Rules.

29 Mar. 1977 Report with H. Rept. 95-130, Amendment, "Providing for the continuation of the Select Committee on Assassinations," 4 pp.; made special order H. Rept. 95-129, "Providing for consideration of H. Res. 433," 1 p.: CR, CXXIII, No. 55, H2724.

30 Mar. 1977 Debated, amended and passed House: CR, CXXIII, No. 56, H2739-53.

73. Providing for consideration of the resolution (H. Res. 433) to provide for the continuation of the Select Committee on Assassinations. H. Resolution 445, 95th Cong., 1st sess., 1977.

29 Mar. 1977 Reported with H. Rept. 95-129, "Providing for consideration of H. Res. 433," 1 p.: CR, CXXIII, No. 55, H2724.

30 Mar. 1977 Debated, agreed to: CR, CXXIII, No. 56, H2730-39.

74. <u>To provide for the expenses of investigations and studies to be conducted by the Select Committee on Assassinations</u>. H. Resolution 465, 95th Cong., 1st sess., 1977.

31 Mar. 1977 Introduced and sent to Committee on House Administration: CR, CXXIII, No. 57, H2870.

26 April 1977 Reported with H. Rept. 95-223, "Providing for the expenses of investigations and studies to be conducted by the Select Committee on Assassinations," 11 pp.: CR, CXXIII, No. 69, H3619.

28 April 1977 Amended and passed House: CR, CXXIII, No. 71, H3722-26.

75. <u>To authorize the Select Committee on Assassinations or any subcommittee thereof to make applications to courts; and to bring and defend lawsuits arising out of subpoenas, orders immunizing witnesses and compelling them to testify, testimony or the production of evidence, and the failure to testify or produce evidence</u>. H. Resolution 760, 95th Cong., 1st sess., 1977.

13 Sept. 1977 Introduced and sent to Committee on Rules: CR, CXXIII, No. 141, H9368.

16 Sept. 1977 Reported with H. Rept.95-606. "Authorizing the Select Committee on Assassinations or any subcommittee thereof to make applications to courts; and to bring and defend lawsuits arising out of subpoenas, orders immunizing witnesses and compelling them to testify, testimony or the production of evidence, and the failure to testify or produce evidence," 3 pp.: CR, CXXIII, No. 144, H9596.

28 Sept. 1977 Debated and agreed to: CR, CXXIII, No. 153, H10254-62.

76. <u>Providing for funds for the Select Committee on Assassinations</u>. H. Resolution 956, 95th Cong., 2d sess., 1978.

19 Jan. 1978 Introduced and sent to Committee on House Administration: CR, CXXIV, No. 1, H51.

25 Jan. 1978 <u>Report of the Select Committee on Assassinations</u> [Budget]. Committee print. 10 pp.

23 Feb. 1978 Reported with H. Rept. 95-898, amendment, "Providing for funds for the Select Committee on Assassinations," 15 pp.: CR, CXXIV, No. 23, H1484.

13 Mar. 1978 Amended and agreed to: statement of Rep. Dodd of Conn.: CR, CXXIV, No. 35, H1962-66, E1219.

77. Providing for the further expenses of the Select
Committee on Assassinations. H. Resolution 1276, 95th Cong.,
2d sess., 1978.

18 July 1978 Introduced and sent to Committee on House
Administration: CR, CXXIV, No. 108, H6936.

27 July 1978 Statement of Committee Chairman Stokes with
budget request: CR, CXXIV, No. 115, H7453-56.

11 Aug. 1978 Statement of Committee Chief Counsel G.
Robert Blakey: CR, CXXIV, No. 126, H8505.

7 Sept. 1978 Reported with H. Rept. 95-1555, "Providing
for the further expenses of the Select Committee on
Assassinations," 12 pp.: CR, CXXIV, H9285-95.

11 Sept. 1978 Budget statement of Committee Chairman
Stokes: CR, CXXIV, No. 140, H9465.

14 Sept. 1978 Bill considered and agreed to: CR,
CXXIV, No. 143, H9811-14.

78. Final Report of the Select Committee on Assassinations.
Summary of Findings and Recommendations. H. Report 95-1828,
95th Cong., 2d sess., Jan. 2, 1979. Committee Print. v,
9 pp.

79. Hearings before the Select Committee on Assassinations.
95th Cong., 2d sess. Committee Print. 1979. 27 volumes.

Investigation of the Assassination of Martin Luther King,
Jr. vols. I-XIII.

Investigation of the Assassination of President John F.
Kennedy. vols. I-XII.

Legislative and Administrative Reforms. vols. I, II.

80. Report of the Select Committee on Assassinations.
Findings and Recommendations. 95th Cong., 2d sess.
Committee Print. 1979.

81. U.S. Congress. Senate. Authorizing the Commission
established to investigate the assassination of President
John F. Kennedy to compel the attendance and testimony of
witnesses and the production of evidence. Public Law 88-202,
88th Cong., 1st sess., Dec. 13, 1963, S. Joint Resolution 137.

6 Dec. 1963 Introduced and Ordered to lie on the table:
CR, CIX, Part 18, 23598.

9 Dec. 1963 Considered and passed Senate: CR, CIX,
Part 18, 23760.

10 Dec. 1963   Considered and passed Senate: CR, CIX,
Part 18, 23941.

11 Dec. 1963   Examined and signed by the Speaker of the
House: CR, CIX, Part 18, 24332.

12 Dec. 1963   Bill presented to the President: CR, CIX,
Part 18, 24332.

13 Dec. 1963   Approved and signed by the President: CR,
CIX, Part 18, 24788.

82.   U.S. Congress.   Senate.   To authorize the Commission
appointed by the President to conduct an investigation of the
facts relating to the assassination of the late President John
F. Kennedy, to compel the attendance of witnesses and the
production of books, papers, and documents, and for other
purposes.   S. Resolution 2358, 88th Cong., 1st sess., 1963.

4 Dec. 1963   Introduced and sent to Committee on Judiciary: CR, CIX, Part 18, 23191.

83.   _____.   To establish a select committee of
the Senate to conduct an investigation and study with respect
to intelligence activities carried out by or on behalf of
the Federal Government.   S. Resolution 21, 94th Cong., 1st
sess., 1975.

21 Jan. 1975   Ordered to be placed on the table: CR,
CXXI, Part 1, 839-44.

27 Jan. 1975   Debated, agreed to, committee members
nominated: CR, CXXI, Part 2, 1416-34.

28 Jan. 1975   Statement of Senator Bayh of Indiana
supporting Bill: CR, CXXI, Part 2, 1566.

29 April 1975   Committee Rules of Procedure: CR, CXXI,
Part 10, 12306-08.

84.   _____.   _____.

20 Nov. 1975   Committee submitted S. Report 94-465,
Alleged Assassination Plots Involving Foreign Leaders:
An Interim Report of the Select Committee to Study
Governmental Operations with Respect to Intelligence
Activities.   94th Cong., 1st sess., xiii, 349 pp.:
recorded CR, CXXI, Part 29, 37557.

26 April 1976   Under authority of April 14, but dated
April 23, 1976, the Select Committee submitted S. Report
94-755, Final Report Intelligence Activities.   94th
Cong., 2d sess. 1976.   6 parts: CR, CXXI, Part 29,
37557.

85. _____ . _____ .

26 May 1976 Select Committee released Book V:
Select Committee to Study Governmental Operations with
respect to Intelligence Activities. The Investigation
of the Assassination of President John F. Kennedy:
Performance of the Intelligence Agencies. S. Report
94-755, 94th Cong., 2d sess., 1976. Final Report,
Book V. v, 106 pp. The Schweiker Report.

Although publicized and entitled an "Investigation of
the Assassination," the introduction states, and the
text affirms, that the report's purpose was neither to
duplicate the efforts made by the WC nor to review evidence nor to address the question of Lee Harvey Oswald's
relationship to the assassination. Rather, they would
review the quality of the CIA's investigation. Since
the CIA did not investigate for the WC but did analyze
data at the request of the WC, the question posed by the
Senators lacked foundation and bordered on the irrelevant. The report is laced with letters substituted for
the names of informants and agents, purportedly to mask
their identity and protect them from harm. Most of the
names, however, had appeared in The Washington Post
several weeks before; moreover, most were well known
to subject matter specialists. The report is ladened
with inaccuracies, incorrect citations, and quotations
carefully changed from the original to reverse the meaning, e.g. a pro-U.S. statement by Premier Castro is
converted into an anti-U.S. statement. The Schweiker
Report, as well as its media coverage, served to provide
the CIA with a public conduit to disseminate its special
views unchecked by objective and open analysis; [See
4799, 4800, 4813, 4818, 4819, 4830, 4832, 4839, 4875-
4878, 4887-4891, 4893, 4896-4899].

86. _____ . Relating to an investigation
of the death of former President John F. Kennedy. S. Resolution 243, 94th Cong., 1st sess., 1975.

8 Sept. 1975 Introduced and sent to Committee on Govern-
ment Operations, statement of Bill sponsor Senator
Schweiker of Pennsylvania, Warren Commission documents:
CR, CXXI, Part 21, 27824-27.

87. U.S. Department of Justice. Attorney General, Letter
of October 31, 1966. "Providing for the Acquisition and
Preservation by the United States of Items of Evidence Pertaining to the Assassination of President John F. Kennedy."
Federal Register, XXXI, No. 212, 1 Nov. 1966, 13968-74.

88. _____ . [Untitled. 1967 Clark
Panel Review of the Photographs, X-Rays, and Other Documents
Related to President Kennedy's Autopsy]. Performed by James
J. Humes, J. Thornton Boswell, and Pierre A. Finck, 20 Jan.
1967. 5 pages typescript. Facsimile reproduced in Weisberg,
Post Mortem [973], 575-579.

Report by three members of the original autopsy team's
secret review of the autopsy documents purporting to
sustain the validity of the "original" autopsy report.
Based on the one hand upon autopsy documents, whose
genuineness is unproven, and on the other hand upon an
"original" that is the severely changed, third autopsy
report, the review seems to serve unclear political ends
of the AG's office.

89. _____. "1968 Panel Review of
Photographs, X-Ray Films, Documents and Other Evidence Pertaining to the Fatal Wounding of President John F. Kennedy
on November 22, 1963 in Dallas, Texas." Performed for
Attorney General Ramsay Clark by William H. Carnes, Russell
S. Fisher, Russell H. Morgan, and Alan R. Moritz in April
and March 1968, but released in Jan. 1969. 16 page typescript. Facsimile reproduced in Weisberg, Post Mortem [973],
580-595.

Report by five forensic specialists on their review of
the JFK autopsy materials requested by AG Clark. Increas-
ing popular disquiet over the official conclusions coupled
with the uncertain direction that the Jim Garrison inquiry
in New Orleans might take engendered the review. Clark
kept the report secret until the last day of his administration when it was released to thwart an effort by
Garrison's office to obtain through court proceedings
the original autopsy materials for his Louisiana trial.
The report was substituted for the evidentiary items
themselves.

90. _____. "Report of Inspection
by Naval Medical Staff on November 1, 1966, at National
Archives of X-Rays and Photographs of Autopsy of President
John Kennedy." Performed by James J. Humes, J. Thornton
Boswell, John H. Ebersole, and John T. Stringer for the
National Archives at the request of the Department of Justice.
1 Nov. 1966. 11 page typescript. Facsimile reproduced in
Weisberg, Post Mortem [973], 565-573.

Report by four members of the original autopsy team purporting to authenticate the photographs and X-rays of the
JFK autopsy being turned over to the National Archives by
the Kennedy family. Their secret review and the subsequent wide use of it by federal publicists as a scientific
imprimatur on the findings of the WC appeared as part of
federal activity on the third anniversary of the assassination, to lay to rest popular discontent with the official conclusions. Neither the genuineness and complete-
ness nor the chain of possession of the autopsy evidence
has ever been established. The subject addressed is thus
erroneously presumed; since the team itself stated under
oath in 1964 that they had never seen the photographs or
X-rays and the WC had not used them during its taking of
witness testimony, the assertion of authenticity must be
questioned.

91. U.S. Federal Bureau of Investigation. Investigation of Assassination of President John F. Kennedy, November 22, 1963. Washington, D.C.: Federal Bureau of Investigation, 9 Dec. 1963. Five volumes.

An error ladened, severely distorted, and deceptive report of the FBI investigation into the assassination that preceded the formation of the WC and became the controversial Procrustean base for its inquiry. The WC assigned it Commission Document number CD 1. Only 450 words appear on the murder, and these exclude the shot that wounded citizen James T. Tague and the wound on President Kennedy's throat. From this paltry base the FBI asserts Oswald was the lone, psychologically disturbed assassin, a conclusory statement. In advance of delivery to the WC the FBI secretly released the findings to the press in a successful effort to mold public opinion. The WC's skepticism, regarding both the validity of the FBI's finding and the presumption of Oswald's guilt, is found in its executive session transcripts [109, 110]. A discussion of CD 1 is found in: [389, 703, 722, 735].

92. _____. Investigation of Assassination of President John F. Kennedy, November 22, 1963. Washington, D.C.: Federal Bureau of Investigation, Jan. 1964. Supplemental Report. Became CD 107.

Factually inaccurate and deceptive supplement to CD 1 demanded by the WC in an attempt to overcome the evidentiary problems presented by the initial FBI report, CD 1. The presumption of Oswald's guilt is maintained and expanded.

93. U.S. President. Executive Order 11128. "Closing Government Departments and Agencies on November 25, 1963." Federal Register, XXVIII, No. 230, 26 Nov. 1963, 12609.

94. _____. Executive Order 11129. "Designating Certain Facilities of the National Aeronautics and Space Administration and of the Department of Defense, in the State of Florida, as the John F. Kennedy Space Center." Federal Register, XXVIII, No. 233, 29 Nov. 1963, 12787; [See 3259, 3613].

95. _____. Executive Order 11130. "Appointing a Commission to Report upon the Assassination of President John F. Kennedy." Federal Register, XXVIII, No. 233, 2 Dec. 1963, 12789; [See 3255].

96. _____. Executive Order 11652. "Classification and Declassification of National Security Information and Material." Federal Register, XXXVIII, No. 48, 9 Mar. 1972, 5209-5218.

97. _____. Executive Order 11828. "Establishing
a Commission on CIA Activities within the United States."
Federal Register, XL, No. 4, 6 Jan. 1975, 1219-1220.

98. _____. Executive Order 11848. "Extending
the Reporting Date for the Commission on CIA Activities within
the United States." Federal Register, XL, No. 65, 1 April
1975, 14885.

99. _____. Letter of November 23, 1964. "Non-
applicability of Declassification Procedures to the Report of
the President's Commission on the Assassination of President
Kennedy." Federal Register, XXIX, No. 232, 27 Nov. 1964,
15893.

100. _____. Proclamation 3561. "National Day of
Mourning, November 25, 1963." Federal Register, XXVIII, No.
230, 26 Nov. 1963, 12607.

101. U.S. President's Commission on CIA Activities Within
the United States. Report to the President. Washington,
D.C.: Government Printing Office, 1975.

The Rockefeller Report.

On 6 June 1975 the special commission chaired by Vice
President Nelson Rockefeller submitted its 299 page
Report on CIA activities. Pages 251-269 are concerned
with the widely circulated allegations that the CIA
assassinated JFK, allegations which were made by critics.
In addition to performing another autopsy review allegedly, the Rockefeller Commission claimed to have examined
film and many documents in support of their conclusion
that the charges were without foundation. The Commission
successfully demolished the critics' allegation that
certain "tramps" captured on film as they were being
escorted past the TSBD by policemen on 22 Nov. 1962 were
CIA assassins. The Commission as well as the segment
of critics making the allegations ignored the findings of
private investigators that demonstrated the "tramps"
were in fact "winos" who were well known to local residents. David Belin, former staff counsel of the WC,
served as executive director. The inquiry was conducted
largely in secret and its records are sealed [12] at the
President Gerald R. Ford Library; [See 714, 1774, 4520,
4524, 4783, 4786, 4788, 4789, 4794, 4796-4798, 4803,
4808-4811, 4822, 4837-4839].

102. U.S. Warren Commission. Investigation of the Assassination of President John F. Kennedy. Hearings Before the
President's Commission on the Assassination of President
Kennedy. Washington, D.C.: Government Printing Office,
1964. 26 volumes.

A 20,000 page, 10,400,000-word body of documents from
the 300 cubic feet assembled by the WC and printed as a

massive appendix to the official Warren Report [684].
Volumes I-XV consist of the printing of verbatim testimony of witnesses who appeared before the WC or its staff
counsel.   In XV, 753-801, is an index to names mentioned
or referred to in I-XV, and 801-826 is an index to
Commission Exhibits 1-1053 mentioned throughout I-XV.

Volumes XVI-XXVI consist of the facsimile reproduction
of exhibits divided into three parts.   XVI-XVIII are
Commission Exhibits 1-1053 referring to various documents
or parts of documents gathered by the Commission that
bear no other classification number.   XIX-XXI are deposition exhibits referred to by name of person, e.g. Allen
Exhibit No. 1.   XXII-XXVI are Commission Exhibits 1054-
3154, exhibit numbers assigned to Commission Documents
numbered 1-1555, or parts of them.   Commission Documents
range in size from a single page to several volumes and
in complexity from a simple statement to an involved
argument.   Before being printed as CE 1054-3154, CD 1-1555
were shuffled and renumbered.   Some CDs were printed in
whole; many were split into parts and selectively printed;
some were neither printed nor made available in unprinted
form for several years in the National Archives.   "A few
of the documents are missing."   Identification and location of CDs is extremely difficult for no effort was made
to cross reference CD numbers with CE numbers.   A cross
reference is important if one is to find a CD in the 26
volumes or if one wishes to analyze any excluded material.
In July, 1968, a private group, The Committee to Investigate Assassinations, compiled a useful research tool from
WC records in an untitled "[Cross List reference for
Commission Exhibits and Commission Documents]," mimeo-
graphed.   In 1973 the National Archives printed this basic
information with some corrections in Johnson Inventory
[11].   This gives the CD number; part or pages; CE number;
description.   It omits several of the CD's available in
the Archives, such as the FBI report, CD 107.

Witness testimony is printed without regard to chronology,
subject matter, or alphabetical principles.   The exhibit
volumes are a subject matter wilderness devoid of a
principle of selection and with documents comprising
basic components of evidence being widely dispersed in
several volumes and interspersed with irrelevant matter
such as reprints of anti-communist diatribes or accounts
of dock loadings in obscure ports.   Some of the exhibits
contain information damaging to the official conclusions
of the WC, e.g. in XXVI an affidavit by T. F. Bowley,
who was never called as a witness and who is not referred
to in the WR, excludes Oswald from the Tippit murder
scene.   The WC staff blocked the printing of a subject
matter index to the 26 volumes.   Two privately printed
indexes have been compiled, however, by private citizens
[696, 697].

(2) NON-FEDERAL

103. Carr, Waggoner. Texas Supplemental Report on the
Assassination of President Kennedy and the Serious Wounding
of Governor John B. Connally, November 22, 1963. Austin,
Texas: Texas Attorney General's Office, 5 Oct. 1964. 20
pages.

> The Texas Court of Inquiry's report: [See 571, 3164,
> 3807].

104. Carrollton Press, Inc. "Central Intelligence Agency.
Kennedy Assassination." Microfiche edition. In The Declassi-
fied Documents Reference System. Retrospective Collection.
Arlington, Va.: Carrollton Press, Inc., 1976, page 33 B.

> 1,049 pages from 325 CIA documents on the JFK assassina-
> tion published in microfiche, but with printed abstract.
> Date of release not given. The abstract contains con-
> clusory statements and controversial descriptions pro-
> vided to the reader as facts, e.g. "Oswald's assassina-
> tion of Pres. J. F. Kennedy;" [See 2].

105. _____. "Federal Bureau of Investigation.
[Kennedy, President John F., assassination. . . .]." Microfiche selection. In Declassified Documents 1978 Annual
Collection. Arlington, Va.: Carrollton Press, Inc., 1978,
pages 156-186.

> 2,505 pages from 469 FBI documents available in the FBI
> Reading Room [5] which were selected from the total files
> released. The professional editors used the criterion
> for selection: "if it was of interest." The Contributing
> Editor, Annadel N. Wile, served for 20 years as the CIA's
> chief of indexing operations.

106. [Jaworski, Leon]. Files of Evidence Connected with
the Investigation of the Assassination of President John F.
Kennedy. N. p., n.d. 21 vols., in two-reel microfilm edition
Washington, D.C.: Microcard Editions, [1967].

> 5,500 page files of the Texas Court of Inquiry containing
> data on the Dallas area, transcripts of radio trans-
> missions, plans and photos of scenes, and related matter.
> On Jaworski's role see Weisberg [736] and Meagher[571];
> [See 109, 172, 4838].

107. Lifton, David (comp.). Document Addendum to the
Warren Report. El Segundo, Cal.: Sightext Publications, 1968

> Contains the early declassified proceedings of WC execu-
> tive sessions; Commission Document 344; transcript of
> tape recordings of the first interrogation of Marina
> Oswald, 22 Nov. 1963; and the Liebeler Memorandum of

6 Sept. 1964, "Galley proofs of Chapter IV of the Report;"
[See 32, 172, 833, 2318].

108. Microfilming Corporation of America. The F.B.I. Files
on the Assassination of President Kennedy. 35 mm microfilm.
New York: Microfilming Corporation of America, A New York
Times Company, 1978.

Microfilm of the first 90,000 pages of FBI Headquarters
Files released in Dec. 1977 and Jan. 1978. Since additional documents as well as some previously deleted portions of sanitized documents have been released and
included in the Files, that term is misleading. The
literature accompanying the microfilm and the advertising
brochures are rife with factual inaccuracies. They offer
conclusory statements, made by persons lacking subject-
matter expertise, for future researchers. Such tangential diversions, from non-FBI evidence already unearthed
and established by scholars, demand that all students use
this collection with special caution; [See 5].

109. Weisberg, Harold. Whitewash IV. JFK Assassination
Transcript. Legal Analysis by Jim Lesar. Frederick, Md.:
By the author, 1974.

Facsimile copy of the 27 Jan. 1964 WC executive session
transcript together with a line by line comparison of it
with the purported verbatim transcript reprinted by WC
member Gerald R. Ford in Portrait of the Assassin [706].
The comparison shows unindicated editing by Ford. Also,
documents relate to the generation of the transcript
via a federal suit [172], including those revealing a
secret meeting of WC with Texas officials; [See 110].

110. Wrone, David R. (ed.) The Legal Proceedings of Harold
Weisberg v. General Services Administration, Civil Action
2052-73, Together with the January 22 and January 27 Warren
Commission Transcripts (The Freedom of Information Act and
Political Assassinations, vol. 1). Stevens Point, Wisconsin:
University of Wisconsin-Stevens Point Foundation Press, Inc.,
1978.

Reprints of the court records of a Freedom of Information
Act suit that released two improperly classified WC executive session transcripts. Included are affidavits by
Archivist James B. Rhoads, WC general counsel J. Lee Rankin, and Harold Weisberg; WC Chairman Earl Warren's letter
re disposition of WC records; WC member Richard Russell's
protest over a faked, official transcript that obliterated
his dissent from the lone assassin theory; and related
issues in a court tested record.

Part III: Local Judicial Records

Dallas.

Legal records associated with the several trials of Oswald's murderer Jack Ruby are found in the courts here. No subject index exists.

New Orleans.

The boundaries of the parish (county) of Orleans and the City of New Orleans are the same.

111. Municipal Court, New Orleans.

The records of Oswald's 9 Aug. 1963 arrest for street brawling are presumably preserved. No finding aids exist and entries are by an arrest "number only."

112. Civil Court Parish of Orleans.

Records of suits for slander, libel, and damages are maintained here. Representative of these is Bringuier v. Canyon Books [126].

113. Criminal Court Parish of Orleans.

Records of the cases of many individuals charged during the complex course of the Garrison inquiry are preserved here. A card file by name exists. Representative instances are:

Andrews, Dean A. Jr.

114. State v. Dean A. Andrews, Jr. No. 197-998. 17 Mar. 1969 Perjury.

115. State v. Dean A. Andrews, Jr. No. 198-483. 12 April 1967 Perjury.

116. State v. Dean A. Andrews, Jr. No. 200-053. 18 July 1967 Perjury.

117. State v. Dean A. Andrews, Jr. No. 208-299. 5 Mar. 1969 Perjury.

McMaines, Mrs. Lilly Mae.

118. State v. Mrs. Lilly Mae McMaines. No. 198-109. n.d. material witness in 198-059.

Novel, Gordon.

119. State v. Gordon Novel. No. 198-066. 23 Mar. 1967. Material witness in 198-059.

120. State v. Gordon Novel. No. 198-198. 31 Mar. 1967.
Conspiracy to burglary.

121. State v. Gordon Novel. No. 198-471. 12 April 1967.
Theft.

Russo, Perry R.

122. State v. Perry R. Russo. No. 216-270. 7 May 1974.
Possession of stolen property.

Shaw, Clay L.

123. State of Louisiana v. Clay L. Shaw. No. 198-059.
Section C 1 Mar. 1967. Judge Edward A. Haggerty, Jr.

District Attorney Jim Garrison charged Shaw with conspiring with David Ferrie and Lee Harvey Oswald "to murder
John F. Kennedy." After numerous appeals and motions in
state and federal courts the trial began on 21 Jan. 1969.
Garrison prosecuted two cases in the guise of one:
(1) he attempted to try the validity of the Warren
Commission's official conclusions; and (2) he tried Shaw
for conspiring to kill JFK. In mid-Dec. 1968 Garrison
appointed his assistant William Alford to prosecute the
case, but Alford had been associated with other duties
in the DA's office and was ill-prepared to conduct a
major, complex trial.

During the trial Alford forced the release of the Zapruder
film from the control of Time-Life and showed it to the
jury; witnesses from the FBI and other governmental agencies testified. Although Judge Haggerty stated that anything in connection with the assassination could be
introduced into the trial proceedings, the DA and Alford
took a restricted approach.

On 1 Mar. 1969, after 51 minutes of deliberation the jury
found Shaw innocent. The members of the jury, individ-
ually polled afterwards, agreed the prosecution had
proven President Kennedy died as a result of a conspiracy,
but that no evidence connected Shaw with it.

124. State of Louisiana v. Clay L. Shaw. No. 208-260.
Section A 3 Mar. 1969. Judge Edward A. Haggerty, Jr.

The first working day following the completion of the
conspiracy trial, Garrison charged Shaw with perjury on
the basis of testimony Shaw had given on the stand in his
own defense at the conspiracy trial. Garrison's only
witnesses were those who had appeared at the conspiracy
trial. Garrison charged that Shaw lied when he denied
knowing Oswald or Ferrie, alleged co-conspirators in
the assassination of JFK. After extended legal appeals
to the state courts Shaw was able to obtain relief from
the United States Court of Appeals which ordered the

United States District Court to hold a hearing. After an extended hearing on 27 May 1971 the court issued a permanent injunction against Garrison and his associates prohibiting trial of Shaw on the perjury charge; [See 4640, 4644].

Part IV: Federal Judicial Records
(1) SUITS INVOLVING PUBLICATION OF EVIDENCE

125.   Jim Braden a/k/a Eugene Hale Brading v. Michael Ewing, Bernard Fensterwald, Jr., the Committee to Investigate Assassinations, Inc., Kensington Publishing Corporation, Peter Noyes, and Pinnacle Books. Law No. 48449. Circuit Court, Montgomery County, Maryland.

A 1978 libel suit against Fensterwald and Ewing, Coincidence or Conspiracy? [2161] and Noyes, Legacy of Doubt [2207].

126.   Dr. Carlos Bringuier v. The Canyon Books and Books Distributing Company, et al. 1968. Civil Court Parish of Orleans.

A suit for damages against Harold Weisberg's publishers alleging inaccuracies and libels in Oswald in New Orleans [1901]. Although successful in this local court, the case had no standing outside the parish; damages were never collected; the entire action merely served to publicize Bringuier's lectures on the assassination. See Bringuier [1890].

127.   John Henry Faulk v. Alpa Productions, Pat Thompson, Lincoln Carl, and Mark Lane. Civil Action No. 3-76-1671-D. United States District Court, Northern District of Texas, Dallas.

Suit to collect monies due on film on JFK assassination [1131] in which Faulk appeared. The check for initial payment was returned by the bank for insufficient funds. Subsequent percentage on gross was never received. Settled by agreement 30 Nov. 1977.

128.   Jacqueline B. Kennedy v. Harper & Row Publishers, Cowles Communications, Inc., and William Manchester. Manhattan Supreme Court, New York. Justice Saul S. Streit.

On 14 Dec. 1966 the widow of JFK filed suit to obtain certain changes in the manuscript of William Manchester's Death of a President [2026]. On 21 Dec. JBK and Look reached an agreement where "passages to which Mrs. Kennedy objected on personal grounds" were deleted. Look had sold rights to West Germany's Stern and on 23 Jan. 1967 filed papers in Hamburg civil court seeking an injunction to halt publication of the material. After publishing

some issues with the serialized material in it, Henri
Nanner, publisher of Stern, had voluntarily agreed to
delete the personal passages in the remaining issues.
On 16 Jan. 1967 JBK, Manchester, and Harper & Row
reached a "mutual agreement" where "certain personal
passages of concern to Mrs. Kennedy have been deleted
or modified."

129. Gordon Novel v. Jim Garrison and HMH Publishing Co.,
Inc., a Delaware Corporation. Civil Action No. 67 C 1895.
United States District Court for the Northern District of
Illinois, Eastern District. Judge Campbell.

In Oct. 1967, Playboy published an interview with
Garrison; Novel sued claiming it libeled him. Garrison
moved for dismissal of the libel action on the ground
the court lacked jurisdiction over his person because
he lived in Louisiana. The Court, refusing Garrison's
motion to dismiss, ruled that the State of Illinois
bore the most substantial relationship to the tortious
act, since the magazine was published in Illinois.
294 F. Supp. 825.

130. Time Incorporated v. Bernard Geis Associates, Bernard
Geis, Josiah Thompson, and Random House, Inc. No. 67 Civ.
4736. United States District Court, Southern District of
New York.

Time held it had a copyright on Abraham Zapruder's motion
picture that had been infringed by Thompson's Six Seconds
in Dallas [732]. The Court held "fair use" of the
Zapruder frames had been made in the book because of
the overriding public interest, in having fullest information available on the assassination. Time Inc. seemed
not to have been damaged by the publication of the
frames. 293 F. Supp. 130.

(2) SUITS CONCERNING OSWALD'S POSSESSIONS

Weapons acquisition

A 6.5mm Mannlicher-Carcano rifle discovered on the sixth
floor of the TSBD and asserted to have been Oswald's,
although he denied it, and a .38 Special S & W revolver
taken from Oswald after his arrest were acquired by the
FBI on 22 Nov. 1963 and held by the Bureau or by the WC
until 7 Nov. 1966. On 2 Nov. 1965 Public Law 89-318
established a national interest in items of evidence
associated with the assassination of President Kennedy.
It required the Attorney General to acquire all right,
title, and interest in the items by determination and
then declaration in the Federal District Court where a
claimant to such items resides. On 1 Nov. 1966 the

Attorney General published in the <u>Federal Register</u> [87] his determination of the national interest in the items and his declaration to acquire title to certain items of WC evidence, including the two weapons. On 8 Nov. 1966 the weapons were deposited in the National Archives. Prior to their deposit, on 29 Mar. 1965 and with extensive press coverage, John J. King of Colorado purchased title to the weapons from Marina Oswald Porter, intending to acquire them from the federal government. The assumption running throughout all the ensuing legal suits and press accounts is that the rifle belonged to Oswald, that the rifle fired the three shots that killed the President, and that the pistol fired the shots that killed Police Officer J. D. Tippit.

I.   Government's attempt to acquire through forfeiture.

131.   <u>United States of America, Libelant, v. One 6.5mm Mannlicher-Carcano Military Rifle, Model 91-38, Serial No. C2766 with Appurtenances, and One .38 Special S & W Victory Model Revolver, Serial No. V510210, with Appurtenances, Respondents</u>.   Civil Action No. 3-1171.   United States District Court for the Northern District of Texas, Dallas Division.   Judge Joe Ewing Estes.

On 10 Sept. 1965 the government filed a libel of information against a rifle and a pistol, asserting they had been previously owned by Oswald and alleging the weapons had been forfeited to the U.S. by virtue of violations of the Federal Firearms Act, viz.:   the weapons' dealers did not keep proper records since Oswald bought the weapons under a false name; therefore, the records were false.   The Court agreed and ordered the weapons forfeited.   250 F. Supp. 410.

II.   Reversal of forfeiture.

132.   <u>John J. King v. United States of America</u>.   5th Cir. No. 23637.   United States Court of Appeals for the Fifth Circuit.   Judges Tuttle, Brown, and Coleman.

King appealed the forfeiture decision.   On 29 July 1966, opinion by Tuttle, the Appeals Court reversed the lower court stating it could not accept the theory that the weapons are a species of Deodands.   No provisions in the Firearms Act required a purchaser to use his true name.   In order to gain title the government would have to resort to condemnation.   364 F. 2d 235.

III.   King seeks compensation.

133.   <u>John J. King v. United States of America</u>.   Civil Action No. 67-C-518.   United States District Court for the District of Colorado.   Judge William E. Doyle.

On 27 Oct. 1967 King filed suit under Pub. L. 89-318
against the U.S. seeking proper compensation for the two
weapons. On 8 Nov. 1968 the court held King was entitled
to bring into evidence only material relating to the
intrinsic value of the weapons, not material relating to
the potential profits for commercial display or their
market value. 292 F. Supp. 767.

IV. Appeal of forfeiture.

134. United States of America v. One 6.5mm Mannlicher-
Carcano Military Rifle, Model 91-38, Serial No. C2766, with
Appurtenances, and One .38 Special S & W Victory Model Re-
volver, Serial No. V510210, with Appurtenances. 5th Cir. No.
26620. United States Court of Appeals for the Fifth Circuit.
Judges Brown, Thornberry, and Morgan.

King appealed the District Court's decision dismissing
the forfeiture judgment claiming it erred in refusing
to adjudicate his claim of ownership. On 23 Jan. 1969,
the court opined that since the issue of ownership was
at that time before the Colorado District Court where
Pub. L. 89-318 required it to be heard, the Texas Court
was correct in not adjudicating the ownership claim.
406 F. 2d 1170.

Compensation suits

Under the terms of Pub. L. 89-318 the widow of Lee Harvey
Oswald attempted to acquire compensation for property
taken by the federal government.

I. The suit.

135. Marina N. Oswald Porter et al. v. United States of
America. Civil Action No. 3-2282. United States District
Court for the Northern District of Texas, Dallas Division.
Judge Estes.

Suit to determine worth. On 16 Sept. 1968 William R.
West, Esq., was appointed Special Master for the purpose
of hearing evidence and making findings on the value of
the property as of 1 Nov. 1966, the date of federal
acquisition. West found the value to be $17,729.37. A
jury having been waived, the court used the findings to
make its decision. Since West's figure included value
accruing to the property from the act of a "depraved
mind," Mrs. Porter was awarded only $3,000. 335 F.
Supp. 498.

II. Appeal.

136. Marina N. Oswald Porter, et al. v. United States of
America. 5th Cir. No. 72-1426. United States Court of
Appeals for the Fifth Circuit. Judges Tuttle, Wisdom, and
Simpson.

On 26 Feb. 1973 the Court of Appeals reversed the District Court's ruling and remanded the case for entry of judgment of $17,729.37. The added value resulting from the interest of collectors had to be taken into consideration. 473 F. 2d 1329.

(3) FEDERAL LITIGATION ASSOCIATED WITH THE GARRISON INQUIRY

137.   United States ex rel. State of Louisiana v. James B. Rhoads. District of Columbia Court of General Sessions, Misc. 825-69A.   Jan. 1969.   Judge Charles W. Halleck, Jr.

After the Department of Justice refused to serve a 9 May 1968 subpoena of New Orleans District Attorney Jim Garrison for the pictures and X-rays of JFK's autopsy, Garrison obtained a second subpoena and moved in the courts to force the National Archives and Archivist Rhoads to release the documents. On 17 Jan. 1969 Garrison's assistant Numa Bertel accompanied by Washington, D.C. attorney Bernard Fensterwald, Jr., and Harold Weisberg, their subject matter expert, argued the case. Eight federal attorneys represented the government. Late the day before, Attorney General Ramsey Clark had filed papers and a Panel Report which was secretly drawn eleven months before by his selected experts. The Panel Report sustained the WC conclusions and the government moved to substitute it for the primary material.

By working through the night, plaintiff prepared to confute the Panel Report and with it the Warren Report. At the critical juncture, when Bertel prepared to place his witness on the stand to give evidence contradicting facts in sworn federal affidavits, the New Orleans District Attorney's office reached the courtroom by phone and directed Bertel not to place witnesses on the stand, in effect blocking the effort to obtain the autopsy material.   Garrison's office later said that the move was designed to halt the trying of a state case in a federal court. While the case suggests confusion in the District Attorney's office and reveals a basic inability to grasp the evidentiary nature of the assassination, it also starkly underlines a certain deviousness consistently practiced by federal agencies. More important, it suggests that the District Attorney and his staff were imbued with a deep pessimism over their ability to meet the power of the highly orchestrated federal resistance to their local criminal case.

138.   Gordon Novel v. Jim Garrison et al. Civil Action No. 67-747. United States District Court for the Eastern District of Louisiana, New Orleans Division. Judge Comiskey.

Garrison's attempt to obtain extradition of Novel from
Ohio to answer an indictment in New Orleans was blocked.
Novel then sued Garrison and others for libel. When
Garrison wished to have his pretrial discovery of Novel
in the libel suit take place in New Orleans, Novel sued
for a protective order to avoid the journey. On 7 June
1967 the court denied Novel's motion, as the Federal Rules
give a broad and powerful right of discovery; Garrison
could depose Novel in New Orleans under oral examination.
No special circumstances exist under the rules. 42 F.R.D.
234.

Shaw I

A suit for an injunction against state prosecution for
conspiracy to commit murder.

139.   Clay L. Shaw v. Jim Garrison et al.   Civil Action No.
68-1063. United States District Court for the Eastern District of Louisiana, New Orleans Division.   Judges Ainsworth,
Heebe, and Comiskey.

On 27 May 1968 Shaw filed suit asking for injunctive
relief from state prosecution for having "willfully and
unlawfully conspire[d]. . . to murder John F. Kennedy."
Edward F. Wegmann, William J. Wegmann, and Salvatore
Panzeca represented Shaw; Shaw based his request for
relief on the illegal search of his premises, the insufficient evidence for his indictment, the prejudicial
nature of the case caused by the publicity, and the
state court's unjust denial of his application. Shaw
also requested the Court declare the Warren Commission's
Report "valid, accurate and correct" and "binding and
controlling upon all courts of the United States, and
admissible in evidence in the state court prosecution."
On 23 July 1968 the court declined to rule on the con-
stitutionality of the numerous state statutes challenged
by Shaw stating that the request was premature and that
he must first seek vindication of his rights in the
state courts. The court refused to declare the Warren
Report binding upon all courts. 293 F. Supp. 937.

140.   Clay L. Shaw v. Jim Garrison et al.   United States
Supreme Court No. 579.   October term, 1968.

On 9 Dec. 1968 the Supreme Court, per curiam, affirmed
the District Court's judgment. The Chief Justice took
no part in the decision. 393 U.S. 220, 89 S.Ct. 453,
21 L. Ed. 2d 392.

Shaw II

Suit to obtain restraining order blocking Garrison's
trial of Shaw for perjury.

141. <u>Clay L. Shaw v. Jim Garrison</u>. Civil Action No. 71-135.
United States District Court for the Eastern District of
Louisiana. Judge Christenberry.

On 1 Mar. 1969 Shaw was found innocent of the charge of
conspiring to murder JFK. On 3 Mar. 1969, the first working day afterwards, Garrison charged Shaw with the crime
of perjury, saying he lied when testifying in his own
defense that he did not know Lee Harvey Oswald or David
Ferrie, alleged co-conspirators in the Garrison-envisioned
plot which killed the president. Garrison's only witnesses were those who testified at the murder trial.
After exhausting state remedies Shaw turned to the federal
system.

On 18 Jan. 1971 Shaw applied to the District Court for a
temporary restraining order to block the perjury trial
scheduled for that day. Because of the imminence of the
trial and the ex parte nature of the temporary restraining order, the court refused.

142. That day Shaw applied to the Appeals Court for emergency relief. A panel of judges directed the District
Court to hear his application for injunctive relief;
the lower court issued a temporary restraining order.

Shaw's attorneys were Edward F. Wegmann, William J.
Wegmann, F. Irvin Dymond, and Salvatore Panzeca; Garrison's attorneys were John P. Volz, Andrew J. Sciambra,
and William R. Alford.

On Jan. 25, 26, 27, Judge Christenberry heard numerous
witnesses and filed into evidence 55 exhibits. Shaw
argued the prosecution was instituted in bad faith and
for the purpose of harassment and that this was the
second of a series of multiple prosecutions to which
he had been and would be subjected. In rebuttal Garrison
argued that he was primarily interested in the forces
behind JFK's assassination and individuals were not
basic to his investigation. In referring to Garrison's
efforts to separate the two issues of JFK and Shaw's
trial, the court stated that Shaw was an integral part
of the probe; there were no grounds for Garrison pro-
ceeding without his arrest.

At the same time the court found substantial weakness
in Garrison's case. The state used drugs, hypnosis,
and other methods to enhance the memory of the key witness, Perry Raymond Russo, who was used to connect Shaw
with Oswald and Ferrie. The court found that the
techniques actually inculcated the desired information
and were incompatible with the American system of justice. Too, Garrison's promotion of the perjury trial
through extensive press conferences related to the promotion of his recently published book <u>Heritage of Stone</u>
[1894], a contract to write three more books, and a need

to repay substantial obligations owed one of his private
financial backers in a local merchants' special fund.

Whereas previously the federal system of constitutional
protection had been typically given a limited application
to a few rights of the individual, the court held that it
applied more widely and spread its protective mantle over
Shaw by permanently enjoining Garrison and his associates
from further prosecution of him.   328 F. Supp. 390.

143.   Clay L. Shaw v. Jim Garrison.   5 CA No. 71-2422.
United States Court of Appeals for the Fifth Circuit.
Judges Wisdom, Godbold, and Roney.

Garrison appealed.   On 31 July 1972 Judge Wisdom delivered
the opinion of the Appeals Court affirming the lower
court's decision.   Extended treatment was given to the
weakness of Garrison's perjury charge and to his severe
conflict with financial interests, while also stressing
serious violations of Shaw's civil rights.   467 F. 2d 113.

144.   Clay L. Shaw v. Jim Garrison.   United States Supreme
Court No. 72-458.   October term, 1972.

The Supreme Court denied certiorari.

93 S.Ct. 467, 409 U.S. 1024, 34 L. Ed. 2d 317.

Shaw III

Suit for damages against Garrison and others who
allegedly conspired to deprive Shaw of his civil rights.

145.   Clay L. Shaw v. Jim Garrison et al.   Civil Action No.
70-466.   United States District Court for the Eastern District of Louisiana.   Judge Frederick Heebe.

In Feb. 1970 Shaw filed suit against Garrison and five
others who, he alleged, had deprived him of his civil
rights under 42 USCS P 1983 when he was prosecuted in
bad faith for conspiring to kill JFK and for perjury
charges connected with the same.   Shaw died 15 Aug.
1974 and left no survivors.   Louisiana law of survivorship would have abated the suit.   On 7 Oct. 1974 the
court granted the motion of Edward F. Wegmann, executor
of Shaw's last will, to be substituted as the plaintiff.
The defendants asked for the case to be dismissed because
of Shaw's death, but the Court found the civil rights
statutes provided broad remedial relief and federal common
law required the suit to survive in favor of the executor
of Shaw's last will.   On 4 Mar. 1975 the Court ruled
against the defendants.   391 F. Supp. 1353.

146. Clay L. Shaw v. Jim Garrison et al. 5 CA No. 75-2019.
United States Court of Appeals for the Fifth Circuit. Judges
Wisdom, Ingraham, and Grooms.

On 24 Jan. 1977 the Appeals Court upheld the lower court's
decision. The brief by Shaw's attorney is lengthy and
profusely documented. 545 F. 2d 980. On 20 June 1977 a
rehearing en banc was denied. 555 F. 2d 1391.

147. Willard E. Robertson v. Edward F. Wegmann, Executor
of the Estate of Clay L. Shaw. United States Supreme Court
No. 77-178. Argued 21 Mar. 1978. Decided 31 May 1978.

The United States Supreme Court reversed the lower court's
opinion. Justice Marshall delivered the opinion of the
Court, in which Chief Justice Burger, and Justices Stewart, Powell, Rehnquist, and Stevens joined. Justice
Blackmun filed a dissenting opinion in which Justices
Brennan and White joined. Robertson was one of the five
other persons in the suit who was alleged to have lent
financial support to Garrison's investigation of Shaw
through an organization known as "Truth and Consequences."
The fact Shaw died without survivors was not sufficient
in itself for the Louisiana law of survivorship to be set
aside as "inconsistent" with the federal laws and the
Constitution. 436 US 584, 98 S. Ct. 1991, 56 L. Ed. 2d 554.

148. Walter Sheridan and Richard Townley v. Jim Garrison
et al. Civil Action No. 67-1147. United States District
Court for the Eastern District of Louisiana, New Orleans
Division. Judge Alvin B. Rubin.

National Broadcasting Company television news reporter
Sheridan and WDSU-TV, New Orleans, news reporter Townley
were charged by District Attorney Garrison with public
bribery of a witness and Townley with intimidating witnesses in June and July 1967. The newsmen appealed to
the federal courts alleging the charges were made in bad
faith to intimidate those who disagreed with the District
Attorney, that he suppressed evidence that demonstrated
the charges false, and that if the charges stood they
would drastically inhibit the freedom of the press.
Judge Rubin, 28 Aug. 1967, granted Garrison summary judgment arguing that the Anti-Injunction Statute, 28 U.S.C.
P 2283, barred the federal courts from intervening in a
local court and that the cases were not extreme enough to
warrant an intervention via other constitutional grounds.
273 F. Supp. 673.

149. Walter Sheridan and Richard Townley v. Jim Garrison
et al. 5 CA No. 25516. United States Court of Appeals,
Fifth Circuit. Judges Thornberry, Dyer, and Fisher.

On 13 Aug. 1969 the Appeals Court reversed and remanded
the lower court stating that the District Attorney was
harassing the reporters and violating their exercise of

free speech. The Anti-Injunction Statute had to give way
before the clear instance of the violations of First
Amendment rights, as the documents filed with the court,
it ruled, showed.   Rehearing denied on 16 Sept. 1969.
415 F. 2d 699.

(4) "FREEDOM OF INFORMATION ACT" LITIGATION

Access to FOIA court records relating to the JFK assassination is difficult.   Records are stored in court facilities, and no subject index exists in a particular court,
let alone at the national level.   Court reporting services
and legal indexes are extremely selective and those reported or listed are not designated by subject matter,
but by legal principles involved.   Approach is by case
number only.   In each District Court an index by case name
and number exists.   This leads to the Court Docket which
lists the filings and proceedings in the case.   Most completed federal case records are typically stored in a
regional records storage facility.   A request takes a few
days to be processed and the materials retrieved.   Some
of the cases are but a few scant pages; others are several
feet thick.

In Wrone, Legal Proceedings [110], a FOIA suit of Harold
Weisberg has been printed, including the complete court
record along with the documents it generated.   The legislative base for FOIA is: Public Law 89-487 (Act of 4
July 1966), 80 Stat. 250, as codified by Public Law 90-23
(Act of 5 June 1967), 81 Stat. 54.   Amended by Public Law
93-502 (Act of 21 Nov. 1974), 88 Stat. 1563.

Allen, Mark A.

150.   Mark A. Allen v. Central Intelligence Agency.   Civil
Action No. 78-1743. United States District Court for the
District of Columbia.   Judge John L. Smith.

Suit to obtain WC document 347, known to the CIA as
number 509-803, brought by a law student who has done
extensive research into the circumstances surrounding
the assassination of President Kennedy, particularly
Oswald's trip to Mexico.   Suit denied.

American Civil Liberties Union.

151.   Mark Lane v. United States Secret Services, Department
of Treasury, et al.   Civil Action No. 76-0227.   United States
District Court for the District of Columbia.

FOIA suit brought by the ACLU for Lane requesting "all
records that are under the control" of the Secret Service
and Treasury Department relating to the JFK assassination.

Despite widespread publicity given by Lane to the releases, most of the records requested and obtained were already in the public domain and many had been published by Weisberg.

152. Mark Lane v. General Services Administration, et al. Civil Action No. 76-0226. United States District Court for the District of Columbia.

FOIA suit brought by the ACLU for Lane requesting all files and records pertaining to Lane found in the WC records in the Archives. With some exceptions copies were provided, but many were already in the public domain.

Exner, Judith Katherine.

Suits by Judith Katherine (Campbell) Exner to obtain FBI records on her.

153. A. Judith Katherine Exner v. Federal Bureau of Investigation et al. Civil Action No. 76-89-S. United States District Court for the Southern District of California. Judge Edward Schwartz.

On 2 Feb. 1976 Exner filed suit to compel the FBI to disclose immediately records she had requested. She had publicly stated that she had had an amorous affair with President Kennedy (when she carried the married name Campbell). She was linked to organized crime by the press. Certain critics have promoted the relationship to the status of "evidence" by concluding organized crime assassinated JFK, although they have never substantiated the claims with documentary proof or even theoretical plausibility. On 9 April and 20 April the Court ordered the federal government to disclose immediately the records.

154. B. Judith Katherine Exner v. Federal Bureau of Investigation et al. 9 CA No. 76-1903. United States Court of Appeals for the Ninth Circuit. Judges Barnes, Goodwin, and Takasugi.

The Department of Justice appealed, pleading the huge number of requests under FOIA and the volume of demands creating a backlog. Exner's requests were placed on a list to be processed when they could get to them. The Appeals Court refused to stay the District Court's order pending appeal and ruled the District Court had not abused its discretion in its orders. The filing of a suit can create a preference, especially when a "federal court orders it." The case was remanded. On 24 June 1976 Exner obtained 200 pages from 85 documents and the Court examined in camera portions of others not released and agreed to the FBI's withholding of them. Later she received additional documents. 542 F. 2d 1121.

155. C. Judith Katherine Exner v. Federal Bureau of Inves-
tigation et al. Civil Action No. 76-89-S. United States
District Court for the Southern District of California.
Judge Edward Schwartz.

Attorney's suit for compensatory fees in accordance with
FOIA stipulations. The Court found the relationship between the lawsuit and the deliverance of information to
be substantial; the government did not show that the
information would have emerged without the lawsuit. 443
F. Supp. 1349.

Fensterwald, Bernard, Jr.

156. Bernard Fensterwald, Jr., v. Department of Justice.
Civil Action No. 861-72. United States District Court for
the District of Columbia. Judge Gerhard Gesell.

Fensterwald sued to obtain copies of three photographs
of an unidentified white male shown by federal agents on
20 Feb. 1964 to Pedro Gutierrez Valencia, Mexico, as the
possible person he had seen entering the Cuban embassy
1 Oct. 1963. The photographs were described in detail
in an FBI report of 24 Feb. 1964 to the WC which became
WC document 566. Fensterwald appeared pro se and Robert
M. Werdig, Assistant United States Attorney, served as
counsel for defendant. After extended delay the government, on 5 July 1972, handed the photographs to Fensterwald during a hearing before Gesell.

157. Bernard Fensterwald, Jr., v. United States Central
Intelligence Agency. Civil Action No. 75-282-A. United
States District Court for the Eastern District of Virginia.
Judge Oren R. Lewis.

Fensterwald sued to obtain a copy of his "Fensterwald
file." The CIA provided him with a copy containing
numerous deletions made on several grounds which, Fensterwald conceded, were proper "except those which the
defendant claims would constitute the clear invasion of
the privacy of a third party." Judge Lewis inspected
the nine documents in camera and opined "the CIA was
justified in deleting the material from the documents
in question before turning them over to the plaintiff."
With an order of 24 Nov. 1975, Lewis dismissed the case.

158. Bernard Fensterwald, Jr., v. United States Central
Intelligence Agency. Civil Action No. 75-897. United States
District Court for the District of Columbia. Judge John
Sirica.

Fensterwald sued to determine the classification status
of several hundred CIA documents relating to JFK's
assassination and after delays got a printout of materials
classified. On 22 Dec. 1977 Judge Sirica responded to
Fensterwald's argument that the CIA's assigned classification status may not be correct by conducting a "prudent"

in camera review of a representative sample of them.
Fensterwald represented himself; Michael Ryan, Assistant
U.S. Attorney, the CIA.   443 F. Supp. 667.

Lane, Mark.

None.   See American Civil Liberties Union.

Levy, Michael.

159.   Michael J. Levy v. U.S. Secret Service et al.   Civil
Action No. 78-0307.   United States District Court for the
District of Columbia.

A successful pro se suit by a private researcher for 99
documents totaling several hundred pages.

Nichols, John.

Suits to study and perform certain scientific tests upon
JFK evidence.

160.   A.   John Nichols v. United States of America.   Civil
Action No. T-4761.   United States District Court for the
District of Kansas.   Judge Templar.

Suit by a physician seeking to study certain items of
evidence in the possession of the National Archives and,
he asserted, in the possession of the U.S. Navy, in order
to perform neutron activation analysis upon some of them.
On 24 Feb. 1971 Judge Templar granted the government
summary judgment emphasizing two factors: the Archives
stated the clothing of JFK lay under Kennedy family
restrictions and could not be examined, and Nichols
failed to challenge the affidavit of Vice Admiral George
M. Davis, commander of Bethesda Naval Hospital, who swore
the Navy did not possess the requested materials.   325 F.
Supp. 130.   For subject matter discussion refer to
Weisberg Post Mortem [973].

161.   B.   John Nichols v. United States of America.   10 CA
No. 71-1238.   United States Court of Appeals for the Tenth
Circuit.   Judges Lewis, Holloway, and Barrett.

On 12 May 1972 the Appeals Court affirmed the lower
court's ruling and dismissed Nichols' suit.   It held
that the 29 Oct. 1966 letter of agreement between the
Kennedy family and the National Archives was a valid,
binding agreement and that restriction on access and
inspection imposed thereby is reasonable.   Further,
since the David affidavit went unchallenged by Nichols
it must stand.   Essentially the Court said that the
FOIA's purpose was to release documents already in
existence, not to generate information such as tests.
460 F. 2d 671.   See Weisberg Post Mortem [973] on the
question of the family's letter of agreement, where

chronological and documentary evidence contradicts the Court on the nature of the relationship of the Kennedy family to the evidence.

162.   C.   John Nichols v. United States of America.   October term, 1973.   The Supreme Court of the United States.

Nichols petitioned the Supreme Court for a writ of certiorari. The Court denied cert. 93 S. Ct. 268, 409 U.S. 966, 34 L· Ed. 2d 232.

163.   D.   Historical note.   Robert M. Brandon v. Jack M. Eckard, Administrator, General Services Administration, et al. DC CA No. 74-1503.   United States Court of Appeals for the District of Columbia.   Judges Wright, Tamm, and Wilkey.

A major reference to Nichols v. United States, Tenth Circuit No. 71-1238, occurs in the opinion of the court by Wright.   Brandon sought to gain access to certain items in the Vice Presidential papers of Nixon but was precluded by the terms of the contract between Nixon and the GSA.   The District Court had denied Brandon access, in part basing its summary judgment upon Nichols, ruling that Brandon was not a party to the agreement and thus had no right to access.   Judge Wright opined, however, that the Tenth Circuit did not cite any authority nor discuss the FOIA's history or purposes in asserting that one who was not a party to an agreement has no standing to object to the agreement or its terms.   "With deference," said Wright, "we reject this attempt to create a novel barrier to FOIA plaintiffs as clearly inconsistent with congressional intent."   On 22 Dec. 1977 the Appeals Court vacated the lower court's judgment and sent the case back for reconsideration of recent legislative and legal developments in the field of FOIA.   569 F. 2d 683.

Smith, Robert P.

164.   Robert P. Smith v. Department of Justice.   Civil Action No. 1840-72.   United States District Court for the District of Columbia.

Critic sought FBI records relating to Oswald and certain FBI laboratory examinations or other reports.   No report handed down.

Weisberg, Harold.

Suits for disclosure of scientific evidence pertaining to the assassination of President John F. Kennedy.

Spectro I

165.   A.   Harold Weisberg v. United States Department of Justice.   Civil Action No. 2301-70.   United States District Court for the District of Columbia.   Judge John Sirica.

In complaint filed in District Court on 3 Aug. 1970,
Weisberg sought the disclosure of the "spectrographic
analysis of bullet, fragments of bullet and other
objects, including garments and part of vehicle and
curbstone said to have been struck by bullet and/or
fragments during assassination of President Kennedy and
wounding of Governor Connally."

Weisberg was represented by Washington, D.C. attorney
Bernard Fensterwald, Jr. The Department of Justice was
represented by Thomas A. Flannery, United States Attorney
for the District of Columbia, and Assistant United States
Attorneys Joseph M. Hannon and Robert M. Werdig, Jr.

Weisberg sought these records in the belief that if the
laboratory tests had been properly done they would disprove key findings of the Warren Commission.

On 6 Oct. 1970 the Department of Justice filed a motion
to dismiss, or, in the alternative, for summary judgment.
The Department contended that Weisberg was not entitled
to copies of these records because they were protected
by the Act's investigatory files exemption. The Department maintained that this exception to the Act's manda-
tory disclosure requirements was a blanket exemption
which protected all of the FBI's investigatory files from
disclosure.

On 9 Nov. 1970 the Department filed an affidavit by FBI
Special Agent Marion E. Williams which claimed that the
release of "raw data" from its investigative files to any
and all persons who requested them "would seriously
interfere with the efficient operation of the FBI and
with the proper discharge of its important law enforcement responsibilities . . . ." It speculated that the
release of such information could lead to "exposure of
confidential informants; the disclosure out of context of
the names of innocent parties, such as witnesses; the
disclosure of the names of suspected persons on whom
criminal justice action is not yet complete; possible
blackmail; and, in general, do irreparable damage." It
concluded by warning that: "Acquiescence to the Plaintiff's request in instant litigation would create a
highly dangerous precedent . . . ."

During oral argument before Judge Sirica on 16 Nov. 1970,
Assistant United States Attorney Robert M. Werdig told
the Court that the Attorney General of the United States
had determined that it was not in the "national interest"
to divulge the spectrographic analyses. This representa-
tion was made even though the Freedom of Information Act
had specifically eliminated "national interest" as a
ground for nondisclosure because it was too vague.

Ruling from the bench and without making any findings of
fact, Judge Sirica granted the Department's motion to
dismiss.

No evidence has ever been produced to substantiate Werdig's claim that the Attorney General had determined that it was not in the national interest to divulge the spectrographic analyses. Several years after Werdig made this assertion, Weisberg obtained records which show that at least by 1972 Department of Justice officials were trying to get the FBI to make a discretionary release of such records in order to avoid a possible adverse legal precedent which would be harmful to the FBI's interests.

 166. B. Harold Weisberg v. United States Department of Justice. DCCA No. 1026. United States Court of Appeals for the District of Columbia Circuit. Judges: Chief Judge David L. Bazelon, Senior Circuit Judge John A. Danaher, Judge Frank R. Kaufman.

This case arose from Weisberg's appeal of Judge Sirica's order granting the government's motion to dismiss in Civil Action No. 2301-70. On appeal Weisberg was again represented by Bernard Fensterwald, Jr., with James H. Lesar serving "of counsel." The Department of Justice was represented by Walter H. Fleischer, Assistant Attorney General L. Patrick Gray, III, Thomas A. Flannery, Harold H. Titus, Jr., Barbara L. Herwig, and Alan S. Rosenthal.

On appeal Weisberg attacked the affidavit of Marion E. Williams as conclusory and far-fetched. He contended that the spectrographic analyses had not been compiled for a "law enforcement purpose," but rather as a result of a request by President Lyndon B. Johnson that the FBI conduct a special investigation for the President; that the Freedom of Information Act's "investigatory files" exemption did not extend blanket protection to all FBI files; and that the Department had failed to show that disclosure of the spectrographic records would result in any harm to the FBI's law enforcement functions.

On 28 Feb. 1973 the Court of Appeals issued its opinion. The majority opinion, written by Judge Kaufman and con- curred in by Chief Judge Bazelon, held that the Williams affidavit was "most general and conclusory" and "in no way explains how the disclosure of the records sought is likely to reveal the identity of confidential informants, or subject persons to blackmail, or to disclose the names of criminal suspects, or in any other way to hinder F.B.I. efficiency." Specifically holding that the Depart- ment had the burden of proving "some basis for fearing such harm," the Court reversed Judge Sirica and remanded the case to him for further proceedings.

Given FOIA's explicit language and criteria, Senior Cir- cuit Judge John A. Danaher curiously but confidently dissented, "it is unthinkable that the criminal investi- gatory files of the Federal Bureau of Investigation are to be thrown open to the rummaging writers of some tele- vision crime series, or, at the instance of some 'party'

off the street, that a court may by order impose a burden
upon the Department of Justice to justify to some judge
the reasons for Executive action involving Government
policy in the area here involved." After offering his
opinion that "the law . . . forfends against [Weisberg's]
proposed further inquiry into the assassination of President Kennedy," he concluded his dissent with a Latin
phrase emblazoned in capital letters: "REQUIESCAT IN
PACE."

The Department of Justice petitioned for a rehearing by
the full court. The Court of Appeals granted the Department's petition and vacated the panel decision. The case
was then orally argued before the nine active members of
the Court, Chief Judge Bazelon and Circuit Judges Wright
McGowan, Tamm, Levanthal, Robinson, MacKinnon, Robb, and
Wilkey, plus Senior Circuit Judge Danaher.

On 24 Oct. 1973, the Court of Appeals upheld Judge
Sirica's original ruling by a 9-1 vote. Senior Circuit
Judge Danaher wrote the majority opinion; Chief Judge
Bazelon filed the lone dissent.

Factually inaccurate where it touched upon the events
surrounding the assassination of President Kennedy, the
Court's en banc opinion held that where Department of
Justice files "were investigatory in nature" and "compiled
for law enforcement purposes," they are exempt from com-
pelled disclosure. 489 F. 2d 1195 (en banc), cert.
denied, 416 U.S. 993. Because this meant that law
enforcement agencies could protect virtually all their
files simply by asserting that they had been compiled as
a result of an investigation made for law enforcement
purposes, this decision eviscerated the Freedom of Information Act. Ultimately, however, Congress amended the
investigatory files exemption and specifically overrode
the decision of the Court of Appeals in the Weisberg case.

167. C. Harold Weisberg v. United States Department of
Justice. United States Supreme Court. No. 73-1138.

Weisberg filed a petition for a writ of certiorari seeking
to have the Supreme Court review the decision of the Court
of Appeals. Weisberg argued that the Court of Appeals'
decision marked the first time that any Court of Appeals
had converted the investigatory files exemption into a
blanket exemption protecting all files said to be (1) investigatory in nature, and (2) compiled for law enforcement purposes, even though the agency had failed to show
any conceivable harm which might result from disclosure.
Weisberg contended that this interpretation of the investigatory files exemption was in direct conflict with the
decisions of other Courts of Appeals and stressed the
important implications the case had for the viability of
the Freedom of Information Act. However, the Supreme
Court denied certiorari, 416 U.S. 993, 94 S. Ct. 2405,

40 L.Ed. 2d 772. Only Justice William O. Douglas voted
to grant certiorari.

Spectro II

168. A. Harold Weisberg v. United States Department of
Justice and United States Energy Research and Development
Administration. Civil Action No. 75-0226. United States
District Court for the District of Columbia. Judge John
Pratt.

In 1974 Congress amended the Freedom of Information Act.
Public Law 93-502 (Act of November 21, 1974), 88 Stat.
1563. In amending the investigatory files exemption,
Congress specified its intention to override the en banc
decision of the United States Court of Appeals for the
District of Columbia Circuit in Weisberg. Senator
Edward Kennedy asked Senator Hart, on the floor of the
Senate, whether Hart's proposed amendment to the investigatory files exemption would override the Weisberg precedent and some other D.C. Circuit cases which followed
it. When Senator Hart replied that it would, Senator
Kennedy announced his support for the measure. It was
then enacted over President Gerald Ford's veto.

On 19 Feb. 1975, the effective date of the Amended
Freedom of Information Act, Weisberg again filed suit
for the spectrographic analyses made in connection with
the investigation into President Kennedy's assassination.
This time he also requested records on or pertaining to
neutron activation analyses and other scientific tests
on the physical evidence associated with the President's
murder.

During the proceedings in front of Judge John Pratt, the
FBI submitted two affidavits by FBI Special Agent John
W. Kilty, who was assigned to the FBI Laboratory. The
first Kilty affidavit swore that the FBI had examined
the President's clothing, the presidential limousine
windshield, and a piece of curbstone allegedly struck
by bullet by means of neutron activation analysis. When
Weisberg sought the records of this testing, Kilty then
executed a second affidavit in which he directly contradicted his first affidavit by declaring that, "upon
further examination" the President's clothing, the windshield, and the curbstone had not been examined by means
of neutron activation analysis. Notwithstanding this
blatant discrepancy, Judge Pratt granted summary judgment
in favor of the government, ruling that the case was moot
because the Department had "substantially complied" with
Weisberg's request. This ruling was based on the government's claim that it had produced "all available" records
sought by Weisberg.

169. B. Harold Weisberg v. United States Department of
Justice et al. DCCA No. 75-2021. United States Court of
Appeals for the District of Columbia Circuit. Judges
Spottswood W. Robinson III, Malcolm R. Wilkey, William
Jameson.

In this appeal Weisberg was represented by James H.
Lesar. Justice Department attorney Michael Stein argued
the case for the appellees. Assistant Attorney General
Rex E. Lee, United States Attorney Earl J. Silbert, and
Justice Department attorney Leonard Schaitman were also
on the brief for appellees.

On appeal Weisberg argued that the government had not
met its burden of showing that each document sought had
been produced and that there were material facts in dispute, particularly as regarded the existence or nonexistence of certain records, which precluded summary
judgment. Weisberg argued that it was essential that he
be allowed to undertake discovery on this issue. District
Judge Pratt had foreclosed Weisberg's attempts to obtain
answers under oath to his interrogatories, labeling them
"oppressive."

The case was argued on 3 June 1976. Barely a month
later, and just three days after the 10th anniversary of
the enactment of the Freedom of Information Act, the
Court of Appeals issued its opinion reversing Judge
Pratt. The opinion, written by Judge Wilkey, held that
there were issues of material fact in dispute, and that
Judge Pratt should not have dismissed Weisberg's interrogatories as oppressive. In remanding the case to the
district court, the Court of Appeals declared that,
"[t]he data which [Weisberg] seeks to have produced, if
it exists, are matters of interest not only to him but
to the nation." Saying that the existence or nonexistence
of these records "should be determined speedily on the
basis of the best available evidence," the Court of
Appeals stated that on remand Weisberg must take the
testimony of live witnesses who had personal knowledge
of events at the time the investigation was made.   177
U.S. App.D.C. 161, 543 F. 2d 308.

In addition to its significance as a legal precedent establishing the right of discovery in Freedom of Information
Act cases, this decision is important because comparison
with its earlier en banc decisions reflects a changed
attitude towards the Freedom of Information Act and a
reversal of the Court's opinion of Weisberg and his work.

170. C. Harold Weisberg v. United States Department of
Justice et al. Civil Action No. 75-0226. United States
District Court for the District of Columbia. Judge John
Pratt.

On remand Weisberg utilized three forms of discovery: interrogatories, depositions, and requests for the production of documents. He took some 400 pages of deposition testimony from four FBI agents who had personally participated in the testing of items of evidence in the assassination of President Kennedy. The evidence developed on remand directly contradicted the affidavit of FBI Agent Kilty in which he swore that neutron activation analysis had not been performed on the presidential limousine windshield. After first testifying that he could not recall whether the windshield scraping had been subjected to neutron activation analysis, FBI Special Agent John F. Gallagher then admitted, when confronted with evidence that the specimen had in fact been submitted to the nuclear reactor, that he had tested it.

Through discovery Weisberg also established that the spectrographic plates and notes on the testing of the curbstone were allegedly missing. This fact had been concealed from Weisberg and the district court when the case had first been before Judge Pratt in 1975. For example, while Kilty's affidavits had asserted that Weisberg had been provided with "all available" records within the scope of his request, they did not provide the essential information that records which had been created had not been provided him because, it was conjectured, they were "destroyed" or "discarded" during "routine housecleaning."

The discovery materials obtained by Weisberg are significant in a number of respects. If the deposition testimony of the FBI agents can be credited, it discloses a picture of the FBI Laboratory as bungling, uncoordinated, amateurish, inept, and anything but thorough, precise, and reliable. It is a portrait quite opposite to the highly-touted reputation that the FBI Lab has cultivated in the press and elsewhere.

The deposition testimony reveals ignorance of fundamental facts by the FBI agents who conducted the investigation of the President's murder. For example, FBI Special Agent Cortlandt Cunningham, who did the original ballistics testing of CE399, did not know that it had been wiped clean before it was sent to the FBI Lab. Agent Gallagher could not remember testing key items of evidence and when asked to circle possible bulletholes on a photograph of the President's shirtcollar, he circled the buttonholes.

The testimony of the FBI agents is suspect at critical points. Their testimony is also marked by extreme personal antagonism towards Weisberg.

In addition to the discovery he undertook, Weisberg also put into the record some important affidavits and exhibits which address both the official version of the

President's assassination and the credibility of the
government's claim that he had been provided all the
records he sought. This included not only the lengthy
affidavits which he himself executed, but an affidavit
by an actual witness to the Kennedy assassination,
James T. Tague, who apparently received a minor wound
on his cheek when a fragment ricocheted off the curbstone
which the FBI tested (seven months after the fact) by
means of spectrographic analysis. The Tague affidavit
ties in with the spectrographic plates and notes on the
curbstone which the FBI claims were destroyed or discarded and with Weisberg's testimony that the curbstone
was patched and that the FBI knew when it tested it that
it had been altered from its original state.

Through the affidavits and exhibits which he submitted
to the district court, Weisberg also maintained that
photographic evidence shows that the alleged bulletholes
in the President's shirtcollar do not overlap and that
the tears in the shirtcollar and the nick in the President's tie were not caused by a bullet but by the fact
that the tie was cut off by a scalpel during emergency
medical efforts. During his deposition, former FBI
Special Agent Robert A. Frazier, who at the time of the
President's assassination was head of the FBI Laboratory,
testified that he had ordered an FBI Agent, he thought
it was Special Agent Paul Stombaugh, to conduct an
examination of the President's shirtcollar to determine
whether the alleged bulletholes overlapped. However,
the FBI has not produced any report or records pertaining to any such examination.

After establishing that records had been created which
he had not been given, Weisberg noted the deposition of
FBI Special Agent John W. Kilty, the agent responsible
for conducting the search for such records. However,
Judge Pratt quashed Kilty's deposition before Weisberg's
counsel had even been served with the motion to quash
the deposition. Subsequently, Judge Pratt granted the
FBI's motion for summary judgment, again finding that
there were no genuine issues of material fact in dispute
and that the FBI had given Weisberg all the documents
it had. 438 F. Supp. 492.

171. D. Harold Weisberg v. United States Department of
Justice et al. DCCA No. 78-1107. United States Court of
Appeals for the District of Columbia. Judges: Chief Judge
David L. Bazelon, Judges Spottswood Robinson III, and
Francis L. Van Dusen.

Case was orally argued before the Court of Appeals on
20 Mar. 1979. James H. Lesar represented Weisberg.
John H. Korns argued the case for the appellees; also
on the brief for appellees were United States Attorney
Earl J. Silbert and Assistant United States Attorneys,
John A. Terry, Michael W. Farrell, and Michael J. Ryan.

In asking the Court of Appeals to reverse Judge Pratt
for the second time, Weisberg's counsel reviewed the
history of the scientific testing of JFK assassination
evidence and presented the evidence for the existence of
records not provided Weisberg. He contended that summary
judgment had been inappropriate because there existed
genuine issues of material facts in dispute; namely,
whether the records said to have been destroyed or discarded had in fact been destroyed or discarded and
whether there had been a thorough search for allegedly
missing records. He pointed out that the government had
not sworn under oath that all relevant files had been
searched and that the records provided Weisberg showed
that only certain files had been searched. He also
asserted that Judge Pratt had violated well-established
principles of summary judgment. Thus, instead of evaluat-
ing the evidence to see whether material facts were in
dispute, Pratt had resolved the factual issues himself.
In addition, he had not applied the principle that matters
of fact are to be viewed in the light most favorable to
the party opposing summary judgment.

While the case was pending before the Court of Appeals,
Weisberg obtained new evidence further discrediting the
government's claims that important JFK assassination
evidence had been "destroyed" or "discarded" during
"routine housecleaning." This evidence, which Weisberg
sought to bring to the attention of the Court of Appeals,
over the government's vehement protests, showed that the
FBI was under instructions not to destroy or discard its
records on its investigation of the assassination of
President Kennedy and that periodic reviews of field
office records had been made to assure that the evidence
was being maintained.

Suits for Warren Commission executive session transcripts.

Transcripts Suit I

172. Harold Weisberg v. General Services Administration.
Civil Action No. 2052-73. United States District Court for
the District of Columbia. Judge Gerhard Gesell.

On 13 Nov. 1973 Weisberg filed suit for the transcript
of the Warren Commission executive session held on 27
Jan. 1964. For several years prior to filing suit,
Weisberg had repeatedly requested disclosure of the
27 Jan. transcript. However, the National Archives and
Records Service, the custodian of the transcript, had
rejected his demands, claiming that the transcript was
classified "Top Secret" on grounds of national security.

Warren Commission member Gerald R. Ford had previously
published parts of the 27 Jan. transcript, including
some extensive and purportedly verbatim quotations, in
his book Portrait of the Assassin [706]. On 5 Nov. 1973

during the Senate hearings on his nomination to be Vice
President, Ford swore that he had used only publicly
available materials in his book. This testimony prompted
Weisberg's suit for the transcript which Ford had used in
his book, but which had been denied him.

In response to Weisberg's suit, the government submitted
two affidavits from high government officials. National
Archivist Dr. James B. Rhoads swore that the 27 Jan.
transcript was classified Top Secret under Executive
Order 10501. J. Lee Rankin, formerly Solicitor General
of the United States and General Counsel of the Warren
Commission, swore that the Warren Commission had instructed
him to classify its records and that he had ordered top
secret classification of the 27 Jan. transcript.

Weisberg met these claims head on. He accused Rhoads and
Rankin of having filed false affidavits and supported his
charges with numerous records taken from the Warren
Commission's own files. He argued that these records
showed that Ward & Paul, the Commission's reporting firm,
had routinely "classified" all records, even housekeeping
records, without regard to the content of the records.

On 3 May 1974 Judge Gesell ruled that the government had
not shown that the 27 Jan. transcript was properly classified. However, he went on to decide the case in the
government's favor, ruling that under the decision of
the Court of Appeals in Weisberg v. U.S. Department of
Justice, 160 U.S.App.D.C. 71, 489 F. 2d 1195 (en banc)
cert. denied, 416 U.S. 993 ("Weisberg I"), it was exempt
from disclosure as an investigatory file compiled for
law enforcement purposes. In a motion for reconsideration, Weisberg pointed out that the government's answers
to interrogatories showed that no law enforcement agency
or official had seen the 27 Jan. transcript until at
least three years after the Warren Commission had ceased
to exist. The motion for reconsideration was promptly
denied.

Weisberg planned to appeal Judge Gesell's decision. But
the National Archives suddenly "declassified" the transcript and, ignoring its court-sanctioned exempt status
as an investigatory file compiled for law enforcement
purposes, made it available to Weisberg on 14 June 1974.
The eighty-six page transcript contained no material
which could have placed the national security in jeopardy
nor any indication that it would be used for law enforcement purposes.

Two years after he obtained the 27 Jan. transcript, Weisberg obtained documents during a subsequent lawsuit which
showed that the National Archives had withheld the transcript at the insistence of the CIA, purportedly to protec
its "intelligence sources and methods." In affidavits
filed in other lawsuits, Weisberg has repeatedly asserted

without contradiction, that the 27 Jan. transcript did
not in fact reveal any such "sources and methods."

The disclosure of the 27 Jan. transcript was followed by
the release of the transcript of the Warren Commission
executive session held on 22 Jan. 1964, for which Weisberg and Dr. Paul Hoch had submitted a new request. The
contents of these two transcripts had a devastating impact
on the credibility of the Warren Commission's findings.
They revealed that the Commission distrusted and feared
the FBI, that it knew that the FBI had reached its conclusion that Oswald was "the lone assassin" without
having made a thorough investigation to determine if there
had been a conspiracy, and that the Commission lacked the
courage to investigate rumors that Oswald had worked for
the FBI.

These revelations ended any lingering questions as to
whether the Warren Commission had conducted a thorough
investigation of the President's assassination and disclosed the whole truth in its Report. They helped create
the climate of opinion which later caused the House of
Representatives to establish a select committee to investigate the assassinations of President John F. Kennedy
and Dr. Martin Luther King, Jr. Case record and transcripts printed verbatim in Wrone [110].

Transcripts Suit II

173. A. Harold Weisberg v. General Services Administration.
Civil Action No. 75-1448. United States District Court for
the District of Columbia. Judge Aubrey E. Robinson.

On 4 Sept. 1975 Weisberg filed suit for copies of all
Warren Commission executive session transcripts which
remained suppressed. These consisted of the complete
transcripts of the 19 May and 23 June 1964 executive
sessions, and pages 63-73 of the transcript of the 21
Jan. 1964 session.

The General Services Administration cited various grounds
for continuing to withhold these transcripts, including
some claims of exemption which had not been made when
Weisberg had requested them in previous years.

The main ground for continuing the suppression of the
21 Jan. and 23 June transcripts rested upon GSA's allegations that making them available would result in the
release of classified information which would endanger
the national security by disclosing "intelligence
sources and methods." The primary justifications for
withholding the 19 May transcript were assertions that
it was exempt from disclosure because: (1) its release
would constitute an unwarranted invasion of the personal
privacy of two Warren Commission staff members whose
continued employment and access to security classified

information were discussed at that session; and (2) it
contained discussions of policy matters which were
immune from disclosure under the Freedom of Information
Act's fifth exemption, which excepts "inter-agency or
intra-agency memorandums or letters" from disclosure.

During the initial discovery phase of the lawsuit, the
government refused to identify the subject of the 23
June transcript on the ground that this was classified
information. When Weisberg produced a letter from the
National Archives to The New Republic which stated that
Soviet defector Yuri Ivanovich Nosenko was the subject
of the 23 June transcript, Judge Robinson ordered the
government to answer Weisberg's interrogatory on this
point. The government then admitted that Nosenko was
indeed the subject of the 23 June transcript.

The government repeatedly resisted Weisberg's attempts
to exercise discovery. Nevertheless, he did obtain some
useful materials. For example, he learned that the 27
Jan. 1964 executive session transcript had been withheld
at the behest of the CIA, purportedly to protect its
intelligence "sources and methods." He also learned
that several copies of the 21 Jan. and 23 June transcripts were missing; and that although they were allegedly classified in the interest of national security,
no attempt to locate the missing copies had been made.

The government submitted two affidavits by a CIA official, Charles A. Briggs, who claimed that the 21 Jan.
and 23 June transcripts had been properly classified in
accordance with the applicable Executive Order and that
the national security would be damaged if they were made
public. Ultimately, Judge Robinson accepted these affidavits at face value and ruled that these two transcripts
were immune from disclosure under Exemption 3 of the
Freedom of Information Act. In his 4 Mar. 1977 order
granting summary judgment to the GSA, he also ruled
that upon in camera inspection of the 19 May transcript,
he found it to be protected by Exemption 5 because it
contained "policy discussions" by members of the Warren
Commission.

174. B. Harold Weisberg v. General Services Administration.
DCCA No. 77-1831. United States Court of Appeals for the
District of Columbia. Judges: Chief Judge David L. Bazelon,
Judges Spottswood W. Robinson III and Edward Tamm.

On appeal Weisberg contended, with respect to the 21 Jan.
and 23 June transcripts, that (1) the district court had
erroneously ruled that they were protected under Exemption
3 by virtue of a statute which requires the Director of
Central Intelligence Agency to protect intelligence
sources and methods from "unauthorized disclosure" without
considering whether they were properly classified; (2) he
had been denied discovery essential to an effective

adversarial testing of the government's claims that the
transcripts were exempt; and (3) the district court
should have examined the transcripts in camera with the
aid of his classification expert to determine whether
they were being properly withheld. With respect to the
19 May transcript, Weisberg also argued that Exemption 5
should not apply because the Warren Commission was de-
funct.

While the case was pending before the Court of Appeals,
Weisberg found new materials relevant to the issues and
attached them as an addendum to his Reply Brief. He
contended that some showed a deep-seated animosity
toward him which gave the GSA a strong motive for withholding nonexempt records from him. In support of this
contention, he submitted records showing that: (a) the
National Archivist had directed that the 27 Jan. 1964
Warren Commission executive session transcript be withheld from Weisberg because releasing it would "encourage
him to increase his demands;" (b) FBI Director J. Edgar
Hoover had ordered the FBI not to respond to Weisberg's
Freedom of Information Act requests; and (c) the Secret
Service and the National Archives had conspired to deny
Weisberg access to a nonexempt record by transferring it
from the former to the latter.

Weisberg also submitted materials undermining the credibility of the CIA's affidavits which declared that the
release of the 23 June transcript would endanger the
national security. Thus, the CIA affidavits had proclaimed that the disclosure of the 23 June transcript
would endanger the life of Soviet defector Yuri Ivanovich
Nosenko. But Weisberg's addendum contained magazine
articles and excerpts from Edward Epstein's newly published book Legend [381] which revealed, with the help
of CIA officials, information about the identity and
whereabouts of Nosenko, information which the CIA had
sworn had to be protected.

The government moved to strike Weisberg's Reply Brief
and/or the Addendum on the grounds that the new materials
were not properly before the Court of Appeals. The Court
of Appeals responded by ordering Weisberg to file a motion
for new trial in the district court. It also ordered the
district court to decide the motion within thirty days of
its filing.

175. C. Harold Weisberg v. General Services Administration.
Civil Action No. 75-1448. United States District Court for
the District of Columbia. Judge Aubrey E. Robinson.

On 12 May 1978 Weisberg filed a motion in district court
asking that it grant him a new trial on the basis of
newly discovered evidence. In addition to the evidence
previously reproduced in the Addendum to his Reply Brief,
Weisberg added the fact that Nosenko's picture had been
published in The Washington Post of 16 April 1978.

The government opposed the motion for new trial, contend-
ing that the "newly discovered evidence" was only irrelevant double or triple hearsay. When Weisberg moved to
take the deposition of the CIA's affiant, Mr. Charles A.
Briggs, the government moved to quash it. Judge Robinson
granted the motion to quash and also denied the motion for
a new trial.

176. D. Harold Weisberg v. General Services Administration.
DCCA Nos. 78-1731 and 77-1831. (Consolidated.) United States
Court of Appeals for the District of Columbia Circuit.
Judges: Chief Judge David L. Bazelon, Judges Spottswood
Robinson III and Edward Tamm.

Weisberg took a separate appeal from Judge Robinson's
denial of his motion for a new trial. This new appeal,
Case No. 78-1731, was consolidated with Case No. 77-1831,
in which briefs had already been submitted to the Court.
Weisberg's brief in this new appeal argued that the district court had abused its discretion in denying his motion
for a new trial on grounds of newly discovered evidence
and fraud on the part of the government.

On the day the government's brief was due in court in this
new appeal, counsel for GSA announced that the 21 Jan. and
23 June transcripts had been "declassified" and would be
made available to Weisberg. The pretext for this action
was that the transcripts had been "declassified" as the
result of a request by the House Select Committee on
Assassinations made in connection with testimony regarding
Nosenko before that committee. At the same time the
government also moved for complete dismissal of Case No.
78-1731 and partial dismissal of Case No. 77-1831, with
which it had been consolidated, on grounds that all issues
save those pertaining to the 19 May transcript were now
moot.

Weisberg opposed the motion to dismiss. However, on 12
Jan. 1979 the Court of Appeals granted it. But the Court
also ordered the district court to vacate its orders with
respect to the 21 Jan. and 23 June transcripts and stated
that the district court might, upon motion, consider such
post-dismissal matters as it thought appropriate.

On 13 Feb. 1979 the only remaining issue before the Court
of Appeals, the status of the 19 May transcript, was
orally argued. On 15 Mar. 1979 the Court issued an order
affirming the district court's finding that the 19 May
transcript was exempt from disclosure.

177. E. Harold Weisberg v. General Services Administration.
Civil Action No. 75-1448. Judge Aubrey E. Robinson.

In May, 1979 Weisberg filed a motion for an award of
attorney fees and costs in district court, arguing that
the release of two of the three transcripts he had sought

meant that he had "substantially prevailed" in this litigation and thus qualified him for such an award. This
issue is still pending in district court at this time.

Suits for Federal Bureau of Investigation records.

FBI Records Suit I

178. Harold Weisberg v. Griffin Bell et al. Civil Action
No. 77-2155. United States District Court for the District
of Columbia. Judge Gerhard Gesell. (Originally assigned to
Judge George Hart.)

Suit under the Freedom of Information Act for preliminary
injunction or other forms of relief, the object of which
was to compel the Department of Justice to provide Weisberg with free copies of approximately 80,000 pages of
FBI Headquarters' records on the assassination of President Kennedy.

The lawsuit was precipitated by an FBI plan to make these
records available to the press in two unmanageable batches
of 40,000 pages each, while effectively excluding Weisberg
from having any meaningful access to them. The first
batch was released on 7 Dec. 1977. Although Weisberg
had requested many of these records as long as ten or
twelve years before, the FBI had not responded to his
requests as required by the Freedom of Information law.
After stalling for many years, the FBI announced release
of these Headquarters' records but told Weisberg that he
had a choice of either purchasing the entire 80,000 pages
for some $8,000 or going to Washington, D.C. to search
for what he had requested in the records placed in the
FBI Reading Room in the J. Edgar Hoover Building. Lacking funds to pay for copies of these records and unable
to drive to Washington, D.C. every day from his home
fifty miles away, Weisberg brought suit instead.

At a hearing held on 16 Jan. 1978 Judge Gerhard Gesell
heard oral argument. James H. Lesar represented Weisberg. The Department of Justice was represented by Paul
Figley, Lynne K. Zusman, Daniel Metcalfe, and Jo Ann
Dolan, attorneys, Department of Justice, Assistant Attorney General Barbara Babcock; and Emil Moschella, Legal
Counsel for the FBI.

At the conclusion of the hearing Judge Gesell found that
Weisberg "has made a unique contribution in the area by
his persistence through the courts and before Congress,
without which there would be no disclosures" of FBI
records on the assassination of President Kennedy. Considering such factors as Weisberg's indigency, the poor
state of his health, the contribution he had made to
public knowledge on the subject, the refusal of the FBI
to even respond to his Freedom of Information Act requests,
and his role in forcing Congress to amend the Freedom of

Information Act so as to make the investigatory records
of the FBI and other law enforcement agencies available
to the public, Judge Gesell ruled that the "equities are
very substantially and overwhelmingly in [Weisberg's]
favor." Accordingly, he ordered the FBI to provide Weisberg with a free copy of the approximately 40,000 pages
of records scheduled to be released on 18 Jan. 1978.

As a result of this decision, Judge June L. Green ordered
the Department of Justice to explain the basis of its
decision to grant Weisberg only a partial waiver of copying costs in Weisberg v. Department of Justice, Civil
Action No. 75-1996, his suit for records pertaining to
the assassination of Dr. Martin Luther King, Jr.
This led to a decision by the Department of Justice to
grant Weisberg a waiver of all search fees and copying
costs for all of its records on both the King and Kennedy
assassinations.

To date Weisberg estimates that he has received more than
200,000 pages of FBI records without charge. This achieve
ment is unique in FOIA litigation.

FBI Records Suit II

179. Harold Weisberg v. Clarence M. Kelley, Griffin Bell,
U.S. Department of Justice. Civil Action No. 78-0249. United
States District Court for the District of Columbia. Judge
John Lewis Smith. (Initially assigned to Judge Louis F. Ober-
dorfer.)

Filed 13 Feb. 1978. Suit to obtain copies of all FBI
Headquarters' worksheets and other records on the JFK
assassination and records related to requests for and
processing and release of those documents. James H.
Lesar represented Weisberg. Emory J. Bailey and Lynne K.
Zusman, attorneys, Department of Justice; Barbara Allen
Babcock, Assistant Attorney General, and Earl J. Silbert,
United States Attorney for the District of Columbia,
attorneys for the government. Several thousand pages
of material is involved. Of the 2,500 pages obtained
in 1978, obfuscation of them was apparent and is now in
litigation.

FBI Records Suit III

180. Harold Weisberg v. William H. Webster, Griffin Bell,
Federal Bureau of Investigation, United States Department of
Justice. Civil Action No. 78-322. United States District
Court for the District of Columbia. Judge John Lewis Smith.
(Initially assigned to Judge Louis F. Oberdorfer.)

Filed 24 Feb. 1978. Suit for disclosure of records of
FBI's Dallas Field Office on the assassination of JFK
and to provide complete and accurate copies of material
released. James H. Lesar, attorney for Weisberg. Daniel

J. Metcalfe and Lynne K. Zusman, attorneys, Department
of Justice; Earl J. Silbert, United States Attorney for
the District of Columbia, Barbara Allen Babcock, Assistant
Attorney General, attorneys for the government. By early
1979 Weisberg and Lesar had uncovered vast quantities of
essential records, including scores of films, suppressed
eyewitness testimony which contradicts the official reconstruction of the crime, reports of tests done of additional possible bullets, and others. Records agreed to
be provided include an index to written communications
for the first two years and an index to their content.

FBI Records Suit IV

181. Harold Weisberg v. Federal Bureau of Investigation,
William H. Webster, United States Department of Justice,
and Griffin Bell. Civil Action No. 78-420. United States
District Court for the District of Columbia. Judge A.
Robinson on the related case rule moved case to Judge John
Lewis Smith.

Filed 10 Mar. 1978. Suit for disclosure of records of
FBI's New Orleans Field Office on assassination of JFK.
James H. Lesar attorney for Weisberg. Daniel J. Metcalfe
and Lynn K. Zusman, attorneys, Department of Justice;
Earl J. Silbert, United States Attorney, Barbara Allen
Babcock, Assistant Attorney General, attorneys for the
government.

Suit for meaningful pictures of JFK's clothing.

182. Harold Weisberg v. General Services Administration.
Civil Action No. 2569-70. United States District Court for
the District of Columbia. Judge Gerhard Gesell.

Suit to obtain meaningful photographs of JFK's clothing
in the National Archives, those available being inadequate
and needlessly unclear. Gesell dismissed the complaint
on the government's request but directed the Archives to
provide Weisberg with photographs of the clothing. Contrary to Court directive and its own rules, the Archives
merely showed some photographs which they selected to
Weisberg, but would not give him copies.

Suits for disclosure of official records pertaining to
the assassination of Dr. Martin Luther King, Jr.

183. Harold Weisberg v. United States Department of Justice,
United States Department of State. Civil Action No. 718-70.
United States District Court for the District of Columbia.
Judge Edward M. Curran.

Filed 11 Mar. 1970. Suit for the disclosure of official
records pertaining to the extradition of James Earl Ray.
Bernard Fensterwald and William G. Ohlhausen, attorneys
for Weisberg. David J. Anderson and Harland F. Anderson,

attorneys, Department of Justice, and William D. Ruckles-
haus, Assistant Attorney General, attorneys for the
government.

184. Harold Weisberg v. United States Department of Justice,
Civil Action No. 75-1996. United States District Court for
the District of Columbia. Judge June L. Green.

Filed 28 Nov. 1975. Suit for disclosure of records per-
taining to the assassination of Dr. Martin Luther King,
Jr. James H. Lesar, attorney for Weisberg. John R.
Dugan and Robert N. Ford, Assistant United States Attor-
neys, Earl J. Silbert, United States Attorney for the
District of Columbia, Barbara Babcock, Assistant Attorney
General, and Lynne K. Zusman and Betsy Ginsberg, attorneys,
Department of Justice, for the government.

185. Harold Weisberg v. Central Intelligence Agency, Na-
tional Security Agency. Civil Action No. 77-1997. United
States District Court for the District of Columbia. Judge
John Lewis Smith.

Filed 21 Nov. 1977. Suit for records pertaining to
Dr. Martin Luther King, Jr., James Earl Ray, and the
assassination of Dr. King. James H. Lesar, attorney
for Weisberg. JoAnn Dolan, Daniel J. Metcalfe, Lynne K.
Zusman, attorneys, Department of Justice, Earl J. Silbert,
United States Attorney for the District of Columbia, and
Barbara Allen Babcock, Assistant Attorney General,
attorneys for the government.

186. Harold Weisberg v. United States Department of Justice.
DCCA No. 78-1641. United States Court of Appeals for the
District of Columbia. Hearing scheduled 6 June 1979.

Appeal from Civil Action No. 75-1996. James H. Lesar,
attorney for Weisberg. Michael L. Limmel and Leonard
Schaitman, attorneys, Department of Justice, Earl J.
Silbert, United States Attorney for the District of
Columbia, and Barbara Allen Babcock, Assistant Attorney
General, attorneys for the government.

Suits for disclosure of official records pertaining to
the assassination of Dr. Martin Luther King, Jr., by
James H. Lesar.

187. James Lesar v. Department of Justice. Civil Action No
77-0692. United States District Court for the District of
Columbia. Judge Gerhard A. Gesell.

Filed 21 April 1977. Suit for disclosure of Report to th
Attorney General by the Office of Professional Responsibility on the FBI's Martin Luther King, Jr., assassinatio
and security investigations and the voluminous appendix
materials thereto. James H. Lesar, pro se. Daniel J.
Metcalfe, Jeffrey Axelrad, and Lynne K. Zusman, attorneys,

Department of Justice, Earl J. Silbert, United States
Attorney for the District of Columbia, and Barbara Allen
Babcock, Assistant Attorney General, attorneys for the
government.

188. James Lesar v. Department of Justice. DCCA No. 78-
2305. United States Court of Appeals for the District of
Columbia. Hearing to be scheduled.

Part V: Photographic Evidence
(1) OSWALD IN NEW ORLEANS

Only a portion of the pre-22 Nov. 1963 photographic record has been assembled by the federal investigative
agencies, the WC and its staff, and New Orleans law
enforcement agencies. Much of the photographic record
was ignored. The critics have not given studied attention to the subject. Listed are just six films of Oswald
in New Orleans that relate to his political activities.

189. Doyle, James Patrick.

Motion picture taken by tourist of Oswald's 9 Aug. 1963
handbill operation depicting those who assisted him and
those who waited in the background as well as another
profile of Oswald. Essential evidence known to the FBI
but not provided WC. Weisberg [1901], pp. 175, 316, 505.

190. Martin, Jack.

Motion picture taken by tourist of Oswald's 9 Aug. 1963
handbill operation. The FBI did not turn over to WC.

191. WDSU-TV (1).

On 12 Aug. 1963 the New Orleans station filmed Oswald's
court appearance outside the Municipal Court of New
Orleans.

192. WDSU-TV (2).

On 16 Aug. 1963 the New Orleans station filmed Oswald
distributing leaflets in front of the Trade Mart.

193. WDSU-TV (3).

On 21 Aug. 1963 the New Orleans station made a sound
film of Oswald at their studio following a radio appearance.

194. WWL-TV.

On 16 Aug. 1963 cameraman Bob Jones of the New Orleans
station filmed Oswald plus another person distributing

handbills in front of the Trade Mart.

(2) THE ASSASSINATION SCENE IN DALLAS

An indeterminate number of slides, still photographs, and motion pictures were taken during and immediately before and after the assassination. Scores of photographers produced tens of thousands of individual frames. Neither the federal investigative agencies nor the WC nor its staff sought to bring these essential, fact-fixing records into the evidentiary base upon which the investigation of JFK's assassination was conducted. On the contrary, they actively discouraged citizens from presenting their film to the WC, often refusing offers, delaying responses for months until the integrity of the particular unit was impaired or destroyed, and in other ways acting to exclude film. For example, the Special Agent in Charge of the Dallas Field Office sent an Airtel cable to Director J. Edgar Hoover on 19 Dec. 1963 stating:

> No effort is being made to set forth the names of news media throughout the country who made photographs or films in Dallas on 11-22-63. [DFO File 100-10461-1478a]

Critics immediately sought to define, preserve, and make known the existence of many of the film records; it is largely through their persistence that portions of photographic records survived. The HSCA's strictly limited use of the photographic records heavily exploited the work of critics for some data. A complex and evolving subject with film still being discovered and little serious work having been done on it, no listing can be complete. The list presented here is restricted to the assassination scene and omits the many photographs found in the WC 26 volumes of Hearings and Exhibits.

M = motion picture   P = still photograph
MC = motion picture color   PC = still photograph
MB = motion picture black   color (slide)
     and white   PB = still photograph
TV = television film   black and white

195. Allen, Richard.

M: Amateur's edited footage which was incorporated into President Kennedy's Last Hour [251].

196. Allen, William.

PB: Dallas Times Herald photographer who snapped 73 shots of Dealey Plaza, the inside of the TSBD, and also three shots of "winos" being taken in for questioning.

197. Altgens, James W.

PB: Associated Press photographer who snapped 73 photos,
seven at the time of the motorcade and the rest that
afternoon. A crucial picture taken from the south side
of Elm depicts JFK clutching his throat with a figure,
said to resemble LHO, standing in the TSBD background.
It is the subject of intense controversy. The FBI
severely cropped the picture, used as evidence by the
WC. Washington Post, 23 Nov. 1963; Shaw [2213] and especially Weisberg [735]; [See 3665].

198. Alyea, Thomas P.

TV: WFAA-TV photographer who at the first sound of
gunfire ran toward the TSBD with his Bell & Howell, 70
DR, 16 mm, filming as he ran. Inside the TSBD he took
five reels as the police made their initial search of
the interior, including the discovery of the alleged
murder weapon, the alleged sniper's nest, etc. The FBI
refused to acquire the 500 feet of film which totaled
25,000 frames until many weeks later, after the studio
had severely edited the reels for a composite single reel
and the integrity of the evidentiary value was impaired.
Remnant frames exist. Weisberg [1075], 39-40, 121-23,
274-75.

199. Atkins.

Listed by Sprague [1098] but unverifiable.

200. Beck.

Listed by Sprague [1098], but unverifiable.

201. Beers, Jack.

PB: Dallas Morning News photographer who snapped 33
shots around and inside the TSBD immediately after the
assassination. Included are shots of the boxes and sash
arrangement inside the alleged sniper's window which clash
with the official findings and shots of "winos" being
taken in for questioning. Weisberg [1058], Shaw [2213].

202. Bell, F. M.

MC: Filmed from the SW corner of Main and Houston.
Thompson map [732].

203. Benell, Albert.

M: Amateur whose edited footage was incorporated into
President Kennedy's Last Hour [251].

204. Betzner, Hugh, Jr.

PB: Citizen who with his Kodak 120 snapped three pictures
of the JFK party turning from Houston into Elm Street,
including one with the TSBD in the background. Weisberg
[1058].

205. Bond, Wilma.

PC: Amateur who snapped nine 35 mm slides as the motorcade moved onto Houston Street, as well as after the
assassination. Some of her slides contain important
factual material obfuscated by the federal investigative
agencies. Weisberg [1075], 42, 46-9 Thompson map [732].

206. Boren, Bryant.

M: Amateur whose edited footage was incorporated into
President Kennedy's Last Hour [251].

207. Bothun, Richard.

PB: Snapped from inside grassy triangle opposite
Zapruder. Thompson map [252], Cutler map [1071].

208. Brenk, Rudy.

M: Amateur whose footage was incorporated into
President Kennedy's Last Hour [251].

209. Bronson, Charles L.

MC: Amateur whose 8mm film of the assassination scene
was discovered in 1978 by critics. Released with a major
news story by Dallas Morning News, 26 Nov. 1978. Film
analyzed and enhanced by optic expert Robert Groden.
Major national coverage impaired by inexpert news
releases by Assassination Information Bureau, 26 Nov.
1978. See also NYT, 28 Nov. 1978.

210. Brown, Joe.

M: Amateur whose footage was incorporated into President
Kennedy's Last Hour [251].

211. Burrows, Henry.

An Associated Press photographer listed by Sprague [1098]
but unverifiable.

212. Cabluck, Jerrold.

PB: Fort Worth Star Telegram photographer who snapped
three pictures of Dealey Plaza from a helicopter as well
as three ground pictures.

213. Cabluck, Harry.

Fort Worth Star Telegram photographer who snapped four
shots of grass on interior triangle of Dealey Plaza where
a bullet possibly hit, and three pictures at Parkland.
Shaw [2213]; [See 714].

214. Cancellare, Frank.

United Press International photographer who snapped
several pictures on Dealey Plaza.

215. Cook, Donald.

A KTTV-TV photographer listed by Sprague [1098] but
unverifiable.

216. Couch, Malcom.

TV: ABC-TV cameraman in motorcade who filmed Dealey
Plaza area immediately after killing. Views of TSBD
front and related subjects.

217. Croft, Robert Earl.

PC: One reel 36 exposures on Kodachrome X film.

218. Daniel, Jack.

MC: Amateur 8mm, ten second, 176 frame movie that
depicts the events immediately after the assassination
including the departure of motorcycle policemen. Discovered in 1978.

219. Darnell, James.

Listed as a WBAP-TV cameraman by Sprague [1098] but
unverifiable.

220. Davis, William.

Listed by Sprague [1098] but unverifiable.

221. Dillard, Thomas C.

PB: Dallas Morning News photographer who snapped at
least five pictures. Immediately after the assassination he took two snaps of the TSBD, one which was reproduced in the WR severely cropped and improperly labeled,
a picture of the triple underpass area which the WC officially refused to admit to its existence, and two shots
which were snapped the next day of the curbstone associated with the wounding of citizen James T. Tague.
Weisberg [1075].

222.   Dorman, Elsie T.

MC: Amateur on the fourth floor TSBD who filmed the
motorcade passing as the assassination occurred.   Film
neither acquired nor examined by the FBI or WC despite
her statement to SS.   Thompson map [732]; Weisberg [1075].

223.   Field, Mr. C.

Listed by FBI in 100-10461-1178 Dallas Field Office
Files.   No description.

224.   Gewertz, Irving.

M: Amateur whose edited footage was incorporated into
President Kennedy's Last Hour [251].

225.   Gray, W. C.

M: Amateur whose edited footage was incorporated into
President Kennedy's Last Hour [251].

226.   Howard, T.

Listed by Sprague [1098] but unverifiable.

227.   Hughes, Robert J.

MC: Amateur standing on the corner of Main and Houston
whose 8mm film recorded the motorcade turning onto Elm
past crowds before the TSBD.   The FBI severely cropped
one frame for presentation in CD 1 [91] by removing information essential for understanding the time and place and
carefully mislabeling it as being taken at 12:20 rather
than the actual 12:30, the time of the assassination.   In
WR 644 the error is continued with the second part in the
footnote reference to a non-existent source, while the
first part is to data other than is claimed.   The two
figures appearing in the windows adjacent to the alleged
sniper's window are presumptively asserted by officials,
and replicated and enhanced by CBS [2690], to be the
central point at issue, but the empty alleged sniper's
window and the empty fifth floor windows where the WC
said the alleged earwitnesses sat at the time the assassi
nation was in progress are the evidentiary points raised.
Thompson's map and discussion [732] ignore the empty
window and FBI misrepresentations and focus on tangential
issues.   Weisberg [1075] is basic.

228.   Jackson, Robert.

P: Dallas Times Herald photographer snapped pictures
after the assassination and over the several days of the
controversy.   His pictures were not introduced when he
testified before the WC and his picture of Oswald's
arrest was excised from the printed record.   WC 26 H
781-2; Weisberg [1075].

229. Jamison, J.

MB: WBAT-TV cameraman mentioned in Weisberg [1075].

230. Kincaid, George.

M: Amateur whose edited footage was incorporated into
President Kennedy's Last Hour [251].

231. KRLD-TV.

TV: Copy of Oswald murder film claimed by Sprague [1098]
but unverifiable.

232. Laird, J.

PB: Dallas Morning News photographer who snapped 47
shots.

233. L'Hoste, A. J.

TV: Professional cameraman for WFAA-TV who filmed the
TSBD immediately after the murder. No official record of
the film exists.

234. McAulay, Joseph.

PB: Fort Worth Star Telegram photographer who snapped
three pictures of a man being apprehended in Fort Worth.

235. MacCammon, Jim.

PB: Snapped pictures of Tippit murder scene and Texas
Theater arrest of Oswald.

236. Martin, John H.

M: Amateur whose edited film of assassionation scene
was incorporated into President Kennedy's Last Hour [251].

237. Mentesana, Ernest.

MC: Amateur located in the freight yard area near the
TSBD who filmed "the turmoil" immediately after the
assassination. Edited version incorporated into President
Kennedy's Last Hour [251].

238. Mester, Earl.

M: Amateur whose edited film was incorporated into President Kennedy's Last Hour [251].

239. Miller, D.

PB: Snapped JFK limousine on Stemmons Freeway on way to
Parkland Hospital.

240.   Moorman, D.

PB: Snapped JFK limousine on Stemmons Freeway on way to Parkland Hospital.

241.   Moorman, Mary.

PB: From the grass on the south side of Elm snapped at least two Polaroid pictures of the assassination, one showing the TSBD and sixth floor window, the other the grassy knoll; [See 1089, 1090].

242.   Muchmore, Mary.

MC: From the grassy interior, an amateur filmed the assassination.   Acquired by UPI.

243.   Murray, James.

PC: Freelance cameraman whose slides include a frontal view of the TSBD about the time of the assassination.

244.   Newman, Justin.

PB: Amateur who snapped the JFK limousine rushing to Parkland Hospital on Stemmons Freeway opposite the Trade Mart where JFK was to have spoken.

245.   Nix, Orville.

MC: Amateur who filmed the assassination from the south of Elm.

246.   Owens, Dan.

TV: Cameraman for WBAP-TV listed by Sprague [1098] but unverifiable.

247.   Parr, Wyman.

M: Amateur whose edited film was incorporated into President Kennedy's Last Hour [251].

248.   Paschall, P.

Listed by Sprague [1098] but unverifiable.

249.   Phenix, George.

Listed by Weisberg [1075].

250.   Powell, James W.

PB: Member of a U.S. Army Intelligence Reserve unit who snapped at least one picture of the full front of the TSBD about 30 seconds after the assassination.   Long

suppressed by the federal government. Shown in Shaw
[2213].

251. President Kennedy's Last Hour.

MC: A 16 mm film produced by Dallas Cinema Associates,
Inc., Dallas, 1964. 175 feet, 8720 frames, 12 minute
composite of 18 Dallas amateurs' edited films of the
motorcade and the assassination and immediate aftermath,
sold commercially first by the amateur group and then
through Wolper Productions, Inc., Dallas. The FBI
refused the edited film and ignored the original films.
The WC ignored it. Weisberg [1075].

252. Randell, Hazel (Gooch).

M: Amateur whose edited film was incorporated into
President Kennedy's Last Hour [251].

253. Reed, S. L.

PC: Snapped three 35 mm pictures of the Texas Theater
arrest scene and related subjects.

254. Reiland, Ronald.

TV: Listed as WFAA-TV cameraman by Sprague [1098] and
Weisberg [1075].

255. Rhodes, Allen.

M: Amateur whose edited film was incorporated into
President Kennedy's Last Hour [251].

256. Rickerby, _____.

PB: Amateur who snapped pictures from the middle of Elm
opposite Zapruder's position a few seconds after the
assassination.

257. Sanderson, _____.

Listed by Sprague [1098] but unverifiable.

258. Seigler, Howard.

M: Amateur whose edited film of the motorcade was
incorporated into President Kennedy's Last Hour [251].

259. Shawver, George.

M: Amateur whose edited film was incorporated into
President Kennedy's Last Hour [251].

260. Similas, Norman Mitchel.

P: Canadian professional photographer who snapped a roll
of film of JFK's assassination from "seven feet" away.
The film was not acquired by the federal government. The
magazine publishing them ceased publication in the midst
of a series. Similas [345] and Weisberg [1075].

261. Smith, George.

P: Fort Worth Star Telegram photographer who snapped
seven pictures of the assassination scene immediately
afterwards.

262. Speigle, _____.

M: Amateur whose edited film was incorporated into
President Kennedy's Last Hour [251].

263. Stoughton, _____.

Listed by Sprague [1098] but unverifiable.

264. Thomas, Larry.

M: Amateur whose edited film was incorporated into
President Kennedy's Last Hour [251].

265. Towner, Jim.

PC: Amateur who snapped twelve pictures of the assassination scene immediately afterwards.

266. Underwood, James.

TV: Photographer for KRLD-TV riding in press car of
motorcade who filmed the TSBD, grassy knoll, and the crowd
as the car moved onto Elm. He left the car and remained
"in front of the building" continuing to photograph all
who entered and left the TSBD. After taking his testimony
the WC declined to examine the film and did not acquire a
copy. Weisberg [1075].

267. Unknown AP.

Sprague [1098] lists four Associated Press photographers,
but this is unverifiable.

268. Unknown DCA-1.

M: Amateur film on list Dallas Cinema Associates supplied
to the FBI of those films making up President Kennedy's
Last Hour [251]. The FBI rendered the name illegible.
Weisberg [1075].

269. Unknown DCA-2.

M: Amateur film on list Dallas Cinema Associates supplied
to the FBI of those films making up President Kennedy's
Last Hour [251]. The FBI rendered the name illegible.
Weisberg [1075].

270. Unknown DFO-FBI.

In the FBI's Dallas Field Office files on JFK since 1963
are "bulky exhibits containing numerous photographs and
other documents . . . located in a secure metal file
cabinet with the total volume . . . being 15 cubic feet."
(DFO 89-43. Serial 9958). Only after a tangled legal
battle did Weisberg discover their existence.

271. Unknown UPI.

Sprague [1098] lists three UPI photographers but this is
unverifiable.

272. Volkland, _____.

Listed by Sprague [1098] but unverifiable.

273. Weaver, Jack A.

PB: One photograph of President's car making the right-
hand turn onto Houston Street from Main showing the TSBD
in the background.

274. Westfall, Mrs. E. H.

PC: Two color photographs of the TSBD, both showing the
pertinent window on the sixth floor as being closed.
Taken 9:00 a.m., 22 Nov. 1963.

275. Willis, Phillip L.

PC: Snapped 18 important slides of the murder scene and
its aftermath which he sells commercially. Slide number
five was taken after the first apparent shot hit JFK and
coordinates with Zapruder frames 202-206. After commercial publication brought them into public view, the WC
interviewed Willis. Weisberg [532, 1075] provides indis-
pensable commentary upon the evidentiary value of the
slides and the relationship of them to the WC's investigation.

276. Winfrey, Bill.

PB: Picture of Oswald handcuffed at Dallas jail, taken
by a professional.

277. Zapruder, Abraham.

MC: Amateur who stood on the pergola north of Elm just
in front of the picket fence and filmed the motorcade from
its entrance into Elm Street until the car bearing the
assassinated President sped away under the triple underpass. Using an 8 mm super Bell & Howell camera his film
has 484 frames running at 18.3 frames per second,
constituting a clock of the assassination, and establishing a time and a place for much evidentiary data. The
FBI and the WC assigned a number to each frame and concluded that trees blocked JFK's car from the alleged
assassin's lair in the TSBD from frame 170 to 210, being
the point where they allege the first shot fired by the
alleged assassin could have hit JFK. The third and last
of the three alleged shots occurred at frame 313. The WR
prints several frames and the Hearings and Exhibits
begins reproduction with 171. The motion picture has
about 25 percent of each frame cropped, removing vital
data; frames 155 and 156 are missing; 207 and 212 are
spliced diagonally being composites; 208, 209, 210, and
211 are missing, reportedly having been destroyed in the
processing lab of Life magazine, who purchased the film.
Black and white copies of the missing frames 208-211 were
made from the poor copy of the Secret Service set.

Photographic expert Robert Groden painstakingly enhanced
the film, slowed down frames, and in other ways improved
it in a major contribution to critical knowledge. See
Groden [1068, 1087].

One edition of the Zapruder film even dubbed the voice of
CBS reporter Dan Rather onto a commercial copy. Rather's
account of the origin of the audio copy [1534] dispels the
misrepresentations effectively.

Individual, high quality slides have also been made of
the film; they serve as an excellent source for study of
the assassination scene. In Weisberg's expanded edition
of Photographic Whitewash [1075], the CIA's records of its
study of Zapruder's film are available in print. These
put the first shot at frames much earlier than WR accepted;
[See 732, 734, 735, 972, 1067, 1075, 1080-1083, 1086, 1087,
1089, 1092, 1094, 1097, 1104, 1108, 1110-1116, 2865, 3219,
3264, 4590, 4598, 4662, 4790].

Section II:
Published Books and Periodicals

Part I: Bibliographies and Research

Books:

279. Committee to Investigate Assassinations. Selective Bibliography on Assassinations (Compiled by Bernard Fensterwald and Associates). Washington, D.C., 1969.

280. _____. American Political Assassinations: a Bibliography of Works Published 1963-1970. Washington, D.C., 1973.

281. Crown, James Tracy. The Kennedy Literature: a Bibliographical Essay on John F. Kennedy. New York: New York University Press, 1968.

282. Irwin, T. H. and Hazel Hale. A Bibliography of Books, Newspaper and Magazine Articles, Published in English Outside the United States of America, Related to the Assassination of John F. Kennedy. Belfast, 1975; Supplementary ed., 1978.

283. Library of Congress, Reference Department. John Fitzgerald Kennedy /1917-1963/ A Chronological List of References. Washington, D.C.: U.S. Government Printing Office, 1964.

284. Miller, Tom. The Assassination Please Almanac. Chicago: H. Regnery Co., 1977.

285. Newcomb, Joan I. John F. Kennedy: An Annotated Bibliography. Metuchen, New Jersey: The Scarecrow Press, Inc., 1977.

286. Rice, William R. John & Robert Kennedy: Assassination Bibliography. Orangevale, California: Published by Author, 1975; rev. ed., 1976.

287. Sable, Martin H. A Bio-Bibliography of the Kennedy Family. Metuchen, New Jersey: The Scarecrow Press, Inc., 1969.

288. Thompson, William Clifton. A Bibliography of Literature Relating to the Assassination of President John F. Kennedy [283 Entries]. San Antonio, Texas: Published by Author, 1968; rev. ed., 1971.

289. Who Killed Kennedy? Bibliography of Assassination Literature. Beaconsfield, Quebec, Canada: Collector's Archives, 1976.

290. Wrone, David R. The Assassination of John Fitzgerald Kennedy: An Annotated Bibliography. Madison, Wisconsin: Historical Society of Wisconsin, 1972 [Originally Published in the Wisconsin Magazine of History, LVI].

Articles by Authors:

291. Baskerville, Donald A. "The Assassination of President John F. Kennedy: Moves to Reopen the Investigation. A Selected List of References," Library of Congress Information Bulletin, XXXV, No. 49 (3 Dec. 1976), 752-757.

292. Calese, Robert S. "Letters: Material Evidence [and the Kennedy Family's Withholding of Evidence]," The Nation, CCIV (2 Jan. 1967), 2.

293. Kubicek, Earl C. "The Legend of John F. Kennedy [An Annotated Bibliography]," American Book Collector, XXI (1970-1971), 25-27.

294. McDade, Thomas M. "The Assassination Industry: a Tentative Checklist of Publications on the Murder of President John F. Kennedy," American Book Collector, XVIII (1968), 8-14.

295. Malow, Richard. "The Kennedy Assassination and the Warren Report: Selected References," Congressional Record, 89th Congress, 2nd Session, CXII, Part 18 (28 Sept. 1966), 24160-24161.

296. Sprague, Richard E. "The Assassination of President Kennedy: Declassification of Relevant Documents from the National Archives," Computers and Automation, XX (Oct. 1971), 41-45.

297. Star, Jack. "The Kennedy Legend [and Preservation of the Evidence]," Look, XXVIII (30 June 1964), 19-21.

298. Winston, Frank. "Connally: Secret JFK Documents Should Be Released Now," The National Tattler, XIX (25 Nov. 1973), 16.

299. Wise, David. "Secret Evidence on the Kennedy Assassination," The Saturday Evening Post, CCXLI (6 April 1968), 70-73.

Anonymous Articles:

300. "Personal Business: Books By---And About---Pres. John F. Kennedy [An Annotated Bibliography]," Business Week, No. 1787 (30 Nov. 1963), 110.

301. "Death of a President: Excerpt from the Introduction to the Annual Report of the Librarian of Congress for the Fiscal Year Ending June 30, 1964," Library Journal, XC (Aug., 1965), 3173-3176.

302. "Suppressed JFK Murder Evidence," The National Enquirer, (28 Jan. 1968), 16-18.

303. "Experts Demand Release of Secret Kennedy Evidence to End Mysteries About JFK Murder," The National Enquirer (2 Dec. 1973), 44.

304. "National Affairs: The JFK Tapes: How It Was," Newsweek, LXXVI (31 Aug. 1970), 23-29.

305. "Biographies of Leading Researchers [and] A Bibliography for JFK Buffs [Cutler to Wrone]," The Saturday Evening Post, CCXLVII (Sept. 1975), 50-53, 110.

306. "75-Year Secrecy for Exhibits in JFK Killing," U.S. News and World Report, LVIII (4 Jan. 1965), 12.

Periodicals Peculiar to JFK Assassination:

307. Clandestine America: Published by Assassination Information Bureau, 1322 18th Street NW, Washington, D.C. 20036.

308. The Continuing Inquiry: Published by Penn Jones Publications, Inc., Midlothian, Texas 76065.

309. The Grassy Knoll Gazette: Published by Intrepid Sports Publications, 903 W. Grace #2, Richmond, Virginia 23220.

310. JFK Assassination Forum: Published by Harry Irwin, 32 Ravensdene Crescent, Belfast, Ireland BT6-ODB.

311. People and the Pursuit of Truth: Published by Berkeley Enterprises, Inc., 815 Washington Street, Newtonville, Massachusetts 02160.

Part II: The Action
(1) DALLAS BEFORE AND AFTER

Books:

312. Jenkins, John H. Neither the Fanatics nor the Faint-Hearted; the Tour Leading to the President's Death and the Two Speeches he Could not Give. Austin, Texas: Pemberton Press, 1963.

313. Kennedy, John F. The Unspoken Speech of John Kennedy at Dallas, Nov. 22, 1963. El Paso, Texas: Privately Printed for Stanley Marcus by Carl Hertzog, 1964.

314. Leslie, Warren. Dallas, Public and Private; Aspects of an American City. New York: Grossman, 1964.

315. Tackett, John Wesley. Nov. 22nd . . . Where It Happened. Fort Worth, Texas: Privately Printed by the author, 1964.

Articles by Authors:

316. [Arnoni, M. S.]. "Dallas Revisited," The Minority of One, VIII (March 1966), 5-6.

317. Bergquist, Laura. "Cover: The President and His Son [Family Photo Story Written Before, and Published After]," Look, XXVII (3 Dec. 1963), 26-36.

318. Boldizsar, Ivan. "Two More Days in Dallas," New Hungarian Quarterly (Budapest), (Autumn 1968), 74-100.

319. _____. "A Taste of Texas: A Hungarian Finds Out for Himself," Atlas, XVII (Feb. 1969), 18-25.

320. Carney, Frederick S. "Crisis of Conscience in Dallas: Soul-Searching vs 'New Faith in Dallas'," Christianity & Crisis, XXIII (23 Dec. 1963), 235-241.

321. Connally, John. "Why Kennedy Went to Texas," Life, LXIII (24 Nov. 1967), 86A-86B, 100A-104.

322. Cook, Fred J. "Radio Right: Hate Clubs of the Air," The Nation, CXCVIII (25 May 1964), 523-527.

323. Daniel, Clifton. "Letters: The [New York] Times on Dallas," Saturday Review, XLVII (11 Jan. 1964), 74.

324. Dudman, Richard. "Commentary of an Eyewitness [The St. Louis Post-Dispatch's Reporter in Dallas]," The New Republic, CXLIX (21 Dec. 1963), 18.

325. Dugger, Ronnie. "Dallas Will Memorialize Itself and JFK: On the Site Where Kennedy Was Slain," The Texas Observer, LVIII (15 April 1966), 8-10.

326. Evans, J. Claude. "Monitoring the 'Monitor': [and the Anti-Kennedy Advertisement in the Dallas Morning News, 22 Nov. 1963]," The Christian Century, LXXXIII (22 June 1966), 796.

327. Friedman, Saul. "Tussle in Texas [The "Rightist Power Structure"]," The Nation, CXCVIII (3 Feb. 1964), 114-117.

328. Harris, T. George. "Memo About a Dallas Citizen [Oil Executive Fired for Critical Remarks after Assassination]," Look, XXVIII (11 Aug. 1964), 64-70.

329. Holmes, William A. "One Thing Worse Than This: a Sermon Delivered at Northaven Methodist Church, Dallas, November 24, 1963," The Christian Century, LXXX (11 Dec. 1963), 1555-1556; [See 3181, 3224].

330. Izakov, Boris. "The Dallas Investigation," New Times (Moscow), 11 Dec. 1963, 10-12.

331. Jones, Wyman. "November in Dallas [a Witness at the Dallas Central Library, Elm Street]," Library Journal, LXXXIX (1 Jan. 1964), 72.

332. Kennedy, Robert F. "Robert Kennedy's Tribute to JFK [and What JFK Did that Morning]," Look, XXVIII (25 Feb. 1964), 37-42.

333. Korolovszky, Lajos. "Fanatizmus és Vallásosság. Gondolatok a Kennedy Gyilkosság Háttéról [Fanaticism and Piety: Thoughts on the Background to the Assassination]," Világosság (Budapest), V (1964), 80-87.

334. Lauzon, A. "Au Banc Accusés, une Ville: Dallas [The Accused in the Dock, One City: Dallas]," Le magazine Maclean (Montreal), IV (March 1964), 13-15, 56-58.

335. McGee, Reece. "Texas: The Roots of the Agony . . . ," The Nation, CXCVII (21 Dec. 1963), 427-431.

336. Montgomery, Ruth. "The Crystal Ball: [Condensed from A Gift of Prophecy: The Phenomenal Jeane Dixon]," Reader's Digest, LXXXVII (July 1965), 235-252.

337. Moulder, John. "A Political Triumph in Fort Worth: On the Very Eve of the Tragedy," The National Tattler, XIX (25 Nov. 1973), 24.

338. Olds, Greg. "In My Opinion: A Good Idea [Proposal to Make Museum of Texas School Book Depository]," The Texas Observer, LXI (10 Jan. 1969), 22.

339. Pacis, Vicente A. "Hate Campaign Did It," Weekly Graphic (Manila), XXX (25 Dec. 1963), 2-3, 98.

340. Prouty, L. Fletcher. "The Guns of Dallas: The Power Conspiracy That Killed JFK," Gallery, (Oct. 1975).

341. Roddy, Jon. "Did This Man Happen Upon John Kennedy's Assassins?" MacLean's, (Toronto) LXXX (Nov. 1967), 2-3.

342. Schüler, Alfred. "Im 'Carousel' sitzen FBI-Agenten. Dallas nach dem Kennedy-Mord [FBI Agents Sit in Ruby's Club, Carousel: Dallas After Kennedy's Murder]," Der Spiegel (Hamburg), XVII, No. 50 (1963), 76.

343. Servan-Schreiber, J.-J. "A Texas Gang [From L'Express, Paris]," Atlas, VII (Feb. 1964), 117.

344. Shea, J. M., Jr. "Memo From a Dallas Citizen [on Hate and Suspicion]," Look, XXVIII (24 March 1964), 88-96.

345. Similas, Norman, with Ken Armstrong. "Dallas Puzzle---by a Canadian Eye-Witness [See H. Weisberg, Photographic Whitewash, 213-240]," Liberty (Toronto), (15 July 1964), 13, 20, 33; [See 261].

346. Sloan, Bill. "Dallas: How a 'City of Hate' Shed Its Burden of Guilt and Is Reborn," The National Tattler, XIX (25 Nov. 1973), 22-24.

347. Smith, Liz. "American Vignettes: Dealey Plaza [On Dallas's Reluctance to Memorialize]," Holiday, XLVI (Nov. 1969), 78-79, 94-96.

348. Turnbull, John W. "A Note From Texas [On Political Feuds]," Commonweal, LXXIX (13 Dec. 1963), 337.

349. Waddell, Les. "Before His Death, JFK Decided to Get Out of Vietnam War, Theodore White Contends [in Reflections on the Assassination]," The National Tattler, XIX (25 Nov. 1973), 25.

350. White, Theodore H. "For President Kennedy: An Epilogue [on Mrs. JFK's Immediate Actions]," Life, LV (6 Dec. 1963), 158-160.

351. Wills, Garry. "Dallas: Out There," National Catholic Reporter, III (4 Jan. 1967), 10.

352. Yarborough, Ralph. "Letters: Sensory Perception [Recalls Smell of Gunpowder at the Scene]," Newsweek, LXIX (16 Jan. 1967), 6.

Anonymous Articles:

353. "Current Comment: Climate of Hate [The Fate of Rev. William A. Holmes]," America, CIX (14 Dec. 1963), 758.

354. "Editorial: Good News from Dallas [on a New Ecumenism]," The Christian Century, LXXXI (17 June 1964), 790.

355. "I Just Heard Some Shots . . . Three Shots," Editor & Publisher, XCVI (30 Nov. 1963), 14-15.

356. "The President Has Been Shot . . . I Saw It Myself [Also Reprints Moorman Photo]," Editor & Publisher, XCVI (30 Nov. 1963), 15, 67.

357. "Letters: Dallas -- City of Patience, Decency . . . Brotherhood in Dallas [on Hate]," Frontier, XVIII (Feb. 1967), 22.

358. "Conspiracy USA: A Plot That Flopped [on Dallas Para-Military Groups]," Look, XXIX (26 Jan. 1965), 28-29.

359. "Editorials: The Dallas Rejoinder ["Don't Blame Dallas"]," The Nation, CXCVIII (25 May 1964), 519.

360. "Man Wounded in Assassination of JFK Finally Talks [James T. Tague]," The National Enquirer (7 April 1968), 16-20.

361. "National Affairs: 'May God Forgive Dallas,'" Newsweek, LXII (9 Dec. 1963), 46-48.

362. "National Affairs: The President: Other Guns [Arrest of Russell McLarry]," Newsweek, LXII (30 Dec. 1963), 15.

363. "National Affairs: Dallas: Living With History," Newsweek, LXVII (18 April 1966), 48-50.

364. "The Periscope: Sniper's Roost For Sale," Newsweek, LXXV (16 March 1970), 23.

365. "Newsmakers: [Texas School Book Depository, Dallas, Purchased by Aubrey Mayhew for $650,000]," Newsweek, LXXV (27 Apr. 1970), 63.

366. "Newsmakers: [Dallas Dedicates Memorial at Place of JFK's Assassination]," Newsweek, LXXVI (6 July 1970), 53.

367. "Where Are They Now?: The Depository's Fate," Newsweek, LXXVIII (22 Nov. 1971), 18-19.

368. "Update: The Book Depository [After Dallas County Paid D.H. Byrd $400,000 For It, But Controversy Continues]," Newsweek, XCI (27 Feb. 1978), 12-13.

369. "The 'Shame of Dallas'," Saturday Review, XLVI (28 Dec. 1963), 26.

370. "And Finally, As to John F. Kennedy," The Texas Observer, LVII (11 June 1965), 19.

371. "Political Intelligence: Good Old Dallas [Dr. Joyce Brothers Tells Dallas that JFK's Murder Could Have Happened "Anywhere, Including South Africa"]," The Texas Observer, LVIII (30 Sept. 1966), 17.

372. "No Action on JFK Commission," The Texas Observer,
LXII (17 April 1970), 15.

373. "Political Intelligence: Depository Bought," The Texas
Observer, LXII (15 May 1970), 6.

374. "Observations: Preserve Assassination Site," The Texas
Observer, LXIII (19 Nov. 1971), 17; LXIII (17 Dec. 1971), 16.

375. "Texas: Little D," Time, LXXXVII (15 April 1966), 25.

376. "President Kennedy Makes a Peace Mission to Texas,"
The Times (London), No. 55,865 (22 Nov. 1963), 10.

377. "In the Kennedy Car--Texas Governor John Connally's
Description of What It Was Like in the President's Limousine
As Assassin's Shots Hit," U.S. News and World Report, LV (9
Dec. 1963), 12.

378. "A Different Look at Dallas, Texas," U.S. News and
World Report, LVI (3 Feb. 1964), 42-46.

379. "Policy Ubil Kennedija? [Did the Police Kill
Kennedy?]," Vecernji Sarajevski list (Sarajevo), XII (24
Dec. 1964), 298-300.

(2) OSWALD THE SUSPECT

Books:

380. Chapman, Gil and Ann. Was Oswald Alone? San Diego:
Publishers Export Co., 1967.

381. Epstein, Edward Jay. Legend: the Secret World of
Lee Harvey Oswald. New York: McGraw, 1978; Ballantine
Paperback, 1978. Condensed Version Serialized in Reader's
Digest, CXII (March 1978), 81-92, 223-258; (April 1978),
154-227; [See 403, 404, 407, 409, 450, 454, 506, 5012, 5087].

382. Hartogs, Renatus, and Lucy Freeman. The Two Assassins.
New York: Thomas Y. Crowell, 1965; Zebra Books, 1976; [See
3996].

383. Joesten, Joachim. Oswald: the Truth. London:
Dawnay, 1967.

384. McBirnie, William Stewart. What Was Behind Lee Harvey
Oswald. Glendale, California: Acare Publications, n.d.

385. Mosby, Aline. The View from Number 13 People's Street
New York: Random House, 1962.

386. Oswald, Marguerite. Aftermath of an Execution---the Burial and Final Rights of Lee Harvey Oswald as Told by His Mother. Dallas: Published by Author, 1964.

387. Ralston, Ross F. History's Verdict: the Acquittal of Lee Harvey Oswald. N.p.: Published by Author, 1975.

388. Ringgold, Gene, and Roger La Manna. Assassin: the Lee Harvey Oswald Biography. Hollywood, California: Associated Professional Services, 1964.

389. Roffman, Howard. Presumed Guilty: Lee Harvey Oswald in the Assassination of President Kennedy. Rutherford, New Jersey: Fairleigh Dickinson University, 1975; A. S. Barnes, 1976; [See 1060].

390. Sites, Paul. Lee Harvey Oswald and the American Dream. New York: Pageant Press, 1967.

391. Thornley, Kerry Wendell. Oswald. Introduction by Albert Ellis. Chicago: New Classics House, 1965.

392. Tonahill, Joe H. Why Lee Oswald Would Have Been Acquitted for the Murder of John F. Kennedy. N.p.: N. publ., 1967.

Articles by Authors:

393. Abrahamsen, David. "A Study of Lee Harvey Oswald: Psychological Capability of Murder," Bulletin of the New York Academy of Medicine, XLIII (1967), 861-888; [See 4451].

394. Ansbacher, Heinz, Rowena R. Ansbacher, David Shiverick and Kathleen Shiverick. "Lee Harvey Oswald: an Adlerian Interpretation," The Psychoanalytic Review, LIII (Fall 1966), 55-68, [379-392].

395. Auchincloss, Kenneth. "Books: Oswald and the Soviets: Legend . . . By Edward Jay Epstein," Newsweek, XCI (10 April 1978), 90.

396. Aynesworth, Hugh. "Oswald's Own Story--As Revealed by His Diary," U.S. News and World Report, LVII (13 July 1964), 54-60.

397. Bachmann, Ida. "Hvem Myrdede Praesident Kennedy? Et Defensorat for Oswald Indleveret [Who Murdered President Kennedy? A Defense of Oswald's Identification]," Frit Danmark (Copenhagen), XXII (1963-4), 1-3.

398. Bagdikian, Ben H. "The Assassin," The Saturday Evening Post, CCXXXVI (14 Dec. 1963), 22-27.

399. Casavantes, Joel [pseudonym]. "Oswald: the Mind of the Assassin," Tallis' Crime and Detection Quarterly, No. 3 (Feb. 1967), 15-33.

400.   Crawford, Curtis.   "Letters: The Second Oswald," The New York Review of Books, VII (6 Oct. 1966), 30-32; [See 727].

401.   Devlin, Patrick (Lord).   "Was Oswald Guilty," New Statesman (London), No. 1774 (12 March 1965), 399-403.

402.   Dunn, Cyril, and Joyce Egginton.   "Das armselige Leben des unseligen Lee H. Oswald [The Miserable Life of the Late Lee H. Oswald]," Die Zeit (Hamburg), XVIII, No. 49 (1963), 3.

403.   Epstein, Edward Jay.   "Reading Oswald's Hand," Psychology Today (April 1978), 97-98, 101-102.

404.   Epstein, Edward Jay, with Susana Duncan.   "The War of the Moles," New York (27 Feb. 1978), 28-38; (6 March 1978), 55-59; (13 March 1978), 12-13.

405.   Evans, M. Stanton.   "Coverup Proved in JFK Murder Probe [About Cuba and Oswald's Marxism]," Human Events, XXXVI (24 July 1976), 13-15.

406.   Freedman, Lawrence Zelic.   "Profile of an Assassin," Police Magazine, X (March-April 1966), 26-30.

407.   Hacker, Andrew.   "Who Was Oswald? . . . The Great Riddle [Review of Epstein, Legend]," The New York Review of Books, XXV (4 May 1978), 3-6.

408.   Harrity, Richard.   "The Face of a Century: Face of Hate: Assassin, 1963," Look, XXIX (12 Jan. 1965), 70.

409.   Heren, Louis.   "Lee Harvey Oswald: Sorting the Truth from the Legend [Review of Epstein]," The Times (London), No. 60,284 (24 April 1978), 14.

410.   Heymann, Stefan.   "Lee H. Oswald--der amerikanische van der Lubbe [Lee H. Oswald--the American van der Lubbe = Convicted for Treason by Nazi Government for Burning the Reichstag, 1933, as Ex-Communist]," Deutsche Aussenpolitik (Berlin), X, No. 1 (1965), 53-57.

411.   Hill, Gladwin.   "The Assassination in Dallas: Case Against Oswald Is a Cinch, Says Police Chief [Captain Willi Fritz]," The Sunday Times (London), No. 7332 (24 Nov. 1963), 2.

412.   Himmelfarb, Gertrude, et al.   "Correspondence: Oswald--The Seed of Doubt," The New Republic, CL (11 Jan. 1964), 28-30.

413.   Holmes, John C.   "The Silence of Oswald," Playboy, XII (Nov. 1965), 101-102, 222-224.

414.   Hunt, George P.   "Editors' Note: Searching the Cold Trail That Oswald Left Behind," Life, LVI (21 Feb. 1964), 3.

415. Irons, Evelyn. "A Lawyer Puts a Case to Exonerate
Oswald [Mark Lane]," The Sunday Times (London), No. 7358
(24 May 1964), 1-2.

416. Jackson, Donald. "The Evolution of an Assassin," Life,
LVI (21 Feb. 1964), 68A-80.

417. Joesten, Joachim. "Lazni Osvald [Fake Oswald]," Oslo-
bodenje (Belgrade), XXI (13 Nov. 1964), 5927-5938.

418. Johnson, Priscilla. "Oswald in Moscow," Harper's
Magazine, CCXXVIII (April 1964), 46-50.

419. Kempton, Murray. "Waiting for the Verdict on Oswald,"
The Spectator (London), No. 7085 (10 April 1964), 472-473.

420. Kennedy, Robert F. "A Misfit in Society," U.S. News
and World Report, LVII (13 July 1964), 60.

421. Lane, Mark. "Lane's Defense Brief for Oswald," National Guardian, XVI (19 Dec. 1963), 5-9.

422. _____. "Oswald Case: Lane in Dallas: Preliminary Investigation Dispels No Doubts, Raises New Ones,"
National Guardian, XVI (9 Jan. 1964), 1, 6-7.

423. _____. "The Oswald Case--All Europe Skeptical:
Mark Lane Back After Tour, Reports on Reaction," National
Guardian, XVI (18 July 1964), 1, 3.

424. Lauzon, A. "Oswald a-t-il tué Kennedy? [Did Oswald
Kill Kennedy?]" Le magazine Maclean (Montreal), IV (March
1964), 1-2.

425. Ludwig, Jack. "Here and There: New York: 'Who
Killed Kennedy?'" Partisan Review, XXXII (1965), 63-69.

426. Lynd, Staughton. "Is the Oswald Inquiry America's
Dreyfus Case?," National Guardian, XVI (27 Feb. 1964), 5.

427. Macdonald, Dwight. "Correspondence: Our Baby [Oswald
Was Marxist, Not Birchite]," The New Republic, CL (25 Jan.
1964), 30.

428. _____. "That Oswald Paternity Case," The
New Republic, CL (29 Feb. 1964), 29-31.

429. Meagher, Sylvia. "Oswald--a Patsy?: from Readers'
Letters," The Minority of One, VII (May 1965), 31.

430. _____. "A Psychiatrist's Retroactive 'Clair-
voyance' [Reviews Hartogs' Book]," The Minority of One, VIII
(June 1966), 25-27.

431. _____. "How Well Did the Non-Driver Oswald
Drive," The Minority of One, VIII (Sept. 1966), 19-21.

432. _____ . "Oswald and the State Department,"
The Minority of One, VIII (Oct. 1966), 22-27; IX (Jan. 1967),
29.

433. Meyer, Karl E. "The Triumph of Caliban," The New
Leader, XLVII (12 Oct. 1964), 4-6.

434. Muggeridge, Malcolm. "A New Kennedy Theory [Oswald Was
a Double Agent, for FBI-CIA and the KGB]," New Statesman
(London), No. 1862 (18 Nov. 1966), 735.

435. O'Brien, Conor Cruise. "No One Else But Him," New
Statesman (London), LXXII (30 Sept. 1966), 479-481.

436. [Oswald, Lee Harvey]. "Lee Oswald's Letters to His
Mother: With Footnotes by Mrs. Oswald," Esquire, LXI (May
1964), 67-73, 75, 162.

437. Palmer, Joel. "The Kennedy Assassination: a Study in
Perversion [and a Victim of a Homosexual Plot]," Confidential,
XVI (Aug. 1968), 14-25, 46-49, 52-54.

438. Plastrik, Stanley. "The Oswald Case Should Be Re-
Opened," Dissent Magazine, XIII (Sept.-Oct. 1966), 469-470.

439. Rifkind, Shepard. "Correspondence: Oswald the Hunter,'
The New Republic, CLI (24 Oct. 1964), 29.

440. Sauvage, Leo. "Oswald in Dallas: a Few Loose Ends,"
The Reporter, XXX (2 Jan. 1964), 24-26; XXX (30 Jan. 1964),
6-10.

441. _____ . "The Oswald Affair," Commentary, XXXVII
(March 1964), 55-65; XXXVIII (July 1964), 16-17.

442. _____ . "Afera Oswald," Vjesnik u srijedai
(Zagreb), XVIII (25 Aug. 1965), 694-695.

443. Slawson, W. David, and Richard M. Mosk. "Discounting
the Critics: . . . the Case Against Oswald Is Still Totally
Convincing," Skeptic, No. 9 (Aug. 1975), 21-23.

444. Smith, Jack A. "Oswald Puzzle Deepens as New Questions
Arise: The Strange Case of the Defector's Passport," National
Guardian, XVI (12 Dec. 1963), 3.

445. _____ . "Did Oswald Fire the Gun? Paraffin Test
Says 'No'," National Guardian, XVI (20 Feb. 1964), 1, 10.

446. Snyder, LeMoyne. "Lee Oswald's Guilt: How Science
Nailed Kennedy's Killer," Popular Science, CLXXXVI (April
1965), 68-73.

447. Specter, Arlen. "'Overwhelming Evidence Oswald Was
Assassin'," U.S. News and World Report, LXI (10 Oct. 1966),
48-50, 53-59, 62-63.

448. Spencer, B. Z. "Assassins! J. W. Booth and L. H. Oswald," The Saturday Evening Post, CCXLIX (July 1977), 72.

449. Sprague, Richard E. "Framing of Lee Harvey Oswald," Computers and Automation, XXII (Oct. 1973), 21-36.

450. Thomas, Hugh. "The Devious Path to Dallas [Review of Epstein, Legend]," The Times Literary Supplement (London), No. 3969 (28 April 1978), 473-474.

451. Thompson, Thomas. "Assassin: the Man Held--and Killed--for Murder," Life, LV (29 Nov. 1963), 37-39.

452. Van Bemmelen, J. M. "Did Lee Harvey Oswald Act Without Help?" New York University Law Review, XL (May 1965), 466-476.

453. Wolk, Robert L., with Arthur Henley. "A Psychologist Probes the Mind of an Assassin," Pageant, XXI (Dec. 1965), 20-25.

454. Wrone, David R. "New Book on Oswald [Legend] Adds to Confusion Surrounding the Kennedy Assassination," The Capital Times (Madison, Wisconsin), (17 April 1978).

455. ZNX. "Oswald Exposé," People's World, XXXVII (7 Dec. 1974), 1.

    Anonymous Articles:

456. "If Oswald Had Lived Could Impartial Jury Have Been Found to Try Him? It's a Sticky Question on Which Experts Split," Broadcasting, LXVI (6 Jan. 1964), 52-53.

457. "Editorial: 'Accused' or 'Assassin' [Especially The New York Times headlining]," Editor & Publisher, XCVI (14 Dec. 1963), 6.

458. "Assassination Story Raised Legal Snares," Editor & Publisher, XCVI (14 Dec. 1963), 12.

459. "Oswald Diary Publication Stirs Furor," Editor & Publisher, XCVII (4 July 1964), 14.

460. "Cover: Lee Oswald, With the Weapons He Used to Kill President Kennedy and Officer Tippett," Life, LVI (21 Feb. 1964), 1.

461. "Lee Oswald Was Headed for Cuba via Mexico," The National Enquirer (8 Dec. 1963), 8.

462. "Did Russian Assassin School Train Oswald?" The National Enquirer (19 Jan. 1964), 8.

463. "Moscow Plotted JFK Assassination--U.S. Government Financed Oswald," The National Enquirer (23 Feb. 1964), 8.

464. "What Happened to Oswald's Hair?" The National Enquirer (12 Apr. 1964), 8.

465. "Link Ruby & Oswald," The National Enquirer (17 May 1964), 16-18.

466. "The Man Who Killed Kennedy," The National Enquirer (30 Aug. 1964), 16-17.

467. "2 Top Psychologists Tell Why Oswald Killed JFK," The National Enquirer (5 Feb. 1967), 16-18.

468. "Fidel Castro Says He Knew of Oswald Threat to Kill JFK," The National Enquirer (15 Oct. 1967), 4-5.

469. "Soviet Leaders Panicked When Oswald Was Arrested for Assassinating JFK," The National Enquirer (15 July 1975), 48.

470. "4 Dallas Policemen Reveal They Saw Evidence Ruby and Oswald Conspired to Kill JFK--On Orders from Castro," The National Enquirer (17 Aug. 1976), 5.

471. "Oswald Would Be Free Today If He Were Alive--So Many of His Rights Were Violated," The National Enquirer (24 Aug. 1976), 33.

472. "Lee Harvey Oswald Did Not Kill JFK," The National Enquirer (26 Apr. 1977), 1, 32-33.

473. "Report to Readers: The Lane Brief--And After," National Guardian, XVI (26 Dec. 1963), 2.

474. "Readers Hail the Lane Brief," National Guardian, XVI (2 Jan. 1964), 6.

475. "Texas Attorney Urges a Defender for Oswald: Mark Lane's Plan Draws Support," National Guardian, XVI (2 Jan. 1964), 7.

476. "Mark Lane Talk in N.Y. on Oswald Case Jan. 24," National Guardian, XVI (16 Jan. 1964), 5.

477. "Lane Speaking Tour Set: Meetings on Oswald Case," National Guardian, XVI (23 Jan. 1964), 4.

478. "Lane Interview on Air," National Guardian, XVI (30 Jan. 1964), 3.

479. "Oswald Case: A Lawyer Barred; a 'Show' on TV: Lane Assails Action," National Guardian, XVI (30 Jan. 1964), 9.

480. "The Oswald Case: Who Wants the Truth Kept Down?" National Guardian, XVI (6 Feb. 1964), 1-2.

481. "Lane Speech on KPFA," National Guardian, XVI (14 March 1964), 7.

482. "A Report on Murder: Dallas and Vietnam [The Oswald Link]," National Guardian, XVI (11 April 1964), 2.

483. "Lane Committee Pressing Inquiry: New Sponsors Announced," National Guardian, XVI (11 April 1964), 6.

484. "Lawyers Urge Kennedy Inquiry: World Group Acts [Mark Lane for Oswald]," National Guardian, XVI (18 April 1964), 4.

485. "Oswald Case--A New Angle: Lane Charges Trickery on News," National Guardian, XVI (9 May 1964), 1, 12.

486. "The Face in the Dallas Doorway: If It Was Oswald, the Assassin Lives," National Guardian, XVI (30 May 1964), 1, 8.

487. "Oswald--Startling New Variation: Official Leak Contradicts FBI, But . . .," National Guardian, XVI (6 June 1964), 1, 9.

488. "On the Left: The Background of the Assassin, Lee Harvey Oswald . . .," National Review, XV (10 Dec. 1963), 2-3.

489. "Cui Bono? . . . How Lone a Loner," National Review, XV (10 Dec. 1963), 4.

490. "The Week: [Oswald and $5,000 from Mexico]," National Review, XV (17 Dec. 1963), 509.

491. "Hypothetical Case: a Letter," National Review, XV (17 Dec. 1963), 515-516; XVI (14 Jan. 1964), 36.

492. "Friends of Lee Oswald, Inc.," National Review, XVI (10 March 1964), 183-185.

493. "The Plot to Clear Lee Oswald," National Review, XVI (7 April 1964), 265.

494. "Oswald: Fiat Lux," National Review, XXII (16 June 1970), 606.

495. "The Man History Forgot: Lee Harvey Oswald's Double [Donald Wayne House]," The National Tattler, XIX (25 Nov. 1973), 21.

496. "The Marxist Marine," Newsweek, LXII (2 Dec. 1963), 27.

497. "Oswald and the Weight of Evidence," Newsweek, LXII (9 Dec. 1963), 36-42.

498. "Medicine: Portrait of a Psychopath [Menninger, Hartogs, etc. on Oswald]," Newsweek, LXII (16 Dec. 1963), 83-84.

499. "National Affairs: Puzzle Picture," Newsweek, LXIII
(1 June 1964), 19.

500. "Letters: The Oswald Diary [by] . . . Mrs. Marina
Oswald," Newsweek, LXIV (10 Aug. 1964), 2.

501. "Medicine: The Presidential Disease [with Oswald as a
Prototype]," Newsweek, LXV (17 May 1965), 67-68.

502. "The Periscope: Diplomatic Pouch: Oswald on Trial
[Staged by Followers of Mark Lane in London]," Newsweek,
LXVI (30 Aug. 1965), 9.

503. "Newsmakers: [Auction of Lee Harvey Oswald's letters
etc.]," Newsweek, LXVI (11 Oct. 1965), 66.

504. "National Affairs: Investigations: Oswald and the
U-2," Newsweek, LXXVII (1 March 1971), 31.

505. "Periscope: Another Oswald Connection?" Newsweek,
LXXXIX (7 March 1977), 13.

506. "The Ultimate Assassination Book [Legend]," New Times
(New York), VIII (6 Feb. 1978), 18; New York (6 Feb. 1978),
9.

507. "Hatred Knows No Logic," The Saturday Evening Post,
CCXXXVII (4 Jan. 1964), 80.

508. "Psychiatry: Oswald Killing Discussed," Science News
Letter, LXXXIV (7 Dec. 1963), 355.

509. "The Gadfly Figure of Lee Harvey Oswald," The Sunday
Times (London), No. 7332 (24 Nov. 1963), 1-2.

510. "Russia Sends a Dossier on Oswald to Aid U.S. Inquiry,"
The Sunday Times (London), No. 7333 (1 Dec. 1963), 1.

511. "Assassin's Trail," The Sunday Times (London), No.
7333 (1 Dec. 1963), 6-7.

512. "The Man Who Killed Kennedy; the Man Who Killed Oswald,
Time, LXXXII (6 Dec. 1963), 33A-35.

513. "Investigations: an Attorney for Oswald," Time,
LXXXIII (6 March 1964), 47.

514. "Historical Notes: A Compendium of Curious Coincidences [Oswald and John Wilkes Booth]," Time, LXXXIV (21 Aug.
1964), 19.

515. "The Sexes: Love Thy Analyst [Lawsuit Against Dr.
Renatus Hartogs]," Time, CV (24 March 1975), 76.

516. "Pacifica Airs Oswald Brief," Tocsin: The West's
Leading Anti-Communist Weekly, V (15 Jan. 1964), 1-2.

517.   "Pro-Oswald Drive Pressed," Tocsin: The West's Leading Anti-Communist Weekly, V (22 Jan. 1964), 1, 4.

518.   "Tocsin Goes to a New York Oswald Defense Meeting," Tocsin: The West's Leading Anti-Communist Weekly, V (4 March 1964), 1, 4.

519.   "The Capture of a Killer [Lee H. Oswald]," U.S. News and World Report, LV (2 Dec. 1963), 10.

520.   "The Assassination - as the Plot Unfolds . . . Case Against Oswald . . . How the President Was Shot," U.S. News and World Report, LV (9 Dec. 1963), 68-71.

521.   "Another Assassination Attempt by Lee Oswald? [Against Major General Edwin Walker]," U.S. News and World Report, LV (16 Dec. 1963), 8.

522.   "Strange World of Lee Oswald: More Light on the Assassination," U.S. News and World Report, LV (16 Dec. 1963), 8.

523.   "A New Clue in Attempt to Shoot General Walker," U.S. News and World Report, LVI (13 Jan. 1964), 10.

524.   "The Oswald Mystery Grows Deeper and Deeper," U.S. News and World Report, LVI (30 March 1964), 45.

525.   "New Light on 'Second Assassin' Theory," U.S. News and World Report, LXII (29 May 1967), 14.

(3) EXECUTIVE INVESTIGATIONS: THE WARREN COMMISSION IN PROGRESS

Books:

526.   Arnoni, M. S. (ed.). The Minority of One: The Death of a President. Passaic, New Jersey: The Minority of One, 1964.

527.   Buchanan, Thomas G. Who Killed Kennedy? New York: Putnam, 1964: Macfadden-Bartell, 1965. Translations in 1964 into French, Dutch, Danish, Finnish, Japanese, Turkish, German and Spanish; [See 3795, 3861].

528.   Curry, Jesse E. Retired Dallas Police Chief Reveals his Personal JFK Assassination File. Dallas: American Poster and Printing Company, 1969.

529.   Joesten, Joachim. Oswald: Assassin or Fall Guy? London: The Merlin Press, 1964; New York: Marzani and Munsell, 1964. [Original title, "Die Verschworung von Dallas [The Dallas Conspiracy]."

530. Tackwood, Louis E. The Glass House Tapes. Center for the Analysis of Law Enforcement Practices. Citizens Research and Investigation Committee. New York: Avon Books, 1973.

531. Warren, Earl. The Memoirs of Earl Warren. Garden City, New York: Doubleday, 1977.

532. Weisberg, Harold. Whitewash II: the FBI-Secret Service Cover-Up. Hyattstown, Md.: Published by Author, 1966; New York: Dell, 1967; [See 4104].

Articles by Authors:

533. A. D. "Sonderkommission untersucht Kennedy-Attentat [Special Commission to Investigate Kennedy's Assassination]," Polizei-Polizeipraxis. Fachzeitschrift für das Sicherheits- und Ordnungswewen (Cologne), LV (1964), 159-160.

534. Abrams, Malcolm. "Ford Spied for FBI in JFK Probe," Midnight Globe, XXV (14 Feb. 1978), 2-3.

535. Amory, Cleveland. "First of the Month [on the Secret Service]," Saturday Review, XLVII (4 Jan. 1964), 6.

536. [Arnoni, M. S.]. "Mr. Warren's Prerogative? [on Suppressing Marina Oswald's Testimony]," The Minority of One, VI (March 1964), 2.

537. Arnoni, M. S. "An Open Letter to Chief Justice Earl Warren," The Minority of One, VI (April 1964), 1-2.

538. [Arnoni, M. S.]. "The Investigation [and Open-Mindedness on the JFK Assassination]," The Minority of One, VI (April 1964), 4.

539. _____. "A Verdict or Propaganda? [By the Warren Commission]," The Minority of One, VI (May 1964), 4-5.

540. _____. "Ripe for the [Warren] Report," The Minority of One, VI (June 1964), 5.

541. _____. "Awaiting the Report," The Minority of One, VI (July 1964), 4-5.

542. Ascoli, Max. "The Reporter's Notes: Interim Reflections," The Reporter, XXXI (22 Oct. 1964), 12.

543. Aynesworth, Hugh. "Oswald Book Filled with Inaccuracies [Review of Joesten]," Editor & Publisher, XCVII (1 Aug. 1964), 40.

544. Bachman, Ida. "Praesident Johnsons Mord-kommission [Pres. Johnson's Commission on the Assassination]," Frit Danmark (Copenhagen), XXIII (1964-1965), 4-6.

545. Belfrage, Cedric. "Four Assassinations: One Pattern [Reviews of Buchanan]," The Minority of One, VI (Oct. 1964), 18-19.

546. Berkeley, Edmund C. "Confirmation of FBI Knowledge 12 Days Before Dallas of a Plot to Kill President Kennedy," Computers and Automation, XIX (July 1970), 32-34.

547. Boeth, Richard. "JFK: What the FBI Found." Newsweek, XC (19 Dec. 1977), 28-33.

548. Bonventre, Peter. "Opening the JFK File [FBI Releases 80,000 Pages]," Newsweek XC (12 Dec. 1977), 34-35.

549. Brandon, Henry, with Tetsuo Tamama. "State of Affairs: Moscow: Questions from Abroad," Saturday Review, XLVII (9 May 1964), 9; (27 June 1964), 21.

550. Brienberg, Mordecai. "The Riddle of Dallas," The Spectator (London), No. 7080 (6 March 1964), 305-306; No. 7084 (3 April 1964), 448-449.

551. Brogan, Patrick. "FBI Chief is Accused of Cover-Up [on Destruction of Oswald's Letter]," The Times (London), No. 59,504 (18 Sept. 1975), 7.

552. Buchanan, Thomas G. "Pravo Porocilo o Umoru v Dallasu [The Rights of Man and Death in Dallas]," Delo (Belgrade), VI (27-29 Feb. 1964), 56-58.

553. _____. "In Defense of a Theory [Replies to Sauvage]," The New Leader, XLVII (9 Nov. 1964), 8-11.

554. Cato. "From Washington Straight: Warren's Men [An Attack on Staff-Member Norman Redlich]," National Review, XVI (21 April 1964), 528.

555. Cipes. Robert M. "The Wiretap War: Kennedy, Johnson and the FBI," The New Republic, CLV (24 Dec. 1966), 16-22.

556. Cross, David. "FBI Makes Kennedy Murder Papers Public," The Times (London), No. 60,181 (8 Dec. 1977), 6.

557. Dempsey, David. "Warren Report in Mass Production," Saturday Review, XLVII (7 Nov. 1964), 25, 38.

558. Feldman, Harold. "Oswald and the FBI," The Nation, CXCVIII (27 Jan. 1964), 86-89.

559. Fensterwald, Bernard, Jr. "The Federal Bureau of Investigation and the Assassination of President Kennedy," Computers and Automation, XX (Sept. 1971), 26-29.

560. Fixx, James F. "As Others See Us: [Concerning the Warren Commission Report]," Saturday Review, XLVII (7 Nov. 1964), 35-37.

561.   Frisell, Bernard. "How to Solve a Murder from Far Away
[Reviews Buchanan], Life International, XXXVI (15 June 1964),
83-85.

562.   Fulks, Bryan. "Letters: Hitting the Targets," The
Nation, CXCVIII (3 Feb. 1964), 108.

563.   Gombrich. Richard, and Martin Gilbert. "Letters: The
Riddle of Dallas," The Spectator (London), No. 7081 (13 March
1964), 343.

564.   Hermann, Kai. "Wer War Kennedys Mörder? [Who Murdered Kennedy?]," Die Zeit (Hamburg), XIX, No. 15 (1964), 7.

565.   Hill, I. William. "Special Teams Pour Over JFK Documents for News [Released by FBI]," Editor & Publisher, CX
(17 Dec. 1977), 7, 28.

566.   Kempton, Murray. "Oswald: May We Have Some Facts
Please? [Criticizes Warren Commission]," The New Republic,
CL (13 June 1964), 13-15.

567.   Macdonald, Neil. "Confidential and Secret Documents
of the Warren Commission Deposited in the U.S. Archives [An
Invaluable List and Index]," Computers and Automation, XIX
(Nov. 1970), 44-47.

568.   Marshall, Eliot. "Aftermath: How the Survivors Feel
Now [About FBI Pre-Emption of State Investigations]," The New
Republic CLXXIII (27 Sept. 1975), 48-51.

569.   Matusow, Harvey. "J. Edgar Hoover--Kennedy's Assassin?
Friends (1 Jan. 1971), 1, 4, 6.

570.   _____. "Hoover FBI Murder Kennedys," Times
Now, II (7 Jan. 1971), 1.

571.   Meagher, Sylvia. "Wheels Within Deals: How the
Kennedy 'Investigation' Was Organized [Federal vs. State],"
The Minority of One, X (July/Aug. 1968), 23-27.

572.   Meisner, P. "JFK Assassination/FBI Knew," Workers
World, XVII (17 Oct. 1975), 4.

573.   Meyer, Karl E., and N. MacKenzie. "Spotlight on
Warren," New Statesman (London), LXVIII (2 Oct. 1964), 474-
476.

574.   Minnis, Jack, and Staughton Lynd. "Seeds of Doubt:
Some questions about the Assassination," The New Republic,
CXLIX (21 Dec. 1963), 14-20; CL (11 Jan. 1964), 28-30.

575.   Packer, Herbert L. "The Warren Report: a Measure
of the Achievement," The Nation, CXCIX (2 Nov. 1964), 295-299

576. Podhoretz, Norman. "The Warren Commission: an Editorial [Requests Public Hearings and Limited FBI Role]," Commentary, XXXVII (Jan. 1964), 24.

577. Possony, Stefan T. "Clearing the Air [Review of Buchanan and Joesten]," National Review, XVII (9 Feb. 1965), 113-116.

578. Rosenberg, Maurice. "The Warren Commission," The Nation, CXCIX (14 Sept. 1964), 110-112.

579. Sauvage, Leo. "Thomas Buchanan: Detective," The New Leader, XLVII (28 Sept. 1964), 10-15.

580. _____. "As I Was Saying [Rejoinder to Buchanan]," The New Leader, XLVII (9 Nov. 1964), 11-13.

581. _____. "Detektiven Thomas Buchanan," Perspektiv, det danske magasin (Copenhagen), XII (1964-5), 7-15.

582. Smith, Jack A. "The Dallas Murders: Motives? Evidence? Guilt?: The Questions Before the Warren Commission," National Guardian, XVI (5 Dec. 1963) 3.

583. _____. "News 'Leaks' Don't End Oswald Mystery: Warren Commission Finds the FBI Report Inadequate," National Guardian, XVI (26 Dec. 1963), 1, 4.

584. _____. "Oswald's Mother Asks Lane to Take Up Case: Before Warren Commission," National Guardian, XVI (16 Jan. 1964), 4.

585. _____. "Presidential Commission: The Men and the Job: 'National Security' vs. the Facts About Oswald," National Guardian, XVI (13 Feb. 1964), 5.

586. _____. "Oswald Commission Invites Lane: Inquiry Board Acts as Public Pressure Mounts," National Guardian, XVI (7 March 1964), 1, 4.

587. _____. "President's Panel Turns to Ruby: Were Oswald and His Slayer Linked?" National Guardian, XVI (21 March 1964), 1, 8.

588. _____. "Nagging Doubts on the 'Crime of the Century': Two Major Books on the Kennedy Assassination [by Buchanan and Joesten]," National Guardian, XVI (22 Aug. 1964), 5.

589. _____. "Oswald Case--the Questions: a Yardstick for Warren Report," National Guardian, XVI (26 Sept. 1964), 1, 8.

590. Spivak, Jonathan. "Warren Panel Assails Secret Service . . . FBI Is Criticized," Wall Street Journal, CLXIV (28 Sept. 1964), 3.

591. Szulc, Tad. "The Death of JFK: an Eye for an Eye?," The New Republic, CLXXIV (5 June 1976), 6-8.

592. Troelstrup, Glenn. "New Light on the Assassination: a Secret Agent's Story [to the Japanese Government]," U.S. News and World Report, LVI (8 June 1964), 38-39; (15 June 1964), 16.

Anonymous Articles:

593. "Editorials: In the Nation's Interest," America, CIX (21 Dec. 1963), 789.

594. "FBI Exposed in Coverup," The Black Panther, XIV (29 Sept. 1975), 11.

595. "So It Can't Occur Again: Safeguarding the President," Business Week, No. 1831 (3 Oct. 1964), 34-36.

596. "The Warren Report," Commonweal, LXXXI (9 Oct. 1964), 59-60.

597. "Johnson Names Commission to Probe Assassination," Congressional Quarterly Weekly Report, XXI (6 Dec. 1963), 2122-2123.

598. "Warren Commission on the Crime in Dallas," The Current Digest of the Soviet Press, XVI (21 Oct. 1964), 30-31.

599. "Who Was to Blame? [LBJ Appoints Warren Commission]," The Economist (London), CCIX (7 Dec. 1963), 1022.

600. "The End of the Tragedy [With Warren Report]," The Economist (London), CCXIII (3 Oct. 1964), 45.

601. "Warren Commission Reports Are Routine [And FBI Planned Leaks]," Editor & Publisher, XCVII (15 Feb. 1964), 66.

602. "Warren Text for All Probable By Sept. 15," Editor & Publisher, XCVII (22 Aug. 1964), 10.

603. "AP Is Rushing Book Containing Warren Report," Editor & Publisher, XCVII (26 Sept. 1964), 11.

604. "The Lead Was Obvious After Reading Was Done," Editor & Publisher, XCVII (3 Oct. 1964), 13.

605. "New York Times Runs 48 Pages of Report," Editor & Publisher, XCVII (3 Oct. 1964), 61.

606. "Recommendation No. 9 [Warren Report's Medical Suggestions]," The Journal of the American Medical Association, CXCI (11 Jan. 1965), 131.

607. "The News: FBI Studies Oswald's Reading at New Orleans Public Library," Library Journal, LXXXIX (1 Jan. 1964), 74.

608. "Cover: The Warren Report: How the Commission Pieced Together the Evidence: Told By One of Its Members," Life, LVII (2 Oct. 1964), 1.

609. "Assassination: The Trail to a Verdict," Life, LVII (2 Oct. 1964), 40-41.

610. "Warren Report: Bureaucratic Blunders Left J.F.K. a Target," Life, LVII (2 Oct. 1964), 50B.

611. "Poročilo Warrenove Komisije [Report of the Warren Commission]," Ljubljanski dnevnik (Ljubljana), XIV (8 Oct. 1964), 268-275.

612. "Editorials: The Warren Commission," The Nation, CXCVII (28 Dec. 1963), 445.

613. "Letters: Trained to Kill . . . The Assassination [And the FBI]," The Nation, CXCVIII (4 Jan. 1964), 1.

614. "Editorials: Task of the Warren Commission," The Nation, CXCVIII (27 Jan. 1964), 81.

615. "Editorials: Hoover the Vulgarian [for Attacking Warren Report]," The Nation, CXCIX (30 Nov. 1964), 394-395.

616. "Warren's Probe May Be Conflict of Interest," The National Enquirer (29 Dec. 1963), 8.

617. "Congressman May Quit Assassination Probe," The National Enquirer (16 Feb. 1964), 8.

618. "Kennedy Assassination Probe Says Connally May Have Been Real Target," The National Enquirer (23 Aug. 1964), 8.

619. "FBI Deliberately Ignored Conspiracy Theory in Murders of JFK, RFK and Martin Luther King," The National Enquirer (6 April 1976), 55.

620. "Right-Wing Extremist Revealed Blueprint for Assassination 13 Days Before It Happened--And the FBI Knew," The National Enquirer (26 April 1977), 34-35.

621. "FBI Files Reveal New Evidence in JFK Assassination," The National Enquirer (7 Feb. 1978), 3.

622. "Warren Group Expected to Duck on Oswald," National Guardian, XVI (23 Jan. 1964), 1, 5.

623. "Lane Cites Curb at Oswald Inquiry: Attorney Denied Right to Cross-Examine Witnesses," National Guardian, XVI (14 March 1964), 4.

624. "Warren Board Will Report: 'Irrational Action By An Individual'," National Guardian, XVI (4 April 1964), 6.

625. "Oswald--Is the Commission in Doubt?: No Final Finding Yet, It Now Says," National Guardian, XVI (13 June 1964), 4.

626. "Mark Lane Challenges Warren to Hear Tape on Disputed Evidence: Oswald Case Testimony [By Mrs. Markham]," National Guardian, XVI (11 July 1964), 4.

627. "Earl Warren's 'Lost Cause'?: Editorial Report to Readers," National Guardian, XVI (29 Aug. 1964), 2.

628. "What's Ahead?: The Warren Commission: Present Questions, Future Answers?," National Review, XV (24 Dec. 1963), 4-5.

629. "Warren's Secret," National Review, XVI (7 April 1964), 265-266; XVI (21 April 1964), 311.

630. "Despite Testimony by J. Edgar Hoover, Warren Group Ignored Fact Jack Ruby Worked for FBI," The National Tattler, Special Edition (Sept. 1975), 8.

631. "Warren Commission," The New Republic, CL (29 Feb. 1964), 4-5.

632. "The Periscope: Inside Story: Dallas [Police Investigations and the FBI]," Newsweek, LXII (16 Dec. 1963), 16.

633. "The Assassination: History's Jury [First Meeting of Warren Commission]," Newsweek, LXII (16 Dec. 1963), 25-27.

634. "The Assassination: Report from the FBI [5 Volume Report to Warren Commission]," Newsweek, LXII (23 Dec. 1963), 19-20.

635. "National Affairs: JFK's Murder: Sowers of Doubt [Lane and Buchanan]," Newsweek, LXIII (6 April 1964), 22-24.

636. "National Affairs: Anniversaries: Nightmare Revisited," Newsweek, LXIII (8 June 1964), 48.

637. "National Affairs: The Assassination: Eye on That Window [Warren Commission in Dallas]," Newsweek, LXIII (22 June 1964), 32-34.

638. "Press: Jumping the Gun [Warren Commission Leaks]," Newsweek, LXIV (13 July 1964), 50.

639. "The Assassination: The Warren Commission Report," Newsweek, LXIV (5 Oct. 1964), 32-64.

640. "Department of Justice: Off Hoover's Chest . . . The Warren Report [And Rev. M. L. King called "the most notorious liar in the country"]," Newsweek, LXIV (30 Nov. 1964), 29-30.

641. "National Affairs: What They Saw That Dreadful Day in Dallas," Newsweek, LXIV (7 Dec. 1964), 28-42.

642. "Education: Instant History [Courses on Warren Report Offered]," Newsweek, LXV (1 Feb. 1965), 47.

643. "Press: Sellout in the Soviet [of the Amerika Reports on JFK and Warren Report]," Newsweek, LXV (5 Apr. 1965), 83.

644. "International: Soviet Union: Banned in Moscow [Russian Translation of Report]," Newsweek, LXVIII (12 Sept. 1966), 40.

645. "Justice: Opening Federal Files [Using the Freedom of Information Act Against Governmental Classification]," Newsweek, XCI (19 June 1978), 85-86.

646. "Kennedy/King/The FBI and CIA," Peoples World, XXXVIII (29 Nov. 1975), 1.

647. "Five Publishers Issue Warren Panel's Report," Publishers Weekly, CLXXXVI (5 Oct. 1964), 43-44.

648. "Warren Report: Paperback Editions Were Produced at Record-Breaking Pace," Publishers Weekly, CLXXXVI (5 Oct. 1964), 80-82; (12 Oct. 1964), 39-40.

649. "Currents: Warren Report in Italian [By Rizzoli Editore: 50,000 Copies]," Publishers Weekly, CLXXXVI (19 Oct. 1964), 23.

650. "Warren Commission Report: Verdict: One Man Alone," Senior Scholastic, LXXXV (7 Oct. 1964), 9-10.

651. "Open Justice," The Spectator (London), No. 7084 (3 April 1964), 435.

652. "Investigations: A Sad and Solemn Duty," Time, LXXXII (13 Dec. 1963), 26-27.

653. "Investigations: Between Two Fires," Time, LXXXIII (14 Feb. 1964), 16-20.

654. "The Warren Commission Report," Time, LXXXIV (2 Oct. 1964), 45-55.

655. "The Secret Service: Trying to Protect the Unprotectable [According to the Warren Report]," Time, LXXXIV (9 Oct. 1964), 28.

656. "The Administration: Off the Chest & Into the Fire [Hoover Defends FBI vs. Warren Report and Rev. M. L. King]," Time, LXXXIV (27 Nov. 1964), 31.

657. "The Warren Commission: the Witnesses," Time, LXXXIV (4 Dec. 1964), 25-27.

658.   "Philadelphia: Republican Specter," Time, LXXXIX (17 March 1967), 26-27.

659.   "FBI: The Oswald Cover-Up," Time, CVI (15 Sept. 1975), 19.

660.   "Investigations: FBI: Shaken By a Cover-Up That Failed [Oswald's Case]," Time, CVI (3 Nov. 1975), 9-10.

661.   "Nation: The FBI Story on J.F.K.'s Death [Release of Documents Under Freedom of Information Act Lawsuits]," Time, CX (19 Dec. 1977), 18-23.

662.   "The United States: The Questions to Be Answered [about Oswald]," Time and Tide (London), XLIV (5-11 Dec. 1963), 11-12.

663.   "United States: Warren's Team," Time and Tide (London), XLIV (12-18 Dec. 1963), 10.

664.   "Who Killed Kennedy?   [Summarizes Buchanan's Arguments]," Time and Tide (London), XLV (30 April - 6 May 1964), 5; (7-13 May 1964), 11; (14-20 May 1964), 10.

665.   "Oswald Note to FBI 'Destroyed' [According to Agent James Hosty]," The Times (London), No. 59,577 (13 Dec. 1975), 5.

666.   "No Kennedy Plot, FBI Files Show," The Times (London), No. 60,182 (9 Dec. 1977), 11.

667.   "American Assassins [Reviews Buchanan's Book]," The Times Literary Supplement (London), No. 3246 (14 May 1964), 407.

668.   "FBI Attacked;   Oswald Defended: Two Communist Papers View the Assassination," Tocsin: The West's Leading Anti-Communist Weekly, V (8 Jan. 1964), 1, 4.

669.   "Redlich Record Under Study: Probe of Warren Commission Prober," Tocsin: The West's Leading Anti-Communist Weekly, V (4 March 1964), 1.

670.   "As the Assassination Inquiry Goes On . . .," U.S. News and World Report, LV (23 Dec. 1963), 10.

671.   "In the JFK Murder Case--Chief Investigator Lee Rankin," U.S. News and World Report, LV (30 Dec. 1963), 10.

672.   "As Warren Inquiry Starts: Latest on the Assassination," U.S. News and World Report, LV (30 Dec. 1963), 28-30.

673.   "Assassination Inquiry: Slow, Careful," U.S. News and World Report, LVI (27 Jan. 1964), 49.

674.   "Back of the Secrecy in the Assassination Probe," U.S. News and World Report, LVI (24 Feb. 1964), 52-55.

675.   "'Counsel' for Oswald: a Top Lawyer Takes Job [With Warren Commission]," U.S. News and World Report, LVI (9 March 1964), 16.

676.   "How FBI, Dallas Police Differ on Oswald Case," U.S. News and World Report, LVI (4 May 1964), 14.

677.   "Latest on Murder of Kennedy: a Preview of the Warren Report," U.S. News and World Report, LVI (1 June 1964), 43-44.

678.   "Warren Findings: Some New Facts," U.S. News and World Report, LVII (6 July 1964), 44.

679.   "Here's What the Warren Report Will Show," U.S. News and World Report, LVII (14 Sept. 1964), 42-43.

680.   "Unravelling the Mystery of the Assassination of John F. Kennedy: the Official Story," U.S. News and World Report, LVII (5 Oct. 1964), 35-42, 70-71, 96-97.

681.   "Rush to Buy the Report on Kennedy Assassination," U.S. News and World Report, LVII (12 Oct. 1964), 20.

682.   "The FBI and Civil Rights: J. Edgar Hoover Speaks Out," U.S. News and World Report, LVII (30 Nov. 1964), 56-58.

683.   "JFK Killing: FBI Files Raise Questions, Give No Answers," U.S. News and World Report, LXXXIII (19 Dec. 1977), 15.

(4) THE WARREN REPORT

684.   United States. President's Commission on the Assassination of President Kennedy. Report of the President's Commission on the Assassination of President Kennedy. Washington, D.C.: U.S. Government Printing Office, 1964 [888 pp.]; [See 3698, 3737, 3740-3742, 3746, 3765, 3823, 3936, 3937, 4041].

685. _____. Investigation of the Assassination of President John F. Kennedy; Hearings Before the President's Commission on the Assassination of President Kennedy. Washington, D.C.: U.S. Government Printing Office, 1964, 26 vols; Reprinted, Washington, D.C.: Zenger Publishing Co., 1975; Film and Fiche Copies, Glen Rock, N.J.: Micro- filming Corp. of America, 1977; [See 3896].

686. _____. "Text of Summary of Warren
Commission Report," Congressional Quarterly Weekly Report,
XXII (2 Oct. 1964), 2332-2340.

687. _____. "The Warren Report on the
Assassination of President John F. Kennedy," Library of Congress, Library Services Division (5 Oct. 1964).

Other Printings:

688. United States. President's Commission on the Assassi-
nation of President Kennedy. A Concise Compendium of the
Warren Commission Report on the Assassination of John F.
Kennedy. Foreword by Robert J. Donovan. New York: Popular
Library, 1964 [637 pp.]; [See 3761].

689. _____. The Official Warren
Commission Report on the Assassination of President John F.
Kennedy. Analysis and Commentary by Louis Nizer; Historical
Afterword by Bruce Catton. Garden City, New York; Doubleday,
1964 [888 pp.]; [See 718, 3681, 4082].

690. _____. Report of the Warren
Commission: the Assassination of President Kennedy. Intro-
duction by Harrison E. Salisbury, for The New York Times.
New York: McGraw-Hill, 1964 [726 pp.].

691. _____. "The Warren Commission
Report," The New York Times, CXIV (28 Sept. 1964), 1A-48A;
[See 3779].

692. _____. The Warren Commission
Report: The Assassination of President Kennedy. With analy-
sis by Miriam Ottenberg. Washington, D.C.: U.S. Information
Agency, 1964.

693. _____. The Warren Report: Report
of the President's Commission on the Assassination of President John F. Kennedy. New York: Associated Press, 1964 [366
pp.].

694. _____. Warren Report über die
Ermordung des Präsidenten John F. Kennedy. Herausgegeben und
kommentiert von Robert M. W. Kempner. Cologne: Kiepenhever
& Witsch, 1964 [703 pp.].

695. _____. The Witnesses: the High-
lights of Hearings Before the Warren Commission on the
Assassination of President Kennedy. Introduction by Anthony
Lewis. New York: Bantam Books, 1964 [626 pp.]; McGraw-Hill,
1965 [634 pp.]; [See 3710].

Separate Indexes:

696. Jones, Penn, Jr. (ed.). "Name Index to 26 Volumes and
Commission Documents," The Continuing Inquiry, I (22 Nov.
1976).

697. Meagher, Sylvia. Subject Index to the Warren Report
and Hearings & Exhibits. Metuchen, New Jersey: Scarecrow
Press, 1966; expanded ed., Ann Arbor, Michigan: University
Microfilms, 1971.

(5) CRITICS AND DEFENDERS OF THE WARREN REPORT

Books:

698. Adler, Bill [pseudonym for Jay David]. The Weight of
the Evidence; the Warren Report and its critics. New York:
Meredith Press, 1968.

699. Belin, David W. November 22, 1963: You are the Jury.
New York: Quadrangle, 1973; [See 1833, 4745]; Excerpts reprinted in Skeptic, No. 9 (Aug. 1975), 12-15, 51-53.

700. Crawford, Curtis, (ed.). Critical Reactions to the
Warren Report. New York: Marzani and Munsell, 1964 [Includes
articles by Murray Kempton, Mark Lane, Thomas Buchanan and
Leo Sauvage].

701. Davis, Marc, and Jim Mathews (eds.). Highlights of
the Warren Report. Covina, Calif.: Collectors Publications,
1967.

702. Eddowes, Michael. The Oswald File. New York: Clarkson N. Potter, distributed by Crown Publishers, 1977.

703. Epstein, Edward Jay. Inquest: the Warren Commission
and the Establishment of Truth. Introduction by Richard H.
Rovere. New York: Viking Press, 1966; Expanded ed., Bantam,
1966; London: Hutchinson & Co., Ltd., 1966; [See 720, 829,
973, 1060, 1901, 4019, 4027, 4028, 4046, 4049].

704. _____. O relatório de mêdo; A Comissao
Warren e a busca da verdade [Translation of Inquest]. Rio de
Janiero: Ed. Inova, 1967. Published in French, Editions
Robert Laffont; in German, S. Fischer Verlag; in Italian,
Rizzoli Editore; and serialized in Der Spiegel and in Spain,
Triunfo.

705. _____. Between Fact and Fiction: the
Problem of Journalism [Essays and Reviews]. New York:
Vintage Books, 1975.

706. Ford, Gerald R., with John R. Stiles. Portrait of the
Assassin. New York: Simon and Schuster, 1965; Ballantine
Paperback, 1966; [See 109, 110, 936, 4055].

707. Fox, Sylvan. The Unanswered Questions About President
Kennedy's Assassination. New York: Award Books, 1965; London: Mayflower-Dell, 1966; [See 4019, 4047].

708. Gauzer, Bernard, and Sid Moody. The Lingering Shadow.
Dallas: Dallas Times-Herald, 1967.

709. Goldberg, Alfred. Conspiracy Interpretations of the
Assassination of President Kennedy: International and Do-
mestic [Air Force Historian and Member of Warren Commission
staff]. Los Angeles, Calif.: University of California
Security Studies Project, Security Studies Paper No. 16, 1968;
[See 4062].

710. In the Shadow of Dallas: A Primer on the Assassination
of President Kennedy. San Francisco: Ramparts Magazine,
Jan. 1967.

711. Jones, Penn, Jr. Forgive My Grief; a Critical Review
of the Warren Commission Report on the Assassination of President John F. Kennedy. Midlothian, Texas: Printed by the
Midlothian Mirror, 1966; [See 4052, 4074].

712. _____. Forgive My Grief. Volume II. A
Further Critical Review of the Warren Commission Report on
the Assassination of President John F. Kennedy. Midlothian,
Texas: Midlothian Mirror, 1967.

713. _____. Forgive My Grief III. Midlothian,
Texas: Published by author, 1969; revised ed., 1976.

714. _____. Forgive My Grief IV. Midlothian,
Texas: Published by author, 1974.

715. Joesten, Joachim. The Biggest Lie Ever Told: the
Kennedy Murder Fraud and How I Helped Expose It. Munich and
New York: Published by the Author, 4 vols., 1968-9.

716. _____. The Gaps in the Warren Report [Re-
prints Part of His Revised Ed. of Oswald]. New York: Marzani and Munsell, [1964].

717. _____. Die Wahrheit über den Kennedy-Mord;
Wie und Warum der Warren Report lügt [The Truth About the
Kennedy Murder; How and Why the Warren Report is Lying].
Zurich: Schweizer Verlagshaus, 1966; Utrecht: Bruna &
Zoon, 1966; [See 4066].

718. Lane, Mark. A Citizen's Dissent; Mark Lane Replies.
New York: Holt, Rinehart and Winston, 1968; [See 1060, 4547].

719. _____. Rush to Judgment; a Critique of the Warren
Commission's Inquiry into the Murder of President John F.
Kennedy, Officer J. D. Tippit, and Lee Harvey Oswald. With
Introduction by Hugh Trevor-Roper. New York: Holt, Rinehart
& Winston, 1966; Fawcett Paperback, 1967; Dell Paperback,
with Lane's new introduction, 1975; [See 689, 797, 799, 812,
840, 852, 1060, 1785, 1900, 2207, 3894, 4019, 4036, 4039,
4049, 4052, 4058, 4074].

720.   Lewis, Richard Warren. The Scavengers and Critics of the Warren Report; the Endless Paradox. With Introduction by Bob Considine. New York: Delacorte Press, 1967; Dell, 1967; [See 718]; Researched by Lawrence Schiller, based on Capitol Records "The Controversy" [See 1134].

721.   Marks, Stanley J. Murder Most Foul! The Conspiracy That Murdered President Kennedy; 975 Questions & Answers. N.p.: Bureau of International Affairs, 1967.

722.   Meagher, Sylvia. Accessories After the Fact: the Warren Commission, the Authorities, and the Report. With Introduction by Leo Sauvage. Indianapolis: Bobbs-Merrill, 1967; New York: Vintage Books, 1976, with Preface by Senator Richard S. Schweiker and Introduction by Peter Dale Scott; [See 290, 4497].

723.   Meunier, Robert F. Shadows of Doubt: the Warren Commission Cover-up. Hicksville, New York: Exposition Press, 1976.

724.   Michel, Armand. L'Assassinat de John Kennedy, le Rapport Warren et ses Critiques. N.p.: Trinckvel, 1968.

725.   Nash, Harry C. Citizen's Arrest: the Dissent of Penn Jones, Jr., in the Assassination of JFK. Austin, Texas: Latitudes Press, 1977.

726.   Newman, Albert H. The Assassination of John F. Kennedy: the Reasons Why [Supplies Chronology and the Strong Defense of Warren Report]. New York: Clarkson N. Potter, 1970.

727.   Popkin, Richard H. The Second Oswald. Introduction by Murray Kempton. New York: Avon Books, 1966; London, 1967; [See 735, 4057].

728.   Sauvage, Leo. L'affaire Oswald: Réponse au Rapport Warren. Paris: Les Editions de Minuit, 1965.

729.   _____. The Oswald Affair; an Examination of the Contradictions and Omissions of the Warren Report. Cleveland: World Publishing Co., 1966; [See 4019, 4036, 4039, 4052, 4074].

730.   Scott, Peter Dale, Paul L. Hoch, and Russell Stetler (eds.). The Assassinations: Dallas and Beyond: a Guide to Cover-ups and Investigations. New York: Random House, 1976.

731.   Sparrow, John Hanbury Angus. After the Assassination: a Positive Appraisal of the Warren Report. New York: Chilmark Press, 1967.

732.   Thompson, Josiah. Six Seconds in Dallas; a Micro-Study of the Kennedy Assassination. New York: Bernard Geis Associates, with Random House, 1967; [See 4460, 4471, 4497, 4510, 4552].

733. Thomson, George C. The Quest For Truth: (a Quizzical Look at the Warren Report) or How President Kennedy Really Was Assassinated. Glendale, Calif.: Privately Printed by G. C. Thomson Engineering Co., 1964.

734. Weisberg, Harold. The Report on the Warren Report; or, The Six Wise Men of Industan. N.p.: Photocopied Type-script by the Author, 1965 [This is the original version of 735].

735. _____ . Whitewash: the Report on the Warren Report. Hyattstown, Md.: H. Weisberg, 1965, 1966; New York: Dell, 1966; [See 4019, 4027, 4052, 4074].

736. _____ . Whitewash IV: Top Secret JFK Assassination Transcript. With Legal Analysis by James Lesar. Frederick, Md.: H. Weisberg, 1974; [See 4776].

737. West, John R. Death of the President. The Warren Commission on Trial. Covina, Calif.: Collectors Publications, 1967.

738. White, Stephen. Should We Now Believe the Warren Report? Preface by Walter Cronkite [Based on 'CBS News Inquiry: the Warren Report' 25-28 June 1967]. New York: Macmillan, 1968; [See 389, 718, 732, 756, 837, 1785, 4405, 4406, 4407, 4410, 4411, 4413].

739. Zwart, Jacques. Invitation to Hairsplitting: A Hypercritical Investigation Into the True Function of the Warren Commission and the True Nature of the Warren Report. Paris & Amsterdam & The Hague, 1970.

Articles by Authors:

740. Amalric, Jacques. "More on the Warren Report [Reviews Sauvage's Oswald]," Atlas, X (Oct. 1965), 249-250.

741. Anson, Robert Sam. "The Man Who Never Was [the Second Oswald]," New Times (New York), V (19 Sept. 1975), 14-16, 21-25.

742. Aronson, James. "Report to Readers: Dallas--Rush to Judgment," National Guardian, XVIII (3 Sept. 1966), 2.

743. _____ . "Report to Readers: The Murder That Will Not Out [Commends Lane and Notes Ruby's Impending Death]," National Guardian, XIX (17 Dec. 1966), 1-2.

744. [Arnoni, M. S.]. "The [Warren] Report," The Minority of One, VI (Nov. 1964), 2-3.

745. _____ . "A Commentator Fights a Reporter [I. F. Stone on the Warren Report]," The Minority of One, VI (Nov. 1964), 5.

746. _____. "The Relevance of an Inquest [By Epstein]," The Minority of One, VIII (July/Aug. 1966), 8-9.

747. _____. "Between Two Assassinations," The Minority of One, VIII (Sept. 1966), 6.

748. _____. "A Dead Brother Is No Brother [Robert Kennedy and the Warren Report]," The Minority of One, IX (Jan. 1967), 6.

749. Belfrage, Cedric. "Books: Assassination Whitewash [Reviews Epstein's Inquest and Weisberg's Whitewash]," National Guardian, XVIII (2 July 1966), 12.

750. Berezhikov, V. "More Light on the Kennedy Assassination [Reviews Joesten, Truth]," New Times (Moscow), 26 Oct. 1966, 28-32.

751. Bickel, Alexander M. "The Failure of the Warren Report [Reviews Epstein, Inquest]," Commentary, XLII (Oct. 1966), 31-39.

752. _____. "Leo Sauvage and the Warren Commission," The New Leader, XLIX (21 Nov. 1966), 19-21.

753. _____. "Re-Examining the Warren Report [Need for Re-Investigation]," The New Republic, CLVI (7 Jan. 1967), 25-28.

754. _____. "Return to Dallas [Reviews Thompson and Meagher]," The New Republic, CLVII (23 Dec. 1967), 34.

755. _____. "Back to the Attack [Reviews Lane]," The New Republic, CLVIII (22 June 1968), 28-29.

756. _____, with W. Lister. "CBS on the Warren Report; How Many Bullets?" The New Republic, CLVII (15 July 1967), 29-30; CLVII (19 Aug. 1967), 30-34.

757. Bonazzi, Robert. "One Man's Grief [On Penn Jones, Jr.]," The Texas Observer, LIX (29 Sept. 1967), 12-13.

758. Brackman, Jacob, and Faye Levine. "Ephemera: Books [A Spoof Review of Epstein, Weisberg, Lane and 2 Fictitious Authors]," Ramparts, V (Nov. 1966), 59-61; V (Jan. 1967), 1, 5-6; [See 2152, 2153].

759. Brandon, Henry. "All too Distressing [on Revived JFK and Warren Report Controversies]," The Sunday Times (London), No. 7474 (21 Aug. 1966), 6.

760. Brill, Steven. "The Case Against Mark Lane; the Conclusions: He Has Only Two Motives--Profit and Headlines," Esquire, XCI (13 Feb. 1979), 48-52.

761. Butterfield, Roger. "Assassination: Some Serious Exceptions to the Warren Report," Harper's Magazine," CCXXXIII (Oct. 1966), 122-126.

762. Campbell, Alex. "Books and the Arts: What Did Happen in Dallas? [Reviews Weisberg and Epstein]," The New Republic, CLIV (25 June 1966), 23-25.

763. Cline, R. A. ""Warren in the Dock: Who Killed Kennedy? [Reviews Epstein and Lane]," The Spectator (London), No. 7213 (23 Sept. 1966), 371-372.

764. _____. "Postscript to Warren [By A. L. Goodhart]," The Spectator (London), No. 7231 (27 Jan. 1967), 99.

765. Cohen, Jacob. "Conspiracy Fever," Commentary, LX (Oct. 1975), 33-42.

766. _____. "The Warren Commission Report and Its Critics," Frontier, XVIII (Nov. 1966), 5-20; [See 831].

767. _____. "What the Warren Report Omits: the Vital Documents," The Nation, CCIII (11 July 1966), 43-49; [See 4029, 4054, 4074].

768. Connolly, Cyril. "Dallas: Pandora's Box Is Opened," The Sunday Times (London), No. 7479 (25 Sept. 1966), 27.

769. _____. "The Death of Innocence [Review of Joesten, The Truth]," The Sunday Times (London), No. 7521 (23 July 1967), 43.

770. Cook, Fred J. "Some Unanswered Questions: the Warren Commission Report," The Nation, CCII (13 June 1966), 705-715.

771. _____. "Testimony of the Eye Witnesses: the Warren Commission Report," The Nation, CCII (20 June 1966), 737-746.

772. _____. "Letters: Cook on Cohen," The Nation, CCIII (22 Aug. 1966), 138, 156.

773. _____. "Books & the Arts: the Warren Report and the Irreconcilables [Review of Josiah Thompson and of Sylvia Meagher]," The Nation, CCVI (26 Feb. 1968), 227-281.

774. _____. "Book Forum: The Assassination of John F. Kennedy, by Albert H. Newman," Saturday Review, LIII (17 Oct. 1970), 29-32.

775. Crawford, Kenneth. "The Warren Impeachers," Newsweek, LXIV (19 Oct. 1964), 40.

776. Cushman, Robert F. "Why the Warren Commission?," New York University Law Review, XL (May 1965), 477-503.

777. Dellinger, Dave. "The Warren Report?: the Death of a President," Liberation, IX (Jan. 1965), 11-12.

778. _____. "Editorials: the Warren Report?" Liberation, X (March 1965), 3-5.

779. Devlin, Patrick [Lord]. "Death of a President: the Established Facts [Warren Report]," The Atlantic Monthly, CCXV (March 1965), 112-118.

780. Drinnon, Richard, with John Jamieson. "War on Violence . . . The Warren Report . . . ." Wilson Library Bulletin, XLV (Sept. 1970), 68-77; XLV (Nov. 1970), 236; XLV (Feb. 1971) 545.

781. Dugger, Ronnie. "November 22, 1963: The Case Is Not Closed: Ten Books in Review," The Texas Observer, LVIII (11 Nov. 1966), 1-2.

782. Ellis, W. "The Warren Report," Jubilee, XII (Dec. 1964), 24-27.

783. Emerson, William A., Jr. "From the Editor [About Josiah Thompson's Book]," The Saturday Evening Post, CCXL (2 Dec. 1967), 3.

784. Emery, Fred. "New Doubts About Kennedy Killing [Harold Weisberg, Post-Mortem]," The Times (London), No. 59,556 (19 Nov. 1975), 6.

785. Epstein, Edward Jay. "Who's Afraid of the Warren Report?" Esquire, LXVI (Dec. 1966), 204, 330-334.

786. Evans, M. Stanton. "A Sober Assessment [Reviews S. Fox]," National Review, XVIII (11 Jan. 1966), 34-37.

787. Fein, Arnold L. "JFK in Dallas: The Warren Report and Its Critics," Saturday Review, XLIX (22 Oct. 1966), 36-47.

788. Fonzi, Gaeton. "Loose Ends: How Many Did the Warren Commission Leave? And Do They Lead Anywhere?" Greater Philadelphia, LVIII (Jan. 1967), 66-69, 88-108.

789. _____. "The Warren Commission, the Truth, and Arlen Specter," Greater Philadelphia, LVII (Aug. 1966), 38-45, 79-91.

790. Ford, Gerald R. "Piecing Together the Evidence," Life, LVII (2 Oct. 1964), 42-51.

791. Fox, Sylvan. "The Hidden Evidence About President Kennedy's Assassination," Saga, XXXIII (Nov. 1966), 12-15, 73-86.

792. _____. "'Mein Gott, sie bringen uns alle um!' Die Rätsel um Kennedys Tod ['My God, You Bring Everything to Us.' The Riddle of Kennedy's Death]." Der Spiegel.

(Hamburg), No. 15 (1967), 88-110; No. 16 (1967), 102-119;
No. 17 (1967), 106-117; No. 18 (1967), 108-124.

793. Freese, Paul L. "The Warren Commission and the Fourth
Shot: a Reflection on the Fundamentals of Forensic Fact-
Finding," New York University Law Review, XL (May 1965), 424-
465.

794. Friedman, Rick. "The Weekly Editor: Assassination
Book [Penn Jones, Jr.]," Editor & Publisher, XCIX (12 Nov.
1966), 100.

795. Gibbons, R. "The Warren Commission," Ave Maria, CIV
(17 Sept. 1966), 16-17.

796. Goodall, Kenneth. "The Warren Commission: The Critics
and the Law: 1. Beyond Reasonable Doubt? [Reviews Epstein
and Lane]," The Reporter, XXXV (15 Dec. 1966), 44-46.

797. Goodhart, Arthur L. "The Warren Commission from the
Procedural Standpoint," New York University Law Review, XL
(1965), 404-423; [See 718].

798. _____. "The Warren Commission: The
Critics and the Law: 2. Legal Ignorance and False Logic
[Against Epstein and Lane]," The Reporter, XXXV (15 Dec.
1966), 47-50.

799. _____. "Three Famous Legal Hoaxes: The
Tichborne Case, the Dreyfus Affair, the Alleged Conspiracy to
Assassinate President Kennedy," Record of the Association of
the Bar of the City of New York, XXII (June 1967), 415-437;
[See 718].

800. Graziani, Gilbert. "Le Mystère Kennedy [and the Tasks
of the Warren Commission]," Paris Match, No. 920 (26 Nov.
1966), 75-86.

801. Griswold, D. "From Warren Commission to CIA," Workers=
World, XVII (17 Jan. 1975), 6.

802. Gross, Alfred A. "Shadows of Doubt [Reviews Lane and
Sauvage]," The Christian Century, LXXXIII (28 Sept. 1966),

803. Habe, Hans. "Die Hälfte der Wahrheit. Der Mörder
gefunden--der Mord ungeklärt. Bemerkungen zum Bericht des
Warren-Ausschusses [Half of the Truth. The Murderer Identi-
fied--the Murder Unexplained. Remarks on the Warren Commission's Report]," Weltwoche (Zürich), XXXII, No. 1614 (1964),
13.

804. Handlin, Oscar. "The Warren Commission [Reviews Epstein, and NBC's Seventy Hours]," The Atlantic Monthly,
CCXVIII (Aug. 1966), 117-118.

805. Hoffman, E. "Warren Commission Frames Oswald," Ann
Arbor Sun, II (6 Dec. 1974), 8.

806. _____. "JFK Murder and Warren Commission Coverup," Ann Arbor Sun, III (9 May 1975), 14.

807. Jacobson, Dan. "Mean Street: Warren Commission Report," New Statesman (London), LXIX (15 Jan. 1965), 76-77.

808. Joesten, Joachim. "Der falsche Oswald. Was der Warren-Bericht enthüllt--aber nicht ausspricht [The Fake Oswald, What the Warren Report Reveals--But Does Not State]," Weltwoche (Zürich), XXXII, No. 1619 (1964), 49.

809. Jones, Penn [Jr.] "Mysterious Deaths in the Long Aftermath of Dallas," The Times (London), No. 56,875 (25 Feb. 1967), 11.

810. Kaplan, John. "The Assassins [Critique of Warren Report and of Its Critics]," The American Scholar, XXXVI (Spring 1967), 271-306.

811. _____. "The Assassin [Expands and Footnotes Above Version]," Stanford Law Review, XIX (1967), 1110-1151.

812. _____. "The Case of the Grassy Knoll: the Romance of Conspiracy [Revised Version of the Above]," in Robin W. Winks (ed.), The Historian as Detective: Essays on Evidence (N.Y.: Harper & Row, 1968), pp. 371-419; [See 718].

813. Karp, Irwin. "Debate Over Dallas: [Theories of John Sparrow and Sylvia Meagher]," Saturday Review, LI (9 March 1968), 113-114.

814. Keisler, J. R. "The Warren Report: from Readers' Letters," The Minority of One, VIII (June 1966), 29.

815. Kempton, Murray. "The Warren Report---Reasonable Doubt," The Spectator (London), No. 7110 (2 Oct. 1964), 428-429.

816. _____. "Warren Report: Case for the Prosecution," The New Republic, CLI (10 Oct. 1964), 13-17.

817. Kerby, Phil. "This Month: The Critics [of the Warren Report]," Frontier, XVIII (Nov. 1966), 2, 26.

818. Kilpatrick, James J. "The Dissenters Ask Too Much [from Warren Report]," Skeptic, No. 9 (Aug. 1975), 29. 61.

819. Knebl, Fletcher. "The Warren Commission Report on the Assassination Is Struck by 'A New Wave of Doubt' [Interviews Epstein]," Look, XXX (12 July 1966), 66-72.

820. Lane, Mark. "Lane on Warren Report: The Doubts Remain," National Guardian, XVI (3 Oct. 1964), 3-6.

821. _____. "The Warren Report: a First Glance," The Minority of One, VI (Nov. 1964), 6-8.

822. _____. "Playboy Interview: Mark Lane," Playboy, XIV (Feb. 1967), 41-68.

823. _____. "A Look At the Evidence--An Answer to John Sparrow [With Sparrow's Reply]," The Times Literary Supplement (London), No. 3,448 (28 March 1968), 319-321.

824. Lipson, D. Herbert. "Off the Cuff [Editorial]: [on the Gaeton Fonzi article]," Greater Philadelphia, LVII (Aug. 1966), 1.

825. Lynd, Staughton. "Comment by Staughton Lynd [Supports Salandria vs. Warren Report]," Liberation, IX (1965), 18.

826. Macdonald, Dwight. "A Critique of the Warren Report," Esquire, LXIII (March 1965), 59-63, 127-138; Reprinted in Gerald Walker (ed.), Best Magazine Articles, 1966 (N.Y.: Crown, 1966), pp. 19-53.

827. McGrory, Mary. "A Controversy That Has Only Just Begun," America, CXVI (7 Jan. 1967), 10.

828. Mailer, Norman. "The Great American Mystery [Reviews Rush to Judgment]," Book Week Washington Post, (28 Aug. 1966), 1, 11-13.

829. Meagher, Sylvia. "On 'Closing Doors, Not Opening Them' or The Limits of the Warren Investigation [Reviews Epstein]," The Minority of One, VIII (July/Aug. 1966), 29-32.

830. _____. "Four Books on the Warren Report: The Summer of Discontent [Epstein, Lane, Sauvage, Weisberg]," Studies on the Left, VI (Sept.-Oct. 1966), 72-84.

831. _____. "Letters: The Warren Commission Report and Its Critics [Specifically Jacob Cohen]," Frontier, XVIII (Jan. 1967), 23-24.

832. _____. "Post-Assassination Credibility Chasm [And the Warren Report]," The Minority of One, IX (March 1967) 21-22.

833. _____. "The Warren Commission's Private Life [Review of Lifton's Book]," The Texas Observer, LXII (3 April 1970), 12-15.

834. _____. "The Curious Testimony of Mr. Givens [With David Belin's Reply]," The Texas Observer, LXIII (13 Aug. 1971), 11-12.

835. _____. "Finishing the [Warren] Commission's Unfinished Business," Skeptic, No. 9 (Aug. 1975), 31-33, 61-62.

836. Meisner, P. "Warren Report Revealed as Fraud," Workers World, XVII (10 Oct. 1975), 2.

837. Mills, Andrew. "Who Killed Kennedy? The Warren Report is Right [The CBS-TV Report]," True, XLVIII (Dec. 1967), 31-32, 72-77.

838. Mitzel, J. "Gay Version of the Warren Report," Fag Rag, No. 13 (Summer 1975), 1.

839. Montague, Ivor. "The Warren Report," Labour Monthly (London), XLVI (Nov. 1964), 449-503.

840. Mosk, Richard M. "The Warren Commission and the Legal Process," Case & Comment Magazine, LXXII (May-June 1967), 13-20; [See 718].

841. Muggeridge, Malcolm. "Books: . . . Inquest, by Edward Jay Epstein," Esquire, LXVI (Oct. 1966), 14-16.

842. Mühlen, Norbert. "Mord und Legende. Die Kritiker des Warren-Reports [Murder and Legend. Critics of the Warren Report]," Der Monat. Internationale Zeitschrift für Politik und geistiges Leben (Frankfurt/Main), CXCIX (17 Jan. 1965), 14-28.

843. Nash, George and Patricia. "The Other Witnesses [Those Not Called or Accepted by Warren Commission]," The New Leader, XLVII (12 Oct. 1964), 6-9.

844. Northcott, Kaye. "Belin Asks Too Much," The Texas Observer, LXIII (13 Aug. 1971), 23.

845. O'Brien, Conor Cruise. "Veto by Assassination? [Review of Sylvia Meagher, Accessories]," The Minority of One, IX (Dec. 1967), 16-18.

846. Olds, Greg. "The Official Doubters [Connally, Senator Richard Russell, Police Chief Curry]," The Texas Observer, LXI (6 Feb. 1970), 9-11.

847. Osterburg, James W. "The Warren Commission: Report and Hearings [On Methods and Criminology]," Journal of the Forensic Sciences, II (July 1966), 261-271.

848. Osvald, Frank. "Kan Man Stole pa Warren? [Can One Trust Warren?]," Verdens Gang (Copenhagen), XVIII (1964), 274-279.

849. Oswald, Marguerite C. "The Warren Report: from Readers' Letters," The Minority of One, VIII (June 1966), 29.

850. Policoff, Jerry. "The Belin Connection," Rolling Stone, No. 185 (24 Aug. 1975), 31.

851. Popkin, Richard H. "The Second Oswald: the Case for a Conspiracy Theory [Reviews Epstein and Weisberg]," The New York Review of Books, VII (28 July 1966), 11-22; (18 Aug. 1966), 31; (8 Sept. 1966), 30; (6 Oct. 1966), 29-34.

852. Raskin, Marcus. "Rush to Judgment: Book Review," Yale Law Journal, LXXVI (1967), 581-597; [See 718].

853. Rosenbaum, Ron. "Turning Point for the Assassination Buffs," Village Voice, XX (5 May 1975), 44, 46, 50, 52.

854. Roszak, Theodore, and Paul Goodman. "Letters . . . [on the Warren Report]," Liberation, X (March 1965), 47; X (April 1965), 30; X (May 1965), 31.

855. Russell, Bertrand. "16 Questions on the Assassination," The Minority of One, VI (Sept. 1964), 6-8.

856. _____. "Letters to the Editor: A Hearing for Oswald [After the Warren Report]," The Sunday Times (London), No. 7388 (20 Dec. 1964), 8; No. 7391 (10 Jan. 1965), 10.

857. Russell, Francis. "Doubts About Dallas," National Review, XVIII (6 Sept. 1966), 887-893.

858. Salisbury, Harrison E. "Who Killed President Kennedy? [Reviews Lane, Epstein and Sauvage]," The Progressive, XXX (Nov. 1966), 36-39.

859. Sauvage, Leo. "As I Was Saying [Reply to Bickel]," The New Leader, XLIX (21 Nov. 1966), 21-22.

860. _____. "Professor Bickel and the Warren Commission [Published in Commentary]," The New Leader, XLIX (7 Nov. 1966), 16-19.

861. _____. "The Duality of the Warren Report [Reviews Epstein's Inquest]," The New Leader, XLIX (20 June 1966), 24-26.

862. _____. "The Case Against Mr. X," The New Leader, XLIX (3 Jan. 1966), 13-18, 33.

863. _____. "Oswald's Case Against the Warren Commission," The New Leader, XLVIII (20 Dec. 1965), 5-10, 30.

864. _____. "The Warren Commission's Case Against Oswald," The New Leader, XLVIII (22 Nov. 1965), 16-21.

865. Schoenmann, Ralph. "Ist der Warren-Bericht über den Tod Präsident Kennedys glaubwürdig? [Is the Warren Report on President Kennedy's Death Believable]," Frankfurter Hefte. Zeitschrift für Kultur und Politik (Frankfurt/Main), XX, No. 1 (Jan. 1965), 15-24.

866. Schwartz, Jay. "A Legal Demurrer to the Report of the Warren Commission," Journal of Forensic Sciences, 11 (1966), 318-329.

867. Scobey, Alfredda. "A Lawyer's Notes on the Warren Commission Report [By a Staff Member]," American Bar Association Journal, LI (Jan. 1965), 39-43.

868. Simpson, Alan W. B. "Letters to the Editor: Postscript to Warren [Critique of R. A. Cline]," The Spectator (London), No. 7232 (3 Feb. 1967), 133.

869. Smith, Jack A. "Oswald Case--Still Mystery: Riddles in the Warren Report," National Guardian, XVI (3 Oct. 1964), 1, 6.

870. _____. "3 Critics of the Warren Report Present Views: Lane, Joesten and Buchanan Assail Commission's Findings on Assassination," National Guardian, XVII (17 Oct. 1964), 3.

871. _____. "Warren Report Target Again: Findings on Shots Challenged [By Salandria]," National Guardian, XVII (2 Jan. 1965), 12.

872. Smith, R. H. "Thinking the Unthinkable: the Warren Commission Books," Publishers Weekly, CXC (10 Oct. 1966), 55.

873. Sparrow, John. "Making Mysteries About Oswald [Against Warren Report Critics, Especially Hugh Trevor-Roper]," The Sunday Times (London), No. 7391 (10 Jan. 1965), 8; Reprinted in Atlas, IX (March 1965), 173-174.

874. _____. "After the Assassination [Wide-Ranging Critique of Warren Report Critics]," The Times Literary Supplement (London), No. 3,433 (14 Dec. 1967), 1217-1222; No. 3,436 (4 Jan. 1968), 12-13; [See 4474, 4475].

875. _____. "John Sparrow's Reply [to Mark Lane]," The Times Literary Supplement (London), No. 3,448 (28 March 1968), 321; No. 3,450 (11 April 1968), 373; No. 3,454 (9 May 1968), 485.

876. Steiner, Stan. "Books: The Politics of Assassination [Reviews Lane]," National Guardian, XX (24 Aug. 1968), 30.

877. Stone, I. F. "The Left and the Warren Commission Report," I. F. Stone's Weekly, XII (5 Oct. 1964), 1-3.

878. Szulc, Tad. "The Warren Commission in Its Own Words; The Documents [Devastating Critique]," The New Republic, CLXXIII (27 Sept. 1975), 9-48.

879. Thompson, Josiah. "Letters: The Second Oswald [Gives Support to Popkin]," The New York Review of Books, VII (6 Oct. 1966), 29-30.

880. _____. "The Cross Fire That Killed President Kennedy," The Saturday Evening Post, CCXL (2 Dec. 1967), 27-31, 46, 50-55.

881.   Towne, Anthony. "The Assassination, the Warren Report and the Public Trust [Reviews Major Critics]," Motive, XXVII (Feb. 1967), 6-14.

882.   Trevor-Roper, Hugh. "Kennedy Murder Enquiry Is Suspect [Warren Report's Flawed Evidence]," The Sunday Times (London), No. 7387 (13 Dec. 1964), 21; [See 3897, 3898, 3903].

883.   _____. "How Was the President Shot: Did Oswald Have Accomplices?," The Sunday Times (London), No. 7390 (3 Jan. 1965), 9.

884.   _____. "The Slovenly Warren Report [Reprint from The Sunday Times (London)]," Atlas, IX (Feb. 1965), 115-118.

885.   Trillin, Calvin. "Reporter at Large: the Buffs [Josiah Thompson, Fox, Lifton, Meagher, Salandria]," New Yorker, XLIII (10 June 1967), 41-71.

886.   Truby, J. David. "Death Curse Haunts Kennedy Investigators [Based on Penn Jones, Jr.]," Midnight Globe, XXV (14 Feb. 1978), 2-3.

887.   Tuchler, Maier I. "Psychiatric Observations on the Warren Commission," Journal of Forensic Sciences, II (1966), 289-299.

888.   Wainwright, Loudon. "The Book for All to Read [Warren Report]," Life, LVII (16 Oct. 1964), 35.

889.   _____. "The Warren Report Is Not Enough [Reviews Popkin and Epstein]," Life, LXI (7 Oct. 1966), 38.

890.   Watson, Allan C. "Realism at the Grassy Knoll," The Christian Century, LXXXIV (13 Dec. 1967), 1596-1597.

891.   Weisberg, Harold. "Kennedy's Murder: Buried Proof of a Conspiracy," Saga, XXXIV (1967), 28-31, 86-96.

892.   Welsh, David, and Penn Jones, Jr. "In the Shadow of Dallas: Editorials from the Midlothian Mirror; The Legacy of Penn Jones, Jr.," Ramparts V (Nov. 1966), 29-50; V (Jan. 1967), 6-7.

893.   Whalen, Richard J. "The Kennedy Assassination," The Saturday Evening Post, CCXL (14 Jan. 1967), 19-25, 69.

894.   Wills, Garry. "The Assassin Seekers," National Catholic Reporter, III (15 Feb. 1967), 8.

895.   Winston, Frank. "Let's Reopen the Case!: 13 Congressmen Still Doubt Warren Verdict: Secret Archives Data Backs Conspiracy Idea," The National Tattler, XIX (25 Nov. 1973), 36.

896. Wrone, David R. "JFK Assassination: A Cover-Up?,"
The Capital Times (Madison, Wisconsin), (1-4 Dec. 1975).

897. Zee, Joe, and James Kerr. "The Oswald Enigma; Warren
Unit Hid Data on Oswald as Foreign Agent," The National
Tattler, XIX (25 Nov. 1973), 8-9.

Anonymous Articles:

898. "None Dare Call It Reason," The Christian Century,
LXXXI (28 Oct. 1964), 1351.

899. "Editorial: 1964's Eventful Non-Event [Applauds
Warren Report]," The Christian Century, LXXXII (13 Jan. 1965),
37.

900. "Letters from Readers: The Warren Report [Bickel Replies to Meager, Weisberg etc.]," Commentary, XLIII (April
1967), 7-28.

901. "Letters from Readers: Assassination Theories [Reply
by Jacob Cohen to Various Letter-Writers]," Commentary, LXI
(Jan. 1976), 4-20.

902. "Was Oswald Alone? [Reviews Epstein and Weisberg],"
The Economist (London), CCXX, No. 6415 (6 Aug. 1966), 544.

903. "N.Y. Times Team Probes JFK's Death," Editor & Publisher, XCIX (10 Dec. 1966), 10.

904. "A Primer of Assassination Theories," Esquire, LXVI
(Dec. 1966), 205-210, 334-335; LXVII (May 1967), 104-107.

905. "Warren Panel Suppressed Report," Intercontinental
Press, XIII (9 June 1975), 772.

906. "Rebuttal by the Protagonist of the One Bullet Verdict [Specter vs. Connally]," Life, LXI (25 Nov. 1966), 48B-
53.

907. "Assassination, a New Book (by Sylvan Fox) Poses Some
Unanswered Questions," Maclean's Magazine (Toronto), LXXIX
(16 April 1966), 18-19.

908. "Editorials: The Warren Commission . . . Did Its Work
Well," The Nation, CXCIX (2 Nov. 1964), 290.

909. "U.S. Seizes British Publications on JFK Assassination
Which . . . Prove Warren Report Wrong," The National Enquirer
(7 May 1967), 15-19.

910. "New Evidence in JFK Assassination Debunks Findings
of the Warren Commission," The National Enquirer (31 May
1970), 16-18.

911. "Warren Report on JFK Assassination Is Wrong," The National Enquirer (7 Oct. 1975), 1, 41.

912. "Charge Warren Commission Error on JFK Bullet," The National Enquirer (5 July 1977), 5.

913. "A Chapter Still Not Closed: Report to Readers [of Warren Report]," National Guardian, XVI (3 Oct. 1964), 2.

914. "Doubt Clings Abroad on Oswald: Warren Report Greeted Skeptically," National Guardian, XVII (10 Oct. 1964), 1, 8.

915. "It's Lane (Doubts) vs. Belli (Faith): Debate on Warren Report," National Guardian, XVII (24 Oct. 1964), 16.

916. "Only in America: [Attorney Percy Foreman, Regarding Oswald and Freedom, on Warren Report]," National Guardian, XVII (31 Oct. 1964), 8.

917. "Oswald--Case Details Add to Doubt: Lane Group Says New Data Do Not Uphold Warren Board Finding," National Guardian, XVII (5 Dec. 1964), 1, 10.

918. "Historian Calls Warren Report a 'Smokescreen': Trevor-Roper Says Commission Presented Only 'The Prosecution Case'," National Guardian, XVII (26 Dec. 1964), 3.

919. "Warren Report Is Challenged Anew on Bullets: Study of Transcript Contradicts the 'Lone Assassin' Theory," National Guardian, XVII (13 March 1965), 7.

920. "Warren Report Veils Data on Shots: Kennedy Assassination Evidence at Odds With Theory," National Guardian, XVII (20 March 1965), 9.

921. "How to Read the Warren Report," National Review, XVI (6 Oct. 1964), 858-859.

922. "For the Record: [Mark Lane's Book Sales, and Robert Kennedy's Support for Hugh Trevor-Roper's Attack on Warren Report]," National Review, XVIII (4 Oct. 1966), 1012.

923. "Confusion Compounded [Arlen Specter Interviewed]," National Review, XVIII (18 Oct. 1966), 1032-1033.

924. "Assassination [Likened to a Growth Industry]," National Review, XVIII (13 Dec. 1966), 1253-1254.

925. "As Member of Warren Commission, Then-Congressman Ford Edited Out Information Linking Oswald to FBI," The National Tattler, Special Edition, (Sept. 1975), 7-8.

926. "Comment: The Ghost Will Not Rest," The New Republic, CLXXIII (27 Sept. 1975), 7-8.

927. "Was Oswald Guilty? A Judicial Summing-Up of the
Warren Report," New Statesman (London), LXIX (12 March 1965),
399-403.

928. "Press: History-or Hysteria? [The Trevor-Roper
Attack]," Newsweek, LXIV (28 Dec. 1964), 35-36.

929. "National Affairs: Inquest: How Many Assassins?"
Newsweek, LXVII (13 June 1966), 36-38.

930. "National Affairs: Again, The Assassination [Rush to
Judgment]," Newsweek, LXVIII (15 Aug. 1966), 30-33.

931. "National Affairs: The Assassination: Deep and Growing Doubts," Newsweek, LXVIII (10 Oct. 1966), 36-41.

932. "National Affairs: Assassination: Any Number Can
Play [About Lane, Jones, etc.]," Newsweek, LXVIII (7 Nov.
1966), 37-38.

933. "The Periscope: Inside Story: Warren on the Warren
Commission Report," Newsweek, LXVIII (28 Nov. 1966), 19.

934. "JFK: the Death and the Doubts," Newsweek, LXVIII (5
Dec. 1966), 25-26.

935. "Notes and Comments [on Josiah Thompson's Book]," New
Yorker, XLIII (9 Dec. 1967), 51.

936. "Tips: A Book About the Warren Commission, 'The Witnesses', Is Being Written by Congressman Gerald R. Ford,"
Publishers Weekly, CLXXXVI (30 Nov. 1964), 42; (7 Dec. 1964),
38; [Title changed to 706].

937. "Lane Says JFK Death is Still Unsolved Murder," Publishers' Weekly, CXC (22 Aug. 1966), 58.

938. "Currents: How Persuasive Are Anti-Warren Books?
[Cites Harris Poll]," Publishers Weekly, CXCI (13 March 1967),
30.

939. "Editorial: November 22, 1966 [on Erosion of Warren
Report's Credibility]," Ramparts, V (Nov. 1966), 3.

940. "A New Warren Commission? [Editorial Following
Whalen's Article]," The Saturday Evening Post, CCXL (14 Jan.
1967), 74; [See 4180].

941. "Kennedy Assassination: Something Rotten . . . [Edi-
torial Again Requests New Investigation]," The Saturday
Evening Post, CCXL (2 Dec. 1967), 88.

942. "Question That Won't Go Away [Call for Fresh Investi-
gation]," The Saturday Evening Post, CCXLVII (Dec. 1975), 38-
39.

943. "Comment: Reaction to the Warren Commission Report,"
Senior Scholastic, LXXXV (14 Oct. 1964), 17.

944. "The Warren Commission and the Death of John F.
Kennedy," Senior Scholastic, LXXXIX (18 Nov. 1966), 14-20.

945. "The Debate on Who Killed John Kennedy?," Senior
Scholastic, LXXXIX (18 Nov. 1966), 21-22, 35.

946. "Zeitgeschichte: Kennedy-Mord: Finstere Mächte
[Contemporary History: Kennedy-Murder: Powers of Darkness],"
Der Spiegel (Hamburg), No. 15 (1967), 82-86.

947. "John Sparrow on the Warren Commission [Critique of
Trevor-Roper's Arguments Against Warren Report]," The Sunday
Times (London), No. 7388 (20 Dec. 1964), 7.

948. "Letters to the Editor: The Warren Report: Right or
Wrong? [From John Sparrow, Serge Zvegintzov, Audrey Williamson, etc.]," The Sunday Times (London), No. 7390 (3 Jan.
1965), 10.

949. "Insight: Kennedy's Death: How the Controversy Was
Re-Born [Buchanan to Lane to Weisberg]," The Sunday Times
(London), No. 7474 (21 Aug. 1966), 6.

950. "Who Killed Kennedy? The Crucial Evidence," The Sunday Times Magazine (London), No. 7481 (9 Oct. 1966), 7-21.

951. "Kennedy Deaths: the Basic Facts [of Unnatural Deaths
of Alleged Witnesses]," The Sunday Times (London), No. 7500
(26 Feb. 1967), 6.

952. "Observations: The Assassination [Josiah Thompson's
Book]," The Texas Observer, LX (12 Jan. 1968), 15.

953. "Books: Inquest: the Warren Commission and the
Establishment of Truth, by Edward Jay Epstein," Time,
LXXXVIII (8 July 1966), 86-E3.

954. "Time Essay: Autopsy on the Warren Commission," Time,
LXXXVIII (16 Sept. 1966), 54-55.

955. "Historical Notes: the Mythmakers [Debunks Penn Jones,
Jr. and Ramparts]," Time, LXXXVIII (11 Nov. 1966), 33-34.

956. "The Press Magazines: Back to Dallas [with Josiah
Thompson]," Time, XC (24 Nov. 1967), 54-55.

957. "The Assassination: The Mystery Makers," Time, XC
(22 Dec. 1967), 21.

958. "The Assassination: Inconceivable Connivance [John P.
Roche Supports John Sparrow]," Time, XCI (12 Jan. 1968), 14.

959. "United States: Kennedy Death Report," Time and Tide (London), XLV (1-7 Oct. 1964), 16.

960. "The Untold Stories--Aftermath of the Assassination; Abroad: Praise--and Doubts," U.S. News and World Report, LVII (12 Oct. 1964), 58-62.

961. "Death of a President: Told in Direct Testimony," U.S. News and World Report, LVII (7 Dec. 1964), 68-70.

962. "To Be Disclosed Soon: More on JFK's Killing," U.S. News and World Report, LVII (17 May 1965), 22.

963. "New Conflict Over the Assassination [Views on Warren Report by John Connally, Sen. Richard Russell, etc.]," U.S. News and World Report, LXI (5 Dec. 1966), 6-8.

964. "Allen Dulles Answers Warren-Report Critics," U.S. News and World Report, LXI (19 Dec. 1966), 20.

965. "JFK Assassination: British Expert's View [A. L. Goodhart's Defense of Warren Report]," U.S. News and World Report, LXII (23 Jan. 1967), 11.

(6) GUNS AND THE JFK AUTOPSY

Books:

966. Bloomgarden, Henry S. The Gun: a "Biography" of the Gun That Killed John F. Kennedy. New York: Grossman Publishers, 1975; Bantam, 1976; [See 389, 3976, 3982, 3986, 3997, 3998, 4031, 4611].

967. Cutler, Robert Bradley. The Flight of CE399: Evidence of Conspiracy. Manchester, Mass.: R. B. Cutler, 1969.

968. _____. Two Flightpaths: Evidence of Conspiracy. Manchester, Mass.: Cutler Designs, 1971.

969. Houts, Marshall. Where Death Delights: the Story of Dr. Milton Helpern and Forensic Medicine. New York: Coward-McCann, 1967.

970. Hoyle, Jeffrey P. Wound Analysis. Swansea, Mass.: Published by Author, 1978.

971. Joesten, Joachim. Panel Review. Munich: Published by Author, 1968.

972. Marcus, Raymond. The Bastard Bullet: a Search for Legitimacy for Commission Exhibit 399. Los Angeles: Rendell Publications, 1966.

973. Weisberg, Harold. Post Mortem: JFK Assassination Cover-Up Smashed. Frederick, Maryland: H. Weisberg, 1975.

974. Wilber, Charles G. Medicolegal Investigation of the President John F. Kennedy Murder. Springfield, Illinois: Charles C. Thomas Publisher, 1978.

Articles by Authors:

975. Askins. "The 6.5 Has a Lot Going for It," Guns, XV (22 June 1969).

976. Braverman, Shelley. "Backfire! The Assassination of J. F. K. [Regarding Firearms and Forensic Ballistics]," Guns, XIII (May 1967), 18-21, 56-57.

977. Breslin, Jimmy. "A Death in Emergency Room No. One," The Saturday Evening Post, CCXXXVI (14 Dec. 1963), 30-31.

978. Brooks, Stewart M. "[John F. Kennedy]," in Our Murdered Presidents: the Medical Story (New York: Frederick Fell, Inc., 1966), pp. 175-202.

979. Cole, Alwyn. "Assassin Forger," Journal of Forensic Sciences, II (July 1966), 272-288.

980. Forman, Robert. "The Wounds of President JFK," People and the Pursuit of Truth, (March 1976).

981. Grahame, Arthur. "Gun Owners Should Switch to the Offense," Outdoor Life, CXXXII (Nov. 1963), 10-11, 88-89.

982. Grichot, Jack. "Cyril H. Wecht: Coroner and Skeptic," Medical Dimensions (March 1975), 19-21.

983. Houts, Marshall. "Dr. Milton Helpern, World's Greatest Expert on Gunshot Wounds, Speaks Out: 1. The Warren Commission Botched the Kennedy Autopsy; 2. Warren Commission One-Bullet Theory Exploded," Argosy, CCCLXV (July 1967), 21-22, 108-116; also printed in part in Medical Economics, (4 March 1968), 249-287.

984. Joesten, Joachim. "Lee Harvey Oswalds Gewehr [Oswald's Gun]," Frankfurter Hefte. Zeitschrift für Kultur und Politik (Frankfurt/Main), XX, No. 9 (Sept. 1965), 596-599.

985. Joling, Robert J. "The JFK Assassination: Still an Unsolved Murder Mystery, Part III," The Saturday Evening Post CCXLVII (Dec. 1975), 44-46, 120.

986. Lattimer, John K. "Similarities in Fatal Woundings of John Wilkes Booth and Lee Harvey Oswald," New York State Journal of Medicine, LXVI (1 July 1966), 1782-1794.

987. _____. "Factors in the Death of President Kennedy," The Journal of the American Medical Association, CXCVIII (24 Oct. 1966), 327, 332-333.

988. _____. "Observations Based on a Review of the Autopsy Photographs, X-Rays, and Related Materials of the Late President John F. Kennedy," Resident and Staff Physician, (May 1972), 34-62; [See 389, 973].

989. Lattimer, John K., and Jon Lattimer. "The Kennedy-Connally Single Bullet Theory: a Feasibility Study," International Surgery, L (Dec. 1968), 524-532; [See 389, 973].

990. _____ and Gary Lattimer. "Could Oswald Have Shot President Kennedy: Further Ballistic Studies," Bulletin of the New York Academy of Medicine, XLVIII (April 1972), 513-524.

991. _____. "The Kennedy-Connally One Bullet Theory: Further Circumstantial and Experimental Evidence," Medical Times (Nov. 1974), 33-56.

992. _____. "An Experimental Study of the Backward Movement of President Kennedy's Head," Surgery, Gynecology & Obstetrics, CXLII (Feb. 1976), 246-254; [See 4874].

993. Meagher, Sylvia. "The Case of the Urologist Apologist," The Texas Observer, LXIV (26 May 1972), 22-24.

994. Meisler, Stanley. "Get Your Gun From the Army," The Nation, CXCVIII (8 June 1964), 568-571.

995. Newcomb, Fred T., and Perry Adams. "Did Someone Alter the Medical Evidence?," Skeptic, No. 9 (Aug. 1975), 25-27, 61.

996. Nichols, John. "President Kennedy's Adrenals," The Journal of the American Medical Association, CCI (10 July 1967), 129-130.

997. _____. "Assassination of President Kennedy," The Practitioner, CCXI (Nov. 1973), 625-633.

998. _____. "The Wounding of Governor John Connally of Texas, November 22, 1963," Maryland State Medical Journal, (Oct. 1977).

999. Roffman, Howard. "Letters to the Editor: New JFK Death Doubts Arise [About Lattimer]," Philadelphia Inquirer (17 Jan. 1972).

1000. Salandria, Vincent J. "A Philadelphia Lawyer Analyzes the Shots, Trajectories and Wounds," Liberation, IX (Jan. 1965), 13-18; [See 3902].

1001. _____. "The Warren Report?: A Phila-
delphia Lawyer Analyzes the President's Back and Neck Wounds;
A Look at the Wounds of Governor Connally," Liberation, X
(March 1965), 14-32.

1002. _____. "The Impossible Tasks of One
Assassination Bullet," The Minority of One, VIII (March 1966),
12-18.

1003. _____. "The Separate Connally Shot,"
The Minority of One, VIII (April 1966), 9-13.

1004. Schweisheimer, W. "Die Wirbelsäulen-Erkrankung Präsi-
dent Kennedys [President Kennedy's Ailing Spinal Injury],"
Medizinische Klinik. Wochenschrift für Klinik und Praxis
(Berlin), LIX, No. 48 (1964), 1927.

1005. Seelye, John. "Mute Witness [Reviews Bloomgarden],"
The New Republic, CLXXII (14 June 1975), 22-24.

1006. Smith, Jack A. "New Break on Oswald's Gun: FBI
'Deal' with Ruby Defense Reported," National Guardian, XVI
(27 Feb. 1964), 1, 8-9.

1007. Snider, Arthur J. "The Assassination: a New Medical
Opinion [Report on Lattimer]," Science Digest, LXI (Feb.
1967), 35-36.

1008. Thomas, Jack. "Tests of Bullet Fail to Prove a JFK
Plot," Boston Globe (30 May 1975), 1, 5.

1009. Warner, Ken. "Big Bargains in Rifles [For the
Mannlicher-Carcano Gun]," Mechanix Illustrated, LX (Oct.
1964), 89-91, 152-153.

1010. Wecht, Cyril H. "A Critique of the Medical Aspects
of the Investigation into the Assassination of President
Kennedy," Journal of Forensic Sciences, II (1966), 300-317.

1011. _____. "Appendix D: A Critique of President
Kennedy's Autopsy," in Josiah Thompson, Six Seconds in Dallas
(N.Y.: Bernard Geis Associates, with Random House, 1967),
pp. 278-284.

1012. _____. "Pathologist's View of JFK Autopsy:
An Unsolved Case," Modern Medicine, XL (27 Nov. 1972), 28-
32; Reprinted in Medical Trial Technique Quarterly, XX
(Summer 1973), 42-52; [See 4711].

1013. _____. "Analysis of the Autopsy on President John F. Kennedy, and the Impossibility of the Warren
Commission's Lone Assassin Conclusion," Computers and Automation, XXII (Feb. 1973), 26-28.

1014. _____. "New Evidence Rekindles Old
Doubts: JFK Assassination: 'a Prolonged and Willful Cover-
Up'," Modern Medicine, XLII (28 Oct. 1974), 40X-40FF.

1015. _____. "A Civilian M.D. In on the Kennedy
Autopsy Says More Than One Gun Killed JFK," Physician's
Management, XV (Oct. 1975), 14-23; XV (Nov. 1975), 37-40,
43-44; [See 973].

1016. Wecht, Cyril H., and Robert P. Smith. "The Medical
Evidence in the Assassination of President John F. Kennedy,"
Forensic Science, III (April 1974), 105-128.

1017. Wheeler, Keith. "'Cursed Gun'---The Track of C2766,"
Life, LIX (27 Aug. 1965), 62-65.

    Anonymous Articles:

1018. "Assassination Gives Impetus to Dodd's Gun Bill,"
Advertising Age, XXXIV (2 Dec. 1963), 1-2.

1019. "[Klein's Sporting Goods, Chicago: Advertisement for
6.5 Italian Carbine]," The American Rifleman, III, No. 1
(Jan. 1963), 61; III, No. 2 (Feb. 1963), 65; III, No. 4
(April 1963), 55.

1020. "[Eastern Firearms Company, New Brunswick, New Jersey: Advertisement for 7.35 Carcano Rifle---Not "the puny
6.5 Carcanos" Offered by Others]," The American Rifleman,
III, No. 3 (March 1963), 59.

1021. "Editorial: Have Gun, Will Kill [Need for Dodd Bill
on Gun Control]," The Christian Century, LXXXII (2 June 1965),
701-702.

1022. "The Warren Report: How to Murder the Medical Evidence," Current Medicine for Attorneys, XII (Nov. 1965), 1-
28.

1023. "Give the Best You Can Buy . . . A Gift from Klein's
[of a 6.5 mm. Italian Carbine, with Scope, for $19.95],"
Field & Stream, LXVIII (Nov. 1963), 97.

1024. "Washington News: Kennedy Shot Twice in the Back,"
The Journal of the American Medical Association, CLXXXVII (4
Jan. 1964), 15.

1025. "Editorials: Those Missing Exhibits," The Nation,
CCIII (14 Nov. 1966), 500.

1026. "Kennedys Hid JFK's Disease," The National Enquirer
(19 Feb. 1967), 3-4.

1027. "JFK Might Be Alive Today---But For His Painful Back,"
The National Enquirer (15 Feb. 1977), 3.

1028. "The Week: [Kennedys Set Rules of Access to JFK's Autopsy Evidence]," National Review, XVIII (29 Nov. 1966), 1199.

1029. "The Week: [John F. Kennedy Was One of Six Presidents Who Have Belonged to National Rifle Association]," National Review, XXI (11 Feb. 1969), 104.

1030. "Where the Shots Came From," The New Republic, CXLIX (28 Dec. 1963), 7.

1031. "Kennedy Assassination [Autopsy Records at National Archives]," The New Republic, CLV (12 Nov. 1966), 8-9.

1032. "Life and Leisure: Right to Bear Arms [with Herblock's Cartoon of Rifle Advertisements]," Newsweek, LXII (9 Dec. 1963), 70-71.

1033. "Medicine: How JFK Died [Navy Pathologists' Report]," Newsweek, LXII (30 Dec. 1963), 55.

1034. "National Affairs: Congress: Misfire [Robert F. Kennedy's Testimony for Gun Control]," Newsweek, LXV (31 May 1965), 22.

1035. "National Affairs: Assassination: The Missing Link [Autopsy Photos]," Newsweek, LXVIII (14 Nov. 1966), 30-31.

1036. "Medicine: Post-mortem on JFK," Newsweek, LXX (24 July 1967), 54.

1037. "Addison's Disease: Pathologist Sleuth Reopens Kennedy Controversy," Science News, XCII (22 July 1967), 79-80.

1038. "Warren Commission Report; Paraffin Test Unreliable," Science News Letter, LXXXVI (10 Oct. 1964), 227.

1039. "General Science: Model of Head Used in Assassination Study," Science News Letter, LXXXVI (10 Oct. 1964), 229.

1040. "Medicine: Kennedy Alive in Hospital," Science News Letter, LXXXVI (10 Oct. 1964), 229.

1041. "Killing Still Mystery; FBI Confused by Oswald's Loose Pistol Barrel," Science News Letter, LXXXVI (10 Oct. 1964), 230.

1042. "Kein Meister traf den Kopf der Puppe. Die Schiess-versuche mit Oswalds Mannlicher-Carcano Gewehr [Not Even a Master-Rifleman Hit the Puppy's Head. Trial Shots with Oswald's Gun]," Der Spiegel (Hamburg), XXI, No. 15 (1967), 104.

1043. "Inquest on Dallas: the Right to Bear Arms," Tablet, CCXVIII (3 Oct. 1964), 1101-1102.

1044.   "Three Patients at Parkland," Texas State Journal of Medicine, LX (1964), 61-74.

1045.   "Medical History: Gunshot Wounds of Four Presidents," Texas State Journal of Medicine, LX (1964), 74-77.

1046.   "The Autopsy," Time, LXXXII (27 Dec. 1963), 18.

1047.   "Historical Notes: Braced for Death? [Arlen Specter's Speculations]," Time, LXXXVI (8 Oct. 1965), 33.

1048.   "Assassinations: the Guns of Dallas [Marina Oswald Sells Guns to John J. King]," Time, LXXXVII (4 March 1966), 28.

1049.   "Historical Notes: Into the Archives," Time, LXXXVIII (11 Nov. 1966), 33.

1050.   "In the Works: Tighter Laws on Gun Sales," U.S. News and World Report, LV (9 Dec. 1963), 4.

1051.   "Problem: What to Do with Rifle That Killed JFK," U.S. News and World Report, LVIII (19 April 1965), 8.

1052.   "Now U. S. Gets JFK Autopsy Photos," U.S. News and World Report, LXI (14 Nov. 1966), 81.

1053.   "The JFK Killing . . . New Findings [the Carnes Autopsy Panel Report]," U.S. News and World Report, LXVI (27 Jan. 1969), 4.

(7) AUDIO-VISUAL MATERIALS: TAPES, PHOTOS, FILMS, RECORDS

Books and Collections:

Assassination Collections, Stevens Point, Wisconsin: Symposium, November, 1976. Office of Educational Services and Innovative Programs; University of Wisconsin - Stevens Point, Wisconsin (Brochure, 1976). Video and Audio Cassettes.

1054.   _____. "The Assassination of President John F. Kennedy and the Impact on the Legal System, the Freedom of Information Act," by James H. Lesar.

1055.   _____. "Lee Harvey Oswald and the Failure of American Justice," by Howard Roffman.

1056.   _____. "The Assassination of John F. Kennedy: Suppression of the Evidence," by Harold Weisberg.

1057.   _____. "The Warren Commission Behind the Scenes---Their Secret Documents," by Harold Weisberg.

1058. _____. "Recent Developments: Schweiker Report, Abzug Report, FBI Revelations," by Harold Weisberg.

1059. _____. "The Assassination of President John F. Kennedy: the Malfunction of Criticism," by David R. Wrone.

Assassination Collections, Stevens Point, Wisconsin: Southern Historical Association Session, 11 Nov. 1977, New Orleans: "The Tools of the Historian and the Assassination of John F. Kennedy," David Brion Davis, Chairman. Audio Cassettes.

1060. _____. "The Evidentiary Base: A Critical Evaluation of 200 Investigators Over the Last Fourteen Years," by David R. Wrone.

1061. _____. "The Medical and Ballistics Evidence: A Matter of Reasonable Doubt," by Michael Kurtz, With "Commentary," by Howard Roffman.

1062. Dallas Police tapes at the Time of the Assassination, Channels 1 and 2, including introductory commentary. [Audio Tape], Distributed by Penn Jones, 197?, 1 reel.

1063. Decade of Assassinations. [Audio-tape], Committee to Investigate Assassinations, 1973; Released by Georgetown University; 12 reels.

1064. Hughes, Robert J. E. "Family Film of Dealey Plaza Background Just Before Shots Fired." Dallas, 1963; 8 mm.

1065. Kennedy Assassination Newsreel Footage. [Motion picture], Collector's Archives, 197?; 8 mm.

1066. Lee Harvey Oswald Interview, New Orleans, La., August, 1963. [Phonotape], Collector's Archives, 197?; 1 cassette.

1067. Life-Itek Kennedy Assassination Film Analysis. Lexington, Mass.: Itek Corporation, 1967; [See 4373].

1068. Model, F. Peter, and Robert J. Groden. JFK: The Case for Conspiracy [Analyzing Zapruder Film]. Introduction by Cong. Thomas N. Downing. New York: Manor Books, Inc., 1976; Expanded ed., 1977; [See 277].

1069. Nix Motion Picture of the Assassination of President John F. Kennedy. [Motion picture], Released by Penn Jones, 1975; 8 mm.

1070. President Kennedy's Assassination. [Slide Set], Released by Assassination Information Bureau, 1975; 31 slides.

1071. Spatial Chart of Northern Half of Dealey Plaza, Dallas, Texas; showing photographers, positions of John F. Kennedy's head, objects and events surrounding 12:30 pm, 22 Nov. 1963. Newtonville, Mass.; Berkeley Enterprizes, Inc., 1971.

1072. United Press International. [Film, Made by] "Mrs. Mary Muchmore, Dallas," 1963; 8 mm.

1073. United Press International. [Film, made by] "Mr. Orville O. Nix, Dallas," 1963; 8 mm.

1074. WDSU: "Oswald-Bringuier Radio Debate." New Orleans, 1963; 1 cassette.

1075. Weisberg, Harold. Photographic Whitewash; suppressed Kennedy assassination pictures. Hyattstown, Maryland, 1967.

1076. WFAA-TV: "The President's Last Hours." Dallas, 1964; 16 mm.

1077. Zapruder and Nix Films with Groden Blow-ups of the Assassination of President John F. Kennedy. [Motion picture], Distributed by Penn Jones, 1976; 16 mm.

1078. Zapruder Motion Picture of the Assassination of President Kennedy. [Motion picture], Distributed by Penn Jones, 1972; 8 mm. [Various Other Distributors, Including Robert J. Groden, Offer Similar Copies.]

1079. CBS News. [Motion picture], n.p., n.d., 16 mm. Zapruder Motion Picture of the Assassination of President John F. Kennedy.

    Articles by Authors:

1080. [Alvarez, Luis]. "New Clues in J.F.K. Assassination Photos: LRL Scientist's Persuasive Theory," The Magnet: Lawrence Radiation Laboratory, XI, No. 7 (July 1967), 1, 6-7.

1081. _____. "A Physicist Examines the Kennedy Assassination [Zapruder] Film," American Journal of Physics, XLIV (1976), 813-827.

1082. Bell & Howell Company. "B&H Camera Used for Assassination Film Now in National Archives," Image Magazine (Jan. 1967), 1.

1083. Diamond, S. A. "Life Loses Copyright Battle on Zapruder Films," Advertising Age, XL (27 Jan. 1969), 55-56.

1084. Epstein, Edward Jay. "Der Tod kam bei Bild 313. Eine neue Untersuchung des Kennedy-Mordes [Death Came at Frame 313. A New Investigation into the Kennedy Murder]," Der Spiegel (Hamburg), XX No. 29 (1966), 63-67.

1085. Friedman, Rick. "Pictures of Assassination Fall to Amateurs on Street," Editor & Publisher, XCVI (30 Nov. 1963), 16-17, 67.

1086. Graves, Florence. "The Mysterious Kennedy Out-Takes
[Zapruder and CBS-TV]," Washington Journalism Review, (Sept.-
Oct. 1978), 24-28.

1087. Groden, Robert. "A New Look at the Zapruder Film,"
Rolling Stone, CLXXXV (24 April 1975), 34-36.

1088. Lane, Mark. "The Man in the Doorway," Film Comment,
IV (1967), 20-21.

1089. Marcus, Raymond. "Mary Moorman Photo Validity," Los
Angeles Free Press, V (19, 26 Jan. 1968).

1090. _____. "Blow-Up! November 22, 1963," Los
Angeles Free Press, IV (24 Nov. 1967), 1-2.

1091. Mezei, Leslie. "Visual Re-Creation of a Scene by
Computer Graphics [Applicable to JFK Assassination]," Computers and Automation, XIX (July 1970), 32.

1092. Olds, Greg. "In My Opinion: The Zapruder Film," The
Texas Observer, LXI (21 Nov. 1969), 16; (19 Dec. 1969), 16;
LXII (20 March 1970), 16.

1093. Olson, Don, and Ralph F. Turner. "Photographic Evidence and the Assassination of President John F. Kennedy,"
Journal of Forensic Sciences, XVI (Oct. 1971), 399-419.

1094. Pilpel, Harriet F., and Kenneth P. Norwick. "But Can
You Do That?: 'Fair Use' Protects Zapruder Film Copies,"
Publishers Weekly, CXCIV (28 Oct. 1968). 26-27.

1095. Quoodle. "Spectator's Notebook: J. F. K. [Reviews
USIA's Film]," The Spectator (London), No. 7131 (26 Feb.
1965), 255.

1096. Salandria, Vincent J. "Life Magazine and the Warren
Commission," Liberation, XI (Oct. 1966), 44.

1097. Shawcross, William. "The Day of the Conspirator:
the Groden Theory," The Sunday Times Magazine (London), No.
7937 (27 July 1975), 19-23.

1098. Sprague, Richard E. "The Assassination of President
John F. Kennedy: the Application of Computers to the Photographic Evidence," Computers and Automation, XIX (May 1970),
29-60; XIX (June 1970), 7; XIX (July 1970), 36; XX (March
1971), 44; XX (May 1971), 27-29.

1100. _____. "The Kennedy Assassination: What
the Photographs Show: Exhibit #1 B," Privately Printed,
15 June 1967.

1101. Stolley, Richard B. "What Happened Next . . .," Esquire, LXXX (Nov. 1973), 134-135, 262-263.

1102. Strafford, Peter. "Oswald Photographs Called Fakes
[His Holding the Rifle Asserted to Be Composite, By Mr. Rusty
Rhodes of the Committee to Investigate Political Assassina-
tions]," The Times (London), No. 59,345 (15 March 1975), 5.

1103. "Assassination Film at UPI Conference ["Four Days in
November"]," Editor & Publisher, XCVII (26 Sept. 1964), 11.

1104. "Cover: Did Oswald Act Alone?: A Matter of Reasonable
Doubt: Frame 230 [Zapruder Film]," Life, LXI (25 Nov. 1966),
1, 38-48A.

1105. "Nov. 22, 1963, Dallas: Photos by Nine Bystanders,"
Life, LXIII (24 Nov. 1967), 87-97.

1106. "Texan's Film Clips Could Implicate U.S. Government
in Murder of Oswald," The National Enquirer (1 Jan. 1965), 8.

1107. "Top Authority on JFK Assassination Photos Says 4 Gun-
men Murdered the President," The National Enquirer (16 Aug.
1970), 16-18.

1108. "Famous Zapruder Film: It Proves Warren Commission
Was Wrong," The National Tattler, Special Edition (Sept.
1975), 10-11.

1109. "Photo Puzzle: Ultimately the Identity of 'The
Tramps' May Lead to Reopening the Kennedy Case," The National
Tattler, Special Edition (Sept. 1975), 13.

1110. "The Periscope: Inside Story: Solved--Mystery of the
Missing Frames [in the Zapruder Film, Cited by Warren Re-
port]," Newsweek, LXIX (6 Feb. 1967), 17.

1111. "Transition: Abraham Zapruder, 66 . . . [Dead] of
Cancer, in Dallas, Aug. 30," Newsweek, LXXVI (14 Sept. 1970),
67.

1112. "Un Document: Dallas, 22 novembre 1963: Kennedy
Marche vers la Mort [Still Photos from Zapruder Film],"
Paris Match, No. 920 (26 Nov. 1966), 69-74.

1113. "JFK Assassination Films: Court Rules Fair Use
[Denies Life's Suit vs. Josiah Thompson for Use of Zapruder
Film]," Publishers' Weekly, CXCIV (14 Oct. 1968), 39.

1114. "USA--Attentat--Film: Zuschlag für Zapruder [USA
Assassination Film: Bonus for Zapruder]," Der Spiegel
(Hamburg), XVII, No. 49 (1963), 88.

1115. "[18 Frames of the Zapruder Colour Film]," The Sunday
Times (London), No. 7337 (29 Dec. 1963), 8-9.

1116. "Milestones: Died: Abraham Zapruder, 65, Dallas,"
Time, XCVI (14 Sept. 1970), 69.

Documentary Films:

1117. A Child's Eyes: November 22, 1963. 8 minutes, color, 16 mm. Group VI Productions: Released by Pathé Contemporary Films, 1968.

1118. The Fateful Trip to Texas: the Assassination of a President. 7 minutes, black & white, 16 mm. Produced by Arthur M. Schlesinger, Jr. and Fred Israel. New York: Chelsea House Educational Communications, 1969.

1119. Four Days in November. 122 minutes, black & white, 16 mm. and 35 mm. Screen Play by Theodore Strauss, Produced and Directed by Mel Stuart; Wolper Productions, Released by United Artists, 6 Oct. 1964; [See 3678, 3739].

1120. John F. Kennedy: Years of Lightning, Day of Drums. 90 minutes. U.S. Information Agency, 17 Oct. 1964. [Translated into thirty languages, 383 copies shown in 117 countries.]

1121. John Fitzgerald Kennedy. 10 minutes, black & white, 16 mm. Capital Film Laboratories, Released by Star Film Co., 1964.

1122. The Kennedy Assassination: What Do We Know Now That We Didn't Know Then? Produced by Witness Productions. New York & Washington: Syndicast Services Inc., 1978.

1123. The President's Last Hours. 30 minutes. Produced by WFAA-TV. Dallas, 1964.

1124. The Private Files of J. Edgar Hoover. Written, Produced and Directed by Larry Cohen. Released by American International Pictures, 1978.

1125. Rush to Judgment. 122 minutes. Produced by Emile de Antonio and Mark Lane, Directed by de Antonio. Impact Films, 1967; [See 23, 4036, 4081, 4102, 4387].

1126. _____. "The Current Cinema," by Penelope Gilliatt. The New Yorker, XLIII (17 June 1967), 95.

1127. _____. "Acquittal for Oswald," by James J. Graham. Commonweal, LXXXVI (21 April 1967), 149-151.

1128. _____. "Rush to Judgement: a Conversation with Mark Lane and Emile de Antonio." Film Comment, IV (1967), 2-18.

1129. _____. "Homo Americanus," by Louis Marcorelles. Film Comment, IV (1967), 19.

1130. _____. "The Periscope: Inside Story: Rush to Riches." Newsweek, LXVIII (28 Nov. 1966), 19.

1131. Two Men in Dallas: John Kennedy and Roger Craig.
60 minutes, videotape. Narrated by Mark Lane. Alpa Productions, 1977.

Long-Play Recordings:

1132. Broadside BR501: "The Oswald Case: Mark Lane's
Testimony to the Warren Commission," 1964.

1133. Broadside: "Lee Harvey Oswald's Letters to His
Mother," 1964.

1134. Capitol KAO 2677: "The Controversy: the Death of
John F. Kennedy: the Warren Report and Controversy," Produced by Lawrence Schiller and Richard W. Lewis, 1966; [see
720].

1135. Capitol: "The Fateful Hours: a Presentation of KLIF
News in Dallas," 1964.

1136. Capitol: [Edward Jay Epstein's Discussion Album Based
on His Book Inquest, Promised in Publishers Weekly, CXCI (16
Jan. 1967), 33].

1137. Capitol: [Jack Ruby's Deathbed Statements, Recorded
by His Brother], 1966-1967.

1138. Colpix CP2500: "The Actual Voices and Events of Four
Days That Shocked the World," Narrated by Reid Collins, Notes
by Merriman Smith, Jan. 1964.

1139. Connie B. Gay Broadcasting Corp.: Matrix No. PB 1495-
1496: "Four Dark Days in November," Presented by WQMR News,
1964.

1140. Evergreen EVR-004: "Mac Bird! A Play by Barbara
Garson; Songs and Music by John Duffy," Feb. 1967.

1141. Happening CA-3210: "Rush to Judgment: with New Insights on the Assassination of President John F. Kennedy,
by Mark Lane," 1967.

1142. Information Council of the Americas (INCA): "Oswald:
Self-Portrait in Red," [2 Record Set Includes Oswald's 21
Aug. 1963 Radio Debate at WDSU, New Orleans, with Carlos
Bringuier and Ed Butler], 1964; [See 2654].

1143. Living History Records: "The Assassination of a President," Written and Narrated by Richard Levitan, Beverly Hills,
California, American Society of Recorded Drama, n.d.

1144. Matrix No. ABC-JFK A-D: "November 22, 1963: an
Historical Document in Sound; Radio Reported to the Nation
Throughout 80 Hours Following the First Broadcast at 1:36
P.M. on the ABC Radio Network," 1963.

1145. <u>Matrix No. N. WBC 2692-2693</u>: "November 22: Dialogue in Dallas; the Assassination of President Kennedy as Reported by Newsmen Malcolm Kilduff, J. F. TerHorst, Robert Donovan, and Sid Davis, with Jim Snyder as Moderator," 1964.

1146. <u>RCA Victor No. LOC-1088</u>: "A Time to Keep: NBC Reporting by Robert MacNeil, Chet Huntley and Tom Pettit," 1963.

1147. <u>Testament Records</u>: "Can't Keep From Crying: Topical Blues on the Death of President Kennedy," 1974.

1148. <u>Truth Records ALM 22-63-B</u>: "Lee Harvey Oswald Speaks: a Personal Interview with Lee Harvey Oswald in New Orleans 17 August 1963," [Interviewed by Bill Stuckey], 1967; [See 4178].

1149. <u>Vanguard VRS 92-42</u>: "Rush to Judgment: the Living Testimony by the Actual Witnesses on the Original Sound Track of the Emile de Antonio and Mark Lane Film," 1967.

Part III: The Reaction
(1) PRESIDENT LYNDON B. JOHNSON'S TRANSITION TO OFFICE

<u>Books</u>:

1150. Amrine, Michael. <u>This Awesome Challenge: the Hundred Days of Lyndon Johnson</u>. New York: Putnam, 1964.

1151. Haley, J. Evetts. <u>A Texan Looks at Lyndon: a Study in Illegitimate Power</u>. Canyon, Texas: Palo Duro Press, 1964; [See 1156, 3732].

1152. Joesten, Joachim. <u>The Case Against Lyndon B. Johnson in the Assassination of President Kennedy. A Special, Privately Published Supplement to the Books: Oswald; the Truth, and Marina Oswald</u>. Gurtweil über Wildshut, 1967, 2 vols. and Munich: Selbstverlag [Published by Author], 1967.

1153. _____. <u>The Dark Side of Lyndon Baines Johnson</u>. London: Dawnay, 1968.

1154. Johnson, Lyndon Baines. <u>The Vantage Point; Perspectives of the Presidency, 1963-1969</u>. New York: Holt, Rinehart, and Winston, 1971.

1155. Schlesinger, Arthur M., Jr. <u>A Thousand Days: John F. Kennedy in the White House</u>. Boston: Houghton Mifflin, 1965; London: A. Deutsch, 1966.

1156. Sherrill, Robert. <u>The Accidental President</u>. New York: Grossman Publishers, 1967.

1157. White, Theodore H. <u>The Making of the President, 1964</u>. New York: Atheneum Publishers, 1965.

1158.   Youngblood, Rufus W.   20 Years in the Secret Service.
My Life With Five Presidents.   New York: Simon and Schuster,
1973; [See 3183].

Articles by Authors:

1159.   Alsop, Stewart.   "Johnson Takes Over: the Untold
Story," The Saturday Evening Post, CCXXXVII (15 Feb. 1964),
17-23.

1160.   Baughman, U. E.   "Can You Really Protect the President?" U.S. News and World Report, LV (23 Dec. 1963), 38-40.

1161.   Collins, Frederic.   "Johnson Consults Cabinet
Ministers," The Sunday Times (London), No. 7332 (24 Nov.
1963), 2.

1162.   .   "President Lyndon B. Johnson,"
The Sunday Times (London), No. 7332 (24 Nov. 1963), 15.

1163.   Cronkite, Walter.   "That Day in Dallas: Lyndon
Johnson . . . Remembers the Assassination of President
Kennedy," The Listener, LXXXIII, No. 2145 (7 May 1970), 612-
614.

1164.   Cutler, Robert B.   "Spotlight on McGeorge Bundy and
the White House Situation Room, November 22, 1963," Computers and Automation, XXI (Jan. 1972), 57-58.

1165.   Davenport, Nicholas.   "A Johnson Boom?," The Spectator (London), No. 7067 (6 Dec. 1963), 766.

1166.   Eisenhower, Dwight David.   "When the Highest Office
Changes Hands," The Saturday Evening Post, CCXXXVI (14 Dec.
1962), 15.

1167.   Knebl, Fletcher.   "After the Shots: the Ordeal of
Lyndon Johnson," Look, XXVIII (10 March 1964), 26-33.

1168.   Meyer, Karl E.   "Echoes of Dallas [the Presidential
Succession]," New Statesman (London), LXVI (13 Dec. 1963),
868-870.

1169.   Mills, George.   "JFK Could Lose [Article Went to
Press Before JFK Murdered]," Look, XXVII (17 Dec. 1963),
94-102.

1170.   Montgomery, Linda, and Constance Powell.   "'Let Us
Continue':   LBJ's Closest Aid [Walter Jenkins] Takes Candid
Look at his First Weeks in White House," The National
Tattler, XIX (25 Nov. 1973), 26.

1171.   Potter, Philip.   "How LBJ Got the Nomination," The
Reporter, XXX (18 June 1964), 16-20.

1172. Schuman, Frederick L. "Schlesinger's JFK," The Minority of One, VIII (March 1966), 19-20.

1173. Sutherland, John P. "200,000 Miles in Safety and Then . . .," U.S. News and World Report, LV (9 Dec. 1963), 60.

1174. Wright, Sylvia. "Parting Shots: Hero Rufus Youngblood Gets the Secret Service Brush-Off [From Nixon White House]," Life, LXXI (5 Nov. 1971), 81.

Anonymous Articles:

1175. "Protecting the President [Secret Service and Federal vs. State Laws]," The Economist (London), CCIX (30 Nov. 1963), 896.

1176. "Hard Road to Publication for Five Kennedy Books and One That Was Untouched [White House Staff Memoirs]," Look, XXXI (4 April 1967), 77.

1177. "JFK Death Car Was Used by Johnson, Nixon and Ford," The National Enquirer (15 Aug. 1978), 32.

1178. "National Affairs: The Most Worried Men [Secret Service]," Newsweek, LXII (9 Dec. 1963), 34.

1179. "Polls: Awful Interval [LBJ's Delayed Announcement of JFK's Death, and Why]," Newsweek, LXIII (6 Jan. 1964), 19-20.

1180. "National Affairs: Ex-Presidents: LBJ on the Assassination," Newsweek, LXXV (11 May 1970), 41.

1181. "Newsmakers: The Limousine in Which President John F. Kennedy Was Assassinated [To Henry Ford Museum, Dearborn, Michigan]," Newsweek, LXXXIX (16 May 1977), 47.

1182. "Johnson Takes Oath as Nation Mourns Kennedy," Senior Scholastic, LXXXIII (6 Dec. 1963), 14.

1183. "Protecting the President: a Job For Superman?," Senior Scholastic, LXXXV (4 Nov. 1964), 6-9.

1184. "The Bodyguards . . . and the Broken First Commandment [Secret Service]," The Sunday Times (London), No. 7332 (24 Nov. 1963), 6.

1185. "The Press: Magazines: Where Was O'Donnell? [When JFK's Body Left Dallas]," Time, LXXXIX (17 Feb. 1967), 78.

1186. "Historical Notes: The Full Record [Full Photo of LBJ's Swearing-In]," Time, LXXXIX (24 Feb. 1967), 19-21.

1187. "Political Skills of Mr. Lyndon Johnson," The Times (London), No. 55,866 (23 Nov. 1963), 9.

1188.   "New Shield Around the President," U.S. News and World
Report, LV (30 Dec. 1963), 29.

1189.   "Why a Plot Was Feared When Kennedy Was Shot," U.S.
News and World Report, LVI (6 Jan. 1964), 7.

1190.   "Campaign Time: When Secret Service Worry Grows,"
U.S. News and World Report, LVI (13 April 1964), 63-64.

1191.   "Was There a [Cuban] Plot to Assassinate LBJ?," U.S.
News and World Report, LVI (27 April 1964), 48-49.

1192.   "The Presidential Car--It's Safer Now," U.S. News and
World Report, LVII (19 Oct. 1964), 14.

1193.   "Fateful Two Hours Without a President: Story of What
Happened Before and After Assassination of Kennedy," U.S.
News and World Report, LXI (14 Nov. 1966), 68-78.

(2) IMMEDIATE REACTIONS: POPULAR AND OFFICIAL

Books:

1194.   Bernières, Luc. Le jour ou Kennedy fut assassiné
[The Day Kennedy Was Assassinated]. Paris: Editions du
Gerfaut, 1963.

1195.   Carlos, Newton. A conspiração. Rio de Janeiro: J.
Alvaro, 1963, 1964.

1196.   Castro, Ruz, Fidel. Comparencia del Comandante Fidel
Castro, ante el pueblo de Cuba sobre los sucesos relacionados
con el asesinato del Presidente Kennedy [Appearance of Comman-
der Fidel Castro, Before the Cuban People Concerning Events
Related to President Kennedy's Assassination]. Havana:
Comisión de Orientacion Revolucionaria, 1963.

1197.   Puché, Ignacio. Asesinato: el asesinato de Kennedy
en todos sus detalles [Assassination: the Assassination of
Kennedy in Full Detail]. Madrid: Gráfica Ruán, 1963.

Articles by Authors:

1198.   Allarey, Monina. "When Night Fell on the U.S."
Philippines Herald Magazine (Manila), (7 Dec. 1963), 12.

1199.   Andrade, Vincente. "The World Resounds: Bogota."
America, CIX (14 December 1963), 769-770.

1200.   Arnoni, M. S. "Who Killed Whom and Why?," The Minority
of One, VI (Jan. 1964), 1, 12-13.

1201. Bailey, George. "The Reporter's Notes: As They See It [in East Germany]," The Reporter, XXIX (19 Dec. 1963), 10-12.

1202. Barbieri, Frane. "Dva Atentata [Two Assassinations]," Vjesnik (Belgrade), XXIV (24 Nov. 1963), 6024.

1204. Becheau, Francois. "The World Resounds: Toulouse," America, (14 Dec. 1963), 771.

1205. Birnbaum, Norman. "Europe After Kennedy [the Reaction to Assassination]," The Correspondent, No. 30 (Jan.-Feb. 1964), 49-57.

1206. Blewett, John. "The World Resounds: Tokyo," America, CIX (14 Dec. 1963), 771.

1207. Boyle, Andrew. "The World Resounds: London," America, CIX (14 Dec. 1963), 771.

1208. Brandon, Henry. "Politics Suffer a Violent Shake-Up," The Sunday Times (London), No. 7332 (24 Nov. 1963), 1.

1209. _____. "The Greatest American Tragedy," The Sunday Times (London), No. 7332 (24 Nov. 1963), 3.

1210. Breig, J. "President Kennedy's Death: Why?," Ave Maria, IC (11 Jan. 1964), 9.

1211. Brigham, Robert. "Russia: 'No, No, This Cannot Be True'," Life, LV (6 Dec. 1963), 129-130.

1212. Buckley, William F., Jr. "On the Right: Do They Really Hate to Hate?," National Review, XV (31 Dec. 1963), 559.

1213. Budimac, Budimir. "Zlocin u Teksasu [Crime in Texas]," Dnevnik (Novi Sad), XXII (23 Nov. 1963), 6124.

1214. Burnham, Walter Dean. "After JFK--What?" Commonweal, LXXIX (13 Dec. 1963), 340-343.

1215. Cameron, J. M. "Human and Sane [Reactions in London]," Commonweal, LXXIX (13 Dec. 1963), 338-339.

1216. Campion, Donald. "The World Resounds: Rome," America, CIX (14 Dec. 1963), 768-769.

1217. Carunungan, C. A. "Grave Dangers Beset Presidents," Weekly Graphic (Manila), XXX (4 Dec. 1963), 3, 86.

1218. Carroll, Nicholas. "A Shift in East-West Relations?" The Sunday Times (London), No. 7332 (24 Nov. 1963), 1.

1219. Ciardi, John. "Manner of Speaking: November 22, 1963 [in New York City]," Saturday Review, XLVI (7 Dec. 1963), 16-18.

1220. Condon, Richard. "'Manchurian Candidate' in Dallas [Attacks Senator Morton's Remarks about Guilt]," The Nation, CXCVII (28 Dec. 1963), 449-451.

1221. Cooke, Alistair. "Death of the Young Warrior," The Listener (London), LXX (28 Nov. 1963), 863-865.

1222. _____. "After the President's Assassination: Letter from America," The Listener (London), LXX (5 Dec. 1963), 907-908.

1223. Daniel, Jean. "Havana: When Castro Heard the News," The New Republic, CXLIX (7 Dec. 1963), 7-9; See 3387 .

1224. Daniel, Price. "Assessing the Blame in the President's Death," U.S. News and World Report, LV (30 Dec. 1963), 73.

1225. Douglas-Home, Alec, Harold Wilson, and Joseph Grimond. "Tributes to President Kennedy," The Listener (London), LXX (28 Nov. 1963), 865-866.

1226. Driver, Tom F. "Thoughts on the Day of the Funeral," Christianity & Crisis, XXIII (23 Dec. 1963), 235-241.

1227. Einzig, P. "How Dallas Tragedy Affected Exchanges," Commercial and Financial Chronicle, CXCVIII (5 Dec. 1963), 2195.

1228. Evans, M. Stanton. "At Home," National Review, XV (10 Dec. 1963), 6.

1229. Falls, Cyril. "A Window on the World: Assassination of a Great President," The Illustrated London News, CCXLIII (30 Nov. 1963), 889-900.

1230. Foltz, Charles, Jr. "Shock and Grief in Russia," U.S. News and World Report, LV (9 Dec. 1963), 42.

1231. Freeman, John. "The Man We Trusted," New Statesman (London), LXVI (29 Nov. 1963), 768-769.

1232. Genet, Jean. "Letter from Paris," The New Yorker, XXXIX (7 Dec. 1963), 133-136.

1233. Hercher, Wilmot W. "'A Thousand Well-Wishers', and One Assassin," U.S. News and World Report, LV (2 Dec. 1963), 34-35.

1234. Holland, Mary. "Failures and Heroes [The Reactions in the Irish Republic]," The Spectator, No. 7071 (3 Jan. 1964), 25.

1235. Howe, Irving. "On the Death of John F. Kennedy [Five Days After]" in, Steady Work: Essays in the Politics of Democratic Radicalism, pp. 187-194. (New York: Harcourt Brace & World, 1966).

1236. Hughes, Everett C. "The Blame [for JFK Assassination]," The Correspondent, No. 30 (Jan.-Feb. 1964), 5-7.

1237. Hughes, H. Stuart. "A Most Unstuffy Man . . . ." The Nation, CXCVII (14 Dec. 1963), 408-409.

1238. Joaquin, Nick. "An American Tragedy," Phillipines Free Press (Manila), LVI (7 Dec. 1963), 2-3, 75.

1239. Kaiser, Horst. "Die Deutschen in der Nachfolge Kennedys [The Germans in the Kennedy Succession]," Gemeinschaft und Politick. Zeitschrift für soziale und politische Gestalt (Bad Godesberg), XI (1963), 343-344.

1240. Kempton, Murray. "The Roman Way," The Spectator (London), No. 7066 (29 Nov. 1963), 683.

1241. Kempton, Murray, and James Ridgeway. "Romans [News Received in Flight, Boston to Washington]," The New Republic, CXLIX (7 Dec. 1963), 9-11.

1242. Larrabee, Eric. "Belgrade: 'So You Too Are Human'," The Correspondent, No. 30 (Jan.-Feb. 1964), 7-8.

1243. Lawrence, David. "Incredible Tragedy," U.S. News and World Report, LV (2 Dec. 1963), 104.

1244. Lerner, Max. "The World Impact," New Statesman (London), LXVI (29 Nov. 1963), 769.

1245. McGill, Ralph Emerson. "Speaking Out: Hate Knows No Direction," The Saturday Evening Post, CCXXXVI (14 Dec. 1963), 8-10.

1246. McGrory, Mary. "After Great Pain, a Formal Feeling . . . ." America, CIX (14 Dec. 1963), 764.

1247. Mannes. Marya. "The Long Vigil," The Reporter, XXIX (19 Dec. 1963), 15-17.

1248. Mayes, Stanley. "What They Are Saying [The Tributes from Non-Western Leaders]," The Listener (London), LXX (28 Nov. 1963), 868; LXX (5 Dec. 1963), 912.

1249. Meyer, Karl E. "History as Tragedy," New Statesman (London), LXVI (29 Nov. 1963), 766-768.

1250. _____. "The Sleepwalkers [Christmas Shoppers in Washington, D.C.]," New Statesman (London), LXVI (20 Dec. 1963), 901-902.

1251. Mihovilovic, Ive. "Snajperski Metak no Savijest Amerike [Sniper's Bullet on America's Conscience]," Vjesnik u srijedu (Zagreb), (27 Nov. 1963), 604.

1252.   Milic, Zivko.   "Ubijen Predsednik SAD Dzon Kenedi
[U.S. President John Kennedy Killed]," Borba (Belgrade),
XXVIII (23 Nov. 1963), 324.

1253.   Milic, Zivko.   "Stravicna Hronika 22.   Novembra [Horri-
fying Chronicle of Nov. 22nd]," Borba (Belgrade), XXVIII (24
Nov. 1963), 325.

1254.   _____.   "Amerika je Povela Istragen nac Samom
Sobom [America Investigates Itself]," Borba (Belgrade), XI
(1 Dec. 1963), 330.

1255.   Morton, Thruston B.   "Collective Guilt? A Senator's
Answer," U.S. News and World Report, LV (23 Dec. 1963), 74.

1256.   Murray, P.   "Report From Mexico on Reaction to John
Kennedy's Tragic Death," Catholic Messenger, LXXXII (5 Dec.
1963), 12.

1257.   Novins, Stuart.   "This 'Heinous Act' Says Khrushchev,"
The Sunday Times (London), No. 7332 (24 Nov. 1963), 1-2.

1258.   _____.   "Shocked Russians Show Their Sympathy," The Sunday Times (London), No. 7332 (24 Nov. 1963),
2.

1259.   O'Gara, James.   "A President Is Buried," Commonweal,
LXXIX (6 Dec. 1963), 308.

1260.   Paetel, Karl O.   "Kennedy und das Andere Kuba [Kennedy
and the 'Other Cuba']," Geist und Tat, Monatsschrift für
Recht, Freiheit und Kultur (Frankfurt/Main), XVIII (1963),
173-175.

1261.   Panter-Downes, Mollie.   "Letter from London," The New
Yorker, XXXIX (7 Dec. 1963), 196-198.

1262.   Quade, Quentin L.   "The World Resounds: Milwaukee,"
America, CIX (14 Dec. 1963), 770-771.

1263.   Quinlan, Sean.   "The World Resounds: Washington,"
America, CIX (14 Dec. 1963), 769.

1264.   Radojcic, Miroslav.   "Kako je Amerika Primila Vest o
Zlocinu Teksasu [How the U.S. Accepted the News About the
Crime in Texas]," Politika (Belgrade), LX (23 Nov. 1963),
18010.

1265.   _____.   "Zasto je Amerika Cutala?" [Why
Was America Silent?]," Politika (Belgrade), (2 Dec. 1963),
18017.

1266.   Royster, Vermont.   "'No Time For Collective Guilt'
[Reprint from editorial, Wall Street Journal, 26 Nov. 1963],
U.S. News and World Report, LV (9 Dec. 1963), 72.

1267. Rubin, Berthold. "Vor dem Toten den Degen senken. Ein
Nachruf auf den Tod des US--Präsidenten John Kennedy [Before
the Sword Was Plunged. A Memorial on the Death of U.S. President John Kennedy]," Schlesische Rundschau (Munich), XV, No.
48 (1963), 3.

1268. Shannon, William V. "The Mood in Washington," Commonweal, LXXIX (13 Dec. 1963), 339-340.

1269. Sheerin, John B. "Editorial: 1. John F. Kennedy and
the New Catholic Image [Impact of Assassination Amongst
American Catholics in Rome for Vatican Council]," The Catholic
World, CXCVIII (Jan. 1964), 203.

1270. Smith, Jack A. "The Assassination Mystery: Kennedy
and Oswald Killings Puzzle Nation," National Guardian, XVI
(28 Nov. 1963), 1, 9.

1271. Stewart, Charles J. "The Pulpit in Time of Crisis:
1865 and 1963," Speech Monographs, XXXII (Nov. 1965), 427-434.

1272. Stone, I. F. "We All Had a Finger on That Trigger,"
Outlook (Sydney), VIII (Feb. 1964), 8-9.

1273. Terry, Anthony. "West and East Germans Mourn," The
Sunday Times (London), No. 7332 (24 Nov. 1963), 2.

1274. Wells, William. "The World Resounds: New York,"
America, CIX (14 Dec. 1963), 767.

1275. White, Theodore H. "One Wished for a Cry, a Sob . . .
Any Human Sound," Life, LV (29 Nov. 1963), 32D-32H.

    Anonymous Articles:

1276. "Current Comment: More Than One Man," America, CIX
(7 Dec. 1963), 722.

1277. "Präsident Kennedy ermordet--Wem nützt das? [President
Kennedy Murdered--Who Benefits?]," Das andere Deutschland,
(Hanover)   No. 24 (1963), 1.

1278. "Editor's Shop Talk [The Assassin "was a crazynut"],"
The Antioch Review, XXIII (Winter 1963-4), 403-404.

1279. "Zum Tode J. F. Kennedys [On J. F. Kennedy's Death],"
Aufrüstung, Moralische. Informationsdienst (Bonn), XI, No.
23 (1963), 90.

1280. "Der Mord von Dallas mahnt die Welt [the Dallas Murder
Warns the World]," Begegnung. Monatsschrift deutschen Katho-
liken (Berlin), III (1963), 1-2.

1281. "'Now the Trumpet Summons Again . . .'," Business Week
No. 1787 (30 Nov. 1963), 21-23.

1282.   "Wall Street Revives Fast After the Crisis," Business Week, No. 1787 (30 Nov. 1963), 28-29.

1283.   "World Weeps and Waits," Business Week, No. 1787 (30 Nov. 1963), 30-31.

1284.   "Shoppers Flock Back to Resume Buying: Merchants See Record Holiday Sales . . ." Business Week, No. 1787 (30 Nov. 1963), 89-90.

1285.   "A Shock, then Recovery [Opinions of U.S. Economists]," Business Week, No. 1787 (30 Nov. 1963), 92-93.

1286.   "It Was the Biggest Spending Binge Ever [In View of JFK Murder]," Business Week, No. 1791 (28 Dec. 1963), 18.

1287.   "SEC's Swipe at Specialists: the Agency's Report on Disorderly Market After Kennedy Assassination Singles Out Relatively Few Offenders," Business Week, No. 1796 (1 Feb. 1964), 73-74.

1288.   "Editorial: Apocalypse and After," The Christian Century, LXXX (4 Dec. 1963), 1487.

1289.   "Editorial: Have We Learned Our Lessons?"   The Christian Century, LXXX (18 Dec. 1963), 1567-1568.

1290.   "The Tragedy in Dallas: Letters to the Editor," The Christian Century, LXXX (18 Dec. 1963), 1588-1589.

1291.   "Reaction to Assassination [in Korea, Venezuela, etc.]," The Christian Century, LXXX (25 Dec. 1963), 1618-1619.

1292.   "Editorial: The Burden of Guilt," The Christian Century, LXXXI (8 Jan. 1964), 37-38; LXXXI (19 Feb. 1964), 243-244.

1293.   "Editorial: . . . [Talbot County, Georgia, School Principal Resigns After His Students Applauded JFK Assassination]," The Christian Century, LXXXI (5 Feb. 1964), 166.

1294.   "Death of the President," Commonweal, LXXIX (6 Dec. 1963), 299-301.

1295.   "Kennedy Assassination--Communist Version," Communist Affairs, I (Nov.-Dec. 1963), 3-6.

1296.   "World After New Year's-America: Minds in Ferment," The Current Digest of the Soviet Press, XVI (8 Jan. 1964), 18-19.

1297.   "Death of President Kennedy: Statements by Sir Robert Menzies and Sir Garfield Barwick on 23rd November [in Australia]," Current Notes on International Affairs (Canberra), XXXIV (Nov. 1963), 38-39.

1298. "The Assassination of President Kennedy," East Europe, XIII (Jan. 1964), 25-26.

1299. "Leader of the West; 'Among Ourselves'; Economic Hazards," The Economist (London), CCIX (30 Nov. 1963), 881-884.

1300. "An American Tragedy--And a Tragedy for Texas," The Economist (London), CCIX (30 Nov. 1963), 895-896.

1301. "'This Is a Great Nation': International Report," The Economist (London), CCIX (30 Nov. 1963), 901-902.

1302. "Conservative After Dallas?" The Economist (London), CCIX (7 Dec. 1963), 995-996.

1303. "Off the Goldwater Standard?" The Economist (London), CCIX (21 Dec. 1963), 1261-1262.

1304. "The Assassination of President Kennedy," Life, LV (29 Nov. 1963), 22-32C.

1305. "Editorial: The 72 Hours and What They Can Teach Us," Life, LV (6 Dec. 1963), 4.

1306. "President Kennedy Is Laid to Rest," Life, LV (6 Dec. 1963), 38-47.

1307. "Sorrow Rings a World," Life, LV (6 Dec. 1963), 117-125.

1308. "Editorials: The American Condition," The Nation, CXCVII (21 Dec. 1963), 425.

1309. "Report to Readers: Assassination--and After," National Guardian, XVI (28 Nov. 1963), 2.

1310. "The Tragedy: J.F.K., 1917-1963," National Review, XV (10 Dec. 1963), 1.

1311. "How Could It Happen?" The New Republic, CXLIX (7 Dec. 1963), 6.

1312. "Uncertainty and Anxiety Abroad: New Delhi, London, Rome," The New Republic, CXLIX (7 Dec. 1963), 11-12.

1313. "Peking: No Love for Kennedy," New Statesman (London) LXVI (6 Dec. 1963), 816.

1314. "Who Killed Kennedy?--Soviet Condolences," New Times (Moscow), 4 Dec. 1963, 5-7.

1315. ". . . And a Child's Yellow Flowers," Newsweek, LXII (2 Dec. 1963), 36-37.

1316. "The Reaction [in Paris, Tokyo, etc.]," Newsweek, LXII (9 Dec. 1963), 2-9; LXII (16 Dec. 1963), 2-10.

1317.   "National Affairs: 'May the Angels, Dear Jack . . .
Lead You Into Paradise . . .'," Newsweek, LXII (9 Dec. 1963),
30-33.

1318.   "The Americas: Cuba: The Grief of a Foe," Newsweek,
LXII (9 Dec. 1963), 53.

1319.   "International: A World Mourns-in Doubt, Fear, Hope,"
Newsweek, LXII (9 Dec. 1963), 56-58.

1320.   "Spotlight on Business: A Renewed Faith," Newsweek,
LXII (9 Dec. 1963), 77-80.

1321.   "The Assassination: X On the Spot [The Malcolm X
Remark]," Newsweek, LXII (16 Dec. 1963), 27-28.

1322.   "International: Assassins: The Imitators [Threats
Against Prime Ministers of Australia, England]," Newsweek,
LXII (23 Dec. 1963), 27.

1323.   "Notes and Comments," The New Yorker, XXXIX (7 Dec.
1963), 45.

1324.   "Book Trade, U.S. and Abroad, Mourns President's
Death," Publishers   Weekly, CLXXXIV (2 Dec. 1963), 27-28.

1325.   "Macmillan Stops Publication of 'JFK' [by Victor Lasky:
Resumed on 7 December 1963]," Publishers   Weekly, CLXXXIV (2
Dec. 1963), 27; (16 Dec. 1963), 22.

1326.   "Statement by the Editors: This Nation, Under God,"
Readers Digest, LXXXIV (Jan. 1964), 37-39.

1327.   "The Reporter's Notes: The Time Between," The Reporter, XXIX (5 Dec. 1963), 14.

1328.   "A Senseless Tragedy," The Saturday Evening Post,
CCXXXVI (14 Dec. 1963), 19.

1329.   "Letters to the Editor: JFK--Reaction from Abroad,"
Saturday Review, XLVI (28 Dec. 1963), 27.

1330.   "Das teuflische Spiel um den Kennedy-Mord.   Der Trick
des Weltkommunismus durchschant und missglückt [The Diabolical
Game of Kennedy's Murder.   The Trick of World Communism Exposed and Aborted]," Schlesische Rundschau (Munich), XV, No.
49 (1963), 1, 3.

1331.   "Beileidsbekundungen zum Tode John F. Kennedys [Public
Condolences on the Death of John F. Kennedy]," Die Sowjetunion
heute.   Zeitschrift über Leben und Arbeit, Kultur, Wirtschaft,
Wissenschaft usw. in der UdSSR, (Bonn), VIII, Heft 23 (1963),
4-5.

1332.   "Death of a Modern [Editorial]," The Spectator (London), No. 7066 (29 Nov. 1963), 681; Reprinted in Atlas, VII
(Feb. 1964), 116-117.

1333.   "Portrait of the Week [Quoting Izvestia]," The Spectator (London), No. 7066 (29 Nov. 1963), 681.

1334.   "Bonn-Kennedy-Begräbnis: 'Was sagen Sie?   [Bonn-Kennedy Burial: 'What Does One Say?']," Der Spiegel (Hamburg), XVII, No. 49 (1963), 21, 23.

1335.   "USA - Kennedy - Attentat: Mord in der Sonne [USA Kennedy Assassination: Murder in Broad Daylight]," Der Spiegel, XVII, No. 49 (1963), 77-83.

1336.   "USA - Attentat - Aufklärung: Weisser Mann gesucht [USA Assassination Clarification: White Man Sought]," Der Spiegel (Hamburg), XVII, No. 49 (1963), 83-86.

1337.   "USA - Präsidentunschutz: Fenster zu [Protecting the US President: Close the Window]," Der Spiegel (Hamburg), XVII XVII, No. 49 (1963), 86-87.

1338.   "The Whole World Mourns Murdered President: Duke of Edinburgh and the Premier [Sir Alec Douglas-Home] Going to U.S. to Join in Last Tributes," The Sunday Times (London), No. 7332 (24 Nov. 1963), 1.

1339.   "Premier [Sir Alec Douglas-Home] Attends Mass in Packed Cathedral," The Sunday Times (London), No. 7332 (24 Nov. 1963), 1.

1340.   "[Editorial]:   In the Line of Heroes: The Man of High Courage," The Sunday Times (London), No. 7332 (24 Nov. 1963),

1341.   "The Presidency: the Government Still Lives," Time, LXXXII (29 Nov. 1963), 21-33.

1342.   "The Nations: How Sorrowful Bad," Time, LXXXII (29 Nov. 1963), 38-39.

1343.   "The Nations: Sympathy & Scrutiny," Time, LXXXII (6 Dec. 1963), 36-37.

1344.   "The Shot That Changed Our Future: A Chronology of Tragedy," Time and Tide (London), XLIV (28 Nov.-4 Dec. 1963), 4, 7-9.

1345.   "Tributes to President Kennedy Pour in From World's Leaders," The Times (London), No. 55, 866 (23 Nov. 1963), 7.

1346.   "President Kennedy Assassinated: Three Shots at Open Car in Texas: Questioned Man's Denial [Oswald]," The Times (London), No. 55, 866 (23 Nov. 1963), 8.

1347.   "The Queen's Message of Sympathy to U.S.:   Gasp of Horror," The Times (London), No. 55, 866 (23 Nov. 1963), 8.

1348.   "[Editorial]:   In the True Line," The Times (London), No. 55, 866 (23 Nov. 1963), 9.

1349. "Obituary: President John F. Kennedy: Courage and Idealism at the White House," The Times (London), No. 55, 866 (23 Nov. 1963), 12.

1350. "World Speculation About the Events in Dallas: Texas to Hold Inquiry into Shootings: Enough Evidence to Convict Oswald Claimed," The Times (London), No. 55,868 (26 Nov. 1963), 10.

1351. "Map Showing Path of Bullet 'Found in Oswald's Room' [According to D.A. Henry Wade]," The Times (London), No. 55,868 (26 Nov. 1963), 10.

1352. "Senate Inquiry Into Shooting of Mr. Kennedy Likely: Ruby Indicted," The Times (London), No. 55,869 (27 Nov. 1963), 11.

1353. "Chinese Anger Over Kennedy Tribute [at Warsaw's World Peace Council]," The Times (London), No. 55,871 (29 Nov. 1963), 9.

1354. "The Moment of Tragedy: When Safeguards Failed After 62 Years," U.S. News and World Report, LV (2 Dec. 1963), 6.

1355. "The Tragic End of John F. Kennedy," U.S. News and World Report, LV (2 Dec. 1963), 31-33.

1356. "'A Thousand Well-Wishers'--And One Assassin," U.S. News and World Report, LV (2 Dec. 1963), 34-35.

1357. "Assassins' Toll: 4 U.S. Presidents," U.S. News and World Report, LV (2 Dec. 1963), 35.

1358. "Foreign Countries, Too Mourn 'First Citizen of World'," U.S. News and World Report, LV (2 Dec. 1963), 48-49.

1359. "From Friend, Foe in America: 'Sense of Shock and Dismay at the Despicable Act'," U.S. News and World Report, LV (2 Dec. 1963), 49.

1360. "Paris Poll: Reasons for Dallas Murders," U.S. News and World Report, LV (9 Dec. 1963), 14.

1361. "Stock-Market Reaction to Kennedy Assassination; How Business Reacted in Past to Death of Pres.," U.S. News and World Report, LV (9 Dec. 1963), 48-50.

1362. "Historic Photo Report: As the World Wept . . ." U.S. News and World Report, LV (9 Dec. 1963), 51-57.

1363. "Collective or Individual Guilt?" U.S. News and World Report, LV (16 Dec. 1963), 10.

1364. "'Collective Guilt' in the U.S.? Take a Look at the World," U.S. News and World Report, LV (23 Dec. 1963), 72-74.

1365. "Assassination Story---the Reaction in Japan," U.S. News and World Report, LV (15 June 1964), 16.

1366. "U.S. 'Guilt' in Assassinations--the Talk and the Facts," U.S. News and World Report, LXIV (24 June 1968), 37.

(3) MEMORIALS AND EULOGIES

Books:

1368. Ballot, Paul. Memorial to Greatness. Island Park, New York: Aspen Corp., 1964.

1369. Bergquist, Laura, and Stanley Tretick. A Very Special President. New York: McGraw-Hill, 1965.

1370. Berry, Wendell, and Ben Shahn. November Twenty Six, Nineteen Hundred Sixty Three. New York: George Braziller, 1964.

1371. Bradlee, Benjamin. That Special Grace. Philadelphia: Lippincott, 1964.

1372. Campbell, Earl Vendryes. Kennedy's Thoughts After He Was Shot. Bigfork, Minnesota and Boston, Mass.: Northwoods Press, 1975.

1373, _____. Last Thoughts of a Dead President. Madison, Wisconsin: Fleetwood Art Studios, 1972.

1374. Chinmoy, Sri. Kennedy: The Universal Heart. Santurce, Puerto Rico: Aum Press, 1973.

1375. Congressional Record, CIX, Part 17 (22-26 Nov. 1963), 22693ff. [Senate], and 22802ff. [House].

1376. Cournos, John. The Lost Leader. New York: Twayne, 1964.

1377. Duheme, Jacqueline. John F. Kennedy: A Book of Paintings. New York: Atheneum, 1967.

1378. Fine, William M. (ed.). That Day With God. Foreword by Richard Cardinal Cushing. New York: McGraw-Hill, 1965.

1379. Gardner, Francis V. Rest Assured, John Kennedy. McLean, Virginia: Published by Author, 1973.

1380.   Garduno, Joseph A.   Museum for a President.   New
York: Carleton, 1966.

1381.   Geer, Candy.   Six White Horses: An Illustrated Poem
About John-John.   Ann Arbor, Michigan: Quill, 1964.

1382.   Glikes, Edwin A. (ed.), with Paul Schwaber.   Of Poetry
and Power: Poems Occasioned by the Presidency and by the
Death of John F. Kennedy.   New York: Basic Books, 1964.

1383.   Goldman, Alex J.   John Fitzgerald Kennedy: The World
Remembers.   New York: Fleet, 1968.

1384.   Gronouski, John S.   Address by John A. Gronouski,
Postmaster General, at the Dedication of the John Fitzgerald
Kennedy Memorial Stamp, Boston, Mass., May 29, 1964.   Washing-
ton, D.C.:   U.S. Post Office Department, 1964.

1385.   John Fitzgerald Kennedy: The Last Full Measure.   Washington, D.C.:   National Geographic, 1964.

1386.   John Fitzgerald Kennedy, A Tribute . . . from the
Youth of the United States for the Youth of the World.
Philadelphia: U.S. National Student Association, 1964.

1387.   A John F. Kennedy Memorial.   New York: MacFadden-
Bartell, 1964.

1388.   John F. Kennedy Memorial Edition: Life.   Chicago:
Time, Inc., 1963.

1389.   John F. Kennedy, 22 november 1963.   Samlet og odsendt
af Danmark-Amerika Fondets stipendiatsektion [A Collection of
Reports of the Danish-American Foundation Scholarship Sec-
tion].   Copenhagen: Nyt Nordisk Forlag, 1965.

1390.   Kazan, Molly.   Kennedy.   New York: Stein and Day,
1963.

1391.   Kellner, Abraham (ed.).   Sunset at Mid-day: A Tribute
to the Late John Fitzgerald Kennedy.   New York: K'Das Publishing Co., 1964.

1392.   Klein, Harry T. (ed.).   President Kennedy Commemorative
Anthology.   Los Angeles: Swordsman Press, n.d.

1393.   Levy, Clifford V. (Compiler).   Twenty-Four Personal
Eulogies on the Late President John F. Kennedy 1917-1963.
San Francisco, 1963.

1394.   Mansfield, Michael J.   John Fitzgerald Kennedy: Eulo-
gies to the Late President Delivered in the Rotunda of the
United States Capitol, November 24, 1963, by Mike Mansfield,
Earl Warren, and John W. McCormack.   Washington, D.C.:   U.S.
Government Printing Office, 1963.

1395. Marten, Paul. Kennedy Requiem. Toronto: Weller, 1963.

1396. Matthews, James P. (ed.). In Memoriam. Los Angeles: Matador Magazine, 1964.

1397. Mayhew, Aubrey. The World's Tribute to John F. Kennedy in Medallic Art. New York: Morrow, 1966.

1398. Murray, Norbert. Legacy of an Assassination. New York: Pro-People Press, 1964.

1399. Nanchant, Frances G. Song of Peace. Francestown, New Hampshire: Golden Quill, 1969.

1400. National Broadcasting Company. 'That Was the Week That Was': A Tribute to John Fitzgerald Kennedy. New York: N. B. C., 1964; [See 2676].

1401. Nyaradi, Nicholas. Memorial Address. Harrogate, Tennessee: Lincoln Memorial University Press, 1964.

1402. Salinger, Pierre, and Sander Vanocur (eds.). A Tribute to John F. Kennedy. Foreword by Theodore C. Sorenson; Dedication by Lyndon B. Johnson. Chicago: Encyclopedia Britannica, 1964; New York: Dell, 1965.

1403. Schmidt, (Sister Mary) Bernadette (ed.). The Trumpet Summons Us---John F. Kennedy. New York: Vantage Press, 1964.

1404. Stewart, Charles J. and Bruce Kendall (eds.). A Man Named John F. Kennedy: Sermons on His Assassination. Glen Rock, New Jersey: Paulist Press, 1964.

1405. Strior, Murray. The Historic Significance of the Assassination of President John F. Kennedy. Flushing, New York: Spinoza Institute of America, 1963.

1406. United Nations. Homage to a Friend: A Memorial Tribute by the United Nations for President John F. Kennedy. New York: The U.S. Commission, with the United Nations Office of Public Information, 1964.

1407. United States Congress. Memorial Addresses in the Congress of the United States and Tributes in Eulogy of John Fitzgerald Kennedy Late President of the United States. Washington, D.C.: U.S. Government Printing Office, 1964.

1408. Vilnis, Aija. The Bearer of the Star Spangled Banner. In Memory of President John Fitzgerald Kennedy. Translated by Lilija Pavars. New York: Speller, 1964.

1409. Walsh, William G. (ed.). Children Write About John F. Kennedy. Brownsville, Texas: Springman-King, 1964.

1410. Warner, Dale G. Who Killed the President? New York:
The American Press, 1964.

1411. Whitbourn, John (ed.). Runnymede Memorial. Ilford,
England: Excel Press, 1965.

Articles by Authors:

1412. Alsop, Joseph. "The Legacy of John F. Kennedy:
Memories of an Uncommon Man," The Saturday Evening Post,
CCXXXVII (21 Nov. 1964), 15-19.

1413. Brother Antoninus. "The Tongs of Jeopardy," Ramparts,
II (Spring 1964), 3-9.

1414. d'Apollonia, L. "Reflexions sur une Tragédie [Reflec-
tions on a Tragedy]," Relations (Montreal), XXIV (Jan. 1964),
27.

1415. Ascoli, Max. "Editorial: The 22nd of November,"
The Reporter, XXIX (5 Dec. 1963), 19.

1416. Attwood, William. "In Memory of John F. Kennedy,"
Look, XXVII (31 Dec. 1963), 11-13.

1417. Augstein, Rudolf. "Der Präsident der Stärke und des
Friedens [The President of the Strong and Peaceful]," Der
Spiegel (Hamburg), No. 48 (1963), 22-23.

1418. Bar-David, M. "Diary of an Israel Housewife,"
Hadassah Magazine, XLV (Jan. 1964), 21-22.

1419. Berendt, John. "A Look at the Record: What the
School Books Are Teaching Our Kids About J.F.K.," Esquire,
LXXX (Nov. 1973), 140, 263-265.

1420. Berger, Kurt Martin. "Das Ende einer 'Führungsmacht'
[The End of a 'Unique Leadership']," Zeitschrift für Geo-
politik (Heidelberg), XXXIV, Hefte 11-12 (1963), 339-342;
also published in Gemeinschaft und Politik. Zeitschrift
für soziale und politische Gestalt (Bad Godesberg), XI (1963),
339-342.

1421. Bergquist, Laura. "John Fitzgerald Kennedy . . .
1917-1963," Look, XXVIII (17 Nov. 1964), 33-35.

1422. Bettiza, Enzo. "The Kennedy Myth [From L'Espresso,
Rome]," Atlas, VII (Jan. 1964), 9.

1423. Booker, Emma. "Frost at Midnight [International Tribute Through the Arts]," The Spectator (London), No. 7075,
(31 Jan. 1964), 146.

1424. Booker, Simeon. "How JFK Surpassed Abraham Lincoln,"
Ebony, XIX (Feb. 1964), 25-34.

1425.   Borch, Herbert von.   "Wird Kennedys Erbe überleben?
[Will the Kennedy Heritage Survive?]," Aussenpolitik Zeitschrift für internationale Fragen (Stuttgart), XV (1964),
1-4.

1426.   Carleton, William G.   "Kennedy in History: an Early
Appraisal," The Antioch Review, XXIV (Fall 1964), 277-299.

1427.   Carter, Manfred A.   "November 22, 1963:   [Four Poems],"
The Christian Century, LXXX (11 Dec. 1963), 1540.

1428.   Chamberlin, Anne.   "The Legacy of John F. Kennedy:
the Commercialization of J. F. K.," The Saturday Evening
Post, CCXXXVII (21 Nov. 1964), 20-21.

1429.   Ciardi, John.   "Manner of Speaking: Of Chaos and
Courage," Saturday Review, XLVI (28 Dec. 1963), 25.

1430.   Clarke, Gerald.   "JFK--Bitter Memories of a Cold Day:
Camelot in Retrospect," The New Republic, CLXIV (16 Jan.
1971), 13-15.

1431.   Clifford, G.   "Warren Report: a New Boost for the
Kennedy Memorabilia Industry," Maclean's Magazine (Toronto),
LXXVII (2 Nov. 1964), 3.

1432.   Cousins, Norman.   "The Legacy of John F. Kennedy,"
Saturday Review, XLVI (7 Dec. 1963), 21-27.

1433.   _____.   "Can Civilization Be Assassinated?"
Saturday Review, XLVI (21 Dec. 1963), 14, 32.

1434.   Dönhoff, Marion (Gräfin).   "Was wird bleiben?   John F.
Kennedys Politik für die Welt von morgen [What Will Remain?
John F. Kennedy's Politics for the World of Tomorrow]," Die
Zeit (Hamburg), XVIII, No. 48 (1963), 1; Translated as "The
Kennedy Legacy," Atlas, VII (Jan. 1964), 8-9.

1435.   Endt, Friso.   "Washington 25 November 1963," Revu
[Netherlands], X (11 March 1967), 18-20.

1436.   Ferlinghetti, Lawrence.   "Assassination Raga [Poems],"
Ramparts, VII (24 Aug. 1968), 38-39.

1437.   Freund, Hugo.   "Zum Tode John F. Kennedys [On the
Death of John F. Kennedy]," Städtehygiene (Freiburg-im-
Breisgau), XV (1964), 1.

1438.   Gappert, Gary.   "Correspondence: Tribute [from Students in Tanganyika]," Atlas, VII (Jan. 1964), 64.

1439.   Götte, Fritz.   "Nach John F. Kennedys Tod [After John
F. Kennedy's Death]," Die Drei. Monatsschrift für Anthro-
posophie, Dreigliederung und Goetheanismus (Stuttgart), XXXIV
(1964), 143-145.

1440. Hart, L. "A Year of Progress With a Sorrowful Close," Columbia, XLIV (Jan. 1964), 16.

1441. Hessel, Dieter. "To Heal the Wounds," The Christian Century, LXXXI (1 Jan. 1964), 15-16.

1442. Joesten, Joachim. "Der Kennedy-Mord als 'politische Walrheit' [Kennedy's Murder as 'Political Truth']," Frankfurter Hefte. Zeitschrift für Kultur und Politik (Frankfurt/Main), XXI, No. 8 (Aug. 1966), 534-540.

1443. Kempton, Murray. "Looking Back on the Anniversary," The Spectator (London), No. 7119 (4 Dec. 1964), 778-779.

1444. Kerr, James. "The Awful Instant That Still Haunts Our World--12:30 P.M., Nov. 22, 1963," The National Tattler, XIX (25 Nov. 1973), 2-6, 31.

1445. Koch, Thilo. "Der Tod des Präsidenten [The Death of the President]," Die Zeit (Hamburg), XVIII, No. 48 (1963), 2.

1446. Krippendorff, Ekkehart. "John F. Kennedy--Rückblick nach einem Jahr [Retrospect on a Year]," Zeitschrift für Politik (Berlin), XI, Heft 4 (1964), 309-322.

1447. Kurnoth, Rudolf. "Gedanken um den Tod John F. Kennedys [Thoughts on the Death of John F. Kennedy]," Frankenstein-Münsterberger Heimatblatt (Lengerich) X, No. 12 (1963), 2.

1448. Levin, Bernard. "The Bell Tolls in Dallas: from BBC-TV 'That Was the Week That Was'," The Listener (London), LXX (5 Dec. 1963), 914.

1449. Logan, Andy. "JFK: the Stained Glass Image," American Heritage, XVIII (Aug. 1967), 4-7, 75-78.

1450. Lohmar, Ulrich. "Kennedys Vermächtnis [Kennedy's Legacy]," Kirche und Mann. Monatszeitung für Männerarbeit der Evangelische Kirche in Deutschland (Gütersloh), XVI, No. 12 (1963), 2.

1451. McLaughlin, M. "Paris, November 22nd, 1963," Immaculate Heart Crusader, XXVIII (Nov. 1964), 8-9.

1452. McNaspy, C. J. "Après la Mort de Kennedy: l'Amérique Devant Elle-Même [After Kennedy's Death: America Facing Herself]," Études: Revue Catholique d'intérêt général, CCCXX (1964), 27-37.

1453. Mayer, Milton. "November 22, 1963," The Progressive Magazine, XXVIII (Dec. 1964), 21-25.

1454. Medved, Michael, and David Wallechinsky. "November 22, 1963 . . . as Remembered by the Class of '65," Senior Scholastic, CIX (18 Nov. 1976), 15, 30.

1455. Moynihan, Daniel Patrick. "The Democrats, Kennedy, and the Murder of Dr. King," Commentary, XLV (1968), 15-29.

1456. Muggeridge, Malcolm. "The Apotheosis of John F. Kennedy," The New York Review of Books, III (28 Jan. 1965), 1, 3-4; IV (11 March 1965), 28.

1457. O'Brien, Conor Cruise. "The Life and Death of Kennedy," New Statesman (London), No. 1818 (14 Jan. 1966), 50-51.

1458. Osbaine, Cecil. "Five Years Later: Kennedy--The Making of a Myth," National Review, XX (5 Nov. 1968), 1113-1114.

1459. Pouillon, Jean. "De l'assassinat à l'enterrement [From the Assassination to the Burial]," Temps modernes (Paris), année 20, No. 218 (1964), 184-192.

1460. Remus, Bernhard. "Erinnerung an John F. Kennedy [Memories of John F. Kennedy]," Weltwoche (Zürich), XXXI, No. 1568 (1963), 1, 3.

1461. Rendulic, Lothar. "Das Erbe nach Kennedy und die Krise des Westens [The Kennedy Heritage and the Western World's Crisis]," Berichte und Informationen des Österreichischen Forschungsinstitutes für Wirtschaft und Politik (Salzburg), XIX, Heft 917 (1964), 1-3.

1462. Roddy, Joseph. "Ireland: They Cried the Rain Down That Night," Look, XXVIII (17 Nov. 1964), 75-79.

1463. Schlesinger, Arthur M., Jr. "A Eulogy: John Fitzgerald Kennedy," The Saturday Evening Post, CCXXXVI (14 Dec. 1963), 32-32a; CCXLVIII (July-Aug. 1976), 74.

1464. Stahl, Walter. "Correspondence: A German Writes About Kennedy," Atlas, VII (Feb. 1964), 127.

1465. Thomas, J. "Le 'monde libre' et le crime de Dallas [The 'Free World' and the Dallas Crime]," La nouvelle revue internationale (Paris), VII (1964), 83-88.

1466. Tschäppät, R. "Das geistige Erbe Kennedys [Kennedy's Spiritual Heritage]," Schweizerisches kaufmännisches Zentralblatt (Zürich), LXVII, No. 48 (1963), 1.

1467. Whittemore, Reed. "Books and the Arts: Poetry of the Assassination," The New Republic, CLI (21 Nov. 1964), 17-19.

Anonymous Articles:

1468. "Memorial Outdoor Boards Are Posted," Advertising Age, XXXIV (2 Dec. 1963), 112.

1469. "Editorials: May He Rest in Peace," America, CIX (7
Dec. 1963), 728-729.

1470. "Zum Tode von Präsident John F. Kennedy [On the Death
of President John F. Kennedy]," Blätter für deutsche und
internationale Politik (Cologne), VIII, Heft 12 (1963), 904-
905.

1471. "Kennedys Vermächtnis [The Kennedy Legacy]," Bulletin
des Presse-und Informationsamtes der Bundesregierung (Bonn),
No. 208 (1963), 1843.

1472. "Editorial: In 1963, We Survived," The Christian Century, LXXX (25 Dec. 1963), 1599-1601.

1473. "Editorial: Birch Society Adopts New Guise," The
Christian Century, LXXXI (1 Jan. 1964), 5.

1474. "Editorial: Cardinal [Cushing] Re-endorses Birch
Society," The Christian Century, LXXXI (6 May 1964), 596.

1475. "The Kennedy Legacy, the People's Task," Commonweal,
LXXIX (13 Dec. 1963), 335-336.

1476. "On the Far Right," Commonweal, LXXIX (27 Dec. 1963),
384-385.

1477. "Backstage [Editorial Tribute to JFK]," Ebony, XIX
(Jan. 1964), 19.

1478. "Ebony Photo-Editorial: A Tribute to John F. Kennedy,"
Ebony, XIX (Jan. 1964), 90-91.

1479. "Letters to the Editor: Death of President Kennedy,"
Ebony, XIX (Feb. 1964), 13-16.

1480. "Letters to the Editor: Kennedy and Lincoln," Ebony,
XIX (April 1964), 10-16.

1481. "Anniversary Fever," The Economist (London), CCXXI (26
Nov. 1966), 914.

1482. "Birch Ads' Response 'Overwhelms' Welch," Editor &
Publisher, XCVII (25 Jan. 1964), 11.

1483. "Ten Years Later: Where were You?:   Nobody Forgets,"
Esquire, LXXX (Nov. 1973), 136-137.

1484. "Ten Years Later: Who Was He?:   Not Everybody Remembers," Esquire, LXXX (Nov. 1973), 138-139.

1485. "In memoriam Kennedy," Forum.   Österreichische Monats-
blätter für Kulturelle Freiheit (Vienna), XI, Heft 125 (1964),
230.

1486. "John F. Kennedy zum Gedächtnis [Memories of John F. Kennedy]," Katholischer Digest. Internationale katholische Monatsrundschan (Aschaffenburg), XVIII (1964), 10-12.

1487. "John F. Kennedy: In Memoriam," The Nation, CXCVII (14 Dec. 1963), 404-405.

1488. "Editorials: Then How About Koch?," The Nation, CXCVIII (2 March 1964), 206-207.

1489. "BB [i.e., B'nai Brith] Overseas Mourn JFK," National Jewish Monthly, LXXVIII (Jan. 1964), 24-26.

1490. "Illinois vs. Oliver," National Review, XVI (7 April 1964), 264-265.

1491. "The Day Kennedy Died," Newsweek, LXII (2 Dec. 1963), 20-26.

1492. "An End and a Beginning," Newsweek, LXII (9 Dec. 1963), 19-20.

1493. "National Affairs: The Right Wing," Newsweek, LXII (30 Dec. 1963), 16-17.

1494. "Business and Finance: Enterprise: Memorial Boom," Newsweek, LXII (30 Dec. 1963), 49-50.

1495. "Music: The Prodigal Returns [Leonard Bernstein's Kaddish, for JFK]," Newsweek, LXIII (10 Feb. 1964), 77.

1496. "The Assassination: Birch View of JFK [by Professor Revilo Oliver, Illinois]," Newsweek, LXIII (24 Feb. 1964), 29-30; (30 March 1964), 73.

1497. "Music: When a Just Man Dies [Igor Stravinsky's Elegy, for JFK]," Newsweek, LXIII (20 April 1964), 75.

1498. "Life and Leisure: Coincidences," Newsweek, LXIV (10 Aug. 1964), 64-65; LXIV (24 Aug. 1964), 2.

1499. "National Affairs: And Then It Was November 22 Again," Newsweek, LXIV (30 Nov. 1964), 25-28.

1500. "Music: Orchestra of Record [Roy Harris's Epilogue, for JFK]," Newsweek, LXVII (21 March 1966), 102-105.

1501. "Where Are They Now?: Black Friday--Five Years Later," Newsweek, LXXII (25 Nov. 1968), 22-23.

1502. "National Affairs: The Kennedy Years: What Endures?" Newsweek, LXXVII (1 Feb. 1971), 20-22.

1503. "Ideas: JFK: Visions and Revisions," Newsweek, LXXXI (19 Nov. 1973), 76-92.

1504. "Newsmakers: [Annual Memorial Ceremonies at Site of JFK Assassination]," Newsweek, LXXXVIII (29 Nov. 1976), 52.

1505. "Kennedys Tod bringt die Welt zur Besinnung [Kennedy's Death Brings the World to Recollection]," Paulinus. Trierer Bistumsblatt (Trier), LXXXIX, No. 48 (1963), 6.

1506. "L'occidente e la morte di Kennedy [The Western World and Kennedy's Death]," Rivista di studi politici internazionali (Florence), XXX, No. 3 (1963), 323-326.

1507. "Letters to the Editor; With Editorial Comment," Senior Scholastic, LXXXIII (10 Jan. 1964), 18.

1508. "This Week in History: Tragic Day in Texas," Senior Scholastic, LXXXIX (18 Nov. 1966), 7.

1509. "Historical Notes: 'Land of Kennedy'," Time, LXXXII (13 Dec. 1963), 27.

1510. "To J.F.K. [Darius Milhand's Musical Ode, for JFK]," Time, LXXXVI (6 Aug. 1965), 69.

1511. "Art: Murals: Assassination in Boston," Time, LXXXVIII (26 Aug. 1966), 60.

1512. "United States: Kennedy Memorial Fund Flop [in Britain Also]," Time and Tide (London), XLV (8-14 Oct. 1964), 18.

1513. "Visitors to the Kennedy Grave--An Endless Line," U.S. News and World Report, LVI (25 May 1964), 79-81.

1514. "For John F. Kennedy: Birthday Tributes," U.S. News and World Report, LVI (8 June 1964), 10-11.

1515. "1963-1973: 10 Years That Shook the World [Triggered by JFK Murder]," U.S. News and World Report, LXXV (26 Nov. 1973), 38-53.

1516. "Nur tausend Tage. Ein Jahr nach der Ermordung John F. Kennedys [Only a Thousand Days. One Year After John F. Kennedy's Murder]," Weltwoche (Zürich), XXXII, No. 1619 (1964), 1.

(4) NEWS MEDIA

Books and Collections:

1517. Armco Microfilming: "Microfilm Documentary Reference File of the Assassination of John F. Kennedy: Articles From 33 Major American and Foreign Newspapers and Magazines, November 22 through November 27, 1963." [35 mm. Film; Armco, 1718 L Street, Fresno 21, California; 1964].

1518. _____: "Microfilm Documentary Reference
File on Oswald and Ruby: a Complete Record of the Historic
Oswald and Ruby Affair Taken From the Pertinent Time Periods
of 9 American Newspapers and Magazines." [35 mm. Film, 1964].

1519. The Assassination Story: Newspaper Clippings from the
two Dallas Dailies, the Dallas Morning News, November 23-
December 11, 1963, the Dallas Times Herald, November 22-
December 10, 1963. Dallas: American Eagle Publishing Co.,
1964.

1520. Associated Press. The Torch is Passed; the Associated
Press Story of the Death of a President. New York: Associated Press, 1963.

1521. Baker, Dean C. The Assassination of President Kennedy:
a Study of the Press Coverage. Ann Arbor, Michigan: University of Michigan Press, Dept. of Journalism, 1965.

1522. Bell & Howell Company. Memorial Collection of Newspapers on Microfilm Chronicling Events of the Assassination
of John F. Kennedy, November 22-26, 1963. Cleveland: Micro-
Photo Division, 1964 [10 reels].

1523. Denegree Vaught, Livingston. La eterna antorcha de
Arlington: Reportajes de un Periodista Mexicano desde Wash-
ington, a la Muerte de John F. Kennedy [Arlington's Eternal
Torch: Reports of a Mexican Journalist from Washington, on
John F. Kennedy's Death]. Mexico City: Editorial Academia
Literaria, 1964.

1524. Denson, R. B. Destiny in Dallas: On-the-Scene Story
in Pictures. Dallas: Denco Corp., 1964.

1525. Duhamel, Morvan. Les Quatre Jours de Dallas [Those
Four Days in Dallas]. Paris: Éditions France-Empire, 1966.

1526. Gross, Gerald (ed.). The Responsibility of the Press.
New York: Fleet Publishing Corp., 1966.

1527. Matthews, James P. Four Dark Days in History: a
Photo History of President Kennedy's Assassination. Los
Angeles: Associated Professional Services, 1963.

1528. Mayo, John B., Jr. Bulletin From Dallas: the President is Dead; the Story of John F. Kennedy's Assassination
as Covered by Radio and TV. Hicksville, New York: Exposition Press, 1967.

1529. National Broadcasting Company. There Was a President:
Illustrated Edition of Seventy Hours and Thirty Minutes.
New York: Random House and Ridge Press, 1966; [See 3645,
4222].

1530. New York Times, Editors. Assassination of a President;
a Chronicle of the Six Days From November 23 to November 28,
1963. New York: Viking Press, 1964.

1531. Pomerantz, Charlotte, with H. H. Wilson. The Mood of
the Nation (November 22-29, 1963): a News Documentary of a
Steadfast Citizenry. New York: Marzani & Munsell, Inc.,
1964.

1532. Rains, Rolen R. (ed.). Editorials, U.S.A. Different
Opinions on Different Subjects. John F. Kennedy Assassination November 22, 1963. Dallas, Texas: Rolen R. Rains, n.d.

1533. Rajski, Raymond B. A Nation Grieved: the Kennedy
Assassination in Editorial Cartoons. Foreword by Arthur
Schlesinger, Jr. Rutland, Vermont: Charles E. Tuttle Co.,
1967.

1534. Rather, Dan, with Mickey Herskowitz. The Camera Never
Blinks: Adventures of a TV Journalist. New York: William
Morrow, 1977; Ballantine, 1978; [See 1785].

1535. Reyes Monroy, Jose Luis (ed.). Ramo de Orquideas; La
Bella Flor Nacional de Guatemala; a La Memoria del Gran
Presidente de los Estados Unidos de América, señor John F.
Kennedy [Bouquet of Orchids; the Beautiful National Flower
of Guatemala: Newspaper Articles to the Memory of the Great
U.S. President, Mr. John F. Kennedy]. Guatemala: Tif
Nacional, 1965.

1536. Schorr, Daniel. Clearing the Air. Boston: Houghton
Mifflin Co., 1977; New York: Berkeley, 1978.

1537. Seigenthaler, John (ed.). He Gave His Life; a News-
paper's Account of the Assassination of a President and the
Two Weeks That Followed. Nashville: the Nashville
Tennessean, 1965.

1538. Smith, A. Merriman. The Murder of the Young President.
United Press International, n.d.

1539. United Press International and American Heritage Maga-
zine (Compilers). Four Days; the Historical Record of the
Death of President Kennedy. Foreword by Bruce Catton. New
York: American Heritage Publishing Co., 1964.

1540. Van Der Karr, Richard K. "Crisis in Dallas: an
Historical Study of the Activities of Dallas Television
Broadcasters During the Period of President Kennedy's Assassi-
nation." Bloomington, Indiana: M.A. Thesis, 1965.

Articles by Authors:

1541. Bell, Jack. "The Wrestling Match For the Scoop of the
Century," The National Tattler, XIX (25 Nov. 1973), 10.

1542. Biskind, Peter. "Larry Flynt Rises Up Angry," Seven Days, II (24 Feb. 1978), 25-27.

1543. Brucker, Herbert. "When the Press Shapes the News," Saturday Review, XLVII (11 Jan. 1964), 75-77, 85.

1544. Conquest, Robert. "A Spectator's Notebook: What Killed Kennedy? The Mythsmiths [The Haste Amongst Some Newsmen to Blame Everyone]," The Spectator (London), No. 7066 (29 Nov. 1963), 684.

1545. Cranberg, Gilbert. "Voluntary Press Codes," Saturday Review, LII (10 May 1969), 71-72.

1546. Cranston, Pat. "Some Historical Newscasts of the American Forces Network," Journalism Quarterly, XLI (1964), 395-398.

1547. David, Paul T. "The TV Image," The Nation, CXCVII (14 Dec. 1963), 413-414.

1548. Diehl, William F., Jr. "The Press: Its Actions and Reactions," New Orleans Magazine, I (April 1967), 12-13, 52-53.

1549. Desrosiers, Bob. "Aynesworth on Hand as History Unfolds," Editor & Publisher, XCVII (11 July 1964), 38.

1550. Dunning, John L. "The Kennedy Assassination as Viewed by Communist Media," Journalism Quarterly, XLI (Spring 1964), 163-169.

1551. Ellison, Jerome. "Television: Stimulant to Violence . . . ," The Nation, CXCVII (21 Dec. 1963), 433-436.

1552. Ephron, Nora. "Media: Twelve Years on the Assassination Beat," Esquire, LXXXV (Feb. 1976), 58-62.

1553. Erwin, Ray. "Columnists Change Copy Immediately," Editor & Publisher, XCVI (7 Dec. 1963), 54.

1554. Friedman, Rick. "The Kennedy Story," Editor & Publisher, XCVI (7 Dec. 1963), 44-46.

1555. Goodhart, Arthur L. "The Mysteries of the Kennedy Assassination and the English Press," The Law Quarterly Review, LXXXIII (1967), 22-63.

1556. Greenberg, Bradley S. "Diffusion of News of the Kennedy Assassination," Public Opinion Quarterly, XXVIII (1964), 225-232.

1557. Grove, Larry. "Did Press Pressure Kill Oswald?" The Quill, LII (March 1964), 16-20.

1558. Heilbroner, Robert.   "The Murder," The Correspondent,
No. 30 (Jan.-Feb. 1964), 3.

1559. Hill, Gladwin. "The Literary Frontier: the Press and
the Assassination--Dispelling Some Illusions," Frontier, XVII
(March 1966), 17-20.

1560. Hill, Richard J., and Charles M. Bonjean. "News
Diffusion: a Test of the Regularity Hypothesis," Journalism
Quarterly, XLI (1964), 336-342.

1561. Hood, Stuart. "Television: The Marathon," The
Spectator (London), No. 7232 (3 Feb. 1967), 131-132.

1562. Horn, John. "What Was Seen and Read [at the Time of
JFK's Assassination]," Columbia Journalism Review, II (Winter
1964), 18-25.

1563. Houston, Darrell. "To SOB or Not to SOB: That's Heady
Question," Editor & Publisher, XCVII (21 March 1964), 46.

1564. Jaffe, Louis L. "Trial by Newspaper," New York University Law Review, XL (1965), 504-524.

1565. Johnson, Bob. "Too Busy for Tears: His Staff During
the Assassination," The AP World, XXIX (Aug. 1972), 14-23.

1566. Johnson, Earl J. "JFK Story Costly to Newspapers,
Too," Editor & Publisher, XCVII (7 March 1964), 12.

1567. Jones, Gerre. "Lesson in Propaganda: How the Communists Reported President Kennedy's Assassination," The Quill,
LII (March 1964), 27-29.

1568. Krueger, Albert R. "Four Days; TV Coverage of Events
Surrounding Death of President Kennedy," Television, XXI (Jan.
1964), 27-33, 54-60.

1569. Lane, Mark. "Who Killed Kennedy? CBS is Wrong,"
True, XLVIII (Dec. 1967), 34, 78-81.

1570. Love, Ruth. "Television and the Kennedy Assassination," New Society (London), (13 Oct. 1966), 567-571.

1571. Maley, Don. "Newsmen Tell How JFK Murder Affects
World," Editor & Publisher, CI (30 Nov. 1968), 36.

1572. Mendelsohn, Harold. "Broadcast vs. Personal Sources
of Information in Emergent Public Crises: the Presidential
Assassination," Journal of Broadcasting, VIII (1964), 147-156.

1573. _____. "Comment on Spitzer's '. . . A
Comparison of Six Investigations'," Journal of Broadcasting,
IX (1964-5), 51-54.

1574.   Perry, George.   "The Man Who Killed Kennedy [The BBC-1 Play of the Month, Written by Felix Lützkendorf for TV from His Theatre Play]," The Sunday Times Magazine (London), No. 7451 (13 March 1966), 44-45;   See 2645 .

1575.   Pett, Saul, et al.   "How the Associated Press Covered the Kennedy Tragedy," The AP World, XVIII (Winter 1963-64), 3-6.

1576.   Policoff, Jerry.   "The Media and the Murder of John Kennedy," New Times (New York), V (8 Aug. 1975), 28-36.

1577.   Porter, William E.   "How the People Heard," Columbia Journalism Review, IV (Winter 1966), 47-48.

1578.   Roberts, Charles.   "Eyewitness in Dallas," Newsweek, LXVIII (5 Dec. 1966), 26-29.

1579.   Rivers, Caryl.   "Warren Report Slaps Press and Calls for Ethics Code; News Media Share in Blame for Killing JFK's Assassin,"   Editor & Publisher, XCVII (3 Oct. 1964), 13, 57.

1580.   Schuyler, Philip N.   "It's Still an Open Book for Dallas City Desks," Editor & Publisher, XCVI (30 Nov. 1963), 18, 66-67.

1581.   Shayon, Robert Lewis.   "The Relevant Question," Saturday Review, XLVI (14 Dec. 1963), 23.

1582.   _____ .   "The Persistent Devils: CBS News Inquiry: the Warren Report," Saturday Review, L (22 July 1967), 46.

1583.   Smith, A. Merriman.   "U.P.I. Reporter, Washington, Nov. 23," Editor & Publisher, XCVI (30 Nov. 1963), 8-10.

1584.   Spitzer, Stephan P.   "Mass Media vs. Personal Sources of Information About the Presidential Assassination: a Comparison of Six Investigations," Journal of Broadcasting, IX (1964-5), 45-50.

1585.   Spitzer, Stephan P., and Norman K. Denzin.   "Levels of Knowledge in an Emergent Crisis," Social Forces, XLIV (Dec. 1965), 234-237.

1586.   Sprague, Richard E.   "American News Media and the Assassination of President John F. Kennedy: Accessories After the Fact," Computers and Automation, XXII (June 1973), 36-40; (July 1973), 31-38.

1587.   Stone, Allen.   "Tunnel Vision at CBS," New Times (New York), V (8 Aug. 1975), 34.

1588.   Thomas, Robert E.   "What 187 Papers Did With Kennedy Story," Editor & Publisher, XCVIII (18 Sept. 1965), 41-42.

1589. Tobin, Richard L. "If You Can Keep Your Head When All About You . . .," Saturday Review, XLVI (14 Dec. 1963), 53-54; XLVII (11 Jan. 1964), 74.

1590. Tuchman, Mitch. "Kennedy Death Films," Take One, VI (May 1978), 18-22.

1591. Waters, Harry F. "Television: Recipe for Paranoia [Reviews ABC-TV's "The Trial of Lee Harvey Oswald"]," Newsweek, XC (3 Oct. 1977), 64-65.

1592. Wicker, Tom. "A Reporter Must Trust His Instinct," Saturday Review, XLVII (11 Jan. 1964), 81-82, 86.

Anonymous Articles:

1593. "Print, Radio-TV Ads, Programs Canceled [sic] After Assassination," Advertising Age, XXXIV (25 Nov. 1963), 8.

1594. "Unprecedented Four-Day Coverage of JFK Death Cost All Media Millions," Advertising Age, XXXIV (2 Dec. 1963), 1.

1595. "Many Advertisers to Accept 'Make-Goods' Where Feasible [That Is, Delayed Broadcasts of Commercials]," Advertising Age, XXXIV (2 Dec. 1963), 112.

1596. "Response Is Slow to Plea by TVB to Reschedule Ads; But Pan Am Waives Rights to Its Canceled [sic] Commercials on Networks," Advertising Age, XXXIV (9 Dec. 1963), 80.

1597. "Editorials: Tribute to Television," America, CIX (7 Dec. 1963), 729; CIX (14 Dec. 1963), 759.

1598. "World Press Comment [on JFK Assassination]," Atlas, VII (Jan. 1974), 7; (Feb. 1974), 69, 75-76.

1599. "A World Listened and Watched," Broadcasting, LXV (2 Dec. 1963), 36-61.

1600. "Make-Goods Still in a Fluid State: Rescheduling of TV Spots Generally Lagging Behind Radio," Broadcasting, LXV (9 Dec. 1963), 32.

1601. "Congress Continues Praise for Industry," Broadcasting, LXV (9 Dec. 1963), 62.

1602. "Media Raked Over the Coals for Oswald Play," Broadcasting, LXV (9 Dec. 1963), 70-71.

1603. "Networks Praised by a Grateful Public," Broadcasting, LXV (9 Dec. 1963), 71.

1604. "73 Per Cent Accept Make-Goods on Major Independent," Broadcasting, LXV (23 Dec. 1963), 38.

1605. "TV's Biggest Audience; Neilsen Reports That 96.1 Per Cent of TV Homes Watched JFK Assassination Coverage for 31.63 Hours," Broadcasting, LXVI (3 Feb. 1964), 54-55.

1606. "Network TV Dropped 8.2 Per Cent; TVB Estimates $9.5 Million Lost in JFK Coverage," Broadcasting, LXVI (24 Feb. 1964), 44.

1607. "Kennedy Coverage a National Service," Broadcasting, LXVI (15 June 1964), 62.

1608. "Aftermath of Warren Report; Radio-TV Joins Mass Effort to Re-Evaluate Media's Position," Broadcasting, LXVII (5 Oct. 1964), 50.

1609. "TV Sees It Now, For Seventy Hours; Massive Effort Pays Off in Rare Drama, Brings Industry New Role," Business Week, No. 1787 (30 Nov. 1963), 34.

1610. "Editorial: Denounces Press and Police," The Christian Century, LXXXI (22 Jan. 1964), 103.

1611. "The Assassination: the Reporter's Story," Columbia Journalism Review, II (Winter 1964), 5-17.

1612. "Journalism's Role: Unresolved Issues [Raised by the JFK Assassination]," Columbia Journalism Review, II (Winter 1964), 26-31.

1613. "The Assassination of President John F. Kennedy," The Current Digest of the Soviet Press, XV (11 Dec. 1963), 3-15.

1614. "Soviet Press Comment Following Kennedy's Death: from Za Rubezhom, Pravda, and Izvestia," The Current Digest of the Soviet Press, XV (18 Dec. 1963), 3-7.

1615. "Aberrations of Bourgeois Democracy: the Right to Deny Rights," The Current Digest of the Soviet Press, XVI (1 Jan. 1964), 25.

1616. "Assassination Edition: The Midlothian [Texas] Mirror," Editor & Publisher, XCVI (30 Nov. 1963), 68.

1617. "Four Days; UPI-Heritage Book," Editor & Publisher, XCVI (7 Dec. 1963), 11.

1618. "Lone Pro on Scene Where JFK Was Shot [James W. Altgens]," Editor & Publisher, XCVI (7 Dec. 1963), 11, 61.

1619. "Assassination Story," Editor & Publisher, XCVI (7 Dec. 1963), 58-59.

1620. "The Torch Is Passed, AP's 100-Page Book," Editor & Publisher, XCVI (14 Dec. 1963), 13.

1621. "UPI-Heritage Book Orders Top 500,000," Editor & Publisher, XCVI (14 Dec. 1963), 13.

1622. "AP's 'Torch' Book Orders Near Million," Editor & Publisher, XCVI (28 Dec. 1963), 10.

1623. "President's Death Tops '63 Stories," Editor & Publisher, XCVI (28 Dec. 1963), 10.

1624. "Second Printing Is Needed to Fill 'Four Days' Order," Editor & Publisher, XCVI (28 Dec. 1963), 10.

1625. "Collector's Club Seeks Assassination Editions," Editor & Publisher, XCVI (28 Dec. 1963), 11.

1626. "Journalism-Students Practiced What Was Preached," Editor & Publisher, XCVI (28 Dec. 1963), 26.

1627. "Orders for Kennedy Books Top 3 Million," Editor & Publisher, XCVII (11 Jan. 1964), 13.

1628. "News Beat: The Weekly Mesquite Texas Mesquiter Claimed a 36-Hour Beat . . . Linking Lee Harvey Oswald With Sniping at Gen. Edwin A. Walker," Editor & Publisher, XCVII (11 Jan. 1964), 38.

1629. "Readers Enjoy Being Told How Big Story Is Handled," Editor & Publisher, XCVII (1 Feb. 1964), 49.

1630. "The Torch Is Passed Orders Are Mounting [from 8 Foreign-Language Editions]," Editor & Publisher, XCVII (1 Feb. 1964), 58.

1631. "Dallas Editors Hit 'Foreigners' [for their JFK Assassination Reports]," Editor & Publisher, XCVII (8 Feb. 1964), 54.

1632. "Kennedy Booklet Sales Continue [for Milwaukee's Newspapers' Booklet = 100,000 Copies]," Editor & Publisher, XCVII (22 Feb. 1964), 34.

1633. "Detroit Reporter Gets Oswald Album Pictures," Editor & Publisher, XCVII (22 Feb. 1964), 61.

1634. "Four Days Tops Best-Seller Lists," Editor & Publisher, XCVII (21 March 1964), 55.

1635. "Book Aids Library [Part of Four Days Profit to JFK Library]," Editor & Publisher, XCVII (28 March 1964), 14.

1636. "ASNE Speakers Condemn 'Mass Coverage' in Dallas," Editor & Publisher, XCVII (18 April 1964), 15, 151; (25 April 1964), 6, 112.

1637. "Papers' Sales Soared When JFK Died," Editor & Publisher, XCVII (18 April 1964), 22.

1638. "Front Page Album on JFK Goes on Sale," Editor & Publisher, XCVII (18 April 1964), 40.

1639. "'The Warren Report': 55 People Given Credit for 9-Month News Probe," Editor & Publisher, C (8 July 1967), 56.

1640. "Dallas Story Examined in 191 Papers [the Dean Baker Book]," Editor & Publisher, XCVII (1 Aug. 1964), 44.

1641. "Editors Will Study News Code Proposal," Editor & Publisher, XCVII (3 Oct. 1964), 12, 57.

1642. "In Dallas--A Year Later: If It All Happened Again," Editor & Publisher, XCVII (21 Nov. 1964), 9-10.

1643. "Editorials: Focus on Chapter V," The Nation, CXCIX (12 Oct. 1964), 205-206.

1644. "Newsmakers," Newsweek, LXII (9 Dec. 1963), 55.

1645. "TV-Radio: As 175 Million Americans Watched . . ." Newsweek, LXII (9 Dec. 1963), 88-90.

1646. "TV-Radio: Priceless Role," Newsweek, LXII (16 Dec. 1963), 56.

1647. "Press: More on JFK," Newsweek, LXIII (13 Jan. 1964), 53.

1648. "Press: A Big Sale," Newsweek, LXIII (2 March 1964), 80.

1649. "Press: '. . . A Little Dignity,'" Newsweek, LXIII (2 March 1964), 80.

1650. "National Affairs: The Assassination: A Piece of the Action," Newsweek, LXIII (9 March 1964), 31-32.

1651. "Press: The 'Mob' of Dallas," Newsweek, LXIII (27 April 1964), 76-77.

1652. "Press: Prize and Prejudice?" Newsweek, LXIII (18 May 1964), 74-76.

1653. "Press: [Harvard Law Dean Erwin Griswold's Critique of Lawyers Involved in JFK Assassination Events]," Newsweek, LXIV (24 Aug. 1964), 53.

1654. "Press: Reporting the Report," Newsweek, LXIV (12 Oct. 1964), 100-101.

1655. "Press: Pooling or Restraint?" Newsweek, LXIV (12 Oct. 1964), 101.

1656. "Press: Code for Justice?" Newsweek, LXV (26 Apr. 1965), 85.

1657.   "Press: Covering Big Jim [Garrison]," Newsweek, LXXIII (17 March 1969), 105.

1658.   "Newsmakers: Mort Sahl [and his Autobiography, Heartland, on the JFK Assassination]," Newsweek, LXXXVIII (9 Aug. 1976), 45.

1659.   "Newsmakers: [the ABC TV-movie 'The Trial of Lee Harvey Oswald']," Newsweek, XC (11 July 1977), 52; XC (15 Aug. 1977), 7-9.

1660.   "And the Advertising Business Stopped," Printers' Ink (Eastern Edition), CCLXXXV (29 Nov. 1963), 5-6.

1661.   "Plans of the Late President's Publisher [Harper & Row]," Publishers Weekly, CLXXXIV (2 Dec. 1963), 27.

1662.   "Plans for Official Book on Kennedy Assassination," Publishers Weekly, CXC (5 Sept. 1966), 40-41.

1663.   "Life Sues to Enjoin Book on Assassination of Kennedy [by Josiah Thompson]," Publishers Weekly, CXCII (25 Dec. 1967), 32.

1664.   "Does TV Crime Reporting Jeopardize Justice? Pro and Con Discussion," Senior Scholastic, LXXXIV (20 March 1964), 6-7.

1665.   "The Press: Covering the Tragedy," Time, LXXXII (29 Nov. 1963), 84.

1666.   "The Press: Editorials; Newspapers," Time, LXXXII (6 Dec. 1963), 81-82.

1667.   "The Press: Publishing: In Memoriam; Broadcasting," Time, LXXXII (20 Dec. 1963), 31-32.

1668.   "The Press: Newspapers: A Jackie Exclusive," Time, LXXXIX (24 March 1967), 63-64.

1669.   "People: That Haunting, Half-Familiar Figure With the Rifle Is Not Lee Harvey Oswald, But Actor John Pleshette . . . ," Time, CX (11 July 1977), 45.

1670.   "Television: Garbling History: 'The Trial of Lee Harvey Oswald,' ABC, Sept. 30 & Oct. 3," Time, CX (3 Oct. 1977), 91.

1671.   "America's Long Vigil," TV Guide, XII (25 Jan. 1964), 19-22.

1672.   "A Permanent Record of What We Watched from November 22-25 1963," TV Guide, XII (25 Jan. 1964), 23-45.

(5) STUDIES OF PUBLIC REACTIONS

Books:

1673.   Bradburn, Norman H., and Jacob J. Feldman. Public Apathy and Public Grief. Chicago: University of Chicago's National Opinion Research Center, 1964.

1674.   Cottrell, John. Assassination: The World Stood Still. London: New English Library, 1964; Muller, 1966.

1675.   Habe, Hans [pseudonym for Jean Bekessy]. The Wounded Land: Journey Through a Divided America. New York: Coward-McCann, 1964.

1676.   . Der Tod in Texas: eine amerikanische Tragödie [The Death in Texas: an American Tragedy]. Munich: K. Desch, 1964.

1677.   Greenberg, Bradley S., and Edwin B. Parker (eds.). The Kennedy Assassination and the American Public; Social Communication in Crisis. Stanford, California: Stanford University Press, 1965.

1678.   Wolfenstein, Martha, and Gilbert Kliman (eds.). Children and the Death of a President; Multi-Disciplinary Studies. Garden City, New York: Anchor Books, 1966; Gloucester, Massachusetts: Peter Smith, 1969.

Articles by Authors:

1679.   Ahler, J., and J. Tamney. "Some Functions of Religious Ritual in a Catastrophe: Kennedy Assassination," Sociological Analysis, XXV (1964), 212-230.

1680.   Appelbaum, Stephen A. "The Kennedy Assassination," The Psychoanalytic Review, LIII (Fall 1966), 69-80 [393-404].

1681.   Back, Kurt W., and Judith Saravay. "From Bright Ideas to Social Research: Studies of the Kennedy Assassination," Public Opinion Quarterly, XXXI (1967), 253-264.

1682.   Banta, Thomas J. "The Kennedy Assassination: Early Thoughts and Emotions," Public Opinion Quarterly, XXVIII (1964), 216-224.

1683.   Cuffaro, H. K. "Reaction of Pre-school Children to the Assassination of President Kennedy," Young Children, XX (Nov. 1964), 100-105.

1684.   Dies, Martin. "Assassination and Its Aftermath," American Opinion, VII (March 1964), 1-10; VII (April, 1964), 33-40.

1685. Fleming, D. F. "Foreword; Postscript [Measuring the Impact of JFK Murder]," The Annals of the American Academy of Political and Social Science, CCCLI (Jan. 1964), x, 180.

1686. Gilman, Richard. "The Fact of Mortality [National Introspection Provoked by JFK Murder]," Commonweal, LXXIX (13 Dec. 1963), 337-338.

1687. Gordon, William E. "World Vistas: The Assassination of President Kennedy," Contemporary Review (London), CCV (Jan. 1964), 8-13.

1688. Kaufman, Richard. "Kennedys Tod als Religionsersatz [Kennedy's Death as a Religion-Substitute]," Christ und Welt (Stuttgart), XX, No. 52 (1967), 28.

1689. Kirschner, David. "The Death of a President: Reactions of Psychoanalytic Patients," Behavioral Science, X (Jan. 1965), 1-6.

1690. Krupp, George R. "The Day the President Died: Its Meaning and Impact," Redbook Magazine, CXXII (March 1964), 49, 98-104.

1691. Langer, E. "Kennedy's Assassination: Study Organized by Social Scientists," Science, CXLII (13 Dec. 1963), 1446-1447.

1692. Levy, Alan. "The Day JFK Died: What People Remember Now," Good Housekeeping, CLXI (Nov. 1965), 84-87, 202-212, 224-226.

1693. Lineberry, William. "The Lingering 'Plot': Foreign Opinion and the Assassination [Arabs and East Europeans]," The New Leader, XLVII (27 April 1964), 21-22.

1694. Lipset, Seymour Martin. "Effects and Perils [in the JFK Assassination]," The Correspondent, No. 30 (Jan.-Feb. 1964), 8-11.

1695. O'Toole, James K. "Mourning a President [Reactions of Emotionally Disturbed Adolescent Females]," Psychiatric Quarterly, XL (1966), 737-755.

1696. Patterson, Samuel C. "Reactions to the Kennedy Assassination Among Political Leaders," Public Affairs (South Dakota), (15 May 1967), 1-5.

1697. Saltz, Eli, and John Wickey. "Resolutions of the Liberal Dilemma in the Assassination of President Kennedy," Journal of Personality, XXXIII (Dec. 1965), 636-648.

1698. Sheatsley, Paul B., and Norman M. Bradburn. "Assassination! How the American Public Responded," American Psychological Association, Los Angeles, (Sept. 1964).

1699. Sheatsley, Paul B., and Jacob J. Feldman. "The Assassination of President Kennedy: a Preliminary Report on Public Reactions and Behavior," Public Opinion Quarterly, XXVIII (1964), 189-215.

1700. Sicinski, Andrzej. "Dallas and Warsaw: the Impact of a Major National Political Event on Public Opinion Abroad," Public Opinion Quarterly, XXXIII (1969), 190-196.

1701. Stencel, Sandra. "How JFK's Murder Changed the Presidency . . . and Your Life," Skeptic, No. 9 (Aug. 1975), 37-42.

1702. Suinn, Richard M. "Note: Guilt and Depth of Reaction to the Death of a President," Psychoanalytic Review, LIII (Fall 1966), 81-82 [405-406].

1703. Tamney, Joseph B. "A Study of Involvement. Reactions to the Death of President Kennedy," Sociologus. Zeitschrift für empirische Soziologie, sozialpsychologische und ethnologische Forschung (Berlin), XIX, Hefte 1 (1969), 66-79.

Anonymous Articles:

1704. "Crime: Were Kennedy, King Conspiracy Victims? [Polled on Dec. 10-13, 1976]," The Gallup Opinion Index, No. 139 (Feb. 1977), 1-4.

1705. "Radio Poll Shows 10-1 Hold Oswald Innocent: After Lane Talk," National Guardian, XVI (29 Aug. 1964), 4.

1706. "The Assassination: Reactions in the South," Newsweek, LXII (16 Dec. 1963), 27.

1707. "Polls: Lingering Doubts," Newsweek, LXIII (6 Jan. 1964), 19.

1708. "National Affairs: Trials: How America Felt," Newsweek, LXIII (16 March 1964), 33.

1709. "Medicine: When Kennedy Died," Newsweek, LXIV (14 Sept. 1964), 61.

1710. "Psychology: Reaction to Killings," Science News Letter, LXXXIV (7 Dec. 1963), 358.

1711. "The Nation: The People: the Mood of the Land," Time, LXXXII (20 Dec. 1963), 9-10.

1712. "Europe: J.F.K.: the Murder & the Myths," Time, LXXXIII (12 June 1964), 44-47.

1713. "Two Presidents [Review of Cottrell, Assassination]," The Times Literary Supplement (London), No. 3,235 (27 Feb. 1964), 169.

1714. "When People Learned of Kennedy's Death," U.S. News and World Report, LV (30 Dec. 1963), 8.

(6) ASSASSINATIONS IN GENERAL: POLITICAL AND PSYCHOLOGICAL STUDIES

Books:

1715. Assassinations: the Murders that Changed History. London and New York: Marshall Cavendish Publications, Ltd., 1975.

1716. Bishop, George V. Executions: the Legal Ways of Death [Chapter XIV: Oswald's Death]. Los Angeles: Sherbourne Press, 1965.

1717. Blumenthal, Sid, and Harvey Yazijian (eds.). Government by Gunplay: Assassination Conspiracy Theories from Dallas to Today. Introduction by Philip Agee. New York: New American Library (Signet), 1976.

1718. Bowart, Walter. Operation Mind Control. New York: Delacorte, 1977.

1719. Crotty, William Joseph (ed.). Assassinations and the Political Order. New York: Harper & Row Torchbook, 1971.

1720. Havens, Murray, Carl Leiden, and Karl M. Schmitt. The Politics of Assassination. Englewood Cliffs, New Jersey: Prentice-Hall, 1970.

1721. Heaps, Willard A. Assassination: a Special Kind of Murder. New York: Meredith Press, 1969.

1722. Kirkham, James F., Sheldon G. Levy, and William J. Crotty. Assassination and Political Violence; a Report to the National Commission on the Causes and Prevention of Violence. Washington, D.C., 1969.

1723. Knight, Janet M. (ed.). Three Assassinations: the deaths of John and Robert Kennedy and Martin Luther King. New York: Facts of File, 1971.

1724. Lawrence, Lincoln. Were We Controlled? New Hyde Park, New York: University Books, 1967.

1725. Leek, Sybil, and Bert R. Sugar. The Assassination Chain. Foreword by Jack Anderson. New York: Corwin Books, 1976; Los Angeles: Pinnacle Books, 1977.

1726. Levine, Isaac D. Eyewitness to History; Memoirs and Reflections of a Foreign Correspondent for Half a Century. New York: Hawthorn Books, 1973.

1727. McConnell, Brian. Assassination. London: Frewin, 1969.

1728. _____. The History of Assassination. Nashville: Aurora Publishers, 1970.

1729. McKinley, James. Assassination in America. New York: Harper & Row, 1977.

1730. Marks, Stanley J. Coup d'état: November 22, 1963; the Conspiracies That Murdered President John F. Kennedy, the Rev. Martin Luther King, and Senator Robert F. Kennedy. Los Angeles: Bureau of International Affairs, 1970.

1731. Murray, Robert. The Great Conspiracy. Hamilton, Montana: Revere Press, 1968.

1732. Oglesby, Carl. The Yankee and Cowboy War: Conspiracies from Dallas to Watergate. Kansas City: Sheed Andrews and McMeel, 1976; New York: Berkeley Publishing Corp, 1977.

1733. Overstreet, Harry. The Strange Tactics of Extremism. New York: W. W. Norton & Co., 1964.

1734. Sparrow, Gerald. The Great Assassins. London: John Long, 1968.

1735. Vuilleumier, John Frédéric. Lincoln-Kennedy, eine tragische Parallele. Basel: Gute Schriften, 1965.

1736. Westerfield, Rex. Assassination. N.p.: Correction Please, Inc., 1968.

1737. Wilkinson, Doris Y. (ed.). Social Structure and Assa Assassination: the Sociology of Political Murder. Cambridge, Mass.: Schenkmen, 1976.

    Articles by Authors:

1738. Allen, Harry C. "Democracy and Violence," The Spectator (London), No. 7067 (6 Dec. 1963), 742-743.

1739. Arrighi, Paul. "L'assassinat d'un homme politique [Assassination of a Politician]," Revue. Littérature, histoire, arts et science des deux mondes (Paris), No. 20 (1965), 509-522.

1740. Berkeley, Edmund C. "Editorial: Computer-Assisted Analysis of Political Assassinations," Computers and Automation, XIX (May 1970), 6.

1741. Biller, Owen A. "Suicide Related to the Assassination of President John F. Kennedy," Suicide & Life-Threatening Behavior, VII (Spring 1977), 40-44.

1742.   Crotty, William S. [J.] "Presidential Assassination,"
Society, IX (May 1972), 18-29, 63.

1743.   [Crotty, William J.]. "Why Do Assassinations Happen?"
Science Digest, LXXIII (April 1973), 88-89.

1744.   Deitsch, David, Ron Freeman, and Edward C. Berkeley.
"'Patterns of Political Assassination'--Comments," Computers
and Automation, XIX (Nov. 1970), 9.

1745.   Douglas, George H. "Dispossessed and Unloved: the
Young Assassins," The Nation, CCXIV (19 June 1972), 778-780.

1746.   Fleming, Thomas J. "Before They Strike," This Week
Magazine (14 Nov. 1965), 2, 12.

1747.   Freedman, Lawrence Zelic. "Assassination: Psychopathology and Social Pathology Postgraduate Medicine," The
University of Chicago School of Medicine, XXXVII (June 1965),
650-658.

1748.   Fromm, Erich. "The Assassin," The Correspondent, No.
30 (Jan.-Feb. 1964), 3-4.

1749.   Herberg, Will. "Political Assassination: Two Historical Types," National Review, XX (2 July 1968), 656, 669.

1750.   Katz, Joseph. "President Kennedy's Assassination,"
Psychoanalytic Review, LI, No. 4 (1964), 121-129.

1751.   McDaniel, Charles-Gene. "The Assassinated," The
Christian Century, LXXXIX (1 Nov. 1972), 1112-1114.

1752.   Nelson, W. H. "Assassination," Canadian Forum, XLIII
(Jan. 1964), 219-220.

1753.   Orren, Karen and Paul Peterson. "Presidential
Assassination: a Case Study in the Dynamics of Political
Socialization," The Journal of Politics, XXIX (May 1967),
388-404.

1754.   Rothstein, David A. "Presidential Assassination Syndrome," Archives of General Psychiatry, XI (1964), 245-254.

1755.   _____. "Psychiatric Implications of
Information Theory," Archives of General Psychiatry, XIII
(1965), 87-94.

1756.   Schreiber, Flora R., and Melvin Herman. "November 22,
1963: a Psychiatric Evaluation," Science Digest, LVIII (July
1965), 39-41.

1757.   Sebastiani, Joseph A., and James L. Foy. "Psychotic
Visitors to the White House," The American Journal of Psychiatry, CXXII (Dec. 1965), 679-686.

1758. Slomich, Sidney J., and Robert E. Kantor. "Social Psychopathology of Political Assassination," Bulletin of the Atomic Scientists, XXV (March 1969), 9-12.

1759. Weinstein, Edwin A., and Olga G. Lyerly. "Symbolic Aspects of Presidential Assassination," Psychiatry, XXXII (1969), 1-11.

1760. Weisz, Alfred E., and Robert L. Taylor. "The Assassination Matrix," Stanford Today, Series II (Winter 1969), 11-17.

Anonymous Articles:

1761. "Psychic Predicted New Mystery Figure in JFK Death Probe," The National Enquirer (5 Sept. 1978), 11.

1762. "International: South Africa: The Mind of an Assassin [Compared to Oswald]," Newsweek, LXVIII (31 Oct. 1966), 56-58.

1763. "Skeptic Backgrounder: Assassinations from Nizam al-Mulk to Robert F. Kennedy," Skeptic, No. 9 (Aug. 1975), 6, 44-48.

1764. "Schwert, Pistolen und Dynamit. Politische Attentate im 20. Jahrhundert [Sword, Pistol, and Explosives. Political Assassination in the Twentieth Century]," Der Spiegel (Hamburg), XVII, No. 49 (1963), 90-99.

1765. "Medicine: Psychiatry: The Kennedy Round [at American Psychiatric Association's Conference]," Time, LXXXIII (15 May 1964), 64.

1766. "Behavior: Is the Victim Guilty?," Time, XCVIII (5 July 1971), 42.

1767. "Time Essay: Did America Shoot Wallace?," Time, XCIX (29 May 1972), 26-27.

1768. "The Nation: Protecting the President," Time, CVI (6 Oct. 1975), 6-11.

1769. "Other Malefactors [Review of McConnell, Assassination]," The Times Literary Supplement (London), No. 3,543 (22 Jan. 1970), 93.

1770. "Red Agitation: How Big a Role in Assassinations?," U.S. News and World Report, LVII (24 Aug. 1964), 13.

1771. "Assassins: Rising Danger in America," U.S. News and World Report, LXVII (10 Nov. 1969), 15.

Part IV: Later Inquiries
(1) EXECUTIVE INVESTIGATIONS: THE ROCKEFELLER COMMISSION, THE CIA AND CUBA

Books:

1772. Alexander, Shana. Talking Woman. New York: Delacorte Press, 1976; Dell, 1977.

1773. Ashman, Charles. The CIA-Mafia Link. New York: Manor Books, 1975.

1774. Canfield, Michael, and Alan J. Weberman. Coup d'état in America: the CIA and the Assassination of John F. Kennedy. Foreword by Henry B. Gonzalez. New York: The Third Press, 1975; [See 4812, 4898].

1775. De Vosjoli, P. L. Thyraud. Lamia. Boston: Little, Brown and Co., 1970.

1776. Hepburn, James. Farewell America. Vaduz, Liechten-stein: Frontiers, 1968. Also published as: Verschworung/ Die Hintergrunde des Politischen Mort in den USA (Düsseldorf: Econ Verlag, 1968); and, L'Amerique Brule (Paris: Nouvelles Frontiers, 1968); [See 1895, 2607, 2650, 2651, 4566].

1777. Johnson, Haynes. The Bay of Pigs: the Leaders Story of Brigade 2506. New York: W. W. Norton & Dell Paperback, 1964.

1778. Munson, Lyle Hugh. Stifle the Legend [Ex-CIA Man Points to Castro]. New York: Bookmailer, 1964.

1779. Powers, Barbara (Moore). Spy Wife. New York: Pyramid Books, 1965.

1780. Prouty, Leroy Fletcher. The Secret Team: the CIA and Its Allies in Control of the United States and the World. Englewood Cliffs, New Jersey: Prentice-Hall, 1973.

1781. Scott, Peter Dale. Crime and Cover-up: the CIA, the Mafia, and the Dallas-Watergate Connection. Berkeley, Calif-ornia: Westworks, 1977.

1782. [U.S. Government.] Commission on CIA Activities Within the United States: the Nelson Rockefeller Report to the Pre-sident. New York: Manor Books, 1975.

Articles by Authors:

1783. Alexander, Shana. "The Assassination of President Kennedy: Real Gardens, Real Toads . . . CIA ," Redbook, CXLVI (Jan. 1976), 77, 109-112.

1784. Alsop, Stewart. "Hogwash About the CIA," The Saturday Evening Post, CCXXXVII (15 Feb. 1964), 15.

1785. Bernstein, Carl. "The CIA and the Media: How America's Most Powerful News Media Worked Hand in Glove . . . ," Rolling Stone, No. 250 (20 Oct. 1977), 55-67.

1786. Brogan, Patrick. "CIA Had No Part in Assassination of President Kennedy, Rockefeller Commission Says: Congress Pressure for Full Report," The Times (London), No. 59,420 (12 June 1975), 5.

1787. Cook, John. "Who Killed King [and JFK]? More FBI-CIA Questions," [National] Guardian, XXVIII (10 Dec. 1975), 4.

1788. Cohen, Jeff, and Donald Freed. "CIA Pins JFK Murder on Castro," [National] Guardian, XXIX (22 Dec. 1976), 7.

1789. Crewdson, John. "Alleged CIA Involvement in Kennedy Murder [Rockefeller Commission Hearings]," The Times (London), No. 59,339 (8 March 1975), 4.

1790. Curtat, Robert. "'America Burns' [Review of Hepburn's Book]," Atlas, XVII (April 1969), 48-49.

1791. Faller, J. "CIA Who-Done-It Thrills Madison," WIN, XI (10 April 1975), 12.

1792. Fensterwald, Bernard, and George O'Toole. "The CIA and the Man Who Was Not Oswald," New York Review of Books, XXII (3 April 1975), 24-25.

1793. Fenton, D. "The Rockefeller Commission," Ann Arbor Sun, III (6 June 1975), 11.

1794. [Flynt, Larry]. "JFK Murder Solved: Killing Coordinated by CIA," Los Angeles Free Press, Special Report Number One, n.d.

1795. Freed, D. "Anti-Castro Cubans/ CIA Labor Pool," Black Panther, XI (26 Jan. 1974), 10.

1796. Hepburn, James. "The Central Intelligence Agency: a Short History to Mid-1963," Computers and Automation, XXI (Nov. 1972), 32-36; XXI (Dec. 1972), 34-37.

1797. Hinckle, Warren, III. "The Mystery of the Black Books [History of the Book by Hepburn]," Esquire, LXXIX (April 1973), 128-131, 170-174.

1798. Hoffman, E. "A Day's Work at the Company," Ann Arbor Sun, III (20 June 1975), 8.

1799. Katz, J. "Kennedy Killing/CIA Connection," New American Movement Newspaper, IV (May 1975), 2.

1800. Lane, Mark. "CIA Killed JFK to Keep War Going," Los Angeles Free Press, VII (7 Aug. 1970), 8.

1801. LF. "Secret Memos Implicate CIA," Workers World, XVII (14 Nov. 1975), 7.

1802. Moldea, Dan E. "The Hoffa Wars [Organized Crime, the CIA, the Teamsters and the JFK Assassination]," Playboy, XXV (Nov. 1978), 140-144, 256-262, 266-274.

1803. O'Toole, George, and Paul Hoch. "Dallas: the Cuban Connection," The Saturday Evening Post, CCXLVIII (March 1976), 44-45, 96.

1804. Popkin, Richard H. "On Daniel Schorr, Castro, the CIA and the Lone Nut Theory of the Kennedy Assassination," Saint Louis Literary Supplement, II (Jan.-Feb. 1978), 3-5.

1805. Rosen, D. "They Shoot People, Don't They?" Liberation, XIX (Sept. 1975), 44.

1806. Russell, Dick. "What Was in the CIA's Declassified JFK File? New Assassination Questions," Village Voice, XXI (26 April 1976), 17-20.

1807. Schulz, Donald E. "Kennedy and the Cuban Connection," Newsweek, LXXXVIII (6 Sept. 1976), 9.

1808. Scott, Peter Dale. "From Dallas to Watergate: the Longest Cover-up," Ramparts, XII (Nov. 1973), 12-17, 20, 53-54.

1809. _____. "Letters: The CIA's Mystery Man," New York Review of Books, XXII (17 July 1975), 44.

1810. Thurston, Samuel F. [pseudonym for Richard E. Sprague]. "The Central Intelligence Agency and The New York Times [The Otepka Case and RFK]," Computers and Automation, XX (July 1971), 51-57.

1811. Viorst, Milton. "The Mafia, the CIA, and the Kennedy Assassination," Washingtonian, XI (Nov. 1975), 113-118.

1812. Wecht, Cyril H. "Why Is the Rockefeller Commission So Single-Minded About a Lone Assassin in the Kennedy Case?" The Journal of Legal Medicine, III (July/Aug. 1975), 22-25.

1813. _____. "A Post-Mortem on the 'Warrenfeller' Commission," Juris: Duquesne University School of Law, (Dec. 1975), 3-7.

1814. Williams, Charles. "The Murder of Malcolm X, the Kennedy Assassination, and the CIA," Black Politics, I (Feb. 1968), 5-15.

Anonymous Articles:

1815. "CIA: Who Killed Kennedy? [Daniel Schorr and L. Fletcher Prouty vs. Richard Helms]," The Economist (London), CCLV (3 May 1975), 80.

1816. "Assassinations of Bobby, JFK and King All Plotted by CIA," The National Enquirer (14 July 1968), 16-17.

1817. "Rocky's Panel Distorted My Evidence in Latest Probe into JFK Assassination [and the CIA]," The National Enquirer (19 Aug. 1975), 17.

1818. "Notes and Comments [On CIA's Assassination Plans]," The New Yorker, LI (8 Dec. 1975), 33.

1819. "National Affairs: JFK: Clean Bill for CIA [the Rockefeller Commission's Conclusions]," Newsweek, LXXXV (23 June 1975), 21.

1820. "On the Trail of the Rogue [CIA]," The Saturday Evening Post, CCXLVIII (25 Dec. 1975), 74.

1821. "Hunt Harassed for JFK Assassination," Takeover, V (23 Jan. 1975), 2.

1822. "CIA and Politics of Assassination," Takeover, V (13 March 1975), 8.

1823. "CIA Jack Off Exposed," Takeover, V (1 Aug. 1975), 14.

1824. "The CIA: The Kennedy Connection [Investigations by Senator Church, and Rockefeller Commission]," Time, CV (2 June 1975), 10.

1825. "CIA: Leaving Murky Murders to the Senate [Previews Rockefeller Commission's Conclusions]," Time, CV (16 June 1975), 9-10.

1826. "Investigations: Rocky's Probe: Bringing the CIA to Heel," Time, CV (23 June 1975), 6-16.

1827. "Those Charges Against the CIA: What the Record Shows," U.S. News and World Report, LXXIX (25 Aug. 1975), 38-41.

(2) CONGRESSIONAL INVESTIGATIONS: SCHWEIKER, ABZUG, PIKE-EDWARDS, AND DOWNING-GONZALEZ-STOKES COMMITTEES

Articles by Authors:

1828. Alpern, David M. "National Affairs: Self-Inflicted Wounds [Gonzales vs. Sprague]," Newsweek, LXXXIX (21 Feb. 1977), 18-21.

1829. _____ . "National Affairs: Are There New
Leads?," Newsweek, LXXXIX (11 April 1977), 32-37.

1830. _____. "JFK: A Telltale Tape?," Newsweek,
XCII (1 Jan. 1979), 21.

1831. Belin, David W. "The Kennedy Assassination: The
Second-Gunman Syndrome," National Review, XXXI (27 April 1979),
534-536, 533-555.

1832. Binyon, Michael. "Feud Splits Committee in Search of
Assassins [Chairman Gonzalez Dismisses Mr. Richard Sprague],"
The Times (London), No. 59,932 (12 Feb. 1977), 4.

1833. Blakey, G. Robert. "Don't Write Off a Second Gunman,"
The Washington Star (16 May 1979).

1834. Brogan, Patrick. "Kennedy Inquiry Finds Oswald Acted
Alone [The Senate Sub-Committee Report Condemning J. Edgar
Hoover's Role]," The Times (London), No. 59,738 (24 June 1976),
6.

1835. _____ . "The Inquiry That Priced Itself Out
[House Committee and Mr. Richard Sprague's Expensive Plans],"
The Times (London), No. 59,919 (28 Jan. 1977), 8.

1836. _____ . "Congress Goes on With Hunt for
Assassins [After George de Mohrenschildt's Suicide]," The
Times (London), No. 59,967 (1 April 1977), 9.

1837. Cadden, Vivian. "The Murder of President Kennedy [The
Church Committee Report]," McCalls, CIV (March 1977), 119-120,
157-172.

1838. Fraker, Susan, and Stephan Lesher. "Investigations:
Back to Square One," Newsweek, LXXXVIII (6 Dec. 1976), 32-35.

1839. Fraker, Susan, and Elaine Shannon. "Hints of the Mob
[Involvement in the JFK Assassination]," Newsweek, XCII (9
Oct. 1978), 44-47.

1840. Gans, Curtis. "Reopening the Warren Commission Investigation," Democratic Review, I (June/July 1975), 30-35.

1841. Gelman, David, and Elaine Shannon. "JFK: Settling
Some Doubts [about Recent Scientific Tests on the Assassination Evidence]," Newsweek, XCII (18 Sept. 1978), 29-30.

1842. _____ . "'A Tremendous
Insanity' [on Fidel Castro's Testimony, Along With Gerald
Ford and Richard Helms]," Newsweek, XCII (2 Oct. 1978), 62.

1843. Hager, Barry. "Law Enforcement and Judiciary: House
Move Reflects Questions on Cost of Assassination Probe," Congressional Quarterly Weekly Report, XXXV (8 Jan. 1977), 46-48.

1844. Jones, Kirby. "Unlikely Assassin [Castro Connection in Schweiker Report]," The New Republic, CLXXV (3 July 1976), 5-6.

1845. Kaiser, Robert B. "The JFK Assassination: Why Congress Should Reopen the Investigation," Rolling Stone, CLXXXV (24 April 1975), 27-28, 30-31, 33, 37-38.

1846. Kipling, Richard E. "Skeptic Forum: Should the Investigation Be Reopened?," Skeptic, No. 9 (Aug. 1975), 34-36, 62-64.

1847. Lardner, George, Jr. "Congress and the Assassinations," Saturday Review, IV (19 Feb. 1977), 14-17.

1848. O'Toole, George (ed.). "The Assassination Probe: Interviews H. B. Gonzales, T. N. Downing, and S. B. McKinley," The Saturday Evening Post, CCXLVII (Nov. 1975), 45-48, 112.

1849. Powers, Thomas. "J.F.K. - R.I.P." Commonweal, CIV (27 May 1977), 337-339; CIV (22 July 1977), 451, 478.

1850. Pringle, Peter. "Why US Wants Another Inquiry on Kennedy Death," The Sunday Times (London), No. 8012 (9 Jan. 1977), 5.

1851. _____. "JFK Story Gains a Mata Hari [Marita Lorenz's Accusations Against Frank Sturgis, Watergate Burglar]," The Sunday Times (London), No. 8055 (6 Nov. 1977), 9.

1852. Segal, Jeff. "Assassination Probe: Counsel Named [Richard Sprague]," [National] Guardian, XXIX (27 Oct. 1976), 11.

1853. _____. "New Leads in Kennedy, King Probe?: Investigators Angle for Big Budget," [National] Guardian, XXIX (12 Jan. 1977), 6.

1854. _____. "JFK, King Probe Falters in Congress," [National] Guardian, XXIX (20 March 1977), 5.

1855. _____. "New Light Shed on J.F.K. Murder [And the De Mohrenschildt Suicide]," [National] Guardian, XXIX (13 April 1977), 3.

1856. Shannon, William V. "Enough is Enough," Commonweal, LXXXV (18 Nov. 1966), 191-192; LXXXV (16 Dec. 1966), 331; LXXXV (13 Jan. 1967), 410-411.

1857. Silber, Irwin. "Fan the Flames [The Schweiker Committee]," [National] Guardian, XXVIII (12 Nov. 1975), 18.

1858. Stetler, Russell. "Can Congress Crack the Kennedy Assassination?," Inquiry (6 March 1978), 11-15.

1859. Ungar, Sanford J. "A New Man on Two Old Cases," The Atlantic Monthly, CCXXXIX (Feb. 1977), 8-14.

1860. ZNS. "Gonzales Reopens JFK Assassination," D.C. Gazette, V (May 1974), 24.

Anonymous Articles:

1861. "The Sprague Circus," The Economist (London), CCLXII (26 Feb. 1977), 49.

1862. "Assassinations: To Be Continued," The Economist (London), CCLXIII (9 April 1977), 31.

1863. "Editorials: Disclose the Evidence," The Nation, CCXXI (13 Dec. 1975), 611-612.

1864. "Lausche to Reopen JFK Assassination Probe," The National Enquirer (10 Jan. 1965), 8.

1865. "Congress Will Probe Kennedy Assassination," The National Enquirer (21 Feb. 1965), 8.

1866. "Congressional Leaders--Ted Kennedy Included--Rally Behind the Cry: 'Give Us All the Facts' [Gonzalez Committee]," The National Tattler, Special Edition (Sept. 1975), 6.

1867. "Washington Diarist: . . . Surely the Assassination of John Kennedy Might Now Be Left to Historians," The New Republic, CLXXIX (23 Sept. 1978), 42.

1868. "Umbrella Cover-Up [Testimony of Louie Steven Witt at JFK Hearings]," The New Republic, CLXXIX (7 Oct. 1978), 7-8.

1869. "Periscope: Pruning the Probers," Newsweek, LXXXIX (31 Jan. 1977), 13.

1870. "National Affairs: Congress: Death Trip," Newsweek, LXXXIX (14 Feb. 1977), 29.

1871. "Update: JFK's 'Close Friend' [on Judith Campbell Exner's Current Litigation]," Newsweek, XCII (18 Sept. 1978), 15.

1872. "The Law: The Tiger [Sprague]," Time, C (17 July 1972), 50-52.

1873. "Investigations: Sprague's Sprawl [House Select Committee on Assassinations]," Time, CIX (10 Jan. 1977), 17.

1874. "Investigations: Shrinking Sprague," Time, CIX (14 Feb. 1977), 24.

1875. "Congress: Assassination: Now a Suicide Talks [George de Mohrenschildt]," Time, CIX (11 April 1977), 20.

1876. "Nation: Dousing a Popular Theory [Gerald Ford and Fidel Castro on the JFK Assassination]," Time, CXII (2 Oct. 1978), 22.

1877. "Nation: The President and the Capo [Trafficante's Denials on the JFK Assassination]," Time, CXII (9 Oct. 1978), 31-32.

1878. "Nation: A Fourth Shot?: New Mystery in the JFK Case," Time, CXIII (1 Jan. 1979), 61-62.

1879. "Call for New Kennedy Death Inquiry [by Senator Richard Schweiker]," The Times (London), No. 59,496 (9 Sept. 1975), 6.

1880. "Cuba Link in Kennedy Assassination Claimed [According to Senator Richard Schweiker]," The Times (London), No. 59,741 (28 June 1976), 5.

1881. "Investigation into Kennedy--King Murders Reopens [Before Congressman Thomas Downing's Committee]," The Times (London), No. 59,812 (18 Sept. 1976), 1.

1882. "Congress Opens Kennedy Assassination File [According to Mr. Richard Sprague]," The Times (London), No. 59,829 (8 Oct. 1976), 10.

1883. "Silent Mafia Witness Rebuffs Committee [Mr. Santos Trafficante]," The Times (London), No. 59,954 (17 March 1977), 6.

1884. "Assassination--Behind Moves to Reopen JFK Case," U.S. News and World Report, LXXVIII (2 June 1975), 30-33.

1885. "Behind the Move to Reopen JFK Case [Senator Schweiker's Committee]," U.S. News and World Report, LXXIX (15 Sept. 1975), 21.

1886. "Charged: a Cover-Up in Kennedy Killing," U.S. News and World Report, LXXXI (5 July 1976), 21.

1887. "Why the JFK Case is Coming Back to Life," U.S. News and World Report, LXXXII (17 Jan. 1977), 28-30.

(3) THE NEW ORLEANS INVESTIGATION: JIM GARRISON

Books:

1888. Almanac of Jim Garrison's Investigation into the Assassination of John F. Kennedy: the Crime of Silence. Austin: Research Publications, 1968.

1889. Brener, Milton E. The Garrison Case. A Study in the Abuse of Power. New York: Clarkson N. Potter, 1969 [See 4638].

1890. Bringuier, Carlos. Red Friday: Nov. 22nd, 1963.
Chicago: Charles Hallberg & Co., 1969.

1891. Davis, William H. Aiming for the Jugular in New
Orleans. Port Washington, New York: Ashley Books, 1976.

1892. Epstein, Edward Jay. Counterplot. New York: Viking
Press, 1969; [See 4545, 4627].

1893. Flammonde, Paris. The Kennedy Conspiracy: An Un-
commissioned Report on the Jim Garrison Investigation. New
York: Meridith Press, 1969.

1894. Garrison, Jim. A Heritage of Stone. New York:
Putnam, 1970; Berkeley Paperback, 1975; [See 4668].

1895. Hinckle, Warren. If You Have a Lemon, Make Lemonade.
New York: G. P. Putnam's, 1974; Bantam, 1976.

1896. James, Rosemary, and Jack Wardlaw. Plot or Politics?
The Garrison Case and Its Cast. New Orleans: Pelican Publishing House, 1967.

1897. Joesten, Joachim. The Garrison Enquiry: Truth &
Consequences. London: Dawnay, 1967.

1898. Kirkwood, James. American Grotesque: An Account of
the Clay Shaw-Jim Garrison Affair in the City of New Orleans.
New York: Simon and Schuster, 1970; [See 4668].

1899. Sahl, Mort. Heartland. New York: Harcourt Brace
Jovanovich, 1976.

1900. Seigenthaler, John. A Search for Justice. Nashville,
Tennessee: Aurora Publishers, 1970; [See 973, 4685].

1901. Weisberg, Harold. Oswald in New Orleans. Case for
Conspiracy With the CIA. Foreword by Jim Garrison. New
York: Canyon Books, 1967.

Articles by Authors:

1902. Allen, Robert L. "New Questions Raised on JFK Killing: New Orleans D.A. Charges Conspiracy," National Guardian,
XIX (18 March 1967), 1, 9.

1903. [Arnoni, M. S.]. "An Assassination's Retroactivity
[and Garrison's Investigation]," The Minority of One, IX
(April 1967), 9.

1904. Arnoni, M. S. "Garrison and Warren: Anything in
Common?" The Minority of One, IX (Oct. 1967), 11-12.

1905. [Arnoni, M. S.]. "Of Demonologists and Eunuchs
[Praising Epstein's Attack on Garrison]," The Minority of
One, X (Sept. 1968), 8-9.

1906. Autry, James. "The Garrison Investigation: How and Why it Began," New Orleans Magazine, I (April 1967), 8-9, 50-51.

1907. Aynesworth, Hugh. "The JFK 'Conspiracy [According to New Orleans D.A. Garrison]," Newsweek, LXIX (15 May 1967), 36-40.

1908. Bennett, Liz. "Mrs. Garrison Talks About Home Life in the Midst of It All," New Orleans Magazine, I (April 1967), 10-11, 48.

1909. Boothby, Paul. "Letters: Abuse of Powers," The Nation, CCVIII (14 April 1969), 450, 468.

1910. Chin, Sylvia Fung. "Federal Courts: Federal Common Law Created To Allow Survival of Section 1983 Action to De-cedant's Executor [Shaw's]," Fordham Law Review, XLIV (Dec. 1975), 666-674.

1911. Cohen, Jerry, and Nicholas C. Chriss. "New Orleans: Act I," The Reporter, XXXVI (6 April 1967), 17-20.

1912. Epstein, Edward Jay. "A Reporter at Large: Garrison," The New Yorker, XLIV (13 July 1968), 35-81; [See 1892].

1913. Feldman, Harold, Maggie Field, Sylvia Meagher, Penn Jones, Jr., and Leo Sauvage. "From Readers' Letters: 'Garrison and Warren: Anything in Common?'," The Minority of One, IX (Dec. 1967), 29-30.

1914. Fensterwald, Bernard. "Jim Garrison, District Attor-ney, Orleans Parish vs. the Federal Government," Computers and Automation, XX (Aug. 1971), 37-42.

1915. Fife, Darlene. "Mark Lane on Oswald [Interview from Garrison's Perspective, New Orleans]," [National] Guardian, XX (6 April 1968), 6.

1916. _____. "Shaw Trial Opens," [National] Guardian, XXI (15 Feb. 1969), 6.

1917. Gifford, Alex. "Clay Shaw Tells His Story," Pub-lished by TV Station WVUE, Channel 12, New Orleans: 11 March 1969, 20 pp.

1918 _____. "Jim Garrison Tells His Story," Pub-lished by TV Station WVUE, Channel 12, New Orleans: 13 March 1969, 14 pp.

1919. Giquel, Bernard. "Bientot Toutes les Preuves [Soon All of the Evidence]," Paris Match, No. 935 (11 March 1967), 44-47.

1920. _____. "Le Mystère Kennedy--Le Procureur Garrison: 'J'irai Jusgu'au Bout' [The Kennedy Mystery:

Attorney Garrison: 'I will go to the bitter end']," Paris Match, No. 934 (4 March 1967), 52-54.

1921. Gun, Nerin E. "Le Mystere Kennedy--La Veille de sa Mort Ferrie m'a dit 'Oswald? Connais pas!' [The Kennedy Mystery: On the Eve of His Death, Ferrie Said to Me: 'Oswald? I Don't Know Him!'], Paris Match, No. 934 (4 March 1967), 67-68.

1922. Hockberg, Sandy, and James T. Valliere. "The Con-spirators: the Garrison Case," New York: Special Ed. of Win Magazine (1 Feb. 1969).

1923. Irons, Evelyn. "'Several Plots' Claims District Attorney," The Sunday Times (London), No. 7500 (26 Feb. 1967), 6.

1924. Jackson, Donald. "Book Review: A Heritage of Smoke [Reviews Garrison, A Heritage of Stone, and Kirkwood, American Grotesque]," Life, LXIX (4 Dec. 1970), 16.

1925. Jackson, John J., III. "State-Federal Relations: Enjoinment of State Criminal Prosecutions," Loyola Law Re-view, XVIII (1972), 207-216.

1926. Joesten, Joachim. "Jim Garrison klagt an. Sieben Jahre nach dem Mord an Präsident Kennedy [Jim Garrison's Litigation Seven Years after Kennedy's Murder]," Stimme der Gemeinde zum kirchlichen Leben, zur Politik, Wirtschaft und Kultur (Frankfurt/Main), XXIII (1971), 10-12.

1927. Kaufman, Allan Martin. "Old Medicine [Review of Hinckle Book]," The New Republic, CLXXII (15 Feb. 1975), 29-30.

1928. Kerby, Phil. "Please Mail Your Check Promptly to the Conspiracy of Your Choice [on Mort Sahl]," Frontier, XVIII (Feb. 1967), 12-13.

1929. Kirkwood, James. "Surviving: So Here You Are, Clay Shaw . . . ," Esquire, LXX (Dec. 1968), 218-221, 254-261.

1930. Knabb, Wayne M. "Shaw's Trial Covered by Reporters in Teams," Editor & Publisher, CII (15 Feb. 1969), 12.

1931. Lane, Mark. "J'espere que Garrison est Fort/ses Ennemis sont sans Pitie" [I Hope That Garrison Is Strong: His Enemies Are Merciless]," Paris Match, No. 934 (4 March 1967), 69.

1932. Lardner, George, Jr. "La. Suspect in JFK 'Plot' Found Dead," Washington Post (23 Feb. 1967).

1933. _____. "Murky, Improbable World of Ferrie," Washington Post (26 Feb. 1967).

1934. Macdonald, Neil. "District Attorney Jim Garrison on The Assassination of President Kennedy: a Review of Heritage of Stone," Computers and Automation, XX (March 1971), 45-46.

1935. Maddox, Henry. "The Plot According to Garrison," New Orleans Magazine, I (July 1967), 18-19, 52-53.

1936. Norden, Eric. "Jim Garrison: a Candid Conversation With the Embattled District Attorney of New Orleans," Playboy, XIV (Oct. 1967), 59-74, 156-176; [See 4444].

1937. Olds, Greg. "In My Opinion: Assassination," The Texas Observer, LX (26 July 1968), 15; (23 Aug. 1968), 15.

1938. Phelan, James. "A Plot to Kill Kennedy? Rush to Judgment in New Orleans," The Saturday Evening Post, CCXL (6 May 1967), 21-25; [See 4362].

1939. _____. "To Old New Orleans: the Vice Man Cometh," The Saturday Evening Post, CCXXXVI (8 June 1963), 67-71.

1940. Popkin, Richard H. "Garrison's Case," New York Review of Books, IX (14 Sept. 1967), 19-29.

1941. Powledge, Fred. "Is Garrison Faking?: The D.A., the CIA and the Assassination," The New Republic, CLVI (17 June 1967), 13-18.

1942. Rogers, Warren. "The Persecution of Clay Shaw," Look, XXXIII (26 Aug. 1969), 53-60.

1943. Ruge, Gerd. "Wie starb John F. Kennedy? Im Prozess von New Orleans geht es um Aufklärung, aber auch um handfeste Interessen [How did Kennedy Die? There Is Clarification from Proceedings in New Orleans - But Also a Sturdy Self-Interest], Die Zeit (Hamburg), XXIV, No. 8 (1969), 2.

1944. Schwelien, Joachim. "'Enthüllungen' über den Kennedy-Mord. Die Kampagne des Staatsanwaltes Garrison ['Disclosures About Kennedy's Murder. District Attorney Garrison's Campaign]," Die Zeit. (Hamburg), XXII, No. 11 (1967), 6.

1945. Shaw, Clay. "Clay Shaw Interviewed," Penthouse, (Nov. 1969), 26-30, 68.

1946. Sprague, Richard E. "Walter Sheridan--Democrats' Investigator? or Republicans' Countermeasure?" Computers and Automation, XXI (Nov. 1972), 29-31.

1947. Theis, William H. "Shaw v. Garrison: Some Observations on 42 U.S.C. §1988 and Federal Common Law," Louisiana Law Review, XXXVI (Winter 1976), 681-691.

1948. Turner, William W. "Assassination: Epstein's Garrison," Ramparts, VII (7 Sept. 1968), 8, 12.

1949. _____. "The Garrison Commission on the Assassination of President Kennedy," Ramparts, VI (Jan. 1968), 2, 43-68.

1950. _____. "The Plot Thickens [in New Orleans]," Ramparts, V (April 1967), 8-9.

1951. _____. "The Inquest [by Garrison]," Ramparts, V (June 1967), 17-29.

1952. _____. "The Press Versus Garrison," Ramparts, VI (Sept. 1967), 8-12.

1953. _____. "Shaw Verdict: Garrison Out, Investigation on," [National] Guardian, XXI (22 March 1969), 15.

1954. W[inston], F[rank]. "Conspiracy?: Undaunted Garrison Won't Rest His Case," The National Tattler, XIX (25 Nov. 1973), 28.

1955. Wood, William. "Ex-CIA Agent Tells His Role in Garrison's Conspiracy Probe," The National Tattler, Special Edition, (Sept. 1975), 4-5, 19.

1956. Young, Roger. "The Investigation: Where It Stands Today," New Orleans Magazine, I (July 1967), 16-17, 54-59.

Anonymous Articles:

1957. "Garrison to Seek Equal Time," Broadcasting, LXXII (26 June 1967), 72-73.

1958. "Will Garrison Take Half of Equal Time?" Broadcasting, LXXIII (10 July 1967), 71.

1959. "Sheridan to Answer Garrison in New Orleans," Broadcasting, LXXIII (17 July 1967), 48.

1960. "New Orleans Portion of the Conspiracy to Assassinate President John F. Kennedy," Computers and Automation, XXII (Apr. 1973), 34-39; XXII (May 1973), 30-32.

1961. "Garrison Under Fire," The Economist (London), CCXXII (25 Feb. 1967), 730.

1962. "Tales of Garrison," The Economist (London), CCXXII (25 March 1967), 1145.

1963. "Plot Thickening?" The Economist (London), CCXXIII (29 April 1967), 468.

1964. "Garrison's Way Out?" The Economist (London), CCXXVIII (20 July 1968), 40.

1965. "Who's on Trial?" The Economist (London), CCXXX (25 Jan. 1969), 21-22.

1966. "Endless Trials," The Economist (London), CCXXX (8 March 1969), 40-43.

1967. "District Attorney Miffed by Scoop on JFK Probe," Editor & Publisher, C (25 Feb. 1967), 10.

1968. "The Theory of an Oswald Conspiracy," Life, LXII (3 March 1967), 33.

1969. "Lenta Disparitie din Scena a lui Jim Garrison [Slow Disappearance from the Scene by Jim Garrison]," Lumea (Bucharest), V (22 June 1967), 97-100.

1970. "Editorials: Verdict in New Orleans," The Nation, CCVIII (17 March 1969), 324-325.

1971. "Key Witness in Garrison Probe Says: I was Offered $50,000 to Kill JFK," The National Enquirer (1 Sept. 1968), 4-5.

1972. "Judge Who Found Clay Shaw Innocent in JFK Plot Is Acquitted of Vice Charge," The National Enquirer (8 March 1970), 32.

1973. "Ex-DA Jim Garrison: I've Been Proved Right At Last About CIA Link With JFK's Death," The National Enquirer (15 June 1976), 47.

1974. "Report to Readers: Death and Intrigue in New Orleans," National Guardian, XIX (4 March 1967), 1-2.

1975. "Shaw Faces Trial in Kennedy Killing: Action by Judge Panel at New Orleans," National Guardian, XIX (1 April 1967), 3.

1976. "Shaw Trial Will Open," [National] Guardian, XXI (21 Dec. 1968), 9.

1977. "New JFK Evidence Unearthed," [National] Guardian, XXVIII (26 Nov. 1975), 7.

1978. "The Week: In a Blaze of Publicity . . . ," National Review, XIX (7 March 1967), 229.

1979. "JFK Assassination [Justice Department Publishes a Report by Doctors]," The New Republic, CLX (1 Feb. 1969), 9-10.

1980. "What Garrison Proved," The New Republic, CLX (15 March 1969), 9.

1981. "National Affairs: Assassination: Carnival in New Orleans," Newsweek, LXIX (6 March 1967), 32-34.

1982. "National Affairs: Assassination: History or Headlines?," Newsweek, LXIX (13 March 1967), 44-47.

1983. "Press: A Taste for Conspiracy," Newsweek, LXIX (20
March 1967), 76.

1984. "National Affairs: The Assassination: Thickening the
Plot," Newsweek, LXIX (27 March 1967), 37-38.

1985. "National Affairs: The Assassination: A Charge of
Conspiracy," Newsweek, LXIX (3 April 1967), 36-37.

1986. "National Affairs: New Orleans: Sleight of Hand,"
Newsweek, LXIX (22 May 1967), 40-42.

1987. "TV-Radio: Two for the Seesaw," Newsweek, LXX (3 July
1967), 82.

1988. "National Affairs: The Assassination: Law Unto Himself," Newsweek, LXXI (8 Jan. 1968), 25-26.

1989. "National Affairs: Investigations: Back in Business,"
Newsweek, LXXII (5 Aug. 1968), 26-27.

1990. "National Affairs: Trials: Curtains for the D.A.,"
Newsweek, LXXIII (27 Jan. 1969), 27.

1991. "National Affairs: Trials: Round One," Newsweek,
LXXIII (3 Feb. 1969), 33.

1992. "National Affairs: Trials: Mardi Gras Season," Newsweek, LXXIII (17 Feb. 1969), 34.

1993. "National Affairs: Trials: What Conspiracy?," Newsweek, LXXIII (24 Feb. 1969), 33.

1994. "National Affairs: Trials: Fact and Opinion," Newsweek, LXXIII (10 March 1969), 36.

1995. "The Periscope: D.A. Garrison's Re-Election Fight,"
Newsweek, LXXIV (18 Aug. 1969), 14.

1996. "National Affairs: New Orleans: Garrison Under Pressure," Newsweek, LXXIV (27 Oct. 1969), 42.

1997. "Newsmakers: [U.S. Justice Dept. Arrests Jim Garrison
on Bribery Charge]," Newsweek, LXXVIII (12 July 1971), 52.

1998. "Newsmakers: [Federal Government Prosecution of Jim
Garrison Continues]," Newsweek, LXXVIII (13 Dec. 1971), 61.

1999. "Newsmakers: [Acquittal of Jim Garrison on Federal
Charges of Bribery]," Newsweek, LXXXII (8 Oct. 1973), 64-65.

2000. "The Periscope: Dallas Revisited?," Newsweek, LXXXII
(22 Oct. 1973), 23.

2001. "Transition: Died: Clay L. Shaw, 60," Newsweek, LXXXIV (26 Aug. 1974), 43.

2002. "The Reporter's Notes: N.O. Evidence," The Reporter, XXXVIII (8 Feb. 1968), 10.

2003. "Kennedy Assassination: New Orleans Plot?" Senior Scholastic, XC (14 April 1967), 18-19.

2004. "JFK Assassination Plot?: Jury Clears Shaw," Senior Scholastic, XCIV (21 March 1969), 16.

2005. "'Kennedy starb im Kreuzfeuer'.   Spiegel-Gespräch mit dem Oberstaatsanwalt von New Orleans Jim Garrison ['Kennedy Died in a Crossfire'.   Interview with D.A. Jim Garrison]," Der Spiegel (Hamburg), XXI, No. 22 (1967), 108-120.

2006. "Political Intelligence: New Orleans," The Texas Observer, LVIII (3 March 1967), 10.

2007. "The Law: The Supreme Court: No Place for Seditious Libel," Time, LXXXIV (4 Dec. 1964), 48.

2008. "Louisiana: Odd Company," Time, LXXXIX (10 March 1967), 24-25.

2009. "The Assassination: Bourbon Street Rococo," Time, LXXXIX (3 March 1967), 26.

2010. "Investigations: The D.A. Wins a Round," Time, LXXXIX (24 March 1967), 17-18.

2011. "Medicine: Drugs: Sifting Fact from Fantasy [Garrison's Use of 'Truth Drugs']," Time, LXXXIX (31 March 1967), 41.

2012. "The Assassination: Closing In," Time, XC (7 July 1967), 17.

2013. "The Law: Trials: Shutting Up Big-Mouth," Time, XC (25 Aug. 1967), 48-51.

2014. "The Law: District Attorneys: Jolly Green Giant in Wonderland," Time, XCII (2 Aug. 1968), 56-57.

2015. "Trials: More Than a Man in the Dock," Time, XCIII (14 Feb. 1969), 26-29.

2016. "Trials: Dallas Revisited," Time, XCIII (21 Feb. 1969), 18-19.

2017. "Trials: Garrison's Last Gasp," Time, XCIII (7 March 1969), 23.

2018. "Trials: Garrison v. Everybody," Time, CII (8 Oct. 1973), 36.

2019. "Kennedy Inquiry Man Criticized: New Orleans Awaits Arrests: Is There Evidence of a Conspiracy?," The Times (London), No. 56,870 (20 Feb. 1967), 1, 12.

2020. "New Controversy on the Kennedy Assassination [Sparrow, Garrison, Lane]," The Times (London), No. 57,212 (28 March 1968), 6.

2021. "JFK Death: a New Investigation, But ---," U.S. News and World Report, LXII (13 March 1967), 16.

2022. "Order for a Trial in Assassination 'Plot'," U.S. News and World Report, LXII (27 March 1967), 10.

2023. "More on the Kennedy Assassination Charges," U.S. News and World Report, LXII (12 June 1967), 55-56.

(4) MANCHESTER-KENNEDY BOOK

Books:

2024. Bennett, Arnold. Jackie, Bobby and Manchester. New York: Bee Line Books, 1967.

2025. Corry, John. The Manchester Affair. New York: G. P. Putnam's Sons, 1967; [See 4431, 4442].

2026. Manchester, William Raymond. The Death of a President, November 20-November 25, 1963. New York: Harper & Row, 1967; Popular Library, n.d.; Baltimore: Penguin, 1978; [See 718, 973, 3604, 4349, 4350].

2027. Van Gelder, Lawrence. The Untold Story: Why the Kennedys Lost the Book Battle. New York: Award Books, 1967.

Articles by Authors:

2028. Anders, Peter. "Das Manchester-Buch [The Manchester-Book]," Zukunft. Sozialist Monatsschrift für Politik und Kultur (Vienna), Hefte XVII-XVIII (1967), 58.

2029. [Arnoni, M. S.] "Any Road That Leads to the White House (A Tragicomic Play in Many Acts) by Robert F. Kennedy," The Minority of One, IX (Feb. 1967), 7.

2030. Bedrick, Stephen B. "Cerf Says Assassination Book to Widen Kennedy-LBJ Rift," Yale Daily News, LXXXVIII (15 Dec. 1966), 1-3.

2031. Bowser, Hallowell. "The Perils of Hasty History," Saturday Review, XLIX (31 Dec. 1966), 14.

2032. Cafiero, L. H. "Manchester Book Alleges Com Lag Day JFK Killed," Electronic News, XII (3 April 1967), 22.

2033. Cannon, James M., and Edward Kosner. "Manchester's Own Story," Newsweek, LXIX (30 Jan. 1967), 21-22.

2034. Churchill, Randolph. "The Manchester Book: Anatomy of the Row With the Kennedy Family: Why Mrs. Kennedy Went to Law," The Times (London), No. 56,864 (13 Feb. 1967), 13; No. 56,865 (14 Feb. 1967), 11.

2035. _____. "Shivs, Kazzazza and Code 4," The Spectator (London), No. 7243 (21 April 1967), 447-449.

2036. Coit, Margaret L. "November 22, 1963," Saturday Review, L (15 April 1967), 30-31.

2037. Collins, R. S. "Kennedy vs. Look, Manchester Harper & Row; an Informal Glossary of Press Relations Techniques," Public Relations Journal, XXIII (April 1967), 13-15.

2038. Corry, John. "The Manchester Papers," Esquire, LXVII (June 1967), 83-91, 124-127, 164-171.

2039. Crawford, Kenneth. "The Holiday Spirit," Newsweek, LXIX (9 Jan. 1967), 25.

2040. Cuneo, Paul K. "Death of a President: Review of the Reviews," America, CXVI (6 May 1967), 684-685.

2041. Cunliffe, Marcus. "A Courtier's Obsequies," New Society (London), 20 Apr. 1967), 580-581.

2042. Dugger, Ronnie. "William Manchester and Texas," The Texas Observer, LVIII (20 Jan. 1967), 18-19; (3 Feb. 1967), 10.

2043. _____. "Manchestered," The Texas Observer, LVIII (17 Feb. 1967), 14-15.

2044. _____. "The Death of a President: The Book: Slanted Morbid, Sentimental, and Valuable; Confusion About LBJ, Youngblood," The Texas Observer, LVIII (14 April 1967), 4-5.

2045. Epstein, Edward Jay. "Manchester Unexpurgated: From 'Death of Lancer' to 'The Death of a President'," Commentary, XLIV (July 1967), 25-31.

2046. Featherstone, Joseph. "Last Flight from Dallas," The New Republic, CLVI (22 April 1967), 20-22.

2047. Fein, Arnold L. "The Legal Right of Privacy," Saturday Review, L (21 Jan. 1967), 26-27.

2048. Galbraith, John Kenneth. "Was Mrs. Kennedy Justified in Bringing Suit?" Saturday Review, L (21 Jan. 1967), 18-21.

2049. Gingrich, Arnold. "The Truth as Personal Property," Saturday Review, L (21 Jan. 1967), 22-23.

2050. _____. "Publisher's Page: The Truth as Private Property," Esquire, LXVII (March 1967), 6-12, 146.

2051. Hardwick, Elizabeth (with Arthur Schlesinger, Jr.). "Blow Up," New York Review of Books, VII (20 April 1967), 11-12; Letters (18 May 1967), 39; (1 June 1967), 34.

2052. Hughes, Emmet John. "The Trials of Government-in-Exile," Newsweek, LXIX (6 Feb. 1967), 20.

2053. Huston, Luther A. "Three Reporters Correct Manchester's Story," Editor & Publisher, C (4 Feb. 1967), 14.

2054. Karp, Irwin. "The Author's Right to Write," Saturday Review, L (21 Jan. 1967), 28-29.

2055. Kempton, Murray. "A Queen and Her Servant," The Spectator (London), No. 7226 (23 Dec. 1966), 806-807.

2056. _____. "America: [Kennedys vs. Look Magazine and William Manchester]," The Spectator (London), No. 7228 (6 Jan. 1967), 5-6.

2057. _____. "A Rage Greater Than Grief," The Atlantic Monthly, CCXIX (May 1967), 98-100.

2058. Kopkind, Andrew. "The Kennedy Book Battle," New Statesman (London), No. 1868 (30 Dec. 1966), 956-957.

2059. Kosner, Edward. "Jacqueline B. Kennedy, Plaintiff . . . ," Newsweek, LXVIII (26 Dec. 1966), 39-43.

2060. _____. "National Affairs: The Assassination: The Book," Newsweek, LXIX (10 April 1967), 34-35.

2061. Krassner, Paul. "The Parts That Were Left Out of the Kennedy Book," The Realist Magazine, LXXIV (May 1967), 1, 18.

2062. _____. "Case History of the Manchester Caper," The Realist Magazine, LXXV (June 1967), 1, 13-16.

2063. Lisagor, Peter. "A Brilliant Mosaic of Events," Panorama Magazine, Chicago Daily News, (8 April 1967), 3.

2064. Little, Stuart W. "Books: Birth Pains of a Book," Saturday Review, L (9 Sept. 1967), 61.

2065. Manchester, William. "The Death of a President [Excerpts]," Look, XXXI (24 Jan. 1967), 36-50; (7 Feb. 1967), 40-56; (21 Feb. 1967), 42-58; (7 March 1967), 50-66.

2066. _____. "Meet the Press: guest," [Merkle Press], XI (12 Feb. 1967), 1-19.

2067. _____. "Wie die Kennedys Mein Buch Bekampften [How the Kennedys Fought Against My Book]," Stern, XIII (26 March 1967), 36-42; also serialized in Match Magazine (Paris, 1967) and in Revu (Netherlands, 1967).

2068. _____. "William Manchester's Own Story," Look, XXXI (4 April 1967), 62-77; (2 May 1967), 18.

2069. _____. "Controversy," in Controversy and Other Essays in Journalism, 1950-1975 (Boston: Little, Brown and Co., 1976), pp. 1-76.

2070. Meagher, Sylvia. "After the Battle, the Book," The Minority of One, IX (June 1967), 25-27.

2071. Murchison, William. "The Man Who Knew Jackie," National Review, XXIX (4 Feb. 1977), 162-164.

2072. Nathan, Paul. "Rights and Permissions: [Details of All Foreign Rights to Manchester's Book]," Publishers Weekly, CXCI (15 May 1967), 34.

2073. Nevins, Allan. "Gargantuan, Honest and Useful, But So Exasperating," Panorama Magazine, Chicago Daily News, (8 April 1967), 2-3.

2074. Passent, Daniel. "Making of a 'Myth'," Atlas, XIII (June 1967), 27-31.

2075. Plumb, J. H. "The Private Grief of Public Figures," Saturday Review, L (21 Jan. 1967), 24-25.

2076. Rovere, Richard H. "Books: A Question of Taste and Something More," The New Yorker, XLIII (8 April 1967), 172-176.

2077. Salinger, Pierre, and William Manchester. "Letters to the Editor: Salinger vs. Manchester," Look, XXXI (16 May 1967), 8.

2078. Sauvage, Leo. "Reviews: The Death of a President by William Manchester," Ramparts, V (June 1967), 51-56.

2079. Schlesinger, Arthur. "On the Writing of Contemporary History," The Atlantic Monthly, CCXIX (March 1967), 69-74.

2080. Smith, R. H. "Suppression Business," Publishers Weekly, CXCI (30 Jan. 1967), 93.

2081. Talese, Gay. "The Corry Papers," Esquire, LXVII (June 1967), 24-38, 92-94.

2082. Tomalin, Nicholas. "Just Read the News, Mr. Manchester," New Statesman (London), LXXIII (21 April 1967), 547-548.

2083. Tuchman, Barbara W. "The Historian's Opportunity," Saturday Review, L (25 Feb. 1967), 27, 31, 71.

2084. West, Rebecca. "Was It Really Like This in Dallas?" The Reporter, XXXVI (18 May 1967), 37-39.

2085. Wills, Garry. "Manchester's Upheaval," National Catholic Reporter," III (29 March 1967), 10.

2086. _____. "Books-Arts-Manners: The Lachrymose Mr. Manchester," National Review, XIX (30 May 1967), 591-592.

2087. Wyndham, Francis. "Manchester and the Kennedys [with Serialization Promised for Next Week's Issue]," The Sunday Times (London), No. 7494 (15 Jan. 1967), 10.

Anonymous Articles:

2088. "Agreement Reached on Changes in Look Kennedy Articles," Advertising Age, XXXVII (26 Dec. 1966), 8.

2089. "Can It Hit One Million?" Business Week, No. 1961 (1 Apr. 1967), 28.

2090. "The Kennedy Book," Commonweal, LXXXV (6 Jan. 1967), 361-362.

2091. "United States: Sensational Announcement [Jacqueline Kennedy Chooses William Manchester to Write Book on JFK Assassination]," The Current Digest of the Soviet Press, XVI (22 April 1964), 25.

2092. "JFK Book: Story Would Fill a Book," Editor & Publisher, XCIX (24 Dec. 1966), 12.

2093. "Washington Report: The Assassination Retold," Life, LVIII (7 May 1965), 48.

2094. "Editorials: The History Makers," The Nation, CCIV, (2 Jan. 1967), 4.

2095. "Editorials: Texas Ueber Alles," The Nation, CCIV (30 Jan. 1967), 132.

2096. "Editorials: The Perils of Overexposure," The Nation, CCIV (6 Feb. 1967), 164-165.

2097. "Mayor of Dallas Blasts Book on JFK's Death," The National Enquirer (12 March 1967), 3.

2098. "Johnson Tells His Side of 'The Death of a President'," The National Enquirer (26 March 1967), 1-5.

2099. "Why Kennedys Picked Manchester to Write 'The Death of a President'," The National Enquirer (9 April 1967), 6.

2100. "The Kennedys Look at History," National Review, XIX (10 Jan. 1967), 12-13.

2101. "The Two Mrs. Kennedys," National Review, XIX (4 April 1967), 335-336.

2102. "Newsmakers: [Manchester's Book Commissioned]," Newsweek, LXIII (6 April 1964), 50.

2103. "National Affairs: Controversies: The Best Kennedy Book?" Newsweek, LXVIII (5 Sept. 1966), 21-22.

2104. "Press: JFK Censored?" Newsweek, LXVIII (3 Oct. 1966), 65-66.

2105. "The Periscope: Ahead of the News: The Kennedys vs. Manchester," Newsweek, LXVIII (7 Nov. 1966), 19.

2106. "National Affairs: Jacqueline Kennedy's Victory," Newsweek, LXIX (2 Jan. 1967), 16-19.

2107. "National Affairs: The Kennedys: Temporary Cease-Fire," Newsweek, LXIX (9 Jan. 1967), 20-21.

2108. "The Periscope: Personal File: Jackie's Deft Editorial Hand," Newsweek, LXIX (16 Jan. 1967), 13.

2109. "The Assassination: Chapter I," Newsweek, LXIX (16 Jan. 1967), 29-30.

2110. "The Assassination: Chapter II," Newsweek, LXIX (30 Jan. 1967), 22-24.

2111. "National Affairs: The Kennedys: How to Lose a War," Newsweek, LXIX (6 Feb. 1967), 34-35.

2112. "Press: The Manchester Story," Newsweek, LXIX (27 March 1967), 95.

2113. "Press: Verdict on Manchester," Newsweek, LXIX (24 April 1967), 90-93.

2114. "National Affairs: The Assassination: 'Death of Lancer'," Newsweek, LXX (17 July 1967), 25.

2115. "National Affairs: History: The LBJ Brand," Newsweek, LXXII (30 Sept. 1968), 28.

2116. "Outdoor Life and The Death of a President," Outdoor Life, CXL (Oct. 1967), 32-33.

2117. "Author Chosen For Story of Assassination," Publishers Weekly, CLXXXV (6 April 1964), 27.

2118. "Media: Look Magazine's Forthcoming Serialization of William Manchester's Book . . . Will Be Sold . . . Abroad," Publishers Weekly, CXC (14 Nov. 1966), 41.

2119. "JFK Book: Accord Reached as Publishers Seek Compromise on Revisions Asked by Kennedys," Publishers Weekly, CXC (26 Dec. 1966), 57-58.

2120. "Mrs. Kennedy and Harper & Row Continue Negotiations on Editorial Content of Death of a President," Publishers Weekly, CXCI (2 Jan. 1967), 33-34.

2121. "Harper & Row, Manchester File Official Answers," Publishers' Weekly, CXCI (16 Jan. 1967), 57.

2122. "Mrs. Kennedy Reaches Accord With Harper & Row and William Manchester," Publishers Weekly, CXCI (23 Jan. 1967), 222.

2123. "Feud Over Death of a President Intensifies as Manchester Attacks Kennedy Family and Aides," Publishers Weekly, CXCI (30 Jan. 1967), 88-89.

2124. "Look, Manchester Sue New York World Journal Tribune," Publishers' Weekly, CXCI (13 Feb. 1967), 53.

2125. "Look Magazine to Print Manchester's Own Story," Pub-lishers Weekly CXCI (13 March 1967), 38.

2126. "Booksellers Assay Sales of Manchester Book," Publishers Weekly CXCI (13 March 1967), 51; (27 March 1967), 52.

2127. "Harpers' Plans for the Manchester Book," Publishers Weekly, CXCI (20 March 1967), 47.

2128. "Currents: Newest Top Sellers for 33 1/3 Cents," Publishers Weekly, CXCI (10 April 1967), 33.

2129. "Currents: Lunch for Mr. Manchester . . . Rush to New Orleans," Publishers Weekly, CXCI (17 April 1967), 25-26.

2130. "Bookstores Report: Manchester Book Sales Mixed," Publishers Weekly, CXCI (5 June 1967), 166.

2131. "Currents: JFK Library Receives First Installment from Manchester and Harper," Publishers Weekly, CXCIV (1 July 1968), 18.

2132. "The Reporter's Notes: The Manchester Book," The Reporter, XXXV (29 Dec. 1966), 8.

2133. "JFK Book Dispute: Widow vs. Author," Senior Scholastic, LXXXIX (6 Jan. 1967), 16.

2134. "Assassination of a President-to-Be," Statist, CXC (23 Dec. 1966), 1521-1522.

2135. "Political Intelligence: More Manchester," The Texas Observer, LVIII (17 March 1967), 8-9.

2136. "The Presidency: Battle of the Book," Time, LXXXVIII (23 Dec. 1966), 15-18.

2137. "The Presidency: Chapter II--or Finis?" Time, LXXXVIII (30 Dec. 1966), 10-12.

2138. "Sequels: Spreading Controversy," Time, LXXXIX (6 Jan. 1967), 16-17.

2139. "The Press: Publishing: Start the Presses [and] What the Fuss Was About," Time, LXXXIX (20 Jan. 1967), 47-48.

2140. "The Press: Magazines: Agony Relived," Time, LXXXIX (27 Jan. 1967), 58.

2141. "The Manchester Book: Despite Flaws and Errors, a Story That Is Larger Than Life or Death," Time, LXXXIX (7 April 1967), 22-23.

2142. "People: [Royalties from the Manchester Book]," Time, XCI (28 June 1968), 31.

2143. "L'Affaire Manchester," Triumph, 11 (Jan. 1967), 7.

2144. "The Book That Has Backfired," U.S. News and World Report, LXI (26 Dec. 1966), 36.

2145. "Battle Over a Book--New Role for Mrs. JFK," U.S. News and World Report, LXII (2 Jan. 1967), 6.

2146. "Growing Rift of LBJ and Kennedys: Behind the Furor Over a Book," U.S. News and World Report, LXII (2 Jan. 1967), 22-27.

2147. "As 'the Book' Appears: a Close Look at the Facts," U.S. News and World Report, LXII (23 Jan. 1967), 50-52.

2148. "JFK and LBJ: More Untold Stories," U.S. News and World Report, LXII (30 Jan. 1967), 36.

2149. "To Help You Keep the Record Straight About That Book," U.S. News and World Report, LXII (6 Feb. 1967), 66-67.

2150. "In the Hours After Dallas: 'the Book' and the Testimony," U.S. News and World Report, LXII (20 Feb. 1967), 51-52.

2151. "The Death of a President," Women's Wear Daily, CXIV (28 March 1967).

(5) OTHER SECONDARY RESEARCH

Faked Books:

2152.   Leboeuf, Ulov G. K.   Time of Assassins.   Levittown,
N.Y.:   Ulov G. H. Leboeuf, n.d., 4 vols;

Rampart's spoof of assassination researchers, especially
directed against Harold Weisberg; [See 758].

2153.   Zaftig, Leopold.   Oswald: Patsy Without Portfolio.
N.p.:   Vanitas, n.d.; same as above.

Books:

2154.   Anson, Robert Sam.   "They've Killed the President!":
the Search for the Murderers of John F. Kennedy.   New York:
Bantam Books, 1975; [See 4865].

2155.   Bane, Bernard M.   The Bane in Kennedy's Existence.
Boston: B.M.B. Publishing Co., 1967.

2156.   _____.   Controlled Brinkmanship.   Boston:
Bernard M. Bane Publishing Co., 1968.

2157.   _____.   Is President John F. Kennedy Alive
and Well?   Boston: Bernard M. Bane Publishing Co., 1977.

2158.   Bebrits, Anna.   Elnökgyilkosságtól elnökválasztásig.
Budapest: Kossuth Konyvkiado, 1964.

2159.   Bonner, Judy Whitson.   Investigation of a Homicide:
the Murder of John F. Kennedy.   Anderson, S.C.:   Droke House,
distributed by Grosset & Dunlap, New York, 1969.

2160.   Bishop, James Alonzo.   The Day Kennedy Was Shot.   New
York: Funk & Wagnalls, 1968; Bantam, 1969 [See 4045, 4052,
4074, 4555, 4560, 4565].

2161.   Committee to Investigate Assassinations.   Coincidence
or Conspiracy?   (Committee to Investigate Assassinations,
directed by Bernard Fensterwald, Jr., and compiled by Michael
Ewing).   New York: Zebra Books, 1977.

2162.   Cutler, Robert Bradley.   Crossfire: Evidence of Conspiracy.   Manchester, Mass.:   Cutler Designs, 1975.

2163,   _____.   The Umbrella Man: Evidence
of Conspiracy.   Manchester, Mass.:   Cutler Designs, 1975.

2164.   Davis, Marc, and Jim Mathews (eds.).   Who Killed
Kennedy?   Covina, Calif.:   Collectors Publications, n.d.

2165. Davis, Nord, Jr. Dallas Conspiracy [Communist Plot].
Hollis, New Hampshire: Published by the author, 1968.

2166. Bi'Bīs, 'Abd al-Jawwād Hamzah. Masra' Kinidī wa-al-
Sihyūnīyah [Zionist Plot]. 1965.

2167. Dunshee, Tom, and Richard Duncan. Motorcade--November
22, 1963. Trenton, New Jersey: Published by authors, 1975.

2168. Eddowes, Michael. November 22: How they Killed
Kennedy. St. Helier, Jersey: N. Spearman Ltd.; London:
Distributed by N. Spearman, 1976. Re-titled The Oswald File,
New York: Clarkson N. Potter, 1977; [See 4990].

2169. Ekko, Egil. Skuddene i Dallas. Oslo: Ekko Forlag,
1974.

2170. Evica, George Michael. And We Are All Mortal: New
Evidence and Analysis in the John F. Kennedy Assassination.
West Hartford, Conn.: University of Hartford, 1978.

2171. Feldman, Harold. Fifty-one Witnesses: the Grassy
Knoll. San Francisco: Idlewild Publishing Co., 1965.

2172. Gilles, Camille. 400,000 (i.e., Quatre cent mille)
Dollars Pour Abattre Kennedy à Paris [$400,000 to Destroy
Kennedy in Paris]. Paris: Julliard, 1973.

2173. Goff, Kenneth. Crackpot or Crack Shot [Communist
Plot]. Englewood, Colorado: Published by author, 1965.

2174. Goranoff, Kyrill. Why Did You Kill Your President?
West Berlin, 1970.

2175. Gordan, Bruce. One and One Make Two Sometimes: The
Kennedy Assassination. Fullerton, Calif., 1968.

2176. Gun, Nerin E. Red Roses from Texas. London: F.
Muller, 1964. Also: Les Roses rouges de Dallas (Paris, 1964)
and Las Rojas rosas de Dallas (Santiago de Chile, 1965).

2177. Hanson, William H. The Shooting of John F. Kennedy;
One Assassin, Three Shots, Three Hits--No Misses. San Antonio,
Texas: Naylor Co., 1969.

2178. Henderson, Bruce, and Sam Summerlin. 1:33. New York:
Cowles, 1968.

2179. Ioĭrysh, Abram Isakovich, and Boris Sergeev. Kuda
vedut sledy . . . [Where the traces lead . . . . .] Moscow,
1964; 2nd ed., 1965.

2180. Idris, Soewardi. Terbunuhnja Presiden Kennedy [How
President Kennedy was Assassinated]. Djakarta: Tekad, 1965.

2181. Irwin, T. Harry. The Harrassment of Roger Craig; the
Case History of an Uncooperative Witness. Belfast: Published
by author, 1977.

2182. Joesten, Joachim. How Kennedy Was Killed: the Full
Appalling Story. London: Dawnay, 1968.

2183. _____. Trilogy of Murder. München: 1968-
70, 5 vols.:

    Reprints revisions of other works, plus a new study,
    Murder Marches On.

2184. Koral, Mark. The Zionist Conspiracy Behind the President Kennedy Assassination. Rochester, New York: Published
by author, 1976.

2185. Kristl, Zvonimir [with Ive Mihovilović and Sead Sara-
cević]. Kennedy. Drama u Dallasu (Tisuću dana nade.--Ivo
Mihovilovic: Životni put.--Sead Saracevic: Atentat u
Dallasu. Treće izdanje.) [Part of: Novinarska i publici-
sticka biblioteka]. Zagreb: Stvarnost, 1964.

2186. Langston, George E. Brothers United Assassinated.
Houston: The King Notsgnal Press, n.d.

2187. Lutz, Tom. Tracking Down Kennedy's Killers. Morton
Grove, Illinois: Newsreal Series, 1977.

2188. McDonald, Hugh C. Appointment in Dallas: the Final
Solution to the Assassination of JFK. As Told to Geoffrey
Bocca. New York: H. McDonald Publishing Corp., and Zebra,
1975; [See 4865].

2189. _____. LBJ and the JFK Assassination Conspiracy. New York: Condor Publishing, 1978.

2190. MacFarlane, Ian Colin A. The Assassination of John F.
Kennedy: a New Review. Melbourne, Australia, 1974.

2191. _____. Proof of Conspiracy in the
Assassination of President Kennedy: Plus 1975 Anthology and
a Resources Directory. Melbourne: Book Distributors, 1975.

2192. Marks, Stanley J. American Dream; American Nightmare.
Los Angeles: Bureau of International Affairs, 1971.

2193. _____. Two Days of Infamy: November 22,
1963 and September 28, 1964. Los Angeles: Bureau of International Affairs, 1969.

2194. Matteo, Pat. This Captive Land [on Anti-Communist
Groups in the U.S.]. Yonkers, New York: Privately Printed,
1968.

2195. Mihilović, Ive. Tko je ubio Kennedyja? [Who Killed
Kennedy?]. Zagreb: Stvarnost, 1967.

2197. Morin, Relman. Assassination: The Death of President
John F. Kennedy. New York: New American Library, 1968.

2198. Morris, W. R. The Men Behind the Guns [Right-Wing
Conspiracies]. Loretto, Tennessee: Angel Lea Books, 1975.

2199. Morrow, Robert D. Betrayal. Chicago: Regnery, 1976;
New York: Warner Books, 1976.

2200. Moses, David. Who Shot Kennedy? England: Church of
God, 1973.

2201. Newcomb, Fred, and Perry Adams. Murder From Within
[by Secret Service]. Santa Barbara, Calif.: Probe, 1974.

2202. Noyes, Peter. Legacy of Doubt. New York: Pinnacle
Books, 1973.

2203. O'Toole, George. The Assassination Tapes: an Elec-
tronic Probe into the Murder of John F. Kennedy and the Dallas
Coverup. New York: Penthouse Press, 1975; rev. ed., with
Foreword by Mark Lane, New York: Zebra, 1977; [See 736].

2204. Pokorný, Dušan. Ulice jilmii [Elm Street]. Prague:
Mlada fronta, 1965.

2205. Rand, Michael, Howard Loxton, and Len Deighton (compilers). The Assassination of President Kennedy. London:
Jackdaw Series, 1967 [See 4304].

2206. Rice, John R. What Was Back of Kennedy's Murder?
[Why Did God Allow It?]. Murfreesboro, Tennessee: Sword of
the Lord Publishers, 1964.

2207. Roberts, Charles. The Truth About the Assassination.
[Views of One White House Correspondent]. With Foreword by
Pierre Salinger. New York: Grosset & Dunlap, 1967; [See
718, 4375].

2208. Rojas, Robinson. ¡Estos Mataron a Kennedy! Reportaje
de un Golpe de Estado [They Killed Kennedy! Report of a
Coup d'etat]. Santiago de Chile: Ediciones Arco, 1964.

2209. Russell, Dick. Closing In: the Search for JFK's
Assassins [Photographs by Richard E. Sprague]. New York:
Dial Press, 1977.

2210. Sagatelyan, Mikhail R. Kto zhe ubil Dzhona Kennedi?
[Who Killed John Kennedy?]. Moscow, 1972.

2211. Sawai, Sirimongkon. Buanglang khattakam prathana-
thipbodi Kennedi [On the Assassination of President Kennedy].
Bangkok, 1964.

2212. The Search For a Master Assassin [White Citizens'
Council's Paper on How the World Jewish Conspiracy Killed
JFK]. Shreveport, Louisiana: Councillor Newspaper, 1972.

2213. Shaw, J. Gary, with Larry R. Harris. Cover-up:
The Governmental Conspiracy to Conceal the Facts about the
Public Execution of John Kennedy. Cleburne, Texas: Shaw,
1976.

2214. Skolnick, Sherman H.   Plaintiff's Brief : Skolnick
vs. National Archives and Records Service: U.S. District
Court, Illinois Eastern Division, 70.C.790. Chicago: Privately printed, 1970;

    [Part of author's attempt to identify a Chicago-based
    plot against JFK].

2215.   . National Archives Lawsuit
[Brought by his Citizen's Committee to Clean up the Courts].
Chicago: Published by author, 1970.

2216. Smith, Gerald L. K. The Mysterious and Unpublicized
Facts Behind the Assassination of John F. Kennedy [Communist
Plot]. Los Angeles: Christian Nationalist Crusade, 1965.

2217. Smith, William R. A Hog Story; from the Aftermire of
the Kennedy Assassination. Washington, D.C.: L'Avant Garde
Books, 1968.

2218.   . Assassination by Consensus: The
Story Behind the Kennedy Assassination. Washington, D.C.:
L'Avant Gards Publications, 1966.

2219. Snyder, George W. Why Did They Assassinate President
Kennedy? N.p.: Privately Printed by the Author, n.d.

2220. Tastmona, Thothnu. It Is As If: Solution of the
President Kennedy Death Mystery. New York: Thothmona Book
Company, 1966.

2221. Venkateswararao, Potluri. Kennedīhatya Kēsu [The
Case of the Assassination of Kennedy, Written in Telugu].
Madras: Balaji Publishers, 1964.

2222. Wise, Dan, and Marietta Maxfield. The Day Kennedy
Died. San Antonio: Naylor Co., 1964.

2223. Zib, William H. Reason Why President John F. Kennedy
Was Murdered. New York: Carlton Press, 1976.

    Articles by Authors:

2224. Anson, Robert S. "The Greatest Cover-Up of All," New
Times (N.Y.), IV (18 April 1975), 16-26, 29; Reprinted in
Skeptic, No. 9 (Aug. 1975), 17-19, 53-61.

2225. _____. "The Man Who Never Was," New Times (N.Y.), V (19 Sept. 1975), 14-16, 21-25.

2226. _____. "Jack, Judy, Sam, & Johnny . . . and Frank, Fidel, Edgar . . . Who Were JFK's Strange Bedfellows, Anyway? If His Weakness for Women Had Been Exploited, By Whom and to What End?" New Times (N.Y.), VI (23 Jan. 1976), 21-23, 27-30, 32-33.

2227. Alexander, John. "Review: The Assassination Tapes, by George O'Toole," Saturday Evening Post, CCXLVII (May 1975), 6, 120.

2228. Andronov, Iona. "On the Trail of a President's Killers," New Times (Moscow), Jan. 1977, No. 1, 27-30; No. 2, 26-30; No. 3, 27-30.

2229. Baxandale, Lee. "The Kennedy Assassination," Views (London), VI (1964), 90-93.

2230. Belin, David W. "'They've Killed the President': the Book You Shouldn't Read," National Review, XXVIII (6 Feb. 1976), 81-85, 88-90; XXVIII (2 April 1976), 303, 306, 345-346.

2231. Berendt, John. "'If They've Found Another Assassin, Let Them Name Names and Produce Their Evidence': Name = Igor 'Turk' Vaganov; Evidence = See Below," Esquire, LXVIII (Aug. 1967), 80-82, 122-126.

2232. Berkeley, Edmund C. "Impact: The May Article [by Richard E. Sprague]: Report No. 2," Computers and Automation, XIX (July 1970), 29-31.

2233. _____. "Patterns of Political Assassination: How Many Coincidences Make a Plot?" Compters and Automation, XIX (Sept. 1970), 39-48.

2234. _____. "Response: [Schwartz vs. Sprague]," Computers and Automation, XX (March 1971), 40-43.

2235. _____. "The Assassination of President Kennedy: the Pattern of Coup d'Etat and Public Deception," Computers and Automation, XX (Nov. 1971), 24-26, 29-30, 48.

2236. Bernert, Philippe, and Camille Gilles. "Le Francais Qui Devait Tuer Kennedy [Frenchman Who Was to Kill Kennedy]," Computers and Automation, XXI (Dec. 1972), 38-40; XXII (Jan. 1973), 37-39.

2237. Besson, Waldemar. "Die Schüsse von Dallas. War eine Verschwörung des Hasses am Werk? [The Shots in Dallas. Was a Conspiracy of Hate at Work?]" Die Zeit (Hamburg), XIX, No. 33 (1964), 6.

2238. Bishop, Jim. "The Day JFK Died," Ladies Home Journal, LXXXV (Nov. 1968), 151-157.

2239. _____. "November 22, 1963: the End of Camelot," Ladies Home Journal, XC (Nov. 1973), 77, 108-113.

2240. Black, Edwin. "The Plot to Kill JFK in Chicago Nov. 2, 1963--Twenty Days Before Dallas," Chicago Independent, I (Nov. 1975), 4-11, 24.

2241. Bloice, C. "Who Shot John," People's World, XXXVIII (8 Feb. 1975), 6.

2242. _____. "Strange Business," People's World, XXXVIII (12 July 1975), 6.

2243. Blumenthal, Sid, and R. D. Rosen. "The Politics of Conspiracy, the Conspiracy of Politics," Computers and People, XXIV (April 1975), 24-26, 31.

2244. Brand, Sergiu. "Şi Totusi Cine? [And Yet, Who?]," Cronica (Bucharest), I (17 Dec. 1966), 12.

2245. Brogan, Denis W. "Death in Dallas--Myths After Kennedy," Encounter, XXIII (Dec. 1964), 20-26.

2246. Brogan, Patrick. "Silence That Weakens Theory of Kennedy Plot," The Times (London), No. 59,007 (6 Feb. 1974), 14.

2247. _____. "'Penthouse' Theory on Kennedy Murder [The George O'Toole Article]," The Times (London), No. 59,341 (11 March 1975), 8.

2248. Brussell, Mae. "Why Was Martha Mitchell Kidnapped?: My Research on Political Assassinations . . . ," The Realist, No. 93 (Aug. 1972), 1, 27-46.

2249. Buckley, William F., Jr. "The Politics of Assassination," Esquire, LXX (Oct. 1968), 163-165, 228-236.

2250. Burnett, Henry B., Jr. "The Question That Keeps Coming Back [Who Killed John F. Kennedy?]," Skeptic, No. 9 (Aug. 1975), 4-5.

2251. Butler, Ed. "The Great Assassin Puzzle," The Westwood Village Square, I (Summer 1968), 21-28; II (1969), 26-27, 37-41.

2252. Charboneau, M. "JFK Assassination Investigator Dead," Workers World, XVI (13 Dec. 1974), 2.

2253. Chester, Lewis. "Angry Decade [and the JFK Assassination According to Michael Eddowes]," The Sunday Times (London), No. 7964 (1 Feb. 1976), 32, 39.

2254. Connally, Mrs. John, with Michael Drury. "Since That Day in Dallas," McCalls, XCI (Aug. 1964), 78-79, 141-142.

2255. Cook, I. "Profile in Courage," Amex-Canada, II (Feb. 1971), 40.

2256. Cook, Fred J. "Assassination Investigations: the Irregulars Take the Field [the Bernard Fensterwald Group]," The Nation, CCXIII (19 July 1971), 40-46.

2257. Crawford, Allan. "Leftists Stoking Fires of 'Conspiracy' Theory in JFK Death," Human Events, XXXV (4 Jan. 1975), 14.

2258. Cross, David. "Court to Hear Kennedy Assassination Allegation [Frank Sturgis, Accused by Marita Lorenz]," The Times (London), No. 60,152 (4 Nov. 1977), 9.

2259. Dahlin, Robert. "Fresh Wave of JFK Assassination Titles Suggests a Host of New Theories," Publishers Weekly, CCVIII (1 Dec. 1975), 50-52.

2260. Dirix, Bob. "Why Was JFK Shot? [Russian Plot]," Atlas, XIII (May 1967), 10-13.

2261. Dunson, J. "Sad Day in Texas," Sing Out, XIV (1964), 26-27.

2262. Evans, M. Stanton. "The Right Books: [on JFK Assassination, by Anson, Fox, and Newman]," National Review, XXVIII (23 July 1976), 796.

2263. Feldman, Harold. "Fifty-one Witnesses: the Grassy Knoll," The Minority of One, VII (March 1965), 16-25; [See 3927].

2264. _____. "The Johnson Murder Charge," The Minority of One, VIII (Dec. 1966), 21-22.

2265. Fensterwald, Bernard, Jr. "'Committee to Investigate Assassinations' Seeks Help from Computer Professionals," Computers and Automation, XIX (May 1970), 13.

2266. _____. "The Right of Equal Access to Government Information [U.S. Civil Action No. 3651-70: Committee to Investigate Assassinations vs. Justice Dept.]," Computers and Automation, XX (April 1971), 32-34, 37.

2267. _____. "The Case of Secret Service Agent Abraham W. Bolden [Alleging Service-Men's Misconduct in Dallas]," Computers and Automation, XX (June 1971), 41-43.

2268. _____. "A Legacy of Suspicion . . . Who Killed John Kennedy?" Esquire, LXXX (Nov. 1973), 141-143, 265.

2269. Fensterwald, Bernard, James Lesar, and Robert Smith. "Report of the National Committee to Investigate Assassinations," Computers and Automation, XX (Feb. 1971), 48-50.

2270. Ferrari, Alfred John. "Kennedy Assassinations and Political Detours: (a Possibly Romantic Posthumous Speculation)," The Minority of One, X (Nov. 1968), 7-9.

2271. Froncek, T. "An American View," Tablet, CCXXI (8 April 1967), 382-383.

2272. Gellner, John. "Who Killed John Kennedy?," Saturday Night (Toronto), LXXIX (July 1964), 11-14.

2273. Goldman, Peter, and John J. Lindsay. "Dallas: New Questions and Answers," Newsweek, LXXXV (28 April 1975), 36-38; [Letters], LXXXV (19 May 1975), 4-7.

2274. Gordon, G. "I Didn't Kill Anyone," Great Speckled Bird, VIII (21 May 1975), 6.

2275. Goulden, Joseph C. "Gun Barrel Politics," The Washingtonian, (Feb. 1975), 46-52.

2276. Heren, Louis. "Kennedy Assassination: All the World Loves a Conspiracy," The Times (London), No. 59,429 (23 June 1975), 9.

2277. _____. "Believing Anything [about the JFK Assassination Books by Michael Eddowes and Robert Sam Anson]," The Times (London), No. 59,620 (5 Feb. 1976), 10.

2278. Herta, A. "Kennedy i druga rewolucja," Kultura, Szkice, opowiadania, sprawozdania (Paris), No. 7-8 (1965), 3-24.

2279. Hoffman, E. "The Assassination of John F. Kennedy," Ann Arbor Sun, II (22 Nov. 1974), 10.

2280. Izakov, Boris. "Echo of Dallas," New Times (Moscow), 21 Dec. 1966, 29-31.

2281. Jakovlev, N. N. "Kak Kennedi stal prezidentom," Voprosy istorii (Moscow), No. 3 (1967), 109-125; No. 4, 117-132; No. 5, 123-131.

2282. Janssen, Karl-Heinz. "Wer ermordete Kennedy? Fakten und Phantome: Suche nach dem zweiten Attentäter [Who Murdered Kennedy? Facts and Fancies: Search for Two Assassins]," Die Zeit (Hamburg) XXI, No. 48 (1966), 7.

2283. Jenkins, Gareth. "Who Shot President Kennedy--or, Fact and Fable in History," Computers and Automation, XXI (Feb. 1972), 43-46.

2284. Jenkins, John A., and Dianne R. Kearns. "Government, Business and the People's Right to Know: A BNA Special Report on the Freedom of Information Act," Media Law Reporter, III (14 Feb. 1978), 2-24.

2285. Kantor, M. "Dear Cousin William," McCalls, XCI (Feb. 1964), 77.

2286. Keisler, J. R. "An Assassin's Motive: from Readers' Letters," The Minority of One, VII (Feb. 1965), 22.

2287. Koehler and Berlet. "Kennedy Assassination/Controversy," College Press Service, No. 59 (21 May 1975), 3.

2288. _____. "Kennedy Assassination/Who Dun It," College Press Service, No. 59 (21 May 1975), 6.

2289. Kopkind, Andrew. "The Kennedy Mystery Re-opened," New Statesman (London), LXXII (29 July 1966), 163.

2290. Lane, Mark. "RFK Implicated: Mark Lane on Bobby's Role in JFK Death--and Since," San Francisco Express Times, I, No. 14 (18 April 1967), 1, 8, 10.

2291. Lurie, Morris. "Johnson's Secret Obsession," Nation Review (Melbourne), (30 Nov. - 6 Dec. 1973), 215.

2292. MacFarlane, Ian. "The Assassination of Truth?" Nation Review (Melbourne), (23-29 Nov. 1973), 177.

2293. McKinley, James. "Playboy's History of Assassination in America: Part IV, The End of Camelot," Playboy, XXIII (April 1976), 125-130, 142, 193-208.

2294. _____. "Playboy's History of Assassination in America: Part V, Cries of Conspiracy," Playboy, XXIII (May 1976), 122-127, 130-132, 200-208.

2295. Mandel, Paul. "End to Nagging Rumors: the Six Critical Seconds," Life, LV (6 Dec. 1963), 52F.

2296. Meagher, Sylvia. "Notes For a New Investigation," Esquire, LXVI (Dec. 1966), 211, 335-336.

2297. _____. "Two Assassinations [JFK-MLK]," The Minority of One, X (June 1968), 9-10.

2298. _____. "Three Assassinations," The Minority of One, X (Sept. 1968), 13-16.

2299. _____. "The Kennedy Conspiracy, by Paris Flammonde [Book Review]," Commonweal, LXXXIX (7 March 1969), 712-714

2300. _____. "Johnnies-Come-Lately to Dealy Plaza [Reviews Books by Newman, Bonner, and McConnell]," The Texas Observer, LXII (24 July 1970), 11-13.

2301. Meisner, P. "U.S. Mercenary Helped Kill JFK," Workers World, XVII (18 July 1975), 10.

2302. _____. "Cracks in JFK Assassination Coverup," Workers World, XVII (12 Sept. 1975), 9.

2303. _____. "Ultraright Conspiracy/JFK," Workers World, XVII (24 Oct. 1975), 9.

2304. _____. "Why JFK Coverup Is Being Exposed," Workers World, XVII (7 Nov. 1975), 9.

2305. _____. "JFK Murderers Are Still Free," Workers World, XVII (21 Nov. 1975), 10.

2306. Mironescu, Emil. "Enigma de la Dallas si Semnele ei de întrebare [Enigma of Dallas and the Vestiges of the Problem]," Pentru apărarea păcii (Bucharest), XII (Dec. 1966), 19-21.

2307. Modesto, Joe. "Contract on Kennedy," St. Louis Outlaw, II (7 May 1971), 9.

2308. Morris, W. R. "The Conspiracy Behind JFK's Slaying," Argosy, No. 384 (Sept. 1976), 42-47.

2309. Moulder, John. "Hall, Nagell, Dean, Augustinovich: These Are the Keys to Unlock JFK Secret," The National Tattler, Special Edition (Sept. 1975), 2-3, 19.

2310. Norden, Eric. "The Death of a President," The Minority of One, VI (Jan. 1964), 16-23.

2311. O'Brien, Conor Cruise. "How Many Conspiracies?" The Minority of One, X (Sept. 1968), 16; X (Nov. 1968), 22.

2312. O'Toole, George, Richard Whalen and Mark Lane. "The Unsolved J.F.K. Murder Mystery," Saturday Evening Post, CCXLVII (Sept. 1975), 44-53, 100-102, 107, 119.

2313. Phyllis. "Dallas Echoes," Good Times, IV (29 Jan. 1971), 13.

2314. PNS/LNS. "Paper Radio/News," Northwest Passage, X (25 March 1974), 28.

2315. Pusateri, C. Joseph. "The Day Kennedy Was Shot, by Jim Bishop," America, CXX (4 Jan. 1969), 22-23.

2316. Ridenour, Ron. "Skeptic Interview: Bernard Fensterwald," Skeptic, No. 9 (Aug. 1975), 8-11, 48-51.

2317. Robert, Peter. "Tragicna pot Stirih Predsednikov," Obzornik (Ljubljana), LXIV (1964), 573-578.

2318. Roffman, Howard. "Freedom of Information: Judicial Review of Executive Security Classifications," University of Florida Law Review, XXVIII (1976), 551-568.

2319. Rothchild, John. "Finding the Facts Bureaucrats Hide," The Washington Monthly, (Jan. 1972), 15-27.

2320. Rowan, Carl T. "How Kennedy's Concern for Negroes Led to His Death," Ebony, XXII (April 1967), 27-34.

2321. Sagatelyan, Mikhail. "Dallas: Who? How? Why?" Sputnik Monthly Digest, VII (June 1971), 111-130; VII (July 1971), 98-120; VII (August 1971), 109-130.

2322. _____. "Dallas: Who, How, Why? [Condensed from Aurora (Leningrad)]," Computers and Automation, XXI (March 1972), 28-32, 34-36; XXI (April 1972), 37-43; XXI (May 1972), 34-40; XXI (June 1972), 34-38, 43.

2323. Saint-Jean, Claude. "Histoire d'un crime [History of a Crime]," Revue. Littérature, histoire, arts et sciences des deux mondes (Paris), No. 10 (1965), 275.

2324. Salandria, Vincent J. "The Assassination of President John F. Kennedy: a Model for Explanation," Computers and Automation, XX (Dec. 1971), 32-40.

2325. _____. "'The Promotion of Domestic Discord'," Computers and Automation, XXI (Jan. 1972), 37-39, 47.

2326. Schonfeld, Maurice W. "The Shadow of a Gunman [and the Grassy Knoll]," Columbia Journalism Review, (July/Aug. 1975), 46-50.

2327. Schwartz, Benjamin L. "Another View [of JFK Assassination, Challenging Richard E. Sprague's]," Computers and Automation, XX (March 1971), 35-39.

2328. Schwelien, Joachim. "Der Mord von Dallas [The Death in Dallas]," Die Zeit (Hamburg), XIX, No. 40 (1964), 3.

2329. Smith, R. P. "Why I Distrust the Romero Story," Computers and Automation, XXII (Jan. 1973), 40.

2330. Sprague, Richard E. "More About Jim Hicks [Alleged Conspirator in JFK Assassination]," Computers and Automation, XIX (July 1970), 32.

2331. _____. "The Second Conspiracy [Cover-Up After JFK's Assassination]," Computers and Automation, XIX (July 1970), 35-36.

2332. _____. "Computer-Assisted Analysis of Evidence Regarding the Assassination of President John F. Kennedy: Progress Report." Computers and Automation, XIX (Sept. 1970), 48.

2333. Stang, Alan. "They Killed the President. Lee Harvey Oswald Wasn't Alone." American Opinion, XIX (Feb. 1976), 1-8, 59-72.

2334. Stapp, A. "JFK Assassination/Indochina Struggle,"
Workers World, XVII (11 April 1975), 9.

2335, Stetler, Russell. "An Agenda for Investigators: Can
Congress Crack the Kennedy Assassination?" Inquiry (6 March
1978), 11-15.

2336. Stevens, Ben. "Did Death Scoop 2 Reporters? [Hunter
and Koethe]; 20 Key 'Conspiracy' Figures Die Mysteriously,"
The National Tattler, XIX (25 Nov. 1973), 21.

2337, Torres, Jose. "Kennedy Shooting Still Haunts Ruling
Circles," [National] Guardian, XXVII (9 April 1975), 8.

2338. Trevor-Roper, Hugh. "Ki Ölte meg Kennedy-t? [Who
Killed Kennedy?]" Kozunk (Cluj), XXV (Nov. 1966), 1601-1609.

2339. Turner, William W. "Some Disturbing Parallels,
[Assassinations of M. L. King and J. F. Kennedy]," Ramparts,
VI (29 June 1968), 33-36.

2340. Veggeberg, S. "Who Killed JFK?" Great Speckled Bird,
VIII (24 April 1975), 3.

2341. Welsh, David, and David Lifton. "The Case for Three
Assassins," Ramparts, V (Jan. 1967), 77-100; V (Feb. 1967),
3 [Letters]; V (March 1967), 2-4.

2342. White, James D. "Skepticism of Official Government'
Explanations: [Parallels Between UFO Sightings and JFK
Assassinations]," Computers and Automation, XX (Aug. 1971),
36.

2343. Wise, David. "It Will Be Many Years . . ." Good
Housekeeping, CLVIII (Feb. 1964), 90-91.

2344. Wiznitzer, L. "Que s'est-il Passé à Dallas? [What
Happened in Dallas?]," Maclean's Magazine (Toronto), VI
(Sept. 1966), 2-3.

Anonymous Articles:

2345. "Die Hintergründe des Kennedy-Mordes [The Background
to the Kennedy Murder]," Das andere Deutschland (Hannover),
No. 3 (1964), 7.

2346. "Break-In at Home of JFK Researcher," Black Panther,
XI (19 Jan. 1974), 5.

2347. "What Conspiracy?" D.C. Gazette, V (Oct. 1974), 7.

2348. "Dallasi Detektivhistoria [Dallas Detective Story],"
Elöre (Bucharest), XVIII (10 April 1964), 3.

2349. "Como E Stato Ucciso Kennedy? [What is the Latest on
the Kennedy Slaying?]," Época (Milan), LXV (23 Oct. 1966),
34-41.

2350. "Who Killed Kennedy?" Fact, III (Nov.-Dec. 1966), 2-17.

2351. "Hvem Myrdede Hven og Hvorfor? [Who Murdered Whom and Why?]," Frit Danmark (Copenhagen), XXII (1963-1964), 3-5.

2352. "Vrae Wat nog Hinder na Kennedy-Moord [A Question Which Still is an Obstacle in the Kennedy Assassination]," Huis en haard (Pretoria), XLII (2 Dec. 1966), 18-21.

2353. "A Dallasi Tragédia," Magyar Szovjet közgazdásagi szemble (Budapest), XXI (14 Oct. 1964), 273-285.

2354. "A Theory on Kennedy Killing: Writer Postulates a Conspiracy Involving 7 Persons [Cites Buchanan]," National Guardian, XVI (28 March 1964), 1, 10.

2355. "Find Cuban Agent Secretly Held by U.S. for 3 Years Who . . . Told of Plot 8 Days Before JFK's Assassination," The National Enquirer (16 Apr. 1967), 2-6.

2356. "Mystery Miami Murder Linked to JFK Plot," The National Enquirer (30 Apr. 1967), 3-4.

2357. "General Walker, the Other Man Oswald Tried to Kill Says . . ." The National Enquirer (21 May 1967), 4-5.

2358. "I Still Get Hate Mail . . . They Blame Me for JFK's Death," The National Enquirer (5 Jan. 1969).

2359. "JFK Slaying Was Part of Military Takeover of the U.S. Govt.," The National Enquirer (14 Sept. 1969), 25-26.

2360. "Group Investigating Assassinations of JFK, RFK and Dr. Martin Luther King Links All Three Murders to the Same Conspiracy," The National Enquirer (20 Sept. 1970), 24.

2361. "Behind the Scenes at JFK's Assassination," The National Enquirer, (27 Sept. 1974), 7-8.

2362. "Enquirer Offers $100,000 Reward for Proof of Conspiracy in JFK Killing," The National Enquirer (2 Sept. 1975), 17.

2363. "JFK & RFK Deaths Were Plotted by Secret & Powerful Group of U.S. Business Leaders," The National Enquirer, (2 Dec. 1975), 48.

2364. "5 Strange Events Prove There Was a Sinister Plot to Kill JFK," The National Enquirer (6 Jan. 1976), 3.

2365. "JFK Was Killed by a Russian Agent," The National Enquirer (4 May 1976), 4.

2366. "1,000,000 Reward . . . For Evidence Leading to Conviction of Conspirators Behind JFK Assassination," The National Enquirer (12 Oct. 1976), 6.

2367. "Enquirer's New JFK Assassination Evidence Is as Good
as Anything the Govt. Has," The National Enquirer (17 May
1977).

2368. "Mystery of JFK Assassination Will Be Solved in 1980,"
The National Enquirer (31 Jan. 1978), 42.

2369. "No Bullets That Hit JFK Were Fired From Front," The
National Enquirer (27 June 1978), 8.

2370. "The Elusive Mr. [Loran Eugene] Hall," The National
Tattler, Special Edition (Sept. 1975), 9, 12, 17-18.

2371. "Same Cast of Characters Has Shaped America's History
from the Bay of Pigs to Watergate," The National Tattler,
Special Edition (Sept. 1975), 14-15.

2372. "With His Death Ex-Deputy Sheriff Craig Becomes 30th
Assassination-Linked Victim," The National Tattler, Special
Edition (Sept. 1975), 16.

2373. "National Affairs: Secret Service: 'Mr. Q' Mystery
[Abraham Bolden]," Newsweek, LXIII (1 June 1964), 20.

2374. "Newsmakers: [Charles de Gaulle's Memoirs on the
Conspiracy Behind Oswald]," Newsweek, LXX (30 Oct. 1967), 49.

2375. "National Affairs: New Assassination Theory," Newsweek, LXX (27 Nov. 1967), 29-35.

2376. "National Affairs: The Assassination: Scene of the
Crime [Where Are They Now?]," Newsweek, LXX (4 Dec. 1967),
31B-32.

2377. "Once Again . . . Once Again [the Parallels of RFK's
Death With JFK]," Newsweek, LXXI (17 June 1968), 20-21.

2378. "Newsmakers: [Notice for Albert H. Newman, The
Assassination of John F. Kennedy: The Reasons Why]," Newsweek, LXXV (8 June 1970), 49.

2379. "Le Mystère Kennedy: Le Témoignage du Gouverneur
Connally [The Kennedy Mystery: Governor Connally's Evi-
dence]," Paris Match, No. 921 (3 Dec. 1966), 64-71.

2380. "JFK," Phoenix, III (2 Feb. 1971), 4.

2381. "Bishop Plans Kennedy Book Despite Family's Objection,"
Publishers' Weekly, CXC (26 Sept. 1966), 107.

2382. "The Editors: Decade of Unanswered Questions," Ramparts, XII (Dec. 1973), 42-44.

2383.   "$250,000 Reward: The Saturday Evening Post Committee to Solve the J.F. Kennedy Assassination," The Saturday Evening Post, CCXLVII (Nov. 1975), 47.

2384.   "Mann Muss immer die Wahrheit sagen [One Must Always Tell the Truth]," SBZ-Archiv. Dokumente, Berichte, Kommentare zu gesamtdeutschen Fragen (Cologne), XIV, Heft 23 (1963).

2385.   "JFK/MLK: Is There More to the Story?"   Senior Scholastic, CIX (18 Nov. 1976), 8-10, 30.

2386.   "Reading Guide [to Books About JFK's Assassination]," Skeptic, No. 9 (Aug. 1975), 43.

2387.   "Kugeln, Köder, und Kubaner.   Theorien über den Kennedy-Mord [Bullet, Decoy, and Cuban.   Theories on Kennedy's Murder]," Der Spiegel (Hamburg), XXI, No. 15 (1967), 97.

2388.   "Kennedy--Tief und Tödlich [Kennedy--Deep and Deadly]," Der Spiegel (Hamburg), XXI, No. 7 (1967), 72-80.

2389.   "The Politics of Murder," Sun, III (5 Nov. 1975), 9.

2390.   "Assassinations/Coups/Conspiracies," Sun, III (19 Nov. 1975), 8.

2391.   "From Bay of Pigs to Dallas," Takeover, IV (1 July 1974), 9.

2392.   "Will Circle Be Unbroken?"   Takeover, IV (4 Sept. 1974), 13.

2393.   "Assassinations, Inc.," Takeover, V (20 Feb. 1975), 7.

2394.   "Who Really Killed JFK?"   Takeover, V (7 April 1975), 2.

2395.   "JFK Big Hit in Town," Takeover, V (11 Dec. 1975), 3.

2396.   "When President Comes Start Clapping," Takeover, VI (1 March 1976), 7.

2397.   "The Assassination: the Phantasmagoria [Dismisses Lane and Connally]," Time, LXXXVIII (25 Nov. 1966), 34-35.

2398.   "The Assassination: Truth v. Death [Review Roberts' Book]," Time, LXXXIX (17 March 1967), 26.

2399.   "The Assassination: Shadow on a Grassy Knoll," Time, LXXXIX (26 May 1967), 21.

2400.   "The Kennedys: Another Death Plot? [Skolnick's Suit and Alleged Chicago Plot vs. JFK]," Time, XCV (20 April 1970), 17-18.

2401. "Investigations: Who Killed J.F.K.? Just One Assassin," Time, CVI (24 Nov. 1975), 32-38.

2402. "Forum: Assassination in Dallas [Includes Letter of E. Howard Hunt from Prison]," Time, CVI (15 Dec. 1975), K4-K6.

2403. "Scandals: J.F.K. and the Mobsters' Moll [Judith C. Exner]," Time, CVI (29 Dec. 1975), 10-11.

2404. "CIA May Have to Publish Kennedy Documents [Judge John Sirica's Order in Suit Brought by Mr. Bernard Fenster-wald]," The Times (London), No. 60,155 (8 Nov. 1977), 8.

2405. "Gunsmoke From Dallas [Reviews Nerin E. Gun, Red Roses from Texas]," The Times Literary Supplement (London), No. 3,255 (16 July 1964), 626.

2406. "Package Deals [Reviews Jackdaw Packet on The Assassi-nation of President Kennedy]," The Times Literary Supplement (London), No. 3,404 (25 May 1967), 463.

2407. "On the Kennedy Assassination," U.S. Farm News, XIX (June 1971), 6.

2408. "Truth About Kennedy Assassination: Questions Raised and Answered," U.S. News and World Report, LXI (10 Oct. 1966), 44-47; [See 389, 735, 973].

2409. "Conspiracy Notes," WIN, X (7 Feb. 1974), 19.

2410. "Is the White Wash Getting Dirty?" Worker's Power, No. 38 (5 Dec. 1975), 2.

Part V: Related Topics
(1) POLICE OFFICER TIPPIT AND HIS FAMILY

Articles by Authors:

2411. Belin, David. "Truth Was My Only Goal [Reply to Sylvia Meagher]," The Texas Observer, LXIII (13 Aug. 1971), 13-15.

2412. Thompson, Thomas. "In Texas a Policeman and an Assassin Are Laid to Rest Too," Life, LV (6 Dec. 1963), 52B-52E.

2413. Thomson, George C. "The Kennedy Hoax [That Tippit Impersonated JFK in the Car]," National Insider (13 Oct. 1968).

2414. Tolbert, Frank X. "The Odd Fate of Oswald's Other Victims," The Saturday Evening Post, CCXXXVII (22-29 Aug. 1964), 68-69.

Anonymous Articles:

2415. "Annenberg Pays Mortgage Debt for Mrs. Tippit [of $12,217]," Editor & Publisher, XCVI (7 Dec. 1963), 61.

2416. "Tippitt [sic] Fund---from $300 to $450,000," Editor & Publisher, XCVII (4 Jan. 1964), 12.

2417. "JFK's Killer Made Me $650,000 Richer . . . But It Can't Bring Me Back My Dear Husband," The National Enquirer, (6 Dec. 1964), 3.

2418. "A New Look at Tippit Killing: Warren Report's Version Challenged," National Guardian, XVII (31 Oct. 1964), 8.

2419. "Money Pours In for Two Dallas Widows," U.S. News and World Report, LV (16 Dec. 1963), 16.

2420. "A Story of Generosity [Donations to Tippit's Family]," U.S. News and World Report, LVI (20 Jan. 1964), 46.

2421. "$650,000 for Family of Man Killed by Oswald," U.S. News and World Report, LVII (2 Nov. 1964), 9.

(2) OSWALD THE FAMILY MAN: MARINA AND MARGUERITE

Books:

2422. Joesten, Joachim. Marina Oswald. London, 1967.

2423. McMillan, Priscilla Johnson. Marina and Lee. New York: Harper & Row, 1977; [See 1901, 3812, 4360, 4665, 4714, 4990].

2424. Oswald, Robert L., with Myrick and Barbara Land. Lee: a Portrait of Lee Harvey Oswald by His Brother. New York: Coward-McCann, 1967; [See 4105, 4476].

2425. Stafford, Jean. A Mother in History [Interviews with Mrs. Marguerite Oswald]. New York: Farrar, Straus and Giroux, 1966; Bantam Paperbacks, 1966; London, 1966; [See 2423, 4000, 4004].

Articles by Authors:

2426. Asbell, Bernard. "10 Years Later: A Legacy of Torment Haunts Those Closest to the JFK Assassination," Todays Health, LI (Oct. 1973), 56-65.

2427. Blake, Patricia. "Books: the Making of an Assassin [Reviews Marina and Lee]," Time, CX (14 Nov. 1977), 106-109.

2428. Gelman, David, and Elaine Shannon. "Marina Oswald's Story," Newsweek, XCII (25 Sept. 1978), 45.

2429. Grove, Larry. "From 'Monkeys in a Cage' to a Quiet Life on a Ranch in Texas: 'My Name is Porter, Not Oswald,'" The National Tattler, XIX (25 Nov. 1973), 7.

2430. Gun, Nerin. "J.F.K.--One Year Later: Mrs. Oswald's Plea: Give My Children a Chance," Pageant, XX (Dec. 1964), 24-31.

2431. McMillan, Priscilla Johnson. "Marina and Lee; Why Oswald Really Killed Kennedy," Ladies Home Journal, XCIV (Oct. 1977), 175-186; XCIV (Nov. 1977), 122-123, 179-196, 200-208, 212-216.

2432. Martin, William C. "Welcome to the Lee Harvey Oswald Memorial Library and Research Institute, Marguerite C. Oswald, Director," Esquire, LXXIX (Jan. 1973), 142-143, 160.

2433. Oswald, Robert L., with Myrick and Barbara Land. "Oswald: He Was my Brother," Look, XXXI (17 Oct. 1967), 62-74.

2434. Sokolov, Raymond. "Books: Dallas Housewife [Review of Marina and Lee]," Newsweek, XC (31 Oct. 1977), 105.

2435. Stafford, Jean. "The Strange World of Marguerite Oswald," McCall's Magazine, XCIII (Oct. 1965), 112-113, 192-202.

2436. Thompson, Thomas. "Exclusive Marina Oswald Interview," People, I (4 Mar. 1974).

2437. West, Jessamyn. "Prelude to Tragedy: the Woman Who Sheltered Lee Oswald's Family Tells Her Story [Ruth Paine of Irving, Texas]," Redbook, CXXIII (July 1964), 53, 84-92.

2438. _____. "Marina Oswald Porter: Seven Years After Dallas," Redbook, CXXXV (Aug. 1970), 57-59, 129-135.

   Anonymous Articles:

2439. "Mrs. Lee Harvey Oswald Watches the Baptism of Her Daughter," Life, LVI (1 May 1964), 36B.

2440. "Cover: Oswald's Full Russian Diary: He and Marina in Minsk," Life, LVII (10 July 1964), 1, 26-31.

2441. "Marina Oswald Becomes a Michigan Coed," Life, LVIII (15 Jan. 1965), 40C.

2442. "Wedding of the Week: in Fate, Texas [Marina Weds Kenneth Porter]," Life, LVIII (11 June 1965), 42.

2443. "FBI Finds Mrs. Oswald's Dad in Red Spy Group," The National Enquirer (5 Jan. 1964), 8.

2444. "Oswald's Widow Isn't Telling Truth About JFK Killing," The National Enquirer (30 Dec. 1977), 4.

2445. "Oswald Panel Hears Mother: First Defense Witness," National Guardian, XVI (13 Feb. 1964), 1, 6.

2446. "How NYU Almost Shut Free Speech Out of Town Hall: Report to Readers [Refusing Podium for Marguerite Oswald]," National Guardian, XVI (20 Feb. 1964), 1-2.

2447. "Overflow at Town Hall: Mother and Mark Lane Speak," National Guardian, XVI (27 Feb. 1964), 9.

2448. "Newsmakers: [Marina Oswald's Interview]," Newsweek, LXIII (10 Feb. 1964), 48.

2449. "National Affairs: Investigation: 'Brave Little Woman' [Marina Oswald Testifies Before Warren Commission]," Newsweek, LXIII (17 Feb. 1964), 17-18.

2450. "The Assassination: Week in the Sun [Marguerite Oswald]," Newsweek, LXIII (24 Feb. 1964), 29.

2451. "Newsmakers: Town Talk . . . Marguerite Oswald [Lectures in New York]," Newsweek, LXIII (2 Mar. 1964), 47.

2452. "TV-Radio: 'Wasn't It Fun?' [a Les Crane Interview with Marguerite Oswald]," Newsweek, LXIV (17 Aug. 1964), 80.

2453. "The Periscope: Inside Story: Dallas [Marina Oswald Plans Book With Harper & Row]," Newsweek, LXIV (21 Sept. 1964), 23-24.

2454. "The Periscope: Cross-Country Wire: Dallas [Marina Oswald's Re-adjustments]," Newsweek, LXIV (5 Oct. 1964), 28; LXIV (19 Oct. 1964), 22; LXIV (30 Nov. 1964), 60.

2455. "Newsmakers: Gift of Gab [Marina Oswald Enrolls in English Language Institute, University of Michigan]," Newsweek, LXV (18 Jan. 1965), 46; LXV (22 Feb. 1965), 46.

2456. "National Affairs: Americana: Love Story [Marina Weds Kenneth Porter]," Newsweek, LXV (14 June 1965), 43-46.

2457. "Newsmakers: Too Much Already [Marina Porter's New Marital Problems]," Newsweek, LXVI (30 Aug. 1965), 48.

2458. "Books: Mama Oswald [Reviews Jean Stafford, A Mother in History]," Newsweek, LXVII (28 Feb. 1966), 93-94.

2459. "Newsmakers: [Marina Oswald Plans Role in Film 'Countdown in Dallas' for $20,000.00 Plus Royalties]," Newsweek, LXX (25 Sept. 1967), 40.

2460. "The Periscope: The Marina Oswald Story," Newsweek, LXXV (12 Jan. 1970), 11.

2461. "Newsmakers: [Marina Oswald Porter's Attempts to Recover Lee Harvey Oswald's Possessions from the Government]," Newsweek, LXXXI (12 Mar. 1973), 42.

2462. "Update: Oswald's Widow," Newsweek, LXXXVI (11 Aug. 1975), 9.

2463. "Newsmakers: [Marina Oswald Porter Plugging Her Book, Marina and Lee]," Newsweek, XC (26 Sept. 1977), 74.

2464. "Investigations: Dear Ma [Excerpts from Oswald to Marguerite]," Time, LXXXII (20 Dec. 1963), 13-14.

2465. "Women: Three Widows," Time, LXXXIII (3 Jan. 1964), 29.

2466. "Investigations: a Mother who Wants to Write," Time, LXXXIII (21 Feb. 1964), 23-24.

2467. "Investigations: The Man Who Wanted to Kill Nixon," Time, LXXXIII (19 June 1964), 21.

2468. "The Presidency: In Remembrance [of JFK]; The Others," Time, LXXXIV (27 Nov. 1964), 32-34.

2469. "People: 'The Eight-Week Crash course at the University of Michigan's English Language Institute': Marina Oswald," Time, LXXXV (1 Jan. 1965), 38.

2470. "[Marina Oswald Re-marries]," Time, LXXXV (11 June 1 1965), 48.

2471. "[Marina Oswald Porter Has Husband Arrested for Assault With a Gun]," Time, LXXXVI (27 Aug. 1965), 28.

2472. "People: 'Auctioning Off the Documentary Remains of Her Son' [for $7,165.00 to Marguerite Oswald]," Time, LXXXVI (8 Oct. 1965), 53.

2473. "Oswald's Widow Says He Tried to Kill Mr. Nixon [in Article in Ladies Home Journal]," The Times (London), No. 60,112 (19 Sept. 1977), 4.

2474. "Lee Oswald's Widow Tells Her Story," U.S. News and World Report, LVI (17 Feb. 1964), 19.

(3) OSWALD'S MURDER: THE RUBY TRIAL

Books:

2475. Belli, Melvin M., with Maurice C. Carroll. Dallas
Justice: the Real Story of Jack Ruby and His Trial. New
York: David McKay Co., 1964; [See 3791].

2476. Gertz, Elmer. Moment of Madness: the People vs. Jack
Ruby. Chicago: The Follett Publishing Co., 1968.

2477. Hunter, Diana, and Alice Anderson. Jack Ruby's Girls.
Atlanta: Hallux, Ind., 1970.

2478. Kaplan, John, and Jon R. Waltz. The Trial of Jack
Ruby: a Classic Study of Courtroom Strategies. New York:
Macmillan, 1965; [See 3981].

2479. Joesten, Joachim. La Verité sur le cas Jack Ruby
[Truth in the Jack Ruby Case]. Paris: Casterman, 1967.

2480. Kantor, Seth. Who Was Jack Ruby? New York: Everest
House, 1978. Originally entitled The Ruby Detail, promised
by Zebra Books but published here instead.

2481. Pottecher, Frédéric. Grands procès, II: Dallas:
affaire Ruby [Great Trials: Dallas]. Paris: Arthaud, 1964,
1965.

2482. _____. Le procès de Dallas [The Trial
in Dallas]. Paris: Librairie Jules Tallandier, 1965.

2483. _____. Dallas: l'affaire Ruby. Genève:
Édito-Service, 1971 [Reprints First Book, with New Preface
and Epilogue].

2484. Stern, R. Le procès Ruby--Dallas [The Trial of Ruby
in Dallas]. Kapellen, Belgium: Beckers, 1967.

2485. Wills, Garry, and Ovid Demaris. Jack Ruby: the Man
Who Killed the Man Who Killed Kennedy. New York: New American Library, 1968.

Articles by Authors:

2486. [Arnoni, M. S.]. "Jack Ruby Cheats History," The
Minority of One, IX (Feb. 1967), 8.

2487. Bedford, Sybille. "The Ruby Trial: a Chance to
Redeem a Tragedy," Life, LVI (28 Feb. 1964), 36-36B.

2488. _____. "'Violence, Froth, Sob Stuff--Was
Justice Done?'" Life, LVI (27 March 1964), 32-34B, 70A-74.

2489. Beers, Jack. "How We Remember That Terrible Time:
Story Behind the Two Most Shocking Photos of All," The
National Tattler, XIX (25 Nov. 1973), 11.

2490. Boroson, Warren. "The Bellicose Mr. Belli," Fact, I
(July-Aug. 1964), 2-13.

2491. Bromberg, Walter, and Elmer Gertz. "Correspondence:
The Last Madness of Jack Ruby," The New Republic, CLVI (25
Feb. 1967), 42-43.

2492. Callahan, John W. "Did Jack Ruby Kill the Wrong Man?"
Argosy, CCCLXV (Sept. 1967), 29, 96-104.

2493. Cartwright, H. L. "Letters: Justice and Oswald," The
Nation, CXCVII (21 Dec. 1963), 424.

2494. Castellano, Lillian. "Oswald Censored: from Readers'
Letters," The Minority of One, VII (March 1965), 30.

2495. Chambliss, Sanford. "Who Killed Jack Ruby?" Real
Magazine, XVIII (April 1967), 40-42.

2496. Cordon [and] Veggeberg. "Ruby/I was Framed to Kill
Oswald," Great Speckled Bird, VIII (29 May 1975), 6.

2497. Dugger, Ronnie. "The Last Madness of Jack Ruby," The
New Republic, CLVI (11 Feb. 1967), 19-23.

2498. Fiddick, Thomas C. "What Ruby Did Not Tell," The
Minority of One, (Nov. 1965), 15-16.

2499. Gertz, Elmer, and Wayne B. Giampietro. "The Trial of
'State Cases': a Postscript on the Jack Ruby Trial," DePaul
Law Review, XVI (1967), 285-308.

2500. Havemann, Ernest. "Defendant Ruby Will Meet the
Ghost of a Long Dead Scot [the McNaughten Rule]," Life, LVI
(21 Feb. 1964), 30-33.

2501. Hegyi, Károly. "A Dallasi Itélethirdetés Után [After
Sentence Was Given at Dallas]," Elöre (Bucharest), XVIII (17
Mar. 1964), 3.

2502. Hitt, Dick. "A Bouncer at History's Door . . . :
Ruby," The National Tattler, XIX (25 Nov. 1973), 12.

2503. Kempton, Murray. "Jack Ruby--Surviving Victim," The
Spectator, (London), No. 7079 (28 Feb. 1964), 270.

2504. _____. "Boy, Don't You Know I'm on Camera?"
The New Republic, CL (29 Feb. 1964), 7.

2505. _____. "Jack Ruby on Trial: 'Leave Me a
Little Dignity'," The New Republic, CL (7 Mar. 1964), 17-20.

2506. _____ . "Who Killed Jack Ruby? [Reviews Book by Kaplan and Waltz]," The New Republic, CLIII (27 Nov. 1965), 25-28.

2507. _____ . "Ruby, Oswald and the State," The Spectator (London), No. 7217 (21 Oct. 1966), 506-507.

2508. _____ . "The Disposable Jack Ruby," The Spectator (London), No. 7229 (13 Jan. 1967), 35.

2509. Kerr, James. ". . . And the Dying Thoughts of Ruby Himself Remain as a Provocative Perplexing Puzzle," The National Tattler, XIX (25 Nov. 1973), 28.

2510. Lane, Mark. "Who Is Jack Ruby?," The Minority of One, VII (April 1965), 8-11.

2511. Lane, Paul R. "Obscure Grave Now Hides His [Ruby's] Secret," The National Tattler, XIX (25 Nov. 1973), 12.

2512. Lewis, Richard Warren. "A Flashy Lawyer for Oswald's Killer [Melvin Belli]," The Saturday Evening Post, CCXXXVII (8 Feb. 1964), 28-30.

2513. Linn, Edward. "Appointment in Dallas: the Untold Story of Jack Ruby," The Saturday Evening Post, CCXXXVII (25 July-1 Aug. 1964), 24-49.

2514. McConal, Jon. "A Grim Note of Comedy Is Struck at Graveside: Reporter Theorized [Oswald's] Body Was Stolen," The National Tattler, XIX (25 Nov. 1973), 8-9.

2515. Malone, William Scott. "The Secret Life of Jack Ruby," New Times (New York), (23 Jan. 1978), 46-51.

2516. Popa, Stefan. "Dallas: Procesul Ruby [Dallas: Ruby's Trial]," Lumea (Bucharest), VIII (20 Feb. 1964), 10-11; (27 Feb. 1964), 8-9.

2517. _____ . "Dallas 'Paziti-l Bine pe Ruby [Dallas Guarding Ruby's Rights]," Lumea (Bucharest), II (26 Mar. 1964), 10-11.

2518. Poznanska, A. "Procès á Dallas [Trial in Dallas]," Cité libre (Montreal), XV (April 1964), 26-28.

2519. Revere, Guy. "Jack Ruby: the Mafia's Man in Dallas," Saga, XXXIII (Mar. 1967), 28-31, 86-90.

2520. Ruby, Jack, with David Welsh. "A Letter from Jail," Ramparts, V (Feb. 1967), 17-21.

2521. Ruby, Jack, with William Read Woodfield. "Why I Kille the Assassin," New York Journal-American, (28 Jan. 1964).

2522.   Szasz, Thomas S.   "Criminal Insanity: Facts or Strategy?"   The New Republic, CLI (21 Nov. 1964), 19-22.

2523.   Tupa, Stefan.   "Dallas: Declaraţii şi Ipoteze," Lumea (Bucharest), XI (12 Mar. 1964), 9-10.

2524.   Tuteur, Werner.   "Dialogue in Dallas: Psychiatric Examination of Jack Ruby [on 12-15 July 1965 in Dallas County Jail]," MH [Mental Hygiene], LVIII (Spring 1974), 6-10.

2525.   Ushakov, G.   "Dallas Merry-Go-Round," New Times (Moscow), (18 Mar. 1964), 27-29.

2526.   Wainwright, Loudon.   "Exit Jack Ruby, a Nobody With One Big Moment," Life, LXII (13 Jan. 1967), 18.

2527.   Watson, Peter.   "Ruby Told Doctor of 'Plot' to Kill Kennedy," The Sunday Times (London), No. 7889 (25 Aug. 1974), 5.

2528.   Wills, Garry, and Ovid Demaris.   "You All Know Me!   I'm Jack Ruby!; The Disposal of Jack Ruby," Esquire, LXVII (May 1967), 79-87, 153-164; LXVII (June 1967), 131-135, 172-184.

2529.   Winston, Frank, and John Moulder.   "Lawyers Wrangle On: Belli, Wade, Alexander," The National Tattler, XIX (25 Nov. 1973), 13, 20.

2530.   Worthington, Peter.   "The Limelight: Why Jack Ruby's First Trial Couldn't Happen Here," Macleans' (Toronto), LXXVII (18 April 1964), 3-4.

     Anonymous Articles:

2531.   "Editorials: The Rights of Men . . . Power and Responsibility," America, CIX (14 Dec. 1963), 761.

2532.   "Hungarian Cartoonists and Jack Ruby," Atlas, VII (Feb. 1964), 113.

2533.   "Radio-TV Barred From Ruby Trial," Broadcasting, LXV (23 Dec. 1963), 56.

2534.   "Radio-TV Newsmen Testify in Ruby Trial," Broadcasting, LXVI (16 Mar. 1964), 74.

2535.   "Murder, Justice and TV; a Newsy Trio," Broadcasting, LXVI (23 March 1964), 90.

2536.   "Filling Out the Jury," Chemical Week, XCIV (7 March 1964), 24.

2537.   "Dallas on Trial," The Economist (London), CCX (22 Feb. 1964), 700-703.

2538. "Dallas in Two Minds," The Economist (London), CCX (21 March 1964), 1107-1108.

2539. "PR Firm Sets Press Rules For Judge at Ruby's Trial," Editor & Publisher, XCVI (28 Dec. 1963), 9.

2540. "Bloom Tells His Public Relations Role in Ruby Case," Editor & Publisher, XCVII (1 Feb. 1964), 58.

2541. "Jack Ruby's Story [written by William Read Woodfield]," Editor & Publisher, XCVII (1 Feb. 1964), 58.

2542. "48 Seats at Ruby's Trial for Press; Protest Filed: Half Are for 'National' Media," Editor & Publisher, XCVII (15 Feb. 1964), 14, 66.

2543. "125 Allowed in Court at Ruby's Trial," Editor & Publisher, XCVII (22 Feb. 1964), 61.

2544. "Ruby Always Around, Acting Like Reporter," Editor & Publisher, XCVII (14 March 1964), 15.

2545. "Ruby Death Verdict: a TV 'Spectacular'," Editor & Publisher, XCVII (21 March 1964), 11, 55.

2546. "Was This Man Sane?" Life, LVI (21 Feb. 1964), 26-29.

2547. "Trauma [Study of Ruby by Forensic Pathologist]," Medico-Legal Journal, VI (Dec. 1964).

2548. "Editorials: The Jack Ruby Case," The Nation, CC (29 March 1965), 323.

2549. "Jack Ruby Was Railroaded into the Death Cell," The National Enquirer (9 Aug. 1964), 14.

2550. "Psychiatrist Reveals His In-Depth Interviews with Jack Ruby," The National Enquirer (21 Jan. 1975), 20.

2551. "A Jack Ruby 'Suicide' Is Predicted: Buchanan Urges [Warren] Panel to Remove Killer From Dallas," National Guardian, XVI (4 April 1964), 6.

2552. "Ruby Is Balked in Plea to Meet Warren Board: Killer Called 'Unstable'," National Guardian, XVI (2 May 1964), 9.

2553. "Belli Charges a Cop Spurred Ruby to 'Lynching' of Oswald: Lane Asks Investigation," National Guardian, XVI (8 Aug. 1964), 5.

2554. "The Dallas Story: [Ruby's Trial and the Dallas Morning News Advertisement 22 Nov. 1963]," The New Republic, CXLIX (21 Dec. 1963), 2.

2555. "Police in Dallas," The New Republic, CL (18 Jan. 1964), 8.

2556. "T.R.B. from Washington: Jack Ruby Died in Dallas of
Cancer," The New Republic, CLVI (14 Jan. 1967), 6.

2557. "National Affairs: 'I Got Principles'," Newsweek, LXII
(9 Dec. 1963), 44-46; [See 3893].

2558. "The Assassination: Day in Court," Newsweek, LXIII
(6 Jan. 1964), 18-19.

2559. "National Affairs: Dallas: Ruby's 'Fugue State',"
Newsweek, LXIII (3 Feb. 1964), 25-26.

2560. "Press: By Jack Ruby," Newsweek, LXII (10 Feb. 1964),
79-80; LXIII (2 March 1964), 5.

2561. "National Affairs: Trials: War of Nerves," Newsweek,
LXIII (2 March 1964), 19.

2562. "National Affairs: Trials: On Camera," Newsweek,
LXIII (16 March 1964), 31-32.

2563. "National Affairs: Trials: The Avenger," Newsweek,
LXIII (23 March 1964), 28-31.

2564. "Medicine: The 'Possessed'," Newsweek, LXIII (23
March 1964), 66.

2565. "National Affairs: Trials: Good-by, Belli," Newsweek,
LXIII (30 March 1964), 19.

2566. "National Affairs: The Assassination: Ruby's Fantasy," Newsweek, LXIII (11 May 1964), 23.

2567. "Press: What's Your Source? [Dorothy Kilgallen's
Scoop on Ruby's Testimony]," Newsweek, LXIV (31 Aug. 1964),
68-69.

2568. "National Affairs: Dallas: Objection Sustained,"
Newsweek, LXVIII (17 Oct. 1966), 31-32.

2569. "The Assassination: 'Who Can Understand?'," Newsweek,
LXIX (16 Jan. 1967), 28-29.

2570. "Playboy Interview: Melvin Belli," Playboy, XII (June
1965), 77-88, 170-172.

2571. "In Jurul Procesului de la Dallas. Răsfoind Presa
Străină [In the Jury Trial at Dallas: Looking through the
Foreign Press]," Scinteia, XXXIII (9 March 1964), 4.

2572. "Jack Ruby: 19. II. 1911--3. I. 1967 [Jack Ruby
19 Feb. 1911-3 Jan. 1967]," Der Spiegel (Hamburg), XXI, No. 3
(1967), 72.

2573. "Can Ruby Tell?," The Sunday Times (London), No. 7481
(9 Oct. 1966), 8.

2574. "Political Intelligence: [U.S. Nazi Leader George
Rockwell's Speech Near JFK Assassination Site; Dallas Police

Lt. Says Jack Ruby "Victim of a Gigantic Plot"]," The Texas Observer, LVII (16 April 1965), 12.

2575. "The Law: Lawyers: Belli for the Defense: a Flamboyant Advocate," Time, LXXXII (20 Dec. 1963), 48.

2576. "Investigations: For the Defense," Time, LXXXIII (31 Jan. 1964), 20-21.

2577. "Investigations: a Defendant Who Wants Attention," Time, LXXXIII (21 Feb. 1964), 23.

2578. "The Law: Juries: 'Like Picking a Wife'," Time, LXXXIII (28 Feb. 1964), 53-54.

2579. "Trials: Another Day in Dallas; The Ruby Jurors," Time, LXXXIII (13 March 1964), 24-25.

2580. "Trials: Death for Ruby," Time, LXXXIII (20 March 1964), 27-28.

2581. "The Law: Lawyers: Casus Belli [After the Ruby Verdict]," Time, LXXXIII (27 March 1964), 34-36.

2582. "The Law: Lawyers: the Ruby Scorecard," Time, LXXXIII (3 April 1964), 68.

2583. "Texas: Trying for the Truth of It," Time, LXXXIII (8 May 1964), 26.

2584. "The Law: Lawyers: And So to Court," Time, LXXXIV (31 July 1964), 62.

2585. "The Press: Reporters: 50,000 Word Leak," Time, LXXXIV (28 Aug. 1964), 40.

2586. "The Law: Trials: The Ruby Circus," Time, LXXXVI (5 Nov. 1965), 86.

2587. "Sequels: A Last Wish," Time, LXXXVIII (30 Dec. 1966), 12.

2588. "The Assassination: A Non-Entity for History," Time, LXXXIX (13 Jan. 1967), 16-17.

2589. "The Law: Criminal Justice: What Does a Change of Venue Gain?," Time, LXXXIX (13 Jan. 1967), 39-40.

2590. "Historical Notes: The Infamous Cobra," Time, LXXXIX (31 March 1967), 23.

2591. "Ruby and the King of Torts," The Times Literary Supplement (London), No. 3,342 (17 March 1966), 221; No. 3,344 (31 March 1966), 263.

2592. "Jack Ruby's Strange Trial--New Chapter in Assassination Story," U.S. News and World Report, LVI (23 March 1964), 70.

2593. "Now, a Chance of Freedom for Jack Ruby," U.S. News and World Report, LXI (17 Oct. 1966), 16.

(4) FICTION RELATED TO EVENTS IN DALLAS: A SELECTION OF NOVELS, PLAYS AND FILMS

Novels:

2594. Agel, Jerome, and Eugene Boe. Twenty-Two Fires [Was Mrs. JFK the Target?]. New York: Bantam, 1977.

2595. Anthony, Evelyn [pseudonym for Eve Stephens]. The Assassin. New York: Coward, 1970.

2596. Barkus, G. Z. A. Incident at Credibility Gap and the Innocent Child. Greenwich, Conn.: Paper Bag Books, 1967.

2597. Bealle, Morris A. Guns of the Regressive Right, or How to Kill a President. Washington, D.C.: Columbia Publishing Co., 1964.

2598. Bourjaily, Vance. The Man Who Knew Kennedy. New York: Dial Press, 1967.

2599. Brammer, William. The Gay Place [Three Novels in One, About Texas Politics and Conspiracies]. New York: Houghton Mifflin, 1961; Fawcett, 1964.

2600. Condon, Richard A. The Manchurian Candidate. New York: McGraw-Hill, 1959.

2601. _____. Winter Kills. New York: Dial Press, 1974.

2602. Davis, Marc. Spector; a novel. New York: Scribner, 1970.

2603. Dimona, Joseph. Last Man at Arlington. New York: Arthur Fields Books, Inc., 1973.

2604. Douglass, William C. The Eagle's Feather. New Orleans, La.: Free Men Speak, Inc., 1966.

2605. Edwards, A. Post-Mortem. New York: Coward-McCann, 1971.

2606. Fox, Victor J. [pseudonym]. The White House Case; a Sequel to the Pentagon Case. Pleasantville, New York: Fargo Press, 1968.

2607. Freed, Donald, and Mark Lane. Executive Action:
Assassination of a Head of State. Introduction by Richard H.
Popkin. New York: Dell, 1973.

2608. Freedman, Nancy (Mars). Joshua Son of None. New
York: Delacorte Press, 1973.

2609. Garrison, Jim. The Star Spangled Contract. New York:
McGraw-Hill, 1976; Warner Books, 1977.

2610. Gosset, Pierre and Renée. L'Homme qui Crut Tuer
Kennedy [The Man Who Thought of Killing Kennedy]. Paris:
Presses de la Cité, 1967.

2611. Harris, Mark. Mark the Glove Boy: or, The Last Days
of Richard Nixon. New York: Macmillan Co., 1964.

2612. Heath, Peter. Assassins From Tomorrow. New York:
Lancer Books, 1967.

2613. Jones, J. Harry, Jr. A Private Army. New York:
Collier Books, 1969; rev. ed. of The Minuteman, New York:
Doubleday, 1968.

2614. Kavanaugh, Paul [pseudonym]. Triumph of Evil. New
York: World, 1971.

2615. King, Mary Paula [Mrs. Edwin O'Donnell]. You Can Hear
the Echo. New York: Simon and Schuster, 1965.

2616. Le Carre, John. The Looking-Glass War. New York:
Coward, 1965.

2617. McCarry, Charles. The Tears of Autumn. New York:
Saturday Review Press, E.P. Dutton & Co., 1974.

2618. Malzberg, Barry N. The Destruction of the Temple.
New York: Pocket Books, 1974.

2619. _____. Scop. New York: Pyramid, 1976.

2620. Marchetti, Victor. Rope Dancer. New York: Grosset
& Dunlap, 1971.

2621. Morris, Wright. One Day: This Being the Day in
November the Word From Dallas Was Heard in Escondido. New
York: Atheneum, 1965.

2622. Names, Larry D. Twice Dead. N.p.: Leisure Books,
1978.

2623. Oates, Joyce Carol. The Assassins. New York: Van-
guard Press, 1975.

2624. Olden, Marc. The Harker File. New York: Signet, 19
1976.

2625. Pearl, Jack. The Plot to Kill the President. New
York: Pinnacle Books, 1972.

2626. Rennert, Maggie. A Moment in Camelot. New York:
Grove, 1968.

2627. Seter, 'Ido [pseudonym for Yeheskel Laufban]. Oz
ya'uz neged rotshe Kenedi [Force Will Move Against Kennedy's
Murderers]. Tel Aviv: N. Tuersky, 1964.

2628. Shea, Robert, and Robert Anton Wilson. The Eye in the
Pyramid. New York: Dell, 1975.

2629. Shrake, Edwin. Strange Peaches. (?)

2630. Singer, Loren. The Parallax View. Garden City, New
York: Doubleday, 1970.

2631. Susann, Jacqueline. Dolores. New York: William
Morrow, 1976.

2632. Syme, Anthony V. The Assassins. London, Melbourne,
Sydney: Horwitz Publications, 1967.

2633. Thurston, Wesley S. The Trumpets of November. New
York: Bernard Geis, 1966.

2634. Uris, Leon. Topaz [Borrowed Heavily from Lamia, by
De Vosjoli]. New York: McGraw-Hill, 1967.

2635. Warren, David M. The Plot to Kill John F. Kennedy.
Chicago: Novel Books, 1965.

2636. Wilgus, Neal. The Illuminoids [Occult Assassination
Conspiracies]. New York: Pocket Books, 1978.

   Plays:

2637. Baker, Paul [Director]. "Macbeth by William Shakes-
peare [Reinterpretation Using JFK's Murder]. Dallas Theater
Center, 29 Nov. 1968.

2638. Collins, Jeremiah, and Mark William. "JFK: a One-Man
Show," Nov. 1971.

2639. DNA Collective. "Sparky and the Truth Detector," San
Francisco, First Unitarian Church, 1975.

2640. Ducovny, Amram, and Leon Friedman. "The Trial of Lee
Harvey Oswald," New York City, Anta Theater, 5 Nov. 1967;
[See 4356, 4456-4458].

2641. Garson, Barbara. MacBird. Berkeley, California:
Grassy Knoll Press, 1966; New York: Grove Press, 1967; [See
4109, 4132, 4277].

2642. Hastings, Michael. Lee Harvey Oswald: a Far Mean
Streak of Independence Brought on by Neglect. Harmondsworth,
England: Penguin Modern Playwrights Series III, 1966; [See
4096].

2643. Logan, John. "Jack Ruby, All American Boy," Dallas
Theater Center, 23 April 1974, Directed by Paul Baker.

2644. Louis, J. C. "A Die-Hard for Dallas," 1976.

2645. Lützkendorf, Felix. Dallas 22 November. Ein Szeni-
scher Bericht [Dallas 22 November. A Scenic Report]. Basel:
Verlag Kurt Desch, 1965; [See 1574, 2677, 3989].

2646. McIntyre, Mark. "J. F. K. Lives," San Francisco, Montgomery Playhouse, Feb. 1977.

2647. Marks, Stanley J. "A Time to Die, A Time to Cry," Los
Angeles, 1971.

2648. Patrick, Robert. Kennedy's Children. New York:
Random House, 1976.

   Films:

2649. The Eternal Frame. 24 minutes. 22 Nov. 1975. Produced by T. R. Uthco and the Ant Farm.

2650. Executive Action. 91 minutes. 1973. Screenplay by
Dalton Trumbo. Directed by David Miller. Based on a novel
by Donald Freed and Mark Lane. Produced by Edward Lewis.
Released by National General Pictures.

   The movie argues extremist businessmen combined with
   dissident intelligence elements to murder JFK who was
   seen as a threat to the continuance of their empires.
   An eight-page leaflet was distributed to patrons asserting to provide the factual background of the movie's
   thesis. In addition to being factually without foundation and logically preposterous, the film's doctrines
   are identical with the doctrines of the book Farewell
   America [1776] an intelligence disinformation operation.
   See the novel Executive Action [2607 and 4733, 4742,
   4763].

2651. Farewell America. Shown 25 Nov. 1968 on UCLA campus.

   Film based on the book Farewell America [1776] and shown
   to a few groups. Originating in France with elements of
   French intelligence associated with it and promoted by
   Herve Lemarre in the U.S., the film's doctrines are
   identical with the book by the same name, an intelligence
   disinformation operation; [See 4632].

2652. Greetings. 88 minutes. 1968. Directed by Brian de
Palma. Distributed by Sigma III.

   Political comedy on the JFK assassination. Contains
   references to Harold Weisberg, the single bullet theory,
   and related subjects.

2653. Lee Oswald, Assassin. 100 minutes. 15 Mar. 1966.
British Broadcasting System. Director Rudolph Cartier.
Adapted from stage work of Munich playwright Felix Lützken-
dorf.

2654. Oswald-Self Portrait. 22 Nov. 1968. Produced by the
Information Council of the Americas. Sponsored by Schick
Safety Razor Co. Narrated by Ed Butler.

   Adapted from the record album of INCA [1142] using documentary scenes. The Procrustes bed of extremist right
   wing political orientation ignores the factual elements
   to force Oswald into a false mold. See Weisberg, Oswald
   in New Orleans [1901].

2655. The Parallax View. 100 minutes. 1974. Directed by
Anthony Pakula. Paramount Pictures.

2656. The Serpent. 90 minutes. 1970. National Educational
Television Playhouse.

   A "ceremony" with a segment of stylized re-enactment of
   the Zapruder film of the JFK murder.

2657. The Two Kennedys: A View from Europe. 120 minutes.
1976. Directed by Gianna Bisiach. Made in Italy.

   Some Critical Reviews:

2658. Aldridge, John W. "The Kennedy Drama: Matrix for
Novelists [Review of Bourjaily's Novel]," Life, LXII (3 Feb.
1967), 8.

2659. Felberbaum, A. "Letter/Executive Action," Cineaste,
VI (Fall 1974), 42.

2660. Hewes, Henry. "The Theater: Atlanta [Michael
Hasting's Play]," Saturday Review, LI (4 May 1968), 40.

2661. Hicks, Granville. "Books: The Generation of the
Assassination [Reviews Bourjaily's Novel]," Saturday Review,
L (4 Feb. 1967), 35-36.

2662. Kerby, Phil. "This Month: the Two 'Macs' [on Dwight
Macdonald's Review of MacBird]," Frontier, XVIII (Jan. 1967),
2, 21-22.

2663. Millen, J. "Executive Action/Politics of Distortion,"
Cineaste, VI (1974), 8.

2664.   Perry, George.   "The Big If [on the ABC-TV's Version
of The Trial of Lee Harvey Oswald]," The Sunday Times Magazine (London), No. 8048 (18 Sept. 1977), 64-69.

2665.   Pickard, Roy.   "Does This Movie Expose the Real Truth
Behind the Kennedy Killing?," Photoplay, (March 1974), 26-28.

2666.   Robach, M.   "Executive Action: Hollywood Rediscovers
Politics," Ramparts, XII (Dec. 1973), 48-50.

2667.   "Who Killed John F. Kennedy?---Executive Action,"
Films and Filming, (Feb. 1974), 37, 42.

2668.   "Books: Melted Snow [Reviews Bourjaily's Novel],"
Newsweek, LXIX (30 Jan. 1967), 94.

2669.   "Theater: Much Ado About Mac," Newsweek, LXIX (27 Feb.
1967), 99; (6 March 1967), 79.

2670.   "Movies: The Killing of JFK [Reviews Executive
Action]," Newsweek, LXXXII (26 Nov. 1973), 104.

2671.   "Periscope: Wrong Target in Dallas? [Preview of
Twenty-Two Fires]," Newsweek, XC (14 Nov. 1977), 29.

2672.   "[Review of MacBird, by Walter Kerr]," The New York
Times (24 Feb. 1967).

2673.   "Books: Intimations of Mortality: The Man Who Knew
Kennedy by Vance Bourjaily," Time, LXXXIX (10 Feb. 1967), 100.

2674.   "Cinema: Tragedy Trivialized [Reviews Executive
Action]," Time, CII (24 Dec. 1973), 71-73.

2675.   "[Review of MacBird, and Later Note on the British
Production]," Time, LXXXIX (3 March 1967), 52; (21 April
1967), 46.

(5) TV SPECIAL PROGRAMS: A SELECTION

BBC-TV (London, England):

2676.   ____, 23 Nov. 1963:   "That Was The Week That Was".

2677.   ____, 15 March 1966:   "Play of the Month: Lee Oswald:
Assassin" [Written by Felix Lutzkendorf]; [See 2645, 3995,
4005].

2678.   ____, 29 Jan. 1967:   "The Death of Kennedy".

2679.   ____, 17 April 1967:   "Panorama: Jim Garrison Interview".

2680. _____, 2 May 1970: "That Day in Dallas: LBJ Speaks".

2681. _____, 22 Nov. 1973: "Midweek: Did Three Assassins Kill Kennedy?"

2682. _____, 6 March 1978: "Panorama: Who Really Killed Kennedy?"

2683. _____, 16 April 1978: "The Trial of Lee Harvey Oswald" [Original Play from ABC-TV].

CBC-TV (Toronto, Canada):

2684. _____, ? 1978: "The Fifth Estate Program: Dallas and After: an Inquiry into the Assassination of John Kennedy" [Produced by Brian McKenna, Hosted by Adrienne Clarkson].

CBS-TV (New York):

2685. _____, 29 Dec. 1963: "The Law and Lee Oswald [Discussion Between Newton E. Minow of the FCC and Professor Paul Freund of Harvard Law School]".

2686. _____, 27 Sept. 1964: "CBS News Extra: November 22 and the Warren Report [Narrated by Walter Cronkite]"; [See 3743, 3745, 3748].

2687. _____, 19 March 1965: "Ruby States Complete Conspiracy".

2688. _____, 18 Feb. 1967: "News Breaks on Garrison Inquiry".

2689. _____, 25-28 June 1967: "CBS News Inquiry: The Warren Commission Report [Four Part Series, Produced by Leslie Midgely, Narrated by Walter Cronkite]"; [See 738].

2690. _____, 25-26 Nov. 1975: "CBS Reports Inquiry: The American Assassins: Lee Harvey Oswald and John F. Kennedy [Two of Four Parts, Executive Producer Leslie Midgely, Narrated by Dan Rather]".

NBC-TV (New York):

2691. _____, 19 June 1967: "The JFK Conspiracy: the Case of Jim Garrison".

2692. _____, 15 July 1967: "Jim Garrison, New Orleans' District Attorney . . . Reply to an NBC News Program Broadcast on June 19th"; [See 4414, 4415, 4417, 4421].

2693. _____, 14 Aug. 1967: "Huntley-Brinkley News: Commentary on Garrison".

Others:

2694. WNEW-TV, New York City, 12 Nov. 1966.

2695. WNYC-TV, New York City, 23 Dec. 1966 and 3 Jan. 1967: "The Barry Gray Show".

2696. KTTV, Los Angeles, Feb. 1967: "Stan Lomax Program".

2697. WFAA-TV, Dallas, 9 Dec. 1967: "Interview with Jim Garrison, by Murphy Martin".

(6) THE SURVIVING KENNEDYS

Books:

2698. Clinch, N. G. The Kennedy Neurosis. Foreword by Bruce Mazlish. New York: Grosset & Dunlop, 1973.

2699. The Complete Kennedy Saga. Hollywood, California: Associated Professional Services, 1967; 4 vols.

2700. Gatti, Arthur. The Kennedy Curse: An Astrologer's View of the Destiny of America's First Family of Politics. Chicago: Henry Regnery Co., 1976.

2701. Gershenson, Alvin H. Kennedy and Big Business. Beverly Hills, California: Book Company of America, 1964.

2702. Joesten, Joachim. The Case Against the Kennedy Clan: In the Assassination of President John F. Kennedy. Munich: Selbstverlag [Published by Author], 1968.

2703. Lasky, Victor. John F. Kennedy; What's Behind the Image? Washington, D.C.: Free World Press, 1960.

2704. _____. J.F.K.: The Man and the Myth. New York: Macmillan, 1963.

2705. Veritas. Everything You Wanted to Know About Jacqueline Kennedy's Behavior at the Moment of the Assassination of President John F. Kennedy in Dallas on Nov. 22, 1963, Including the Way the News Media Described It at the Time and the Way Mrs. Kennedy Described It Three Years Later. Washington, D.C.: Published by Author, n.d.

Articles by Authors:

2706. Bergquist, Laura. "Valiant Is the Word for Jacqueline," Look, XXVIII (28 Jan. 1964), 72-78.

2707. Davidson, Bill. "A Profile in Family Courage," The Saturday Evening Post, CCXXXVI (14 Dec. 1963), 32b-35.

2708. Goldman, Peter. "National Affairs: A Shadow Over Camelot [the Mistresses and the Mafia]," Newsweek, LXXXVI (29 Dec. 1975), 14-16; LXXXVII (26 Jan. 1976), 18-19; (1 March 1976), 32; (23 Aug. 1976), 38; XC (11 July 1977), 52.

2709. Granton, E. Fannie. "The Lady in Black: U.S. Negroes Look With Nostalgia on Former First Lady's White House Reign," Ebony, XIX (Feb. 1964), 81-86.

2710. Gun, Nerin. "J.F.K.---One Year Later: A Special Report [Jacqueline, Caroline, Robert]," Pageant, XX (Dec. 1964), 24-31.

2711. Hamblin, Dora Jane. "Mrs. Kennedy's Decisions Shaped All the Solemn Pageantry," Life, LV (6 Dec. 1963), 48-49.

2712. Kennedy, Edward M. "Letters to the Editor: Rushing to Judgement," The Saturday Evening Post, CCXLVIII (Jan./Feb. 1976), 4.

2713. Kennedy, Jacqueline. "Mrs. Kennedy Says 'Thank You' to 800,000 Friends," Life, LVI (24 Jan. 1964), 32B-32C.

2714. Moore, Thomas. "Parting Shots: A J.F.K. Impersonator Tries to Be a Funny Man Again [Vaughan Meader's Career]," Life, LXXII (21 Jan. 1972), 68.

2715. O'Neil, Paul. "The Kennedys: 'They Draw the Lightning'," Life, LXIV (14 June 1968), 75-87.

2716. Sparks, Fred. "Jackie: Wife, Widow, Woman," The National Tattler, XIX (25 Nov. 1973), 17-19.

    Anonymous Articles:

2717. "Report JFK Took Out $1 Million Policy," The National Enquirer (29 March 1964), 8.

2718. "The Kennedy Curse," The National Enquirer (13 Aug. 1967), 16-17.

2719. "Details of JFK's Personal Estate Are Finally Revealed," The National Enquirer (15 Feb. 1970), 27.

2720. "Jackie's Secret Testimony on JFK Assassination," The National Enquirer (26 Aug. 1975), 13.

2721. "National Affairs: In Her Time of Trial," Newsweek, LXII (9 Dec. 1963), 29.

Section III:
THE NEW YORK TIMES
Daily Reports, 1963-1978,
Supplemented by
THE WASHINGTON POST, 1978

The New York Times

Volume CXIII

2722. 21 Nov. 1963: "President's Wife as Hostess Again; Resumes Her Social Duties at White House Fete [and to Include a Trip to Texas With the President Tomorrow]," Marjorie Hunter, p. 29.

2723. 22 Nov. 1963: "Kennedy Pledges Space Advances; Opens Texas Tour . . . Party Split Evidenced: Yarborough Scores Connally and Refuses to Accompany Johnson on [San Antonio and Houston] Motorcade," Tom Wicker, pp. 1, 20.

2724. _____: "'64 Plan is Denied by Robert Kennedy," p. 27.

2725. _____: "Nixon Finds Record of Kennedy Weak: Dallas, Nov. 21 (UPI)," p. 27.

2726. _____: "Catholics Can Eat Meat at Kennedy Lunch Today: Dallas, Nov. 21 (UPI)," p. 35.

2727. _____: "Business: Market Plummets: Sharp Stock Downturn Linked to Suspension of Wall Street Houses," pp. 53, 56.

2728. _____. "Seven Days in May: An Eternity of Suspense! [Film Advertisement]," p. 76.

2729. 23 Nov. 1963: "Kennedy Is Killed by Sniper as He Rides in Car in Dallas; Governor Connally Shot; Mrs. Kennedy Safe," Tom Wicker, pp. 1-2.

2730. 23 Nov. 1963:   "Johnson Sworn in on Plane: Texan
Asks Unity," Felix Belair, Jr., pp. 1, 11.

2731. _____: "Leftist Accused: Figure in a Pro-
Castro Group Is Charged--Policeman Slain," Gladwin Hill, pp.
1, 4.

2732. _____: "Why America Weeps: Kennedy Victim
of Violent Streak He Sought to Curb in the Nation," James
Reston, pp. 1, 7.

2733. _____: "President's Body Will Lie in State,"
Jack Raymond, pp. 1, 9.

2734. _____: "City Goes Dark," Robert C. Doty, pp.
1, 5.

2735. _____: "Parties Outlook for '64 Confused:
Republican Prospects Rise--Johnson Faces Possible Fight
Against Liberals," Warren Weaver, Jr., pp. 1, 6.

2736. _____: "The President's Death: the Scene,
Return to Washington, a Stunned New York," p. 3.

2737. _____: "Career of Suspect Has Been Bizarre:
U.S. Loan Enabled Oswald to Return from Soviet," Peter Kihss,
p. 4.

2738. _____: "Oswald, When a Marine, was Not a
Crack Shot," p. 4.

2739. _____: "Nasser Says [JFK] Death Is Humanity's
Loss," p. 4.

2740. _____: "Border [with Mexico] Closed and Re-
opened [after Several Hours after JFK Assassination]," p. 4.

2741. _____: "Truman Calls Slaying a Tragedy for
Country," p. 4.

2742. _____: "Kennedy Photo Requests Flood Party
Office Here," p. 4.

2743. _____: "First, 'Is It True?' Then Anger and
Anguish Among New Yorkers and Visitors: News of Tragedy
Spreads Quickly," George Barrett, p. 5.

2744. _____: "Eyewitnesses Describe Scene of
Assassination: Sounds of Shooting Brought Cars to Halt--
Motorcade Sped Kennedy to Hospital," Jack Bell, p. 5.

2745. _____: "Memories of Visit [by JFK] Add to
Irish Grief," p. 5.

2746. _____: "Jagan Sends Condolences to Mrs.
Kennedy and Nation [from British Guiana]," p. 5.

2747.   23 Nov. 1963:   "Senate, Stunned and Confused by Word
of the Shooting, Adjourns Until Monday: Brother in Chair
as News Arrives--Edward Kennedy Leaves the Dais Quickly:
Party Leaders Voice Grief," Cabell Phillips, p. 6.

2748.   _____ :   "Throng Gathers at White House:
Capital Church Bells Toll--Embassy Flags Lowered," Nan
Robertson, p. 6.

2749.   _____ :   "Foreign Policy Role: As Kennedy
Grew in the Presidency Effective Diplomacy Was His Forte,"
Max Frankel, p. 6.

2750.   _____ :   "Racial Hostility Ignored by South:
Many Who Fought Policies of Kennedy Voice Grief," Claude
Sitton, p. 6.

2751.   _____ :   "All New York Police Are Placed on
Alert," p. 6.

2752.   _____ :   "6 Cabinet Members Turn Back After
Getting News Over Pacific [of JFK Assassination]," Henry
Raymont, p. 6.

2753.   _____ :   "West Point in Mourning," p. 6.

2754.   _____ :   "Financial and Commodities Markets
Shaken; Federal Reserve Acts to Avert Panic: Stocks Plunge
in a Sudden Rush of Sales, But Prices Are Mixed Elsewhere,"
John M. Lee, p. 7.

2755.   _____ :   "Texas Governor a Self-Made Man:
Connally, a Johnson Friend, Was Born on Small Farm," p. 7.

2756.   _____ :   "The Final Hours of Kennedy's Life:
President Began Day With Talk in a Parking Lot," p. 7.

2757.   _____ :   "Rockefeller and Wagner Order a 30-Day
Period of Mourning," p. 7.

2758.   _____ :   "Pope Paul Will Say Mass for Kennedy,"
p. 7.

2759.   _____ :   "Right-Wing Senator [Tower, of Texas]
Receives Threats," p. 7.

2760.   _____ :   "Princess Radziwill Due in U.S.,"
p. 7.

2761.   _____ :   "Dallas Bishop Is Shocked," p. 7.

2762.   _____ :   "World Leaders Voice Sympathy and
Shock as Their Countries Mourn President," p. 8.

2763.   _____ :   "Soviet People and Leaders Grieved for
Kennedy," Henry Tanner, p. 8.

2764.   23 Nov. 1963:   "Ambush Building Chosen With Care:
Looms Over Kennedy Route--6th Floor Little Used," p. 8.

2765. _____ : "Tributes Cite Loss to U.S. and
World," p. 8.

2766. _____ : "Huey Long's Slaying in '35 Recalled
by Son, a Senator," p. 8.

2767. _____ : "Priest Describes How He Administered
Last Rites After the President's Death," Ronald Sullivan, p. 9.

2768. _____ : "News Withheld from 2 Children:
They Leave the White House Without Seeing Mother," Eileen
Shanahan, p. 9.

2769. _____ : "Kennedy Car Built for Security,"
p. 9.

2770. _____ : "Agents Checked Kennedy's Route:
Dallas Police Also Helped in Security Precautions," John
Herbers, p. 9.

2771. _____ : "Kennedys Gather at Hyannis Port:
Senator and Sister Join President's Parents," p. 9.

2772. _____ : "Kennedy's Wife Kept Composure:
Accompanied His Body to Bethesda Naval Hospital," Marjorie
Hunter, p. 9.

2773. _____ : "Hagerty Tells of Plots to Slay
Eisenhower," p. 9.

2774. _____ : "Kennedy Denied Talk of Dropping
Johnson," p. 9.

2775. _____ : "Tighter Security Seen [as Result
of JFK Assassination]," Ben A. Franklin, p. 9.

2776. _____ : "James Roosevelt to Urge Medal of
Honor for Kennedy," p. 9.

2777. _____ : "Grandmother Not Told," p. 9.

2778. _____ : "Kennedy Fourth President Killed
by an Assassin; Attacks on Two Others Failed," p. 10.

2779. _____ : "Arts Encouraged by the Kennedys:
Frost's Poem at Inaugural Showed Family's Intent," Milton
Esterow, p. 10.

2780. _____ : "Visit to New York [Last Week]
Disturbed Police: They Protested President's Removal of
Cycle Escort," Martin Arnold, p. 10.

2781. 23 Nov. 1963: "Networks Drop Regular Shows: News and Solemn Music Heard on Radio and TV," Val Adams, p. 10.

2782. _____: "Captain of Japanese Ship That Sank PT-109 Mourns," p. 10.

2783. _____: "West Berliners Gather in Dark," p. 10.

2784. _____: "Adenauer Cables Mrs. Kennedy," p. 10.

2785. _____: "Lasky, Critic of Kennedy, Says Book Sale Is Halted [and Lecture Tour Cancelled]," p. 10.

2786. _____: "Deaths in Office Show a 20-year Coincidence," p. 10.

2787. _____: "Sister Sees Dallas Telecast," p. 10.

2788. _____: "McCormack, Next in Line of Succession to the Presidency, Is Given Security Guard: . . . He and Other House Officials Meet Plane as Coffin Is Taken to Washington," John D. Morris, p. 11.

2789. _____: "Kennedy was Called Man Subject to Moods [by Theodore C. Sorensen]," p. 11.

2790. _____: "Setback to Unity of Europe Feared: Allied Diplomats See Peril of Weakened U.S. Backing," Drew Middleton, p. 11.

2791. _____: "People Across U.S. Voice Grief and Revulsion: Chicago, Los Angeles, Philadelphia," p. 11.

2792. _____: "Churches Fill Up on News of Death," Paul L. Montgomery, p. 11.

2793. _____: "Eshkol [Premier of Israel] Condemns 'Dastardly' Crime," p. 11.

2794. _____: "[Cardinal] Spellman Gets News in Rome," p. 11.

2795. _____: "Mississippian Resigns Post [in State Democratic Party Because of Hate for J.F.K.]," p. 11.

2796. _____: "Robert Kennedy May Keep Cabinet Post as Attorney General Under Johnson: Capital Expects Offer to Be Made," Anthony Lewis, 12.

2797. _____: "U. N. Mourns Loss; Session Adjourns," Sam Pope Brewer, p. 12.

2798. _____: "New Phase Opens in U.S. - Soviet Ties: Johnson Relatively Unknown to Moscow Leaders," Harry Schwartz, p. 12.

2799. 23 Nov. 1963: "Capitals of Asia Express Sorrow:
Sleeping Cities Awaken to News of Assassination," p. 12.

2800. _____ : "Kennedy Impact Felt in Moscow," Theodore Shabad, p. 12.

2801. _____ : "Military to Fire Salutes Every Half
Hour Today," p. 12.

2802. _____ : "A Tribute by Eisenhower," Dwight D.
Eisenhower, p. 12.

2803. _____ : "Group Here Denies a Tie With Suspect
in Kennedy Killing," p. 12.

2804. _____ : "G.O.P. Meeting [of Midwestern Confer-
ence] Cancelled; Miller Decries Shooting," p. 12.

2805. _____ : "Red China Report is Brief [and without
Comment]," p. 12.

2806. _____ : "Kennedy Family Asks Flowers Be
Omitted," p. 12.

2807. _____ : "Mrs. Lawford Flies East," p. 12.

2808. _____ : "Truce in Toledo News Strike [Because
of JFK Assassination]," p. 12.

2809. _____ : "Kennedy Boyhood and Youth Were Often
a Tale of Sharp Rivalry of 2 Brothers: Joseph Jr. Ruled
John With Fists," p. 13.

2810. _____ : "Death of Brother in War Thrust Kennedy
into Career of Politics," p. 13.

2811. _____ : "Coconut Shell in the White House
Recalled Rescue in World War II," p. 13.

2812. _____ : "'There is Only Prayer' Nassau [County]
Executive Says," p. 13.

2813. _____ : "Assassination 'Celebrator' Held in
Wisconsin Capital," p. 13.

2814. _____ : "Visitors to Family [Kennedy] Were
Advised to Be Ready for Football Game," p. 13.

2815. _____ : "Book on 'Courage' and '56 Convention
Role Put Kennedy on Road to White House: Volume Written
During '55 Illness," p. 14.

2816. _____ : "Irish Wards of Boston Forged Kennedy's
Political Weapons," p. 14.

2817.   23 Nov. 1963:   "Kennedy Concentrated on Domestic
Issues After Showdown Over Cuba in '62:   Major Programs Met
Frustration," p. 15.

2818. _____ :   "Death Came as Kennedy Sought to Shape
a New Foreign Policy Geared to Changes in the World Outlook,"
p. 15.

2819. _____ :   "Constitution Vague on President's
Successor," p. 16.

2820. _____ :   "Editorial: John Fitzgerald Kennedy,"
p. 28.

2821. _____ :   "Foreign Affairs: At the End of a
Sudden Day," C. L. Sulzberger, p. 28.

2822. _____ :   "College Football Curtailed; New York
Racing Off Until President's Funeral," Steve Cady and Gerald
Eskenazi, p. 33.

2823. _____ :   "Market Activity Halted Abruptly:
Little Panic Evident," Phillip Shabecoff, p. 36.

2824. _____ :   "U.S. Dollar Steady in Spite of Tragedy," p. 36.

2825. _____ :   "$11 Billion Lost in Hectic Trading:
Market Closed at 2:07 P.M.--Volume Advances to 6.63 Million
Shares," Robert Metz, pp. 36, 38.

2826. _____ :   "Wall Street Is Shaken by Grief
Following Death of President," Edward Cowan, pp. 36, 40.

2827. _____ :   "Federal Reserve System, in Official
Statement, Assures Public of 'No Need' for Special Action,"
pp. 36, 40.

2828. _____ :   "Retail Shoppers Stunned by News:
Sorrow and Shock Spread Quickly Through Stores," Leonard
Sloan, pp. 36, 41.

2829. _____ :   "Sidelights: Canada Markets Close
Early [Following the NYSE]," p. 37.

2830. _____ :   "Bonds: Death of President Halts
Trading in U.S. Securities: Federal Reserve Requests Closing," p. 40.

2831. _____ :   "Commodities: Trading Halted on New
York Markets; Price Pattern Mixed at Close," p. 42.

2832. _____ :   "All Prices Dive in Grain Market: News
of Attack on Kennedy Spurs Active Selling [in Chicago]," p.
42.

2833.   23 Nov. 1963:   "Radio and TV Cancel Regular Broadcasts [on CBS, ABC, and NBC Networks and Affiliates]," p. 59.

2834.   24 Nov. 1963:   "Kennedy's Body Lies in White House; . . . Police Say Prisoner is the Assassin: Rites Tomorrow," Jack Raymond, pp. 1, 3.

2835.   _____: "Johnson at Helm With Wide Backing: Cabinet Convenes," James Reston, pp. 1, 7.

2836.   _____: "Johnson Orders Day of Mourning: A Proclamation," E. W. Kenworthy, pp. 1, 7.

2837.   _____: "Capital Weighing Political Effect: Party Chiefs Expect Johnson to Push Kennedy Program and Be Nominee in '64," Warren Weaver, Jr., pp. 1, 4.

2838.   _____: "Evidence Against Oswald Described as Conclusive," Gladwin Hill, pp. 1-2.

2839.   _____: "Khruschev Pays Special Respects; Texts of Soviet Messages," Henry Tanner, pp. 1, 6.

2840.   _____: "Oswald Wrote to Connally About 'Injustice'," Peter Kihss, p. 2.

2841.   _____: "Marxism Called Oswald Religion: Suspect 'Refused to Eschew Violence,' Friend Says [Irving, Texas]," Donald Janson, p. 2.

2842.   _____: "Dallas Asks Why It Happened; Worry Over 'Image' Is Voiced," p. 2.

2843.   _____: "F.B.I. Reports to Johnson on Assassination Inquiry," p. 2.

2844.   _____: "Police Relate Story of Swift Capture," p. 2.

2845.   _____: "Connally Effort to Delay Texas Trip Is Reported," p. 2.

2846.   _____: "Jamming Continues in Eastern Europe," p. 2.

2847.   _____: "Author Says Kennedy Felt He'd Break 20-Year Jinx," p. 2.

2848.   _____: "New Drive Pledged for Mental Health [in Tribute to JFK]," p. 2.

2849.   _____: "Children Learn Father Is Dead; Mother Returns to White House: . . . Mrs. Kennedy Stays Most of the Night at Bethesda Naval Hospital," Nan Robertson, p. 3.

2850.   24 Nov. 1963:   "Father Informed of Death of Son,"
John H. Fenton, p. 3.

2851. _____: "List of Foreign Dignitaries to Attend
Funeral," p. 3.

2852. _____: "Killing of President Not a U.S.
Offense; States' Laws Apply," p. 3.

2853. _____: "Kennedy Will Lie in a Quiet Cemetery
That He Knew Well," p. 3.

2854. _____: "Connally's Son to Attend Rites," p. 3.

2855. _____: "2,500 Crowd Into Saint Patrick's
Cathedral for a Pontifical Requiem Mass: Mourners Weep at
Sound of Taps," Paul L. Montgomery, p. 4.

2856. _____: "Jews Here Recite Mourning Prayer:
1,100 in Temple Say Kaddish in Tribute to Kennedy," McCandlish
Phillips, p. 4.

2857. _____: "Connally Gains, Doctors Report: Turn
May Have Saved Life--Full Recovery Likely," John Herbers,
p. 4.

2858. _____: "Political Prospects for 1964 Are
Changed in City and State," Richard P. Hunt, p. 4.

2859. _____: "U.S. Communists Condemn Killing: Call
It Action of Madman or 'Enemy of Democracy'; Tass Accuses
Racists," p. 4.

2860. _____: "Armed Forces Get M'Namara Message,"
p. 4.

2861. _____: "How to Display the Flag in Mourning
Described," p. 4.

2862. _____: "Secret Service Faces Changes in Its
Procedures as a Result of the Assassination," Felix Belair,
Jr., p. 5.

2863. _____: "Goldwater Holds to Course for '64:
Indicates Tragedy Will Not Alter His Political Plans," p. 5.

2864. _____: "The Kennedy Wound: Fatal Shot Struck
Base of His Skull Causing Immediate Unconsciousness," Howard
A. Rusk, (M.D.), p. 5.

2865. _____: "Movie Amateur Filmed Attack; Sequence
Is Sold to Magazine [Zapruder and Time-Life]," Richard J. H.
Johnston, p. 5.

2866. _____: "Walker Says Assassination Shows the
'Internal Threat'," p. 5.

2867.   24 Nov. 1963:   "Two Bullets Reported to Have Hit Kennedy," p. 5.

2868.   _____ :   "Voice of America Alters Its Format," p. 5.

2869.   _____ :   "London Statue of Kennedy Is Goal of a Memorial Fund," p. 5.

2870.   _____ :   "A Mass of Requiem Can Be Said Today [by Vatican Permission]," p. 5.

2871.   _____ :   "[General] Strike in Palermo [Sicily] Postponed," p. 5.

2872.   _____ :   "Pope and Council Join in Mourning: Spellman Officiates at Mass for Kennedy in Rome," Milton Bracker, p. 6.

2873.   _____ :   "Many Nations Share America's Grief: [Foreign Dispatches]," p. 6.

2874.   _____ :   "British to Sound Johnson on Ties: [Sir Alec Douglas] Home to Accompany Philip on Trip to U.S. Today," Sydney Gruson, p. 6.

2875.   _____ :   "Peking Ignores Killing; Papers Note It Briefly," p. 6.

2876.   _____ :   "Regime in [South] Vietnam Expresses Sorrow," p. 6.

2877.   _____ :   "Torch-Bearing Swiss Mourn," p. 6.

2878.   _____ :   "Supreme Court [Monday] Session Off," p. 6.

2879.   _____ :   "President [Macapagal] of Philippines Calls Kennedy a Martyr," p. 6.

2880.   _____ :   "Cambodia Bars Attack on U.S. for Three Days," p. 6.

2881.   _____ :   "Ireland Mourns 'Death in Family'," p. 7.

2882.   _____ :   "Policeman's Family to Get Aid [Arkansas State Police Aid Tippits], p. 7.

2883.   _____ :   "Travel to Capital to Be Heavy Today," p. 7.

2884.   _____ :   "4 Calls to Houston Police Threatened Kennedy's Life," p. 7.

2885.   24 Nov. 1963:   "Carriers Won't Deliver Regular Mail Tomorrow," p. 7.

2886.   _____: "2 Films Have Dealt With Assassination [Plus Soon to Be Released Seven Days in May]," p. 8.

2887.   _____: "Negro Women's Group Postpones Its cotillion," p. 8.

2888.   _____: "March Will Honor Kennedy [by Conference on Religion and Race, St. Louis]," p. 8.

2889.   _____: "TV Will Continue a Sober Approach: Restrained Period Indicated in Regular Programming," Val Adams, p. 9.

2890.   _____: "City to Observe Day of Mourning: Changes in Listed Events," Homer Bigart, p. 9.

2891.   _____: "Life Here Goes On with Muted Tone: Few Have Adjusted to Loss of the President," Robert C. Doty, p. 9.

2892.   _____: "Dutch Fly Flags for Kennedy," p. 9.

2893.   _____: "TV Personalizes Grief: Millions Feel Full Impact of Tragedy and Witness History's Grim Unfolding," p. 9.

2894.   _____: "Sukarno Expresses Grief of Indonesians Over Loss," p. 9.

2895.   _____: "Repercussions of Assassination Continue to Spread Through Business and Finance: Officials Move to Ease Impact--Stock Market Closed," Edward Cowan, p. 10.

2896.   _____: "Editorial Reactions to Kennedy's Death [in U.S. Newspapers]," p. 10.

2897.   _____: "Loss of Strong Friend Alarms Latins: Ferment Testing Policies," Henry Raymont and Tad Szulc, p. 10.

2898.   _____: "A Midwest View: Johnson Is Able: Despair Begins to Lift in the City of Janesville, Wisconsin," Austin C. Wehrwein, p. 10.

2899.   _____: "Castro Mourns 'Hostile' Leader: Deplores Slaying But Says Kennedy Courted War," p. 10.

2900.   _____: "Nixon Voices Grief Before TV Audience," p. 10.

2901.   _____: "U.N. Memorial on Tuesday," p. 10.

2902.   _____: "Dallas [Police] Switchboard Jammed," p. 10.

2903.   24 Nov. 1963:   "Threats to Premier [Erlander] Stir Swedish Alert," p. 10.

2904. _____ :   "Widow of Texas Policeman [Tippit] Hears from New President," p. 10.

2905. _____ :   "Harvard Honors John Kennedy, '40, With a Memorial Service at University Church," R. W. Apple, Jr., p. 11.

2906. _____ :   "California Finds Outlook Shifting: Leaders Expect Johnson to Cost Democrats Strength; Change in Mountain States," Lawrence E. Davies and Wallace Turner, p. 11.

2907. _____ :   "Erhard Pledges to Back Johnson: Berlin in Mourning," Arthur J. Olsen, p. 11.

2908. _____ :   "In South Boston, Angry Silence Reflects the Passing of a Hero," Gay Talese, p. 11.

2909. _____ :   "De Gaulle Will Attend Funeral; Hopes to Meet With Johnson: Gaullists Study Succession," Drew Middleton and Henry Giniger, p. 11.

2910. _____ :   "Phoenix Jolted; '64 Talk Stilled: Goldwater's City Expresses Grief Over Assassination," p. 11.

2911. _____ :   "Death of President Brings Pact Ending Toledo News Strike," p. 11.

2912. _____ :   "13 Still Unaware of Slaying [as Jurors in Tennessee Case]," p. 11.

2913. _____ :   "[Herbert] Hoover Jr. Will Represent Father at Funeral Service," p. 11.

2914. _____ :   "A Kennedy Trademark Leaves White House [with JFK Belongings]," p. 11.

2915. _____ :   "Audubon Stamp [Issuance] Delayed," p. 11.

2916. _____ :   "News Numbs G.I.'s; Many Incredulous," p. 11.

2917. _____ :   "Pennsylvania Homage [to JFK] Set," p. 11.

2918. _____ :   "Texts of Kennedy's Address in Fort Worth and of His Undelivered Dallas Speech," p. 12.

2919. _____ :   "Kennedy and Reporters: Daily Contact with President Formed Personal Bond Beyond Formal One," Tom Wicker, p. 12.

2920.   24 Nov. 1963:   "Dallas Times Herald Asks Prayer to End
Bitterness and Hate," p. 12.

2921.   _____: "Markets Assess Kennedy's Death: . . .
Expansion in Activity Is Still Going Strong With No Fear of
Downturn at Hand," M. J. Rossant, pp. 1F, 5F.

2922.   _____: "The Week in Finance: Stunning News of
President's Death Casts Shadow on the Financial Markets,"
Thomas E. Mullaney, pp. 1F, 5F.

2923.   _____: "The Merchant's View: President's
Death Spreads a Pall as Merchants Plan Holiday Selling,"
Herbert Koshetz, p. 11F.

2924.   _____: "The News of the Week in Review:
Grief," pp. 1E-2E.

2925.   _____: "In His Own Words--Kennedy's Creed and
His Basic Policies," p. 3E.

2926.   _____: "The World Impact: Report from Eight
Capitals," p. 4E.

2927.   _____: "The Presidency: Johnson and Kennedy
Compared," Tom Wicker, p. 6E.

2928.   _____: "Editorial: The Accused; The Death of
the President," p. 8E.

2929.   _____: "The Continuum: Kennedy's Death Points
Up Orderly Progression in U.S. Government," Arthur Krock,
p. 9E.

2930.   _____: "Sadness in the U.N.," Thomas J.
Hamilton, p. 9E.

2931.   _____: "Opinion of the Week: At Home and
Abroad," p. 9E.

2932.   _____: "Sports Schedule Drastically Cut,"
Leonard Koppett, p. 1S.

2933.   _____: "Giants Face Cards Today, and Some Angry
Fans Will Stay Home: Vocal Critics Upset that N.F.L. Will
Play a Full Slate," Joseph M. Sheehan, pp. 1S-2S.

2934.   _____: "Service Classic Up to Pentagon:
Schools Await Word [on Army vs. Navy Football Game]," Allison
Danzig, pp. 1S, 5S.

2935.   _____: "Michigan State--Illini Thursday: Game
Is Postponed," Michael Strauss, pp. 1S-2S.

2936.   _____: "Westbury Cancels Racing Tomorrow Night
and Reschedules $50,000 Stakes: Slate to Resume on Tuesday
Night," p. 3S.

2937. 24 Nov. 1963: "Phone Threats Cause Postponement of
Game [Between Wilmington and Scranton]," p. 3S.

2938. _____: "U.S. Riders Sit Out Toronto Show, Lose
[in International Show-Jumping]," p. 4S.

2939. _____: "Yale to Play Harvard [Next Saturday],"
William N. Wallace, pp. 1S, 5S.

2940. _____: "Boston Dog Show Begins with Officials
Aware They Are Open to Criticism: Top Skye Terrier Is Among
Victors," John Rendel, p. 14S.

2941. 25 Nov. 1963: "Grieving Throngs View Kennedy Bier:
Crowd Is Hushed: Mourners at Capital File Past the Coffin
Far into the Night," Tom Wicker, pp. 1-2.

2942. _____: "Mrs. Kennedy Will Walk Behind the
Caisson to Mass at Cathedral," Jack Raymond, pp. 1, 6.

2943. _____: "World Leaders to Attend Requiem Today
in Capital: Officials at Nearly 100 Lands in U.S.--They Will
Meet Johnson; List of Dignitaries Expected . . ." Max Frankel,
pp. 1, 6.

2944. _____: "President's Assassin [sic] Shot to
Death in Jail Corridor by a Dallas Citizen: One Bullet
Fired," Gladwin Hill, pp. 1, 10.

2945. _____: "Mrs. Kennedy Leads Public Mourning,"
Marjorie Hunter, pp. 1-2.

2946. _____: "Johnson Affirms Aims in Vietnam:
Retains Kennedy's Policy of Aiding War on Reds--Lodge
Briefs President," E. W. Kenworthy, pp. 1, 5.

2947. _____: "Millions of Viewers See Oswald Killing
on 2 TV Networks," Jack Gould, pp. 1, 10.

2948. _____: "Johnson Spurs Oswald Inquiry: President Orders F.B.I. to Check Death--Handling of Case Worries
Capital; Evidence Offered," Anthony Lewis with Fred Powledge,
pp. 1, 11.

2949. _____: "Business of City Will Halt Today:
Mayor Says Only Essential Services Will Be Provided," Leonard
Ingalls, pp. 1, 9.

2950. _____: "Pope Paul Warns That Hate and Evil
Imperil Civil Order," pp. 1, 4.

2951. _____: "Johnson Scored by Chinese Reds: Views
Called 'Reactionary' [as Kennedy's] --Taiwan Aid Attacked,"
pp. 1, 7.

2952.   25 Nov. 1963:   "Kennedy's Mother Visits Altar Dedicated to Son Killed in War; Grandmother [Aged 98] Not Told,"
p. 2.

2953. _____ :   "Thousands Pass Bier at Night Despite
the Cold and Long Wait," p. 2.

2954. _____ :   "U.N. Will Be Closed Today," p. 2.

2955. _____ :   "A Widow's Courage Catches at the Heart
of a Nation as Kennedy Lies in State," p. 3.

2956. _____ :   "Cushing Eulogizes Kennedy as Both a
Great Leader and a Family Man of Warmth; . . . Cardinal
Describes Him as a 'Youthful Lincoln' Who Gave the World
Hope: Transcript," John H. Fenton, p. 4.

2957. _____ :   "Eulogies Given by Leaders: by Speaker
McCormack; by Chief Justice Warren; by Senator Mansfield
[Texts]," p. 4.

2958. _____ :   "Cushing to Offer Pontifical Mass:
Cardinal to Be Celebrant at Simple Requiem Service," Paul L.
Montgomery, p. 4.

2959. _____ :   "Britons to See Funeral on TV [via
Telstar Satellite]," p. 4.

2960. _____ :   "Tokyo Stocks Drop Sharply," p. 4.

2961. _____ :   "They Came to Bid a Friend Good-By:
'I Feel as If a Member of My Family Had Died'," Nan Robertson,
p. 5.

2962. _____ :   "A Portion of Guilt for All: New
Violence Underlines Need to Fix Public as Well as Private
Responsibility," James Reston, p. 5.

2963. _____ :   "Johnsons Go to Church on Capital
Hill; [Rector] Deplores U.S. Attitudes," p. 5.

2964. _____ :   "Boston Ceremony Is Planned Today,"
p. 5.

2965. _____ :   "Woman Brings a Tribute of Single
Chrysanthemum," p. 5.

2966. _____ :   "Night of Stars Show Will Honor
Kennedy," p. 5.

2967. _____ :   "St. Louis Mourns Kennedy at Rally
for Equal Rights," p. 5.

2968. _____ :   "Street to Honor Kennedy: Foggia,
Italy," p. 5.

2969. 25 Nov. 1963: "U.S. Forces Abroad to Join in Kennedy Tribute Today," p. 5.

2970. _____: "List of Dignitaries Expected at Kennedy's Funeral," p. 6.

2971. _____: "Britons See Hope of Leading West: Lord Avon Says [Prime Minister] Home Has Experience 'to Play Part'," Sydney Gruson, p. 6.

2972. _____: "[Blackfeet] Indian Tribe Mourns Loss," p. 6.

2973. _____: "Macmillan Will Lead the House of Commons in Its Tribute to Kennedy Today: Home and Others to Be at Funeral," Lawrence Fellows, p. 7.

2974. _____: "Dignitaries Pose Big Security Task," Ben A. Franklin, p. 7.

2975. _____: "Excerpts from Castro Talk: Castro Declares U.S. May Change," p. 7.

2976. _____: "Mikoyan Flies to Washington as Russians Praise Kennedy: Moscow Television Broadcasts Special Program on Years in White House and Newscasts of Ceremonies," Henry Tanner, p. 7.

2977. _____: "Macapagal Is in U.S. for Kennedy Rites," p. 7.

2978. _____: "U.S. Servicemen in Japan Mourn Death at All Bases," p. 7.

2979. _____: "10,000 Attend a Memorial Outside Independence Hall," p. 7.

2980. _____: "Mrs. Nhu Recalls Saigon Coup in a Message to Mrs. Kennedy," p. 7.

2981. _____: "Memorial Services Are Held in Thronged Churches Throughout the City: Loss to Nation Told in Sermons," p. 8.

2982. _____: "The Muted City: Children Gambol; But Parents Sit Quietly in Sad, Bright Sunshine," Philip Benjamin, p. 8.

2983. _____: "Theaters On and Off Broadway Cancel Performances for Today," Richard F. Shepard, p. 8.

2984. _____: "Sad Harlem Faithful Pay Tribute to 'Our Man'," p. 8.

2985. _____: "Oswald Made a Visit in September to Mexico (Laredo, Texas)," p. 8.

2986. 25 Nov. 1963: "New Yorkers Are Horrified by Slaying of Oswald," Guy Talese, p. 8.

2987. _____: "London Bobby Stops a Car to Express Britons' Grief," p. 8.

2988. _____: "Changes in Listed Events and Activities," p. 8.

2989. _____: "Texas Increases Connally Guard: Connally Leaves Bed," p. 9.

2990. _____: "Masefield Poem Honors Kennedy [Text]," p. 9.

2991. _____: "Right-Wing Group in Dallas Debut: Assailed Kennedy with Ad on Day of His Death," p. 9.

2992. _____: "Lone Assassin the Rule in U.S.; Plotting More Prevalent Abroad," Foster Hailey, p. 9.

2993. _____: "Experts Favor Telling Children About Death," Martin Arnold, p. 9.

2994. _____: "Even Blind Visit Coffin," p. 9.

2995. _____: "Knight Denounces the Dallas Police," p. 9.

2996. _____: "Pharmacist Says He Gave F.B.I. a Tip on the Rifle," p. 9.

2997. _____: "Dallas Policeman's Widow Also Weeps for Husband," p. 9.

2998. _____: "Any Aid to Oswald Is Denied by Tower," p. 9.

2999. _____: "Boston Banks To Be Open," p. 9.

3000. _____: "Dallas Is Groping for a Reason Why: Some Say 'Crackpots' Have Touched Off Violence," John Herbers, p. 10.

3001. _____: "A British Program Honoring Kennedy Shown Over N.B.C.," p. 10.

3002. _____: "Irish Cousin of Kennedy Is Asked to Attend Rites," p. 10.

3003. _____: "Friend Offers to Take Oswald's Family Into Her Home Again," Donald Janson, p. 10.

3004. _____: "Airlines in Capital Expect Rush of Outbound Traffic," p. 10.

3005. 25 Nov. 1963: "TV Coverage in Capital Starts at 7 A.M. Today," p. 10.

3006. _____ : "Oswald, a Man of Many Troubles, Took Marxism as His Gospel While a Teen-Ager: Onetime Marine Hated the Corps: Assassin [sic], Always Poor, Once Tried Life in Soviet Union--Backed Castro's Rule," Peter Kihss, p. 11.

3007. _____ : "Oswald's Killer Described as Emotional Man Who 'Hates Anything Done' to U.S.: Ruby Is Regarded as 'Small-Timer'," Joseph A. Loftus, p. 12.

3008. _____ : "'62 Ruling Upset Dallas Gun Curb: U.S. and Texas Codes Say Citizens May Bear Arms," Oscar Godbout, p. 12.

3009. _____ : "South, in Its Grief for Kennedy, Finds a Spirit of National Unity," Claude Sitton, p. 12.

3010. _____ : "Negroes Ponder Next Rights Step: 'What's Going to Happen to Us?' One Woman Asks," Layhmond Robinson, p. 12.

3011. _____ : "Chicagoans Recall Jack Ruby as Ticket Scalper and Chiseler," Austin C. Wehrwein, p. 12.

3012. _____ : "Assassins' Fate: Death or Prison: Only One, Who Tried to Kill Truman, Is Still Alive," p. 12.

3013. _____ : "A Kennedy Message Is Heard in Vienna," p. 12.

3014. _____ : "Editorial: Spiral of Hate; the President's Security," p. 18.

3015. _____ : "Foreign Affairs: Instant Grief and Instant Terror," C. L. Sulzberger, p. 18.

3016. _____ : "Wagner Now Bears a Heavier Political Burden," Clayton Knowles, p. 20.

3017. _____ : "Oistrakh Offers Subdued Recital: Violinist's Program Includes a Tribute to Kennedy," Raymond Ericson, p. 23.

3018. _____ : "Pro Football Attendance Unaffected," Leonard Koppett, p. 24.

3019. _____ : "Sports: a Strange Afternoon," Arthur Daley, p. 24.

3020. _____ : "Eagles Collect Money for Slain Officer's Kin (Philadelphia)," p. 24.

3021. _____ : "Titles and Bowl Bids at State in Heavier-than-Ever Late-Season Schedule: Decision Awaited on Army vs. Navy," Allison Danzig, p. 26.

3022.   25 Nov. 1963:   "City Banks Decide to Close for Day:
Action Taken Hesitantly--Institutions Puzzled by the Authority
of Proclamation," John H. Allan, p. 27.

3023. _____ :   "Economists Predict Brief Doubt: But
They Also Say Expansion Will Be Resumed," John M. Lee, pp.
27, 40.

3024. _____ :   "Europeans Voice Uncertainty Over
Possible Economic Crisis [Caused by JFK Assassination],"
Richard E. Mooney, pp. 27, 40.

3025. _____ :   "Calm Is Expected on London Board:
Brokers Believe Sales Will be Mild at Reopening," Clyde H.
Farnsworth, p. 27.

3026. _____ :   "Market Letters Recommending Caution
to Investors in Stocks," Alexander R. Hammer, p. 27.

3027. _____ :   "Brokers Are Attempting to Untangle
Mix-Up," pp. 27-28.

3028. _____ :   "Deadline Extended on Weekly Bill Sale
[by U.S. Treasury]," p. 27.

3029. _____ :   "Exchanges to Be Closed in the U.S. and
Canada," p. 27.

3030.   26 Nov. 1963:   "Kennedy Laid to Rest in Arlington;
Hushed Nation Watches and Grieves: A Hero's Burial," Tom
Wicker, pp. 1-2.

3031. _____ :   "New York Like a Vast Church," R. W.
Apple, Jr., pp. 1, 8.

3032. _____ :   "Mrs. Kennedy Puts Flowers on Grave in
Nighttime Visit," p. 2.

3033. _____ :   "The Texts of Eulogy at the Funeral
Service and Prayer by the Side of the Grave," p. 2.

3034. _____ :   "Hymn in Procession Work of Cardinal,"
p. 2.

3035. _____ :   "Requiem Mass Communion Called No
Longer Unusual [in Roman Catholic Church]," p. 2.

3036. _____ :   "John Fitzgerald Kennedy Takes His
Place Among the Dead of the Nation's Wars," p. 3.

3037. _____ :   "Silence Is Everywhere as Thronged
Capital Bids Farewell to President Kennedy: Crowd Is Muted,
Grief All Spent," Russell Baker, p. 4.

3038. _____ :   "The Anonymous Also Pay Homage: Thousands Travel to Capital for Funeral on Impulse," Nan Robertson, p. 4.

3039.   26 Nov. 1963: "Transcript of Commentary at Requiem Mass for Kennedy in Washington; Timetable of the Kennedy Funeral and Procession," p. 4.

3040. _____ : "Timetable of the Kennedy Funeral and Procession," p. 4.

3041. _____ : "Britain's Chief Rabbi Hails Kennedy Moral Leadership," p. 4.

3042. _____ : "Mrs. Kennedy Maintains a Stoic Dignity Throughout Final Hours of Public Grief: Walks 8 Blocks to the Cathedral," Anthony Lewis, p. 5.

3043. _____ : "John Jr., on 3d Birthday, Salutes His Father's Passing Coffin," p. 5.

3044. _____ : "Stunned Silence in Massachusetts: Memorial Services Times with Rites at Arlington," John H. Fenton, p. 5.

3045. _____ : "2 Kennedy Children Got [President] Johnson's First Letters," p. 5.

3046. _____ : "Joseph Kennedy Controls Grief; Sees Part of Proceedings on TV," p. 5.

3047. _____ : "Kennedy Is Honored in Mississippi Mass," p. 5.

3048. _____ : "Tributes Offered at 'Night of Stars'," p. 5.

3049. _____ : "Crewmate Eulogizes Kennedy," p. 5.

3050. _____ : "'Eternal Flame' at Arlington Will Be Only Temporary Setup," p. 5.

3051. _____ : "Taps Sounded on [Pennsylvania Railroad] Train," p. 5.

3052. _____ : "Additional List of Dignitaries at President Kennedy's Funeral," p. 6.

3053. _____ : "Both Houses of Congress Meet to Adopt Resolutions of Sorrow on Kennedy Death: A Red Rose Shows Senate's Regard," John D. Morris, p. 7.

3054. _____ : "Transcripts of Eulogies by Mansfield and Dirksen," p. 7.

3055. _____ : "'A Time to Heal': Change Discerned in Capital Politics from Sharp Conflict to Moderation," James Reston, p. 7.

3056. 26 Nov. 1963: "Protocol Chiefs Rely on Alphabet: Problem of Procedence for Dignitaries Is Solved," p. 7.

3057. _____: "Resolutions of Congress [Texts]," p. 7.

3058. _____: "Integrated Tribute at Cambridge, Md. [Scene of Racial Conflicts]," p. 7.

3059. _____: "Kennedy Is 6th President to Lie in Capital Rotunda," p. 7.

3060. _____: "Funeral Traffic Delays Leaders: Dignitaries Wait at Church Half an Hour for Cars," p. 8.

3061. _____: "Shriver Decided Funeral Details: Selected Rituals That Were Followed by the Military," p. 8.

3062. _____: "28 New York Policemen Stand Guard at Funeral," p. 8.

3063. _____: "Jamaican Praises Kennedy," p. 8.

3064. _____: "Delayed Telegram Keeps Envoy Friend From Rites," p. 8.

3065. _____: "Grieving People Flock to Kennedy Memorial Services Here and Across the Nation: Speakers Warn Against Discord," McCandlish Phillips, p. 9.

3066. _____: "U.N. Leaders and Staff Mourn at St. Patrick's," George Dugan, p. 9.

3067. _____: "Episcopal Service Uses a Part of Catholic Mass," p. 9.

3068. _____: "[Prayer] Card Distributed at Service," p. 9.

3069. _____: "250,000 Mourners File Silently Past Coffin in Capital's Rotunda During 18 Hours . . . 3,000 Unable to Get In," Ben A. Franklin, p. 10.

3070. _____: "Carrier's Crew Tosses a Wreath: Silent Ritual Pays Tribute to 'a Good Shipmate'," John Sibley, p. 10.

3071. _____: "Irish Cousin Flies In Just in Time," p. 10.

3072. _____: "Riderless Horse an Ancient Tradition," Jack Raymond, p. 10.

3073. _____: "Kennedy Visited Arlington Nov. 11: He Led Nation in Homage to War Dead 2 Weeks Ago," p. 10.

3074. _____: "Bagpipers Who Pleased Kennedy Return to Funeral Procession," Marjorie Hunter, p. 10.

3075. 26 Nov. 1963: "A 50-Gun Salute Is Fired in Ceremony at Albany," p. 10.

3076. _____: "Montreal Lights Show Grief," p. 10.

3077. _____: "Philadelphia Police Mourn," p. 10.

3078. _____: "Exiles Say Cubans Admired Kennedy," p. 10.

3079. _____: "Lincoln's Funeral and Burial Were Separated by 15 Days and Journey of 1,700 Miles: U.S. Was Minor Power and Europe's Chief Did Not Come to Washington," Paul L. Montgomery, p. 11.

3080. _____: "Television Pools Camera Coverage: Measures Set a Record for Distance and Duration," Richard F. Shepard, p. 11.

3081. _____: "TV: A Chapter of Honor: Millions Join in Rites Through Sensitive and Tasteful Camera Coverage," Jack Gould, p. 11.

3082. _____: "Hospital Is Urged in Kennedy Honor: Baptists Endorse Interfaith Health Group's Project," p. 11.

3083. _____: "Most Presidents Buried at Home: Only 2, Kennedy and Taft, in Arlington Cemetery," p. 11.

3084. _____: "G.O.P. Leaders Ask Halt in Campaign," Homer Bigart, p. 11.

3085. _____: "Stadium Renaming Proposed [for Washington, D.C.]," p. 11.

3086. _____: "Connally Sees Funeral on TV; Tight Security Guard Continued," p. 11.

3087. _____: "People Around the World Join Americans in Mourning Death of Their President: . . . Great and Small Visit U.S. Embassies to Express their Condolences," p. 12.

3088. _____: "Dallas in Europe's Eyes: Paris Is Disquieted by Thought of the U.S. as Lawless," Drew Middleton, p. 12.

3089. _____: "Dallas in Europe's Eyes: London Awaits Proof That No Plot Was Behind Deaths," Sydney Gruson, p. 12.

3090. _____: "Parliament Pays Unusual Tribute: Britain's Honors Like Those After Roosevelt's Death," Lawrence Fellows, p. 12.

3091. _____: "[Italian President] Segni Attends Mass Celebrated by Spellman to Honor Kennedy [in Rome]," p. 12.

3092.   26 Nov. 1963: "Pro-China Papers Assail Kennedy: Two in Hong Kong Assert Policies Were Aggressive," p. 12.

3093. _____: "Talk With Robert Kennedy on Johnson Oath Reported," p. 12.

3094. _____: "U.S. Troops at Korean Outposts Pay Final Respects to the Chief," p. 12.

3095. _____: "[House] Doorkeeper Is at Cathedral," p. 12.

3096. _____: "Soviet Promises U.S. Cooperation: Izvestia calls on Johnson to Continue Peace Effort; Communist Links Denied [to Assassination]:   Text of Izvestia Editorial," Henry Tanner, p. 13.

3097. _____: "Soviet Bloc Shows Uncertainty on Johnson's Political Policy: Poles Mourn for Kennedy: Yugoslaves [sic] Attend Service," p. 13.

3098. _____: "Johnson Tells Israelis Close Ties Will Remain," p. 13.

3099. _____: "Wife of Slain Japanese Consoles Mrs. Kennedy," p. 13.

3100. _____: "Georgia Governor [Sanders] Assails Talk That Spurs Violence," p. 13.

3101. _____: "Kennedy's Rescuer in Wartime Mourns," p. 13.

3102. _____: "Texan to Give 2d Eulogy to a Slain U.S. President," p. 13.

3103. _____: "[Buffalo] G.O.P. Urges Kennedy Honor," p. 13.

3104. _____: "Oswald Told Untrue Story of His Soviet Stay, Says Man Who Aided Him on Return," Peter Kihss, p. 14.

3105. _____: "Dallas Is Willing to Bare Evidence: But Oswald Case Is Delayed at Suggestion of U.S.," Fred Powledge, p. 14.

3106. _____: "Dallas Prosecutor's News Conference [Transcript from WBC-TV, Dallas]," p. 14.

3107. _____: "Oswald Is Buried in Texas in a Wooden Coffin," Donald Janson, p. 14.

3108. _____: "Latins Say Kennedy Instituted New Era in Hemispheric Ties," Henry Raymont, p. 14.

3109. _____: "Fund Begun for Mrs. Oswald," p. 14.

3110.   26 Nov. 1963:   "Oswald Visited Mexico Seeking Visas,"
Paul P. Kennedy, p. 14.

3111.   _____ :   "Ruby Is Transported Secretly from City
to County Jail at Midday Without Incident: Death Sentence to
Be Demanded . . . --No Link With Oswald Found," Gladwin Hill,
p. 15.

3112.   _____ :   "Johnson Pledges Facts in Killings:
Orders Full Investigation--Texas Plans Inquiry," Cabell
Phillips, p. 15.

3113.   _____ :   "Ruby Linked to Chicago Gangs; . . .
Police Say He Was Friendly With Several Who Were Slain, But
Never Made 'Big Time' --Had Union Ties," Austin C. Wehrwein,
p. 15.

3114.   _____ :   "[Jack Ruby] Traced to Coast," Joseph A.
Loftus, p. 15.

3115.   _____ :   "Doctors Question Oswald's Sanity:
Leaving Clues for Pursuit a Psychopathic Trait," Walter
Sullivan, p. 15.

3116.   _____ :   "Slain Policeman [Tippit] Is Honored by
Dallas," John Herbers, p. 15.

3117.   _____ :   "Text of the Tass Dispatch on Dallas,"
p. 15.

3118.   _____ :   "U.N. Assembly Will Honor Kennedy in
Session Today," p. 15.

3119.   _____ :   "Leaflets Linked to Rifle [and name of
A. J. Hidell]," p. 15.

3120.   _____ :   "Pennsylvania Salutes Kennedy," p. 15.

3121.   _____ :   "Guevara Says Cuba Must Remain Alert,"
p. 15.

3122.   _____ :   "Latin Citizens Honor Kennedy [in Hous-
ton]," p. 15.

3123.   _____ :   "400 - Game [Chess] Match Put Off; New
[Bobby] Fischer Date Sought," p. 34.

3124.   _____ :   "Editorial: The Whole Truth," p. 36.

3125.   _____ :   "Observer: The Old Passes," Russell
Baker, p. 36.

3126.   _____ :   "In the Nation: The Modern Miracle and
the Ancient Curse," Arthur Krock, p. 36.

3127.   26 Nov. 1963:   "Mourning for a President [Letters to the Editor]," p. 36.

3128.   _____: "Music Programs Are Rescheduled: Over 30 Were Called Off Because of Kennedy's Death," p. 52.

3129.   _____: "Broadway Totals a Loss of $275,000: 51 Performances Cancelled Because of Mourning," p. 53.

3130.   _____: "Racing Will Resume Today at Aqueduct and Tonight at Westbury," Joe Nichols, p. 53.

3131.   _____: "Wood, Field and Stream: Sportsmen Fear New Curbs on Guns Following Slaying of President," Oscar Godbout, p. 54.

3132.   _____: "Sports: A Day of Mourning," Arthur Daley, p. 55.

3133.   _____: "American Dollar Continues Steady: U.S. Currency Is Unshaken as Reserve Intervenes in Foreign Exchange," Edward Cowan, pp. 57, 61.

3134.   _____: "Europeans Calm as Trading Opens: Price of Gold Edges Up: Central Banks Avert Crisis Simply by Declaring an Intent to Intervene," Richard E. Mooney, pp. 57, 60.

3135.   _____: "Wall Street Resumes Work Today; Plans Made for Heavy Volume," Elizabeth M. Fowler, pp. 57, 60.

3136.   26 Nov. 1963:   "Europe Is Wary in Stock Trades;   Violent Selling Wave Absent: Tokyo Markets Decline Sharply," p. 60.

3137.   _____: "Commodity Markets Close Early Abroad . . . Out of Respect for the Late President Kennedy," p. 63.

3138.   _____: "Back to Normal for Radio and TV: Special Network Programs Filled 60 to 71 Hours," Val Adams, p. 75.

3139.   27 Nov. 1963:   "Stock Market up $15 Billion on Record Day: Big Loss Erased: Wall Street Attributes Rally to Confidence in New President," Vartanig G. Bartan, pp. 1, 51.

3140.   _____: "Ruby Is Indicted as Oswald Killer: Could Receive Death Penalty--Trial Is Expected to Begin in Mid-January," Gladwin Hill, pp. 1, 20.

3141.   _____: "Mrs. Kennedy Likely to Reside in Capital," Marjorie Hunter, pp. 1, 18.

3142.   _____: "Congressional Record Mourns [Eight Page Eulogies]," p. 16.

3143.   27 Nov. 1963:   "Senator Margaret Smith Cancels '63 Appearances," p. 16.

3144. _____: "Refuge to Honor Kennedy [on Nassau County's South Shore]," p. 16.

3145. _____: "Cuba Attributes Murder to 'Right': 'Provocation Against Peace' Is Charged by Havana," p. 17.

3146. _____: "Indiana Tightens Security [for Governor]," p. 17.

3147. _____: "Governor Love [of Colorado] Urges a Limit on Heads of State at Rites," p. 17.

3148. _____: "U.N. Mourning Sets Work Back by Week," p. 17.

3149. _____: "Medal Urged for Kennedy [Congressional Medal of Honor]," p. 17.

3150. _____: "Text of Statements by 2 U.N. Leaders Honoring Kennedy, and Stevenson's Expression of Gratitude," p. 17.

3151. _____: "A Saddened City Resumes Its Workaday Pace, But With Overtones of Mourning: Tempo Picks Up; Schools Reopen," R. W. Apple, Jr., p. 18.

3152. _____: "Hundreds Visit Kennedy Grave: Some Foreign Dignitaries Return to Arlington," Nan Robertson, p. 18.

3153. _____: "Izvestia Says TV on Kennedy Stirred Sympathy of Russians: But . . . Contempt for 'Detective Thriller' Events That Occurred in Dallas," Theodore Shabad, p. 18.

3154. _____: "Kennedys to Gather [for Thanksgiving Day at Hyannis Port]," John H. Fenton, p. 18.

3155. _____: "Foreign Notables Depart for Home: Frederika and Beatrix Hail Mrs. Kennedy's Courage," p. 18.

3156. _____: "City Hall Memorial for Kennedy Monday [Next]," p. 18.

3157. _____: "Caroline [Kennedy] Returns to School Desk in White House," p. 18.

3158. _____: "Democrats Delay Meetings on Nominating Convention [to January],   p. 18.

3159. _____: "Mrs. Kennedy Pays Visit to Grave With Caroline," p. 18.

3160.   27 Nov. 1963:   "Detroit Memorial Urged," p. 18.

3161. _____ :   "Mrs. Kennedy's Opposition to Open Coffin Explained," p. 18.

3162. _____ :   "Movie ['Take Her, She's Mine'] Is Deleting Scenes That Refer to Kennedy," p. 18.

3163. _____ :   "Senate Committee to Investigate Assassination of Kennedy and Killing of Oswald: Eastland Panel to Make Inquiry," John D. Morris, p. 19.

3164. _____ :   "Texas Is Planning a Public Hearing: Hopes Assassination Inquiry Will End All Doubts: [London] Suspicions Are Voiced: Arabs Blame Zionists," p. 19.

3165. _____ :   "Goldwater Drive Set Back in South: Observers Cite the Senator's Prior Attacks on Kennedy," Claude Sitton, p. 19.

3166. _____ :   "Text of Tass Dispatch on Dallas Police," p. 19.

3167. _____ :   "[California Gov. Edmund] Brown Hopes for 'Cleansing'," p. 19.

3168. _____ :   Tufts [University] Creates an Award as Memorial to Kennedy," p. 19.

3169. _____ :   "Kennedy Struck by Two Bullets, Doctor Who Attended Him Says: Physician Reports One Shot Remained in President's Body After Hitting Him at Level of His Necktie Knot," John Herbers, p. 20.

3170. _____ :   "Cuba Exile Tells of Oswald Boast: Reports He Said He Would Aid Castro Against U.S.," Fred Powledge, p. 20.

3171. _____ :   "Oswald's Widow and Relatives Kept in Hiding by U.S. Agents," Donald Janson, p. 20.

3172. _____ :   "Trail of Oswald in Mexico Vague: Officials Doubt He Crossed Border in Sailor's Uniform," Paul P. Kennedy, p. 20.

3173. _____ :   "Tippitt [sic] Family Is Getting Help: 'People Are So Good' Says Widow--Donations Grow," p. 20.

3174. _____ :   "Navy Pay Owed to Kennedy [for Retirement Disability]," p. 20.

3175. _____ :   "Negroes Ask Rights in Name of Kennedy," p. 20.

3176. _____ :   "Alarm in Capital Brings Roof Search [at IRS Building]," p. 20.

3177.   27 Nov. 1963: "Broadcasts of Fulton Lewis and George Combs Halted [for Week's Moratorium]," p. 20.

3178. _____ : "[Civil] Rights Plea by [Arkansas] Women," p. 20.

3179. _____ : "Tests Show Rifle Like Assassin's [sic] Might Be Able to Get Off 3 Shots in 5 Seconds," Oscar Godbout, p. 21.

3180. _____ : "Accused Assassin Belied Tenets of Marxism, Experts Here Agree," Peter Kihss, p. 21.

3181. _____ : "Cleric Denounces Dallas in Slaying: 'What Kind of City Have We Become?' He Asks on TV [Rev. Holmes]," Martin Arnold, p. 21.

3182. _____ : "City Police Study Tighter Laws for Users of Pistols and Rifles," Philip Benjamin, p. 21.

3183. _____ : "Johnson Says Agent [Youngblood] in Dallas Screened Him With His Body," p. 21.

3184. _____ : "Kennedy Dinner Fund Unused [$300,000 in Austin, Texas for 22 November 1963]," p. 21.

3185. _____ : "National Symphony Gives Concert for 'Neighbor': Tribute to Kennedy Is Played in Empty Constitution Hall Across from Arlington," p. 22.

3186. _____ : "How to Fly Flag During Mourning: Civilians Advised to Display It Only During Daylight," p. 22.

3187. _____ : "Auchincloss Family at Rites," p. 22.

3188. _____ : "Hospital in Illinois to Name Its New Branch for Kennedy," p. 22.

3189. _____ : "Kennedy Praised on Civil Rights [by The Rev. Dr. Martin Luther King, Jr.]," p. 24.

3190. _____ : "Mournful Britons Dedicate a Chapel [at Wellington Barracks, London, in JFK's Memory]," p. 24.

3191. _____ : "Publishers Rush President Books: Revised Works on Kennedy and Johnson Planned," Harry Gilroy, p. 35.

3192. _____ : "A President Mourned [Letters to the Editor]: [Includes Editorial Apology for Prejudice Against Oswald]," p. 36.

3193. _____ : "Press Scored [by Indiana Governor] for Printing Utterances of Extremists," p. 41.

3194. 27 Nov. 1963: "Army-Navy Game Postponed to December
7; Usual Ceremonies Will be Eliminated: Decision Is Made
By the Pentagon," Leonard Koppett, p. 44.

3195. _____: "[Illinois] Democrats Cancel Events,"
p. 49.

3196. _____: "Suicide Laid to Funeral on TV," p. 49.

3197. _____: "Sadness Haunts the City's Shops:
Traffic Lighter Than Usual, Customers Are Subdued," Leonard
Sloane, p. 50.

3198. _____: "Commodities: Prices for Futures
Climb as Confidence Grows," p. 50.

3199. _____: "All Prices Gain in Grain Market
[Chicago]: Confidence Is Shown in New Administration,"
p. 50.

3200. _____: "Shipping Industry Honoring Kennedy,"
p. 74.

3201. _____: "Government Praised Networks for TV
Coverage of Tragedy," Jack Gould, p. 75.

3202. 28 Nov. 1963: "Connally Account Recalls First Lady's
'Jack! Jack!' [Transcript of Interview]," Joseph A. Loftus,
pp. 1, 23.

3203. _____: "Clues to Oswald Traced in Books: He
Borrowed Library Texts on Kennedy, Communists and Huey Long
Slaying," Fred Powledge, pp. 1, 23.

3204. _____: "Mrs. Kennedy Accepts a Loan of
Harriman Georgetown Home," Marjorie Hunter, pp. 1, 22.

3205. _____: "Desk Kennedy Used May Go to Harvard,"
p. 18.

3206. _____: "Teamsters Ask Holiday Pay for the
'Day of Mourning'," p. 18.

3207. _____: "Late Changes Made by 2 Encyclopedias
[to Include JFK Assassination for 1964 Editions]," p. 20.

3208. _____: "Needy to Eat Kennedy [Donated] Turkey,"
p. 20.

3209. _____: "Billboard Industry Pays a Tribute to
Kennedy," p. 21.

3210. _____: "Parade Trying to Withhold Issue with
Kennedy Story [Entitled: Is Jackie Kennedy Tired of the
White House?]," p. 21.

3211.   28 Nov. 1963:   "Drives Under Way for Kennedy Memorials: Funds Also Set Up to Help the Widow of Policeman," Philip Benjamin, p. 22.

3212. _____: "Hundreds Vent Grief in Poetry: Young and Old Are Driven to Write of Kennedy's Death," Thomas Lask, p. 22.

3213. _____: "District Attorney Doubts Ruby's Tale of Vengeance," p. 22.

3214. _____: "Kennedy Service in Athens," p. 22.

3215. _____: "Kennedys Gathering for Sad Thanksgiving Reunion at Hyannis Port," Homer Bigart, p. 22.

3216. _____: "Oswald Unable to Keep $50 Job: Dismissed as Incompetent in Unskilled Work [in Graphic Arts Company]," p. 23.

3217. _____: "Tough Texas Prosecutor: Henry Menasco Wade," p. 23.

3218. _____: "Physician Tells of Aiding Oswald: Says He Almost Survived But Kennedy Had No Chance," p. 23.

3219. _____: "Tippitt's Widow Gets $25,000 Paid for Assassination Movies [by Abraham Zapruder]," p. 23.

3220. _____: "2 Plans to Honor Kennedy Drawn in Oslo and Bangkok," p. 23.

3221. _____: "San Francisco Bar Decries News Media in Dallas Case," p. 23.

3222. _____: "London Sets Memorial Service [for St. Paul's Cathedral]," p. 23.

3223. _____: "Stamp to Honor Kennedy," p. 23.

3224. _____: "Dallas Police Guard Cleric Who Assailed Intolerance in Sermon and on TV [Rev. Holmes]," Donald Janson, p. 26.

3225. _____: "Letters to Caroline and Poems Reflect Pupils' Grief Here," Gay Talese, p. 26.

3226. _____: "Dallas Divided Over Its Future: Leaders Disagree On Need to Alter Political Climate," John Herbers, p. 27.

3227. _____: "Johnson 'Shield' Described Action: Agent [Youngblood] Says He Didn't Know Kennedy Had Been Shot,' p. 28.

3228. 28 Nov. 1963: "Havana Accuses Mexico of 'Plot':
Says Regime Tries to Link Castro to Assassination," Henry
Raymont, p. 29.

3229. _____: "State Department Scored on Slaying
[by Congressman John Ashbrook, Ohio Republican]," p. 31.

3230. _____: "Nixon Cancels Speech [in New York
Because of Assassination]," p. 31.

3231. _____: "Dallas Worries Press in France: Papers
Believe Assassin of Kennedy had Accomplice; [Text of Tass
Dispatch]," p. 32.

3232. _____: "Indians [in New Delhi] Believe Oswald
Was Only a 'Tool': Left and Right Question Actions of Dallas
Police," Thomas F. Brady, p. 33.

3233. _____: "Alabamian Declares State Shares
Assassination Guilt," p. 44.

3234. _____: "Pickets at the White House Demand
Invasion of Cuba," p. 47.

3235. _____: "Fulton Lewis Jr. Restored to WOR:
Show Had Been Withdrawn After Program on Kennedy," Val Adams,
p. 79.

3236. 29 Nov. 1963: "Kennedy's Words Provide Keynote for
Thanksgiving: His Proclamation Stressing 'Great Unfinished
Tasks' Is Read from Pulpits," McCandlish Phillips, pp. 1, 40.

3237. _____: "Canaveral Space Center Renamed Cape
Kennedy," Cabell Phillips, pp. 1, 20.

3238. _____: "Kennedys Gather at Hyannis Port:
President's Wife Returns to Cape Cod for Thanksgiving Reunion with Family," Homer Bigart, pp. 1, 21.

3239. _____: "Ministers in Dallas Ask an End to
Hate," Joseph A. Loftus, pp. 1, 21.

3240. _____: "Spain Tightens [Political] Curbs,
Citing Murder of Kennedy," Paul Hofmann, p. 11.

3241. _____: "Chinese Protest Kennedy Tribute:
Peking Delegation Angered by Homage in Warsaw," p. 18.

3242. _____: "World Red Cross Bars Plea to Aid
Kennedy Memorial," p. 18.

3243. _____: "Connally Gains; Has New Surgery," p.
20.

3244. _____: "[Archbishop of] Canterbury Lauds
Kennedy's Example," p. 20.

3245.   29 Nov. 1963:   "[Cardinal] Cushing Urges a Shrine for Kennedy in Boston," p. 20.

3246.   _____ :   "Candlelight Rites for Kennedy Urged," p. 20.

3247.   _____ :   "Mass in Bonn for Kennedy," p. 20.

3248.   _____ :   "Thousands View Kennedy's Grave," p. 21.

3249.   _____ :   "F.B.I. Studying Oswald's Stay in New Orleans: Agents Are Piecing Together Chronology of 20 Weeks --Many Details Missing," Fred Powledge, p. 21.

3250.   _____ :   "Flame at Kennedy Grave Studied by Army Engineers," p. 21.

3251.   _____ :   "Gunsmith Attached Sight for Man Named Oswald," John Herbers, p. 22.

3252.   _____ :   "Prayers Reflect Nation's Tragedy: Worshipers Ask Help of God to Eradicate Hatred," George Dugan, p. 41.

3253.   _____ :   "Kennedy's Death Cancels Premiere of 'Strangelove' [by Film Producer-Director, Stanley Kubrick]," p. 48.

3254.   _____ :   "The Legacy of John F. Kennedy: an Editorial Condensed from the Current Issue of Saturday Review," Norman Cousins, p. 76.

3255.   30 Nov. 1963:   "Johnson Names a 7-Man Panel to Investigate Assassination; Chief Justice Warren Heads It: Texas Offers Aid," John D. Morris, pp. 1, 12.

3256.   _____ :   "Oswald Planned a Book on Russia: Stenographer in Fort Worth Tells of Typing His Notes Criticizing Soviet Life," John Herbers, pp. 1, 9.

3257.   _____ :   "Kennedy Chose Site at Harvard for Presidential Library October 19," pp. 1, 14.

3258.   _____ :   "Johnson Answers Nigerian's Rebuke [by President Azikiwe on Racism as Cause of JFK's Death]," Lloyd Garrison, p. 5.

3259.   _____ :   "Executive Order Renames Center [at Cape Canaveral]:   Mrs. Kennedy Made Request," p. 8.

3260.   _____ :   "French Post Urged for Mrs. Kennedy [to Become Ambassador]," p. 8.

3261.   _____ :   "White House Receives 235,000 Condolences," p. 8.

3262. 30 Nov. 1963: "Protests Called Off at Cambridge, Maryland, in Mourning Period," p. 8.

3263. _____: "Kennedy Portrait Planned [by Count de Bouvier de Cachard]," p. 8.

3264. _____: "Motion Picture Film Sequence Relates in Detail the Assassination of Kennedy," p. 9.

3265. _____: "Policeman's Widow Expresses Gratitude for Aid: Donations Sent to Mrs. Tippitt in Dallas Exceed $50,000--Some Still Uncounted," p. 9.

3266. _____: "Oswald Opposed Child's Baptism: His Wife Arranged a Secret Ceremony for Daughter," p. 9.

3267. _____: "F.B.I. Checks Reported Oswald--Rightist Link: [Greenwich] 'Village' Residents Are Asked About Mississippian Called Accused Assassin's Friend," Edith Evans Asbury, p. 9.

3268. _____: "Congress Tributes to Kennedy Printed," p. 9.

3269. _____: "Fund to Be Raised for Oswald's Wife," p. 9.

3270. _____: "Germans Plan Security Steps [Because of JFK Assassination]," p. 9.

3271. _____: "Team of 15 Doctors Strove to Save Kennedy at the Hospital: Events in Emergency Room Reconstructed--Time of Death Fixed at 1 P.M.," Bryce Miller, p. 10.

3272. _____: "Activities of Oswald Before the Death of President; Ruby Chronology," p. 10.

3273. _____: "Ruby's Family Denies Link Between Him and Oswald," p. 10.

3274. _____: "Ad in Dallas Paper Is Put Up to F.B.I. [for Investigation]," p. 10.

3275. _____: "Business and Zest Have Declined at Ruby's Club," Donald Janson, p. 11.

3276. _____: "A Kennedy Coin Proposed [by Congressman Henry Gonzalez]," p. 11.

3277. _____: "Presidential Inquiries Left Marks on History," p. 12.

3278. _____: "Kennedy's Son to Get [British Naval] Film That Was Gift to Father," p. 12.

3279. 30 Nov. 1963: "Mrs. Kennedy Chooses an Architect to Design Husband's Tomb: Crowds Defy Rain In Visiting Grave," p. 13.

3280. _____: "Mrs. Kennedy Spends Rainy Day in Seclusion," Homer Bigart, p. 13.

3281. _____: "Special Book of Condolence Signed by East Berliners," p. 13.

3282. _____: "White House Considers Kennedy's Will Private," p. 13.

3283. _____: "House to Act Monday on Bill Giving Mrs. Kennedy a Staff," p. 13.

3284. _____: "More Changes in Place Names Urged as Kennedy Memorials," Martin Tolchin, p. 13.

3285. _____: "Robert Joffrey Ballet in Moscow Dedicated Program to Kennedy," Theodore Shabad, p. 18.

3286. _____: "Meader Is Dropping Kennedy Imitation," p. 18.

3287. _____: "Kennedy's Death Affects Movies: Some Films to Be Changed and Others Withdrawn," Eugene Archer, p. 18.

3288. _____: "[Howard] Hanson Bases Work on Kennedy Address [for National Symphony, Commissioned in Part by Joan Baez]," p. 19.

3289. _____: "Student Play [in Bedford Village, New York] to Benefit Tippitt Education Fund," p. 20.

3290. _____: "Half-Brother of Oswald an Air Force Sergeant," p. 53.

3291. _____: "Russians Aiding Oswald Inquiry; Turn Over Files: Soviet Action Unusual: It Is Regarded as Reflecting Fear That Assassination Could Increase Tension," Jack Raymond, p. 57.

3292. 1 Dec. 1963: "Oswald, As Boy, Had Mental Test: Was Reportedly Diagnosed as 'Potentially Dangerous' by Psychiatrist Here," pp. 1, 57.

3293. _____: "Oswald, While Idle, Led a Frugal Life," Donald Janson, pp. 1, 57.

3294. _____: "Assassination Held Result of Timidity and Torpor," p. 56.

3295. _____: "J. Edgar Hoover Asks U.S. to Re-Examine Standards [of Morality]," p. 57.

3296. 1 Dec. 1963: "Oswald Sought A.F.L.-C.I.O. Job, Acting Like 'Fellow-Traveler'," Fred Powledge, p. 57.

3297. _____: "Ruby's Attorney May Seek to Move Trial from Dallas," p. 57.

3298. _____: "TV Risked Profits in Kennedy Shows: At First Many Advertisers Refused to Share Costs," Jack Gould, p. 61.

3299. _____: "History Is Seen: Home Screen Records Tragic Events During Nation's Anxious Hours," Jack Gould, p. 15X.

3300. _____: "News of TV and Radio: Good Taste: Networks Check Future Shows to Cut Works Offensive to Mourning Nation," Val Adams, p. 15X.

3301. _____: "The Dallas Mystery: Large Questions Remain Unanswered About Oswald and Ruby Following Kennedy's Assassination," Donald Janson, p. 5E.

3302. _____: "Editorial: The Ruby Trial; The Assassination Inquiry [7 Harvard Law Professors Condemn Oswald Publicity]," p. 10E.

3303. 2 Dec. 1963: "Oswald's Mother Places Blame on Federal and Dallas Officers: Queries Son's Surveillance--Says Before His Death She Saw Ruby's Photo," Jack Langguth, p. 16.

3304. _____: "[Senator] Douglas Critical of Dallas Police," p. 16.

3305. _____: "Mail Commending Ruby is Shown by His Lawyer: Messages Hail Him as Patriot and Enclose Funds--He Eats Well and Jokes," Donald Janson, p. 18.

3306. _____: "Russians Dwell on Rightist Plot: Most Commentators Insist Ruby Was Part of It," Henry Tanner, p. 20.

3307. _____: "Malcolm X Scores U.S. and Kennedy: Likens Slaying to 'Chickens Coming Home to Roost'," p. 21.

3308. _____: "Footnotes to the Assassination: the Kennedy Sense of History--Widow on Return to Capital, Asked Protocol Chief: Find How Lincoln Was Buried," p. 22.

3309. _____: "[Major General Edwin A.] Walker Is Quoted as Saying Assassination Was Red Plot," p. 23.

3310. _____: "Oswald Was 'Loner', Ex-Marine Recalls," p. 41.

3311. 3 Dec. 1963: "Oswald's Trip to Mexico in September Was a Lonely Venture, Inquiry Shows: 7 Day Visit's Cost Put at Under $30," Peter Kihss, p. ?⁴.

3312.   3 Dec. 1963:   "F.B.I. Hopes to Compile Assassination
Data Soon," p. 34.

3313. _____ :   "Judges Asked Aid for Oswald at 13:   4
Here Called for Intensive Psychiatric Treatment," Martin Tolchin, p. 34.

3314. _____ :   "Oswald's Mother Talks About Money and
'Class'," Jack Langguth, p. 34.

3315. _____ :   "F.B.I. Denies Showing Mrs. Oswald Ruby
Photo: [Izvestia Implicates F.B.I. in Assassination]," p. 34.

3316. _____ :   "Oswald Below Average in Junior High,"
Fred Powledge, p. 34.

3317. _____ :   "War Crime Prosecutor [Leon Jaworski]
to Head Texas Investigation of Kennedy's Assassination:
Federal Commission to Get Results of Its Hearings--F.B.I.
Report Awaited," Joseph A. Loftus, p. 35.

3318. _____ :   "Guards for Kennedy Accused of Drinking
[by Senator Young, Ohio]," p. 35.

3319. _____ :   "'Silent' Citizens Blamed for Hate:
Alabamian at Harvard, Says They Tolerate Evil," p. 35.

3320. _____ :   "Threats Against Oswald Grave Pose
Problem for Fort Worth," John Herbers, p. 35.

3321. _____ :   "100 Advertisers Receive TV Plea:
Telegram Cites Problem of Cancelled Announcements," Jack
Gould, p. 87.

3322.   4 Dec. 1963:   "Hero's Medal Given Secret Service Man
[Clinton J. Hill] for Dallas Bravery," pp. 1, 19.

3323. _____ :   "Panel on Slaying Meets Tomorrow:
Assassination to Be Studied--F.B.I. 'Probably' Will Find
Oswald Acted Alone," Ben A. Franklin, pp. 1, 18.

3324. _____ :   "Ruby Trial Date Reset to February 3:
Postponement Granted After Both Sides Ask for Time," Donald
Janson, p. 18.

3325. _____ :   "Mental Study of Oswald [By Dr. Renatus
Hartogs] at 13 Found Him Angry," Martin Arnold, p. 18.

3326. _____ :   "Ex-Marine Lieutenant Calls Oswald
'Wise Guy'," p. 18.

3327. _____ :   "[Oswald] Loved Dogs as Boy," Jack
Langguth, p. 18.

3328. _____ :   "U.S. Hails Mexico for Oswald Data:
Expects to Get All the Facts When Inquiry Is Finished,"
Peter Kihss, p. 18.

3329. 4 Dec. 1963: "Gun Experts Dispute Doubters; Say Assassin Could Fire Fast," Fred Powledge, p. 18.

3330. _____: "Scoffer at Kennedy in Ad Quits Dallas [i.e. Bernard Weissman]," p. 18.

3331. _____: "Dallas City Leaders Admit Excesses," Joseph A. Loftus, p. 18.

3332. _____: "Mother Will Receive $863 As Oswald's Insurance," p. 19.

3333. _____: "Youth Is Accused in Kennedy Threat," p. 19.

3334. _____: "Pan Am Waves Claims to Cancelled TV Ads," p. 95.

3335. 5 Dec. 1963: "Malcolm X Silenced for Remarks on Assassination of Kennedy: Head of Muslims Suspends Second Most Powerful Figure in Movement," R. W. Apple, Jr., p. 22.

3336. _____: "Killer Had 6 Days to Plot Ambush: Early Data Indicated Route of Kennedy Motorcade," Joseph A. Loftus, p. 32.

3337. _____: "Johnson Praises Agent's [Youngblood] Bravery: Honors Guard Who Shielded Him in Dallas Shooting," p. 32.

3338. _____: "Funeral Honor Guard Chief Is Eulogized in the House," p. 32.

3339. _____: "Head of Bar Group Says Oswald Was 'Lynched'," p. 32.

3340. _____: "Schoolmate Recalls Oswald as Teaser," Jack Langguth, p. 33.

3341. _____: "Cremation of Oswald Suggested to Avert Assaults on Grave," p. 34.

3342. _____: "Oswald Studied Russian in Corps: Marine Officer Gives Clue to Preparation for Flight," p. 36.

3343. 6 Dec. 1963: "Warren Inquiry in Assassination Begins Its Work: Calls for Subpoena Power, Raising the Possibility of Public Hearings," Anthony Lewis, pp. 1, 18.

3344. _____: "Police Reproved on Oswald Rights: Liberties Union Also Indicts TV, Radio and the Press," Homer Bigart, p. 18.

3345. _____: "Connally Leaves Dallas Hospital: He Will Recuperate at Home--Pupils' Cheers Denied," Fred Powledge, p. 18.

3346. 6 Dec. 1963: "Kennedy Slaying Is Reconstructed:
Simulated Ride Is Filmed by U.S. Investigators in Dallas,"
Joseph A. Loftus, p. 18.

3347. _____ : "Mother Seeks to Clear Oswald; Finds
Gaps in Reconstruction," Jack Langguth, p. 18.

3348. _____ : "Fulbright Deplores Spirit of Absolutism
and Vigilante Rule," p. 18.

3349. _____ : "[Dr. Karl] Menninger Assails Spirit of
Violence," p. 18.

3350. _____ : "New Yorker Is Held for Tricking F.B.I.,"
p. 18.

3351. _____ : "Donations to Tippit's Widow in Dallas
May Be $200,000; [Donations Also for Mrs. Lee Oswald]," p.
18.

3352. _____ : "Malcolm [X] Expected to Be Replaced
[as Minister of Mosque]," p. 27.

3353. 7 Dec. 1963: "Oswald Linked to a Shot Fired at General
Walker: Said to Have Told Someone, Thought to Be His Wife,
of Dallas Attack in April: Bullet Pieces Studied," Joseph A.
Loftus, pp. 1, 12.

3354. _____ : "Anti-Semitic Tract Traced in Toronto
[Linking Jews with JFK Assassination]," p. 5.

3355. _____ : "Mother Recalls Plea on Oswald: Cites
'61 Appeal to Kennedy on Locating Son in Soviet," Jack Langguth, p. 12.

3356. _____ : "Oswald Spurned Social Aid in '53:
Mother Also Saw Little Need for a Father-Like Friend," Thomas
Buckley, p. 12.

3357. _____ : "Congressional G.O.P. Deplores Linking
Assassination to 'Hate': Says 'Teachings of Communism' Could
Have Moved Killer--Simpson Charges Some Seek to Blame Conser-
vatives," Anthony Lewis, p. 12.

3358. _____ : "Texas Investigation into Kennedy Death
Put Off Indefinitely," Fred Powledge, p. 12.

3359. _____ : "Mrs. Oswald Wants to Stay in the U.S.,"
p. 12.

3360. _____ : "Many Seek to Get Rifle Like One Oswald
Bought," p. 12.

3361. _____ : "Macmillan Frees Book on Kennedy [by
Victor Lasky]," p. 13.

3362. 8 Dec. 1963: "F.B.I. Gets Oswald Letters Sent to Pro-Castro Group: . . . He Wrote of 'Stirring Things Up'; Texts of Oswald's Six Letters," Peter Kihss, pp. 1, 73.

3363. _____: "Rightists' Blame in Killing Denied: Kennedy Critic [Bernard Weissman] Sees Move to Shift Responsibility," p. 59.

3364. _____: "Dallas Schools Suspend Teacher Critical of City [For Saying Dallas Was Also Responsible for JFK Murder]," p. 60.

3365. _____: "Analyst Studies Oswald and Ruby: Sees Vengefulness Pattern Linked to Childhood," Emma Harrison, p. 62.

3366. _____: "'Mad Dog' Actions Scored by Cleric: Mueller Says U.S. Has Not Assessed Kennedy Death," George Dugan, p. 62.

3367. _____: "Oswald's Wife Plans to Stay in Dallas," Donald Janson, p. 63.

3368. _____: "Girl's Worry for Dallas Brings Tolerance Plea [from LBJ]," p. 68.

3369. _____: "Lee Harvey Oswald--the Man and the Mystery: Suspended Assassin of Kennedy Was Withdrawn and Friendless: Turned to Marx in High School," Donald Janson, p. 4E.

3370. _____: "Succession Problem: the Death of Kennedy Again Points Up the Need to Devise Solution," Arthur Krock, p. 9E.

3371. _____: "What Kind of Nation Are We? In the Wake of the Stunning Events in Dallas . . . ," Andrew Hacker, pp. 23, 120: NYT Magazine.

3372. 9 Dec. 1963: "Computer Is Suggested to Detect Assassins," p. 14.

3373. _____: "Oswald Chafed at Life in Soviet: He Wrote Mother He Was Eager to Return to U.S.," Jack Langguth, p. 38.

3374. _____: "Dallas Suspends Critical Teacher: She Says View on Climate of Hate Led to Ouster," p. 38.

3375. _____: "Kennedy's Guard Brings Questions: Ex-Chief of Secret Service [U. E. Baughman] Raises Queries in Slaying," p. 38.

3376. _____: "Critic of Kennedy Had Protest Role: [Bernard Weissman] Picketed Stevenson in Dallas Before Drawing Up Ad," R. W. Apple, Jr., p. 38.

3377. 9 Dec. 1963: "Texts of 6 Oswald Letters to Mother on Trip to the Soviet Union," p. 38.

3378. _____: "Kennedy Death Laid to World Failing [by Rev. Joseph McCulloch, St. Mary-le-Bow Church, London]," p. 39.

3379. 10 Dec. 1963: "Oswald Assassin Beyond a Doubt, F.B.I. Concludes: He Acted Alone and Did Not Know Ruby, Says Report to Warren Inquiry Panel," Joseph A. Loftus, pp. 1, 30.

3380. _____: "Slur by Cambodia Shocks Washington [Celebrating JFK's Death and That of Thailand's Premier]," p. 13.

3381. _____: "Witnesses Recall Oswald Firing at a Rifle Range Near Dallas," Fred Powledge, p. 30.

3382. _____: "F.B.I.'s 'Risk' List Omitted Oswald: Secret Service Got Names Before Kennedy's Trip," p. 31.

3383. _____: "Dallas Teacher Retains Her Job: Suspension for Letter Citing Hate in City Is Revoked," p. 31.

3384. _____: "Oswald Met Offers of Friendship with Surliness," Donald Janson, p. 31.

3385. _____: "Oswald's Mother Received Letters Attacking Her Handling of Son," Jack Langguth, p. 32.

3386. _____: "Hoffa Says Remarks After Assassination Were Misconstrued [That RFK "was now just another lawyer"]," p. 32.

3387. 11 Dec. 1963: "Two Interviews: Castro's Reply to Kennedy Comments on Cuba: Texts," Jean Daniel, pp. 1, 16.

3388. _____: "Oswald Assailed Right-Wing Views: Spoke Out in Public After Attending Dallas Rally," Donald Janson, p. 40.

3389. _____: "A Troubled Marine [Oswald]," Bill Becker, p. 40.

3390. _____: "2 California Lawyers Will Defend Ruby in Trial: Join 2 Texas Attorneys--Visit Client in Dallas Jail: Plan to Plead Temporary Insanity in Oswald Death," Fred Powledge, p. 40.

3391. _____: "Rankin to Assist Warren's Panel: Ex-Solicitor Named Counsel in Assassination Inquiry [Biography Appended]," Anthony Lewis, p. 41.

3392. _____: "[Representative Gerald Ford] Sees Report by February," p. 41.

3393. 11 Dec. 1963: "[Major General] Walker Ignores Mourning, Flies His Flags Full Staff," p. 41.

3394. _____: "Jersey Church Sends $4,000 to Help Widow of Oswald," p. 43.

3395. 14 Dec. 1963: "Christmas Toys Sent to Oswalds: Gifts Show Compassion for Accused Slayer's Family," Donald Janson, p. 19.

3396. _____: "[Long Island] Teacher Backed on Kennedy 'Jest': Nassau Colleagues Defend Remark on Assassination," p. 19.

3397. 15 Dec. 1963: "Ruby's Chicago Acquaintances Depict Him as the Victim of Stunted Adolescence," Austin C. Wehrwein, p. 83.

3398. _____: "6th Lawyer Joins in Ruby's Defense: Chief Attorney Says Bond of $100,000 Is Arranged," Donald Janson, p. 83.

3399. _____: "The Time Has Come [The John Birch Society Full-Page Ad Citing JFK Assassination]," p. 5E.

3400. 16 Dec. 1963: "Connally Leaves Hospital," p. 22.

3401. 17 Dec. 1963: "Bail Asked to Give Ruby 'Psychiatric Treatment'," p. 25.

3402. _____: "Anti-Kennedy Ad in Dallas Still Draws Mail, Mostly Critical of Right Wing," Donald Janson, p. 30.

3403. _____: "Magazine Halted by Birch Society: Issue Containing Criticism of Kennedy Withdrawn," John H. Fenton, p. 31.

3404. _____: "Warren Inquiry to Fill All Gaps: Plans to Settle Doubts Left by F.B.I. on Assassination," p. 31.

3405. _____: "Ford Bulletproofing Kennedy Limousine [in Dearborn, Michigan] for Use by Johnson," p. 35.

3406. _____: "Editorial: Lesson fron an Assassination," p. 38.

3407. 18 Dec. 1963: "Tippit Fund Up to $277,951," p. 16.

3408. _____: "2d Shot Reported Fatal to Kennedy: First Hit No Vital Organs, Autopsy Said to Disclose," p. 27.

3409. _____: "L.I. Teacher Accused of Slur Kept in Job," p. 28.

3410. 18 Dec. 1963: "Birch Society Spent $35,000 on Ads
Asking Funds [to Aid Contention That Communists Killed JFK],"
John H. Fenton, p. 29.

3411. 19 Dec. 1963: "Officials Silent on Kennedy Shots:
Autopsy Said to Show Both Hit Him from the Rear: Bullets'
Course Not Traced [in Dallas Hospital]," p. 23.

3412. _____: "Lawyer Urges Defense for Oswald at
Inquiry: Ex-State Assemblyman [Mark Lane] Files Brief With
Warren Unit: He Charges Many Gaps Exist in Data on Assassi-
nation," Peter Kihss, p. 24.

3413. _____: "Photo Ban Urged for Ruby's Trial:
Group of Dallas Judges Map a Statement of Policy," Donald
Janson, p. 27.

3414. 20 Dec. 1963: "Kennedy Threat Is Laid to Texan:
Dallas Machinist Held--Remarks Made November 21," Donald
Janson, p. 19.

3415. _____: "Donations to Tippit Family at $312,250
and Still Rising," p. 19.

3416. _____: "Editorial: The Birch Advertisement,"
p. 28.

3417. 21 Dec. 1963: "Slaying of Kennedy Is Deplored by Chou
[En-Lai, Premier of China]," pp. 1, 4.

3418. _____: "Oswald's Widow Kept in Seclusion: Few
Other Than F.B.I. Men Are Allowed to See Her," Donald Janson,
p. 12.

3419. _____: "Kennedy Albums Selling Briskly: Five
Million Disks Reported Bought Across Country [Promoted by
Decca, Twentieth Century Fox, Premier Albums, Documentary
Unlimited, and Newark Synthetic Plastic Co.]," p. 15.

3420. 22 Dec. 1963: "Ruby Is Examined by Psychiatrists: 2
Doctors for Defense See Oswald's Slayer in Jail," Donald Janson, p. 22.

3421. _____: "F.B.I. Agent Waited in Vain for an
Oswald Confession," p. 22.

3422. 23 Dec. 1963: "Ruby's Attorney Scoffs at Critics:
Colorful Lawyer Defends His Courtroom Style," Lawrence E.
Davies, p. 17.

3423. _____: "Reflective Spirit Marks Season:
Assassination Casts a Shadow Over All but Midtown Glow,"
Fred Powledge, pp. 27-28.

3424. 24 Dec. 1963: "Ruby Bail Ruling Off Until January 10
as Lawyers Spar," Jack Langguth, pp. 1, 6.

3425.   24 Dec. 1963:   "Wife and 2 Children Get Kennedy Estate [will Filed for Probate in Boston]," pp. 1, 6.

3426. _____: "Red Party Offers Oswald Letters: Correspondence Has Been Sent to Inquiry Board," Peter Kihss, p. 6.

3427. _____: "Oswald Sought to Study Russian in Language School as a Marine," p. 6.

3428. _____: "Johnson Feared a Plot in Dallas: Held Up Report on Kennedy During Return to Plane," p. 6.

3429.   25 Dec. 1963:   "Birch Group Lists $2 Million Outlay: Welch Gives 1963 Figure--Kennedy 'Glorification' Hit," p. 20.

3430. _____: "Mrs. Tippit Sees Slain Husband's Family; Oswald's Wife Visits His Grave," Jack Langguth, p. 21.

3431. _____: "President Calls on Governor Connally: Also Hunts Deer (No Luck) on Christmas Trip Home," p. 22.

3432.   26 Dec. 1963:   "Ruby Has Christmas Dinner," p. 18.

3433. _____: "Thousands in Dallas Pass Site of the Assassination [on Christmas Day]," p. 19.

3434.   28 Dec. 1963:   "Santa Barbara Investigates Hanging of Warren Effigy [as 'Head of the Oswald Whitewash Committee']," p. 3.

3435. _____: "Pro-Castro Group Disbanding; Oswald Episode the Fatal Blow," Will Lissner, p. 44.

3436. _____: "Inquiry to Hear Oswald's Widow: One of Warren Panel and Rankin to Go to Dallas," Jack Langguth, p. 44.

3437.   30 Dec. 1963:   "Oswald Counsel at Inquiry Asked: Lawyer [Percy Foreman] Says Public Interest Requires a Defense," p. 22.

3438. _____: "Cushing Says Death Followed Kennedy," p. 28.

3439.   31 Dec. 1963:   "Oswald Note Held Walker Case Link," p. 20.

3440.   1 Jan. 1964:   "Secretary Sorts Kennedy Papers: Mrs. Lincoln Says She Had Even Saved His 'Doodles'," p. 11.

3441. _____: "Widow Says Oswald Admitted Firing at Walker," Jack Langguth, p. 11.

3442. _____: "Tippit Fund at $445,297," p. 11.

3443.   2 Jan. 1964:   "Dallas Urged to Reject 'Absolutism':
[Warren] Panel to Hear [Oswald's] Widow," Jack Langguth, p.
21.

3444.   4 Jan. 1964:   "Dallas Supports Moderation Plea:
Response to Ad Is Termed Good by Nieman-Marcus," Jack Langguth, p. 16.

3445.   _____: "Ruby Bond Hearing Delayed 3 Weeks,"
p. 47.

3446.   5 Jan. 1964:   "Youth Problems Restudied in Light of
Oswald Case [by Dr. Renatus Hartogs]," John Sibley, p. 75.

3447.   7 Jan. 1964:   "Oswald's Mother Cites New Letter: Son
Told Her How to Help Him Get Early Discharge; Ruby-Police
Tie Denied," Jack Langguth, p. 7.

3448.   8 Jan. 1964:   "Oswald's Widow Now Reported Convinced
of Husband's Guilt: Rejects Suggestions That She Sue Ruby
or Dallas for Her Husband's Death," Jack Langguth, p. 18.

3449.   _____: "Warren Panel to Consider Brief in
Oswald's Defence [by Mark Lane]," p. 28.

3450.   _____: "Actors to Waive One Day's Pay for 2
Kennedy Cancellations [in November 1963]," Sam Zolotow, p. 41.

3451.   10 Jan. 1964:   "Dallas Letters Abuse Johnson: One
Paper Stops Publishing Hate Correspondence," Jack Langguth,
p. 41.

3452.   _____: "Oswald's Wife to Testify [to Warren
Commission]," Jack Langguth, p. 41.

3453.   _____: "[Robert] Morris Sees Legal Problem
on Warren's Inquiry Role," p. 41.

3454.   11 Jan. 1964:   "Oswald's Widow Bars Interviews: Note
to Civil Liberties Union Says F.B.I. Occupies Time," Jack
Langguth, p. 10.

3455.   _____: "Youth Cleared in Kennedy Threat [i.e.,
Russel W. McLarry]," p. 10.

3456.   12 Jan. 1964:   "Six-Phase Inquiry on Assassination
Charted by Panel: Aides Chosen for Detailed Study of Kennedy
Slaying and Security Agencies," Anthony Lewis, p. 46.

3457.   14 Jan. 1964:   "Taped Oral History of Kennedy to Go
in Projected Library," Anthony Lewis, p. 17.

3458.   15 Jan. 1964:   "Mrs. Kennedy Thanks 800,000 Who Ex-
pressed Their Sympathies," Nan Robertson, pp. 1, 13.

3459. 15 Jan. 1964: "Mrs. Oswald Picks New York Lawyer [Mark Lane] to Defend Her Son: Rankin's Position [Against Lane as Oswald's Lawyer]," p. 14.

3460. 17 Jan. 1964: "Ruby's Attorneys Ask Venue Change, Cite 'Hostile Press'," p. 15.

3461. _____: "Negro Who Laid Plot to Muslims Is Held [in JFK Assassination]," p. 15.

3462. 19 Jan. 1964: "Posthumous Police Award [For J. D. Tippit]," p. 37.

3463. _____: "Action Suggested on Ill Presidents: Two Legal Experts Call for Commission on Inability," Austin C. Wehrwein, p. 50.

3464. _____: "Group of Businessmen Rules Dallas Without a Mandate from the Voters," Jack Langguth, p. 58.

3465. _____: "A Portrait of Marina Oswald: She Is Expected to Shed Light on Kennedy's Alleged Assassin," Jack Langguth, p. 10E.

3466. 20 Jan. 1964: "Ruby Defense Based on a Mental Report," Jack Langguth, pp. 1, 85.

3467. 21 Jan. 1964: "Defense Maintains Ruby Can't Remember Shooting," Jack Langguth, pp. 1, 19.

3468. 22 Jan. 1964: "Ruby Disclaims Knowing Oswald: Tells of Trip to Cuba--Drops Request for Bond," Jack Langguth, p. 29.

3469. _____: "Mrs. Tippit Thanks Nation for $600,000," p. 29.

3470. 23 Jan. 1964: "Visit With Oswald's Wife Sought by Lawyer [Mark Lane] Here," p. 18.

3471. _____: "Judge [in Ruby Trial] Helped Ruby Join Chamber [of Commerce] in '59," p. 24.

3472. 24 Jan. 1964: "[Advertisement]: Appeal for Fair Play; Save Jack Ruby: Funds for His Defense Needed," p. 16.

3473. _____: "[Advertisement]: Mark Lane Discusses the Oswald Case Tonight, 8:30 p.m. Contrib. $1; Henry Hudson Hotel . . . Ausp. Militant Labor Forum," p. 22.

3474. _____: "Group Seeks Funds for Ruby's Defense," p. 57.

3475. _____: "Hospitals in Dallas Refuse to Test Ruby," p. 57.

3476.   25 Jan. 1964:   "Dallas Doctors Tell of Desperate
Fight for Kennedy's Life," p. 10.

3477.   _____: "Doubt Voiced at Meeting on Oswald
Guilt in Slaying [by Mark Lane]," p. 10.

3478.   26 Jan. 1964:   "12 Perplexing Questions About Kennedy
Assassination Examined," Jack Langguth, p. 58.

3479.   _____: "Wife of Connally Recalls Shooting:
Thought He Was Dead After Assassin's Bullet Hit Him," p. 60.

3480.   27 Jan. 1964:   " Advertisement :   Jack Ruby Tells His
Strange Story . . . "Why I Killed President Kennedy's
Assassin" . . . in Tomorrow's Journal-American," p. 6.

3481.   28 Jan. 1964:   "Widow of Oswald to Be Called First by
Warren Panel," pp. 1, 28.

3482.   29 Jan. 1964:   "Connally Returns to Office in Austin
[for First Time Since JFK Assassination]," p. 16.

3483.   30 Jan. 1964:   "Mother of Oswald Scores F.B.I.
Inquiry," p. 13.

3484.   1 Feb. 1964:   "Kennedy's Death Found Exploited: Extremists Held Capitalizing on 'Need' to Fix Blame [According
to Anti-Defamation League]," Peter Kihss, p. 19.

3485.   2 Feb. 1964:   "Warren Panel Will Hear Oswald's Wife
Tomorrow [at 10:00 A.M.]," p. 75.

3486.   _____: "Jack Ruby--Profile of Oswald's
Assassin," Jack Langguth, p. 10E.

3487.   3 Feb. 1964:   "Mrs. [Marina] Oswald in Capital," p. 7.

3488.   4 Feb. 1964:   "Warren Panel Hears Mrs. [Marina] Oswald;
Blame for Texas Rejected [by John Connally]," William M.
Blair, pp. 1, 23.

3489.   5 Feb. 1964:   "Warren Commission Will Ask Mrs. [Marina]
Oswald to Identify Rifle Used in the Kennedy Assassination;
Ruby Defense Call 165 [Witnesses]," William M. Blair, p. 19.

3490.   6 Feb. 1964:   "Kennedy Memorial Sought in Dallas," p.
15.

3491.   _____: "Oswald's Widow, in Testimony for Panel,
Confirms Her Earlier Statements," William M. Blair, p. 17.

3492.   7 Feb. 1964:   "Rifle Identified by Mrs. [Marina] Oswald: She Says Husband Owned Assassination Weapon," William
M. Blair, p. 37.

3493. 8 Feb. 1964: "Widow Says Oswald Changed on Return
from Soviet in 1962: Found Him 'Normal' When They Married--
Can't Give Reason for Assassination," William M. Blair, p.
10.

3494. 9 Feb. 1964: "Oswald's Mother Ready to Testify:
Presents Data Tomorrow Before Warren Panel," Jack Langguth,
p. 43.

3495. 10 Feb. 1964: "A Movie Is Made of Oswald 'Trial':
Film of 'Court Proceedings' Completed on Dallas Sites [by
Harold Hoffman and Larry Buchanan]," A. H. Weiler, p. 21.

3496. _____: "Ruby Will Press for Shift in Trial:
Effort Begins Today to Move Proceedings from Dallas," p. 53.

3497. 11 Feb. 1964: "Oswald's Mother Tells Her Story:
Carries a Bag of Documents Before Warren Panel," William M.
Blair, p. 18.

3498. _____: "Kennedy Target of Birch Writer:
Article [By Revilo P. Oliver] Says He Was Killed for Fumbling
Red Plot," Peter Kihss, p. 18.

3499. _____: "Dallas Impugned by Ruby Lawyers:
Leaders Said to Seek Death Penalty to Vindicate City," Jack
Langguth, p. 19.

3500. _____: "Briefcase of Witness Opened [in
Dallas, Belonging to a Yale University Psychologist Testifying in Ruby Trial]," p. 78.

3501. 12 Feb. 1964: "Oswald's Mother Detailing His Life:
She Also Tells Panel of Her Relationship With Him," William
M. Blair, p. 14.

3502. _____: "Dallas's Leaders Doubt Ruby Can Get
Fair Trial," Jack Langguth, p. 15.

3503. 13 Feb. 1964: "Ruby Judge's Aide Is Cross-Examined,"
Jack Langguth, p. 10.

3504. 13 Feb. 1964: "Mrs. [Marguerite] Oswald Says Son Is
Scapegoat: Thinks He Was C.I.A. Agent 'Set Up to Take
Blame'," William M. Blair, p. 11.

3505. _____: "Illinois Professor [Revilo P. Oliver]
Scored and Defended on Article," p. 64.

3506. 14 Feb. 1964: "Oswald Never With C.I.A., Chief of
the Agency [John A. McCone] Asserts," p. 11.

3507. _____: "Ruling Due Today on Trial for Ruby:
41 Heard on Plea for Change of Venue from Dallas," Jack
Langguth, p. 12.

3508. 15 Feb. 1964: "Ruby Trial Opens in Dallas Monday:
Question of Change of Venue Awaits Jury Selection," Jack
Langguth, pp. 1, 10.

3509. _____: "Inquiry Will Hear Oswald's Brother,"
p. 9.

3510. 16 Feb. 1964: "Sister Declares She Is Certain Ruby
Was Insane," Jack Langguth, p. 43.

3511. _____: "Ruby Case--Is the City of Dallas on
Trial Too?" Jack Langguth, p. 6E.

3512. 17 Feb. 1964: "Ruby Trial Opens in Dallas Today:
Efforts to Select Jury from Panel of 900 to Begin," Jack
Langguth, p. 13.

3513. 18 Feb. 1964: "Plea to Free Ruby Denied by Judge:
Ruling of Insanity Refused--Choosing of Jury Starts," Homer
Bigart, p. 23.

3514. _____: "Judge for Ruby Trial: Joseph Brantley
Brown," p. 23.

3515. 18 Feb. 1964: "Ruby Tests Find Seizure Disorder:
Court Report Lists Brain-Injury Possibility," Jack Langguth,
p. 23.

3516. _____: "Pro-Oswald Data Claimed by Lane: He
Says Police Documents Bolster Defense Stand," Peter Kihss,
p. 23.

3517. 19 Feb. 1964: "1,500 Here Cheer Oswald's Mother:
Town Hall Insisted on Bond Before Allowing Meeting," Peter
Kihss, p. 30.

3518. _____: "Oswald With Weapons: Picture of
Lee H. Oswald . . . April, 1963 . . . Published by Detroit
Free Press and Dallas Morning News," p. 30.

3519. _____: "Four Are Barred as Ruby Jurors: Defense Uses Up 2 of Its Arbitrary Challenges," Homer Bigart,
p. 30.

3520. _____: "Law Bars Jurors Who Saw Shooting on
TV, Ruby Says," Jack Langguth, p. 30.

3521. _____: "Warner to Reissue Film About Kennedy
['PT-109', in Dallas; Also, 'The Manchurian Candidate'],"
p. 35.

3522. 20 Feb. 1964: "Ruby's Attorneys Fail in Maneuver:
Judge Stops Move to Call Venireman as Witness," Homer Bigart,
p. 13.

3523. 21 Feb. 1964: "First Ruby Juror Chosen at Trial:
Engineer Accepted After 23 on Panel Are Rejected," Homer
Bigart, p. 15.

3524. _____ : "Oswald's Brother Is Heard at [Warren
Commission] Inquiry," Anthony Lewis, p. 15.

3525. _____ : "Defense Phones Neighbors [of Prospec-
tive Ruby Jurors]," Jack Langguth, p. 15.

3526. 22 Feb. 1964: "A 2d Juror Sworn for Trial of Ruby:
37 Dismissed After 5 Days--Case Resumes Today," Homer Bigart,
p. 22.

3527. 22 Feb. 1964: "Ruby Jurors Begin Leading Life More
Solitary Than Defendant's," Jack Langguth, p. 22.

3528. _____ : "Russian Training of Oswald Hinted:
Brother Believes Suspect May Have Been Agent," Anthony Lewis,
p. 22.

3529. 23 Feb. 1964: "Oswald's Widow Dismisses 2 Aides:
She Ends Agreements With Lawyer [John Thorne] and Adviser
[James H. Martin]," Jack Langguth, p. 38.

3530. _____ : "Times Article [by Anthony Lewis, on
Robert Oswald's Testimony] Disputed," p. 38.

3531. _____ : "Court Dismisses 9 for Ruby Jury:
Defense Gets Through Day Without Using Challenges," Homer
Bigart, p. 39.

3532. _____ : "Dallas Citizens Propose Assassination
Site Marker," p. 59.

3533. 24 Feb. 1964: "Menninger Rejects Ruby Defense Plea
to Testify at Trial," p. 11.

3534. 25 Feb. 1964: "Ruby Fails in Bid to Move His Trial:
High Court in Texas Rejects Motion on TV Witnesses," Homer
Bigart, p. 18.

3535. _____ : "Mrs. [Marina] Oswald's Ex-Attorney
Threatens Contract Suit," Jack Langguth, p. 18.

3536. 26 Feb. 1964: "Bar Head Will Represent Oswald in
Warren Inquiry [i.e., Walter E. Craig, President of American
Bar Association]," pp. 1, 17.

3537. _____ : "Ruby Trial Seats Two More Jurors:
Sharp Words Exchanged by Defense and Prosecution," Homer
Bigart, p. 17.

3538. 27 Feb. 1964: "8th Juror Picked at Trial of Ruby:
Early Completion of Panel Foreseen by Both Sides, Homer
Bigart, p. 39.

3539. 27 Feb. 1964: "Mrs. [Marina] Oswald Gets Offer by
Adviser: He Will Release Her from Pact for Share of Funds,"
p. 39.

3540. 28 Feb. 1964: "Commission Hears Mrs. [Marina] Oswald
Aide [James Martin]," p. 10.

3541. _____: "Ruby Maps Appeal on TV 'Witnesses':
May Ask High Court to Bar Jurors Who Viewed Killing," Homer
Bigart, p. 12.

3542. 29 Feb. 1964: "Ruby Judge Calls Saturday Session:
Hopes 2 Remaining Jurors Can Be Picked Today," Homer Bigart,
p. 10.

3543. 1 March 1964: "'Hate' Again Cited by Ruby Counsel:
He [Belli] Shows Paper Impugning Kennedy's Character," Homer
Bigart, p. 72.

3544. _____: "Attitudes Change in Polls on Ruby:
Defense Pleased by Growth of Sympathetic Response," Jack
Langguth, p. 72.

3545. _____: "Ruby Case--Who Is a Witness?: Whether
TV Viewers of Shooting Can Serve on Jury Is Debated," Jack
Langguth, p. 6E.

3546. 2 March 1964: "Ruby to Testify, Lawyers Decide
Appearance Will Expose Him to Cross-Examination," Homer
Bigart, pp. 1, 12.

3547. 3 March 1964: "Ruby's Counsel Denied Mistrial: Out-
burst Flares Over 'Fact Sheet' by Epilepsy League," Homer
Bigart, p. 25.

3548. 4 March 1964: "Jury Completed for Ruby's Trial:
State to Open Case Today--Judge, Ill, Is Replaced [by Judge
J. Frank Wilson]," Homer Bigart, p. 28.

3549. 4 March 1964: "Ruby Is Reported to Lack Remorse:
Psychiatrist for the Defense Makes Findings Available," Jack
Langguth, p. 28.

3550. 5 March 1964: "Witness Ascribes Malice to Ruby:
Quotes Him as Saying He Hopes Oswald Would Die," Homer
Bigart, p. 12.

3551. _____: "Lane Gives Views to Warren Panel:
Public Hearing Is Held at Request of Lawyer," p. 13.

3552. 6 March 1964: "Police Say Ruby Planned 3 Shots: 2
Detectives Testify to His Words After Slaying," Homer Bigart,
p. 12.

3553. 7 March 1964: "7 Flee Dallas Jail, Passing the Door
of Ruby Courtroom," Jack Langguth, pp. 1, 11.

3554. 7 March 1964: "Jury Hears Ruby Pondered Killing: He Thought of It Two Days Earlier, Sergeant Testifies," Homer Bigart, p. 11.

3555. _____: "Most of U.S. Wept at Assassination [Based on National Opinion Research Center, Chicago]," p. 11.

3556. _____: "Warren Commission Calls Assassination Eyewitnesses [including 4 Secret Service Agents]," p. 19.

3557. 8 March 1964: "Dallas Amused by Escape at Jail: 5th Fugitive Is Recaptured--12 Deputies Suspended," Jack Langguth, p. 40.

3558. _____: "Widow [of Oswald] Opposed Execution [for Ruby]," p. 40.

3559. _____: "The Nation: Dallas' Trials," p. 2E.

3560. 10 March 1964: "Warren Panel Views Kennedy Windshield," p. 26.

3561. _____: "Yale Psychologist Testifies That Ruby Suffered a Rare Form of Epilepsy," Homer Bigart, p. 27.

3562. 11 March 1964: "Mind Expert Says Ruby Was Insane: He Asserts Defendant Had a 'Psychotic' Experience [Dr. Manfred Guttmacher]," Homer Bigart, p. 35.

3563. _____: "Oswald's Mother Balked at Trial: Texas Subpoena Bars Her From Ruby Courtroom," Jack Langguth, p. 35.

3564. 12 March 1964: "2 Psychiatrists Call Ruby Sane: State Rebuttal Opens After Defense Suddenly Rests," Homer Bigart, p. 31.

3565. _____: "Oswald's Car Mate [Buell Wesley Frazier] Is Heard by [Warren] Inquiry," p. 31.

3566. 13 March 1964: "Ruby Plea Scored by Neurologists: Expert Says Brain Charts Show Slight Abnormality," Homer Bigart, p. 16.

3567. _____: "Two Drivers Heard at Warren Inquiry [Bus Driver Cecil J. McWatters and Cab Driver William W. Whaley]," p. 21.

3568. 14 March 1964: "Ruby Jury Gets Case After a Long Delay," Homer Bigart, pp. 1, 27.

3569. _____: "Ruby Judge [Brown] to Let TV Cover Verdict: Disregards Wide Objections to Cameras in Courtrooms," Jack Langguth, p. 27.

3570. 14 March 1964: "Warren Unit Hears 3 Who Knew Oswald [Mr. and Mrs. Declan Ford, and Peter Paul Gregory]," p. 27.

3571. 15 March 1964: "Ruby Sentenced to Death Speedily by Dallas Jury; Oswald Killer to Appeal: Defense Angered--Calls Verdict Triumph for Bigotry--Millions Watch on Television," Homer Bigart, pp. 1, 82.

3572. 15 March 1964: "Dallas Is Shaken by Death Penalty: Guilty Verdict No Surprise, but Sentence Shocks Many--City's Mood Somber," Jack Langguth, pp. 1, 82.

3573. _____: "University of Illinois Trustees Ponder Role of Birchite Classics Scholar [Revilo P. Oliver]," Austin C. Wehrwein, p. 57.

3574. _____: "Bailiff Reports Jurors Got Along Well," p. 82.

3575. _____: "Ruby Wants a Lie Test," p. 82.

3576. _____: "Ruby Case Virtually Retried Over Coast-to-Coast Television," Jack Gould, p. 83.

3577. _____: "Chronology of Ruby Trial," p. 83.

3578. _____: "The Nation: Verdict on Ruby," p. 2E.

3579. _____: "Science: On Epilepsy: Ruby Trial Focuses Attention on Seizures and Their Effects," Walter Sullivan, p. E7.

3580. 16 March 1964: "Ruby Trial Leaves Some With Unresolved Doubts: Question of a Previous Link to Oswald Raised Although Evidence Indicates None," Jack Langguth, p. 22.

3581. _____: "Belli Says Ruby Is in Peril in Jail: Others Advise Precautions, Defense Lawyer Reports," Homer Bigart, p. 23.

3582. _____: "Mark Lane Says 9 [Witnesses] Dispute Evidence [Against Oswald]," p. 28.

3583. 17 March 1964: "Bar Group Head Criticizes Belli: Suggest Inquiry in Conduct of Counsel for Ruby," p. 14.

3584. _____: "'Cover-Up' Charged Again [over Moscow and Prague Radios]," p. 14.

3585. _____: "3 Doctors Who Performed Kennedy Autopsy Testify [Drs. Boswell, Humes, and Finck at Warren Inquiry]," p. 15.

3586. 18 March 1964: "Bar Asked to Act on Belli Conduct: Morris, a Senate Candidate, Assails Ruby's Lawyer," p. 19.

3587.   19 March 1964:   "Belli Is Dismissed as Ruby's Counsel,"
pp. 1, 37.

3588.   _____: "Illinois U. Backs Birchite's Academic
Freedom: Trustees Say Professor [Oliver] Who Wrote About
Kennedy Has Right to Be 'Offensive'," Austin C. Wehrwein, p.
27.

3589.   _____: "2 Held in Threat [Against John
Connally]," p. 37.

3590.   _____: "Bar Head [Walter Craig] Clarifies
Role [with Warren Panel]," Wallace Turner, p. 37.

3591.   _____: "Warren Panel Questions Two Who Aided
Oswalds [Mr. and Mrs. Michael Paine]," p. 37.

3592.   20 March 1964:   "Ruby Family Hire New Top Counsel
[Percy Foreman]," p. 14.

3593.   _____: "Oswald Is Linked to Shot at Walker,'"
p. 14.

3594.   21 March 1964:   "Warren Panel Hears Texan [Mrs. Ruth
Paine]," p. 12.

3595.   _____: "Belli Resigning from Bar Group:
Former Ruby Lawyer Calls Dallas 'Murder Capital'," Wallace
Turner, p. 53.

3596.   22 March 1964:   "Oswald's Captor [Maurice McDonald]
to Testify [before Warren Panel]," p. 31.

3597.   23 March 1964:   "Ruby Talks With New Lawyer," p. 26.

3598.   24 March 1964:   "Foreman Resigns as Ruby Counsel:
Says Sister of Condemned Man Disputed His Tactics," p. 22.

3599.   _____: "Warren Panel Meets Today [with 4
Employees of Texas School Book Depository Building]," p. 25.

3600.   25 March 1964:   "5 Assassination Witnesses Testify at
Investigation [including Howard Brennan and Ray Truly]," p.
23.

3601.   25 March 1964:   "Law School Aide Retained as Ruby
Defense Counsel [Dr. Hubert Winston Smith]," p. 24.

3602.   26 March 1964:   "More Tests for Ruby Are Sought," p.
27.

3603.   _____: "Oswald Is Viewed as a Fame-Seeker
[by Priscilla Johnson, in Harper's April Issue]," p. 27.

3604.   27 March 1964:   "Author Is Chosen by Mrs. Kennedy:
Manchester Will Write Book About the Assassination," p. 10.

3605.   27 March 1964: "Warren Panel Told of Officer's Death [J. D. Tippit]," p. 15.

3606.   _____: "Stanton Scores TV on Ruby Trial: New Standards for Press Urged by C. B. S. Head," Jack Gould, p. 49.

3607.   28 March 1964: "Kennedy, Vietnam Topped '63 News: A.P. Says Press Rose to Its 'Finest Hour' on Slaying," p. 16.

3608.   30 March 1964: "Warren Inquiry Believed Ready to Start on Report," p. 26.

3609.   31 March 1964: "Texas Bar Asks for Ban on Belli: Moves in Court to Keep Him from Practicing in State," p. 16.

3610.   _____: "Warren Panel Sees 2 Kennedy Doctors [Charles Carrico and Malcolm Perry of Dallas]," p. 16.

3611.   2 April 1964: "Mother of Oswald Ends Tie With Lane," p. 37.

3612.   3 April 1964: "Tens of Thousands Go to Kennedy Gravesite [Daily]," p. 14.

3613.   _____: "Name of Cape Kennedy is Finally Made Official," p. 18.

3614.   4 April 1964: "Ruby Lawyer Gets Leave [from University of Texas]," p. 20.

3615.   _____: "Kennedy [Death] Stirred Teen-Agers' Grief: . . . 'Paradox' Is Discerned; Young Children Preoccupied by Violence of Murder, Psychiatrists Say Here," Joseph Lelyveld, p. 29.

3616.   5 April 1965: "[Dallas] Police Say Warren Inquiry Bars Oswald Data Release," p. 48.

3617.   6 April 1964: "TV Role Assessed in Kennedy Grief: It Deepened Feelings of All, Psychotherapists Agree," p. 5.

3618.   _____: Assassination Bullets Tested [in Philadelphia Crime Laboratory]," p. 28.

3619.   7 April 1964:   "Bar Unit Head [Walter Craig] Backs Court Press Code [Proposed by Frank Stanton, President of CBS]," p. 19.

3620.   11 April 1964:   "Oswald's Mexico Trip Studied [by Warren Commission]," p. 16.

3621.   12 April 1964:   "TV or No TV in Court? . . . as a Result of the Ruby Trial," pp. 16, 101-104:   NYT Magazine.

3622.   14 April 1964:   "Ruby Refused Delay in Hearing; New Session Ordered April 29," p. 28.

3623.   16 April 1964:   "2 Ruby Trial Rivals Split on News Curbs," p. 41.

3624.   17 April 1964:   " Justice Arthur Goldberg Warns the Press on Ethics [after Dallas Killings]," p. 26.

3625.   22 April 1964:   "Connallys Testify in Warren Inquiry," p. 30.

3626.   23 April 1964:   "End to Hate [that Killed JFK] Is Urged by Senator Kennedy," p. 35.

3627.   _____ :   "Ruby's Lawyer Asks More Mental Tests," p. 45.

3628.   24 April 1964:   "Paper Reports F.B.I. Knew Oswald Peril [According to Dallas Morning News]," p. 16.

3629.   25 April 1964:   "Article on Oswald [in the Dallas Morning News] Is Disputed by F.B.I.," p. 10.

3630.   _____ :   "Ruby Said to Show Signs of Delusion: Fears Being Thrown in Pit and Beaten With Chains," Jack Langguth, p. 11.

3631.   _____ :   "Dallas Jail Calm After Rioting By 160 on the Floor Above Ruby," p. 11.

3632.   26 April 1964:   "Ruby Pens Notes for His Defense: Tells of Events Leading to the Slaying of Oswald," Jack Langguth, p. 59.

3633.   27 April 1964: "Ruby Rams Head into Cell Wall:
Suffers Cut--X-Rays Show No Internal Damage," p. 21.

3634.   28 April 1964: "Ruby Sanity Trial Is Won by Defense:
His 'Mind Is Falling Apart,' Lawyers Tell Court," p. 24.

3635.   29 April 1964: "Coast Psychiatrist Hired to Treat
Ruby," p. 83.

3636.   30 April 1964: "Ruby Judge Refuses to Grant New
Trial," p. 21.

3637.   _____: "Lane Files Protest on F.B.I. Questioning [about Oswald Documents]," p. 21.

3638.   2 May 1964: "Grief of Prisoners [in East Germany]
for Kennedy Told," p. 8.

3639.   _____: "Mrs. Kennedy Will Give Data for Warren
Inquiry," p. 25.

3640.   3 May 1964: "Belli Asserts That Dallas Harbors
'Spirit of Hatred'," p. 40.

3641.   5 May 1964: "Pulitzer Prizes . . . [to Merriman
Smith, U.P.I., for JFK Assassination Reporting]," Peter
Kihss, pp. 1, 39.

3642.   _____: "Winning Photograph [Pulitzer Award to
Robert Jackson for Photo of Ruby Shooting Oswald]," pp. 1,
39.

3643.   7 May 1964: "New Warren Panel Aide [Norman Redlich]
Held a Defender of Reds," p. 33.

3644.   _____: "N.B.C. Preparing 'White Paper' on Oswald
Assassination Role," Val Adams, p. 75.

3645.   9 May 1964: "News-Media Role in Trials Studied:
Brookings Report May Lead to Year-Long Survey [in Wake of
Ruby's Trial]," p. 55.

3646.   10 May 1964: "Warren Panel Told of Dallas Rifleman
[by Unnamed Part-Time College Student]," p. 81.

3647.   13 May 1964: "Warren Panel to Hear Hoover [and John
McCone, Director of C.I.A.]," p. 43.

3648.   14 May 1964: "Warren Panel Hears Three [an F.B.I.
Laboratory Expert and Two Dallas Policemen]," p. 4.

3649. 14 May 1964: "News Writers Here Present 4 Awards
[includes Jimmy Breslin for Accounts of Attempts to Save JFK's
Life]," p. 20.

3650. _____: "Birch [Society] Head Disputes Attack
on Kennedy [by Revilo Oliver]," p. 42.

3651. 15 May 1964: "Hoover and M'Cone Warren Witnesses,"
p. 20.

3652. _____: "Mrs. Kennedy's View on Dallas Is Given,"
[Regarding Memorials]," p. 23.

3653. 20 May 1964: "Ruby Is Treated for Mental Upset:
Dallas Judge Says Prisoner Receives Pills in Cell," pp. 1,
35.

3654. _____: "Secret Service Man [Abraham Bolden]
Accused of Attempt to Sell Covert Data [on Counterfeiting
Plot]," p. 35.

3655. 21 May 1964: "District Attorney Denies Ruby Gets Any
Medication," p. 17.

3656. _____: "Accused Agent [Abraham Bolden] Sees
Laxity on Kennedy [in Dallas by Secret Service]," p. 38.

3657. 22 May 1964: "M'Kelway Questions a 'Code' for Press
[after JFK Assassination]," p. 12.

3658. _____: "Agent [Abraham Bolden] Indicted in Plot
to Sell Secret Service Document," p. 22.

3659. 23 May 1964: "10,000 at Kennedy's Grave [on Friday,
Six Months after Death]," p. 6.

3660. _____: "Threat to President [LBJ] Denied [by
ex-Marine Corps Sharpshooter]," p. 11.

3661. _____: "Judge Will Discuss a Hearing for
Ruby," p. 12.

3662. _____: "Post Office Prints Poems on Kennedy
[Death] by Jersey Employee," p. 25.

3663. 24 May 1964: "Latvian Recalls 'Dzons Kenedijs': Book
Tells About Kennedy's Ties to the Baltic People," p. 38.

3664. _____: "Louisville Jaycees Drop Drive to Help
Oswald's Children [After Abusive Public Reactions]," p. 56.

3665. _____: "Texan Calls Assassination Photo His
[Billy Lovelady Identified]," p. 57.

3666. 25 May 1964: "F.B.I. Men Re-Enact Kennedy's Shooting,"
p. 25.

3667.   26 May 1964:   "Ruby Sanity Hearing Delayed," p. 24.

3668.   28 May 1964:   "Commission Traces Fatal Dallas Shots," p. 21.

3669.   29 May 1964:   "Dallas Sheriff Says Ruby Acted Violently in His Cell," p. 8.

3670.   _____: "Rite for Kennedy [Birthday] Is Led by Johnson: President Visits Grave After White House Ceremony," Tom Wicker, p. 12.

3671.   30 May 1964:   "Kennedy's Birthday Marked in Sorrow; Widow at a Mass [Photo]: Mourning in Dallas," Nan Robertson, pp. 1, 5.

3672.   _____: "Killer's First Shot Reportedly Struck Kennedy and Texan [Governor Connally]," p. 5.

3673.   _____: "De Valera [President of Eire] Lays Wreath on Kennedy's Grave," p. 5.

3674.   _____: "Bar Association Transfers Belli Hearing to the Coast [after Ruby's Trial]," p. 42.

3675.   1 June 1964:   "Panel to Reject Theories of Plot in Kennedy Death: Warren Inquiry Is Expected to Dispel Doubts in Europe That Oswald Acted Alone [with Reports from Britain, Moscow, Paris, Vienna, Warsaw]," Anthony Lewis, pp. 1, 19.

3676.   2 June 1964:   "Book Depository Is Sought as a Kennedy Memorial," p. 27.

3677.   _____: "Judge Sets Hearing for Ruby on June 19," p. 42.

3678.   3 June 1964:   "Films on Kennedy Planned for Fall: 2 Color Documentaries Will Tell of Life and Death [One by David Wolper and Another by Harry Rasky]," Eugene Archer, p. 36.

3679.   _____: "Warren Panel Calls Oswald's Wife Again [Plus F.B.I. Agents, Dallas Law Officers, and State Department Employees]," p. 87.

3680.   4 June 1964:   "Embassy Aide [Richard E. Snyder] to Testify on Oswald Years in Soviet," p. 10.

3681.   _____: "Doubleday to Issue Warren Panel Book [One Month After Report's Release]," p. 34.

3682.   6 June 1964:   "Warren Commission Hears Mrs. Kennedy," p. 20.

3683.   7 June 1964:   "Closer Check Is Planned on Members of Rifle Clubs Obtaining U.S. Arms [after JFK's Death]," Jack Raymond, p. 41.

3684. 8 June 1964: "Books on C.I.A. and Bay of Pigs Disturb Officials [Written by Haynes Johnson, and by David Wise and Thomas Ross, Respectively]," Jack Raymond, p. 14.

3685. _____: "Warren Meets Ruby for 3 Hours in Jail [in Dallas]," p. 21.

3686. _____: "Letters to the Times: Theories on Assassination [and European Obsessions for Conspiracies]," Kenneth Nary, p. 28.

3687. 9 June 1964: "Dallas Prosecutor [Henry Wade] Testifies Before Warren Commission," p. 27.

3688. 10 June 1964: "Chief of Dallas Bar [Clayton Fowler, Now] Heads Ruby Defense," p. 34.

3689. _____: "C.I.A. Said to Charge Book [by Wise and Ross] Is Inaccurate [and Unpatriotic]," p. 48.

3690. 11 June 1964: "Johnson Reported to Feel Kennedy Had Premonition," p. 22.

3691. _____: "New Book to Cover 'The Kennedy Years' [to be Published by Viking Press on 22 November 1964 by Harold Faber]," p. 30.

3692. 12 June 1964: "Mrs. [Marina] Oswald Gives Data About Nixon [to Warren Panel]," p. 19.

3693. 13 June 1964: "Letters to the Times: Habe Defends Views: Failure to Probe Assassination's Political Background Charged," Hans Habe, p. 22.

3694. 14 June 1964: "Kennedy Limousine Redone for Johnson," p. 49.

3695. 16 June 1964: "Ruby's Side Opposes Hearing on Sanity," p. 12.

3696. 17 June 1964: "Ruby Hearing Postponed," p. 5.

3697. _____: "[Warren] Inquiry Calls [Major-General] Walker's Aide," p. 40.

3698. 19 June 1964: "Inquiry Is Ended by Warren Panel: Secret Service Chief Is Last of Hundreds to Testify [Report Scheduled for 30 June 1964]," p. 13.

3699. 20 June 1964: "Psychiatrist Visits Ruby and Urges Hospital Care," p. 14.

3700. 23 June 1964: "Medical Aid for Ruby Asked," p. 30.

3701. 28 June 1964: "Paid by Russians, Oswald Reported: Said to Have Left Notes on Link to Soviet Police [Based on His Diary]," p. 56.

3702. 29 June 1964: "Warren Panel Will Inquire Into Oswald
Diary Article [with Report Scheduled for Issuance in Four
Days]," p. 10.

3703. 30 June 1964: "Robert Kennedy Says Oswald Acted on
Own in Assassination [Replying to Polish Questioner in
Cracow]," Arthur J. Olsen, pp. 1-2.

3704. _____: "F.B.I. To Check on [Oswald] Diary [and
Warren Report Now Due After Republican Convention]," p. 2.

3705. 3 July 1964: "Mark Lane Silent at Warren Inquiry
[about Jack Ruby]," p. 7.

3706. 4 July 1964: "Warren Doubtful of Lane Testimony on
Assassination," p. 5.

3707. 8 July 1964: "Warren Committee Challenged by Lane
[Who Invites Justice Department to Charge Him With Perjury],"
p. 25.

3708. 12 July 1964: "Yugoslav's Ballad Salutes Kennedy as
a Folk Hero [Text Translated Here, Concerning JFK's Assassination, by Ramo Ramovic]," David Binder, p. 45.

3709. _____: "Secret Service Man's Jury Is Dismissed
After Impasse [Re: Abraham Bolden]," p. 60.

3710. 16 July 1964: "Books and Authors: Warren Report in
Paperback [Planned by Bantam Books, with The New York Times],"
p. 28.

3711. 21 July 1964: "Belli Sues U.S. Bar Head [Walter
Craig] in $5 Million Libel Case," p. 28.

3712. _____: "[Les] Crane Invites Mrs. [Marguerite]
Oswald [for TV Talk Show, 5 August]," Paul Gardner, p. 67.

3713. 22 July 1964: "Striking Teamsters Win Pay on Kennedy
Mourning Day [25 November 1963 in New Jersey Local 701],"
p. 12.

3714. 23 July 1964: "Warren Unit Plans September Report;
[Ruby's Polygraph Test Showed Killing Oswald Was Spur-of-
Moment Decision]," p. 28.

3715. 24 July 1964: "Ruby Retains His Lawyers Over Family's
Objections," p. 16.

3716. 28 July 1964: "Salinger Says Kennedy Balked at Dallas
Trip [from Weariness]," p. 26.

3717. 29 July 1964: "Ruby Appeal Battle Is Opened in
Dallas," p. 18.

3718. 31 July 1964: "Mrs. [Marina] Oswald Settles Suit
Against Former Advisers," p. 6.

3719. _____: "Goldwater Says He Almost Quit: JFK
Assassination Caused Him to Lose Interest in Race [for Presi-
dency]," p. 10.

3720. 3 Aug. 1964: "Guarding President Stressed by [Allen]
Dulles," p. 22.

3721. 4 Aug. 1964: "Warren Panel Expected to Rebut Plot
Theory [According to The Washington Evening Star]," p. 16.

3722. 5 Aug. 1964: "Kennedy Threat Case Ends [Against 77
Year Old New Hampshire Man Made in 1960]," p. 68.

3723. 6 Aug. 1964: "Curbing Sent to Warren Panel [with
Bullet Markings]," p. 7.

3724. 8 Aug. 1964: "Ruby Is Rebuffed by Judge Brown: Defense Now Can Take Plea to Texas's High Court," p. 7.

3725. 9 Aug. 1964: "Mrs. John F. Fitzgerald Is Dead;
Kennedy's Grandmother was 98: Widow of Honey Fitz, Boston's
Ex-Mayor, Was Not Told of President's Assassination," p. 77.

3726. 10 Aug. 1964: "Communism Cited in Kennedy Death:
House Panel Calls Agitation Cause of Assassination [i.e.
HUAC]," p. 4.

3727. _____: "Film on Death of Kennedy Shown at
Venice Festival ['Faces of November,' Directed by Robert
Drew]," p. 23.

3728. 13 Aug. 1964: "U.S. Agent [Abraham Bolden] Is Guilty
in Bid to Sell Data," p. 19.

3729. 18 Aug. 1964: "Was the Kennedy Assassination Engi-
neered? [Advertisement for] 'The Green Mirror,' L'Avant
Garde Publications," p. 29.

3730. 19 Aug. 1964: "Reports on Ruby Distress Inquiry:
Testimony to Warren Panel Appears in Two Papers [by Dorothy
Kilgallen]," p. 38.

3731. 28 Aug. 1964: "Radioactive Tests Used in Oswald Case,"
p. 32.

3732. 3 Sept. 1964: "Sales of Anti-Johnson Book [by J.
Evetts Haley, Over 7 Million, and Especially Good in John
Birch Society Bookstores]," p. 6.

3733. 5 Sept. 1964: "3 to Question Oswald Widow [i.e.,
Senators John Cooper and Richard Russell, and Cong. Hale
Boggs, All Part of Warren Commission]," p. 11.

3734. 5 Sept. 1964: "50% in U.S. Wept at Assassination:
Reaction to Kennedy Death Reported by Psychologists [Sheat-
sley and Bradburn Report]," Gladwin Hill, p. 16.

3735. 8 Sept. 1964: "A Kennedy Plaza Planned by Dallas on
Full City Block [as Assassination Memorial]," p. 31.

3736. _____: "Bar Group Names TV Study Panel: Rules
to Protect Defendant Will Be Recommended [After Ruby Trial],"
p. 59.

3737. 13 Sept. 1964: "Warren Findings Are Due in 'Days':
Report on Kennedy Slaying May Be Issued September 27," p. 46.

3738. _____: "Parallels Are Noted in Oswald History
and 10 Other Cases [of Persons Jailed for Threats Against
Presidents; Study by David A. Rothstein]," Emma Harrison,
p. 46.

Volume CXIV

3739. 18 Sept. 1964: "Film on the Assassination of Kennedy
to Open October 6 [i.e., 'Four Days in November', Produced by
David Wolper and U.P.I.]," p. 27.

3740. 20 Sept. 1964: "Warren Report Will Go to Johnson
Tomorrow [According to Congressman Gerald Ford]," p. 44.

3741. 22 Sept. 1964: "Warren Panel Reports to Johnson
Thursday [24 September]," p. 26.

3742. 23 Sept. 1964: "Warren Findings Due Next Sunday:
Assassination Report to Be Made Public at 6:30 P.M. [27
September]," p. 20.

3743. 24 Sept. 1964: "[TV] Warren Report Specials [on
Sunday Night, 27 Sept., on All Networks]," Val Adams, p. 83.

3744. 25 Sept. 1964: "Johnson Gets Assassination Report,"
Charles Mohr, pp. 1, 30.

3745. _____: "Networks to Offer Sunday Analyses of
Warren Report," George Gent, p. 83.

3746. 27 Sept. 1964: "Nation Awaiting Warren Report:
Assassination Data to Have a Worldwide Distribution," Jack
Raymond, pp. 1, 48.

3747. _____: "Kennedy's Widow Loses Her Listing in
Capital Society ['Social List', after Move to New York City],"
p. 75.

3748. 27 Sept. 1964: "[Full-Page Ad]: His Wife, His Mother,
His Best Friend . . . the Arresting Officer . . . Will Reveal
Today . . . What they Know of Lee Harvey Oswald [on CBS-TV
Today, 5-7 pm]," p. 5E.

3749. 28 Sept. 1964: "Warren Commission Finds Oswald Guilty
and Says Assassin and Ruby Acted Alone; Panel Unanimous:
Theory of Conspiracy by Left or Right Is Rejected," Anthony
Lewis, pp. 1, 14.

3750. _____: "[Warren Commission] Rebukes Secret
Service, Asks Revamping: F.B.I. Is Criticized: Security
Steps Taken by Secret Service Held Inadequate," Felix Belair,
Jr., pp. 1, 15.

3751. _____: "Johnson Names 4 to Act on Report:
Commission Calls for Action to Increase the Security of the
Presidency [Dillon, Katzenbach, McCone, McG. Bundy]," pp.
1, 17.

3752. _____: "A New Chapter Unfolds in the Kennedy
Legend," James Reston, pp. 1, 15.

3753. _____: "'Myths' of Case Denied in Detail:
Panel Says Misinformation on the Assassination Led to 'Distorted' Views [Challenges Doubters by Name]," Peter Kihss,
pp. 1, 16.

3754. 28 Sept. 1964: "Campaign Impact Believed Likely:
'Kennedy Legacy' Could Aid Democrats at the Polls," Tom
Wicker, pp. 1, 15.

3755. _____: "Scientific Police Work Traced Bullets
to Rifle Oswald Owned," John Finney, pp, 1, 16.

3756. _____: "Dallas Absolved, Civil Leaders Say:
Report Called an Answer to 'City of Hate' Charges," p. 14.

3757. _____: "Chief of Inquiry, Earl Warren: He
Was Moved by a Simple Appeal to Patriotic Duty," p. 14.

3758. _____: "Secrets of Many Bared by Inquiry:
Dozens Were Drawn Into Scope of Investigation," p. 14.

3759. _____: "Oswald's Mother Still Unconvinced
[Widow Unavailable for Comment]," p. 14.

3760. _____: "Identity of Some Sources Shielded by
Commission [e.g., in Mexico]," p. 14.

3761. _____: "Paperback Version Is Fast Seller
Here [Published by Popular Library, Foreword by Robert J.
Donovan]," p. 14.

3762. _____: "Oswald's Act Held Consistent with
Personality," Joseph A. Loftus, p. 15.

3763. 28 Sept. 1964: "Aide Kept Mrs. Kennedy from Falling Off Car: Hill, a Secret Service Agent, Pushed Her Back from Auto's Rear Deck," Marjorie Hunter, p. 15.

3764. _____: "Warren Commission Found No Foreign Power Involved in Kennedy's Assassination: Soviet and Cuba Furnished Data: Inquiry Got Moscow's File on Oswald's Stay in Russia--Rusk Backs Conclusion," Max Frankel, p. 16.

3765. _____: "Report Goes on Sale in Washington Today," p. 16.

3766. _____: "20 Volumes of Testimony to Be Made Public Later," p. 16.

3767. _____: "Press and Dallas Police Blamed for Confusion That Permitted Slaying of Oswald: Panel Suggests a Code of Ethics: Statements from Officials Are Called Prejudicial to Fair Trial for Assassin," Jack Raymond, p. 17.

3768. _____: "Commission Says Ruby Acted Alone in Slaying," John D. Pomfret, p. 17.

3769. _____: "Autopsy Showed 2 Bullet Wounds: Shot Through Brain Fatal, Medical Report Says," Harold M. Schmeck, Jr., p. 17.

3770. _____: "Robert Kennedy Says He Won't Read Report," p. 17.

3771. _____: "Shot at Walker Laid to Oswald: But Report Discounts Any Plan to Attack Nixon," p. 17.

3772. _____: "British Papers Highly Praise Detail of Commission's Report," p. 17.

3773. _____: "Projectile Pierces a Pane at Site of Kennedy Exhibit [in Houston, Possibly a Bullet]," p. 17.

3774. _____: "[Warren Panel's] Detective Effort Termed 'Massive' [by Un-Named 'Historians and Archivists']," p. 17.

3775 _____: "Belli to File Ruby Appeal at the Slayer's Request," p. 17.

3776. _____: "[Editorial] The Warren Commission Report," p. 28.

3777. _____: "[Editorial] The Police, Press, and Fanaticism," p. 28.

3778. _____: "TV: Networks Cover Warren Report Thoroughly," Jack Gould, p. 47.

3779. 28 Sept. 1964: "THE WARREN COMMISSION'S REPORT [Text and Photos in Full]," pp. 1A-48A.

3780. 29 Sept. 1964: "New Panel Plans to Act Speedily on Warren Data: Hopes to Start Work Today--Will Study Proposals on Secret Service: . . . Senators Weighing Measure to Make a Presidential Slaying a Federal Crime," Anthony Lewis, pp. 1, 29.

3781. _____: "[Robert] Kennedy, Disturbed by Memory of Tragedy, Cancels Rally Here," Homer Bigart, pp. 1, 36.

3782. _____: "Text of the Warren Report's Appendix on the History of Presidential Protection," pp. 28-29.

3783. _____: "Pooling of News Asked in Covering Major Events," Peter Kihss, p. 29.

3784. _____: "Khrushchev Given Copy of the Report [as well as 100 Other Soviet Officials]," p. 29.

3785. _____: "Printing Shop Denies Role in Anti-Kennedy Handbills [in Dallas]," p. 29.

3786. _____: "Warren Report Denounced by Leftist as a 'Cover-Up' [the Workers World Party]," p. 29.

3787. _____: "Many in Europe Skeptical About Warren Report: Findings Widely Publicized--Left Tends to Doubt Them, Right to Accept Them," Drew Middleton, p. 29.

3788. _____: "2 Stravinsky Works to Have Premieres [Includes 'Elegy to J.F.K.']," p. 50.

3789. 30 Sept. 1964: "Panel Takes Up Warren Report: Plans on Presidential Safety Are Studied by Committee Appointed by Johnson," Anthony Lewis, pp. 1, 33.

3790. _____: "Soviet Papers Call Warren Data False," p. 31.

3791. _____: "Kennedy's Mother Declines to Read the Warren Report," p. 31.

3792. _____: "F.B.I. Said to Punish 2 Agents in Charge of the Oswald Case," p. 33.

3793. 1 Oct. 1964: "Procedures in Defectors' Cases Revised by the State Department [as a Result of the Lee Harvey Oswald Case]," Max Frankel, p. 22.

3794. _____: "Publishers Rush Warren Report: 6 Editions of Findings Meet Large Public Demand," Harry Gilroy, p. 32.

3795. 1 Oct. 1964: "Books-Authors: [Thomas] Buchanan Book Here ["Who Killed Kennedy?" To Be Published by Putnams]," p. 32.

3796. 2 Oct. 1964: "[Advertisement]: Last 2 Times Prior to Tour; Nightly at 8 P.M.: 'Mark Lane on Who Killed Kennedy?': Jan Hus Theater--351 E. 74 St.," p. 32.

3797. _____ : "Books-Authors: A Defense of Ruby ["Dallas Justice" by Melvin M. Belli and Maurice G. Carroll to Be Published Oct. 19 by McKay Publ.]," p. 34.

3798. _____ : "Letters to the Times: News Problems in Dallas: Reporter Comments on Press Role During Oswald Detention," Gladwin Hill, p. 36.

3799. 3 Oct. 1964: "F.B.I. Chief Sees a Limit to Protection of President [J. Edgar Hoover Criticizes Warren Report]," Anthony Lewis, pp. 1, 16.

3800. _____ : "Oswald Findings Doubted Abroad: U.S. Reports Many Papers Reject the Conclusion That Assassin Acted Alone," Max Frankel, pp. 1, 16.

3801. 4 Oct. 1964: "The News of the Week in Review: The Nation: The Warren Report," p. 1E.

3802. _____ : "Presidential Security--Warren Report Raises Large Questions," Anthony Lewis, p. 3E.

3803. _____ : "[Editorial]: Ten Months After Tragedy,' p. 10E.

3804. _____ : "The F.B.I. Position: Warren Commission's View Following Hoover's Testimony Is Analyzed," Arthur Krock, p. 11E.

3805. _____ : "Opinion of the Week: At Home and Abroad: Warren Report," p. 11E.

3806. 6 Oct. 1964: "Johnson Uses Rebuilt Kennedy Car, Now Bulletproof," pp. 1, 19.

3807. _____ : "Texas Affirms Oswald's Guilt: Report Also Finds Slaying Was Not Result of Plot [According to Attorney General Waggoner Carr]," p. 19.

3808. 7 Oct. 1964: "Artists at Odds on Kennedy Tomb: They Argue Over Design--Plans to Be Unveiled Soon," p. 58.

3809. 8 Oct. 1964: "Move Against Belli [by State Bar Association] Is Beaten in Texas," p. 39.

3810. _____ : "F.B.I. Bid To Cover Up on Oswald Report ed [by Dallas Police Chief, Jesse Curry]," p. 60.

3811. 9 Oct. 1964: "News Media Act to Study Charges:
Meeting to Weigh Warren Report's Criticisms [on 17 Oct.,
by American Society of Newspaper Editors]," p. 21.

3812. _____: "Books-Authors: A Study of Marina
[Oswald to Be Published by Harper & Row Next Year, Written
by Priscilla Johnson]," p. 36.

3813. 10 Oct. 1964: "Letters to the Times: Scope of
Warren Report [Favorably Contrasted to the Roberts Report
in 1942 on Pearl Harbor]," Donald G. Brownlow, p. 28.

3814. 12 Oct. 1964: "Security Remains a Major Problem [for
Presidential Secret Service]," p. 17.

3815. 13 Oct. 1964: "Johnson to Visit Dallas First Time
Since November 22: Guard for Trip Next Monday Has Been
Intensified Since the Murder of Kennedy," p. 34.

3816. _____: "Kennedy Monument Unveiled [in Dallas
at the Trade Mart by the Bishop of Coventry, England]," p.
34.

3817. 14 Oct. 1964: "Plot on Johnson Hinted in Texas . . .
Motorcade Dropped [for Dallas]," Donald Janson, p. 30.

3818. 15 Oct. 1964: "Warren Report Summary Printed by
Soviet Weekly [Za Rubezhom, Prepared by U.S. Information
Agency]," p. 2.

3819. _____: "Dallas [Chief Curry] Denies F.B.I.
Asked for Cover-Up," p. 35.

3820. _____: "Czech Writes Kennedy Play [on First
Anniversary of Assassination, by Jiri Puda]," p. 54.

3821. 18 Oct. 1964: "Newsmen Wary on Warren Code: But
They Note Problems in Mass Coverage of Events," Jack Raymond,
p. 53.

3822. _____: "The Case of 'Trial by Press' [the Ruby
Trial and the Warren Report]," Anthony Lewis, pp. 31, 94-100:
NYT Magazine.

3823. 19 Oct. 1964: "Random Notes from All Over: Warren
Report Sells [at Record Pace for Government Printing Office:
97,000 Copies in Three Weeks]," p. 10.

3824. 22 Oct. 1964: "$650,000 Is Given to Tippit Family:
Donations Honor Patrolman Slain by Oswald in Dallas," p. 24.

3825. 25 Oct. 1964: "[Commemorative Stamps for 22 Novem-
ber] Issued by Bonn," p. 28.

3826. 27 Oct. 1964: "Letters to the Times: Mass Media's
Role in Dallas [criticizing Earlier Letter by Gladwin Hill],"
Stanley M. Cohen, p. 38.

3827.   31 Oct. 1964:   "Mrs. Kennedy Is Appointed Guardian of Her Children," p. 26.

3828.   1 Nov. 1964:   "An Oswald Alias Seen as Anagram: The Name of 'Alek J. Hidell' Linked to Jekyll and Hyde," p. 50.

3829.   2 Nov. 1964:   "Dallas Leaders Oppose G.O.P.'s Alger [for Congress, in Aftermath of JFK Assassination]," Gladwin Hill, p. 27.

3830.   3 Nov. 1964:   "President Kennedy's Widow Says 'He Is Free, We Must Live' [in Look Magazine's Memorial Issue]," p. 19.

3831.   3 Nov. 1964:   "Mass for Kennedy Set [by Cardinal Cushing in Boston on First Anniversary of Assassination]," p. 20.

3832.   4 Nov. 1964:   "[Advertisement]:   Four Assassinated Presidents Honored on Postage Stamps [The JFK Stamps in Argentina, Colombia, Paraguay, Togo, Yemen, Jordan]," p. 30.

3833.   10 Nov. 1964:   "Ousted F.B.I. Man's Plea Is Refused by High Court [That William W. Turner was Improperly Dismissed]," p. 41.

3834.   13 Nov. 1964:   "Model of Grave Memorial Approved by Mrs. Kennedy [and Over Two Million Have Visited JFK Grave]," p. 19.

3835.   14 Nov. 1964:   "Tomb for Kennedy Is of Simple Design," Nan Robertson, pp. 1, 15.

3836.   15 Nov. 1964:   "What Was Killed Was Not only the President But the Promise," James Reston, pp. 24-25, 126-127: NYT Magazine.

3837.   17 Nov. 1964:   "The Kennedy Tomb: Simple Design Outlined: Flame and a Tablet Will Mark Grave at Arlington," Nan Robertson, pp. 1, 34.

3838.   _____ :   "The Screen: Tribute to a President: Kennedy Documentary Is Shown in Capital ['John F. Kennedy: Years of Lightning, Day of Drums']," Bosley Crowther, p. 47.

3839.   19 Nov. 1964:   "Hoover Assails Warren Findings: Says F.B.I. Was Criticized Unfairly on Oswald Check--Calls Dr. King a 'Liar'," Ben A. Franklin, pp. 1, 28.

3840.   _____ :   "Widow of Oswald in Dallas Hospital; Reported Resting," p. 47.

3841.   _____ :   "TV: . . . 'Burden and the Glory': [CBS Recapitulation of JFK's Presidency]," Paul Gardner, p. 79.

3842. 20 Nov. 1964: "Johnson Proclaims Sunday a Day to Honor Kennedy [Text]," pp. 1, 22.

3843. _____ : "Data Due Nov. 30 on Assassination: Warren Inquiry Transcripts Will Be Made Public," p. 22.

3844. _____ : "Hospital Report on Mrs. [Marina] Oswald: A Stomach Ailment and Fatigue," Fred Powledge, p. 22.

3845. _____ : "Daniel [Managing Editor, New York Times] Cautions on Press Codes: Puts Stress on Freedom in Reply to Warren Panel," p. 76.

3846. 21 Nov. 1964: "Kennedy Tribute Asked by Wagner: Minute of Silence at 1 P.M. Tomorrow Is Urged Here," p. 11.

3847. _____ : "German Stamp Honors Kennedy," p. 11.

3848. _____ : "Sister of Castro Assails Him Here: Says He Is Indirect Cause of Kennedy's Death," Tania Long, p. 11.

3849. _____ : "Many Faiths Plan Kennedy Services: Churches Throughout City to Conduct Memorials," George Dugan, p. 26.

3850. 22 Nov. 1964: "Panel Opposes New F.B.I. Role in Johnson Guard: Cabinet Study Rejects Shift of Investigating Function from Secret Service: Warren Data Weighed," Felix Belair, Jr., pp. 1, 76.

3851. _____ : "Kennedy Epilogue: A Shocked Dallas Changing Its Ways," Fred Powledge, pp. 1, 74.

3852. _____ : "Thousands Expected to Pay Respects at Grave: Senator-Elect Kennedy and Cabinet Aides to Appear at Arlington Cemetery," Nan Robertson, p. 74.

3853. _____ : "Tributes Throughout the World to Mark Anniversary of Death," p. 74.

3854. _____ : "Musical Tributes Listed for Today: Concerts, Services, TV and Radio to Honor Kennedy," Theodore Strongin, p. 75.

3855. _____ : "Johnson, Ending Year in Office, to Hear Tributes to Kennedy," Marjorie Hunter, p. 75.

3856. _____ : "Kennedy Memorial of Simple Design Planned in Britain [at Runnymede, Site of Signing of Magna Carta, 1215]," p. 75.

3857. _____ : "The News of the Week in Review: A Year Later: Day of Remembrance," pp. 1E-2E, 8E.

3858.   22 Nov. 1964:   "Opinion of the Week: At Home and Abroad: One Year Later [The JFK Assassination]," p. 9E.

3859.   23 Nov. 1964:   "The Nation Remembers Its Slain President: Robert Kennedy Leads the Family as 40,000 Pay Tribute at Arlington," Nan Robertson, pp. 1, 28.

3860.   _____: "Cushing Recalls 'His Noble Deeds'; World's Capitals Join in Tribute [to JFK]," pp. 1, 28.

3861.   _____: "[Advertisement]:   The Report Is Out. The Question Remains.   Who Killed Kennedy?   By Thomas G. Buchanan," p. 27.

3862.   _____: "Minute of Prayer Silences Dallas: Traffic Halts as City Recalls Assassination of Kennedy," Fred Powledge, p. 28.

3863.   _____: "Johnsons Attend Kennedy Service: Connallys Go With Them to Austin Memorial Rites," Marjorie Hunter, p. 28.

3864.   _____: "Tributes Paid Here to Kennedy; City Observes Minute of Silence," p. 28.

3865.   _____: "It Was Their Anniversary, Too: Mrs. J. D. Tippit and Her Children," p. 28.

3866.   _____: "Mrs. Kennedy Spends Day at Long Island Residence," p. 28.

3867.   _____: "Canadian TV Shows Film Paying Tribute to Kennedy ['Years of Lightning, Day of Drums']," p. 28.

3868.   _____: "Oswald's Widow Expresses Sorrow for Kennedy Family," p. 28.

3869.   _____: "TV: Memorial Programs: NBC and ABC Present Documentary Tributes to President Kennedy," Jack Gould, p. 75.

3870.   24 Nov. 1964:   "Kennedy Slaying Relived in Detail in Warren Files: Testimony of 552:   Widow's Recollections Among the Poignant Passages Published," Anthony Lewis, pp. 1, 28.

3871.   _____: "Friend of Oswalds Knew Mrs. Kennedy [George S. de Mohrenschildt]," Tad Szulc, pp. 1, 33.

3872.   _____: "Kennedy Barred Car-Step Guards: 4 Days Before His Death He Asked Secret Service Men Not to Ride on Auto," Felix Belair, Jr., pp. 1, 33.

3873.   _____: "Testimony of Witnesses Before Warren Commission During Assassination Inquiry: Mrs. John F. Kennedy's Account," p. 28.

3874. 24 Nov. 1964: "F.B.I. Aide Puts Rights of the Individual First [in Testifying Before Warren Commission]," p.
28.

3875. _____: "Warren Panel Data Sold by U.S. for $76
a Set [of 26 Volumes]," p. 28.

3876. _____: "Oswald Said to Say He Broke Single
Law [Only When He Struck Arresting Officer in Cinema]," p.
28.

3877. _____: "[Excerpts from Testimony of LBJ, John
Connally, Secret Service Agents, J. Edgar Hoover, and Oswald's
Diary]," pp. 28-32.

3878. _____: "Oswald's Wife Says He Developed 2d
Personality: She Recalls His Irritability After Return from
Soviet: Believes He Shot Kennedy to Achieve Notoriety,"
John W. Finney, p. 32.

3879. _____: "3 Witnesses Saw Assassin Fire; One
Gave Description of Oswald [Evins, Brennan, and Worrell],"
p. 32.

3880. _____: "Mrs. Oswald Says F.B.I. Threatened to
Deport Her," p. 32.

3881. 24 Nov. 1964: "Mrs. Johnson Taped Impressions [on
30 Nov. 1963]: Dictated Notes Show a Flash of Anger by Mrs.
Kennedy," Nan Robertson, p. 33.

3882. 25 Nov. 1964: "All Tips Run Down by Warren Panel:
Doubts May Remain Despite Checking of Plot Theories," p. 19.

3883. _____: "White House Staff Lacks Taster for
the President [According to Warren Report]," p. 19.

3884. 26 Nov. 1964: "Counsel Explains Absence of Quote in
Warren Report [Made by Mrs. Kennedy to Mrs. Johnson After
Assassination]," p. 34.

3885. _____: "15 Noted Dancers Present Kennedy Tribute in Dallas [Ballet]," p. 52.

3886. _____: "Mother Visits Oswald's Grave [at Rose
Hill Cemetery, Fort Worth]," p. 76.

3887. 27 Nov. 1964: "Oswald's Wife Visits Relative [Robert
Oswald in Wichita Falls]," p. 26.

3888. _____: "Books and Authors: Warren Inquiry
Sidelights [in Book by Gerald Ford to Be Published by Simon
& Schuster]," p. 33.

3889. 28 Nov. 1964: "Secret Service Acts to Bolster Johnson's Guard: Dillon Tells of Plan to Hire 75 Agents as First
Step in $3 Million Project," Felix Belair, Jr., pp. 1, 16.

3890.   29 Nov. 1964:   "Collectors Shun Warren Volumes [380 Sets Sold in First Week]," p. 63.

3891.   30 Nov. 1964:   "Letters to the Times: Hoover Stand on Report: F.B.I. Head's Criticism of Warren Commission Is Defended [by A.C.L.U. Lawyer]," Nanette Dembitz, p. 32.

3892.   7 Dec. 1964:   "Random Notes from All Over: A Wierd Book [The Warren Report's Testimony by Nelson Delgado, Oswald's Friend in the Marine Corps]," p. 16.

3893.   9 Dec. 1964:   "Ruby Lawyer Sues Magazine [Newsweek for 9 Dec. 1963 Article on Tom Howard]," p. 30.

3894.   12 Dec. 1964:   "Mark Lane Writing Book to 'Expose' Warren Report ["Rush to Judgment" Scheduled for March 1965 Publication by Grove Press]," p. 22.

3895.   13 Dec. 1964:   "Rankin Reports 'Many Oswalds':   Warren Commission Aide Says Society Is to Blame," Fred Powledge, p. 76.

3896.   14 Dec. 1964:   "Random Notes from All Over: Volume Sales [Warren Commission Hearings Sell 846 of 2500 Printed]," p. 10.

3897.   _____ :   "Briton Questions Warren Findings: Historian Calls the Kennedy Death Report 'Suspect' [i.e., Professor Hugh Trevor - Roper in The Sunday Times]," Clyde H. Farnsworth, p. 30.

3898.   17 Dec. 1964:   "Critic Is Disputed on Warren Group: Oxford Professor's Doubts Dismissed in Capital," Anthony Lewis," p. 23.

3899.   24 Dec. 1964:   "Oswald's Widow to Study English [at University of Michigan, Ann Arbor]," p. 12.

3900.   25 Dec. 1964:   "Ruby Gets $100 Present [from a Sunday School Class]," p. 32.

3901.   28 Dec. 1964:   "Random Notes from All Over: Wife-Beating Puzzles Bachelor [i.e., Senator Richard Russell's Curiosity About the Oswald Marriage, from Warren Commission Testimony]," p. 32.

3902.   3 Jan. 1965:   "Lawyer Disputes Warren Findings: Article Says at Least Two Persons Fired at Kennedy [Vincent J. Salandria, in Liberation, Jan. 1965]," p. 38.

3903.   4 Jan. 1965:   "Warren Findings Again Questioned: But Trevor-Roper Concedes an Error on One Point," p. 30.

3904.   5 Jan. 1965:   "Widow of Oswald Enrolls at College [University of Michigan]," p. 19.

3905. 6 Jan. 1965: "Mrs. [Marina] Oswald Attends Classes,"
p. 30.

3906. 7 Jan. 1965: "[Senator Wayne] Morse Seeking Curb on
Pretrial Reports [after Oswald-Ruby Cases]," p. 17.

3907. 9 Jan. 1965: "2 Agents Removed from White House by
Secret Service [Behn and Boring, Replaced by Two Who Were
With JFK in Dallas: Youngblood and Kellerman]," p. 10.

3908. 10 Jan. 1965: "News of the Week in Law: Law and
Press [after JFK Assassination]," John D. Pomfret, p. 8E.

3909. 11 Jan. 1965: "Lawyer Assays Warren Report as Trial
Evidence [Alfredda Scobey, Staff-Member of Warren Panel],"
Austin C. Wehrwein, p. 23.

3910. 12 Jan. 1965: Bar Head [Lewis F. Powell, Jr.] Warns
Law and Press: Says Right to Free Trial Is Being Endangered
[Citing JFK Assassination for Prejudicial Pre-Trial Publi-
city]," p. 34.

3911. 14 Jan. 1965: "Philadelphia Bar Answers Press:
Lawyers Say News Policy Aims Only at Fair Trials," p. 47.

3912. 16 Jan. 1965: "Ruby's Appeal Date Set for March 10
in Texas," p. 25.

3913. 21 Jan. 1965: "[American] Bar Association to Weigh
U.S. Assassination Law [Making It a Federal Offense]," p. 28.

3914. 4 Feb. 1965: "Publishers Plan Fair-Trial Study:
Will Explore Relationship of Press and Courts [the American
Newspaper Publishers Association]," p. 26.

3915. _____ : "Belli to File Ruby Briefs [for Texas
Appeal]," p. 62.

3916. 6 Feb. 1965: "News Curbs Decried by Head of TV
Group [Against Warren Commission Suggestions]," p. 53.

3917. 7 Feb. 1965: "News Curb Asked to Aid Fair Trials:
Telford Taylor Says Law Is Needed to Protect Rights," p. 80.

3918. 13 Feb. 1965: "Law Firm Here Steps Out of Ruby Case
[William Kuntsler's Firm]," Alfred E. Clark, p. 50.

3919. 17 Feb. 1965: "Publishers Initiate News-Justice
Study [by American Newspapers Publishers Association, Following Warren Commission Suggestions]," p. 46.

3920. 18 Feb. 1965: "Ruby Family Bid Ignored by Texas
Appeals Court [for New Lawyers]," p. 26.

3921. 21 Feb. 1965: "Katzenbach [U.S. Attorney General] Preparing an Order to Limit Pretrial Data to Press," Fred P.
Graham, p. 57.

3922.   23 Feb. 1965:   "Voluntary Backing of News Code Seen [by Clifton Daniel, Managing Editor, The New York Times]," p. 14.

3923.   23 Feb. 1965:   "Pretrial Publicity Issue in Cleveland," p. 27.

3924.   25 Feb. 1965:   "A Sanity Ruling Sought on Ruby: Appeals Court Delays Case Pending a Decision," p. 63.

3925.   27 Feb. 1965:   "Ruby Sanity-Trial Hearing Is Postponed to March 8," p. 11.

3926.   _____: "Mrs. [Marina] Oswald Cries at Her Graduation With English Class," p. 11.

3927.   1 March 1965:   "Study Says 2 Men Shot at Kennedy: 51 Witnesses Linked Firing to Knoll, Writer Finds [Harold Feldman, in The Minority of One]," p. 17.

3928.   9 March 1965:   "Jury Trial on Ruby's Sanity Is Set for March 29:   Tonahill Named an Attorney Over Slayer's Objections: Family's Lawyer Will Seek Order to Disqualify Judge [Joe B. Brown]," p. 21.

3929.   _____: "Capital Gets Bill on Assassination: Congress Asked to Make Attacks a Federal Offense," p. 21.

3930.   15 March 1965:   "Plot on Kennedy Still Suspected: Theory Persists in Europe Despite Warren Report," p. 11.

3931.   18 March 1965:   "Official Asks End of Death Penalty: District Attorney's Leader Calls It Worthless [and Press Freedoms Debated Concerning Oswald-Ruby]," Sydney E. Zion, p. 24.

3932.   20 March 1965:   "Ruby Plea Loses in Federal Court: Case Sent Back to State for Hearing on His Sanity," p. 9.

3933.   21 March 1965:   "Syndrome Found in Threat Cases: Would-Be Assassins Said to Show Pattern of Rebellion [According to Dr. David Rothstein]," Walter Sullivan, p. 66.

3934.   23 March 1965:   "U.S. Court Gets Ruby Plea [on Sanity U.S. Court of Appeals, Fifth Circuit, New Orleans]," p. 20.

3935.   _____: "Oswald Widow Petitions to Administer Property," p. 22.

3936.   26 March 1965:   "Warren Report Still Selling [140,233 Copies, to Date]," p. 27.

3937.   4 April 1965:   "U.S.I.A. Drops Plan on Warren Data: Idea of Distributing Russian Version in Soviet Cancelled p. 55.

3938. 10 April 1965: "Stabbing of Seward in 1865 Is Recalled [by Dr. John K. Lattimer, Regarding JFK Assassination]," p. 59.

3939. 11 April 1965: "Nixon, Back in Moscow, Debates Again: Issue of Kennedy's Slaying Raised by University Aide," Henry Tanner, pp. 1, 13.

3940. 14 April 1965: "100 Years Ago Tonight: The Tragedy at Ford's Theatre: Parallels Are Noted in Lincoln's Death and Kennedy's," Homer Bigart, pp. 1, 28.

3941. _____: "Booth and Oswald: 2 Assassins Very Little Alike," p. 28.

3942. 15 April 1965: "Editors Oppose Crime News Curbs as Dangerous [American Society of Newspaper Editors]," p. 40.

3943. 17 April 1965: "[U.S. Attorney General] Katzenbach Defines Standards for Information on Defendants: Tells What Will and Will Not Be Disclosed Before Trial in U.S. Criminal Cases [After Oswald-Ruby]," E. W. Kenworthy, pp. 1, 20.

3944. 17 April 1965: "Letters to the Editor of the Times: Nixon's Reply to Russian Criticized [Rejects His Parallel of JFK's Fate With That of Trotsky and Beria]," Letitia Upton, p. 18.

3945. 18 April 1965: "News of the Week in Law: Press Code," p. 12E.

3946. 24 April 1965: "Court Bars a Delay in Ruby Sanity Case," p. 12.

3947. 27 April 1965: "Press and Bar Unit Discuss Crime News [on Pre-Trial Publicity]," p. 24.

3948. 7 May 1965: "White House Intruders Said to Be Driven by Fears and Illusions [by Drs. J. Sebastiani and J. L. Foy]," Raymond H. Anderson, p. 7.

3949. 9 May 1965: "Author Relives Days of Kennedy Assassination for New Book [William Manchester]," p. 43.

3950. 10 May 1965: "U.S. Will Seek Possession of the Rifle Used by Oswald [Permanently]," p. 29.

3951. 18 May 1965: "Humphrey Visits a Vigilant Dallas: Ringed by Police--Forth Worth Watches Oswald's Mother [Under Police Surveillance She Calls 'Asinine']," p. 17.

3952. 25 May 1965: "Ruby Testifies to Taking Pills: Tells Hearing About Actions Before He Shot Oswald," p. 21.

3953. _____: "Ruby Beanie Caps Proposed by Lawyer [as Fund-Raiser for Defense]," p. 21.

3954.   26 May 1965:   "Judge [Joe B. Brown] Doubts Ruby Will
Be Executed," p. 21.

3955.   27 May 1965:   "Hearing Reviews Kennedy Murder: 2
House Chiefs [Boggs and Ford] Back Move for Federal Jurisdiction [in Assassination Cases]," p. 40.

3956.   28 May 1965:   "C.B.S. Will Keep Confessions, Defendants' Records Off the Air," Val Adams, p. 67.

3957.   2 June 1965:   "Oswald's Widow Weds a Neighbor: She
Marries an Electronics Worker, 27, in Texas [Kenneth Jess
Porter]," pp. 1, 18.

3958.   6 June 1965:   "Bar Group to Ask a New Ruby Trial:
New York Court Association Will File Brief in Texas," p. 77.

3959.   _____: "Reports from Other News Fronts:
Personal: The New Marina [Oswald Porter]," p. 4E.

3960.   7 June 1965:   "F.B.I. Academy Is Accused of Barring
Dallas Police [Since JFK Assassination]," p. 34.

3961.   9 June 1965:   "U.S. Law on Killing a President Gains
[House Judiciary Committee Approval]," p. 2.

3962.   10 June 1965:   "Book Views Role of Oswald's Wife
[Ford-Stiles, 'Portrait of the Assasin', That Her Rejection
of Him Goaded Him to Kill JFK]," p. 18.

3963.   13 June 1965:   "Kilduff, Press Aide, Quits White House
Post to Be Consultant: [Was Aid Who Officially Announced
JFK's Death]," Robert B. Semple, Jr., p. 67.

3964.   18 June 1965:   "U.S. Urged to Keep Assassination Gun
[by U.S. Attorney General Katzenbach]," p. 15.

3965.   22 June 1965:   "Brown Withdraws as Ruby Case Judge,"
p. 70.

3966.   21 July 1965:   "Senate Committee [Judiciary] Backs
Assassination Legislation [Creating Federal Crime]," p. 6.

3967.   23 July 1965:   "TV: 'Young Man From Boston', a
Kennedy Tribute: WABC-TV Shows New Home-Movie Selection:
Prying Into Private Life Found Objectionable [Sponsored by
Plymouth Motor's Souvenir Book]," Jack Gould, p. 57.

3968.   24 July 1965:   "Ruby Bid on Hearing Over Judge [Brown]
Denied," p. 8.

3969.   8 Aug. 1965:   "News Unit Scores Chaotic Coverage:
Asks Officials to Draft Plans for Press Before Event [in
Aftermath of JFK Killing]," p. 24.

3970.   14 Aug. 1965:   "Hearing Ordered for Ruby [by Judge
Louis Holland, on Habeas Corpus Hearing]," p. 9.

3971.   17 Aug. 1965:   "Kennedy Called Tense Near End: But
Secretary [Evelyn Lincoln] Says He Was Fatalistic About
Death," p. 19.

3972.   19 Aug. 1965:   "Oswald's Widow Says New Husband Hit
Her," p. 13.

3973.   _____: "U.S. Judge [William F. Smith, Newark]
Backs Trial News Curb: But He Asks for a Change in Measure's
Language: Belli Opposes Bill," p. 21.

3974.   20 Aug. 1965:   "Widow of Oswald and New Husband End
Family Spat," p. 26.

3975.   1 Sept. 1965:   "Attacks on President Now Federal
Crime [Signed by LBJ]," p. 14.

3976.   8 Sept. 1965:   "House Votes to Put Assassination Rifle
in Keeping of U.S.,", p. 28.

3977.   11 Sept. 1965:   "Ruby Loses Plea for New Trial Based
on Disqualifying of Judge," p. 15.

3978.   21 Sept. 1965:   "United States Scene: Oswald Letters
on Auction [by His Mother]," p. 3:   NYT International Edition.

VOLUME CXV

3979.   2-3 Oct. 1965:   "N.Y. Book Dealer [David Kirschenbaum]
Buys Letters by Oswald and Mrs. J. F. Kennedy," p. 3:   NYT
International Edition.

3980.   14 Oct. 1965:   "Self-Rule By Press Urged as Court Aid
[at Center for the Study of Democratic Institutions]," p. 50.

3981.   18 Oct. 1965:   "2 Lawyers Term Ruby Trial Unfair:
392-Page Study Is Critical of the Presiding Judge--Cites His
Book Contract [Kaplan and Waltz]," Will Lissner, pp. 37, 42.

3982.   19 Oct. 1965:   "Measure on Kennedy Rifle Sent to
Johnson by Senate [to Retain Oswald's Rifle Permanently],"
p. 22.

3983.   _____: "Ruby Sanity Hearing Postponed in
Texas," p. 37.

3984.   22 Oct. 1965:   "Dallas to Mark the Site of Kennedy's
Slaying," p. 40.

3985.   31 Oct. 1965:   "Kennedy Is Hero No. 1 for German
Children . . . followed closely by an Apache Indian named
Winnetou," p. 83.

3986.   3 Nov. 1965:   "Johnson Signs Bill to Keep Control of
Kennedy Rifle," p. 28.

3987. 5 Nov. 1965: "Ruby Prosecutor Backs Life Term: Dallas Official [Henry M. Wade, D.A.] Is Willing to Commute Death Sentence," p. 12.

3988. 11 Nov. 1965: "Philadelphia Bar Asks Press Curbs: Urges Withholding of Data on Crimes Until Trial," p. 32.

3989. 12 Nov. 1965: "Events of Kennedy Assassination Become a Play in West Germany ["Dallas--November 22d" by Felix Lützkendorf]," p. 54.

3990. 21 Nov. 1965: "Johnson to Mark Kennedy's Death: Plans Family Observance on Anniversary Tomorrow," Robert B. Semple, Jr., p. 37.

3991. 28 Nov. 1965: "Ruby Judge Thinks Oswald Was Firing Only at Connally [Judge Joe B. Brown]," p. 69.

3992. 9 Dec. 1965: "Ruby's Lawyers Drop Bid for Federal Court Hearing [on Sanity]," p. 27.

3993. 12 Dec. 1965: "Dallas Picks Design of Kennedy Memorial: Monument by Philip Johnson to Stand Near Death Spot [Photo of Model]," pp. 1, 39.

3994. 19 Dec. 1965: "Oswald Figure Is Killed [William W. Whaley, Taxi Driver]," p. 47.

3995. 14 Jan. 1966: "B.B.C. Plans Drama on Oswald [in March, Entitled "Lee Oswald, Assassin"]," p. 5.

3996. 23 Jan. 1966: "Alienated and Neglected: [Review of The Two Assassins, by R. Hartogs and L. Freeman]," Francis J. Braceland, pp. 30-31: NYT Book Review.

3997. 1 Feb. 1966: "6 Letters Linked to Assassins Sold [2 Written by Ruby, 4 by John Wilkes Booth]," p. 8.

3998. 19 Feb. 1966: "Ownership of Rifle of Oswald Disputed [Claims of John J. King vs. U.S. for Rifle and Pistol He Paid Marina Oswald $10,000 For]," p. 11.

3999. 22 Feb. 1966: "Court Rules Oswald Weapons are U.S. Property [Federal Judge Joe E. Estes, Dallas]," Martin Waldron, p. 10.

4000. 23 Feb. 1966: "Books of the Times: How Oswald Happened [Review of A Mother in History, by Jean Stafford]," Eliot Fremont-Smith, p. 37.

4001. 26 Feb. 1966: "Experts Find Gaps in Warren Report [at American Academy of Forensic Sciences, Meeting in Chicago]," p. 9.

4002. 27 Feb. 1966: "Jack Ruby Draws and Colors to While Away Time in Jail: Slayer of Oswald Is Reported to Be Much Calmer Than After Conviction in '64," Martin Waldron, p. 72.

4003. 8 Mar. 1966: "Kennedy Memorial Approved [by Dallas Park Board, an $8,000 Plaque at Site of Assassination]," p. 30.

4004. 13 Mar. 1966: "Mom Talks: [Review of A Mother in History, by Jean Stafford]," Annette Baxter, pp. 16-18: NYT Book Review.

4005. 16 Mar. 1966: "TV: Britons See the First Play About Lee Oswald: Adaptation of a German Work [by Felix Lützen-dorff] Disappointing: But Individual Nature of Crime Is Stressed," Jack Gould, p. 89.

4006. 11 Apr. 1966: "Kennedy Grave Visitors Are Undaunted by Cold," p. 30.

4007. 12 Apr. 1966: "First Stones Placed at Permanent Site of Kennedy Grave," Nan Robertson, pp. 1, 24.

4008. 17 Apr. 1966: "Thousands Pay Visit to Kennedy Grave [in Easter Week]," p. 13.

4009. _____: "Assassination Marker Delayed [Indefi-nitely by Dallas Park Board at Assassination Site]," p. 68.

4010. 28 Apr. 1966: "Ruby Nightclub to Become Gymnasium for Dallas Boys [Given Rent-Free to Police by Owner, Houston N. Nichols]," p. 50.

4011. 12 May 1966: "High Court in Texas Hears Ruby Appeal [Regarding Judge Brown's $5000 Book Advance Before Trial]," p. 12.

4012. 19 May 1966: "Early Sanity Trial for Ruby Ordered by Appeals Court [and Declines to Rule on Judge Brown's Book Advance for Now]," p. 40.

4013. 23 May 1966: "Ruby's Sanity Trial Is Set for June 13 by U.S. Judge [Louis T. Holland, Dallas]," p. 19.

4014. 29 May 1966: "John Fitzgerald Kennedy: From Harvard to History [Previews NBC-TV's "The Age of Kennedy" Broadcast 29 May, 6:30-7:30 pm]," Steven V. Roberts, p. 15D.

4015. 30 May 1966: "Service Held in Capital on Kennedy's Birthday [at Shrine of the Immaculate Conception]," p. 6.

4016. _____: "TV: 'The Age of Kennedy,' Chapter 1: N.B.C. Covers Period to 1960 Nomination: Last of 2 Programs Is Set Next Sunday," Jack Gould, p. 37.

4017. 3 June 1966: "Stay of Ruby Sanity Hearing Is Asked
in Supreme Court [by William Kunstler in Washington, D.C.],"
p. 24.

4018. 4 June 1966: "[Associate Justice Hugo L.] Black Bars
a Stay on Ruby's Hearing [Concerning Sanity]," p. 18.

4019. 5 June 1966: "Warren Report on Assassination Challenged Again [by Epstein, Lane, Weisberg, Sauvage, Fox Brooks],"
p. 42.

4020. 6 June 1966: "TV: 'Age of Kennedy' [2nd Part, Re-
viewed]," Jack Gould, p. 83.

4021. 11 June 1966: "Ruby Sanity Trial Ordered to Proceed
[by District Judge Holland]," p. 12.

4022. 14 June 1966: "Ruby Ruled Sane by a Texas Jury:
Oswald Slayer, Guards and Prison Doctor Testify," Martin
Waldron, p. 27.

4023. 25 June 1966: "Lawyers for Ruby Dispute 'Errors':
Texas Appeals Court Gets Many Pleas for New Trial," p. 34.

4024. 30 June 1966: •"Court Hears Pleas on Oswald's Guns
[John J. King vs. U.S.]," p. 23.

4025. 1 July 1966: "Warren in Israel for Kennedy Rite:
Will Dedicate a Memorial and Forest on July 4 [Defends Report
on Assassination]," James Feron, p. 3.

4026. 2 July 1966: "Agent [William R. Greer] Who Drove
Kennedy Car in Dallas Retires: Did Not Know the President
Had Been Hit by Bullet," Robert B. Semple, Jr., p. 10.

4027. 3 July 1966: "Reports on the Report: [Reviews Epstein's Inquest and Weisberg's Whitewash]," Fred Graham, pp.
3, 22: NYT Book Review.

4028. 6 July 1966: "Books of the Times: Pandora's Box
[Review of Epstein's Inquest]," Eliot Fremont-Smith, p. 43.

4029. 8 July 1966: "A Study of X-Rays of Kennedy Is Urged
[by Jacob Cohen in The Nation]," p. 7.

4030. 24 July 1966: "Former Kennedy Aide [Richard N. Good-
win] Suggests Panel to Check Warren Report," Edith Evans
Asbury, p. 25.

4031. 31 July 1966: "Court Holds U.S. Must Pay for Assassination Weapons [as Reimbursement to John J. King, Who Paid
$10,000 to Marina Oswald]," p. 52.

4032. 1 Aug. 1966: "Warren Unit Backed by Edward Kennedy,"
p. 25.

4033. 5 Aug. 1966: "Big Bid Reported for Book on Kennedy
[$650,000 by Look for Manchester's Serial Rights]," Homer
Bigart, p. 29.

4034. 13 Aug. 1966: "Ruby Appeal [on Murder Conviction]
Goes to Supreme Court," p. 10.

4035. _____: "Abstract Mural Stirs Bostonians:
Viewers Link Motherwell Work to Kennedy Death [Entitled:
New England Elegy]," John H. Fenton, p. 22.

4036. 16 Aug. 1966: "Books of the Times: Rush to the
Warren Committee Report [Reviews Lane and Sauvage]," Christopher Lehmann-Haupt, p. 37.

4037. 23 Aug. 1966: "Film to Examine Kennedy Inquiry:
'Rush to Judgment' Assails Warren Group Findings," p. 32.

4038. 27 Aug. 1966: "Pressure Denied on Kennedy Book:
Family Said to Be Concerned Over Its Serialization," Homer
Bigart, p. 27.

4039. 28 Aug. 1966: "Round Two [Review of Lane and Sauvage
Books]," Fred Graham, pp. 3, 28-29: NYT Book Review.

4040. 29 Aug. 1966: "Mrs. Kennedy Sent Kremlin Peace Plea
[on Her Last Night in White House]," p. 21.

4041. 1 Sept. 1966: "The Warren Report Is Barred in Soviet,"
pp. 1, 2.

4042. _____: "Aid Due for Study of Warren Report
[$2000 from Historical Research Foundation, and William F.
Buckley, Jr.]," p. 2.

4043. _____: "[Editorial] Slander in Moscow: [By
Banning Warren Report]," p. 34.

4044. 11 Sept. 1966: "No Conspiracy, But--Two Assassins,
Perhaps?" Henry Fairlie, pp. 52-55, 154-159: NYT Magazine.

VOLUME CXVI

4045. 18 Sept. 1966: "Jim Bishop Asserts Kennedys Tried to
Bar Book: Reports Pressure by Family After He Rejected
Requests by Former First Lady," p. 41.

4046. _____: "Letters to the Editor: 'Inquest',"
Edward Jay Epstein, p. 52: NYT Book Review.

4047. 25 Sept. 1966: "Letters to the Editor: Warren Report
[Criticisms of Fred Graham's Earlier Review]," Sylvan Fox,
et al., p. 55: NYT Book Review.

4048. _____: "The Right of Appeal for Lee Oswald,"
Tom Wicker, p. 10E.

4049. 26 Sept. 1966: "London Debates Warren Report: Critics Are Split on Issues Raised by 2 U.S. Books [by Epstein and Lane]," Anthony Lewis, p. 14.

4050. _____ : "U.S. Inquiry Is Urged on Warren Report [by Rep. Theodore R. Kupferman]," p. 26.

4051. 3 Oct. 1966: "Lawford Plans to Make Series of Documentaries on Kennedy," Val Adams, p. 94.

4052. 5 Oct. 1966: "Warren Report's Critics to Appear on TV Program [Lane, Sauvage, Weisberg, Jones, and Jacob Cohen, with Jim Bishop as Moderator]," George Gent, p. 95.

4053. 6 Oct. 1966: "Texas Court Voids Ruby's Conviction in Oswald Death: Orders Retrial Outside Dallas--Cites the Publicity and Inadmissible Evidence," Martin Waldron, pp. 1, 31.

4054. _____ : "Truculent Texan: Jack Ruby [Biographical Profile]," p. 31.

4055. _____ : "Rep. Ford Defends Warren Unit Report [That No New Evidence, Only Doubts, Have Appeared]," p. 31.

4056. _____ : "Text of Judge's Order on New Ruby Trial [in Texas Court of Criminal Appeals, Presiding Judge W. A. Morrison]," p. 31.

4057. 7 Oct. 1966: "Books of the Times: More Doubts, and a New Conspiracy Theory [Reviews Richard H. Popkin's Book]," Eliot Fremont-Smith, p. 41.

4058. 9 Oct. 1966: "French Editions Due on Kennedy's Death [for Books by Epstein and Lane]," p. 20.

4059. _____ : "The News of the Week in Review: New Trial for Ruby [with Photo of Oswald Shooting]," p. 2E.

4060. 19 Oct. 1966: "Army Engineers Deny Plan to Move Kennedy Body in '66 [to a New Grave]," p. 11.

4061. 21 Oct. 1966: "Dallas [District Attorney] Charges 4 Errors in Ruby Sentence Reversal," p. 37.

4062. 23 Oct. 1966: "2 Groups Analyze Kennedy Murder: Warren Unit Critics Scored by U.C.L.A. Project Head [Wesley Liebeler, Assistant Counsel to Warren Commission]," Peter Bart, p. 36.

4063. 25 Oct. 1966: "Ruby Freedom Step Studied [for Bail]," p. 3.

4064. 27 Oct. 1966: "Hearing in Ruby Case Nov. 9 [Over Ruby's Death Sentence]," p. 54.

4065. 2 Nov. 1966: "Autopsy Photos Put in Archives by the Kennedys: Access to Negatives, Slides and X-Rays of President's Body Will Be Restricted: Open to Law Agencies," Fred P. Graham, pp. 1, 33.

4066. _____: "Soviet Praises Book on Oswald-C.I.A. Tie [by Joachim Joesten, The Truth About Kennedy's Death] . . . ," p. 33.

4067. _____: "John F. Kennedy Birthplace Returned to Kennedy Family [in Brookline, Mass., for Memorial]," p. 33.

4068. 3 Nov. 1966: "Photos and X-Rays of Kennedy Autopsy Will Be Barred to All Private Persons for at Least Five Years," Fred P. Graham, p. 20.

4069. 5 Nov. 1966: "Transcript of the President's News Conference . . . 12: Data on Kennedy's Death," p. 10.

4070. _____: "Johnson Backs Warren Report as Thorough and Reasonable," p. 11.

4071. 6 Nov. 1966: "All Neatly Stacked Away [an Oliphant Cartoon on Warren Report]," p. 11E.

4072. 7 Nov. 1966: "Books of the Times: The Effect of Books [with Warren Report Controversy as Case in Point]," Eliot Fremont-Smith, p. 45; (9 Nov. 1966,) 37.

4073. 9 Nov. 1966: "Rights to Book on Kennedy Sold [by Manchester to The Sunday Times, London]," p. 3.

4074. 13 Nov. 1966: "4 Critics and 2 Defenders Debate Warren Report on Television [Lane, Weisberg, Sauvage, Jones vs. Jacob Cohen, Bishop]," Peter Kihss, p. 80.

4075. _____: "France Broadcasts Criticism [of Warren Report by Roland Mehl on the Government Radio]," p. 80.

4076. _____: "The Dallas 'Plot' Opens in Belgium: Conspiracy Idea Is Debated in Theatrical Report [by Jean Francis]," p. 80.

4077. 14 Nov. 1966: "TV: Warren Commission's Foes Get 3 Hours: 'A Minority Report' [Reviews 13 Nov. Debate]," Jack Gould, p. 83.

4078. 15 Nov. 1966: "Photo Taken When Kennedy Was Assassinated Sets Off Controversy [in Esquire, Dec., Claim of Second Rifleman]," Peter Kihss, p. 35.

4079. 16 Nov. 1966: "Letters to the Editor of the Times: Custody of X-Rays [Asks How the Official Autopsy Records Came to Kennedy Family in First Place?]," Alfred M. Rossum, p. 46.

4080. 17 Nov. 1966: "Kennedy Plaques Put Up in Dallas:
Bronze Marker Is Erected Near Assassination Site," p. 24.

4081. _____: "Mark Lane's Film Shown [in Paris,
'Rush to Judgment']," p. 24.

4082. _____: "Nizer Calls Criticism of Warren Report
'an Outrage'," Ralph Blumenthal, p. 25.

4083. _____: "Court Reaffirms Ruby Trial Ruling
[for a New Trial]," p. 25.

4084. _____: "Music: Memorial to John F. Kennedy:
Work by [William] Sydeman Has New York Premiere," Harold
C. Schonberg, p. 56.

4085. 18 Nov. 1966: "Lawyers Clash on Warren Panel: Aides
of Commission Debate Mark Lane and Author [Epstein vs. Wesley
Liebeler and Joseph A. Ball for the Warren Report]," p. 26.

4086. 19 Nov. 1966: "Serial Rights Sold for Kennedy Book
[by Look in Britain, Ireland, France, Italy, Germany: 'The
Manchester Book']," p. 7.

4087. _____: "Lane Seeks Debates with Aides of
[Warren] Panel," p. 43.

4088. 21 Nov. 1966: "Life Magazine Urges 2d Inquiry into
Kennedy Killing: Holds Doubts Exist That Oswald Was Sole
Assassin: [Sen.] Hart Would Oppose Inquiry," Peter Kihss,
p. 18.

4089. 22 Nov. 1966: "Warren Panel, Under Attacks, Stands
Firm on Its Findings in Kennedy Death 3 Years Ago," Peter
Kihss, p. 22.

4090. _____: "Mass at Tufts [University] Pays Tribute to Kennedy 'In Word and Song'," p. 22.

4091. 23 Nov. 1966: "House Chiefs Back Warren Commission
as Criticism Grows," Peter Kihss, pp. 1, 25.

4092. _____: "Throng at Grave Salutes Kennedy:
Visitors Stream to Site as Work Proceeds on Tomb: Edward
Kennedy in Algiers: 300 Turn Out in Dallas," Nan Robertson,
p. 25.

4093. 24 Nov. 1966: "Connally Backs the Warren Report:
Text of Governor Connally's Statement: Lane Replies,"
Martin Waldron, pp. 1, 58.

4094. 25 Nov. 1966: "Autopsy Surgeon Says Photos Support
Warren Report on Wound in Neck; Pre-Dallas Fears Reported
[Cancelled Atlanta Trip]," Peter Kihss, p. 30.

4095.   25 Nov. 1966:   "[Editorial]:   Unanswered Questions [for Warren Panel]," p. 36.

4096.   _____: "Play About Oswald Offered in London ["The Silence of Lee Harvey Oswald" by Michael Hastings]," p. 47.

4097.   26 Nov. 1966:   "Hoover Says Facts Show Oswald Alone Was Kennedy Killer: Text of Statement by Hoover on the Warren Report; Hundreds Visit Oswald Grave," Fred P. Graham, pp. 1, 25.

4098.   27 Nov. 1966:   "Publicity Foreseen on Kennedy Autopsy [If Pressure Continues, According to Arlen Specter, of the Warren Investigation]," p. 75.

4099.   _____: "The News of the Week in Review: The Nation: New Questions on Assassination," p. 2E.

4100.   _____: "[Cartoon by Conrad]:   'The Assassins'," p. 13E.

4101.   28 Nov. 1966:   "Warren Panel Member Suggests Independent Group Study Kennedy X-Rays [Rep. Hale Boggs]," Peter Kihss, p. 29.

4102.   1 Dec. 1966:   "B.B.C. Buys Movie on Warren Panel: Pays $40,000 for Lane Film--Will Show It Jan. 29:   Oswald's Mother in Debt," p. 33.

4103.   7 Dec. 1966:   "Second Ruby Trial Will Be Held in Wichita Falls Sometime in '67," p. 39.

4104.   8 Dec. 1966:   "Critic of Warren Commission Disputes Film Timing of Assassination Shots [Harold Weisberg, in White-wash II]," Peter Kihss, p. 40.

4105.   9 Dec. 1966:   "Oswald's Brother is Planning a Book," p. 28.

4106.   10 Dec. 1966:   "Ruby Seriously Ill in Dallas Hospital [with Pneumonia]," Martin Waldron, pp. 1, 22.

4107.   11 Dec. 1966:   "Widow Dismayed by Kennedy Book: Personal Material in 'Death of President' Upsets Her [Manchester's Book]," pp. 1, 39.

4108.   _____: "Ruby Has Cancer; Outlook in Doubt," Martin Waldron, pp. 1, 40.

4109.   12 Dec. 1966:   "Books of the Times: Experiments and Fashions [Reviews Mac Bird by Barbara Garson]," Eliot Fremont-Smith, p. 45.

4110.   _____: "Friends of the Oswalds Believe Assassination Had No Rationale: Couple Tie Death of Kennedy, Whose

Kin They Also Know, to a Domestic Quarrel [Photo of George de Mohrenschildt]," p. 57.

4111.   12 Dec. 1966:   "Ruby Takes Tests for Cancer Today: Doctors Hope to Find Source of Spreading Malignancy," p. 57.

4112.   14 Dec. 1966:   "Mrs. Kennedy Gives Publishers Notice of Court Move on Book [by Manchester]," John Corry, pp. 1,

4113.   _____: "Ruby's Cancer Is Widespread: Drugs Called His Only Chance," Martin Waldron, p. 42.

4114.   _____: "Man Held in Threat to Kennedy Is Freed [Richard P. Pavlick, 79 Year Old Retired Postal Clerk, Arrested in Florida in 1960]," p. 52.

4115.   15 Dec. 1966:   "Mrs. Kennedy Will Seek an Injunction to Block Book About the Assassination: Suit to Be Filed Against Harper and Row, Author, and Look Magazine," John Corry, pp. 1, 36.

4116.   _____: "Statements by Mrs. Kennedy, Look and Harper & Row on Book Dispute [Texts]," p. 36.

4117.   _____: "Manchester's Foreword to 'The Death of a President'," William Manchester, p. 36.

4118.   _____: "Diagnostic Report on Ruby Will Be Released Today," p. 54.

4119.   16 Dec. 1966:   "Kennedy Book Fight Prompting Feelers to Avoid Court Test," John Corry, pp. 1, 41.

4120.   _____: "Doctors Can't Find Prime Ruby Cancer," p. 36.

4121.   _____: "[Editorial]:   'Authorized' History," p. 46.

4122.   17 Dec. 1966:   "Mrs. Kennedy Sues to Hold Up Book on Assassination: State Justice Sets a Hearing for Dec. 27 and Orders 3 Defendants to Appear," John Corry, pp. 1, 19.

4123.   _____: "Mock Trial Acquits Oswald [at Oshkosh State University, Wisconsin]," p. 3.

4124.   _____: "Texts of Documents Filed by Lawyers for Mrs. Kennedy in Move to Block Book," pp. 18-19.

4125.   _____: "Beleaguered Author: William Raymond Manchester," p. 19.

4126.   _____: "[Texts]:   Letter by Manchester Memorandum of Understanding [Signed by Manchester and RFK]," p. 19.

4127.   _____: "Manchester Assured Magazine Kennedys Approved Publication: Copy of Accord with Cowles, Publisher of Look, Is Filed in Suit Over the Book," Sidney E. Zion, p. 19.

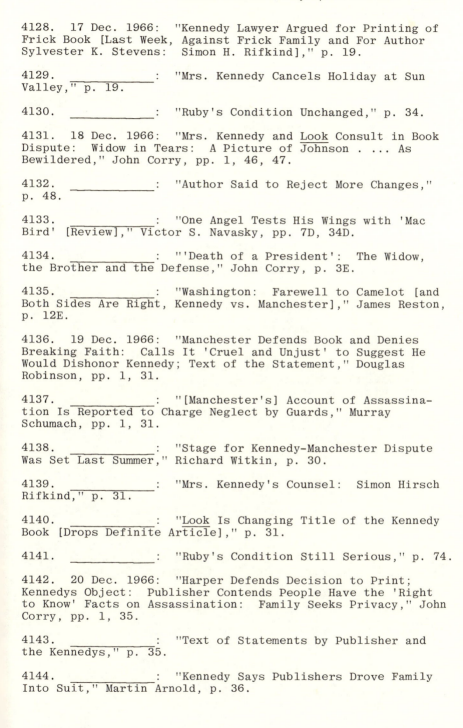

4128. 17 Dec. 1966: "Kennedy Lawyer Argued for Printing of
Frick Book [Last Week, Against Frick Family and For Author
Sylvester K. Stevens: Simon H. Rifkind]," p. 19.

4129. _____ : "Mrs. Kennedy Cancels Holiday at Sun
Valley," p. 19.

4130. _____ : "Ruby's Condition Unchanged," p. 34.

4131. 18 Dec. 1966: "Mrs. Kennedy and Look Consult in Book
Dispute: Widow in Tears: A Picture of Johnson . ... As
Bewildered," John Corry, pp. 1, 46, 47.

4132. _____ : "Author Said to Reject More Changes,"
p. 48.

4133. _____ : "One Angel Tests His Wings with 'Mac
Bird' [Review]," Victor S. Navasky, pp. 7D, 34D.

4134. _____ : "'Death of a President': The Widow,
the Brother and the Defense," John Corry, p. 3E.

4135. _____ : "Washington: Farewell to Camelot [and
Both Sides Are Right, Kennedy vs. Manchester]," James Reston,
p. 12E.

4136. 19 Dec. 1966: "Manchester Defends Book and Denies
Breaking Faith: Calls It 'Cruel and Unjust' to Suggest He
Would Dishonor Kennedy; Text of the Statement," Douglas
Robinson, pp. 1, 31.

4137. _____ : "[Manchester's] Account of Assassination Is Reported to Charge Neglect by Guards," Murray
Schumach, pp. 1, 31.

4138. _____ : "Stage for Kennedy-Manchester Dispute
Was Set Last Summer," Richard Witkin, p. 30.

4139. _____ : "Mrs. Kennedy's Counsel: Simon Hirsch
Rifkind," p. 31.

4140. _____ : "Look Is Changing Title of the Kennedy
Book [Drops Definite Article]," p. 31.

4141. _____ : "Ruby's Condition Still Serious," p. 74.

4142. 20 Dec. 1966: "Harper Defends Decision to Print;
Kennedys Object: Publisher Contends People Have the 'Right
to Know' Facts on Assassination: Family Seeks Privacy," John
Corry, pp. 1, 35.

4143. _____ : "Text of Statements by Publisher and
the Kennedys," p. 35.

4144. _____ : "Kennedy Says Publishers Drove Family
Into Suit," Martin Arnold, p. 36.

4145.   20 Dec. 1966:   "Ruby Asks World to Take His Word:
Dying, He Claims Sole Guilt for the Murder of Oswald," p. 36.

4146.   _____: "Hearing Asked on [Warren] Report [by
Rep. John W. Wydler]," p. 36.

4147.   _____: "Mrs. Kennedy Reported to Have Rebuked
de Gaulle [After the Funeral for His Obstacles to Good Diplomatic Relations, According to Manchester's Book]," Robert
Alden, p. 37.

4148.   _____: "Issues in Book Dispute: Kennedy Suit
Raises Legal Problems Beyond Question of a Broken Promise,"
Sidney E. Zion, p. 38.

4149.   21 Dec. 1966:   "Mrs. Kennedy Is Reported Nearing
Accord with Look," John Corry, pp. 1, 29.

4150.   _____: "Decisions Traced to Mrs. Kennedy:
She Made Up Her Own Mind on Deletions, Friend Says [Richard
N. Goodwin]," Martin Arnold, p. 29.

4151.   _____: "Letters to the Editor of the Times:
Suit on Kennedy Book [on Publishers Premature Leaks and Publications; by the Chairman of the American Society of Magazine Editors]," Robert Stein, p. 38.

4152.   22 Dec. 1966:   "Kennedys Reach Accord With Look on
Serialization: Widow Says Magazine Will 'Remove or Modify'
Parts Regarding Personal Life: 1,600 Words Taken Out," John
Corry, pp. 1, 24.

4153.   _____: "Dispute Detailed on Earlier Book:
Mrs. Kennedy Objected to 'White House Nannie' [by Maude
Shaw, English Nurse to Kennedy Infants]," Edith Evans
Asbury, p. 24.

4154.   _____: "Statements by Mrs. Kennedy and Cowles,"
p. 24.

4155.   _____: "[Editorial]: The Kennedy Post-Mortem,"
p. 32.

4156.   _____: "Letters to the Editor of the Times:
Issues in Kennedy Suit Enjoining Publishers [Disagrees With
Reston, Defends Mrs. Kennedy]," Theodore H. White, p. 32.

4157.   23 Dec. 1966:   "Harper Hopeful of Accord to Publish
Kennedy Book," John Corry, pp. 1, 22.

4158.   24 Dec. 1966:   "Night Talks Held on Kennedy Book:
Both Sides Hoping for an Accord by Christmas," Douglas Robinson, p. 20.

4159.   _____: "Taiwan Assures U.S. on Kennedy Book
[to Halt Pirate Editions]," John W. Finney, p. 20.

4160.   24 Dec. 1966:   "German Defiant on Book Changes: Editor of Stern Vows to Run Original Manchester Text," Philip Shabe-coff, p. 20.

4161.   25 Dec. 1966:   "'Problems' Arise in Kennedy Talks: Accord on Book Termed Not Likely Before Tomorrow," Douglas Robinson, p. 40.

4162.   _____ :   "Taiwan Pledges Effort to Ban Pirate Edition of Kennedy Book [at Suggestion of Its Washington Embassy]," p. 40.

4163.   _____ :   "The News of the Week in Review: The Nation: Compromise on 'The Book'," p. 1E.

4164.   _____ :   "A New Inquiry Is Needed," Herbert Mitgang, p. 14:   NYT Magazine.

4165.   26 Dec. 1966:   "Letters to the Editor of The Times: Manchester Defends His Book," William Manchester, p. 20. .

4166.   _____ :   "Johnson Termed Unhappy on Book: Newsweek Issues a Report on Manchester's Work," Robert E. Dallos, p. 30.

4167.   _____ :   "Manchester in Hospital; High Fever Is Reported," p. 30.

4168.   _____ :   "2 Polygraph Experts Urge Lie Detector for Ruby," p. 30.

4169.   27 Dec. 1966:   "Johnson Aide Disputes Newsweek Report of President's Comments on Kennedy Book Controversy: Man-chester Improving: Court Hearing Today," p. 26.

4170.   _____ :   "In the Nation: William Manchester's Sponsors," Tom Wicker, p. 34.

4171.   28 Dec. 1966:   "Hearing Put Off on Kennedy Book: Publisher and Widow Agree to Move Trial to January and Press for Accord," Douglas Robinson, pp. 1, 17.

4172.   _____ :   "Johnson Described Events on Plane [at Dallas, 22 Nov. 1963]," Charles Grutzner, p. 17.

4173.   29 Dec. 1966:   "Hostility by Mrs. Kennedy Is Denied [by Arthur M. Schlesinger, Jr.]," Douglas Robinson, p. 15.

4174.   _____ :   "Lie Test for Ruby Backed [by Col. Homer Garrison, Head of Texas Department of Public Safety]," p. 23.

4175.   30 Dec. 1966:   "Johnson Kindness to Widow Is Cited: [U.S. News & World Report] Magazine Tells of Moves to Console Mrs. Kennedy: Kennedy Quoted on Risk," p. 12.

4176.   31 Dec. 1966:   "Ruby Weaker, Losing Weight," p. 12.

4177.   _____: "Kennedy Book Talks Put Off to Tuesday,"
p. 24.

4178.   1 Jan. 1967:   "Court Holds Up Oswald Record: Dispute
Delays Distribution of Interview Taped in '63 [17 Aug. by
William Kirk Stuckey, to Be Sold by Audio Fidelity Records],"
p. 32.

4179.   _____: "Manchester Is Home After Six Days in
Hospital," Robert E. Dallos, p. 32.

4180.   3 Jan. 1967:   "Saturday Evening Post Asks for Warren
Review: Joins Life in Call for a New Study of Kennedy Find-
ings: It Says Possibility of a Plot Must Not Be Left to
Gossip," p. 12.

4181.   _____: "Ruby in Recording Denies Conspiracy,"
p. 12.

4182.   4 Jan. 1967:   "Ruby, Oswald Slayer, Dies of Blood Clot
in Lungs: Shot Kennedy Assassin [sic] as Millions Watched
on TV--in Prison 3 Years," Martin Waldron, pp. 1, 20.

4183.   _____: "New Manchester Text in Spain," p. 6.

4184.   _____: "Ruby, Who Wanted Esteem, Won a Place
in History," p. 20.

4185.   4 Jan. 1967:   "Ruby Says in Tape No Plan Existed: He
Denies in Recording That Oswald Had Been in Club: Excerpts
from Ruby Tape," p. 20.

4186.   _____: "A Warren Lawyer Says Ruby's Death Can't
Alter Report [Joseph A. Ball]," p. 20.

4187.   _____: "Belli Scores Dallas Over Death of
Ruby [for Negligence]," p. 21.

4188.   _____: "[Editorial]: Death of a Nobody," p. 42.

4189.   5 Jan. 1967:   "Publishers and City Bar Group Oppose
Crime News Restrictions: Report by A.N.P.A.: Study by Lawyers [of New York City]," Sidney E. Zion and Edward Ranzal,
pp. 1, 20.

4190.   _____: "Ruby Funeral Tomorrow Is Private
[in Chicago, Burial in Westlawn Cemetery]," p. 27.

4191.   _____: "In the Nation: Unplanned Left Turn
Into History [Ruby-Oswald]," Tom Wicker, p. 36.

4192.   _____: "Attorneys Discuss Manchester Suit," p.
44.

4193. 6 Jan. 1967: "Responses Filed in Kennedy Suit:
Harper and Manchester Say Widow Approved Book," John Corry,
p. 33.

4194. 7 Jan. 1967: "Ruby Buried in Chicago Cemetery Along-
side Graves of His Parents," p. 15.

4195. 8 Jan. 1967: "Manchester's Book Says Oswald 'Was
Going Mad': The 'Private Nightmare' of Assassin Pictured
in Article in Look," John Corry, pp. 1, 77.

4196. _____: "Kennedy-Johnson Clash on the Eve of
Killing Is Related in Series [in Look of Manchester's Book],"
Tom Wicker, pp. 1, 77.

4197. _____: "Progress Is Reported in Book Negotiations [by Simon H. Rifkind, Mrs. Kennedy's Lawyer]," p. 55.

4198. _____: "Hands of Kennedy Reported Shaking on
Eve of Slaying," p. 76.

4199. 9 Jan. 1966: "Plea from Kennedy Rejected by Stern
[to Delete Parts of Serialized Manchester Book]," p. 27.

4200. _____: "Mrs. Kennedy Back Home [from Two Weeks
in Caribbean]; Declines Comment on Book," p. 27.

4201. _____: "Kennedy's Texas Trip Opposed by
Connally [According to Dallas Times-Herald]," p. 47.

4202. 10 Jan. 1967: "Stern Publishes Kennedy Version: It
Prints Letter from Wife That Was Cut by Look," p. 16.

4203. 11 Jan. 1967: "Connally Rebuts Manchester; Plans Own
Version," p. 10.

4204. _____: "A Ruby Plot Theory [Letter from Jail
That Johnson Plotted Kennedy's Killing]," p. 10.

4205. _____: "Look 'Bombarded' [With Requests for
Copies of Manchester Issue]," p. 64.

4206. 12 Jan. 1967: "Gallup Poll Shows a [7%] Gain in
Belief Oswald Was Alone," p. 23.

4207. _____: "Kennedy's Lawyer [William Vanden
Heuvel] Going to Germany [to Stern Magazine Editors]," p. 43.

4208. _____: "Tehran, Iran: The Weekly Magazine
Ettelaat Haftegi [Prints Original, Full Text of Manchester's
Book, Unauthorized and in Persian]," p. 43.

4209. 13 Jan. 1967: "A Kennedy Friend Joins Stern Talks:
Magazine Will Be Asked to Revise Its Serialization," John
Corry, p. 11.

4210. 13 Jan. 1967: "Book Assailed in Texas [State Legis-
lature Passes Resolutions Condemning Manchester's Book and
Praising Connally]," p. 11.

4211. _____ : "A Correction [29%, Not the 39% Reported Yesterday, Responded to Gallup Poll in Nov. 1963 on
JFK Assassination]," p. 13.

4212. 14 Jan. 1967: "Stern Refuses Cuts in Kennedy Article,"
p. 16.

4213. _____ : "Rep. Gonzalez Tells of Kennedy Death
[and Johnson's Condition at Parkland Hospital]," p. 26.

4214. 15 Jan. 1967: "Warren Unit's Foes Scored in Britain
[by Professor Goodhart in The Law Quarterly Review]: Epstein
Defends Book," Anthony Lewis, p. 56.

4215. _____ : "Dallas Ex-Mayor [Earle Cabell]
Challenges Book: Says Manchester Account Tries 'to Distort
History'," p. 57.

4216. _____ : "Look Acts to Sue Stern Over Book:
Breach of Contract Is Laid to German Magazine: 2 Other Magazines Cited [Paris Match, Epoca]," Philip Shabecoff, p. 58.

4217. _____ : "Letters: Death of a President--But
Which One? [Lincoln in Herbert Mitgang's Earlier Article],"
p. 21.

4218. 16 Jan. 1967: "[Advertisement]: Dallas: City of
Patience, Decency; An Editorial from The Dallas Times Herald,"
p. 15.

4219. _____ : "A Dallas Editorial Is Reprinted As
Ad," p. 18.

4220. _____ : "Stern Describes Kennedy Parting:
Tells of Night Before Slaying in Uncut Version of Book," p.
18.

4221. _____ : "Accord Near in Kennedy Book Dispute,"
Douglas Robinson, p. 18.

4222. _____ : "Books of The Times: End Papers
[Reviews There Was A President by N.B.C. News]," Eliot
Fremont-Smith, p. 39.

4223. _____ : "Letters to the Editor of The Times:
Ruby's Death," Paul R. Clarkson, p. 40.

4224. 17 Jan. 1967: "Accord Reached on Kennedy Book; Suit
Withdrawn: Publisher and Author Agree to Changes in Passages
Offensive to Widow," Douglas Robinson, pp. 1, 25.

4225. 17 Jan. 1967: "Stern Bars Kennedy Book Censorship,"
p. 24.

4226. _____: "Texts of Statements on Accord on
Kennedy Book," p. 25.

4227. _____: "[Historian Allen] Nevins Backs Publisher [Against Kennedys]," p. 25.

4228. 18 Jan. 1967: "Johnson Is Leaving Decision on Letters
to Mrs. Kennedy [That He Wrote to Her and Children After
Assassination]," p. 40.

4229. 19 Jan. 1967: "Look Sues Chicago Daily News and Stern
Over Kennedy Serial," Sidney E. Zion, p. 32.

4230. _____: "Advertising: What Manchester Did to
Look," Philip H. Dougherty, p. 45.

4231. 20 Jan. 1967: "Court in Hamburg to Hear Look Suit:
A Bar on Kennedy Series in Stern to Be Sought Today," p. 40.

4232. _____: "Warren Report Show [on WOR for 3 Hours,
42 Minutes: Louis Nizer, Charles Roberts, Leo Sauvage, Harold
Weisberg]," Val Adams, p. 87.

4233. 22 Jan. 1967: "Paper in Lisbon to Begin Kennedy Book
This Week [in Diario Popular, by Agreement with Manchester],"
p. 30.

4234. 23 Jan. 1967: "Manchester Assails Kennedy 'Politics',"
John Corry, pp. 1, 26.

4235. _____: "Author Expects $500,000 Net for '3
Years' Agony' [Manchester]," p. 26.

4236. _____: "Stern Gets Appeal from Manchester
[Not to Publish Uncut Version]," p. 26.

4237. 24 Jan. 1967: "Manchester Says Kennedy Guards Might
Have Balked Assassin," p. 24.

4238. _____: "Look Loses Book Suit in Germany [for
Injunction]," p. 24.

4239. 25 Jan. 1967: "Stern Prints Passage Mrs. Kennedy
Opposed," p. 7.

4240. _____: "Oswald's Mother Threatens to Sue
Manchester on Book," p. 32.

4241. 26 Jan. 1967: "Stern Will Defer to Mrs. Kennedy:
Will Delete Parts of Book as a 'Personal Gesture'," p. 12.

4242. _____: "Published in Soviet [Excerpts from
Uncut Version in Literaturnaya Gazeta Published from Stern,
But Omit References to Oswald in Russia]," p. 12.

4243.   26 Jan. 1967:   "B.B.C. to Spend Evening on Assassination Doubt [Includes Showing of Lane's 'Rush to Judgment' Film]," p. 14.

4244.   27 Jan. 1967:   "Manchester Book Has Big Advance: Orders Indicate Work Will Be One of Great Sellers," Harry Gilroy, p. 42.

4245.   _____: "Manchester Reported Raising New Objection [to Specific Cuts]," p. 42.

4246.   28 Jan. 1967:   "Kennedy Book Gets Final Corrections," p. 25.

4247.   30 Jan. 1967:   "The Story of the Kennedy-Look Battle," John Corry, pp. 1, 22.

4248.   _____: "Life to Release Today Part of Kennedy Film [the Four Frames, Nos. 208-211, of Zapruder Film Missing in Later Copies]," p. 22.

4249.   _____: "Widow of 2d Oswald Victim [sic] Wed [Mrs. Marie Tippit, to Police Lt. Harry Dean Thomas; Final Tax-Free Donations Were $647,579]," p. 22.

4250.   _____: "British TV Reviews Warren Dispute [Patrick Lord Devlin and Alexander Bickel Debate]," p. 23.

4251.   31 Jan. 1967:   "Kennedy Is Assailed by Editor of Stern [Says RFK Acted with 'Hectic Clumsiness']," p. 18.

4252.   _____: "Ruby's Murder Case Dismissed in Texas [by District Judge Louis Holland, Wichita Falls]," p. 18.

4253.   1 Feb. 1967:   "Polls Say Dispute Hurt Mrs. Kennedy [and RFK]," p. 36.

4254.   _____: "Statement on Kennedy Book Is Denied by Siegenthaler [That He Had Permitted Serialization Rights]," p. 36.

4255.   3 Feb. 1967:   "World Journal Is Sued by Look: $700,000 Action Cites Use of Manchester Material," Douglas Robinson, p. 29.

4256.   4 Feb. 1967:   "Chicago Daily News and Look Magazine Settle Book Dispute," p. 25.

4257.   5 Feb. 1967:   "Coins: The Honest Value of a Dallas Dollar [Quash Rumors That 1963 Series from Federal Reserve Bank in Dallas Have Special Assassination Value]," Herbert C. Bardes, p. 33D.

4258.   7 Feb. 1967:   "Manchester Says Kennedy Aides Showed Hostility to Johnson on Flight from Dallas to the Capital," Richard Witkin, p. 20.

4259.   7 Feb. 1967:   "Stern Runs Look Version," p. 20.

4260.   9 Feb. 1967:   "Observer: A Crisis in Identity [The Mania for Name-Changes in Memory of JFK]," Russell Baker, p. 38.

4261.   10 Feb. 1967:   "Photo Rebuts Manchester on Johnson Swearing-In [The Boston Globe Produces Uncropped Photo With K. P. O'Donnell Present]," John H. Fenton, p. 15.

4262.   11 Feb. 1967:   "Manchester Book Excerpts Stir 3 East Europe Nations [in Czechoslavkia, Hungary, and Bulgaria in State Newspapers, to Support Conspiracy Theories]," p. 32.

4263.   12 Feb. 1967:   "'Puny Nit-Picking' Charged to Critic of Warren Report [by Louis Nizer About Mark Lane, on WNEW-TV]," p. 34.

4264.   13 Feb. 1967:   "Manchester Concedes That Kennedy Aides Could Have Been at Johnson Swearing-In," Douglas Robinson, p. 28.

4265.   _____: "TV: 'The Warren Report: Nizer and 2 Commission Aides Rebut Lane's Theory of a Conspiracy' [on WNEW-TV, 12 Feb. 1967]," Jack Gould, p. 67.

4266.   14 Feb. 1967:   "[Sen. Strom] Thurmond Says a Red Plot Led to Death of Kennedy," p. 24.

4267.   _____: "O'Donnell Says Manchester Pledged to Delay Book to '68," p. 40.

4268.   16 Feb. 1967:   "Ruby Appeal Off Court Docket [in U.S. Supreme Court]," p. 23.

4269.   _____: "Letters to the Editor of The Times: Deletions in Kennedy Book," William Manchester, p. 38.

4270.   18 Feb. 1967:   "New 'Plot' Inquiry Reported on Kennedy Assassination [by New Orleans States Item, Led by Local District Attorney's Office]," p. 19.

4271.   _____: "An Unsigned Will of Ruby Disclosed [Probated in Precedence Over 1949 Will, in Wayne County, Michigan]," p. 19.

4272.   19 Feb. 1967:   "New Oswald Clue Reported Found: New Orleans Official Vows Arrests Will Be Made," p. 43.

4273.   20 Feb. 1967:   "Data Are Requested on Oswald Inquiry [Rep. Gerald Ford Says New Orleans Officials Should Be Sent to U.S. Attorney General]," p. 28.

4274.   _____: "Manchester Book Says Schlesinger Conferred With Aides on '64 Replacement for Johnson," Edward C. Burks, p. 29.

4275. 21 Feb. 1967: "Arrests in Kennedy Case Delayed for
Months, New Orleans Prosecutor Says [Because of Premature
Publicity]: Lane Sees Truth Blocked: [Sen.] Dodd Asks New
Inquiry," Gene Roberts, p. 20.

4276. _____: "Time Says Pictures of '63 Oath-Taking
show [5] Kennedy Men," p. 21.

4277. 22 Feb. 1967: "'M' Bird!' Gets Off to Flying Start:
It Will 'Open' Tonight After a Profitable Month," Dan Sullivan, p. 22.

4278. _____: "Senator [Russell B. Long] Thinks Prosecutor Has New Assassination Data," p. 22.

4279. 23 Feb. 1967: "Ruby Case Death Sifted in Florida:
Suicide Doubled by Brother of Stripper's Husband [Thomas
Henry Killam, of Pensacola, Whose Wife Wanda Worked for
Ruby]," p. 22.

4280. _____: "Figure in Oswald Inquiry Is Dead in
New Orleans: Garrison Links Him to a Plot, an Idea He'd
Called a Joke: Apparent Suicide Note Found---Brain Hemorr-
hage Cited," Gene Roberts, p. 22.

4281. 24 Feb. 1967: "Death of Ferrie Called Natural:
Autopsy Doctor Rules Out Suicide in New Orleans," Gene
Roberts, p. 21.

4282. _____: "Story of an Oswald-Ferrie Link Shown
by Archives to Be False," Nan Robertson, p. 21.

4283. 25 Feb. 1967: "Archives Detail Ferrie's Travels: He
Told Agents He Was in New Orleans Nov. 22," Nan Robertson,
p. 56.

4284. _____: "Flashy Prosecutor: Jim Garrison:
Man in the News," p. 56.

4285. _____: "Businessmen Aid Inquiry on 'Plot':
50 Give $100 a Month--Case 'Solved,' Says Garrison: Con-
spiracy Called Possible [by Dallas D.A., Henry Wade]:
Connally Has Doubts," Gene Roberts, p. 56.

4286. 26 Feb. 1967: "Oswald Inquiry Now Centered on Cuban
Refugees [in New Orleans]," Gene Roberts, p. 56.

4287. _____: "Johnson Reported Sworn Minus Bible
[with Hand on a Roman Catholic Missal]," p. 87.

4288. 27 Feb. 1967: "Production Halted on Kennedy Book to
Fix Error," p. 16.

4289. 28 Feb. 1967: "Letters to the Editor of the Times:
Postmaster General in Dallas [and Personally Witnessed
Johnson's Oath--Taking in Air Force One]," Lawrence F.
O'Brien, p. 36.

4290. 1 March 1967: "[Robert] Kennedy Delays Book of
Speeches: Move Attributed to Dispute with Harper and Row,"
Henry Raymont, pp. 1, 25.

4291. _____: "Ramsey Clark Nominated to Be Attorney
General . . . Backs Warren Report," pp. 1, 24.

4292. _____: "Subpoena Is Issued in Garrison Inquiry [for 'James Lawallen']," p. 27.

4293. 2 March 1967: "Garrison Arrests an Ex-Major in 'Conspiracy' to Kill Kennedy [Clay Shaw]," p. 24.

4294. 3 March 1967: "Transcript of the President's News
Conference: . . . 6. Warren Commission Report [and New
Orleans]," p. 14.

4295. _____: "Suspect in 'Plot' Linked to Oswald:
Clandestine Meeting Alleged in New Orleans Document," Gene
Roberts, p. 22.

4296. _____: "[Acting Attorney General] Clark Discounts a Shaw Conspiracy," Robert B. Semple, Jr., p. 22.

4297. 4 March 1967: "4th Man Queried in Louisiana in
Assassination Investigation: Dante Marachini and Oswald
Worked for the Same Coffee Combine in Summer of '63," Gene
Roberts, p. 25.

4298. _____: "Warren Satisfied With Conclusions in
Kennedy Report," p. 25.

4299. 5 March 1967: "New Orleans Strip Joint [Cartoon by
Herblock on Garrison as a Publicity-Seeker]," p. 9E.

4300. _____: "In and Out of Books: Jacket Copy
[Proposed by Manchester]," Lewis Nichols, p. 8: NYT Book
Review.

4301. 7 March 1967: "Louisiana A.C.L.U. Scores Garrison:
Says Investigation Into Plot Becoming 'Roman Circus'," Gene
Roberts, p. 21.

4302. 9 March 1967: "Garrison Blocks Plea to Give Data:
Need Not Produce Evidence on Shaw Until Hearing: Vatican
Paper's View [Many Questions Unanswered]," Gene Roberts, p.
25.

4303. 10 March 1967: "Grand Jury Opens Hearing on 'Plot':
2 Witnesses Subpoenaed in Inquiry on Assassination [Dean
Andrews, Jr., and Mrs. Josephine Hug]," Gene Roberts, p. 27.

4304. _____: "Packets on Assassination Held Up in
Customs: U.S. Publisher [Dial] Protests Delay of 'Educa-
tional' Material--Explanation Disputed [Packets Part of
'Jackdaw' Series for History Students]," p. 27.

4305.   11 March 1967:   "Garrison's Aides Said to Plan Use of Hypnosis on Witnesses," Gene Roberts, p. 26.

4306.   12 March 1967:   "4 Kennedy Issues Set Mark at Look: Sales of 9.5 Million at Peak of Series Reported," Henry Raymont, p. 43.

4307.   13 March 1967:   "[Attorney General] Ramsey Clark Calls Garrison's Inquiry Disturbing [for Creating Further Doubt and Publicity]," p. 28.

4308.   14 March 1967:   "New Orleans Hearing Today May Clarify Charges of Assassination 'Plot'," Gene Roberts, p. 40.

4309.   15 March 1967:   "Bodies of Kennedy, Children Are Moved to Permanent Grave," p. 1.

4310.   _____: "Witness Says He Heard Oswald and 2 New Orleans Men Plot to Kill Kennedy [Perry Raymond Russo]," Gene Roberts, p. 33.

4311.   16 March 1967:   "Johnson at Grave with the Kennedys . . . As [New] Grave Was Consecrated," Robert B. Semple, Jr., pp. 1, 25.

4312.   _____: "Witness Says Beard Painted on a Photo Enabled Him to Link Oswald to Kennedy Slaying 'Plot' [Perry Raymond Russo]," Gene Roberts, p. 39.

4313.   17 March 1967:   "[Richard Cardinal] Cushing Doubts One Man Carried Out Assassination," p. 13.

4314.   _____: "3 Changes Made in Original Design of Kennedy Grave," p. 22.

4315.   _____: "Witness in Assassination 'Plot' Says That He Was Hypnotized," Gene Roberts, p. 24.

4316.   _____: "Atlanta: The Kennedys--Power and Publicity," James Reston, p. 40.

4317.   18 March 1967:   "Kennedy 'Plot' Trial Ordered by Judges," Gene Roberts, pp. 1, 13.

4318.   _____: "Book Reply Avoided by Secret Service [to Manchester's Criticisms]," p. 15.

4319.   19 March 1967:   "Figure in Kennedy Inquiry Is in New Orleans Hospital [Clay Shaw Has Back Trouble]," p. 95.

4320.   _____: "The 'Oswald Plot,' or Something," Gene Roberts, p. 4E.

4321.   _____: ""In and Out of Books: Sweet and Sour [Advance Orders for Manchester's Book Multiply]," Lewis Nichols, p. 8:   NYT Book Review.

4322. 20 March 1967: "Manchester Adds Epilogue on Fight:
Article Relates More Details of Kennedy Book Dispute," John
Corry, p. 19.

4323. 21 March 1967: "Jack Ruby Estate Includes Pistol
Used to Kill Oswald [an Offer of $50,000 Made]," p. 33.

4324. 23 March 1967: "New Orleans Jury Indicts Shaw on
Assassination Plot Charges: Says He, Oswald and Others
Conspired to Kill Kennedy--Russo Testifies Again," Martin
Waldron, p. 21.

4325. 24 March 1967: "Garrison Seeking Witness's Arrest:
Judge Issues a Warrant for a Former Bar Owner [Gordon Novel],"
Martin Waldron, p. 19.

4326. _____: "Judge Acts on Ruby Will [in Dallas,
an Administrator Appointed]," p. 64.

4327. 26 March 1967: "'Plot Witness' Given Lie Test:
Novel, Sought by Garrison, Examined in McLean, Va. [Passes
Test Given Near C.I.A. Headquarters]: Denies Attending
Party [Sandra Moffit]," p. 48.

4328. 26 March 1967: "[Cartoon by Haynie on Garrison's In-
vestigation] But, on the Other Hand, They Just Might Have
Something," p. 11E.

4329. 28 March 1967: "Mistrial Ruled in Midwest Insurance
Fraud Case [Defendant David R. Kroman Claims Documents
Proving JFK Conspiracy Were Seized at Gunpoint]: Garrison
Issues Warrant [for former Sandra Moffit]," p. 36.

4330. 29 March 1967: "Garrison Witnesses Taken Into Custody
[in Omaha, Mrs. Lillie Mae McMaines, formerly Sandra Moffit],"
p. 12.

4331. _____: "Manchester Says Johnson Was Unbriefed
on Atom Attack Code," Homer Bigart, p. 40.

4332. 30 March 1967: "Grand Jury in Plot Recesses for Week,"
p. 29.

4333. _____: "Manchester Book Removed from Counter
in Pittsburgh [After Premature Availability]," p. 41.

4334. 31 March 1967: "Jet Kills 9 Girls as It Hits Motel
[One Pilot Was George Piazza 2d, the Lawyer for James Lawallen, Garrison's Suspect]," p. 22.

4335. _____: "Sorenson Disputes Article by Manchester on Kennedy [Says No Truth in M.'s Claimed Meeting
With Him in Which M. Begged Him to Stand Up to Kennedys],"
p. 35.

4336. 1 April 1967: "Garrison Obtains 2 New Warrants [for Gordon Novel and Sergio Arcacha Smith]," p. 47.

4337. 2 April 1967: "Oswald Mock Trial Splits Jury, 6 to 6 [at Yale Law School]," Sidney E. Zion, pp. 1, 37.

4338. _____: "Witness in Kennedy 'Plot' Is Seized by Ohio Police [Gordon Novel, Near Columbus]," p. 55.

4339. _____: "Letters to the Editor of The Times: Jurisdiction in Assassinations [the Garrison Lesson Is Need for Federal Control]," Marshall P. Jones, Jr., p. 11E.

4340. 3 April 1967: "Books of The Times: At Last, the Whole Book -- and Worth Having [Reviews Manchester]," Eliot Fremont-Smith, p. 31.

4341. 4 April 1967: "Witness in Plot Investigation Hints a Cuban Link [Gordon Novel]," p. 19.

4342. 5 April 1967: "An Affable Shaw Is Host to Press: Gives a Cocktail Party and Talks of Many Things: Novel Freed on Bail," Gene Roberts, p. 29.

4343. 6 April 1967: Manchester Book Causes a Price War," p. 18.

4344. _____: "Shaw Pleads Not Guilty to Plotting Kennedy Death [Photo of Layton Martens, Ex-Room-mate of David Ferrie]," Gene Roberts, p. 24.

4345. 7 April 1967: "$45,637 in Taxes Is Sought from Ruby Estate by U.S.," p. 22.

4346. 8 April 1967: "Garrison Spurns Witness's Terms [Novel Would Return If Kept Free of Harassment]," p. 16.

4347. _____: "Manchester Says Profit Is Limited," Harry Gilroy, p. 29.

4348. 9 April 1967: "Garrison Acts to Extradite Man Sought in 'Plot' Inquiry [Gordon Novel]," p. 74.

4349. _____: "November 22, 1963 [Reviews Manchester]," Tom Wicker, pp. 1-3, 28: NYT Book Review.

4350. _____: "In and Out of Books: A Visit with Bill [Manchester]," Lewis Nichols, p. 8: NYT Book Review.

4351. 11 April 1967: "Witness in Garrison Inquiry Is Ordere to New Orleans [Mrs. Sandra Moffit McMaines]," p. 29.

4352. 13 April 1967: "[Rep. Theodore R.] Kupferman Asks Congress to Investigate Assassination," p. 18.

4353. 13 April 1967: "Lawyer Reindicted in Kennedy Inquiry
[Dean Andrews]," p. 30.

4354. 18 April 1967: "Pentagon Moves Hats from Grave:
Kennedy Library to Receive Caps of Servicemen: Kennedy Birthplace Honored," p. 25.

4355. _____: "Britons Criticize Manchester's Book'
[Dame Rebecca West, Malcolm Muggeridge, Alistair Cooke [sic],
Bernard Levin and Cyril Connolly]," p. 25.

4356. _____: "Play to Imagine Trial of Oswald:
Courtroom Drama, Due in Fall, Avoids Conclusion ['The Trial
of Lee Harvey Oswald' by Amram Ducovny and Leon Friedman],"
Louis Calta, p. 34.

4357. 19 April 1967: "Suit for $100,000 Against Garrison
Filed in Louisiana [by Dean Andrews]," p. 27.

4358. 22 April 1967: "Manchester Wins Prize [the Dag
Hammarskjold Prize, at Stresa, Italy]," p. 2.

4359. _____: "Puerto Rican Tells of a Kennedy 'Plot'
[Luis Angel Castillo, in Custody of Philippine National
Bureau, as Cuban-Trained Guerrilla]," p. 36.

4360. 23 April 1967: "Translator Met Writer in Soviet
[Also, Mrs. Priscilla Johnson MacMillan Met With Lee Harvey
Oswald in Moscow]," p. 23.

4361. 24 April 1967: "Hammarskjold Book Prize Is Awarded
to Manchester," p. 30.

4362. 25 April 1967: "Garrison Office Accused of Prompting
Witness [in Saturday Evening Post, May 6, Concerning Perry R.
Russo]," p. 32.

4363. 26 April 1967: "A Newspaper Links 'Plot' Figure to
C.I.A. [Gordon Novel, in The New Orleans States Item]," p. 19.

4364. _____: "1959 Kennedy Letter Discussed Death
of Presidents," p. 44.

4365. 29 April 1967: "New Orleans Grand Jury Hears Warren
Report Critic [Harold Weisberg]," p. 24.

4366. 5 May 1967: "2 Networks Give Newsfilm on Kennedy to
Family: Footage Covering 1952-63 Gift of C.B.S. and N.B.C.,
Destined for Library," Robert E. Dallos, p. 78.

4367. 10 May 1967: "Garrison Charges C.I.A. and F.B.I. Conceal Evidence on Oswald," Martin Waldron, p. 27.

4368. 11 May 1967: "Garrison Subpoenas Helms to Testify on
C.I.A. Investigation of Oswald," Martin Waldron, p. 35.

4369. 13 May 1967: "'Code' in an Address Book Called Ruby-Oswald Link," p. 20.

4370. 14 May 1967: "Investigations: Some Say It's Garrison Who's in Wonderland," Martin Waldron, p. 5E.

4371. 18 May 1967: "F.B.I. Agent Balks Garrison Inquiry: Invokes Executive Privilege Before Jurors on Plot [Regis Kennedy]: Explanation for 'Code'," p. 32.

4372. _____: "Advertising: A Look at a Magazine Survey [Manchester's Book's Impact on Sales]," Philip H. Dougherty, p. 67.

4373. 19 May 1967: "Study of Dallas Film Disputes Theory of an Assassin on Knoll [the Itek Corporation's Analysis]," p. 19.

4374. 21 May 1967: "The Case of Jim Garrison and Lee Oswald," Gene Roberts, pp. 32-40: NYT Magazine.

4375. _____: "In Brief: The Truth About the Assassination. By Charles Roberts," p. 48: NYT Book Review.

4376. 22 May 1967: "Garrison Says Five Were the Assassins: [Gordon Novel Wounded by Sniper in Nashville]," p. 84.

4377. 23 May 1967: "Garrison Says C.I.A. Knows the Slayers," p. 20.

4378. 24 May 1967: "Garrison Says Kennedy Was Killed in Crossfire," p. 50.

4379. 25 May 1967: "'Plot' Witness Sues Garrison in South [Gordon Novel, for $50 Million Damages]," p. 14.

4380. _____: "Manchester Sales Are Generally Good," p. 44.

4381. 26 May 1967: "Garrison Witness Worked for C.I.A., Lawyer Says [G. Novel]," p. 44.

4382. 27 May 1967: "Bar Groups Asked to Oust Garrison: Ruby's Lawyer Seeks End to Kennedy 'Exploitation'," p. 25.

4383. _____: "Guerrilla Theory Discounted [by Dallas Officials]," p. 25.

4384. 29 May 1967: "Garrison Answers Attorney for Ruby [Sol Dann]," p. 11.

4385. 30 May 1967: "O'Brien Asserts Hero Worship May Obscure Kennedy's Deeds: Widow Attends Mass [JFK's 50th Birthday]," p. 19.

4386.   30 May 1967:   "66% in Poll Accept Kennedy Plot View
[7 Out of 10 Find Warren Report Inadequate]," p. 19.

4387.   3 June 1967:   "The Screen: Mark Lane vs. the Warren
Report: 'Rush to Judgment' at Carnegie Hall Cinema: Inter-
views Contradict Official Findings [But "Rather Sketchy and
Speculative"]," Bosley Crowther, p. 18.

4388.   6 June 1967:   "Manchester Book Sold Out; Second Edition on Press [First Edition Was 600,000 With 25,000 for
Second]," p. 55.

4389.   _____: "Garrison Says Ruby Had Role in a Plot
to Slay Kennedy," p. 95.

4390.   9 June 1967:   "Garrison Is Told to List Backers:
Shaw's Lawyers Win Fight on Private Group's Rolls [Novel
Withdraws Suit to Avoid Appearance]," p. 32.

4391.   12 June 1967:   "Two Convicts Cite Proposition to Aid
Garrison in Plot Inquiry [Miguel Torres and John Cancler],"
Gene Roberts, pp. 1, 88.

4392.   13 June 1967:   "Rulings Deferred at Shaw's Hearing
[No Trial Before August or September]," p. 40.

4393.   16 June 1967:   "Lawyer for Ruby Indicted on Tax Evasion Charges [Joe Tonahill, for $124,732 in Austin, Texas],"
p. 24.

4394.   18 June 1967:   "Garrison Disputes Finding That Oswald
Acted Alone [in Talk in Monticello, New York]," p. 57.

4395.   19 June 1967:   "New Witness Alleges That He Was
Offered Money to Aid Garrison in Investigation of Assassination [Fred Leemans]," Robert E. Dallos, p. 27.

4396.   20 June 1967:   "Statements of 2 on 'Plot' Doubted:
N.B.C. Says Lie Detectors Weaken Garrison's Case [in Testimony
of Russo and V. Bundy]," Robert E. Dallos, p. 7.

4397.   _____: "TV: N.B.C. Questions Assassination
Inquiry [Last Night's Hour Long 'The J.F.K. Conspiracy: The
Case of Jim Garrison']," Jack Gould, p. 79.

4398.   21 June 1967:   "Witness in Kennedy 'Plot' Says N.B.C.
Tried to Wreck Inquiry [Perry R. Russo]," p. 19.

4399.   22 June 1967:   "Judge in Shaw Case Cautions Newsmen,"
p. 22.

4400.   23 June 1967:   "Investigation of Garrison by Louisiana
Is Urged [by Metropolitan Crime Commission of New Orleans],"
p. 6.

4401.   24 June 1967:   "Plea for Inquiry on Garrison Fails: Louisiana Attorney General Says He Lacks Authority," p. 13.

4402. _____: "Aide Declines Comment [William Gurvich, Garrison's Chief Investigator, on Visit and Conversation with Senator Robert F. Kennedy]," Robert E. Dallos, p. 13.

4403.   25 June 1967:   "Garrison Charges Pressure by U.S.: Declares 'Federal Power' Won't Stop Plot Inquiry," Martin Waldron, p. 2.

4404.   26 June 1967:   "Aide Will Ask Garrison to Take A New Look Into Kennedy 'Plot' [William Gurvich]," Robert E. Dallos, p. 36.

4405. _____: "C.B.S. Study Calls Oswald Assassin: Network's 7-Month Inquiry Finds He Shot Kennedy [Produced by Leslie Midgely]," p. 36.

4406. _____: "TV: C.B.S. Program Views Warren Report [First Hour of Four Hour Program Last Night]," Jack Gould, p. 67.

4407.   27 June 1967:   "Surgeon Depicts Kennedy's Wounds: Tells C.B.S. Pictures Refute Critics of Warren Report [Capt. James J. Humes, Chief Surgeon at Bethesda's Autopsy]," p. 25.

4408. _____: "Investigator Quits Garrison's Staff and Assails Inquiry into Plot [William H. Gurvich]," Gene Roberts, p. 25.

4409.   28 June 1967:   "Plan to Raid F.B.I. Laid to Garrison: Gurvich Says He will Tell Grand Jury of 'Travesties'," Gene Roberts, p. 6.

4410. _____: "Garrison Labels Oswald a 'Decoy': Says Real Assassins Hoped Police Would Kill Suspect [on C.B.S. Third Broadcast in Series]," Peter Kihss, p. 7.

4411.   29 June 1967:   "McCloy Regrets One Aspect of Warren Inquiry: Wishes Panel Had Studied Photographs and X-Rays: But He Supports Findings in Slaying of Kennedy," Martin Gansberg, p. 18.

4412. _____: "Garrison Critics Fail to Sway Jury: Panel Holds Investigation of Assassination Inquiry," Gene Roberts, p. 18.

4413. _____: "TV: Useful View of Warren Report: C.B.S. Programs Are Antidote for Critics: Time and Money Go Into a Public Service," Jack Gould, p. 87.

4414.   4 July 1967:   "N.B.C. Offers Garrison a Show to Defend Inquiry: Would Give District Attorney Time to Reply to Criticism of Assassination Study," p. 41.

4415. 5 July 1967: "Garrison Sets Up Conditions for TV:
Asks Hour on NBC to Reply -- Balks at Panel Format: Charges
Against Garrison," p. 83.

4416. 6 July 1967: "Garrison Requests Early Trial for Shaw
in Conspiracy Case: Second Extradition Fails [for Sergio
Arcacha Smith, as for Gordon Novel]," p. 24.

4417. 8 July 1967: "Garrison Goes on N.B.C. Next Week:
Bribery Laid to N.B.C. Man [Walter Sheridan for Alleged Offer
to Perry Russo]: Two Subpoenaed by Garrison [Gurvich and
Cancler]," p. 51.

4418. 9 July 1967: "Warren Commission Challenged on Photos:
Author Says Panel Failed to Examine Picture Evidence [Harold
Weisberg, Photographic Whitewash]," Peter Kihss, p. 51.

4419. 12 July 1967: "TV Newsman Named in Garrison Charges
[Against Richard Townley of WDSU-TV, on Public Bribery and
Intimidation]," p. 50.

4420. 13 July 1967: "Convict is Silent in Garrison Case:
Refuses to Confirm or Deny Story He Told on TV [John Cancler],"
Martin Waldron, p. 27.

4421. 16 July 1967: "Garrison Calls Warren Report 'Fairy
Tale' in TV Appearance: Statement by N.B.C.," p. 64.

4422. 19 July 1967: "N.B.C. Man Gives Up in Garrison Case:
Bond Is Posted on Charges of Attempted Bribery [Walter J.
Sheridan]," Martin Waldron, p. 17.

4423. 22 July 1967: "Garrison and Jury Receive Subpoenas
[in Walter Sheridan Case]," p. 6.

4424. 28 July 1967: "Newsman for N.B.C. Loses Plea on 'Plot'
[Must Testify]," p. 62.

4425. 29 July 1967: "N.B.C. Newsman Wins Court Stay: Grand
Jury Appearance in 'Plot' Inquiry Delayed," p. 51.

4426. 6 Aug. 1967: "39 Subpoenaed by Defense in Perjury
Trial on 'Plot' [in Case Against Dean A. Andrews Jr.]," p. 9.

4427. 7 Aug. 1967: "A Warren Commission Aide Eludes Louisiana Summons [Wesley J. Liebeler, for the Andrews Perjury
Trial]," p. 26.

4428. 8 Aug. 1967: "N.B.C. Suit Rejected by Louisiana
Court: [Novel Offers Testimony If Under Hypnosis]," p. 28.

4429. 10 Aug. 1967: "Garrison Scored at Perjury Trial:
Andrews Attacks Prosecutor After Losing Bid for Delay," p. 18.

4430. 11 Aug. 1967: "Andrews Loses Dismissal Plea: Perjury
Defendant Renews His Attack on Garrison," Martin Waldron, p.
29.

4431.   11 Aug. 1967:   "Books of The Times: The Battle of
the Book; or, a Case of Other Commitments [Reviews John
Corry, The Manchester Affair]," Eliot Fremont-Smith, p. 29.

4432.   12 Aug. 1967:   "Assistant to Garrison Tells Jury
Andrews Lied About Clay Shaw [Richard Burnes]," Martin Waldron, p. 11.

4433.   13 Aug. 1967:   "A Garrison 'Deal' Charged at Trial:
Andrews Tells of Accord on Identity of Bertrand," Martin
Waldron, p. 33.

4434.   14 Aug. 1967:   "Lawyer Convicted of Perjury in Kennedy
Inquiry: 5-Man Panel in New Orleans Finds Andrews Accused by
Garrison, Guilty," Martin Waldron, p. 15.

4435.   15 Aug. 1967:   "Garrison Inquiry Buoyed by Andrews
Conviction," Martin Waldron, p. 25.

4436.   17 Aug. 1967:   "A September Trial for Shaw Pressed,"
p. 14.

4437.   19 Aug. 1967:   "Andrews Sentenced in New Orleans Case
[18 Months]," p. 22.

4438.   21 Aug. 1967:   "Kennedy's Grave Is Site of Scuffle
in Rights Protest [by Open-Housing Advocates]," p. 38.

4439.   24 Aug. 1967:   "Oswald Case Aids Adoption Reform:
Rule on Religious Pairing Is Eased by Convention [in New
York's State Constitutional Convention]," Sydney H. Schan-
berg, p. 19.

4440.   29 Aug. 1967:   "Garrison Rebuffed on Calling Witness
[in Walter Sheridan Case]," p. 26.

4441.   1 Sept. 1967:   "Kennedy 'Plot' Figure Loses Fight to
Get New Testimony [Clay Shaw]," p. 12.

4442.   3 Sept. 1967:   "In Brief: The Manchester Affair: By
John Corry," pp. 18-19:   NYT Book Review.

4443.   10 Sept. 1967:   "News of the Rialto: You're the
Judge [Reviews 'The Trial of Lee Harvey Oswald' by Ducovny
and Friedman]," Lewis Funke, p. 9D.

4444.   11 Sept. 1967:   "Garrison Increases His Kennedy Total
to 7 Conspirators [in Playboy, October]," p. 14.

4445.   14 Sept. 1967:   "Dallas Group Begins Producing Film
on Kennedy Assassination [Produced by Robert Larsen, Flag-
Star Co. Raising $500,000]," p. 52.

VOLUME CXVII

4446. 19 Sept. 1967: "Shaw Loses Court Bid to Quash Indictment in Assassination Plot," p. 42.

4447. 22 Sept. 1967: "Garrison Says Some Policeman in
Dallas Aided Kennedy Plot," p. 21.

4448. 29 Sept. 1967: "[Letter from JFK to Charles H. Percy,
Later Senator from Illinois, Withdrawn at Auction]," Sandra
Knox, p. 53.

4449. 4 Oct. 1967: "Garrison Objects to Delay or Venue
Shift for Shaw," p. 40.

4450. 9 Oct. 1967: "Dallas Sets a 1969 Target for Its
Kennedy Memorial," p. 20.

4451. 12 Oct. 1967: "Oswald a Loner, Researcher Says: 3-
Year Study Contends He Conspired Against Himself [David Abra-
hamsen, in Bulletin of the New York Academy of Medicine],"
Martin Arnold, p. 25.

4452. 14 Oct. 1967: "Clark Aide Denies Move on Garrison
[by U.S. Attorney General's Office]," p. 8.

4453. 17 Oct. 1967: "Conspiracy Trial of Shaw Is Delayed
Until February [After Defense Requested Delay Until Spring
1968]," p. 95.

4454. 20 Oct. 1967: "De Gaulle Said to Blame Police in
Kennedy Death: Book by a French Historian Says He Feels
They Also Wanted Oswald Killed [Jean-Raymond Tournoux, La
Tragédie du Général]," p. 14.

4455. 31 Oct. 1967: "U.S. Sued by Widow for Oswald Items
[in $500,000 Claim]," p. 38.

4456. 6 Nov. 1967: "Theater: 'The Trial of Lee Harvey
Oswald' Arrives: Taste of Sensationalism in Dramatic Method:
Audience Becomes Jury for Fictional Case [at the ANTA Theater,
by Ducovny and Friedman]," Clive Barnes, p. 64.

4457. _____ : "Theater Petitions Ask Assassination
Inquiry [at ANTA Theater]," p. 64.

4458. 10 Nov. 1967: "'Oswald Trial' Closing [after 4 Pre-
views and 9 Performances at ANTA Theater]," p. 54.

4459. 12 Nov. 1967: "American Notebook: That Book Revisited
[Disappointing Sales of Manchester's Book, But He's Pleased],"
Lewis Nichols, pp. 60-61: NYT Book Review.

4460. 16 Nov. 1967: "New Book on Warren Report Argues 3 Men,
Probably Excluding Oswald, Joined in Killing Kennedy [Josiah
Thompson, Six Seconds in Dallas]," Sylvan Fox, p. 50.

4461.   19 Nov. 1967:   "Connally Denies Kennedy Went to Texas to Help Out Johnson [But to Help Himself Politically]," Edith Evans Asbury, p. 46.

4462.   21 Nov. 1967:   "Johnson Hails Legacy of President Kennedy," p. 26.

4463.   22 Nov. 1967:   "Cathedral Offers a Mass Today to Kennedy, Slain 4 Years Ago," p. 8.

4464.   23 Nov. 1967:   "Dallas Mayor Bids the Living Pursue Kennedy Goals: Rite at Dealey Plaza Marks Anniversary of Assassination: 300 Attend Service -- Brothers Visit Arlington Grave," p. 55.

4465.   _____: "Granite Marker Is Stolen from the Grave of Oswald," p. 55.

4466.   24 Nov. 1967:   "Memorials to Kennedy Still Rising Around the World," p. 44.

4467.   25 Nov. 1967:   "Headstone on Oswald Grave Is Recovered In Oklahoma," p. 36.

4468.   29 Nov. 1967:   "Oswald's Tombstone Back," p. 28.

4469.   1 Dec. 1967:   "Books of the Times: [Reviews A Nation Grieved, Edited by Raymond B. Rajski]," Eliot Fremont-Smith, p. 45.

4470.   6 Dec. 1967:   "Three Lawyers Say Convict Told Them of Plot on Kennedy [Mark Lane, Richard Burnes, John Hosmer Reporting Ex-Secret Serviceman Abraham Bolden's Testimony]," p. 26.

4471.   9 Dec. 1967:   "Life Sues to Halt Book on Kennedy: Magazine Charges Misuse of Its Assassination Film [by Josiah Thompson]," p. 61.

4472.   11 Dec. 1967:   "Mrs. Kennedy Aids State Democrats: Fund Dinner Here Marks First Political Appearance Since Husband's Death," Clayton Knowles, pp. 1, 36.

4473.   _____: "Garrison Says Assassin Killed Kennedy from Sewer Manhole," p. 28.

4474.   14 Dec. 1967:   "Scholar Upholds Warren Report: Briton Says Its Critics Are Reckless and Foolish [John Sparrow, in The Times Literary Supplement]," Anthony Lewis, p. 34.

4475.   17 Dec. 1967:   "Another Opinion: In Defense of the Warren Report [Excerpts from John Sparrow's Article in TLS]," p. 11E.

4476.   17 Dec. 1967:   "Pattern of Defeat [Reviews Lee, By Robert L. Oswald et al.]   Peter Kihss, p. 10:   NYT Book Review.

4477. 21 Dec. 1967: "Garrison Accuses Coast Man, Who Denies Kennedy Plot Role [Edgar Eugene Bradley]," p. 25.

4478. 22 Dec. 1967: "Garrison Scored on New Charge:
Right-Wing Church Leader Defends Accused Aide [Dr. Carl
McIntire Defends Bradley]," p. 11.

4479. 24 Dec. 1967: "Garrison's Charges on Assassination
a Thorn to New Orleans," p. 34.

4480. 27 Dec. 1967: "Garrison Says Oswald Gave F.B.I. a
Tip Before Assassination: Bradley's Arrest Ordered," p. 28.

4481. 28 Dec. 1967: "Suspect in 'Plot' Gives Up on Coast:
Will Start Move to Prevent Extradition to Louisiana [E. E.
Bradley in Los Angeles]," Gladwin Hill, p. 10.

4482. 30 Dec. 1967: "Garrison Record Shows Disability:
It Led to His Release from Active Duty, Pentagon Says: 3
'Witnesses' Subpoenaed," p. 28.

4483. 3 Jan. 1968: "Educator Scorns 'Plot' on Kennedy:
Johnson Aide Is Critical of Conspiracy Theorists [John P.
Roche, in London]," Anthony Lewis, p. 18.

4484. 5 Jan. 1968: "U.S. Worker Called in Kennedy 'Plot'
[James Hicks, Civilian Employee in Air Force, Present in
Dallas Near Assassination]," p. 33.

4485. 7 Jan. 1968: "Arrests for Threats to the President
Up Sharply Since the Assassination [425 Against LBJ in Fiscal
Year 1967, Ending 30 June]," Fred P. Graham, p. 59.

4486. 20 Jan. 1968: "Oswald's Widow Summoned in Suits on
His Possessions," p. 12.

4487. 25 Jan. 1968: "Garrison Subpoenas Widow of Oswald,"
p. 17.

4488. 27 Jan. 1968: Court Balks Return of Witness in 'Plot'
[Lawrence Howard Jr. of Bel Monte, California]," p. 34.

4489. 29 Jan. 1968: "President Kennedy Praised on Soviet
TV as a Realist [4 Minutes Devoted to Assassination]," p.
12.

4490. 30 Jan. 1968: "Marina Oswald Summoned to Inquiry in
New Orleans: [Thomas E. Beckham of Omaha Sought as Witness],"
p. 28.

4491. 31 Jan. 1968: "Garrison Witness Gets Order [Thomas E.
Beckham]," p. 10.

4492. 1 Feb. 1968: "Garrison Declares Ruby Was Sighted Near
Assassination [in Interview With Johnny Carson on the "Tonight" Show]," p. 75.

4493.   2 Feb. 1968:   "'63 Patient Quoted on Kennedy 'Plot' [on 19 Nov. 1963 at Jackson Memorial Hospital, According to The Capital Times, Madison, Wisconsin]," p. 11.

4494.   9 Feb. 1968:   "Oswald's Widow Tells a Jury of Poor Times in New Orleans," Martin Waldron, p. 52.

4495.   14 Feb. 1968:   "Garrison Objects to Shift in Trial [Out of New Orleans]," p. 44.

4496.   17 Feb. 1968:   "Dulles Subpoenaed in Garrison Inquiry [as Former Director of C.I.A.]," p. 57.

4497.   18 Feb. 1968:   "Studies in Disbelief [Reviews Books By Josiah Thompson and by Sylvia Meagher]," Fred Graham, pp. 16-18:   NYT Book Review.

4498.   21 Feb. 1968:   "Judge Joe Brown of Ruby Case Dies: Sentenced Oswald's Killer to Death After Stormy Trial [Age 59]," p. 47.

4499.   22 Feb. 1968:   "Garrison Charges Perjury to Former Oswald Friend [Kerry Thornley, A Marine Corps Friend]," p. 62.

4500.   23 Feb. 1968:   "Kennedy Book Prize Won By a Newsman [Louis Heren, Washington Reporter for The Times, London, for a Book: The New American Commonwealth]," p. 47.

4501.   28 Feb. 1968:   "President Urges Firmness on War: In First Visit to Dallas Since Assassination, He Sees a Turning Point in Vietnam: An Unmarked Car," Roy Reed, pp. 1, 33.

4502.   3 March 1968:   "Oswald Letters to Be Sold Here: MSS. Lead Week's Auction -- Ceramics Also Listed," p. 8.

4503.   17 March 1968:   "District Attorneys Pay for a Dinner; Garrison Cancels It [Because Not Allowed to Speak Against LBJ and Federal Courts]," p. 78.

4504.   19 March 1968:   "Shift of Shaw Trial Weighed at Hearing," p. 44.

4505.   25 March 1968:   "Warren Sought Kennedy Photos: Articl Depicts Panel's Bid to See Autopsy Pictures [in Saturday Even ing Post, 6 April, by David Wise]," p. 6.

4506.   26 March 1968:   "Kennedy Cheered by Watts Negroes: Backs Warren Report," John Herbers, p. 24.

4507.   _____ :   "Oswald Case Figure Called [Mrs. Ruth Paine]," p. 39.

4508.   29 March 1968:   "Garrison Charges Ex-Aide With Theft [William H. Gurvich]," p. 45.

4509. 30 March 1968: "Delay on 'Plot' Extradition [of
Edgar E. Bradley, from Los Angeles to New Orleans]," p. 21.

4510. 31 March 1968: "Letters to the Editor: In Dallas
[Against Fred Graham's Earlier Review, from Josiah Thompson
and George Lakoff]," pp. 20-22: NYT Book Review.

4511. 4 April 1968: "Shaw Judge Denies Motion to Reopen
Venue Hearing," p. 50.

4512. 5 April 1968: "Judge Denies Shaw a Change of Venue,"
p. 40.

4513. 6 April 1968: "Europe Dismayed; Fearful for U.S.:
Murder of Dr. King Evokes Doubts Over Stability of the
American Society," Anthony Lewis, pp. 1, 28.

4514. 19 April 1968: "Radar to Raise Shield Planned by
Engineers [to Prevent Future Assassination Successes]," p. 12.

4515. _____: "Play on Lee Oswald Given Its U.S.
Pemier [sic] in Atlanta [by Michael Hastings]," p. 35.

4516. 29 April 1968: "Ruby's Grave Vandalized," p. 61.

4517. 9 May 1968: "Garrison Schedules Trial of Clay Shaw
for June 11," p. 38.

4518. 13 May 1968: "Choral Work Built on Kennedy Words
[Composed by Louise Talma at Hunter College and Premiered
Saturday, 11 May, There]," p. 52.

4519. 16 May 1968: "Manchester's Book Is Due in Paperback
[Hardcover = 548,500 Distributed by Publisher and 686,909 by
Book-of-the-Month Club]," p. 44.

4520. 24 May 1968: "Photos Cited by Research Group in
Kennedy Death [The Kennedy Assassination Inquiry Committee,
Chairman Trent Gough, on the 'Dallas Tramps']," Peter Kihss,
p. 41.

4521. _____: "Books of The Times: Congress, Consensus and Two Presidents [Reviews JFK and LBJ, by Tom Wicker],"
Eliot Fremont-Smith, p. 45.

4522. 25 May 1968: "Amended Subpoena Issued by Garrison in
Shaw Case [for Dr. James B. Rhoades, U.S. Archivist]," p. 71.

4523. 26 May 1968: "Intentions and Achievements [Reviews
JFK and LBJ by Tom Wicker]," James MacGregor Burns, pp. 2-3:
NYT Book Review.

4524. 27 May 1968: "Garrison Offers $1000 for Identification
of Photo [of 'Dallas Tramp']," p. 28.

4525.   29 May 1968:   "Letter by Oswald Is Sold for $1,050
[to His Mother from Russia]," p. 20.

4526.   _____: "Judge Restrains Shaw Prosecutor:
Issues a Temporary Order Barring Action in Case," p. 28.

4527.   30 May 1968:   "Mrs. Kennedy Attends Mass on Date of
Husband's Birth [51st]," p. 11.

4528.   2 June 1968:   "The Haunting of Robert Kennedy: For
Many Voters . . . Look at R.F.K. and They See J.F.K.:   The
Specter [of National Guilt]," Victor S. Navasky, pp. 26-27,
78-83:   NYT Magazine.

4529.   6 June 1968:   "[Robert] Kennedy Is Dead, Victim of
Assassin: Surgery in Vain: President Calls Death Tragedy,
Proclaims a Day of Mourning   Mrs.[J.F.K. Also at Deathbed],"
Gladwin Hill, pp. 1, 20, 25.

4530.   _____: "Robert Francis Kennedy: Attorney
General, Senator and Heir of the New Frontier," Alden Whitman, p. 26; (7 June 1968), 18.

4531.   7 June 1968:   "Senator Will Be Buried Near His Slain
Brother: Arlington Cemetery Gravesite to Be in Area of
President's -- Flow of Tourists Rises," Richard L. Madden,
p. 20; (8 June 1968), p. 12.

4532.   8 June 1968:   "Jail Chapel Used as Court to Bar
'Another Dallas':   Sirhan's Arraignment Set Up While the
Grand Jury Is Still Hearing Witnesses," Terry Robards, p.
13.

4533.   _____: "Assassination and Law: Yorty Statements on Notebook Said to Complicate Issue of Police and
Press," Sidney E. Zion, p. 13.

4534.   _____: "Soviet Criticizes U.S. on Suspect:
Sees an Effort to Deflect Guilt to Foreign Circles [Repeated
from Dallas]," p. 14.

4535.   9 June 1968:   "Thousands in Last Tribute to Kennedy;
Service at Arlington Is Held at Night," Anthony J. Lukas,
pp. 1, 53.

4536.   _____: "Suspect in Assassination of Dr. King
Is Seized in London: Ray Found Armed: Arrested at the Air-
port by Scotland Yard on Way From Lisbon," Fred P. Graham,
pp. 1, 74.

4537.   _____: "President Joins Kennedys in Tribute
at Graveside [for Robert Kennedy's Burial]," Tom Wicker, pp.
1, 55.

4538.   _____: "The Kennedy Legend: A Nation Mourns
Again," William V. Shannon, p. 1E.

4539. 9 June 1968: "American Tragedy: The Terrible Toll of Violence," Tom Wicker, p. 1E.

4540. _____: "Guns and Assassins: 'In the Name of Sanity'," John W. Finney, p. 2E.

4541. 12 June 1968: "Grandson to Finish Work on Churchill [Late Robert Kennedy Had Approached Randolph Churchill to Author Biography of JFK]," p. 50.

4542. 16 June 1968: "[Full-Page Advertisement for Gun-Control Legislation: That Since 1900 Over 750,000 Americans Killed by Private Guns]," p. E7.

4543. 21 June 1968: "Manchester and Harper Donate $750,000 to the Kennedy Library," Henry Raymont, pp. 1, 38.

4544. 29 June 1968: "Warren Still Firm on Oswald's Guilt," p. 10.

4545. 11 July 1968: "Warren Panel Critic Scores Garrison [Edward Jay Epstein, in The New Yorker, 13 July]," Peter Kihss, p. 44.

4546. 12 July 1968: "Garrison Claims Foreign Spy Link: Says He Exchanged Data About President Kennedy," p. 64.

4547. 14 July 1968: "One Man's Doubts: [Reviews Mark Lane, A Citizen's Dissent]," Victor S. Navasky, pp. 32-33: NYT Book Review.

4548. 19 July 1968: "Court's Technical Custody of Oswald's Weapons Ended," p. 6.

4549. 14 Aug. 1968: "A Delay In Shaw's Plot Trial Ordered by Federal Court [Until Decision Made on Shaw's Countersuit]," p. 19.

4550. 29 Aug. 1968: "Film on J. F. Kennedy Will Be Set in West [and Depict Assassination, in Spanish-Italian Production by Tonino Baldi]," p. 40.

VOLUME CXVIII

4551. 28 Sept. 1968: "Shaw Appeals to High Court on Sanctuary from Garrison: [D.A. Subpoenas Diary of Seymore Gelber, Florida's Assistant Attorney General]," p. 22.

4552. 1 Oct. 1968: "Time Inc. Loses Suit on 'Dallas' Photos [by Abraham Zapruder, Alleging Infringement of Copyright by Josiah Thompson]," p. 22.

4553. 21 Oct. 1968: "'Very Happy' Mrs. Kennedy and Onassis Married [on Island of Skorpios by Greek Orthodox Prelate]," Alvin Shuster, pp. 1, 51.

4554. _____ : "[Robert] Kennedy Memoir Details Cuba Crisis: President's Mind Turned to Lincoln at Crisis' End," Bernard Gwertzman, pp. 1, 4.

4555. 24 Oct. 1968: "New Kennedy Book Is Set for Release [Jim Bishop's The Day Kennedy Was Shot for Release on 22 Nov. After Excerpts in The Ladies Home Journal]," p. 95.

4556. 26 Oct. 1968: "Cushing Irate at Onassis Furor, Says He Will Retire This Year [After Defending Marriage]," John H. Fenton, pp. 1, 43.

4557. 8 Nov. 1968: "Kennedy Trustee Named [Mrs. Patricia Lawford Replaces RFK as Trustee for JFK's Estate]," p. 44.

4558. 9 Nov. 1968: "Reagan Declines Extradition of Figure in Kennedy 'Plot' [Edgar E. Bradley, Business Representative to Dr. Carl McIntire, Evangelist]," p. 29.

4559. 22 Nov. 1968: "Coast Commentator Heard by Garrison Grand Jury [Fred Lee Crisman of Tacoma, Washington, Says He Knows Nothing]," p. 28.

4560. 22 Nov. 1968: "Books of The Times: Kennedy: Memorials and Assaults [Reviews Jim Bishop's Book, Alex. J. Goldman on JFK, and 1:33. In Memoriam]," Eliot Fremont-Smith, p. 45.

4561. 23 Nov. 1968: "John F. Kennedy Remembered Five Years After Death: Before Gates Open: Ceremony in Dallas," Nan Robertson, pp. 49, 95.

4562. 10 Dec. 1968: "Louisiana Trial of Shaw Assured: High Court Refuses to Block Action in Kennedy's Death: January Trial Planned," p. 42.

4563. 12 Dec. 1968: "Clay Shaw Trial Is Slated Jan. 21: Garrison Sets Date in Case Charging Plot on Kennedy," p. 48.

4564. 18 Dec. 1968: "Mrs. Onassis in Capital Visit [with Mrs. Ethel Kennedy, at Birth of 11th Child to Her and Late Senator Robert F. Kennedy]," p. 45.

4565. 29 Dec. 1968: "The Day Kennedy Was Shot. By Jim Bishop," John Corry, p. 6: NYT Book Review.

4566. 1 Jan. 1969: "Book on Kennedy Sees a Wide Plot: Origin of French Bestseller Remains a Mystery [Farewell America by James Hepburn]," John L. Hess, p. 12.

4567. 11 Jan. 1969: "Garrison's Effort to Subpoena Kennedy Photos Faces Hurdles: Archives, Citing Proviso Set by Family, Opposes Use of Assassination Items," p. 16.

4568. 12 Jan. 1969: "Cuban Film 'L.B.J.' Accuses Johnson of Assassinations [of JFK, Martin Luther King, Jr., and RFK]," p. 63.

4569. 14 Jan. 1969: "Judge Bars Delay in Trial of Shaw [After Defense Again Asks]," p. 17.

4570. 15 Jan. 1969: "Garrison Role in Shaw Trial [Will Not Personally Prosecute]," p. 24.

4571. 17 Jan. 1969: "Inquiry Upholds Warren Report: Finds Autopsy Photos Show 2 Shots Killed President [Panel of 4 Medical Experts for Justice Dept.]," Fred P. Graham, pp. 1, 17.

4572. _____: "Conclusions of the Panel [Text: Study of JFK Autopsy Photos by Drs. William Carnes, Russell Fisher, Russell Morgan, and Alan Moritz]," p. 17.

4573. 18 Jan. 1969: "A U.S. Judge Denies Kennedy Photos to Garrison [After Attorney General Ramsey Clark Releases Four-man Medical Panel's Report]," Fred P. Graham, p. 25.

4574. _____: "Trial Delay Asked [This Time by D.A. Jim Garrison's Office]," Martin Waldron, p. 25.

4575. 19 Jan. 1969: "Speculation Rises That Garrison May Abandon the Investigation of President Kennedy's Assassination [After Request for Indefinite Delay for Shaw Trial]," Martin Waldron, p. 27.

4576. _____: "Thirteen Days [Reviews Robert Kennedy's A Memoir of the Cuban Missile Crisis]," David Schoenbrun, pp. 1, 30-32: NYT Book Review.

4577. 21 Jan. 1969: "Garrison Staff Ready for Shaw Trial," Martin Waldron, p. 19.

4578. 22 Jan. 1969: "Shaw's Conspiracy Trial Opens; 2 Jurors Chosen," Martin Waldron, p. 16.

4579. 23 Jan. 1969: "2 Negroes Among 4 Named to Shaw Jury," p. 55.

4580. 24 Jan. 1969: "Veniremen Added for Trial of Shaw," p. 44.

4581. 25 Jan. 1969: "Two Jurors Added for Trial of Shaw [Justice Dept. Permits F.B.I. Analyst to Testify]," p. 30.

4582. 26 Jan. 1969: "Shaw's Trial Is Adjourned as Jury Panels Are Sought [as Addition to Chosen Panel]," p. 27.

4583.   26 Jan. 1969:   "Garrison's Case: At Long Last, the
Shaw Trial," Martin Waldron, p. 2E.

4584.   28 Jan. 1969:   "New Juror Picked for Trial of Shaw,"
p. 21.

4585.   29 Jan. 1969:   "Last of Shaw Jury May Be Named Today,"
p. 18.

4586.   30 Jan. 1969:   "11th Juror in Trial of Shaw Selected
in New Orleans," p. 20.

4587.   31 Jan. 1969:   "Shaw Jury One Short; New Lists Are
Drawn," p. 18.

4588.   1 Feb. 1969:   "Washington   Judge Presses Garrison for
Data on 'Plot' [Before U.S. Judge Charles Halleck Rules on
Request for Autopsy Photos]," p. 25.

4589.   2 Feb. 1969:   "12th Juror Seated for Trial of Shaw,"
p. 47.

4590.   5 Feb. 1969:   "Garrison Subpoenas Film of Kennedy
Assassination [Made in Color by Abraham Zapruder, Now Owned
by Life], p. 20.

4591.   7 Feb. 1969:   "Garrison Tells Shaw Jury He Will Prove
Plot in Kennedy's Death, With Fatal Shot Fired From Front,"
Martin Waldron, p. 19.

4592.   8 Feb. 1969:   "Witness Relates Shaw Discussion: Says
Murder of Kennedy Was Topic at a Party [Charles I. Spiesel,
a New York Accountant]," Martin Waldron, p. 18.

4593.   9 Feb. 1969:   "Shaw Jury Visits French Quarter:
Witness [Spiesel] Shows Court Scene He Links to Assassination," Martin Waldron, p. 32.

4594.   10 Feb. 1969:   "Hypnosis a Factor in New Orleans Trial
of Shaw [for Witnesses Spiesel and Russo]," Martin Waldron,
p. 30.

4595.   11 Feb. 1969:   "Shaw Trial Hears of '63 Meeting:
Witness [Russo] Is Unsure If Kennedy Discussion Was Serious:
Judge Rejects Move of the Defense to Curb Testimony," Martin
Waldron, p. 8.

4596.   12 Feb. 1969:   "Witness Relates Doubts on Shaw's Conspiracy Role [Russo]," Martin Waldron, p. 22.

4597.   13 Feb. 1969:   "Shaw Trial Turns to Texas and Assassination Alibis," Martin Waldron, p. 22.

4598.   14 Feb. 1969:   "Zapruder Film of Kennedy Shown at Shaw
Trial: Garrison Seeks to Disprove Warren Panel Conclusion of
a Single Assassin," Martin Waldron, p. 20.

4599. 15 Feb. 1969: "Shaw Jury Told of Oswald Flight: Ex-
Deputy in Dallas Says a Second Man Drove Car [Roger Dean
Craig = Witness]," Martin Waldron, p. 13.

4600. _____: "X-Rays Released for Witness [Dr.
Cyril H. Wecht, by U.S. Judge Charles Halleck, Washington,
D.C.]," p. 13.

4601. 16 Feb. 1969: "Weather Delays Shaw Witnesses: Texans
Unable to Fly In --- Only 3 Persons on Stand [James Simmons,
Mrs. Frances Gail Newman, Mrs. Mary Moorman]," p. 32.

4602. 17 Feb. 1969: "Garrison Puts Off Calling Connally,"
p. 22.

4603. 18 Feb. 1969: "Data on Autopsy Freed by Court:
Garrison Request Granted, But U.S. Plans Appeal," Fred P.
Graham, p. 29.

4604. _____: "Two Jurors Ill, Shaw Trial Halts; a
Witness Says Kennedy May Have Been Shot in Front [Dr. John M.
Nichols]," Martin Waldron, p. 29.

4605. 19 Feb. 1969: "It's Fat Tuesday in New Orleans and
500,000 Enjoy, Enjoy: Shaw Jurors See Parades," Martin Waldron, p. 43.

4606. 20 Feb. 1969: "Shaw Judge Impugns State Witness:
Denies Mistrial [Claims Policeman A. W. Habighorst Not to Be
Believed: Judge Edward A. Haggerty, Jr.]," Martin Waldron,
p. 25.

4607. 21 Feb. 1969: "Shaw Asks Acquittal After Prosecution
Rests: Request for Photos Dropped [by Garrison]," Martin
Waldron, p. 24.

4608. 22 Feb. 1969: "Widow of Oswald Testifies He Did Not
Know Shaw or Ferrie [Spent Every Night But One at Home While
in New Orleans]," Martin Waldron, p. 21.

4609. 23 Feb. 1969: "F.B.I. Arms Expert Tells Shaw Trial
Kennedy Was Shot from Behind: Refers to 'Sonic Booms' [to
Explain Anyone's Hearing More Than Three Shots Fired],"
Martin Waldron, p. 28.

4610. 25 Feb. 1969: "Kennedy Autopsy Doctor Tells Shaw
Jury Shots Came from Rear [Col. Pierre A. Finck, U.S. Army],"
Martin Waldron, p. 18.

4611. _____: "Jury Bars Payment for Oswald's Rifle
[Remains in National Archives But John J. King Reimbursed
$350. for Oswald's Pistol]," p. 18.

4612. 26 Feb. 1969: "Lawyer Testifies He Made Up Story
About Oswald [Dean A. Andrews, Jr.]," Martin Waldron, p. 16.

4613.   27 Feb. 1969:   "2 At Shaw Trial Rebut Russo Story
[Lt. Edward M. O'Donnell, and James R. Phelan, Author of
Saturday Evening Post Article on Garrison]," Martin Waldron,
p. 28.

4614.   28 Feb. 1969:   "Shaw Denies Kennedy Murder Plot,"
Martin Waldron, p. 14.

4615.   1 March 1969:   "Shaw Acquitted of 'Kennedy Plot':
Jury Out 50 Minutes After Summation by Garrison [to Fight
"Power of the Secret Police, the Admirals and Generals"],"
Martin Waldron, pp. 1, 16.

4616.   2 March 1969:   "Jury, Acquitting Shaw, Deals Blow to
Garrison 'Plot' Theory," Martin Waldron, p. 56.

4617.   _____: "Garrison Flops on the Conspiracy
Theory," Sidney E. Zion, p. 6E.

4618.   _____: "[Editorial] Justice in New Orleans,"
p. 12E.

4619.   4 March 1969:   "Shaw Is Charged With Lie at Trial:
Garrison Files Perjury Writ Against Freed Defendant [for Saying He Never Knew Oswald and Ferrie]," p. 19.

4620.   5 March 1969:   "Garrison Accuses Ex-Aide of Stealing
Shaw Trial Plan [Against Thomas Bethell]," p. 24.

4621.   15 March 1969:   "Garrison Says Evidence Rules Cost Him
Verdict [and Details His Own Errors of Judgment]," p. 20.

4622.   16 March 1969:   "Garrison, Undaunted by Criticism,
Continuing Inquiry into Murder of Kennedy," Martin Waldron,
p. 59.

4623.   17 March 1969:   "241 in New Orleans Sign Ad Endorsing
Garrison," p. 19.

4624.   23 March 1969:   "Clay Shaw Finds Life 'Pretty Much'
the Same as Before Charge by Garrison," Martin Waldron, p. 71.

4625.   26 March 1969:   "A Texas Kennedy Memorial [Senate
Creates 9-Member Commission, by 25 to 4 Vote]," p. 41.

4626.   11 April 1969:   "[Truman] Capote Denounces Kennedy
Article Attributed to Him ['Dead or Alive' Circulated in
Mid-West Tabloids]," p. 41.

4627.   20 April 1969:   "The Final Chapter in the Assassination
Controversy? [About Mort Sahl, Mark Lane, Jim Garrison, Penn
Jones, and Harold Weisberg]," Edward Jay Epstein, pp. 30-31,
115-120:   NYT Magazine.

4628.   18 May 1969:   "Letters: How Many Bullets?" Josiah
Thompson, and Edward Jay Epstein, p. 133:   NYT Magazine.

4629. 30 May 1969: "Kennedy's Birthplace Made a National Shrine: Family Gathers in Brookline [Mass.] on Nostalgic Day [52 Years Ago]," Robert Reinhold, p. 29.

4630. 22 June 1969: "Dallas Kennedy Monument Promised by First of Year," p. 34.

4631. 7 Aug. 1969: "Shyre Assails Ford's Theater Board [for Rejecting "The President Is Dead," a Play About Lincoln With Parallels to JFK, Written in 1967]," Louis Calta, p. 28.

4632. 6 Sept. 1969: "A Kennedy Film Cancelled in Paris: Director Says United Artists Blocked Sept. 17 Premier ["Mort d'un President" by Herve Lamarre, the Publisher of Farewell America]," p. 22.

VOLUME CXIX

4633. 19 Oct. 1969: "A Talk With Warren on Crime, the Court, the Country: [His Unhappiest Day? JFK's Death]," Anthony Lewis, pp. 34-35, 122-136 [esp. pp. 133-134]: NYT Magazine.

4634. 26 Oct. 1969: "Garrison Faces Fight in Election: 3 Press Shaw Prosecutor in Bid for Third Term," Roy Reed, p. 78.

4635. 10 Nov. 1969: "Garrison Crossed Racial Lines to Win New Orleans Primary," Roy Reed, p. 16.

4636. 22 Nov. 1969: "Topics: Since Nov. 22, 1963," Theodore C. Sorensen, p. 36.

4637. 23 Nov. 1969: "John F. Kennedy Jr. Assists at Services in Honor of Father [Serves Mass at Hyannis Port]," p. 45.

4638. 30 Nov. 1969: "New Orleans Enjoyed the Circus: The Garrison Case, by Milton E. Brener," Alexander M. Bickel, p. 73: NYT Book Review.

4639. 5 Dec. 1969: "President Kennedy Left $1.8-Million in Property," p. 90.

4640. 19 Dec. 1969: "Shaw Case Judge Seized by 'Stag Show' Raiders [Criminal District Judge Edward A. Haggerty Jr.: for Assault Against Police, Soliciting for Prostitution and Conspiracy for Obscenity]," p. 37.

4641. 21 Dec. 1969: "Judge Bids U.S. Pay for Oswald Items [Documents, Including Diary, Totaling 500 Items Seized for the Government, But Not the Rifle]," p. 45.

4642. 17 Jan. 1970: "Ex-Police Chief of Dallas Finds Data on Kennedy Death Unclear: Jesse Curry, in a Book About the Murder, Cites Varying Accounts of Witnesses," Martin Waldron, p. 14.

4643.   20 Jan. 1970:   "Senator Clarifies His View on Oswald
[Sen. Richard B. Russell, That Oswald Had to Have Some En-
couragement from Someone]," p. 16.

4644.   27 Jan. 1970:   "Judge [Haggerty] in Shaw Trial Is Found
Not Guilty [Because Party Was Private and Police Thus Had No
Right to Raid It: Case Heard Without Jury, Before Fellow
Judge]," p. 18.

4645.   28 Feb. 1970:   "Clay Shaw Sues Garrison and Others
for $5 - Million," p. 12.

4646.   1 March 1970:   "Detective in Death of Kennedy Retires
[Capt. Will Fritz, Dallas]," p. 87.

4647.   7 April 1970:   "Archives Charged With Suppressing
Assassination Data [by Sherman Skolnick of Chicago: That
Conspiracy Started in Chicago]," p. 29.

4648.   17 April 1970:   "Building from Which Oswald Fired
[sic] Brings $650,000 [Sold by D. Harold Byrd, Oil Million-
aire, to Aubrey Mayhew of Nashville]," B. Drummond Ayres,
Jr., p. 26.

4649.   29 April 1970:   "Johnson TV Interview Abridged at His
Request: Deletion Is Said to Have Cast Doubt on Findings of
the Warren Commission [for C.B.S. Next Saturday, 2 May],"
Christopher Lydon, p. 83.

4650.   3 May 1970:   "Johnson Accuses Some of '63 Staff: On
TV, He Asserts Kennedy Holdovers 'Undermined' Him Early in
Term," Warren Weaver, Jr., pp. 1, 79.

4651.   4 May 1970:   "Johnson 'Undermining' Charge Denied
[by Pierre Salinger]," Paul L. Montgomery, p. 32.

4652.   25 May 1970:   "Oswald's Hatred Linked to Castro:
Book Says Critics of Cuba Aroused Him to Anger [by Albert H.
Newman]," p. 34.

4653.   30 May 1970:   "At Arlington National Cemetery:
[Photo of Sen. Edward Kennedy, on JFK's 53rd Birthday]," p.
20.

4654.   13 June 1970:   "Kennedy Memorial Slated [for Dedication in Dallas June 24 Within Sight of Assassination Site],"
p. 16.

4655.   25 June 1970:   "Dallas Memorial Dedicated to Kennedy
200 Yards from Site of Slaying [Cenotaph; No Member of Kennedy
Family Present]," Martin Waldron, pp. 1, 27.

4656.   1 July 1970:   "Clay Shaw Case Continued [Motion to
Dismiss Perjury Charge]," p. 20.

4657. 10 July 1970: "A Federal Evaluator Puts $17,654 Value on Oswald's Papers [Compared with $500,000 Claim by Mrs. Marina Oswald Porter and $3000 Claimed by U.S. Government]," p. 37.

4658. 17 Aug. 1970: "Kennedy Archives Illuminate Cuba Policy [Opens to Scholars and Researchers, 15 Million Pages of Documents and Oral-History Interviews]," Henry Raymont, pp. 1, 16.

4659. 18 Aug. 1970: "Khrushchev, in Letter for Archives, Extolled John Kennedy as Statesman [Harold Macmillan and Charles de Gaulle Never Replied to Requests for Oral-History Interviews]," Henry Raymont, p. 4.

4660. 19 Aug. 1970: "Library's Tapes Detail Luce's Ambivalent Relationship With John Kennedy," Henry Raymont, p. 10.

4661. 23 Aug. 1970: "Witness in Clay Shaw case Held on 3 Burglary Counts [Perry R. Russo]," p. 60.

4662. 31 Aug. 1970: "Abraham Zapruder Dies; Filmed Kennedy Death: Footage of Tragedy in Dallas Had Role in Shaw Trial and Warren Commission Report," p. 27.

VOLUME CXX

4663. 27 Sept. 1970: "Clay Shaw Is Touring Colleges Lecturing on 'Erosion of Rights' [Fee Is $1000]," p. 58.

4664. _____: "Perry Russo Convicted [of Possession of Stolen Property]," p. 58.

4665. 20 Nov. 1970: "The Real Lee Harvey Oswald [Psychoanalyzed]," Priscilla McMillan, p. 41.

4666. 23 Nov. 1970: "Moment of Prayer [Photo: Sen. Edward Kennedy and Mrs. Ethel Kennedy and Their Children at JFK's Grave]," p. 1.

4667. 24 Nov. 1970: "Shaw Judge Is Ordered Ousted Over His Arrest in a Vice Raid [by Louisiana Supreme Court: Judge Edward A. Haggerty, Jr. to Apply for Re-Hearing]," p. 24.

4668. 1 Dec. 1970: "Books of The Times: The Shaw-Garrison Affair [Reviews James Kirkwood, American Grotesque, and Jim Garrison, A Heritage of Stone]," John Leonard, p. 45.

4669. 14 Jan. 1971: "Shaw Loses Plea to Delay Perjury Trial in Louisiana," p. 50.

4670. 20 Jan. 1971: "Prosecution of Clay Shaw Is Blocked by Court Order," p. 53.

4671. 4 Feb. 1971: "Mrs. Onassis Returns for White House Visit [First Since Dec. 1963]," p. 19.

4672.   5 Feb. 1971: "Kennedy Portraits Go on View at White House [Painted by Aaron Shikler]," Nan Robertson, p. 38; (8 Feb. 1971), p. 20; (16 Feb. 1971), p. 67.

4673.   26 March 1971: "$11,000 Paid at Auction for Part of Letter by President Kennedy," p. 32; (26 May 1972), p. 31.

4674.   11 April 1971: "L.B.J. Library Near Completion [with Public Dedication Soon]," Martin Waldron, pp. 1, 47; (23 April 1971), p. 36.

4675.   28 April 1971: "Rival Banquet Protests Law Day Speech Official [Robert Mardian; Who Says F.B.I.'s Lax Security Aided JFK's Assassination; Judge John Sirica Pictured With Him]," Fred P. Graham, p. 26.

4676.   21 May 1971: "Johnson Library Doors to Open on Everybody: Johnson Ceremony on TV [for Saturday Dedication; President Nixon to Attend, Under Elaborate Security Precautions in Austin, Texas]," Nan Robertson, p. 45; (22 May 1971), p. 35; (23 May 1971), pp. 1, 39.

4677.   23 May 1971: "Kennedy Library to Be Scaled Down [I. M. Pei's Design Still Only a Partial Model; Documents Available in Storage at Waltham, Mass.]," Henry Raymont, p. 39.

4678.   28 May 1971: "U.S. Judge [Herbert W. Christenberry] Orders Garrison to Stop Prosecuting Shaw [Because of Garrison's Financial Interest in the Continuation of Case]," p. 10.

4679.   30 May 1971: "At Arlington Cemetery [Photo of Sen. Edward Kennedy and Family at JFK's Grave for President's 54th Birthday]," p. 40; (7 June 1971), p. 16.

4680.   10 June 1971: "Notes of People [Retirement of Rufus Youngblood, Secret Service Agent at JFK Assassination]," p. 37.

4681.   29 June 1971: "Notes on People: Mrs. Rose Kennedy Said She Was 'Never Particularly Incensed' at the Assassins of Her Two Sons," p. 43.

4682.   2 July 1971: "Garrison Links Arrest [for Bribery] to a Move to Hide Kennedy Death 'Truth'," Roy Reed, p. 30; (4 July 1971), 3E.

4683.   27 July 1971: "Plans for Book Depository [in Dallas, to Become Museum for More Than 150,000 Items Associated With JFK]," p. 65.

4684.   2 August 1971: "Kennedy Library Opens Most of Its Files [at Temporary Location in Federal Records Center, Waltham, Mass.]," Henry Raymont, pp. 1, 6; (3 Aug. 1971), p. 26.

4685.   15 August 1971:   "Book Casts Doubt on Justice in U.S.:
Raises Questions on Trials of Shaw, Ray and Sirhan [Edited by
John Siegenthaler, A Search for Justice]," p. 46.

VOLUME CXXI

4686.   26 Sept. 1971:   "Dallas Depository to Open to Tourists
[for $2.00 Each, by Owner, Aubrey Mayhew, for JFK Assassina-
tion Visitors]," Martin Waldron, p. 66.

4687.   8 Oct. 1971: "Notes on People: Dan H. Fenn [a Harvard
Instructor, Has Been Named the First Director of the John F.
Kennedy Library to Be Built in Cambridge, Mass.]," p. 25;
(16 Nov. 1971), 52.

4688.   17 Oct. 1971:   "[Photo] Nov. 22, 1963:   President
Kennedy, Vice President Johnson and Gov. John Connally of
Texas Arrive in Dallas: By Lyndon B. Johnson: 'The Vantage
Point' [Autobiography]," pp. 1, 40.

4689.   19 Oct. 1971:   "J.F.K. in Retrospect [and the Use of
Force]," William V. Shannon, p. 43.

4690.   9 Nov. 1971:   "Johnson Announces Texas Symposium on
U.S. Education [24-25 Jan. 1972, to Coincide With First
Release of Presidential Papers to Public]," p. 10.

4691.   21 Nov. 1971:   "The Site of the Most Shocking Single
Event of Our Time [Dallas, the Memorials and the Commerciali-
zation]," Gary Cartwright, 1XX, 20xx-21XX; (12 Dec. 1971),
4XX.

4692.   22 Nov. 1971:   "The Warren Commission Was Right,"
David W. Belin, p. 39.

4693.   _____: "Theater: 'JFK' Recalled [a One-Man
Show, by Actor Jeremiah Collins]," Howard Thompson, p. 50.

4694.   23 Nov. 1971:   "Thousands Visit Kennedy's Grave [Photo
of Sen. Edward Kennedy at Site]," p. 57.

4695.   3 Dec. 1971:   "Letters to the Editor: Facts on J.F.K.'s
Death [Criticizes David Belin's Earlier Article and Governmental Secrecy]," Marvin Frankel, p. 40.

4696.   16 Dec. 1971:   "Garrison Pleads Not Guilty; Says He
Is Being Repressed [on Federal Bribery and Gambling Charges,
Before Judge Herbert W. Christenberry]," p. 71.

4697.   22 Dec. 1971:   "Ruling on Oswald's Effects [Federal
District Judge Joe E. Estes, That U.S. Need Pay $3,000 Only
to Widow]," p. 71.

4698. 9 Jan. 1972: "Doctor Inspects Kennedy X-Rays [John K. Lattimer Supports Warren Report on Bullets]," Fred P. Graham, pp. 1, 44.

4699. 20 Jan. 1972: "Horse That Followed Kennedy Coffin Ages Friskily [Black Jack, Age 25]," Nan Robertson, p. 45.

4700. 21 March 1972: "Garrison Petition Rejected [by U.S. Supreme Court, to Block Clay Shaw's $5 Million Damage Suit]," p. 35.

4701. 30 April 1972: "Nightclub Furnishings of Jack Ruby Are Sold [at Public Auction in Athens, Texas]," p. 53.

4702. 2 May 1972: "Jack Ruby's Club Safe Stolen Before Auction [Was Never Opened After Ruby Shot Oswald]," p. 17.

4703. 21 May 1972: "Bremer's Way of Life [Before Shooting Gov. George Wallace] Likened to 3 Assassins [Oswald, Ray, Sirhan, in Study by Dr. David Abrahamsen]," Boyce Rensberger, pp. 1, 48.

4704. 31 May 1972: "Kennedy Library Notes [55th] Birthday of President," p. 8.

4705. 6 June 1972: "Mrs. Onassis, in First Visit to Kennedy Center, Sees Bernstein Mass," Nan Robertson, p. 33.

4706. 7 June 1972: "Rites Held at Robert Kennedy's Grave [4 Years After Killing; Entire Family Then Visit JFK's Grave]," p. 30.

4707. 11 June 1972: "New Perjury Trial Ordered [by Louisiana Supreme Court for Dean A. Andrews, Jr., on Petition by Garrison and Andrews]," p. 34.

4708. 9 July 1972: "In Kabul, Connally Meets His Nov., '63, Dallas Doctor [from Parkland Hospital, James H. Duke, Now at Nangrahar University]," James P. Sterba, p. 15.

4709. 21 July 1972: "Fire Damages Texas Building Used in Kennedy Shooting [Arsonists' Damage of $5000]," p. 28.

4710. 3 Aug. 1972: "Texas Book Depository Reverts to Original Owner [D. Harold Byrd, After Foreclosure Against Aubrey Mayhew]," p. 31.

4711. 27 Aug. 1972: "Mystery Cloaks Fate of Brain of Kennedy [in Study by Dr. Cyril H. Wecht, Forensic Pathologist]," Fred B. Graham, pp. 1, 57.

4712. 12 Sept. 1972: "New Plan for Dallas Site [Citizens Committee Will Try to Buy Texas School Book Depository for Public]," p. 33.

4713.   15 Sept. 1972:   "Schmitz [American Party Candidate for President] Says U.S. Hides Data on Plot to Slay Wallace [and Likens This to JFK, MLK, and RFK Murders]," James T. Wooten, p. 24.

VOLUME CXXII

4714.   19 Oct. 1972:   "The Presidency: Too Soon [Since JFK] to Love Again," Priscilla McMillan, p. 47.

4715.   25 Oct. 1972:   "High Court Bars Doctor's Plea to See Kennedy Autopsy Data [by John Nichols, University of Kansas Pathologist, Suing Under Freedom of Information Act]," p. 10.

4716.   26 Oct. 1972:   "Mrs. Shriver Visits Brother's Memorial in Dallas [as First Visitor in Family to Assassination Site]," Christopher Lydon, p. 34.

4717.   8 Nov. 1972:   "Notes on People: [Sketch Alleged to Be Drawn by JFK and Signed Valued at $25,000]," p. 43.

4718.   17 Nov. 1972:   "Notes on People: [Mrs. Marina Oswald Porter Presses Federal Appeals Court in New Orleans for $500,000 from U.S. for Oswald's Confiscated Property; Denies He Was Assassin, Criminal or Wrongdoer]," p. 55.

4719.   21 Nov. 1972:   "Notes on People: [Mrs. RFK and Family Visit Both Kennedy Graves]," p. 39.

4720.   _____: "Actions Taken by the Supreme Court: Harassment: Refused to Consider Setting Aside a Court Order Barring Jim Garrison [from Perjury Prosecution Against Clay Shaw: No. 72-460, Shaw v. Garrison]," p. 39.

4721.   22 Nov. 1972:   "'With Your Guns and Drums and Drums and Guns Hurroo, Hurroo . . . Johnny, We Hardly Knew Ye [on Events the Morning of 22 Nov. 1963]," Kenneth P. O'Donnell, p. 35.

4722.   23 Nov. 1972:   "On Anniversary in Dallas: Mayor Wes Wise [Photo Inside New Memorial; Other Tributes at Arlington, Moscow and Elsewhere]," p. 38.

4723.   9 Dec. 1972:   "Johnson Feared War at Kennedy Death, Earl Warren Says," p. 25.

4724.   12 Jan. 1973:   "Books of The Times: Tears and Thoughts for J.F.K. [Review of Kenneth P. O'Donnell & David F. Powers Book, Also Henry Fairlie's The Kennedy Promise]," Christopher Lehmann-Haupt, p. 31.

4725.   10 Feb. 1973:   "[E. Howard] Hunt Linked to Talk of Spy on Kennedy [3 Brothers, for Nixon White House]," p. 38.

4726. 11 Feb. 1973: "Conspirator Lancaster [Shooting Begins on Film 'Executive Action' in May]," A. H. Weiler, p. 15D.

4727. 27 Feb. 1973: "Oswald Papers Valued at $17,700 by Court [Overturns Earlier Texas Court's Ruling of $3000]," p. 14.

4728. 27 March 1973: "Briefs on the Arts: Marginalia: Film on Kennedy Given [to LBJ Library, Austin, Accepts WFAA-TV's Complete Coverage of JFK's Murder]," p. 56.

4729. 30 March 1973: "Notes on People: [Repr. Bertram L. Podell Introduces U.S. Bill Moving Thanksgiving Day to 29 Nov. When It Falls on Anniversary of JFK Killing]," p. 35; (25 April 1973), p. 42.

4730. 12 May 1973: "Notes on People: A Government Settlement of $17,729 Was Awarded to Marina Oswald Porter [as Compensation for Oswald's Belongings]," p. 39.

4731. 25 May 1973: "Shaw-Garrison Suit Put Off [Indefinitely by U.S. District Judge Frederick J. R. Heebe; for $5 Million Damages]," p. 40.

4732. 30 May 1973: "At President's Grave: Mrs. Evelyn Lincoln, President Kennedy's Personal Secretary [on His 56th Birthday; Photo]," p. 14.

4733. 12 June 1973: "Film to Detail 'Plot' to Kill Kennedy ['Executive Action' Stars Burt Lancaster, Robert Ryan, Will Geer; Written by Dalton Trumbo, Donald Freed and Mark Lane]," Stephen Farber, p. 40.

4734. 19 Aug. 1973: "Items in Kennedy Death Are Going to Archives [Parkland Hospital's Equipment Used on JFK in Dallas Sent to Washington, for $1000 Compensation]," p. 64.

VOLUME CXXIII

4735. 16 Oct. 1973: "Notes on People: [Notices Article by Mrs. Onassis Remembering JFK, in McCall's, Nov.]," p. 39.

4736. 19 Oct. 1973: "Notes on People: [Notices Letter to The Miami Herald from Sen. Edward Kennedy Acknowledging Return of Cape Kennedy's Name to Canaveral; Thanks Locals for the Ten Year 'Honor']," p. 39.

4737. 4 Nov. 1973: "1963: Then [Events Prior to JFK's Murder]," William Manchester, pp. 37, 123-136: NYT Magazine.

4738. _____: "1963: Where They Are Now: The Camelotians [O'Donnell, Sorensen, Powers, McNamara, O'Brien, Salinger]," Donald Smith, pp. 38-39, 137-142, 150: NYT Magazine.

4739. 4 Nov. 1973: "1963: Formal Elegy," John Berryman,
pp. 40-41: NYT Magazine.

4740. 6 Nov. 1973: "Ford Favors Role for Congress [Nominee
for Vice-President Admits Book and Article Profits from Warren
Commission But Denies Documents He Used Were Classified],"
Marjorie Hunter, p. 22.

4741. 8 Nov. 1973: "N.B.C. Sued on Ads for Kennedy Film:
Makers of 'Executive Action' Ask Cancellation Damages," Louis
Calta, p. 48.

4742. _____: "Suspense Film Dramatizes Kennedy
Assassination [Reviews 'Executive Action']," Nora Sayre, p.
60.

4743. 9 Nov. 1973: "Notes on People: [Italian TV to Tape
10th Anniversary Program on JFK's Murder: Includes Salinger,
Schlesinger, Eugene McCarthy and John J. Marchi]," p. 37.

4744. 17 Nov. 1973: "President's Proclamation [Text Marks
Thanksgiving Day, 22 Nov., and Recalls JFK's Contribution],"
p. 22.

4745. 18 Nov. 1973: "November 22, 1963 [Review Book by
Daniel [sic] W. Belin]," George McMillan and Priscilla
Johnson, pp. 35-38: NYT Book Review.

4746. 21 Nov. 1973: "Notes on People: [Mrs. RFK and Family
at Arlington Commemorate Both Kennedy Graves: Photo]," p.
34.

4747. _____: "Mansfield [Senate Majority Leader]
Reads Senate His Elegy for John Kennedy," p. 39.

4748. 22 Nov. 1973: "Kennedy's Role in History: Some
Doubts [Amongst Scholars: Thomas Cronin, James MacGregor
Burns, Richard Neustadt, J. David Barber, etc.]," Robert
Reinhold, pp. 1, 46.

4749. _____: "[Editorial] Ten Years Later [JFK
Killing Ended Era of Optimism and Confidence]," p. 36.

4750. _____: "That Time We Huddled Together in Disbelief," Priscilla McMillan, p. 37.

4751. _____: "That Time We Huddled Together in Disbelief, Theodore C. Sorensen, p. 37.

4752. _____: "[Excerpts from] John Fitzgerald
Kennedy -- On the Day He Was Shot," Paul Engle, p. 37.

4753. _____: "Time Remembered: Abroad at Home,"
Anthony Lewis, p. 37.

4754. 22 Nov. 1973: "Kennedy, Nixon: 2 Faces of One Era,"
Clifton Daniel, p. 46.

4755. _____: "Critics Still Doubt Slayer Was Alone,"
Martin Waldron, p. 46.

4756. _____: "On Campus, Magic of Camelot Fades,"
p. 46.

4757. _____: "After 10 Years: W. Kemp Clark, Marina
Pruskova Oswald, Mrs. Marguerite Oswald, Mrs. Marie Tippit,
Sarah T. Hughes," p. 46.

4758. _____: "300 Honor Kennedy at Dallas Ceremony,"
p. 46.

4759. 23 Nov. 1973: "Kennedy Family Pays Tribute to
Murdered Brothers [Photo at Arlington Cemetery]," pp. 1, 70.

4760. _____: "Microfilm on Kennedy's Life to Be Presented to Library [19 Rolls of Over 30,000 Newspaper Clip-
pings]," p. 31.

4761. _____: "Gains by Gun Foes Few Over Decade
[Since JFK Murder]: Efforts for Stricter Control Laws Have
Produced Mostly Frustration," Ben A. Franklin, p. 70.

4762. 24 Nov. 1973: "Change, More Than a Sense of Tragedy,
Now Dominates Dallas," Anthony Ripley, p. 33.

4763. 25 Nov. 1973: "A Shabby Fiction About JFK [Reviews
'Executive Action' Film]," Vincent Canby, pp. 1D, 37D.

4764. 28 Nov. 1973: "[Pentagon Denies Rumor It Will Extin-
guish JFK Grave-Site Flame]," p. 32.

4765. _____: "Notes on People: [Caroline Kennedy
Loses Secret Service Guard on 16th Birthday]," p. 51.

4766. 10 March 1974: "Protecting the Fairness of a Trial:
Can It Be Overdone? [Using the Oswald Case as One Example],"
Anthony Lewis, p. 5E.

4767. 27 March 1974: "Garrison Not Guilty of U.S. Tax
Evasion [Acquitted Earlier of Bribery Charges]," p. 70

4768. 22 April 1974: "Kennedy's Opinion Polling Baffles
Moscow Audience [and Senator Voices Agreement With Warren
Report But Admits He Has Never Read It]," Hedrick Smith,
pp. 1, 16.

4769. 14 May 1974: "[U.S. Supreme] Court Backs Denial of
Kennedy Reports [on Freedom of Information Act Lawsuit by
Harold Weisberg Against F.B.I.: No. 73-1138, Justice Douglas
Dissenting]," p. 18.

4770.   30 May 1974:   "Honors His Brother [Sen. Edward Kennedy at Arlington on JFK's 57th Birthday: Photo]," p. 18.

4771.   2 June 1974:   "Psychiatrist Asserts Ruby Was Too Ill for '67 Trial [Dr. Tuteur of Loyola University, Chicago, in Current Issue of MH]," p. 38.

4772.   16 Aug. 1974:   "Clay Shaw Is Dead at 60; Freed in Kennedy 'Plot':   New Orleans Businessman Accused of Planning President's Murder," David Bird, p. 32.

VOLUME CXXIV

4773.   10 Nov. 1974:   "Program to Weigh Slaying of Kennedy ['Who Killed Kennedy?' to Be Presented at Rutgers University by Assassination Information Bureau of Cambridge, Mass.]," p. 107.

4774.   21 Nov. 1974:   "Notes on People: [Mrs. Ethel Kennedy and 4 Children Visit Graves of Murdered Brothers]," p. 59.

4775.   23 Nov. 1974:   "Notes on People: [Senator Edward Kennedy and Mrs. Ethel Kennedy at JFK's Grave on 22 Nov.; Mayor Wes Wise Gives Eulogy in Dallas]," p. 19.

4776.   _____ :   "C.I.A. and F.B.I. Had a Policy on Lying: Hid Identities of Agents, Allen Dulles Said in '64 [Admitted that Knowledge of Oswald Would Never Be Conceded: Reported by Harold Weisberg in Whitewash IV]," p. 48.

4777.   23 Jan. 1975:   "[Obituary] Rev. Oscar Huber, 81, Gave John Kennedy Last Rites," p. 36.

4778.   31 Jan. 1975:   "Boggs Says Father [Cong. Hale Boggs] Left F.B.I. Dossiers [That Had Been Collected to Discredit Critics of Warren Commission]," p. 31.

4779.   3 Feb. 1975:   "Critics of Warren Report Meet to Ask New Study [Sponsored by the Assassination Information Bureau in Cambridge, Mass., With Mark Lane as Overseer]," John Kifner, p. 14.

4780.   13 Feb. 1975:   "F.B.I. Director [Clarence Kelley] Bars New Dallas Inquiry," p. 40.

4781.   23 Feb. 1975:   "Data on Oswald Apparently Withheld from Key Warren Investigation Aides [J. Edgar Hoover's Memorandum and State Dept. Memoranda]," Ben A. Franklin, p. 32.

4782.   23 Feb. 1975:   "Kennedys Are Satisfied on Murder Findings [According to Eunice Kennedy Shriver]," p. 33.

4783.   8 March 1975:   "Rockefeller Unit Said to Check Report of C.I.A. Link to Kennedy Assassination," John M. Crewdson, p. 11.

4784. 10 March 1975: "6 Democrats Here Critical of C.I.A.:
Representatives Draw 800 to East Side Meeting [on Connections
with JFK Assassination]," Paul L. Montgomery, p. 49.

4785. 20 March 1975: "The Kennedy Transcripts [Reviews
Benjamin Bradley's Conversations With Kennedy, in Attempt to
Make JFK Appear More Manipulative Than Ex-President Nixon],"
William Safire, p. 39; (1 April 1975), p. 34; (17 April 1975),
p. 39; (29 Oct. 1975), p. 34.

4786. 27 March 1975: "[Dick] Gregory Testimony Cited [Before
Rockefeller Commission on C.I.A.'s Complicity in JFK Murder],"
p. 28.

4787. _____: "TV: Two Programs Exploit Subjects:
Dallas Assassination Viewed by Rivera," John J. O'Connor, p.
61.

4788. 4 April 1975: "President [Gerald R. Ford] Upholds The
Warren Report on Oswald's Guilt," p. 13.

4789. 5 April 1975: "Panel Aide Discounts Evidence of C.I.A.
Link in Kennedy Death [David W. Belin, Executive Director to
Rockefeller Commission]," p. 15.

4790. 10 April 1975: "'Time' Yielding Custody of Kennedy-
Death Film [Returns Original to Zapruder Heirs According to
Original Contract and They Will Place It in National Ar-
chives]," p. 35.

4791. 21 April 1975: "A.D.A. Urges Jobs and Indochina Aid
[as Well as Reopening of JFK Murder Investigation]," p. 17.

4792. 23 April 1975: "Books of The Times: John F. Kennedy's
Table Talk [Reviews Benjamin Bradley, Conversations With
Kennedy]," Christopher Lehmann-Haupt, p. 41.

4793. 26 April 1975: "Johnson in '69 Suspected Foreign Ties
With Oswald," Murray Illson, p. 12.

4794. _____: "Autopsy Studied Again [of JFK, by Lt.
Col. Robert McMeekin and Werner U. Spitz for Rockefeller
Commission in Response to Dick Gregory's Allegations]," p.
12.

4795. 27 April 1975: "The Nation: One More Theory on
Assassination [from Marianne Means, Confidante to LBJ]," p.
4E.

4796. 29 April 1975: "Helms [Ex-Director C.I.A.] Terms
Newsman [Daniel Schorr] 'Killer' for Hint of Murders by
C.I.A.," p. 10.

4797. 4 May 1975: "Assassination Is a Subject That Just
Won't Go Away: The Rockefeller Commission Has Been Forced
to Add It to the Agenda," Daniel Schorr, p. 3E.

4798. 4 May 1975: "Sunday Observer: Past Shock [and the JFK Murder as "Surefire for Nostalgia Salesmen" and "the Myth of a Golden Moment Lost in an Instant,"]," Russell Baker, p. 6: NYT Magazine.

4799. 8 May 1975: "Castro Urges U.S. to Ease Embargo [and Categorically Denies Any Cuban Involvement in JFK Murder]," p. 11.

4800. 9 May 1975: "[Sen] McGovern's Plan Scores With Cubans [in Cuba, Where Premier Castro Again Denies Cuban Connections With JFK's Death]," p. 2.

4801. 10 May 1975: "CBS Reports K.G.B. Held Oswald Unstable [According to Defector to U.S., Lt. Col. Yuri Nosenko]," p. 10.

4802. _____ : "[Sen. Edward Kennedy Quoted on Satisfaction with Governmental Investigations But Will Support Review If New Evidence Appears]," p. 10.

4803. 12 May 1975: "3 Men Studied in Kennedy Assassination Photos: 2 'Vagrants' in Picture Said to Resemble Watergate's Hunt and Sturgis: [Study for Rockefeller Commission]," p. 10.

4804. 13 May 1975: "Wide C.I.A. Spying at Home Is Denied: But Dillon, on Rockefeller's Panel, Says There Were One or Two Exceptions [But That Won't Alter Warren Report]," Nicholas M. Horrock, pp. 1, 13.

4805. 16 May 1975: "Warren Commission Backed by Surgeon [Dr. James Carrico, Who Attended JFK in Dallas After Shooting]," p. 13.

4806. 5 June 1975: "Nixon Never Did [the Dirty Deeds That Modern Democratic Presidents Have Done---And Gotten Away With!]," William Safire, p. 37.

4807. 8 June 1975: "Tough Guys in the Years of Kennedy's Presidency: 'Hard-Nosed' Was Good; 'Idealistic' Was Scorned [Breeding a Culture That Condoned Selective Violence]," Richard J. Walton, p. 3E.

4808. 10 June 1975: "Ford Will Submit [Rockefeller] Report on C.I.A. to Attorney General for Review, With Data on Assassination Issue . . . Public Release Is Curbed," James M. Naughton, pp. 1, 20.

4809. 11 June 1975: "C.I.A. Panel [Rockefeller Commission] Finds 'Plainly Unlawful' Acts That Improperly Invaded American Rights [Also Finds Support for Warren Report: Full Text]," Nicholas M. Horrock, pp. 1, 18-20, 21.

4810. _____ : "Democrats Accuse President of Avoiding Major Questions in C.I.A. Investigation: Omissions on Issues of Killings Noted," Christopher Lydon, p. 21.

4811. 12 June 1975: "Doctor [Cyril H. Wecht] Says Rockefeller Panel Distorted His View on Kennedy," p. 23.

4812. 20 July 1975: "Luck and the C.I.A. [Announces Publication of Coup d'Etat in America, by Michael Canfield and
Alan J. Weberman]," p. 5F.

4813. 21 July 1975: "New Study Urged in Kennedy Death:
[Sen.] Schweiker Sees Evidence of Castro Involvement," Edward
Cowan, p. 27.

4814. 24 Aug. 1975: "Conspiracy to the Left of US! Paranoia to the Right of US!: . . . the Defects of Education
That Let Their Theories Flourish," Mark Harris, pp. 12-13,
49-54: NYT Magazine.

4815. 31 Aug. 1975: "F.B.I. Says Oswald Threatened Agent,"
p. 24.

4816. 2 Sept. 1975: "Dallas Ex-Police Chief [J. E. Curry]
Alleges an F.B.I. Cover-Up on Oswald," p. 12..

4817. 5 Sept. 1975: "Letters to the Editor: Of Jack Ruby
and His Connections [with Chicago Union Leaders]," Mark
Lane, p. 28.

4818. 8 Sept. 1975: "Schweiker Seeking Inquiry on Kennedy
[and Warren Report]," p. 12.

4819. 9 Sept. 1975: "A Poison Linked to C.I.A. Reported
Found at Base: [Senator Schweiker Again Asks JFK Inquiry
But Sen. Church and Sen. Tower Oppose It]," Nicholas M.
Horrock, pp. 1, 27.

4820. _____ : "President Kennedy's Birthplace Damaged
in Apparent Busing Protest [in Brookline, Mass.]," p. 28;
(26 Oct. 1975), 5XX.

4821. 11 Sept. 1975: "Assassination Study Bid Blocked by
Coast Senate [California Assembly Supports Move to Reopen
JFK Case But Senate Defeats Same 27 to 6]," p. 47.

4822. 14 Sept. 1975: "Ford Vows Curb on Social Outlays:
[in Dallas Amidst Tight Security, Also Rejects Reopening of
JFK Investigation]," James M. Naughton, pp. 1, 32.

4823. 16 Sept. 1975: "Ex-Texas Official Seeking Study of
F.B.I. - Oswald Ties [Former Attorney General Waggoner Carr,
in Letters to Both Texas Senators]," p. 19.

4824. 17 Sept. 1975: "F.B.I. Chiefs Linked to Oswald File
Loss," Martin Waldron, pp. 1, 21.

VOLUME CXXV

4825.   21 Sept. 1975:   "Oswald Calls to Embassies Reported
Taped by C.I.A. [Eight Weeks Before JFK Killed, to Cuban and
Russian Embassies in Mexico City]," Nicholas M. Horrock, pp.
1, 49.

4826.   22 Sept. 1975:   "Texas Depository Offered for Sale
[Again, by D. Howard Byrd, After 1972 Foreclosure on Aubrey
Mayhew by Republic National Bank of Dallas]," p. 36.

4827.   10 Oct. 1975:   "Senators Raise New Doubts on Warren
Report Relating to Purported Soviet Defector [Lt. Col. Yuri
Nosenko, Suspect as KGB 'Plant']," John M. Crewdson, p. 19.

4828.   12 Oct. 1975:   "The Warren Commission Didn't Know
Everything: But Withheld Information Is Unlikely to Change
the Conclusion," Nicholas M. Horrock, p. 4E.

4829.   14 Oct. 1975:   "Panel Studies F.B.I. Links to Oswald
and Ruby in '63 [the U.S. House Sub-Committee, Rep. Don
Edwards, Chairman]," Nicholas M. Horrock, pp. 1, 16.

4830.   16 Oct. 1975:   "Schweiker Predicts Collapse of Warren
Report on Kennedy," p. 28.

4831.   19 Oct. 1975:   "The Nation: One More Probe of
Assassination [of JFK, by Rep. Don Edwards, Chairman of
House Civil and Constitutional Rights Subcommittee]," p. 4E.

4832.   20 Oct. 1975:   "Schweiker Joins Attack on Warren
Report as Clamor for New Inquiry Rises [Reports on Convention
of Warren Critics at University of Hartford, 10-12 Oct., With
Lane and Garrison]," Martin Waldron, p. 16.

4833.   22 Oct. 1975:   "Justice Department Decides Against
Prosecution [of F.B.I. Agents] in Destruction of Note from
Oswald," John M. Crewdson, p. 25.

4834.   26 Oct. 1975:   "The Nation: Nothing Is Clear on Oswald
Letter [and the F.B.I.'s Contradictory Statements]," p. 3E.

4835.   30 Oct. 1975:   "Tap on Marina Oswald's Room Reported by
Ex-F.B.I. Official: He Says Warren Commission Was Not Told
of Action After Kennedy Death," John M. Crewdson, p. 34.

4836.   _____: "About the Evidence [Against Oswald and
Now Against Warren Commission, By a Staff-Member]," John Hart
Ely, p. 39.

4837.   3 Nov. 1975:   "Ford Acts to Bar Death Plot Data: Asks
Senators Not to Reveal Details of U.S. Activities Against
Foreign Chiefs [and Protects Secrecy of C.I.A. File for 22
Nov. 1963]," Nicholas M. Horrock, pp. 1, 11.

4838.   8 Nov. 1975:   "Jaworski Says He Cleared Bush: Defends C.I.A. Nominee in 1970 Fund-Raising Issue [Also, That a Blow-Up of JFK Assassination Photo Disproves E. Howard Hunt's Presence]," James P. Sterba, p. 28.

4839.   ]2 Nov. 1975:   "Church Urges Senate to Reject Ford's Nomination of Bush as Intelligence Chief and Strongly Backs C.I.A.:   Testimony on Castro Plots [and JFK Killing, Given by David W. Belin]," Nicholas M. Horrock, p. 31.

4840.   13 Dec. 1975:   "Kennedy Bomb Suspect Dies [Richard Pavlick, 88, Who Plotted to Make Himself a Human Bomb in Dec. 1960 in Palm Beach, to Blow-Up JFK]," p. 44.

4841.   16 Nov. 1975:   "Defending the Dollar When Kennedy Was Shot [Excerpt from 'The Arena of International Finance,' to be Published July 1976 by John Wiley & Sons, Inc.]," Charles A. Coombs, pp. 1F, 16F.

4842.   23 Nov. 1975:   "Senator Edward M. Kennedy and Mrs. Robert F. Kennedy Visiting the Grave of President John F. Kennedy [Photo]," p. 1.

4843.   _____: "Warren Panel Aide Calls for 2d Inquiry into Kennedy Killing [David W. Belin Confident It Would Not Upset Warren Commission on Oswald]," Nicholas M. Horrock, pp. 1, 49.

4844.   _____: "Students Lay Wreath [from John F. Kennedy High School, San Antonio, Where JFK on 21 Dec. 1963 Promised to Return for School's Dedication]," p. 49.

4845.   _____: "The Assassination That Will Not Die [Because of "Irresponsible Polemics" by Critics of Warren Report]," James R. Phelan, pp. 28-29, 109-111, 120-132:   NYT Magazine.

4846.   26 Nov. 1975:   "Film Analysis Backs Warren Report [by Itek Corp., Lexington, Mass.]," p. 37.

4847.   27 Nov. 1975:   "Ford Would Sift New Data in Kennedy, King Slayings [Text of Presidential Conference]," Nicholas M. Horrock, pp. 1, 17, 42-43.

4848.   _____: "Kennedy Death Inquiry Urged [by Mass. House on Voice Vote]," p. 68.

4849.   1 Dec. 1975:   "[Editorial for New JFK Inquiry]: Restoring Faith," p. 30.

4850.   _____: "Schlesinger and Kissinger [Also, the Failure of "American Judicial Authorities to Uncover the Assassins and to Clear Up the Crime" of JFK's Murder]," Alexander I. Solzhenitsyn, p. 31.

4851.   4 Dec. 1975: "Notes on People: Eunice Kennedy Shriver Joined the Kennedy Family Members on Record Against Reinvestigation [of JFK's Murder]," p. 82.

4852.   6 Dec. 1975: "A Critic's View of the Warren Commission Report," Jerry Policoff, p. 29.

4853. 10 Dec. 1975: "Kennedy and Castro: 'No Smoking Gun But . . .' [Kennedy's "Machismo" and the Sen. Smather's Interview 4 Months After JFK's Death]," Richard J. Walton, p. 47.

4854. 11 Dec. 1975: "F.B.I. Chief Asks Accounting in Harrassment of King [and Links of JFK with the Mafia by way of Girlfriend, Judith Campbell]," p. 27.

4855. 13 Dec. 1975: "Agent Tells Fate of Oswald Note: [James P. Hosty, Jr.] Says He Flushed It Down Drain on Order of Chief of F.B.I. in Dallas [J. Gordon Shanklin]," p. 56.

4856. 15 Dec. 1975: "The President's Friend [Unnamed Female Connected with Mafia]," William Safire, p. 31; (27 Dec. 1975), p. 16.

4857. 16 Dec. 1975: "[Sen.] Church Denies Cover-Up of a Kennedy Friendship [Text of Senate Select Committee on Intelligence's Report Pertinent to JFK]," John M. Crewdson, pp. 1, 45.

4858. 18 Dec. 1975: "Kennedy Friend Denies Plot Role [Judith Campbell Exner Interviewed]," John M. Crewdson, pp. 1, 52.

4859. 20 Dec. 1975: "More Disclosures by Kennedy Friend Promised [Judith Campbell Exner's Proposed Book or TV Interview]," p. 28.

4860. 21 Dec. 1975: "Addendum to the Kennedy Years [the Murder and the Girl Friend]," p. 1E.

4861. 22 Dec. 1975: "Murder Most Foul: Essay [on JFK-Mafia Relations and the Murder of Sam Giancana on Eve of His Testifying to Sen. Church's Committee]," William Safire, p. 29.

4862. 23 Dec. 1975: "Presidential Privacy: A Question: Kennedy Disclosure Raises Problem for Reporters," Martin Arnold, p. 23.

4863. 24 Dec. 1975: "Notes on People: Kenneth P. O'Donnell [Asserts Disclosure of JFK's Girl-Friend Part of Campaign to Get the Kennedys]," p. 27.

4864.   4 Jan. 1976: "Letters: Uncomfortable Doubts; Bullet Proof? [Provoked by James Phelan's Earlier Article, with His Reply]," Kristin W. Henry, and Carl [sic] H. Wecht, p. 40: NYT Magazine.

4865.   4 Jan. 1976:   "More Arguments on the Assassination
[Reviews Robert Sam Anson, 'They've Killed the President!',
and Hugh C. McDonald, Appointment in Dallas,]," David C.
Anderson, pp. 18-20:   NYT Book Review.

4866.   5 Jan. 1976:   "Put Your Dreams Away: The Sinatra
Connection: Essay [on Judith Campbell Exner and JFK and the
Mafia]," William Safire, p. 29;   (26 Jan. 1976) p. 23; (29
Jan. 1976), p. 33.

4867.   15 Jan. 1976:   "Mrs. Exner Plans a Book on Kennedy
Friendship," John M. Crewdson, p. 14.

4868.   29 Jan. 1976:   "Slain Kennedys Called 'Most Dangerous
Men' [by William M. Kunstler, Who Is 'Not Entirely Upset' by
Assassinations]," p. 28.

4869.   1 Feb. 1976:   "[Editorial, Attacking Kunstler's Re-
mark]: Condoning Murder," p. 16E.

4870.   6 Feb. 1976:   "[Sen. James] Buckley Asks Bar to Find
Kunstler Unfit to Practice," p. 59.

4871.   10 Feb. 1976:   "Letters to the Editor: Kunstler on
Violence," William M. Kunstler, p. 36.

4872.   14 Feb. 1976:   "Notes on People: Judith Campbell
Exner [Sues F.B.I. for File on Her]," p. 17; (6 March 1976),
p. 13.

4873.   24 Feb. 1976:   "Remarks on Kennedys Explained by
Kunstler [Emphasizing His Grief]," p. 27.

4874.   25 Feb. 1976:   "Oswald's Gun Fired 2 Shots, Expert
Says [Dr. John K. Lattimer]," p. 16.

4875.   4 March 1976:   "Inside Church's Bunker [Previews
Senate Committee Report]," William Safire, p. 31.

4876.   21 March 1976:   "C.I.A. Memo Says Warren Unit Slighted
Leads on Foreign Plot [Cuban]," p. 36.

4877.   22 March 1976:   "Cuban Defector, Cited by C.I.A.,
Hinted Oswald Link to Havana [Unnamed]," p. 23.

4878.   25 March 1976:   "C.I.A. Held Russian With Oswald Data
[Yuri Nosenko]," p. 11.

4879.   1 April 1976:   "House Panel Rejects Assassination Inquiry [Rules Committee, 9 to 6, Proposed by Thomas N. Downing
and Henry B. Gonzalez]," p. 38.

4880.   6 April 1976:   "[New Jersey Senate Passes Resolution
Supporting New JFK Murder Inquiry]," Alfonso A. Narvaez, p.
75.

4881.   10 April 1976:   "Notes on People: Judith Campbell
Exner [Sued by Lawyer for Breach of Contract Over Book]," p.
21.

4882.   12 April 1976:   "Link of Kennedy Friend to Mafia Is
Still a Puzzle," Nicholas Gage, pp. 1, 26; (13 April 1976)
pp. 1, 22; (14 April 1976) pp. 1, 18.

4883.   13 April 1976:   "[Obituary] Sol A. Dann, Who Won
Reversal of Ruby's Death Sentence, Dies," p. 36.

4884.   22 April 1976:   "Government Appeals Order to Turn
Over Exner Files," p. 30.

4885.   25 April 1976:   "Court Refuses Mrs. Exner Quick
Access to F.B.I. File," p. 28.

4886.   13 May 1976:   "Oswald Not in 1963 Million-Name Secret
Service File," Peter Kihss, p. 10.

4887.   14 May 1976:   "Panel Says It Has New Evidence on Why
Oswald Shot Kennedy [Senate Select Committee, Sen. Frank
Church, Chairman]," p. 10.

4888.   15 May 1976:   "Senator [Schweiker] Says Agencies
Lied to Warren Panel," p. 13.

4889.   21 May 1976:   "Data Said to Show F.B.I. Knew of
C.I.A. Plot on Castro in '63," p. 10.

4890.   27 May 1976:   "Report on Oswald to Be Made Public
[by Senate Intelligence Committee, 8 to 2]," p. 38.

4891.   28 May 1976:   "Senate Unit Defers Inquiry on Kennedy
[Murder, 6 Months, According to Sen. Daniel Inouye]," p. 13D.

4892.   30 May 1976:   "President Kennedy Is Remembered:
Evelyn Lincoln [His Personal Secretary, at Arlington on His
59th Birthday: Photo]," p. 1.

4893.   24 June 1976:   "F.B.I.-C.I.A. Laxity on Kennedy Found:
Senate Unit Sees No Proof of '63 Assassination Plot, But
Asks New Study," David Binder, pp. 1, 8.

4894.   25 June 1976:   "Kennedy and Castro: Reports of
Possible Cuban Links to 1963 Assassination Seen as Basis
for Study [in Senate Report]," David Binder, p. 12.

4895.   _____: "Johnson Is Quoted on Kennedy Death
[by Howard K. Smith, ABC-TV, That Cuban Connection Existed],"
p. 12.

4896.   27 June 1976:   "The Nation: C.I.A. and F.B.I.
Accused in the J.F.K. Inquiries," p. 3E.

4897.   2 July 1976:   " Editorial on Senate Committee's Report : Burglaries, Lies . . .," p. 26.

4898.   29 July 1976: "Notes on People: In Miami, E. Howard
Hunt Filed a $2.5 Million Lawsuit [Against Canfield and
Weberman, for Book Alleging He Planned JFK Murder]," p. 37.

4899.   15 Sept. 1976: "House Inquiry Into Killing of
Kennedys and King Due [According to Speaker Carl Albert],"
p. 24; (16 Sept. 1976) p. 30; CXXVI, (18 Sept. 1976) p. 1.

VOLUME CXXVI

4900.   19 Sept. 1976: "The Nation: Congress Votes JFK
Probe," p. 2E.

4901.   5 Oct. 1976:   "Assassination Panel Names Top Counsel:
Lawyer Who Sent Boyle to Prison Will Head Inquiry Into Kill-
ing of President Kennedy and Dr. King [Richard A. Sprague],"
Ben A. Franklin, p. 17.

4902.   10 Oct. 1976: "Ford Presses Drive to Gain Texas Votes
[Rides Through Dallas in Open Limousine]," Charles Mohr, p.
1.

4903.   13 Nov. 1976: "Hoover Is Said to Have Been Told
Oswald Disclosed Plans to Cubans: 1964 Memo Reportedly
Quotes an Informant on Talk With Castro About Assassination,"
p. 9.

4904.   14 Nov. 1976: "House Unit Will Get Memo Saying Oswald
Planned to Kill Kennedy," Nicholas M. Horrock, p. 30.

4905.   16 Nov. 1976: "House Panel Picks 170 to Investigate
Kennedy and King Slayings," p. 20.

4906.   18 Nov. 1976: "House Panel Issues Subpoenas in Inquiry on 2 Assassinations," p. 17.

4907.   _____: "Dallas Cancels Kennedy Memorial [Mayor
Robert Folsom Cites "Declining Local Interest"]," p. 20.

4908.   19 Nov. 1976: "House Panel on Assassinations Denies
Planning Visit to Cuba," p. 12.

4909.   21 Nov. 1976: "[Judge Harold R.] Medina Warns Press
Not to Accept Bar Group's Fair-Trial Guidelines [Drafted in
Wake of JFK Murder]," Deirdre Carmody, p. 62.

4910.   _____: "Why Another Assassination Inquiry?:
Suspicions of Bungling and Coverup Still Linger," David
Binder, p. 4E.

4911.   21 Nov. 1976:   "Assassination Panel Organizing," p. 4E.

4912.   23 Nov. 1976:   "[Photo] The 13th Anniversary of President John F. Kennedy's Assassination [Family at Arlington; Observances at Boston and Dallas]," p. 16.

4913.   26 Nov. 1976:   "[Editorial on House Inquiry]: The Truth Heals," p. 22.

4914.   6 Dec. 1976:   "2 Named to Assassination Study [from N.Y. County District Attorney's Office]," p. 38.

4915.   10 Dec. 1976:   "Assassination Study Requests $13 Million: House Panel Supports Bid for Funds to Investigate the Slayings of President Kennedy and Dr. King," David Burnham, p. 19.

4916.   15 Dec. 1976:   "3 More New York Investigators to Join Assassination Inquiry [from District Attorney's Office and Homicide Police Division]," p. 29.

4917.   19 Dec. 1976:   "Kennedy Home Is Reopened [After Firebombing Year Ago in Brookline, Mass.]," p. 38; (2 Jan. 1977), 3XX, 13XX.

4918.   1 Jan. 1977:   "House Panel Seeks to Continue Inquiry Into Assassinations," David Burnham, p. 4.

4919.   2 Jan. 1977:   "Counsel in Assassination Inquiry Often Target of Criticism [Richard A. Sprague]," David Burnham, p. 38; (9 Jan. 1977), p. 2.

4920.   6 Jan. 1977:   "Assassination Panel Is Warned on Its Techniques," David Burnham, p. 18.

4921.   _____: "Bullet to Be Tested [Found at JFK Murder Site 2 Years Ago]," p. 18.

4922.   _____: "[Editorial on House Committee's JFK Inquiry]: Blank Checks and Fearful Fantasies," p. 28.

4923.   7 Jan. 1977:   "House Assassination Panel Unlikely to Get 6.5 Million [Dollars]," p. 8.

4924.   12 Jan. 1977:   "New Assassination Panel Is Blocked," David Burnham, p. 6B.

4925.   22 Jan. 1977:   "[President] Carter Chooses Desk Once Used by Kennedy," p. 11.

4926.   25 Jan. 1977:   "Assassination Panel Facing Budget Trim: House Majority Leader Predicts Inquiry Will Be Continued, But Not With 'Grandiose' Funds," David Burnham, p. 17.

4927. 25 Jan. 1977: "Letters: How Not to Investigate
Assassination," Paul G. Wallach, p. 34.

4928. 26 Jan. 1977: "Assassination Action Delayed By House
Unit," p. 14.

4929. 29 Jan. 1977: "Sprague Denies Conflict in Roles as
Prosecutor [of W. A. Boyle for Murder in 1974]," p. 17.

4930. 1 Feb. 1977: "Inquiry on Assassinations Losing Favor
in House: Electronic Surveillance Opposed," David Burnham,
p. 15.

4931. 2 Feb. 1977: "House Panel Limits Assassinations Inquiry to 2 Months [with Budget of $84,000 Per Month]," David
Burnham, p. 9.

4932. 3 Feb. 1977: "House Gives Assassination Panel
Authority to Continue Temporarily," David Burnham, p. 21.

4933. 4 Feb. 1977: "Assassination Panel Head [Rep. Henry B.
Gonzalez] Cites Conspiracy Data," p. 8.

4934. 5 Feb. 1977: "Qualms About the House's Assassination
Investigation," George McMillan, p. 19.

4935. 6 Feb. 1977: "The Nation: Assassination Panel Extended," p. 2E.

4936. 11 Feb. 1977: "Sprague Ouster Is Upset by Panel on
Assassination: Counsel Told to Ignore Chairman's Order [from
Rep. Gonzalez]," David Burnham, pp. 1, 28.

4937. 12 Feb. 1977: "Assassination Panel's Fate in Doubt
as Sprague Faces New Allegations," David Burnham, p. 11.

4938. _____: "[Editorial]: Assassination Probe,
Revisited," p. 20.

4939. 15 Feb. 1977: "Gonzalez Claims Key Support in Bid to
Oust Sprague," Juan Vasquez, p. 12.

4940. 17 Feb. 1977: "Panel Delays Action on Sprague; Gonzalez Terms Him 'Deceitful'," David Burnham, p. 24.

4941. 23 Feb. 1977: "Letters: Assassination Inquiry:
'To Find the Truth'," Henry B. Gonzalez, p. 22.

4942. 25 Feb. 1977: "Mafia Said to Have Slain Rosselli
Because of His Senate Testimony [about the C.I.A. and Cuban
Connections]," Nicholas Gage, pp. 1, 12.

4943. 26 Feb. 1977: "Compromise Offered in Inquiry Dead-
lock: House Leader [Jim Wright] Moves to Patch Up Quarrel
on Assassination Panel," Martin Tolchin, p. 10.

4944. 3 March 1977: "Gonzalez, Assailing His Committee,
Quits as Assassination Inquiry Head," David Burnham, pp. 1,
14.

4945. 4 March 1977: "Assassination Panel Wants 3 to Testify: O'Neill Says Move Is Seen as Way to Shore Up Dr. King
Inquiry--Witnesses Are Not Identified," David Burnham, p. 12.

4946. 5 March 1977: "Spokesman Denies That [the Late] H. L.
Hunt Ever Communicated With Oswald," p. 17.

4947. 6 March 1977: "Assassination Panel Mired in Problems:
Dissension That Imperils Inquiry Provides Insight into Workings of House and Its Staff System," David Burnham, p. 19.

4948. 9 March 1977: "Resignation of Gonzalez from
[Assassination's Inquiry] Panel Is Accepted," p. 14.

4949. 17 March 1977: "Underworld Figure Refuses to Talk
Before a House Assassination Panel [Santos Trafficante, Jr.],"
p. 23.

4950. 22 March 1977: "House Assassination Panel Cuts Budget
by Over Half for Year [From $6.5 to $2.5 Million]," p. 22.

4951. 29 March 1977: "Ray's Report of Bounty Checked [Also,
Oswald's Connections With F.B.I. and Anti-Castro Groups],"
p. 62.

4952. 30 March 1977: "Kennedy Inquiry Witness Is an Apparent
Suicide in Mansion in Florida [George de Mohrenschildt, Age
65]," p. 18.

4953. 31 March 1977: "House Votes to Keep Assassination
Panel After Sprague Quits: Inquiry Into Kennedy-King Slayings
Extended Through '78--Group Compliments Ex-Counsel," Richard
L. Madden, pp. 1, 13.

4954. _____: "Professor, 65, Who Killed Himself May
Have Been Oswald Confidant [George de Mohrenschildt's Death
Follows That of Giancana and Rosselli]," p. 14.

4955. 1 April 1977: "Ruby Introduced Oswald as C.I.A.
Agent, Woman Tells House Inquiry: [Also] Suicide Time Pin-
pointed," p. 6.

4956. 2 April 1977: "Witness Ties Oswald to Oilmen and
Cubans: [Willem Oltmans] Newsman Tells Panel That Suicide
Had Related Conspiracy Story," Wendell Rawls, Jr., pp. 1, 12.

4957. _____: "Sprague to Return to Yablonski Case
[in Re-Trial of W. A. Boyle]," p. 12.

4958. 3 April 1977: "Lawyer Says Texan Told Him Oswald Had
Aid in '63 Plot [Pat S. Russell, Attorney for George de
Mohrenschildt]," p. 17.

4959.   3 April 1977:   "Experts Examine Letter [Oswald to
H. L. Hunt, 8 Nov. 1963]," p. 17.

4960.   4 April 1977:   "Assertions About Oswald Confronting
House Group [Photo of Letter from Oswald to "Mr. Hunt"],"
Martin Waldron, p. 50.

4961. _____ :   "Reporter Who Testified Spent a Decade
Studying Kennedy's Assassination [Willem Oltmans]," p. 50.

4962.   5 April 1977:   "Warren Study Influence Laid to F.B.I.
by O'Neill [House Speaker]," p. 16.

4963.   7 April 1977:   "A 'McCarthy Era' Tactic in the
Assassination Committee [Staging Trafficante's Refusal to
Testify]," James Hamilton, p. 25.

4964.   11 April 1977:   "Interim Counsel Named to Assassinatio
Panel [Alvin B. Lewis, Jr., Replaces Sprague]," p. 12.

4965.   12 April 1977:   "Sprague Urges Carter to Set Up Inquiry into the Murders of Kennedy and Dr. King [By Special
Prosecutor]," Ben A. Franklin, p. 18.

4966. _____ :   "Dutch Journalist in Kennedy Case Is
'Half Showman', Colleague Says [Peter d'Hamacourt About
Willem Oltmans]," Wendell Rawls, Jr., p. 18.

4967.   24 April 1977:   "Reporters Are Criticized in Assassination Inquiry [Rep. Walter Fauntroy Says Some Might Be C.I.A
Operatives]," p. 18.

4968.   29 April 1977:   "House Adopts Budget of Assassination
Unit [213 to 192, for $2.5 Million]," p. 17.

4969.   1 May 1977:   "Book Ends: Marina and Lee [Reports
Publication of Priscilla McMillan's Book]," Richard R. Lingeman, p. 71:   NYT Book Review.

4970.   5 May 1977:   "Museum Acquires Kennedy Death Car [Henry
Ford Museum, Dearborn, Michigan Will Not Display It For
Several Years]," p. 17.

4971.   6 June 1977:   "House Inquiry Reported Fruitless on
Kennedy-King Assassinations," Wendall Rawls, Jr., pp. 1, 20.

4972.   8 June 1977:   "Ex-Castro Soldier Balks at House Heari
on Assassination of Kennedy [Loran E. Hall]," Wendall Rawls,
Jr., p. 15.

4973. _____ :   "[Editorial] Topics: Reprise [Calls fo
End of House Assassination Panel's "Charade" and Withdrawal
of Funds]," p. 20.

4974.   12 June 1977:   "Levels of Intelligence: Lane's Persistence [Mark Lane's Influence Behind Origins and Support
for Current House Assassinations' Inquiry]," p. 1E.

4975. 13 June 1977: "Ceremony for Kennedy Library [Spade-Turning By Entire Family for Building on Boston Harbor: Photo]," pp. 1, 18.

4976. _____ : "Frank & Jack & Sam & Judy [Reviews Judith Campbell Exner's Book, My Story, In Context of Sinatra, JFK and Giancana]," William Safire, p. 29.

4977. 21 June 1977: "Cornell Professor Is Named as Assassinations Panel Counsel [G. Robert Blakey, Introduced by Chairman Louis Stokes]," Wendall Rawls, Jr., p. 21.

4978. 24 June 1977: "Advertising: Agency Resigns Grove Press Account [Because of Potential for Litigation Over Judith Campbell Exner's Book, My Story]," Philip H. Dougherty, p. 9D.

4979. 3 July 1977: "Nonfiction in Brief: My Story by Judith Exner. As Told By Ovid Demaris," Jeff Greenfield, p. 10: NYT Book Review.

4980. 3 Sept. 1977: "Former Kennedy Aide Critically Ill [Kenneth P. O'Donnell, Age 53; Obituary Quotes Him About Third Shot That Struck JFK]," p. 38; (5 Sept.) p. 29; (7 Sept.) p. 12B; (9 Sept.) p. 6B; (10 Sept.) p. 28.

4981. 13 Sept. 1977: "Service for Kennedy Aide: Members of the Kennedy Family [in Boston for Kenneth O'Donnell's Funeral: Photo]," p. 34.

4982. 14 Sept. 1977: "[G. Gordon] Liddy Scores Lack of Secrecy in U.S. in Magazine Article [in Chic, "American Nightmare," Says Oswald May Have Acted for Castro]," p. 13.

VOLUME CXXVII

4983. 20 Sept. 1977: "ABC's Scheduling of Oswald Film Forces CBS to Hold Off Its Version ['The Trial of Lee Harvey Oswald' vs. 'Ruby and Oswald']," Les Brown, p. 81.

4984. 30 Sept. 1977: "'Oswald' As Imagined by ABC-TV [Review]," John J. O'Connor, p. 26C.

4985. 3 Oct. 1977: "[Editorial]: Fact, Fabrication and Docu-Drama [ABC Program on Oswald Condemned]," p. 30.

4986. 6 Oct. 1977: "Notes on People: [Former French Ambassador Herve Alphand, in His Published Diary, Notes JFK Vulnerable for His Amorous Behavior]," p. 2C.

4987. 9 Oct. 1977: "TV View: Playing Fast and Loose With Recent History [Reviews ABC Program on Oswald]," John J. O'Connor, p. 39D.

4988.   13 Oct. 1977:   "Oswald's Widow Tells of 'Very High
Level of Anger' at Him for the Legacy of Shame," Carey Winfrey, p. 12B; (21 Oct.) p. 30.

4989.   17 Oct. 1977:   "Assassination Panel Is Given Right to
Bypass House [for Powers of Subpoena from Courts]," Wendall
Rawls, Jr., p. 15.

4990.   30 Oct. 1977:   "The Heart of the Story [Reviews Pris-
cilla Johnson McMillan, Marina and Lee, and Michael Eddowes,
The Oswald File]," Thomas Powers, pp. 10, 46-47:   NYT Book
Review.

4991.   2 Nov. 1977:   "Watergate Burglar Arrested on Charge
of Coercion [Frank Sturgis Charged by Marita Lorenz, Who
Reports That He Was Linked With Oswald]," David Bird, p. 16;
(3 Nov.) p. 18.

4992.   4 Nov. 1977:   "F.B.I. Is Ready to Release File on
Slaying of President Kennedy [After More Than 50 Suits under
Freedom of Information Act: Over 30,000 Documents]," p. 17.

4993.   _____: "Police Studying Arrest of Sturgis, Who
Denies Threatening Accuser," Laurie Johnston, p. 2B.

4994.   5 Nov. 1977:   "Sturgis Is Cleared of Coercion Charges:
No Evidence Found That Watergate Figure Threatened Ex-Spy
[Marita Lorenz]," p. 24.

4995.   8 Nov. 1977:   "Court May Seek C.I.A. Kennedy File
[Federal District Judge John J. Sirica, on Plea by Bernard
F. Fensterwald]," p. 65.

4996.   23 Nov. 1977:   "Graveside Remembrance: The 14th
Anniversary [of JFK Murder: Photo at Arlington Cemetery],"
p. 10.

4997.   2 Dec. 1977:   "F.B.I. Records Trace Oswald and Bullets
Newly-Released Files Describe Inquiry into Kennedy Death,"
p. 17.

4998.   6 Dec. 1977:   "Supreme Court Roundup: Civil Rights
[To Review Right of Clay Shaw's Executor to Continue Suit
Against Garrison]," Warren Weaver, Jr., p. 34.

4999.   8 Dec. 1977:   "Hoover Was Certain Oswald Was Killer:
F.B.I. Files Don't Dispute Finding That Assassin Acted Alone:
Excerpts from Memo by Hoover," pp. 1, 20B.

5000.   _____: "Few Show Up to Read Files on the
Assassination [at F.B.I. Building; News Reporters and 4 from
Assassination Information Bureau Inc., Cambridge, Mass.],"
Marjorie Hunter, p. 20B.

5001.   8 Dec. 1977:   "Schoolgirl Makes F.B.I. List [Diane Fleddermann of St. Louis Wrote Hoover for Data on Oswald: F.B.I. File Created on Her]," p. 9B.

5002.   9 Dec. 1977:   "Around the Nation: F.B.I. Still Checks Tips on Kennedy Assassination," p. 18.

5003.   11 Dec. 1977:   "The Nation: Back to Basics and Lee Oswald," p. 3E.

5004.   15 Dec. 1977:   "F.B.I. Files Disclose Letter on Kennedy: Hoover Gave His Brother Report on Alleged Settlement of Suit and Sealing of Records [Jilted Woman Sued JFK in 1951 for $500,000]," Wendall Rawls, Jr., p. 20.

5005.   _____: "J. Edgar's Private Files [on JFK, the Jilted Lady and the Judith Campbell Affair]," William Safire, p. 31.

5006.   16 Dec. 1977:   "Letters: Kennedy Assassination: An 'Industry's' Promise," H[enry] D. Fairlie, p. 30.

5007.   22 Dec. 1977:   "New Files Released on Kennedy Death: Records Disclose Secret Service's Inquiry into the Assassination Concentrated on Cuban Aspect," p. 13.

5008.   26 Dec. 1977:   " C.I.A.   Cable Sought to Discredit Critics of Warren Report [Especially Edward Jay Epstein and Mark Lane]," p. 37.

5009.   8 Jan. 1978:   "[Advertisement]:   Help Solve JFK's Murder: $1,000,000 Reward: Americans for a Free Press, Columbus, Ohio: Larry Flynt, p. 45.

5010.   19 Jan. 1978:   "Files Show F.B.I. Rift With Warren Panel: Newly Released Data on Inquiry into President Kennedy Slaying Tell of Mistrust and Feuds [and Rep. Gerald Ford as J. Edgar Hoover's Spy on Panel]," p. 16.

5011.   8 Feb. 1978:   "TV: 'Ruby and Oswald' on CBS [Review]," John J. O'Connor, p. 20C.

5012.   5 March 1978:   "Oswald and the Russian Defector [Reviews Legend by Edward Jay Epstein]," Kevin Buckley, pp. 7, 35:   NYT Book Review.

5013.   25 March 1978:   "House Panel Is Pressing Inquiries on Assassinations Amid Secrecy [Public Hearings Begin in September, Another for November]," Marjorie Hunter, p. 6.

5014.   27 March 1978:   "Oswald Link to C.I.A. Reported at Inquiry: Ex-Employee of Agency [James B. Wilcott] Tells Panel That he Heard Figure in Kennedy Killing Was an Agent in Japan," Nicholas M. Horrock, p. 14.

5015.   12 May 1978:   "TV Weekend: [Reviews WOR Program]
'The Assassination of President Kennedy: What Do We Know
Now That We Didn't Know Then?'" John J. O'Connor, p. 29C.

5016.   23 May 1978:   "Notes on People: [Robert Kennedy's
Note to His Oldest Daughter on JFK's Burial Day]," p. 4C.

5017.   16 June 1978:   "Notes on People: Jim Garrison [Sworn
in as Judge on State Court of Appeals in Louisiana's 4th Circuit, Makes 'Final' Self-Exculpatory Comment on JFK Case],"
p. 16.

5018.   20 June 1978:   "[Editorial]:   Clay Shaw's Lost Cause
[Criticizes U.S. Supreme Court's Ruling That Case Against
Garrison Ended With Shaw's Death]," p. 16.

5019.   1 Aug. 1978:   "Help Asked in Locating Assassination
Witnesses [By U.S. Congressional Committee, Specifically for
JFK Murder]," p. A13.

5020.   3 Aug. 1978:   "Cuba Says C.I.A. Fabricated Evidence
on Kennedy [Assassination, According to Charges Made at
Eleventh International Youth Festival, Havana]," Alan Riding,
p. A3.

5021.   8 Aug. 1978:   "Fund Request Under Fire [in U.S. Congress for House Committee on Assassinations, for an Extra
$790,000]," p. A10.

5022.   9 Aug. 1978:   "Around the Nation: House Holds Up
Funds for Assassination Panel," p. A16.

THE NEW YORK TIMES, STRIKE SUPPLEMENT

5023.   10 Aug. 1978:   "The House Select Committee on Assassinations Has Asked for Additional Funds [to Test Acoustical
Evidence in JFK Murder]," pp. 74-75.

5024.   13 Aug. 1978:   "The House Select Committee on Assassinations [and Contradictory Evidence with Warren Report],"
Nicholas M. Horrocks, p. 135.

5025.   15 Aug. 1978:   "Rep. Louis Stokes . . . as the Chairman of the House Select Committee on Assassinations [a Biographical Sketch]," Richard D. Lyons, pp. 8-9.

5026.   17 Aug. 1978:   "[Biographical Sketch of G. Robert
Blakey, Chief Legal Counsel for the House Select Committee
on Assassinations]," Edward C. Burks, pp. 17-18.

5027.   18 Aug. 1978:   "[The Tape That Threatens the Warren
Report's One-Gun Theory]," Bob Wieland, pp. 18-19.

5028. 18 Aug. 1978: "The Pistol That Police Say Jack Ruby
Used to Kill Lee Harvey Oswald. . .," p. 40.

5029. 19 Aug. 1978: "The House Select Committee on Assassinations Ended Its Initial . . . [Public Hearings, to Resume
in Sept.]," Nicholas M. Horrock, pp. 116-117.

5030. 20 Aug. 1978: "Authorities Will Try to Keep the Area
Around Dealey Plaza as Quiet as Possible Sunday Morning When
Acoustics Experts Record Gunfire . . .," p. 25.

5031. _____: "[House Committee Plans September
Hearings on JFK Murder]," Nicholas M. Horrock, p. 117.

5032. 21 Aug. 1978: "Shots Rang From the Old Texas School
Book Depository . . . as Acoustical Experts Tested . . .
[Theory of More Than One Rifle]," pp. 17-19.

5033. 22 Aug. 1978: "The Assassinations That Would Not Die,"
p. 27.

5034. _____: "CIA Director Stansfield Turner Says
the Agency Has Been Unable to Find a Supposed Memo [Linking
E. Howard Hunt with JFK in Dallas]," Tom DeCola, p. 79-80.

5035. 28 Aug. 1978: "The Dallas Morning News Said . . .
That at Least Five People Claim to Have Met Men Who Identi-
fied Themselves as Secret Service Agents in Dealey Plaza Just
Before . . . [JFK Killing]," pp. 22-23.

5036. 29 Aug. 1978: "Rep. Richardson Preyer of North
Carolina [Conducts Fact-Finding Tour to Havana on JFK Mur-
der]," p. 109.

5037. 30 Aug. 1978: "Rep. L. Richardson Preyer, D-N.C.,
. . . Said Tuesday His Fact-Finding Trip to Cuba Was Successful [Interviewing Witnesses Regarding JFK Murder]," p. 41.

5038. 4 Sept. 1978: "Fidel Castro . . . Has Denied Any
Complicity [in JFK's Death]; . . . Public Testimony by Yuri
Nosenko [Promised]," Nicholas M. Horrock, pp. 10-13.

5039. 7 Sept. 1978: "[The Zapruder Film Shown to House
Select Committee, and the Connallys Testify]," Nicholas M.
Horrock, pp. 123-124.

5040. 8 Sept. 1978: "John Connally of Texas . . . Re-Telling
the Ghoulish Story of President Kennedy's Murder [And JFK's
Political Plans]," James Reston, pp. 110-111.

5041. _____: "Eight Medical Experts Backed the
Warren Commission's Conclusion That There Was No Conspiracy
Behind John F. Kennedy's Assassination [But Dr. Cyril H.
Wecht Dissents on 'Magic Bullet' Theory]," pp. 124-126.

5042.   9 Sept. 1978: "A Ballistics Expert [Dr. Vincent P. Guinn Testifies That Neutron Activation Method Tends to Vindicate Warren Report on Bullet Fragments]," Jim Adams, pp. 11-13.

5043.   10 Sept. 1978: "Relying Heavily on Science, House Investigators Are Answering Some of the Nagging Questions About President John F. Kennedy's Assassination," Margaret Gentry, pp. 10-14.

5044.   11 Sept. 1978: "For Three Days Last Week, a House Select Committee on Assassinations Minutely Re-Examined [JFK's Murder]," Nicholas Horrock, pp. 64-65.

5045.   12 Sept. 1978: "[Dispute Over Tape-Recording and Possible Fourth Gun Shot at JFK According to Expert, James E. Barger]," Nicholas M. Horrock, pp. 24-25.

5046.   _____: "The Panel of Medical Experts . . . [Begin to Break Down Conspiracy Theories on JFK's Murder]," Tom Wicker, pp. 113-114.

5047.   13 Sept. 1978: "Former President Gerald R. Ford Is Expected to Testify Before the House Assassinations Committee," p. 51.

5048.   _____: "A Space Engineer and a Photo Analyst [Tom Canning and Calvin McCamy] Told Congress [Their Studies Support Warren Report's Single-Bullet Theory]," Margaret Gentry, pp. 90-91.

5049.   14 Sept. 1978: "[Marina Oswald Porter's Testimony to House Select Committee]," Nicholas M. Horrock, pp. 12-13.

5050.   15 Sept. 1978: "Lee Harvey Oswald's Widow . . . Believes He Did Murder the President," Jim Adams, pp. 9-10.

5051.   _____: "[House Select Committee Hears That Oswald Sent Picture of Himself With Rifle and Pistol to George de Mohrenschildt, Five Days Before Major General Walker Was Shot At]," Jim Davis, p. 104.

5052.   16 Sept. 1978: "Kennedy Hearings: Photograph Analysts [McCamy and Kirk] . . . Proved the Authenticity of Three Snapshots [of Oswald with Rifle]," Margaret Gentry, pp. 1-2.

5053.   _____: "Kennedy Hearings: The CIA Kept a Soviet Defector [Nosenko] Who Said He Had Information About Lee Harvey Oswald in Isolation for Three Years," Jim Adams, pp. 14-15.

5054.   17 Sept. 1978: "House Investigators Are Pointing Out Major Flaws in the Warren Commission's Work," Margaret Gentry, pp. 5-6.

5055.   19 Sept. 1978:   "The House Assassination Committee
. . . Told There May Be Some Support for a Report That Fidel
Castro Knew in Advance [of Threat to JFK]," Jim Adams, pp.
2-4.

5056.   20 Sept. 1978:   "Cuban President Fidel Castro Says It
Would Have Been 'a Tremendous Insanity' for Cuba to Have
Plotted [JFK's Murder]," Margaret Gentry, p. 1.

5057.   21 Sept. 1978:   "The Late J. Edgar Hoover Disciplined
17 FBI Employees for Not Having Lee Harvey Oswald on a List
of Subversives," Jim Adams, p. 3.

5058.   _____ :   "The House Select Committee on Assassinations [Links Ex-President Ford as FBI Informant on Warren
Commission]," Nicholas M. Horrocks, pp. 24-25.

5059.   22 Sept. 1978:   "Former Pres. Gerald Ford Denies He
Agreed to Secretly Inform FBI About Warren Commission Activities," p. 18.

5060.   23 Sept. 1978:   "Former CIA Director Richard Helms
Acknowledged Friday He Approved Three Years of Solitary Con-
finement [for Defector Nosenko, Regarding Oswald]," Jim
Adams and Margaret Gentry, pp. 7-10.

5061.   _____ :   "[CIA's Helms Asked Why Data Was Withheld from Warren Commission]," Margaret Gentry, pp. 24-26.

5062.   25 Sept. 1978:   "A Key Member of the House Assassina-
tions Committee [Rep. Richardson Preyer, Interviewed:
Committee Will Make Warren Report 'Persuasive']," William
Kronholm, p. 21.

5063.   _____ :   "Soviet Television Viewers Were Told
Sunday That JFK Assassination Was Part of Large Conspiracy,"
p. 29.

5064.   26 Sept. 1978:   "The 'Umbrella Man' . . . Testifies
[to House Committee, on JFK Murder]," Jim Adams, p. 9.

5065.   27 Sept. 1978:   "Earl Ruby Testified Tuesday That
[Brother Jack Ruby Killed Oswald Purely on Impulse]," p. 2.

5066.   28 Sept. 1978:   "A Cuban Exile [Jose Aleman, Talks
About Connections Between Mafia and Cuban Exiles and JFK
Murder]," Jim Adams, pp. 3-4.

5067.   29 Sept. 1978:   "Reputed Mafia Boss Santo Trafficante
Testified Thursday He Took Part in a CIA Plot to Murder Fidel
Castro [But Not JFK]," Jim Adams, pp. 11-12.

5068.   30 Sept. 1978:   "House Investigators Say They've Made
Little Headway [on Mafia's Connection to JFK Murder]," Margaret Gentry, p. 49.

5069.   23 Oct. 1978:   "[Ex-CIA Chief Helms and Ex-Attorney
General Katzenbach Policies Toward Soviet Defector Nosenko,
and Legend by Edward Jay Epstein]," William Safire, pp. 37-
38.

THE NEW YORK TIMES
VOLUME CXXVIII

5070.   16 Nov. 1978:   "Editorial: On Laying Murders to Rest
[of J. F. Kennedy and M. L. King]," p. A26.

5071.   22 Nov. 1978:   "Editorial: November 22," p. A18.

5072.   _____: "Notes on People: Judge at '63 Swear-
ing in Looks Back in Candor [Sarah T. Hughes, now 82, Federal
District Judge]," p. C8.

5073.   23 Nov. 1978:   "[Photo]:   Senator Edward M. Kennedy
at the Grave of President John F. Kennedy . . . ." p. C18.

5074.   26 Nov. 1978:   "New Evidence Is Hinted in Assassination
Film [Taken By Charles L. Bronson of Ada, Oklahoma, and Reported in The Dallas Morning News]," p. 35.

5075.   27 Nov. 1978:   "Film Said to Show Oswald Had Help:
But Footage Shot By an Amateur Prior to the Kennedy Murder
Is Inconclusive to Some," Wendell Rawls, Jr., p. B15.

5076.   29 Nov. 1978:   "Federal Agencies Creating a Plan for
Inquiries into Assassinations [Specifically, the F.B.I.],"
Wendell Rawls, Jr., p. A23.

5077.   18 Dec. 1978:   "Assassinations Study May Be Inconclusive," p. A15.

5078.   22 Dec. 1978:   "Panel Told of 4 Shots at Kennedy," p.
A16.

5079.   23 Dec. 1978:   "House Panel Plans Public Hearing on
Hint of a 2d Kennedy Gunman," p. 19.

The Washington Post
VOLUME CI

5080.   8 Jan. 1978:   "[Advertisement by Larry Flynt]:   Help
Solve JFK's Murder: $1,000,000 Reward," p. A5.

5081.   17 Jan. 1978:   "Critic to Get Free FBI Set of JFK
Files [Harold Weisberg]," George Lardner, Jr., A4.

5082.   19 Jan. 1978:   "FBI Weighed Posters Depicting Oswald
as a Marxist [Plan to Distribute Anonymously, Two Months
After Assassination, Approved by J. Edgar Hoover, Rejected
by His Aide]," George Lardner, Jr., A8.

5083.   20 Jan. 1978:   "Documents Show Ford Promised FBI Data
- Secretly - About Warren Probe [After Commission's First
Meeting]," George Lardner, Jr., p. A10.

5084.   1 Feb. 1978:   "A Return to the Garrison Probe [by
House Select Committee, on Plots in New Orleans Against JFK],"
Jack Anderson, p. B15.

5085.   8 Feb. 1978:   "Hey Diddle Diddle, Fiddling With His-
tory: in 'King' and 'Ruby and Oswald', Real-Life Figures
Become Comic-Strip Cutouts [Reviews NBC and CBS TV Dramas],"
Tom Shales, pp. B1, B3.

5086.   19 Feb. 1978:   "Spy Allegedly Duped Hoover [According
to Edward Jay Epstein, Legend]," Jack Egan, p. A9.

5087.   23 April 1978:   "Agents, Assassins, and Moles [Review
of Legend by Edward Jay Epstein]," George Lardner, Jr., p.
E4.

5088.   4 July 1978:   "Panel Plans Hearings on Kennedy, King:
House Assassination Investigations," George Lardner, Jr., p.
A6.

5089.   31 July 1978:   "Panel Releases Pictures Linked to
Kennedy, King Assassinations [in Hope That Witnesses May
Come Forward]," p. A10.

5090.   8 Aug. 1978:   "Assassinations Probes Survive: More
House Funding Likely," George Lardner, Jr., p. A7.

5091.   13 Aug. 1978:   "House Assassinations Hearings: Circus
or Catharsis?" George Lardner, Jr., p. A18.

5092.   21 Aug. 1978:   "Acoustics Experts Reenact '63 Kennedy
Assassination in Dallas," Nancy Smith, p. A3.

5093.   23 Aug. 1978:   "The Assassination Quandry [the Need
to Reassure Versus the Need to Know About JFK Murder]," Meg
Greenfield, p. A15.

5094.   6 Sept. 1978:   "Hill Unit to Open Hearings on JFK:
No Conspiracy Found," p. A6.

5095.   _____: "Hunt Sues to Obtain Data Linking Him
to Assassin [E. Howard Hunt Suing Author Tad Szulc in His
$2 Million Libel Suit Against Alan Weberman]," Jane Seaberry,
p. A6.

5096.   6 Sept. 1978:   "Questions of Conspiracy: A Commentary [on Knowing "the Unknowable" About JFK's Murder]," Nicholas von Hoffman, p. C15.

5097.   7 Sept. 1978:   "Connallys Tell of 'Terrible Ride'," George Lardner, Jr., pp. A1, A6.

5098.   8 Sept. 1978:   "2 Warren Commission Findings Backed [the Single-Bullet Explanation, Originating from Behind Kennedy]," George Lardner, Jr., pp. A1, A2.

5099.   9 Sept. 1978:   "New Tests Said to Match Fragments in Kennedy, Connally [to Support Further the Single-Bullet Explanation]," George Lardner, Jr., p. A3.

5100.   _____: "Assassination Theorists [Both Present and Absent at House Committee Hearings]," Myra MacPherson, pp. B1, B3.

5101.   12 Sept. 1978:   "50-50 Chance of a 4th Shot In Dallas, JFK Panel Is Told [by Acoustical Scientists]," George Lardner, Jr., p. A2.

5102.   13 Sept. 1978:   "Expert Backtraces Dallas Bullets for House Assassinations Hearing [NASA Expert Traces Bullets Back to Book Depository]," p. A2.

5103.   14 Sept. 1978:   "Oswald Widow Says She Lied to the FBI [By Not Reporting His Trip to Mexico, By Denying Seeing Rifle Ammunition at Home, But Says She Told the Truth to Warren Panel]," George Lardner, Jr., p. A2.

5104.   15 Sept. 1978:   "More Oswald Photo Evidence Said to Be Found [Including One Photo From Oswald to George de Mohrenschildt]," p. A3.

5105.   16 Sept. 1978:   "CIA Ignored Defector's Data on Oswald [the Nosenko Information]," George Lardner, Jr., pp. A1, A4.

5106.   17 Sept. 1978:   "JFK Unit Reportedly Didn't Seek CBS Film [of Interviewed Witnesses]," Larry Kramer, p. A18.

5107.   19 Sept. 1978:   "Ex-Diplomat Denies Oswald Told Cubans He Might Kill JFK [Cuban Consul in Mexico City, Eusebio Azcue]," George Lardner, Jr., p. A3.

5108.   _____: "Soviet Writer Suggests Peking Role in JFK Death [Because Oswald Was a Chinese Agent]," p. A3.

5109.   20 Sept. 1978:   "Castro, on Tape, Denies Complicity in JFK's Murder," George Lardner, Jr., pp. A1, A7.

5110.   21 Sept. 1978:   "[Ex-President] Ford Expected to Testify on Warren Panel Role," George Lardner, Jr., p. A3.

5111.   22 Sept. 1978:   "Ford Stands by Warren Panel Findings [and Says His Informing for FBI Lasted One Week]," George Lardner, Jr., p. A2.

5112.   23 Sept. 1978:   "[Ex-CIA Chief] Helms Clashes With Probe Panel [in His Lingering Doubts About Nosenko]," George Lardner, Jr., pp. Al, A6.

5113.   26 Sept. 1978:   "'Umbrella Man' Was Heckler [at Dealey Plaza, Dallas]," George Lardner, Jr., p. A2.

5114.   27 Sept. 1978:   "Assassinations Committee Turns to Tantalizing Leads [Concerning the Mafia, Anti-Castro Cubans and Connections Between Oswald and Ruby]," George Lardner, Jr., p. A2.

5115.   28 Sept. 1978:   "Mafioso Told Him JFK Would Be 'Hit', Cuban Exile Testifies [About Santo Trafficante's Words]," George Lardner, Jr., p. A3.

5116.   29 Sept. 1978:   "Reputed Godfather [Trafficante] Tells About Plot to Murder Castro [and Explains His Words About JFK]," p. A3.

5117.   14 Oct. 1978:   "On the Confusing Trail of Jack Ruby [Reviews Seth Kantor's Biography]," Bob Katz, p. B4.

5118.   _____ :   "Judge Orders Author [Tad Szulc] to Reveal Sources [Regarding Link Between E. Howard Hunt and Oswald in Mexico City]," Jane Seaberry, p. C5.

5119.   19 Oct. 1978:   "Warren Report Ignored Soviet Defector's Claims [That Is, Nosenko's Statements on Oswald, in Documents Released to Harold Weisberg]," George Lardner, Jr., p. A14.

5120.   23 Oct. 1978:   "Late Mobster's View of JFK Killing [John Roselli Told Details to His Lawyer Before Gangland Death]," Jack Anderson, p. C27.

5121.   24 Oct. 1978:   "JFK Assassination and a Mafia Hit [John Roselli's Story, Continued]," Jack Anderson, p. Fll.

5122.   4 Nov. 1978:   "Data on Howard Hunt Shielded: Judge Cites First Amendment [for Tad Szulc in Hunt's Libel Suit Against Alan J. Weberman]," Jane Seaberry, p. A3.

5123.   5 Nov. 1978:   "Role in Murder of JFK Denied By Hunt Again [in Miami News Conference]," Merwin Sigale, p. A3.

5124.   26 Nov. 1978:   "'63 Film Hints at Two Dallas Assassins [Taken by Charles L. Bronson of Ada, Oklahoma, and Reported in The Dallas Morning News]," p. A19.

5125.   27 Nov. 1978:   "Film in JFK Assassination Reassessed: Second Figure With Oswald?" George Lardner, Jr., p. A8.

THE WASHINGTON POST
VOLUME CII

5126. 12 Dec. 1978: "FBI Chief [William H. Webster] Backs Death Penalty for Presidential Assassinations [and How FBI Would Organize Future Investigations]," George Lardner, Jr., p. A13.

5127. 13 Dec. 1978: "Crime Fighters Divide on Assassination Risk in Limiting Probers [Disagreement Between Secret Service and Justice Department]," p. A7.

5128. 21 Dec. 1978: "JFK Panel Gets Evidence of Conspiracy [in Acoustical Evidence, for Fourth Shot]," George Lardner, Jr., pp. A1, A35.

5129. 22 Dec. 1978: "Experts Track Mystery JFK Bullet [in New Evidence Supporting 'Grassy Knoll' Origin]," George Lardner, Jr., pp. A1, A8.

5130. 23 Dec. 1978: "Assassination Unit to Announce Verdicts Jan. 3, Evidence Later," George Lardner, Jr., p. A2.

5131. _____: "[Editorial]: Biting the Fourth Bullet," p. A16.

5132. 30 Dec. 1978: "Second JFK Gunman Experts Say: Findings on Tape 'Beyond a Reasonable Doubt'," George Lardner, Jr., pp. A1, A4.

5133. _____: "For Conspiracists, Vindication Day: 'Government Is Beginning to Acknowledge What Really Happened' [Says Carl Oglesby, co-director of Assassination Information Bureau]," Bill Peterson, p. A4.

5134. 31 Dec. 1978: "JFK-King Panel Finds Conspiracy Likely in Slayings [Conclusion Made Yesterday]," George Lardner, Jr., pp. A1, A4.

Index of Names
(Sections I, II, and III)

A

Abrams, Malcolm: 534.

Abrahamsen, David: 393, 4451, 4703.

Abzug, Bella S.: 32.

Adams, James B.: 34.

Adams, Perry: 995, 2201.

Adenauer, Konrad: 2784.

Agee, Philip: 1717.

Agel, Jerome: 2594.

Ahler, J.: 1679.

Albert, Carl: 4899.

Aldridge, John W.: 2658.

Aleman, Jose: 5066.

Alexander, John: 2227.

Alexander, Shana: 1772, 1783.

Alford, William: 123, 142.

Allarey, Monina: 1198.

Allen, Harry C.: 1738.

Allen, Mark A.: 150.

Allen, Richard: 195.

Allen, Robert L.: 1902.

Allen, William: 196.

Alpern, David M.: 1828-1830.

Alphand, Herve: 4986.

Alsop, Joseph: 1412.

Alsop, Stewart: 1159, 1784.

Altgens, James W.: 197, 1618.

Alvarez, Luis: 1080-1081.

Alyea, Thomas P.: 198.

Amalric, Jacques: 740.

Amory, Cleveland: 535.

Amrine, Michael: 1150.

Anders, Peter: 2028.

Anderson, Alice: 2477.

Anderson, David J.:   183.

Anderson, Harland F.:   183.

Anderson, Jack: 1725.

Andrade, Vincente: 1199.

Andrews, Dean A., Jr.:   114-
   117, 4303, 4353, 4357,
   4426-4427, 4429-4430, 4432-
   4435, 4437, 4612, 4707.

Andronov, Iona: 2228.

Annenberg, Walter: 2415.

Ansbacher, Heinz: 394.

Ansbacher, Rowena R.:   394.

Anson, Robert Sam: 741,
   2154, 2224-2226, 2230,
   2262, 2277, 4865.

Anthony, Evelyn: 2595.

Brother Antoninus: 1413.

d'Apollonia, L.:   1414.

Appelbaum, Stephen A.:   1680.

Armstrong, Ken: 345.

Arnoni, M. S.:   316, 526,
   536-541, 744-748, 1200,
   1903-1905, 2029, 2486.

Aronson, James: 742-743.

Arrighi, Paul: 1739.

Askell, Bernard: 2426.

Ascoli, Max: 542, 1415.

Ashman, Charles: 1773.

Askins,   :   975.

Atkins,   :   199.

Attwood, William: 1416.

Auchincloss, Kenneth: 395.

Augstein, Rudolf: 1417.

Autry, James: 1906.

Axelrad, Jeffrey: 187.

Aynesworth, Hugh: 396, 543,
   1907.

Azcue, Eusebio: 5107.

B

Babcock, Barbara: 178-181,
   184-187.

Bachmann, Ida: 397, 544.

Back, Kurt W.:   1681.

Baez, Joan: 3288.

Bagdikian, Ben H.:   398.

Bailey, Emory J.:   179.

Bailey, George: 1201.

Baker, Dean C.:   1521, 1640.

Baker, Paul: 2637, 2643.

Ball, Joseph A.:   4085,
   4186.

Ballot, Paul: 1368.

Bane, Bernard M.:   2155-2157.

Banta, Thomas J.:   1682.

Barbieri, Frane: 1202.

Bar-David, M.:   1418.

Barger, James E.:   5045.

Barkus, G. Z. A.:   2596.

Barnard, D. Douglas, Jr.:
66.

Barwick, Garfield: 1297.

Baskerville, Donald A.:   291.

Baughman, U. E.:   1160, 3375.

Bauman, Robert E.:   65.

Baxandale, Lee: 2229.

Bayh, Birch: 83.

Bazelon, (Judge) David L.:
166, 171, 174, 176.

Bealle, Morris A.:   2597.

Bebrits, Anna: 2158.

Becheau, François: 1204.

Beck,   : 200.

Beckham, Thomas E.:   4490-
4491.

Bedford, Sybille: 2487-2488.

Bedrick, Stephen B.:   2030.

Beers, Jack: 201, 2489.

Belfrage, Cedric: 545, 749.

Belin, David W.:   32, 101,
699, 834, 844, 850, 1831,
2230, 2411, 4695, 4789,
4839, 4843.

Bell, F. M.:   202.

Bell, Griffin: 178-181.

Bell, Jack: 1541.

Belli, Melvin: 25, 915,
2475, 2512, 2529, 2553,
2565, 2570, 2575, 2581,
2591, 3543, 3581, 3583,
3586-3587, 3595, 3609,
3640, 3674, 3711, 3775,
3797, 3809, 3915, 3973,
4187, 4745.

Benell, Albert: 203.

Bennett, Arnold: 2024.

Bennett, Liz: 1908.

Berendt, John: 1419, 2231.

Bergquist, Laura: 317,
1369, 1421, 2706.

Berkeley, Edmund C.:   546,
1071, 1740, 1744, 2232-
2235.

Bernert, Philippe: 2236.

Bernières, Luc: 1194.

Bernstein, Carl: 1785.

Bernstein, Leonard: 1495,
4705.

Berry, Wendell: 1370.

Bertel, Numa: 137.

Besson, Waldemar: 2237.

Bethell, Thomas: 4620.

Bettiza, Enzo: 1422.

Betzner, Hugh, Jr.:   204.

Bickel, Alexander M.:   751-
756, 859-860, 900, 4250.

Biller, Owen A.:   1741.

Billings, Richard: 6, 21.

Binyon, Michael: 1832.

Birnbaum, Norman: 1205.

Bishop, George V.:   1716.

Bishop, James Alonzo: 2160,
2238-2239, 2381, 4045,
4052, 4074, 4555, 4560,
4565.

Bisiach, Gianna: 2657.

Biskind, Peter: 1542.

Black, Edwin: 2240.

Black, (Judge) Hugo L.: 4018.

Blackwell, J. A.: 69:

Blake, Patricia: 2427.

Blakey, G. Robert: 77, 1833,
  4977, 5026.

Blewett, John: 1206.

Bloice, C.: 2241-2242.

Bloomgarden, Henry S.: 966,
  1005.

Blumenthal, Sid: 1717, 2243.

Bocca, Geoffrey: 2188.

Boe, Eugene: 2594.

Boeth, Richard: 547.

Boggs, Hale: 3733, 3955,
  4101, 4778.

Bolden, Abraham W.: 2267,
  2373, 3654, 3656, 3658,
  3709, 3728.

Boldizsar, Ivan: 318-319.

Bonazzi, Robert: 757.

Bond, Wilma: 205.

Bonjean, Charles M.: 1560.

Bonner, Judy Whitson: 2159,
  2300.

Bonventre, Peter: 548.

Booker, Emma: 1423.

Booker, Simeon: 1424.

Booth, John Wilkes: 448,
  514, 986, 3941, 3997.

Boothby, Paul: 1909.

Borch, Herbert von: 1425.

Boren, Bryant: 206.

Boroson, Warren: 2490.

Boswell, J. Thornton: 88,
  90, 3585.

Bothun, Richard: 207.

Bourjaily, Vance: 2598,
  2658, 2661, 2668, 2673.

Bowart, Walter: 1718.

Bowley, T. F.: 102.

Bowser, Hallowell: 2031.

Boyle, Andrew: 1207.

Brackman, Jacob: 758.

Bradburn, Norman H.: 1673,
  1698, 3734.

Braden, Jim (alias Eugene
  Hale Brading): 125.

Bradlee, Benjamin: 1371,
  4785, 4792.

Bradley, Edgar E.: 4477-
  4478, 4480-4481, 4509,
  4558.

Brammer, William: 2599.

Brand, Sergiu: 2244.

Brandon, Henry: 549, 759,
  1208-1209.

Brandon, Robert F.: 163.

Braverman, Shelly: 976.

Breig, J.: 1210.

Bremer, Arthur: 4703.

Brener, Milton E.: 1889,
  4638.

Brenk, Rudy: 208.

Brennan, Howard: 3600.

Breslin, Jimmy: 977,3649.

Brienberg, Mordecai: 550.

Briggs, Charles A.: 173, 175.

Brigham, Robert: 1211.

Brill, Steven: 760.

Bringuier, Carlos: 112, 126, 1074, 1142, 1890.

Brogan, Denis W.: 2245.

Brogan, Patrick: 551, 1786, 1834-1836, 2246-2247.

Bromberg, Walter: 2491.

Bronson, Charles L.: 209, 5074, 5124.

Brooks, Stewart M.: 978.

Brothers, Joyce: 371.

Brown, Joe: 210.

Brown, (Judge) Joe B.: 25, 3514, 3569, 3724, 3928, 3954, 3965, 3968, 3991, 4011-4012, 4498.

Brucker, Herbert: 1543.

Brussell, Mae: 2248.

Buchanan, Larry: 3495.

Buchanan, Thomas G.: 527, 545, 552-553, 561, 577, 579-581, 588, 635, 664, 667, 700, 870, 949, 2354, 2551, 3795, 3861.

Buckley, William F., Jr.: 1212, 2249, 4042.

Budimac, Budimir: 1213.

Bundy, MacGeorge: 1164, 3751.

Burger, Kurt Martin: 1420.

Burnes, Richard: 4432, 4470.

Burnett, Henry B., Jr.: 2250.

Burnham, Walter Dean: 1214.

Burrows, Henry: 211.

Butler, Ed: 1142, 2251, 2654.

Butterfield, Roger: 761.

Byrd, D. Harold: 368, 4648, 4710, 4826.

C

Cabell, Earle: 4215.

Cabluck, Harry: 213.

Cadden, Vivian: 1837.

Cafiero, L. H.: 2032.

Calese, Robert S.: 292.

Callahan, John W.: 2492.

Cameron, J. M.: 1215.

Campbell, Alex: 762.

Campbell, Earl Vendryes: 1372-1373.

Campbell, Judith Katherine: (see Exner).

Campion, Donald: 1216.

Cancellare, Frank: 214.

Cancler, John: 4391, 4420.

Canfield, Michael: 1774, 4812, 4898.

Canning, Tom: 5048.

Cannon, James M.: 2033.

Capote, Truman: 4626.

Carrico, Charles James: 3610, 4805.

Carl, Lincoln: 127.

Carlos, Newton: 1195.

Carleton, William G.: 1426.

Carnes, William H.: 89, 1053, 4571-4572.

Carney, Frederick S.: 320.

Carr, Waggoner: 18, 103, 3807, 4823.

Carroll, Maurice C.: 2475, 3797.

Carroll, Nicholas: 1218.

Carter, Manfred A.: 1427.

Cartier, Rudolph: 2653.

Cartwright, H. L.: 2493.

Carunungan, C. A.: 1217.

Casavantes, Joel: 399.

Castellano, Lillian: 2494.

Castillo, Luis Angel: 4359.

Castro, Fidel: 85, 468, 470, 1196, 1223, 1777-1778, 1842, 1844, 1876, 2731, 2899, 2975, 3006, 3121, 3145, 3170, 3228, 3362, 3387, 3435, 3848, 4652, 4658, 4799-4800, 4813, 4839, 4853, 4889, 4894, 4903, 4972, 5007, 5020, 5036-5038, 5055-5056, 5066-5067, 5107, 5109, 5116.

Catton, Bruce: 689, 1539.

Cerf, Bennett: 2030.

Chamberlin, Anne: 1428.

Chambliss, Sanford: 2495.

Chapman, Ann: 380.

Chapman, Gil: 380.

Charboneau, M.: 2252.

Chester, Lewis: 2253.

Chin, Sylvia Fung: 1910.

Chinmoy, Sri: 1374.

Chou, En-Lai: 3417.

Chriss, Nicholas: 1911.

Christenberry, (Judge) Herbert W.: 4678, 4696,

Church, Frank: 1824, 1837, 4819, 4839, 4857, 4861, 4875, 4887.

Churchill, Randolph: 2034-2035, 4541.

Ciardi, John: 1219, 1429.

Cipes, Robert M.: 555.

Clark, Ramsay: 88-89, 137, 4291, 4296, 4307, 4452, 4573.

Clarke, Gerald: 1430.

Clarkson, Adrienne: 2684.

Clifford, G.: 1431.

Clinch, N. G.: 2698.

Cline, R. A.: 763-764, 868.

Cohen, Jacob: 765-767, 772, 831, 901, 4029, 4052, 4074.

Cohen, Jeff: 1788.

Cohen, Jerry: 1911.

Cohen, Larry: 1124.

Coit, Margaret L.:   2036.

Cole, Alwyn: 979.

Collins, Frederic: 1161-1162.

Collins, Jeremiah: 2638, 4693.

Collins, R. S.:   2037.

Collins, Reid: 1138.

Condon, Richard: 1220, 2600-2601.

Connally, John B.:   103, 321, 377, 618, 846, 906, 963, 989, 991, 998, 1001, 1003, 2379, 2723, 2729, 2755, 2840, 2845, 2854, 2857, 2989, 3086, 3202, 3243, 3345, 3400, 3431, 3451, 3482, 3488, 3589, 3625, 3672, 3863, 3877, 4093, 4201, 4203, 4210, 4285, 4461, 4602, 4708, 5040, 5097, 5099.

Connally, Mrs. John B.:   2254, 3479, 3625, 5040, 5097.

Connolly, Cyril: 768-769, 4355.

Conquest, Robert.   1544.

Considine, Bob: 720.

Cook, Donald: 215.

Cook, Fred J.:   322, 770-774, 2256.

Cook, I.:   2255.

Cook, John: 1787.

Cooke, Alistair: 1221-1222, 4355.

Cooper, John Sherman: 3733.

Corry, John: 2025, 2038, 2081, 4431, 4442.

Cottrell, John: 1674, 1713.

Couch, Malcolm: 216.

Cournos, John: 1376.

Cousins, Norman: 1432-1433.

Craig, Roger: 1131, 2372, 4599.

Craig, Walter E.:   3536, 3590, 3619, 3711.

Cranberg, Gilbert: 1545.

Crane, Les: 2452, 3712.

Cranston, Pat: 1546.

Crawford, Allan: 2257.

Crawford, Curtis: 400, 700.

Crawford, Kenneth: 775, 2039.

Crewdson, John: 1789.

Crisman, Fred Lee: 4559.

Croft, Robert Earl: 217.

Cronkite, Walter: 1163, 2686, 2689.

Cross, David: 556, 2258.

Crotty, William Joseph: 1719, 1722, 1742-1743.

Crown, James Tracy: 281.

Cuffaro, H. K.:   1683.

Cuneo, Paul K.:   2040.

Cunliffe, Marcus: 2041.

Cunningham, Cortland: 170.

Curran, (Judge) Edward M.:   183.

Curry, Jesse: 528, 846,
3810, 3819, 4642, 4816.

Curtat, Robert: 1790.

Cushing, Richard (Cardinal):
1474, 2956, 2958, 3245,
3438, 3831, 3860, 4313,
4556.

Cushman, Robert F.: 776.

Cutler, Robert Bradley: 6,
22, 967-968, 1164, 2162-
2163.

D

Dahlin, Robert: 2259.

Danaher, (Judge) John A.:
166.

Daniel, Clifton: 323, 3845,
3922.

Daniel, Jack: 218.

Daniel, Jean: 1223.

Daniel, Price: 1224.

Dann, Sol: 4382, 4384,
4883.

Darnell, James: 219.

Davenport, Nicholas: 1165.

David, Jay (alias Bill Adler): 698.

David, Paul T.: 1547.

Davidson, Bill: 2707.

Davis, David Brion: 1060-
1061.

Davis, Marc: 701, 2164,
2602.

Davis, Nord, Jr.: 2165.

Davis, Sid: 1145.

Davis, William: 220.

Davis, William H.: 1891.

De Antonio, Emile: 23,
1125-1130, 1149, 4387.

Deighton, Len: 2205, 2406.

Deitsch, David: 1744.

Delaney, James J.: 65.

Dellinger, Dave: 777-778.

Dellums, Ronald V.: 65.

Demaris, Ovid: 2485, 2528,
4979.

Dempsey, David: 557.

Denegree Vaught, Livingston:
1523.

Denson, R. B.: 1524.

Denzin, Norman K.: 1585.

Desrosiers, Bob: 1549.

Devlin, (Lord) Patrick:
401, 779, 4250.

De Vosjoli, P. L. Thyraud:
1775, 2634.

Diamond, S. A.: 1083.

Di'Bīs, 'Abd al-Jawwād Hamzah: 2166.

Diehl, William F., Jr.:
1548.

Dies, Martin: 1684.

Dillard, Thomas C.: 221.

Dillon, Douglas: 3751,
3889, 4804.

Dimona, Joseph: 2603.

Dirix, Bob: 2260.

Dirksen, Everett: 3054.

Dodd, Christopher, J.: 76.

Dodds, C.: 63.

Dolan, Jo Ann: 178, 185.

Dönhoff, Marion (Gräfin): 1434.

Donovan, Robert J.: 688, 1145, 3761.

Dorman, Elsie T.: 222.

Douglas, George H.: 1745.

Douglas Home, Alec: 1225, 1338-1339, 2874, 2971, 2973.

Douglass, William C.: 2604.

Downing, Thomas N.: 63, 1068, 1848, 1881, 4879.

Doyle, James Patrick: 189.

Drew, Robert: 3727.

Drinnon, Richard: 780.

Driver, Tom F.: 1226.

Drury, Michael: 2254.

Ducovny, Amram: 2640, 4356, 4443, 4456-4458.

Dudman, Richard: 324.

Duffy, John: 1140.

Dugan, John R.: 184.

Dugger, Ronnie: 325, 781, 2042-2044, 2497.

Duhamel, Morvan: 1525.

Duheme, Jacqueline: 1377.

Duke, James H.: 4708.

Dulles, Allen W.: 24, 964, 3720, 4496, 4776.

Duncan, Richard: 2167.

Duncan, Susana: 404.

Dunn, Cyril: 402.

Dunning, John L.: 1550.

Dunshee, Tom: 2167.

Dunson, J.: 2261.

Dymond, F. Irvin: 142.

E

Ebersole, John H.: 90.

Eckard, Jack M.: 163.

Eddowes, Michael: 702, 2168, 2253, 2277, 4990.

Edwards, A.: 2605.

Edwards, Don: 34, 4829, 4831.

Egginton, Joyce: 402.

Einzig, P.: 1227.

Eisenhower, Dwight David: 1166, 2802.

Ekko, Egil: 2169.

Elizabeth II: 1347.

Ellis, W.: 782.

Ellison, Jerome: 1551.

Emerson, William A., Jr.: 783.

Emery, Fred: 784.

Endt, Friso: 1435.

Ephron, Nora: 1552.

Epstein, Edward Jay: 9, 174, (continued...)

(Epstein, continued)
381, 395, 404, 407, 409,
450, 454, 506, 703-705,
746, 749, 751, 758, 762-
763, 785, 796, 798, 804,
819, 829-830, 841, 851,
858, 861, 889, 902, 953,
1084, 1136, 1892, 1905,
1912, 1948, 2045, 4019,
4027-4028, 4046, 4049,
4058, 4085, 4545, 4628,
5008, 5012, 5069, 5086-
5087.

Erhard, Ludwig: 2907.

Erwin, Ray: 1553.

Eshkol, Levi: 2793.

Estes, Joe Ewing: 131, 135,
3999, 4697.

Evans, J. Claude: 326.

Evans, M. Stanton: 405,
786, 1228, 2262.

Evica, George Michael: 2170.

Ewing, Michael: 125, 2161.

Exner, Judith Katherine
(Campbell): 153-155,
1871, 2403, 4854, 4856-
4863, 4866-4867, 4872,
4881-4882, 4884-4885,
4976, 4978-4979, 5005.

F

Fairlie, Henry D.: 4724.

Faller, J.: 1791.

Falls, Cyril: 1229.

Farrell, Michael W.: 171.

Faulk, John Henry: 127.

Fauntroy, Walter: 4967.

Featherstone, Joseph: 2046.

Fein, Arnold L.: 787, 2047.

Felberbaum, A.: 2659.

Feldman, Harold: 558, 1913,
2171, 2263-2264, 3927.

Feldman, Jacob J.: 1673,
1699.

Fenn, Dan H.: 4687.

Fenner, Nancy Lee: 34.

Fensterwald, Bernard, Jr.:
125, 137, 156-158, 165-
166, 183, 279, 559, 1792,
1914, 2161, 2256, 2265-
2269, 2404, 4995.

Fenton, D.: 1793.

Ferlinghetti, Lawrence:
1436.

Ferrari, Alfred John: 2270.

Ferrie, David: 123-124,
141-142, 1921, 1932-1933,
4280-4283, 4344, 4608,
4619.

Fiddick, Thomas C.: 2498.

Field, C.: 223.

Field, Maggie: 1913.

Fife, Darlene: 1915-1916.

Figley, Paul: 178.

Finck, Pierre A.: 88, 3585,
4610.

Fine, William M.: 1378.

Fisher, Russell S.: 89,
4571-4572.

Fixx, James F.: 560.

Flammonde, Paris: 1893,
2299.

Flannery, Thomas A.: 165-
166.

Fleischer, Walter H.:   166.

Fleming, D. F.:   1685.

Fleming, Thomas J.:   1746.

Flynt, Larry: 1794, 2366, 5009, 5080.

Folsom, Robert: 4907.

Foltz, Charles, Jr.:   1230.

Fonzi, Gaeton: 788-789, 824

Ford, Declan: 3570.

Ford, Gerald R.:   12, 101, 109, 168, 172, 534, 706, 790, 925, 936, 1842, 1876, 3392, 3740, 3888, 3955, 3962, 4055, 4273, 4740, 4788, 4808, 4822, 4837, 4839, 4847, 4902, 5010, 5047, 5058-5059, 5083, 5110-5111.

Ford, Robert N.:   184.

Foreman, Percy: 916, 3437, 3592, 3598.

Forman, Robert: 980.

Fowler, Clayton: 3688.

Fox, Sylvan: 707, 786, 791-792, 885, 907, 2262, 4019.

Fox, Victor J.:   2606.

Foy, James L.:   1757, 3948.

Fraker, Susan: 1838-1839.

Frazier, Buell Wesley: 3565.

Frazier, Robert A.:   170.

Freed, Donald: 1788, 1795, 2607, 2650, 4733.

Freedman, Lawrence Zelic: 406, 1747.

Freedman, Nancy (Mars):   2608.

Freeman, John: 1231.

Freeman, Lucy: 382, 3996.

Freeman, Ron: 1744.

Freese, Paul L.:   793.

Freund, Hugo: 1437.

Freund, Paul: 2685.

Friedman, Leon: 2640, 4356, 4443, 4456-4458.

Friedman, Rick: 794, 1085, 1554.

Friedman, Saul: 327.

Frisell, Bernard: 561.

Fritz, Willi: 411, 4646.

Fromm, Erich: 1748.

Froncek, T.:   2271.

Fulbright, J. William: 3348.

Fulks, Bryan: 562.

G

Galbraith, John Kenneth: 2048.

Gallagher, John F.:   170.

Gans, Curtis: 1840.

Gappert, Gary: 1438.

Gardner, Francis V.:   1379.

Garduno, Joseph A.:   1380.

Garrison, Jim: 6, 21, 24, 25, 31, 89, 113-124, 129, 137-149, 1657, 1888-2023, 1894, 1901, 2609, 2679, (continued...)

(Garrison, continued)
2688, 2691-2693, 2697,
4270, 4275, 4278, 4280-
4286, 4292-4297, 4299,
4301-4303, 4305, 4307-4308,
4310, 4312, 4315, 4317,
4319-4320, 4324-4325, 4327-
4330, 4332, 4334, 4336,
4338-4339, 4341-4342, 4344,
4346, 4348, 4351, 4353,
4357, 4362-4363, 4365,
4367-4371, 4374, 4376-4379,
4381-4384, 4389-4392, 4394-
4404, 4408-4410, 4412,
4414-4417, 4419-4430, 4432-
4437, 4440-4441, 4444,
4446-4447, 4449, 4451-4453,
4473, 4477-4484, 4486-4488,
4490-4492, 4494-4496, 4499,
4503-4504, 4507-4509, 4511-
4512, 4517, 4522, 4524,
4526, 4545-4546, 4549,
4551, 4558-4559, 4562-4563,
4567, 4569-4570, 4573-4575,
4577-4610, 4614-4624, 4627,
4634-4635, 4638, 4645,
4668, 4678, 4682, 4696,
4700, 4707, 4720, 4731,
4767, 4832, 4998, 5017,
5084.

Garson, Barbara: 1140, 2641,
2662, 2669, 2672, 2675,
4109, 4133, 4277.

Gatti, Arthur: 2700.

Gaulle, Charles de: 2374,
2909, 4147, 4454, 4659.

Gauzer, Bernard: 708.

Geer, Candy: 1381.

Geis, Bernard: 130, 732,
1011.

Gellner, John: 2272.

Gelman, David: 1841-1842,
2428.

Genet, Jean: 1232.

Gershenson, Alvin H.: 2701.

Gertz, Elmer: 25, 2476,
2491, 2499.

Gesell, (Judge) Gerhard:
156, 172, 178, 182, 187.

Gewertz, Irving: 224.

Giampietro, Wayne B.: 2499.

Giancana, Sam: 4861, 4954,
4976.

Gibbons, R.: 795.

Gifford, Alex: 1917-1918.

Gilbert, Martin: 563.

Gilles, Camille: 2172,
2236.

Gilliatt, Penelope: 1126.

Gilman, Richard: 1686.

Gingrich, Arnold: 2049-2050.

Ginsberg, Betsy: 184.

Giquel, Bernard: 1919-1920.

Glikes, Edwin A.: 1382.

Goff, Kenneth: 2173.

Goldberg, Alfred: 709.

Goldberg, Arthur: 3624.

Goldman, Alex J.: 1383.

Goldman, Peter: 2273, 2708.

Goldwater, Barry: 1303,
2863, 2910, 3165, 3719.

Gombrich, Richard: 563.

Gonzalez, Henry B.: 43, 45,
46, 1774, 1828, 1832, 1848,
1860, 1866, 3276, 4213,
4879, 4933, 4936, 4939-
4941, 4944, 4948.

Goodall, Kenneth: 796.

Goodhart, A. L.:   764, 797–799, 965, 1555, 4214.

Goodman, Paul: 854.

Goodwin, Richard N.:   4030, 4150.

Goranoff, Kyrill: 2174.

Gordan, Bruce: 2175.

Gordon, G.:   2274.

Gordon, William E.:   1687.

Gosset, Pierre: 2610.

Gosset, Renée: 2610.

Götte, Fritz: 1439.

Gough, Trent: 4520.

Goulden, Joseph C.:   2275.

Graham, James J.:   1127.

Grahame, Arthur: 981.

Granton, E. Fannie: 2709.

Graves, Florence: 1086.

Gray, Barry: 2695.

Gray, L. Patrick: 166.

Gray, W. C.:   225.

Graziani, Gilbert: 800.

Green, (Judge) June L.:   178, 184.

Greenberg, Bradley S.:   1556, 1677.

Greer, William R.:   4026.

Gregory, Dick: 4786, 4794.

Gregory, Peter Paul: 3570.

Grichot, Jack: 982.

Grimond, Joseph: 1225.

Griswold, D.:   801.

Griswold, Erwin: 1653.

Groden, Robert J.:   278, 1068, 1078, 1087, 1097.

Gronouski, John S.:   1384.

Gross, Alfred A.:   802.

Gross, Gerald: 1526.

Grove, Larry: 1557, 2429.

Guinn, Vincent P.:   5042.

Gun, Nerin E.:   1921, 2176, 2405, 2430, 2710.

Gurvich, William: 4402, 4404, 4408–4409, 4508.

Guttmacher, Manfred: 3562.

H

Habe, Hans (pseudonym for Jean Bekessy):   803, 1675–1676, 3693.

Habighorst, A. W.:   4606.

Hacker, Andrew: 407.

Hager, Barry: 1843.

Hagerty, James: 2773.

Haggerty (Judge) Edward A., Jr.:   123–124, 1972, 4606, 4640, 4644, 4667.

Hale, Hazel: 282.

Haley, J. Evetts: 1151, 3732.

Hall, Loran Eugene: 2370, 4972.

Halleck, (Judge) Charles,
    Jr.:   4588, 4600.

d'Hamacourt, Peter: 4966.

Hamblin, Dora Jane: 2711.

Handlin, Oscar: 804.

Hannon, Joseph M.:   165.

Hanson, Howard: 3288.

Hanson, William H.:   2177.

Hardwick, Elizabeth: 2051.

Harris, Herbert E., II: 44.

Harris, Larry R.:   2213.

Harris, Mark: 2611.

Harris, Roy: 1500.

Harris, T. George: 328.

Harrity, Richard: 408.

Hart, L.:   1440.

Hart, Philip: 168.

Hartogs, Renatus: 382, 430,
    498, 515, 3325, 3445,
    3996.

Hastings, Michael: 2642,
    2660, 4096, 4515.

Havemann, Ernest: 2500.

Havens, Murray: 1720.

Haziyian, Harvey: 1717.

Heaps, Willard A.:   1721.

Heath, Peter: 2612.

Heebe, (Judge) Frederick J.
    R.:   4731.

Hegyi, Károly: 2501.

Heilbroner, Robert: 1558.

Helms, Richard: 1815, 1842,
    4796, 5060-5061, 5069,
    5112.

Helpern, Milton: 969, 983.

Henderson, Bruce: 2178.

Henley, Arthur: 453.

Hepburn, James: 1776, 1796-
    1797, 4566, 4632.

Herberg, Will: 1749.

Hercher, Wilmot W.:   1233.

Heren, Louis: 409, 2276-
    2277, 4500.

Herman, Melvin: 1756.

Hermann, Kai: 564.

Herskowitz, Mickey: 1534.

Herta, A.:   2278.

Herwig, Barbara L.:   166.

Hessel, Dieter: 1441.

Hewes, Henry: 2660.

Heymann, Stefan: 410.

Hicks, Granville: 2661.

Hicks, James: 4484.

Hill, Clinton J.:   3322,
    3763.

Hill, Gladwin: 411, 1559.

Hill, I. William: 565.

Hill, Richard J.:   1560.

Himmelfarb, Gertrude: 412.

Hinckle, Warren, III: 1797,
    1895, 1927.

Hitt, Dick: 2502.

Hoch, Paul L.:   172, 730, 1803.

Hockberg, Sandy: 1922.

Hoffa, James R.:   1802, 3386.

Hoffman, E.:   805-806, 1798, 2279.

Hoffman, Harold: 3495.

Holland, (Judge) Louis T.:   3970, 4013, 4021, 4252.

Holland, Mary: 1234.

Holmes, John C.:   413.

Holmes, William A.:   329, 353, 3181, 3224.

Holt, Marjorie S.:   65.

Hood, Stuart: 1561.

Hoover, J. Edgar: 174, 551, 569-570, 615, 630, 640, 656, 682, 1124, 1834, 3295, 3647, 3651, 3799, 3804, 3839, 3877, 3891, 4097, 4781, 4903, 4999, 5001, 5004-5005, 5010, 5057, 5082, 5086.

Horn, John: 1562.

Hosmer, John: 4470.

Hosty, James P., Jr.:   34, 665, 4855.

House, Donald Wayne: 495.

Houston, Darrell: 1563.

Houts, Marshall: 969, 983.

Howard, Lawrence, Jr.:   4488.

Howard, T.:   226.

Howe, Irving: 1235.

Howe, Kenneth C.:   34.

Hoyle, Jeffrey P.:   970.

Huber, Oscar: 4777.

Hug, Josephine: 4303.

Hughes, Emmet John: 2052.

Hughes, Everett C.:   1236.

Hughes, H. Stuart: 1237.

Hughes, Robert J.:   227.

Hughes, Robert J. E.:   1064.

Humes, James J.:   88, 90, 3585, 4407.

Hunt, E. Howard: 1821, 2402, 4725, 4803, 4838, 4898, 5034, 5095, 5118, 5122-5123.

Hunt, George P.:   414.

Hunt, H. L.:   4946, 4959-4961.

Hunter, Diana: 2477.

Huntley, Chet: 1146.

Huston, Luther A.:   2053.

I

Idris, Soewardi: 2180.

Ioĭrysh, Abram Isakovich: 2179

Irons, Evelyn: 415, 1923.

Irwin, T. H.:   282, 310, 2181.

Israel, Fred: 1118.

Izakov, Boris: 330, 2280.

J

Jackson, Donald: 416, 1924.

Jackson, John J., III: 1925.

Jackson, Robert: 228, 3642.

Jacobson, Dan: 807.

Jaffe, Louis L.: 1564.

Jagan, Cheddi: 2746.

Jakovlev, N. N.: 2281.

James, Rosemary: 1896.

Jamieson, John: 780.

Jamison, J.: 229.

Janssen, Karl-Heinz: 2282.

Jaworski, Leon: 106, 3317, 3358, 4838.

Jenkins, Gareth: 2283.

Jenkins, John A.: 2284.

Jenkins, John H.: 312.

Jenkins, Walter: 1170.

Joaquin, Nick: 1238.

Joesten, Joachim: 383, 417, 529, 543, 577, 588, 715-717, 750, 769, 808, 870, 971, 984, 1152-1153, 1442, 1897, 1926, 2182-2183, 2422, 2479, 2702, 4066.

Johnson, Bob: 1565.

Johnson, Earl J.: 1566.

Johnson, Haynes: 1777, 3684.

Johnson, Lady Bird: 3881, 3884.

Johnson, Lyndon Baines: 13, 166, 544, 1150-1193, 1402, 2680, 2723, 2730, 2735, 2755, 2798, 2835-2837, 2843, 2874, 2898, 2906- 2907, 2909, 2927, 2943, 2946, 2948, 2951, 2963, 3093, 3096-3098, 3112, 3183, 3255, 3258, 3337, 3368, 3405, 3428, 3431, 3670, 3690, 3694, 3732, 3740-3741, 3744, 3751, 3806, 3815, 3817, 3842, 3855, 3863, 3877, 3889, 3975, 3986, 3990, 4069-4070, 4131, 4166, 4169, 4172, 4175, 4196, 4204, 4213, 4228, 4258, 4261, 4264, 4274, 4287, 4289, 4311, 4331, 4461-4462, 4485, 4501, 4537, 4568, 4649-4651, 4674, 4676, 4688, 4690, 4723, 4728, 4793, 4895, 5072.

Johnson, Marion: 11, 32.

Johnson, Philip: 3993.

Johnson, Priscilla: (see McMillan, Priscilla Johnson).

Joling, Robert J.: 985.

Jones, Gerre: 1567.

Jones, J. Harry, Jr.: 2613.

Jones, Kirby: 1844.

Jones, Penn, Jr.: 26, 308, 696, 711-714, 725, 757, 794, 809, 886, 892, 932, 951, 955, 1062, 1069, 1077-1078, 1616, 1913, 4052, 4074, 4627.

Jones, Wyman: 331.

K

Kaiser, Horst: 1239.

Kaiser, Robert B.: 1845.

Kantor, M.:   2285.

Kantor, Robert E.:   1758.

Kantor, Seth: 2480, 5117.

Kaplan, John: 25, 810-812,
  2478, 2506, 3981.

Karp, Irwin: 813, 2054.

Katz, J.:   1799.

Katz, Joseph: 1750.

Katzenbach, Nicholas: 3751,
  3921, 3943, 3964, 5069.

Kaufman, Allan Martin: 1927.

Kaufman, (Judge) Frank R.:
  166.

Kaufman, Richard: 1688.

Kavanaugh, Paul: 2614.

Kazan, Molly: 1390.

Kearns, Dianne R.:   2284.

Keisler, J. R.:   814, 2286.

Kelley, Clarence M.:   179,
  4780.

Kellner, Abraham: 1391.

Kempner, Robert M. W.:   694.

Kempton, Murray: 419, 566,
  700, 727, 815-816, 1240-
  1241, 1443, 2055-2057,
  2503-2508.

Kendall, Bruce: 1404.

Kennedy: Edward: 168, 1866,
  2712, 2747, 3626, 4032,
  4092, 4464, 4653, 4666,
  4679, 4694, 4736, 4770,
  4775, 4802, 4842, 5073.

Kennedy, Jacqueline Bouvier:
  128, 1317, 1668, 2024-
  2151, 2091, 2101, 2106,
  2108, 2120, 2122, 2711,
  2713, 2716, 2720-2722,
  2729, 2772, 2784, 2849,
  2942, 2945, 2955, 3032,
  3042, 3099, 3141, 3155,
  3159, 3204, 3210, 3238,
  3259-3261, 3279-3283, 3308,

3425, 3458, 3604, 3618,
  3639, 3652, 3671, 3682,
  3747, 3763, 3827, 3830,
  3834, 3866, 3870-3871,
  3873, 3881, 3884, 3979,
  4040, 4045, 4107, 4112,
  4115-4116, 4119, 4124-4129,
  4131, 4134-4135, 4138-4139,
  4143-4144, 4147-4163, 4171,
  4173, 4175, 4177, 4192-
  4193, 4200, 4202, 4224,
  4226, 4228, 4241, 4253,
  4385, 4472, 4527, 4529,
  4553, 4556, 4564, 4671,
  4705, 4735, 4765.

Kennedy, John F.:   14, 37-
  62, 78-82, 85-92, 94-95,
  99, 102, 106, 108, 313,
  1368-1516, 2729, 2732-
  2733, 2744, 4756, 2809-
  2811, 2814-2820, 2834,
  2864, 2866, 2918, 2925,
  3030, 3036-3041, 3169,
  3271, 3336, 3346, 3408,
  3411, 3476, 3478-3479,
  3585, 3672, 3769, 4026,
  4029, 4065, 4068, 4078-
  4079, 4094, 4196, 4198,
  4311, 4364, 4571-4572,
  4639, 4677, 4684, 4734,
  4746-4760, 4794, 4992,
  4997.

Kennedy, Regis: 4371.

Kennedy, Robert F.:   43, 45,
  46, 49, 51, 56, 59, 286-
  287, 332, 420, 748, 922,
  1034, 1723, 1730, 1763,
  1816, 2029, 2290, 2360,
  2363, 2377, 2724, 2796,
  3093, 3386, 3703, 3770,
  3781, 3852, 3859, 4126,
  4134-4135, 4144, 4148,
  4207, 4251, 4253, 4290,
  4402, 4464, 4506, 4528-
  4535, 4537-4541, 4554,
  4564, 4576, 4706, 4719,
  4746, 4774, 4842, 5004,
  5016.

Kerby, Phil: 817, 1928,
  2662.

Kerr, James: 897, 1444,
  2509.

Kevin, Art: 20.

Khrushchev, Nikita: 2839,
3784, 4659.

Kilduff, Malcolm: 1145,
3963.

Kilgallen, Dorothy: 2567,
3730.

Kilpatrick, James J.: 818.

Kilty, John W.: 168, 170.

Kincaid, George: 230.

King, John J.: 61, 132-134,
1048, 3976, 3986, 3998,
4024, 4031, 4611.

King, Martin Luther, Jr.:
20, 43, 45, 46, 49, 51,
56, 59, 62, 78-80, 183-
188, 640, 656, 1723, 1730,
1787, 1816, 2339, 2360,
2385, 3189, 4513, 4847,
4854, 4901, 4905, 4915,
4945.

King, Mary Paula: 2615.

Kipling, Richard E.: 1846.

Kirkham, James F.: 1722.

Kirkwood, James: 1898,
1924, 1929, 4668.

Kirschner, David: 1689.

Klein, Harry T.: 1392.

Kliman, Gilbert: 1678.

Knabb, Wayne M.: 1930.

Knebl, Fletcher: 819, 1167.

Knight, Goodwin: 2995.

Knight, Janet M.: 1723.

Koch, Edward I.: 45.

Koch, Thilo: 1445.

Kopkind, Andrew: 2058,
2289.

Koral, Mark: 2184.

Korns, John H.: 171.

Korolovszky, Lajos: 333.

Kosner, Edward: 2033, 2059-
2060.

Koster, Charles: 69.

Krassner, Paul: 2061-2062.

Krippendorff, Ekkehart:
1446.

Kristl: Zvonimir: 2185.

Kroman, David R.: 4329.

Krueger, Albert R.: 1568.

Krupp, George R.: 1690.

Kubicek, Earl C.: 293.

Kunstler, William: 3918,
4017, 4868-4871, 4873.

Kupferman, Theodore R.:
4050, 4352.

Kurnoth, Rudolf: 1447.

Kurtz, Michael L.: 17, 27,
1061.

L

Lagomarsino, Robert J.: 48.

Laird, J.: 232.

La Manna, Roger: 388.

Land, Barbara: 2424, 2433.

Land, Myrick: 2424, 2433.

Lane, Mark: 23, 25, 34, 63,
127, 151-152, 415, 421-
423, 473-485, 502, 518,
586, 623, 626, 635, 700,
718-719, 742-743, 755,
758, 760, 763, 796, 798,
802, 820-823, 828, 830,
851, 858, 870, 875-876,
915, 917, 922, 930, 932,
937, 949, 1088, 1125-1132,
1141, 1149, 1569, 1705,
1800, 1915, 1931, 2020,
2203, 2290, 2312, 2447,
2510, 2607, 2650, 3412,
3449, 3459, 3470, 3473,
3477, 3516, 3551, 3582,
3611, 3637, 3705-3707,
(continued...)

(Lane, continued)
3796, 3894, 4019, 4036-
4037, 4039, 4049, 4052,
4058, 4074, 4081, 4085,
4087, 4093, 4102, 4243,
4263, 4265, 4275, 4387,
4470, 4547, 4627, 4726,
4733, 4763, 4779, 4832,
4974, 5008.

Lane, Paul R.: 2511.

Langer, E.: 1691.

Langston, George E.: 2186.

Lardner, George, Jr.: 1847,
1932-1933.

Larrabee, Eric: 1242.

Lasky, Victor: 1325, 2703-
2704, 2785, 3361.

Lattimer, Gary: 990-992.

Lattimer, John K.: 986-992,
999, 1007, 3938, 4698,
4874.

Lattimer, Jon: 989-992.

Lausche, Frank: 1864.

Lauzon, A.: 334, 424.

Lawallen, James: 4292,
4334.

Lawrence, David: 1243.

Lawrence, Lincoln: 1724.

Leboeuf, Ulov G. K.: 2152.

Le Carre, John: 2616.

Lee, Rex E.: 169.

Leek, Sybil: 1725.

Leemans, Fred: 4395.

Leiden, Carl: 1720.

Lemarre, Herve: 2651, 4632.

Lerner, Max: 1244.

Lesar, James H.: 20, 28,
32, 109, 166, 169, 171,
178-181, 184-188, 736,
1054, 2269.

Lesher, Stephan: 1838.

Leslie, Warren: 314.

Levin, Bernard: 1448, 4355.

Levine, Faye: 758.

Levine, Isaac D.: 1726.

Levitan, Richard: 1143.

Levy, Alan: 1692.

Levy, Clifford V.: 1393.

Levy, Michael J.: 159.

Levy, Sheldon: 1722.

Lewis, Alvin B., Jr.: 4964.

Lewis, Anthony: 695.

Lewis, Edward: 2650.

Lewis, (Judge) Oren R.:
157.

Lewis, Richard Warren: 720,
1134, 2512.

L'Hoste, A. J.: 233.

Liddy, G. Gordon: 4982.

Liebeler, Wesley: 9, 107,
4062, 4085, 4427.

Lifton, David: 107, 833,
885, 2341.

Limmel, Michael L.: 186.

Lincoln, Abraham: 1480,
1735, 2956, 3079, 3308,
3940-3941, 4164, 4217,
4554, 4631.

Lincoln, Evelyn: 3440, 3971,
    4732, 4892.

Lindsay, John J.:   2273.

Lineberry, William: 1693.

Linn, Edward: 2513.

Lipset, Seymour Martin:
    1694.

Lipson, D. Herbert: 824.

Lisagor, Peter: 2063.

Little, Stuart W.:   2064.

Lodge, Henry Cabot, Jr.:
    2946.

Logan, Andy: 1449.

Logan, John: 2643.

Lohmar, Ulrich: 1450.

Lomax, Stan: 2696.

Long, Huey: 2766.

Long, Russell: 4278.

Lorenz, Marita: 1851, 2258,
    4991, 4994.

Louis, J. C.:   2644.

Love, Ruth: 1570.

Lovelady, Billy: 3665.

Loxton, Howard: 2205, 2406.

Ludwig, Jack: 425.

Lurie, Morris: 2291.

Lutz, Tom: 2187.

Lützkendorf, Felix: 1574,
    2645, 2653, 2677, 3989,
    4005.

Lyerly, Olga G.:   1759.

Lynn, Staughton: 426, 574,
    825.

M

Macapagal, Ramon: 2879, 2977.

McAulay, Joseph: 234.

McBirnie, William Stewart:
    384.

MacCammon, Jim: 235.

McCamy, Calvin: 5048, 5052.

McCarry, Charles: 2617.

McCloy, John J.:   13, 4411.

McConal, Jon: 2514.

McCone, John A.:   3506,
    3647, 3651, 3751.

McConnell, Brian: 1727-1728,
    1769, 2300.

McCormack, John W.:   1394,
    2788, 2957.

McDade, Thomas M.:   294.

McDaniel, Charles-Gene:
    1751.

Macdonald, Dwight: 427-428,
    826.

McDonald, Hugh C.:   2188-
    2189, 4865.

McDonald, Maurice: 3596.

Macdonald, Neil: 567, 1934.

MacFarlane, Ian Colin A.:
    2190-2191, 2292.

McGee, Reece: 335.

McGill, Ralph Emerson:
    1245.

McGrory, Mary: 827, 1246.

McIntire, Carl: 4478, 4558.

McIntyre, Mark: 2646.

McKenna, Brian: 2684.

MacKenzie, N.:   573.

McKinley, James: 1729, 2293-
   2294.

McKinley, S. B.:   1848.

McLarry, Russell: 362, 3455.

McLaughlin, M.:   1451.

McMaines, Lilly Mae (alias
   Sandra Moffit):   118, 4327,
   4329-4330, 4351.

McMeekin, Robert: 4794.

McMillan, Priscilla Johnson:
   418, 2423, 2427, 2431,
   2434, 2463, 3603, 3812,
   4360, 4665, 4745, 4750,
   4969, 4990.

McNamara, Robert: 2860,
   4738.

McNaspy, C. J.:   1452.

MacNeil, Robert: 1146.

McWatters, Cecil J.:   3567.

Maddox, Henry: 1935.

Mailer, Norman: 828.

Malcolm X: 1321, 1814,
   3307, 3335, 3352.

Maley, Don: 1571.

Malone, William Scott: 2515.

Malow, Richard: 295.

Malzberg, Barry N.:   2618-
   2619.

Manchester, William: 128,
   2024-2151, 3604, 3949,
   4033, 4038, 4073, 4086,
   4107, 4112, 4115-4117,
   4119, 4121-4122, 4125,
   4131-4132, 4134-4140,
   4142-4143, 4147-4163,
   4165-4167, 4169-4171,
   4177, 4179, 4183, 4192,
   4195-4203, 4205, 4207-
   4210, 4212, 4216, 4220-
   4221, 4224, 4226, 4230,
   4233-4237, 4240, 4244-
   4247, 4255, 4258, 4264,
   4269, 4300, 4318, 4321-
   4322, 4331, 4333, 4335,
   4340, 4343, 4347, 4349-
   4350, 4355, 4358, 4361,
   4372, 4380, 4388, 4431,
   4442, 4459, 4519, 4543.

Mandel, Paul: 2295.

Mannes, Marya: 1247.

Mansfield, Michael J.:
   1394, 2957, 3054.

Marachini, Dante: 4297.

Marchetti, Victor: 2620.

Marcorelles, Louis: 1129.

Marcus, Raymond: 972, 1089-
   1090.

Mardian, Robert: 4675.

Markham, Mrs.:   626.

Marks, Stanley J.:   721,
   1730, 2192-2193, 2647.

Marshall, Eliot: 568.

Marten, Paul: 1395.

Martin, Jack: 190.

Martin, John J.:   236.

Martin, Murphy: 2697.

Martin, William C.:   2432.

Masefield, John: 2990.

Mathews, James P.:   1396,
1527.

Mathews, Jim: 701, 2164.

Matteo, Pat: 2194.

Matusow, Harvey: 569-570.

Maxfield, Marietta: 2222.

Mayer, Milton: 1453.

Mayes, Stanley: 1248.

Mayhew, Aubrey: 365, 1397,
4648, 4683, 4686, 4709-
4710, 4826.

Mayo, John B., Jr.:   1528.

Mazlish, Bruce: 2698.

Meader, Vaughan: 2714,
3286.

Meagher, Sylvia: 106, 429-
432, 571, 697, 722, 754,
773, 813, 829-835, 845,
885, 900, 993, 1913, 2070,
2296-2300, 2411, 4497.

Means, Marianne: 4795.

Medina, (Judge) Harold R.:
4909.

Medved, Michael: 1454.

Meisler, Stanley: 994.

Meisner, P.:   572, 836,
2301-2305.

Mendelsohn, Harold: 1572-
1573.

Menninger, Karl: 498, 3349,
3533.

Mentesana, Ernest: 237.

Menzies, Robert: 1297.

Mester, Earl: 238.

Metcalfe, Daniel J.:   178,
181, 185, 187.

Meunier, Robert F.:   723.

Meyer, Karl E.:   433, 573,
1168, 1249-1250.

Mezei, Leslie: 1091.

Michel, Armand: 724.

Midgely, Leslie: 2689-2690,
4405.

Mihovilović, Ive: 1251,
2185, 2195.

Mikoyan, Anastas: 2976.

Milhaud, Darius: 1510.

Milic, Zivko: 1252-1254.

Millen, J.:   2663.

Miller, D.:   239.

Miller, David: 2650.

Miller, Tom: 284.

Mills, Andrew: 837.

Mills, George: 1169.

Mineta, Norman Y.:   44.

Minnis, Jack: 574.

Minow, Newton: 2685.

Mironescu, Emil: 2306.

Mitchell, Martha: 2248.

Mitzel, J.:   838.

Model, F. Peter: 1068.

Modesto, Joe: 2307.

Mohrenschildt, George de:
1836, 1855, 1875, 3871,
4110, 4952, 4954, 4958,
5051, 5104.

Moldea, Dan E.:   1802.

Montague, Ivor: 839.

Montgomery, Linda: 1170.

Montgomery, Ruth: 336.

Moody, Sid: 708.

Moore, Thomas: 2714.

Moorman, D.:   240.

Moorman, Mary: 241, 356,
    1089, 4601.

Morgan, Russell H.:   89,
    4571-4572.

Morin, Relman: 2197.

Moritz, Alan R.:   89, 4571-
    4572.

Morris, W. R.:   2198, 2308.

Morris, Wright: 2621.

Morrison, (Judge) W. A.:
    4056.

Morrow, Robert D.:   2199.

Morse, Wayne: 3906.

Morton, Thruston B.:   1220,
    1255.

Mosby, Aline: 385.

Moschella, Emil: 178.

Moses, David: 2200.

Mosk, Richard M.:   443, 840.

Moulder, John: 337, 2309,
    2529.

Moynihan, Daniel Patrick:
    1455.

Muchmore, Mary: 242, 1072.

Muggeridge, Malcolm: 434,
    841, 1456, 4355.

Mühlen, Norbert: 842.

Munson, Lyle Hugh: 1778.

Murchison, William: 2071.

Murray, James: 243.

Murray, Norbert: 1398,
    1731.

Murray, P.:   1256.

N

Names, Larry D.:   2622.

Nanchant, Frances G.:   1399.

Nanner, Henri: 128.

Nash, George: 843.

Nash, Harry C.:   725.

Nash, Patricia: 843.

Nasser, Gamal Abdel: 2739.

Nathan, Paul: 2072.

Nelson, W. H.:   1752.

Nevins, Allan: 2073, 4227.

Newcomb, Fred T.:   995,
    2201.

Newcomb, Joan I.:   285.

Newman, Albert H.:   726,
    774, 2262, 2300, 2378,
    4652.

Newman, Frances Gail: 4601.

Newman, Justin: 244.

Nichols, John M.:   160-163,
    996-998, 4604, 4715.

Nix, Orville: 245, 1069,
  1073, 1077.

Nixon, Richard M.:   2431,
  2467, 2473, 2725, 2900,
  3230, 3692, 3771, 3939,
  3944, 4725, 4754, 4785,
  4806.

Nizer, Louis: 689, 4082,
  4232, 4263, 4265.

Norden, Eric: 1936, 2310.

Northcott, Kaye: 844.

Norwick, Kenneth P.:   1094.

Nosenko, Yuri I.:   173-175,
  4801, 4827, 4878, 5038,
  5053, 5060, 5069, 5105,
  5112, 5119.

Novel, Gordon: 25, 119-121,
  129, 138, 4325, 4327, 4336,
  4338, 4341, 4346, 4348,
  4363, 4376, 4379, 4381,
  4390, 4416, 4428.

Novins, Stuart: 1257-1258.

Noyes, Peter: 125, 2202.

Nyaradi, Nicholas: 1401.

O

Oates, Joyce Carol: 2623.

O'Brien, Conor Cruise: 435,
  845, 1457, 2311.

O'Brien, Lawrence F.:   4289,
  4385, 4738.

O'Donnell, Edward M.:   4613.

O'Donnell, Kenneth P.:
  1185, 4261, 4267, 4724,
  4738, 4863, 4980-4981.

O'Gara, James: 1259.

Oglesby, Carl: 1732, 5133.

Ohlhausen, William G.:   183.

Oistrakh, David: 3017.

Olden, Marc: 2624.

Olds, Greg: 338, 846, 1092,
  1937.

Oliver, Revilo P.:   1488,
  1490, 1496, 3498, 3505,
  3573, 3588, 3650.

Olson, Don: 1093.

Oltmans, Willem: 4956,
  4961, 4966.

O'Neil, Paul: 2715.

Orren, Karen: 1753.

Osbaine, Cecil: 1458.

Osvald, Frank: 848.

Oswald, Lee Harvey: 34, 63,
  71, 85, 91-92, 102, 111,
  123-124, 131, 135, 141-
  142, 150, 164, 189-194,
  380-525, 436, 984, 986,
  1041-1042, 1066, 1074,
  1133, 1142, 1148, 1350-
  1351, 1367, 1628, 1633,
  1659, 1669-1670, 1705,
  1716, 1762, 1968, 2357,
  2422-2474, 2475-2593,
  2737-2738, 2838, 2840-
  2841, 2944, 2947-2948,
  2985-2986, 2998, 3003,
  3006, 3104-3107, 3110-
  3111, 3115, 3119, 3163-
  3164, 3170, 3172, 3179-
  3180, 3192, 3203, 3216,
  3218, 3232, 3249, 3251,
  3256, 3266-3267, 3272,
  3290-3294, 3296, 3301-
  3304, 3310-3316, 3320,
  3323, 3325-3328, 3336,
  3339-3342, 3344, 3353,
  3360, 3362, 3365, 3369,
  3373, 3377, 3379, 3381-
  3382, 3384, 3388-3389,
  3412, 3421, 3426-3427,
  3435, 3437, 3439, 3446,
  (continued...)

(Oswald, continued)
3459, 3473, 3477, 3506,
3516, 3518, 3528, 3536,
3580, 3582, 3591, 3593,
3596, 3603, 3616, 3620,
3628-3629, 3632, 3637,
3644, 3675, 3680, 3701-
3704, 3731, 3738, 3748-
3749, 3755, 3762, 3764,
3767, 3771, 3798, 3800,
3807, 3810, 3828, 3871,
3876-3877, 3879, 3901,
3950, 3978-3979, 3982,
3986, 3995, 3998-4000,
4024, 4031, 4048, 4088,
4123, 4185, 4195, 4206,
4242, 4272-4273, 4295,
4297, 4310, 4312, 4324,
4356, 4360, 4367-4369,
4374, 4394, 4439, 4451,
4460, 4465, 4467-4468,
4502, 4525, 4548, 4599,
4610, 4619, 4640, 4643,
4648, 4652, 4657, 4665,
4703, 4718, 4727, 4730,
4766, 4776, 4781, 4801,
4815-4816, 4823-4825,
4829, 4833-4834, 4855,
4877, 4886-4887, 4890,
4903-4904, 4946, 4951,
4955-4960, 4982-4985, 4991,
4997, 4999, 5001, 5003,
5011-5013, 5082, 5104-
5105, 5118-5119, 5125.

Oswald, Marguerite: 386,
436, 849, 1133, 2425,
2432, 2435, 2446-2447,
2450-2452, 2458, 2464,
2466, 2472, 3303, 3314-
3315, 3332, 3347, 3355-
3356, 3377, 3385, 3447,
3459, 3483, 3494, 3497,
3501, 3504, 3517, 3563,
3611, 3712, 3759, 3886,
3951, 3978, 4102, 4240,
4525, 4757.

Oswald, Marina [Porter]:
107, 135-136, 500, 1048,
1152, 2422-2474, 3109,
3171, 3266, 3269, 3315,
3351, 3353, 3359, 3367,
3394-3395, 3418, 3430,
3435, 3441, 3443, 3448,
3452, 3454, 3465, 3470,

3481, 3485, 3487-3489,
3491-3493, 3529, 3535,
3539-3440, 3558, 3664,
3679, 3692, 3718, 3733,
3812, 3840, 3844, 3868,
3878, 3880, 3887, 3899,
3901, 3904-3905, 3926,
3935, 3957, 3959, 3962,
3972, 3974, 3998, 4031,
4455, 4486-4487, 4490,
4494, 4608, 4657, 4718,
4727, 4730, 4757, 4835,
4969, 4988, 4990, 5049-
5050, 5103.

Oswald, Robert L.: 2424,
2433, 3509, 3524, 3528,
3530, 3887, 4105, 4476.

Osterburg, James W.: 847.

O'Toole, George: 1792,
1803, 1848, 2203, 2227,
2312.

O'Toole, James K.: 1695.

Ottenburg, Miriam: 692.

Overstreet, Harry: 1733.

Owens, Dan: 246.

P

Pacis, Vicente A.: 339.

Packer, Herbert: 575.

Paetel: Karl O.: 1260.

Paine, Ruth: 2437, 2841,
3003, 3591, 3594, 4507.

Pakula, Anthony: 2655.

Palma, Brian de: 2652.

Palmer, Joel: 437.

Panter-Downes, Mollie: 1261.

Panzeca, Salvatore: 139, 142.

Parker, Edwin B.: 1677.

Parr, Wyman: 248.

Paschall, P.: 249.

Passent, Daniel: 2074.

Patrick, Robert: 2648.

Patterson, Samuel C.: 1696.

Pavars, Lilija: 1408.

Pavlick, Richard P.: 4114,
  4840.

Pearl, Jack: 2625.

Percy, Charles H.: 4448.

Perry, George: 1574, 2664.

Perry, Malcolm: 3610.

Peterson, Paul: 1753.

Pett, Saul: 1575.

Pettit, Tom: 1146.

Phelan, James: 1938-1939,
  4613.

Phenix, George: 250.

Pickard, Roy: 2665.

Pilpel, Harriet F.: 1094.

Plastrik, Stanley: 438.

Plumb, J. H.: 2075.

Podell, Bertram L.: 4729.

Podhoretz, Norman: 576.

Pokorný, Dušan: 2204.

Policoff, Jerry: 850, 1576.

Pomerantz, Charlotte: 1531.

Popa, Stefan: 2516-2517.

Pope Paul VI: 2758, 2872,
  2950.

Popkin, Richard H.: 400,
  727, 741, 851, 879, 889,
  1804, 1940, 2607, 4057.

Porter, Kenneth J.: 2442,
  2456, 2470-2471, 3957,
  3972, 3974.

Porter, William E.: 1577.

Possony, Stefan T.: 577.

Pottecher, Frédéric: 2481-
  2483.

Potter, Philip: 1171.

Pouillon, Jean: 1459.

Powell, Constance: 1170.

Powell, James W.: 251.

Powell, Lewis F., Jr.:
  3910.

Power, David F.: 4724,
  4738.

Powers, Barbara (Moore):
  1779.

Powers, Thomas: 1849.

Powledge, Fred: 1941.

Poznanska, A.: 2518.

Pratt, (Judge) John: 168,
  170-171.

Preyer, L. Richardson:
  5036-5037, 5062.

Pringle, Peter: 1850-1851.

Prouty, Leroy Fletcher: 340,
  1780, 1815.

Puché, Ignacio: 1197.

Puda, Jiri: 3820.

Pusateri, C. Joseph: 2315.

Q

Quade, Quentin L.:   1262.

Quinlan, Sean: 1263.

Quoodle,   :   1095.

R

Radojcic, Miroslav: 1264-
    1265.

Rains, Rolen R.:   1532.

Rajski, Raymond B.:   1533,
    4469.

Ralston, Ross F.:   387.

Ramovic, Ramo: 3708.

Rand, Michael: 2205, 2406.

Randell, Hazel (Gooch): 253.

Rankin, J. Lee: 34, 110,
    172, 671, 3391, 3435,
    3459, 3895.

Raskin, Marcus: 852.

Rather, Dan: 278, 1534,
    2690.

Ray, James Earl: 183, 185,
    4536, 4685, 4703, 4951.

Redlich, Norman: 554, 669,
    3643.

Reed, S. L.:   254.

Reiland, Ronald: 255.

Remus, Bernhard: 1460.

Rendulic, Lothar: 1461.

Rennert, Maggie: 2626.

Revere, Guy: 2519.

Reyes Monroy, Jose Luis:
    1535.

Rhoads, James B.:   32, 33,
    110, 137, 172, 4522.

Rhodes, Allen: 256.

Rhodes, Rusty: 1102.

Rice, John R.:   2206.

Rice, William R.:   286.

Rickerby,   :   257.

Ridenour, Ron: 2316.

Ridgeway, James: 1241.

Rifkind, Shepard: 439.

Rifkind, Simon H.:   4128,
    4139, 4197.

Ringgold, Gene: 388.

Rivers, Caryl: 1579.

Robach, M.:   2666.

Robert, Peter: 2317.

Roberts, Charles: 1578,
    2207, 2398, 4232, 4375.

Robertson, Willard E.:   147.

Robinson, (Judge) Aubrey E.:
    173, 175, 177.

Robinson, (Judge) Spottswood
    W.:   171, 174, 176.

Roche, John P.:   958, 4483.

Rockefeller, Nelson W.: 45,
    101, 1782, 1772-1827,
    2757, 4783, 4786, 4789,
    4797, 4803-4804, 4808-
    4810.

Rockwell, George: 2574.

Roddy, Jon: 341.

Roddy, Joseph: 1462.

Roffman, Howard: 389, 999, 1055, 1061, 2318.

Rogers, Warren: 1942.

Rojas, Robinson: 2208.

Roosevelt, James: 2776.

Rosen, D.: 1805.

Rosen, R. D.: 2243.

Rosenbaum, Ron: 853.

Rosenberg, Maurice: 578.

Rosenthal, Alan S.: 166.

Ross, Thomas: 3684, 3689.

Rosselli/Roselli, John: 4942, 4954, 5120-5121.

Roszak, Theodore: 854.

Rothchild, John: 2319.

Rothstein, David A.: 1754- 1755, 3738, 3933.

Rovere, Richard H.: 703, 2076.

Rowan, Carl T.: 2320.

Royster, Vermont: 1266.

Rubin, Berthold: 1267.

Ruby, Earl: 5065.

Ruby, Jack: 25, 34, 342, 465, 470, 587, 630, 1137, 1352, 2475-2593, 2520- 2521, 2944, 3007, 3011- 3012, 3111-3114, 3140, 3213, 3272-3273, 3275, 3297, 3301-3306, 3365, 3390, 3397-3398, 3401, 3413, 3420, 3422, 3424, 3432, 3445, 3447-3448,
3460, 3466-3468, 3471- 3472, 3474-3475, 3480, 3486, 3489, 3496, 3499- 3500, 3502-3503, 3507- 3508, 3510-3515, 3519- 3520, 3522-3523, 3525- 3527, 3531, 3533-3534, 3537-3538, 3541-3550, 3552-3554, 3558-3559, 3561-3564, 3566, 3568- 3569, 3571-3572, 3574- 3581, 3597, 3602, 3606, 3621-3623, 3627, 3630- 3636, 3653, 3655, 3661, 3667, 3669, 3677, 3685, 3688, 3695-3696, 3699- 3700, 3714-3715, 3717, 3730, 3767-3768, 3797, 3900, 3912, 3915, 3918, 3920, 3924-3925, 3928, 3932, 3934, 3946, 3952- 3954, 3958, 3968, 3970, 3977, 3981, 3983, 3991- 3992, 3997, 4002, 4010- 4013, 4017-4018, 4021- 4023, 4034, 4053-4054, 4056, 4059, 4061, 4063- 4064, 4083, 4103, 4106, 4108, 4111, 4113, 4118, 4120, 4130, 4141, 4145, 4168, 4174, 4176, 4181- 4182, 4184-4188, 4190, 4194, 4204, 4252, 4268, 4271, 4279, 4323, 4326, 4345, 4369, 4389, 4492, 4516, 4701, 4771, 4817, 4955, 5028, 5065, 5117.

Ruckelshaus, William D.: 183.

Ruge, Gerd: 1943.

Russell, (Lord) Bertrand: 23, 855-856.

Russell, Dick: 1806, 2209.

Russell, Francis: 857.

Russell, Richard B.: 16, 110, 846, 963, 3733, 3901, 4643.

Russo, Perry R.: 122, 142, (continued...)

(Russo, continued)
  4310, 4312, 4324, 4362,
  4396, 4398, 4594-4596,
  4613, 4661, 4664.

Ryan, Michael: 158, 171.

                S

Sable, Martin H.: 287.

Sagatelyan, Mikhail R.:
  2210, 2321-2322.

Sahl, Mort: 1658, 1899,
  1928, 4627.

Saint-Jean, Claude: 2323.

Salandria, Vincent: 825,
  871, 885, 1000-1003, 1096,
  2324-2325, 3902.

Salinger, Pierre: 1402,
  2077, 2207, 3716, 4651,
  4738, 4743.

Salisbury, Harrison E.:
  690, 858, 3192.

Saltz, Eli: 1697.

Sanderson,   : 258.

Saracevic, Sead: 2185.

Saravay, Judith: 1681.

Sauvage, Leo: 440-442, 553,
  579-581, 700, 722, 728-
  729, 740, 752, 802, 830,
  858-864, 1913, 2078, 4019,
  4036, 4039, 4052, 4074,
  4232.

Sawai, Sirimongkon: 2211.

Schaitman, Leonard: 169,
  186.

Schiller, Lawrence: 1134.

Schlesinger, Arthur M., Jr.:
  1118, 1155, 1172, 1463,

1533, 2051, 2079, 4173,
  4274, 4743.

Schmidt, (Sister Mary)
  Bernadette: 1403.

Schmitt, Karl M.: 1720.

Schoenmann, Ralph: 865.

Schonfeld, Maurice W.:
  2326.

Schorr, Daniel: 1536, 1815,
  4796-4797.

Schreiber, Flora R.: 1756.

Schüler, Alfred: 342.

Schulz, Donald E.: 1807.

Schuman, Frederick L.:
  1172.

Schuyler, Philip N.: 1580.

Schwaber, Paul: 1382.

Schwartz, Benjamin L.:
  2327.

Schwartz, (Judge) Edward:
  153, 155.

Schwartz, Jay: 866.

Schweiker, Richard S.: 85-
  86, 722, 1844, 1857,
  1879-1880, 1885, 4813,
  4818-4819, 4830, 4832,
  4888.

Schweisheimer, W.: 1004.

Schweben, Joachim: 1944,
  2328.

Sciambra, Andrew J.: 142.

Scobey, Alfredda: 867,
  3909.

Scott, Peter Dale: 722,
  730, 1781, 1808-1809.

Sebastian, Joseph A.:   1757,
   3948.

Seelye, John: 1005.

Segal, Jeff: 1852-1855.

Seigenthaler, John: 1537,
   1900, 4254, 4685.

Seigler, Howard: 259.

Sergeev, Boris: 2179.

Servan-Schreiber, J.-J.:
   343.

Seter, 'Ido: 2627.

Shahn, Ben: 1370.

Shanklin, J. Gordon: 34,
   4855.

Shannon, Elaine: 1839,
   1841-1842, 2428.

Shannon, William V.:   1268,
   1856.

Shaw, Clay: 25, 123-124,
   139-147, 197, 201, 1898,
   1916-1917, 1929-1930,
   1942, 1945, 1947, 1953,
   1972, 1975-1976, 2001,
   4293, 4319, 4324, 4342,
   4344, 4390, 4392, 4399,
   4432, 4436, 4441, 4446-
   4447, 4449, 4453, 4504,
   4511-4512, 4526, 4549,
   4551, 4562-4563, 4577-
   4587, 4589-4610, 4614-
   4624, 4640, 4645, 4656,
   4661-4663, 4667-4670,
   4678, 4685, 4700, 4720,
   4731, 4772, 4998, 5018.

Shaw, J. Gary: 2213.

Shawcross, William: 1097.

Shawver, George: 260.

Shayon, Robert Lewis: 1581-
   1582.

Shea, J. M., Jr.:   344.

Shea, Robert: 2628.

Sheatsley, Paul B.:   1698-
   1699, 3734.

Sheerin, John B.:   1269.

Sheridan, Walter J.:   148-
   149, 1946, 1959, 4422-
   4425, 4440.

Sherrill, Robert: 1156.

Shiverick, David: 394.

Shiverick, Kathleen: 394.

Shrake, Edwin: 2629.

Sicinski, Andrzej: 1700.

Silber, Irwin: 1857.

Silbert, Earl J.:   169, 171,
   179-181, 184-187.

Similas, Norman M.:   261,
   345.

Simmons, James: 4601.

Simpson, Alan W. B.:   868.

Singer, Loren: 2630.

Sirhan, Sirhan: 4532-4533,
   4685, 4703.

Sirica, (Judge) John: 158,
   165-166, 2404, 4675, 4995.

Sites, Paul: 390.

Skolnick, Sherman H.:   2214-
   2215, 2400, 4647.

Slawson, W. David: 443.

Sloan, Bill: 346.

Slomich, Sidney J.:   1758.

Smathers, George: 4853.

Smith, A. Merriman: 1138,
    1538, 1583, 3641.

Smith, George: 262.

Smith, Gerald L. K.:   2216.

Smith, Howard K.:   4895.

Smith, Hubert Winston:
    3601, 3614.

Smith, Jack H.:   444-445,
    582-589, 869-871, 1006,
    1270.

Smith, (Judge) John L.:
    150, 179-181, 185.

Smith, Liz: 347.

Smith, R. H.:   872, 2080.

Smith, Robert P.:   164,
    1016, 2269, 2329.

Smith, Sergio Arcacha:
    4336, 4416.

Smith, William R.:   2217-
    2218.

Snider, Arthur J.:   1007.

Snyder, George W.:   2219.

Snyder, Jim: 1145.

Snyder, Le Moyne: 446.

Snyder, Richard E.:   3680.

Sokolov, Raymond: 2434.

Sorenson, Theodore C.:
    1402, 2789, 4335, 4738.

Sparks, Fred: 2716.

Sparrow, Gerald: 1734.

Sparrow, John H. A.:   731,
    813, 823, 873-875, 947-948,
    958, 2020, 4474-4475.

Specter, Arlen: 447, 658,
    789, 906, 923, 1047, 4098.

Speigle,   :   263.

Spellman, Francis (Cardi-
    nal):   2794, 3091.

Spellman, Gladys N.:   43.

Spencer, B. Z.:   448.

Spiesel, Charles I.:   4592-
    4594.

Spitz, Werner U.:   4794.

Spitzer, Stephan P.:   1573,
    1584-1585.

Spivak, Jonathan: 590.

Sprague, Richard A.:   1828,
    1832, 1835, 1852, 1861,
    1872-1874, 1882, 4901,
    4919, 4929, 4936-4937,
    4939-4940, 4953, 4957,
    4964-4965.

Sprague, Richard E.:   6, 29,
    296, 449, 1098-1100,
    1586, 1810, 1946, 2209,
    2232, 2234, 2327, 2330-
    2332.

Stafford, Jean: 2425,
    2435, 2458, 4000, 4004.

Stahl, Walter: 1464.

Stang, Alan: 2333.

Stanton, Frank: 3606,
    3619.

Stapp, A.:   2334.

Star, Jack: 297.

Stein, Michael: 169.

Steiner, Stan: 1005.

Stencel, Sandra: 1701.

Stern, R.:   2484.

Stetler, Russell: 730, 1858, 2335.

Stevens, Ben: 2336.

Stevens, Sylvester K.: 4128.

Stewart, Charles J.: 1271, 1404.

Stiles, John R.: 706, 3962.

Stokes, Louis B.: 66, 71, 77, 4977, 5025.

Stolley, Richard B.: 1101.

Stombaugh, Paul: 170.

Stone, Allan: 1587.

Stone, I. F.: 745, 877, 1272.

Stoughton,   : 264.

Strafford, Peter: 1102.

Strauss, Theodore: 1119.

Stravinsky, Igor: 1497, 3788.

Streit, Saul S.: 128.

Stringer, John T.: 90.

Strior, Murray: 1405.

Stuart, Mel: 1119.

Stuckey, Bill: 1148, 4178.

Sturgis, Frank: 1851, 2258, 4803, 4991, 4993-4994.

Sugar, Bert R.: 1725.

Suinn, Richard M.: 1702.

Sukarno, Achmed: 2894.

Summerlin, Sam: 2178.

Susann, Jacqueline: 2631.

Sutherland, John P.: 1173.

Sydeman, William: 4084.

Syme, Anthony V.: 2632.

Szasz, Thomas S.: 2522.

Szulc, Tad: 591, 878, 5095, 5118, 5122.

T

Tackett, John Wesley: 315.

Tackwood, Louis E.: 530.

Tague, James T.: 91, 170, 221, 360.

Talese, Gay: 2081.

Talma, Louise: 4518.

Tamama, Tetsuo: 549.

Tamm, (Judge) Edward: 174, 176.

Tamney, Joseph B.: 1679, 1703.

Tastmona, Thothnu: 2220.

Taylor, Robert L.: 1760.

Taylor, Telford: 3917.

TerHorst, J. F.: 1145.

Terry, Anthony: 1273.

Terry, John A.: 171.

Theis, William H.: 1947.

Thomas, Hugh: 450.

Thomas, J.: 1465.

Thomas, Jack: 1008.

Thomas, Larry: 265.

Thomas, Robert E.:   1588.

Thompson, Josiah: 130, 732,
754, 773, 783, 879-880,
885, 935, 952, 956, 1011,
1663, 4460, 4471, 4497,
4510, 4552, 4628.

Thompson, Pat: 127.

Thompson: Thomas: 451,
2412, 2436.

Thompson, William Clifton:
288.

Thomson, George C.:   733,
2413.

Thone, Charles: 63.

Thornley, Kerry Wendell:
391, 4499.

Thurmond, Strom: 4266.

Thurston, Samuel F.:   (alias
for Richard E. Sprague).

Thurston, Wesley S.:   2633.

Tippit, J. D.:   102, 460,
2411-2421, 2882, 2904,
2997, 3020, 3116, 3173,
3211, 3219, 3265, 3289,
3351, 3407, 3415, 3430,
3442, 3462, 3469, 3605,
3824, 3865, 4249, 4757.

Titus, Harold H., Jr.:   166.

Tobin, Richard L.:   1589.

Tolbert, Frank X.:   2414.

Tomalin, Nicholas: 2082.

Tonahill, Joe H.:   392,
3928, 4393.

Torres, Jose: 2337.

Torres, Miguel: 4391.

Tower, John: 2759, 2998,
4819.

Towne, Anthony: 881.

Towner, Jim: 266.

Townley, Richard: 148-149,
4419.

Trafficante, Santo, Jr.:
69, 70, 1877, 1883, 4949,
4963, 5067, 5115-5116.

Tretick, Stanley: 1369.

Trevor-Roper, Hugh: 719,
873, 882-884, 918, 922,
928, 2338, 3897-3898,
3903.

Trillin, Calvin: 885.

Troelstrup, Glenn: 592.

Truby, J. David: 886.

Truly, Ray: 3600.

Truman, Harry S :   2741.

Trumbo, Dalton: 2650,
4733.

Tschäppät, R.:   1466.

Turnbull, John W.:   348.

Tuchler, Maier I.:   887.

Tuchman, Barbara W.:   2083.

Tuchman, Mitch: 1590.

Tupa, Stefan: 2523.

Turner, Ralph F.:   1093.

Turner, Stansfield: 5034.

Turner, William W.:   1948-
1953, 2339, 3833.

Tuteur, Werner: 2524, 4771.

U

Underwood, James: 267.

Ungar, Sanford J.:   1859.

Uris, Leon: 1775, 2634.

Ushakov, G.:   2525.

Uthco, T. H.:   2649.

V

Valencia, Pedro Gutirrez:
    156.

Valliere, James T.:   1922.

Van Bemmelen, J. M.:   452.

Van Der Karr, Richard K.:
    1540.

Van Dusen, (Judge) Francis
    L.:   171.

Van Gelder, Lawrence: 2027.

Vanocur, Sander: 1402.

Veggeberg, S.:   2340, 2496.

Venkateswararas, Pothuri:
    2221.

Veritas: 2705.

Vilnis, Aija: 1408.

Viorst, Milton: 1811.

Volkland,   :   273.

Volz, John P.:   142.

Vuillemier, John Frédéric:
    1735.

W

Waddell, Les: 349.

Wade, Henry: 1351, 2529,
    3106, 3213, 3217, 3687,
    3987, 4061, 4285.

Wainwright, Loudon: 888-
    889, 2526.

Walker, Edwin A.:   521,
    1628, 2357, 2866, 3309,
    3393, 3439, 3441, 3593,
    3697, 3771, 5051.

Walker, Gerald: 826.

Wallace, George C.:   43, 45,
    46, 49, 51, 56, 59, 1767,
    4713.

Wallechinsky, David: 1454.

Walsh, William G.:   1409.

Walters, William: 34.

Waltz, Jon R.:   25, 2478,
    2506, 3981.

Wardlaw, Jack: 1896.

Warner, Dale G.:   1410.

Warner, Ken: 1009.

Warren, David M.:   2635.

Warren, Earl: 13, 110,
    531, 536-537, 627, 629,
    1394, 2957, 3255, 3434,
    3453, 3685, 3757, 4025,
    4298, 4544, 4633, 4723.

Waters, Harry F.:   1591.

Watson, Allan C.:   890.

Watson, Peter: 2527.

Weaver, Jack A.:   274.

Weberman, Alan J.:   1774,
    4812, 4898, 5095, 5122.

Webster, William H.:   180-
    181, 5126.

Wecht, Cyril H.:   982, 1010-
    1016, 1812-1813, 4600,
    4711, 4811, 5041.

Wegmann, Edward F.:   139,
142, 145, 147.

Wegmann, William J.:   139,
142.

Weinstein, Edwin A.:   1759.

Weisberg, Harold: 2, 5, 20,
30, 31, 32, 34, 63, 88-90,
106, 109, 110, 126, 137,
151, 160-161, 165-186, 189,
197-198, 201, 278, 345,
532, 734-736, 749, 758,
762, 784, 830, 851, 891,
900, 902, 949, 973, 1056-
1058, 1075, 1901, 2152,
2652, 2654, 4019, 4027,
4052, 4074, 4104, 4232,
4365, 4418, 4627, 4769,
4776, 5081, 5119.

Weissman, Bernard: 3330,
3363, 3376.

Weisz, Alfred E.:   1760.

Wells, William: 1274.

Welsh, David: 892, 2341,
2520.

Werdig, Robert M., Jr.:
156, 165.

West, Jessamyn: 2437-2438.

West, John R.:   737.

West, Rebecca: 2084, 4355.

West, William R.:   135.

Westerfield, Rex: 1736.

Westfall, Mrs. E. H.:   275.

Whalen, Richard J.:   893,
940, 2312.

Whaley, William W.:   3567,
3994.

Wheller, Keith: 1017.

Whitbourn, John: 1411.

White, James D.:   20, 30,
2342.

White, Jenifer: 20, 30.

White, Stephen: 738.

White, Theodore H.:   349-
350, 1157, 1275.

Whittemore, Reed: 1467.

Wicker, Tom: 1592, 4521,
4523.

Wickey, John: 1697.

Wilber, Chalres G.:   974.

Wilcott, James B.:   5014.

Wile, Annadel N.:   105.

Wilgus, Neal: 2636.

Wilkinson, Doris Y.:   1737.

William, Mark: 2636.

Williams, Charles: 1814.

Williams, Marion E.:   165-
166.

Williamson, Audrey: 948.

Willis, Phillip L.:   276.

Wills, Garry: 25, 351,
894, 2085-2086, 2485,
2528.

Wilson, H. H.:   1531.

Wilson, Harold: 1225.

Wilson, J. Frank: 3548.

Wilson, Robert Anton: 2628.

Winfrey, Bill: 277.

Winks, Robin W.:   812.

Winston, Frank: 298, 895,
1954, 2529.

Wise, Dan: 2222.

Wise, David: 299, 2343,
    3684, 3689, 4505.

Wise, Wes: 4722, 4775.

Witt, Louie Steven: 1868.

Wiznitzer, L.: 2344.

Wolfenstein, Martha: 1678.

Wolk, Robert L.: 453.

Wolper, David: 1119, 3678,
    3739.

Wood, William: 1955.

Woodfield, William Read:
    2521, 2541.

Worthington, Peter: 2530.

Wright, Sylvia: 1174.

Wrone, David R.: 20, 28,
    30, 31, 110, 290, 454,
    896, 1059-1060.

Wydler, John W.: 4146.

Wyndham, Francis: 2087.

X

Y

Yarborough, Ralph: 352,
    2723.

Young, Roger: 1956.

Youngblood, Rufus W.: 1158,
    1174, 2044, 3183, 3227,
    3337, 3907, 4680.

Z

Zaftig, Leopold: 2153.

Zapruder, Abraham: 123,
    130, 278, 1068, 1077-
    1079, 1081, 1083, 1086-
    1087, 1092, 1094, 1104,
    1108, 1110-1116, 2656,
    2865, 3219, 4248, 4471,
    4552, 4590, 4598, 4662,
    4790, 5039.

Zee, Joe: 897.

Zib, William H.: 2223.

Zusman, Lynne K.: 178-181,
    184-185, 187.

Zvegintzov, Serge: 948.

Zwart, Jacques: 739.

Index of Correspondents:
THE NEW YORK TIMES

Adams, Jim: 5042, 5050, 5053, 5055, 5057, 5060, 5064, 5066-5067.

Adams, Val: 2781, 2889, 3138, 3235, 3300, 3644, 3743, 3956, 4051, 4232.

Alden, Robert: 4147.

Allan, John H.: 3022.

Anderson, David C.: 4865.

Anderson, Raymond H.: 3948.

Apple, R. W., Jr.: 2905, 3031, 3151, 3335, 3376.

Archer, Eugene: 3287, 3678.

Arnold, Martin: 2780, 2993, 3181, 3325, 4144, 4150, 4451, 4862.

Asbury, Edith Evans: 3267, 4030, 4153, 4461.

Ayres, B. Drummond, Jr.: 4648.

Baker, Russell: 3037, 3125, 4260, 4798.

Bardes, Herbert C.: 4257.

Barnes, Clive: 4456.

Barrett, George: 2743.

Bart, Peter: 4062.

Baxter, Annette: 4004.

Becker, Bill: 3389.

Belair, Felix, Jr.: 2730, 2862, 3750, 3850, 3872, 3889.

Belin, David W.: 4692.

Bell, Jack: 2744.

Benjamin, Philip: 2982, 3182, 3211.

Berryman, John: 4739.

Bickel, Alexander M.: 4638.

Bigart, Homer: 2890, 3084,
3215, 3238, 3280, 3344,
3513, 3519, 3522-3523,
3526, 3531, 3534, 3537-
3538, 3541-3543, 3546-3548,
3550, 3552, 3554, 3561-
3562, 3564, 3566, 3568,
3571, 3581, 3781, 3940,
4033, 4038, 4331.

Binder, David: 3708, 4893-
4894, 4910.

Bird, David: 4772, 4991.

Blair, William M.:   3488-
3489, 3491-3493, 3497,
3501, 3504.

Blumenthal, Ralph: 4082.

Braceland, Francis J.:   3996.

Bracker, Milton: 2872.

Brady, Thomas F.:   3232.

Brewer, Sam Pope: 2797.

Brown, Les: 4983.

Brownlow, Donald G.:   3813.

Buckley, Kevin: 5012.

Buckley, Thomas: 3356.

Burks, Edward C.:   4274,
5026.

Burnham, David: 4915, 4918-
4920, 4924, 4926, 4930-
4932, 4936-4937, 4940,
4944-4945, 4947.

Burns, James MacGregor:
4523.

Cady, Steve: 2822.

Calta, Louis: 4356, 4631,
4741.

Canby, Vincent: 4763.

Carmody, Dierdre: 4909.

Cartwright, Gary: 4691.

Clark, Alfred E.:   3918.

Clarkson, Paul R.:   4223.

Cohen, Stanley M.:   3826.

Coombs, Charles A.:   4841.

Corry, John: 4112, 4115,
4119, 4122, 4131, 4134,
4142, 4149, 4152, 4157,
4193, 4195, 4209, 4234,
4247, 4322, 4565.

Cousins, Norman: 3254.

Cowan, Edward: 2826, 2895,
3133, 4813.

Crewdson, John M.:   4783,
4827, 4833, 4835, 4857-
4858, 4867.

Crowther, Bosley: 3838,
4387.

Daley, Arthur: 3019, 3132.

Dallos, Robert E.:   4166,
4179, 4366, 4395-4396,
4402, 4404.

Daniel, Clifton: 4754.

Daniel, Jean: 3387.

Danzig, Allison: 2934,
3021.

Davies, Lawrence E.:   2906,
3422.

Davis, Jim: 5051.

DeCola, Tom: 5034.

Dembitz, Nanette: 3891.

Doty, Robert C.:   2734,
2891.

Dougherty, Philip H.:   4230,
4372, 4978.

Dugan, George: 3066, 3252,
3366, 3849.

Eisenhower, Dwight D.:   2802.

Ely, John Hart: 4836.

Engle, Paul: 4752.

Epstein, Edward Jay: 4046,
4627-4628.

Ericson, Raymond: 3017.

Eskenazi, Gerald: 2822.

Esterow, Milton: 2779.

Fairlie, Henry D.:   4044,
5006.

Farber, Stephen: 4733.

Farnsworth, Clyde H.:   3025,
3897.

Fellows, Lawrence: 2973,
3090.

Fenton, John H.:   2850,
2956, 3044, 3154, 3403,
3410, 4035, 4261, 4556.

Feron, James: 4025.

Finney, John W.:   3755, 3878,
4159, 4540.

Fowler, Elizabeth M.:   3135.

Fox, Sylvan: 4047, 4460.

Frankel, Marvin: 4695.

Frankel, Max: 2749, 2943,
3764, 3793, 3800.

Franklin, Ben A.:   2775,
2974, 3069, 3323, 3839,
4761, 4781, 4901, 4965.

Fremont-Smith, Eliot: 4000,
4028, 4057, 4072, 4109,
4222, 4340, 4431, 4469,
4521, 4560.

Funke, Lewis: 4443.

Gage, Nicholas: 4882, 4942.

Gansberg, Martin: 4411.

Gardner, Paul: 3712, 3841.

Garrison, Lloyd: 3258.

Gent, George: 3745, 4052.

Gentry, Margaret: 5043,
5048, 5052, 5054, 5056,
5060-5061, 5068.

Gilroy, Harry: 3191, 3794,
4244, 4347.

Giniger, Henry: 2909.

Godbout, Oscar: 3008, 3131,
3179.

Gonzalez, Henry B.:   4941.

Gould, Jack: 2947, 3081,
3201, 3298-3299, 3321,
3576, 3606, 3778, 3869,
3967, 4005, 4016, 4020,
4077, 4265, 4397, 4406,
4413.

Graham, Fred P.:   3921, 4027,
4039, 4065, 4068, 4097,
4485, 4497, 4536, 4571,
4573, 4603, 4675, 4698,
4711.

Greenfield, Jeff: 4979.

Gruson, Sydney: 2874, 2971,
3089.

Grutzner, Charles: 4172.

Gwertzman, Bernard: 4554.

Habe, Hans: 3693.

Hacker, Andrew: 3371.

Hailey, Foster: 2992.

Hamilton, James: 4963.

Hamilton, Thomas J.:   2930.

Hammer, Alexander R.:   3026.

Harris, Mark: 4814.

Harrison, Emma: 3365, 3738.

Henry, Kristin W.:   4864.

Herbers, John: 2770, 2857,
  3000, 3116, 3169, 3226,
  3251, 3256, 3320, 4506.

Hess, John L.:   4566.

Hill, Gladwin: 2731, 2838,
  2944, 3111, 3140, 3734,
  3798, 3829, 4481, 4529.

Hofmann, Paul: 3240.

Horrock, Nicholas M.:   4804,
  4809, 4819, 4825, 4828-
  4829, 4837, 4839, 4843,
  4847, 4904, 5014, 5024,
  5029, 5031, 5038-5039,
  5044-5045, 5049, 5058.

Hunt, Richard P.:   2858.

Hunter, Marjorie: 2722,
  2772, 2945, 3074, 3141,
  3204, 3763, 3855, 3863,
  4740, 5000, 5013.

Illson, Murray: 4793.

Ingalls, Leonard: 2949.

Janson, Donald: 2841, 3003,
  3107, 3171, 3224, 3275,
  3293, 3301, 3305, 3324,
  3367, 3369, 3384, 3388,
  3395, 3398, 3402, 3413-
  3414, 3418, 3420, 3817.

Johnston, Laurie: 4993.

Johnston, Richard J. H.:
  2865.

Jones, Marshall P., Jr.:
  4339.

Kennedy, Paul P.:   3110,
  3172.

Kenworthy, E. W.:   2836,
  2946, 3943.

Kifner, John: 4779.

Kihss, Peter: 2737, 2840,
  3006, 3104, 3180, 3311,
  3328, 3362, 3412, 3426,
  3484, 3498, 3516-3517,
  3641, 3753, 3783, 4074,
  4078, 4088-4089, 4091,
  4094, 4101, 4104, 4410,
  4418, 4476, 4520, 4545,
  4886.

Knowles, Clayton: 3016,
  4472.

Knox, Sandra: 4448.

Koppett, Leonard: 2932,
  3018, 3194.

Koshetz, Herbert: 2923.

Krock, Arthur: 2929, 3126,
  3370, 3804.

Kronholm, William: 5062.

Kunstler, William M.:   4871.

Lane, Mark: 4817.

Langguth, Jack: 3303, 3314,
  3327, 3340, 3347, 3355,
  3373, 3385, 3424, 3430,
  3436, 3441, 3443-3444,
  3447-3448, 3451-3452,
  3454, 3464-3468, 3478,
  3486, 3494, 3499, 3502-
  3503, 3507-3508, 3510-
  3512, 3515, 3520, 3525,
  3527, 3529, 3535, 3544-
  3545, 3549, 3553, 3557,
  3563, 3569, 3572, 3580,
  3630, 3632.

Lask, Thomas: 3212.

Lee, John M.:   2754, 3023.

Lehmann-Haupt, Christopher:
4036, 4724, 4792.

Lelyveld, Joseph: 3615.

Leonard, John: 4668.

Lewis, Anthony: 2796, 2948,
3042, 3343, 3357, 3391,
3456-3457, 3524, 3528,
3530, 3675, 3749, 3780,
3789, 3799, 3802, 3822,
3870, 3898, 4049, 4214,
4474, 4483, 4513, 4633,
4753, 4766.

Lingeman, Richard R.: 4969.

Lissner, Will: 3435, 3981.

Loftus, Joseph A.: 3007,
3114, 3202, 3239, 3317,
3331, 3336, 3346, 3353,
3379, 3762.

Long, Tania: 3848.

Lukas, Anthony J.: 4535.

Lydon, Christopher: 4649,
4716, 4810.

Lyons, Richard D.: 5025.

McMillan, George: 4745,
4934.

McMillan, Priscilla (Johnson): 4665, 4714, 4745,
4750.

Madden, Richard L.: 4531,
4953.

Manchester, William: 4117,
4165, 4269, 4737.

Metz, Robert: 2825.

Middleton, Drew: 2790,
2909, 3088, 3787.

Miller, Bryce: 3271.

Mitgang, Herbert: 4164,
4217.

Mohr, Charles: 3744, 4902.

Montgomery, Paul L.: 2792,
2855, 2958, 3079, 4651,
4784.

Mooney, Richard E.: 3024,
3134.

Morris, John D.: 2788,
3053, 3163, 3255.

Mullaney, Thomas E.: 2922.

Narvaez, Alfonso A.: 4880.

Nary, Kenneth: 3686.

Naughton, James M.: 4808,
4822.

Navasky, Victor S.: 4133,
4528, 4547.

Nichols, Joe: 3130.

Nichols, Lewis: 4300, 4321,
4350, 4459.

O'Brien, Lawrence F.: 4289.

O'Connor, John J.: 4787,
4984, 4987, 5011, 5015.

O'Donnell, Kenneth P.:
4721.

Olsen, Arthur J.: 2907,
3703.

Phelan, James R.: 4845.

Phillips, Cabell: 2747,
3112, 3237.

Phillips, McCandlish: 2856,
3065, 3236.

Policoff, Jerry: 4852.

Pomfret, John D.: 3768,
3908.

Powers, Thomas: 4990.

Powledge, Fred: 2948, 3105,
   3170, 3203, 3249, 3296,
   3316, 3329, 3345, 3358,
   3381, 3390, 3423, 3844,
   3851, 3862, 3895.

Ranzal, Edward: 4189.

Rawls, Wendell, Jr.:   4956,
   4966, 4971-4972, 4977,
   4989, 5004, 5075-5076.

Raymond, Jack: 2733, 2834,
   2942, 3072, 3291, 3683-
   3684, 3746, 3767, 3821.

Raymont, Henry: 2752, 2897,
   3108, 3228, 4290, 4306,
   4543, 4658-4660, 4677.

Reed, Roy: 4501, 4634-4635,
   4682.

Reinhold, Robert: 4629,
   4748.

Rendel, John: 2940.

Rensberger, Boyce: 4703.

Reston, James: 2732, 2835,
   2962, 3055, 3752, 3836,
   4135, 4316, 5040.

Riding, Alan: 5020.

Ripley, Anthony: 4762.

Robards, Terry: 4532.

Roberts, Charles: 4375.

Roberts, Gene: 4275, 4280-
   4281, 4285-4286, 4295,
   4297, 4301-4303, 4305,
   4308, 4310, 4312, 4315,
   4317, 4320, 4342, 4344,
   4374, 4391, 4408-4409,
   4412.

Roberts, Steven V.:   4014.

Robertson, Nan: 2748, 2849,
   2961, 3038, 3152, 3458,
   3671, 3835, 3837, 3852,
   3859, 3881, 4007, 4092,

   4282-4283, 4561, 4672,
   4676, 4699, 4705.

Robinson, Douglas: 4136,
   4158, 4161, 4171, 4173,
   4221, 4224, 4255, 4264.

Robinson, Layhmond: 3010.

Rossant, M. J.:   2921.

Rossum, Alfred M.:   4079.

Rusk, Howard A.:   2864.

Safire, William: 4785,
   4806, 4856, 4861, 4866,
   4875, 4976, 5005, 5069.

Sayre, Nora: 4742.

Schanberg, Sydney H.:   4439.

Schmeck, Harold M., Jr.:
   3769.

Schoenbrun, David: 4576.

Schonberg, Harold C.:   4084.

Schorr, Daniel: 4797.

Schumach, Murray: 4137.

Schwartz, Harry: 2798.

Semple, Robert B., Jr.:
   3963, 3990, 4026, 4296,
   4311.

Shabad, Theodore: 2800,
   3153, 3285.

Shabecoff, Philip: 2823,
   4160, 4216.

Shanahan, Eileen: 2768.

Shannon, William V.:   4538.

Sheehan, Joseph M.:   2933.

Shepard, Richard F.:   2983,
   3080.

Shuster, Alvin: 4553.

Sibley, John: 3070, 3446.

Sitton, Claude: 2750, 3009,
3165.

Sloan, Leonard: 2828, 3197.

Smith, Donald: 4738.

Smith, Hedrick: 4768.

Solzhenitsyn, Aleksandr I.:
4850.

Sorenson, Theodore C.:
4751.

Stein, Robert: 4151.

Sterba, James P.: 4708,
4838.

Strauss, Michael: 2935.

Strongin, Theodore: 3854.

Sullivan, Dan: 4277.

Sullivan, Ronald: 2767.

Sullivan, Walter: 3115,
3579, 3933.

Sulzberger, C. L.: 2821,
3015.

Szulc, Tad: 2897, 3871.

Talese, Gay: 2908, 2986,
3225.

Tanner, Henry: 2763, 2839,
2976, 3096, 3306, 3939.

Thompson, Howard: 4693.

Thompson, Josiah: 4628.

Tolchin, Martin: 3284,
3313, 4943.

Turner, Wallace: 2906,
3590, 3595.

Upton, Letitia: 3944.

Vartan, Vartanig G.: 3139.

Vasquez, Juan: 4939.

Waldron, Martin: 3999,
4002, 4022, 4053, 4093,
4106, 4108, 4113, 4182,
4324-4325, 4367-4368,
4370, 4403, 4420, 4422,
4430, 4432-4435, 4494,
4574-4575, 4577-4578,
4583, 4591-4599, 4604-
4610, 4612-4616, 4622,
4624, 4642, 4655, 4674,
4686, 4755, 4824, 4832,
4960.

Wallace, William N.: 2939.

Wallach, Paul G.: 4927.

Walton, Richard J.: 4807,
4853.

Weaver, Warren, Jr.: 2735,
2837, 4650, 4998.

Wecht, Carl [Cyril] H.:
4864.

Wehrwein, Austin C.: 2898,
3011, 3113, 3397, 3463,
3573, 3588, 3909.

Weiler, A. H.: 3495, 4726.

White, Theodore H.: 4156.

Whitman, Alden: 4530.

Wicker, Tom: 2723, 2729,
2919, 2927, 2941, 3030,
3670, 3754, 4048, 4170,
4191, 4196, 4349, 4537,
4539, 5046.

Wieland, Bob: 5027.

Winfrey, Carey: 4988.

Witkin, Richard: 4138,
4258.

Wooten, James T.: 4713.

Zion, Sidney E.: 3931,
    4127, 4148, 4189, 4229,
    4337, 4533, 4617.

Zolotow, Sam: 3450.

Index of Correspondents:
THE WASHINGTON POST

Anderson, Jack: 5084, 5120–5121.

Egan, Jack: 5086.

Greenfield, Meg: 5093.

Hoffman, Nicholas von: 5096.

Katz, Bob: 5117.

Kramer, Larry: 5106.

Lardner, George, Jr.: 5081–5083, 5087–5088, 5090–5091, 5097–5099, 5101, 5103, 5105, 5107, 5109–5115, 5119, 5125–5126, 5128–5130, 5132, 5134.

MacPherson, Myra: 5100.

Peterson, Bill: 5133.

Seaberry, Jane: 5095, 5118, 5122.

Shales, Tom: 5085.

Sigale, Merwin: 5123.

Smith, Nancy: 5092.

ABOUT THE AUTHORS

DeLloyd J. Guth is a specialist in pre-Reformation legal history, with an avocation for bibliography and historiography. He compiled and edited *Late-medieval England 1377-1485* (Cambridge University Press, 1976) and has published numerous scholarly articles and reviews, mainly on topics in English history. An undergraduate at Marquette University, he did post-graduate work at Creighton University and completed doctoral studies at the University of Pittsburgh (1967), after two years as a research student in Clare College, Cambridge University.

David R. Wrone received his B.S. (1958), M.A. (1959) and Ph.D. (1964) in American history from the University of Illinois, Urbana. His chief scholarly concerns are the ideas and institutions for reform, especially the philosophical foundations for them in the modern era. Among his publications are books on the American Indian, *Who's the Savage?* (Fawcett, 1973), which he co-edited, and on the Freedom of Information Act, plus articles on the press, evolution of modern transportation, Abraham Lincoln, and the assassination of President John F. Kennedy.